NORTHERN ROCKIES

A BEST PLACES® GUIDE
TO THE OUTDOORS

SUSAN ENGLISH AND
KATHY WITKOWSKY

SASQUATCH
BOOKS
SEATTLE

Dedication

This book is dedicated to all of those public servants and volunteers—you know who you are—who spend their lives preserving and protecting the integrity of the Northern Rocky Mountain region. Thank you.

Copyright © 1997 by Sasquatch Books
All rights reserved. No portion of this book may be reproduced or utilized in any form, or by any electronic, mechanical, or other means, without the prior written permission of the publisher.
Printed in the United States of America
Distributed in Canada by Raincoast Books Ltd.

First Edition

Library of Congress Cataloging in Publication Data
English, Susan.
        Inside out. Northern Rockies : a best places guide to the outdoors / by Susan English and Kathy Witkowsky.
        p.   cm.
        Includes index.
        ISBN 1-57061-092-4
        1. Outdoor recreation—Rocky Mountains—Guidebooks. 2. Rocky Mountains—Guidebooks. I. Witkowsky, Kathy. II. Title.
        GV191.42.R63E54   1997   97-7472
                                        CIP

Cover Photo: Douglass Dye, Kalispell MT
Cover Design: Karen Schober
Interior Design: Lynne Faulk, Vashon Island WA
Maps: Rohani Design, Edmonds WA
Copy editor: Noelle Sullivan
Proofreader: Karen Parkin
Composition: Patrick David Barber Design

Important Note: Please use common sense. No guidebook can act as a substitute for experience, careful planning, and appropriate training. There is inherent danger in all the outdoor activities described in this book, and readers must assume responsibility for their own actions and safety. Changing or unfavorable conditions in weather, roads, trails, waterways, etc. cannot be anticipated by the authors or publisher, but should be considered by any outdoor participants. The authors and the publisher will not be responsible for the safety of users of this guide.

The information in this edition is based on facts available at press time and is subject to change. The authors and publisher welcome information conveyed by users of this book, as long as they have no financial connection with the area, guide, outfitter, organization, or establishment concerned. A report form is provided at the end of the book.

Sasquatch Books
615 Second Avenue, Suite 260
Seattle, Washington 98104
(206)467-4300
http://www.sasquatchbooks.com

Contents

Acknowledgments

As with every project of this magnitude, many, many people contributed to this book. Stephanie Irving gets credit for coming up with the idea and shepherding us through the process, even after it was no longer her job to do so. Thanks to Todd Wilkinson who researched and wrote the Bozeman and Environs chapter, and to Brooks Tisch and John Gunter who both wrote about Boise and the Sun Valley-Ketchum area. The authors also wish to thank their numerous friends, new and old, who accompanied them on their often exhaustive travels, and those who shared their opinions and sometimes even their secrets in the hope of making this book more useful. In particular, we wish to express our sincerest gratitude to the countless Forest Service and National Park Service rangers and state and provincial authorities who freely contributed their time to ensure the manuscript's accuracy and integrity.

Introduction

When the explorers Lewis and Clark ventured west in 1805, seeking the fastest overland route to the Pacific, they knew they faced a daunting challenge in crossing the Rocky Mountains. The defining feature of the West and the birthplace of the continent's rivers, the Rockies are comprised of not one but dozens of mountain ranges, a vast expanse of peaks, rivers, forests, and canyons. For centuries, Native Americans have considered the Rockies to be sacred: vision quests and spiritual journeys took them deep into glacial-carved valleys and high onto alpine slopes. It's no surprise, then, that in 1872 when the first US National Park was established, it was an area in the Rocky Mountains with ten thousand hot springs, geysers, mud volcanoes, and fumaroles. Yellowstone National Park became the cornerstone of our US parks system.

Millions of visitors travel to the Rockies each year, inspired and awed by the naked grandeur and abundance of stunning natural attractions in these mountains that span the North American continent. In this book, we have concentrated on the rugged northern portion of the range, which features Yellowstone, as well as Glacier, Jasper, and Banff National Parks—meccas for outdoor enthusiasts. The desire for authentic wilderness experiences and the devotion to healthful living and rigorous exercise have increased markedly over the last ten years. As such, in the following pages, we have offered suggestions for what we think are the very best outdoor experiences in the region, for both local recreationalists and active travelers.

Today, the Northern Rockies are experiencing a population boom, a backwash from the wave of earlier West Coast migration that initially skipped over this beautiful but harsh land, concentrating instead on more hospitable coastal terrain. While the growth brings with it all the concerns typically associated with such population increases—socioeconomic stratification, environmental degradation, and questions of property rights—it also is making the region a more diverse, interesting, and tolerant place to live. We now have Thai cafes alongside our burger joints; reggae bands featured in our Western bars; foreign films playing in our movie houses; and of course, roadside espresso stands *everywhere*. Hopefully, the region can withstand pressure to become homogenized and predictable, and the individuality on which Westerners pride themselves can continue to flourish, even amidst this rapidly changing society. With this hope in mind, we have enthusiastically recommended restaurants and lodgings, the bulk of them individually owned, that we feel reflect the spectrum of personalities and tastes that make the Northern Rockies special.

One thing, and one thing alone, remains the common denominator for inhabitants of the Northern Rockies, whether third-generation ranchers or so-called "modem-cowboys" who relocated within the last year: we all live here by choice, rather than necessity. And it is this dedication to our extraordinary quality of life—and the determination to preserve it— that binds us. Whether you live here or are just visiting, we invite you to celebrate, cherish, and preserve the splendor.

—*The Editors, June 1997*

How to Use
This Book

We have tried to make *Inside Out: Northern Rockies* an entertaining, informative, and easy-to-use guidebook. The regions covered in this book are divided into eight sections and reflect the portions of Idaho, Montana, Wyoming, and Alberta, Canada, that flank the Rocky Mountain range. Basic reference maps are featured at the beginning of each section. Each section is then subdivided into smaller, more manageable areas (or chapters) that are represented in the following manner.

Introduction

The introduction to each chapter offers a general description of the area and its primary towns and features. These sections should provide you with a sense of place and history, as well as give you an idea of what to expect when you visit. Directions to the area and transportation information are included in the **Getting There** sections, which are followed by **Adjoining Areas** to your destination that are found in this book.

inside out

The Inside Out sections make up the bulk of the book. We go to great pains to discover what the best year-round options are for outdoor activities in each area. We talk to locals, rangers, guides, and outdoor store owners to get the scoop on the most popular trails, lakes, stretches of river, climbs, ski slopes, and more. And we reveal some lesser-known gems as well.

These sections are divided into individual sports and activities, listed in order of prominence and appeal, from **Hiking** and **Skiing** to **Wildlife** viewing and **Fishing**. Here, you can select your adventure and discover how to get out into the wilderness, outside, out-of-doors, just out!

The "Northern Rockies Outdoor Primer," found at the beginning of the book, also provides safety tips and essential information on outdoor recreation and travel.

outside in

After a long day of hiking, biking, rafting, or skiing, you need to know where to go for some inside fun. The **Attractions** sections tell you about museums, hot springs, shops, and other sights in the area that will distract the kids, get you out of inclement weather, or are just plain interesting places. In **Calendar of Events**, you'll find out what's going on in the area and what events locals are attending.

The **Restaurants** and **Lodgings** sections provide star-rated reviews of the best places to eat and sleep. (See the "About *Best Places* Guidebooks" segment in the beginning of this book for a description of how we rate and choose our restaurants and lodgings.) These listings are supplemented by **Ranches and Resorts** and **Backcountry Cabins,** which offer some additional unrated lodging options.

More Information

Finally, we wrap up each chapter with a list of useful phone numbers specific to that area. Ranger districts, chambers of commerce, visitors centers, and more are all included for your convenience.

Northern Rockies Outdoor Primer

The newfound popularity of backcountry recreation reemphasizes the pricelessness of our wildlands, and our responsibility to protect them. Take full advantage of the outdoor playground that is the Northern Rockies, but, please, be a responsible steward to the land and practice appropriate backcountry etiquette. Think about the importance of these precious places, and when you see them threatened, speak out. Remember: they will only stay wild if there's enough public support to keep them that way.

All the activities in this guidebook were researched to the best of our ability. Keep in mind, however, that any outdoor activity—whether it's hiking, kayaking, rafting, climbing, biking, or skiing—carries with it inherent risks. The natural world is a dynamic world and conditions can change quickly. We strongly encourage you to speak with US Forest Service and National Park Service rangers or Parks Canada officials before you set out. It is their job to help you enjoy the outdoors in a safe and responsible manner. Many forest service districts offer a brochure with regional highlights, detailing the best of their district's offerings. Rangers are familiar with current trail conditions and can assist you in planning a trip suited to your needs.

General Information

Wilderness Designations

The US Forest Service emphasizes a **multi-use** approach to forest service lands, and you are likely to encounter motorcycles, ATVs, and snowmobiles in many of these areas. Within national forests there are **designated wildernesses**, managed with an eye toward more solitude. Wilderness lands are off-limits to all but human and pack use. Motorized vehicles, bicycles, and motorized engines (such as chainsaws) are prohibited within designated wilderness boundaries. For more information, contact the US Forest Service Northern Region headquarters in Missoula, Montana (see below), or any district office. Also, look for information to become available on the Internet; access the Forest Service Home Page at www.fs.fed.us.

Phone Numbers

We've listed specific phone numbers at the end of each chapter, under **More Information,** geared toward the areas covered within that chapter.

The following numbers are useful for more general information:

US Forest Service Northern Region, Missoula, MT: *(406) 329-3511; for information about National Forest Service lands in Montana and northern Idaho.*

US Forest Service Intermountain Region, Ogden, UT: *(801) 625-5306; for information about National Forest Service lands in northwestern Wyoming and southern Idaho.*

Alberta Environmental Protection: *(403) 310-0000; for information about public lands in Alberta.*

Yellowstone National Park: *(307) 344-7381.*

Grand Teton National Park: *(307) 739-3300.*

Banff National Park: *(403) 762-1500.*

Jasper National Park: *(403) 852-6176 or (403) 852-6162.*

Idaho Travel Council, Boise, ID: *(800) 635-7820; for general travel information on Idaho.*

Travel Montana, Helena, MT: *(800) 847-4868 out-of-state, (406) 444-2654 in-state; for general travel information on Montana, ask for either the "Travel Planner," which lists hotels, motels, campgrounds, and outfitters, or the "Winter Guide," which details ski resorts, cross-country ski trails, and snowmobile routes.*

Wyoming Division of Tourism, Cheyenne, WY: *(303) 777-7777; for general travel information on Wyoming, ask for the "Wyoming Vacation Guide," which lists lodgings, dude ranches, and campgrounds.*

Travel Alberta, Edmonton, AB: *(800) 661-8888; for general travel information on Alberta.*

Camping

Reservations

Call the national parks or ranger districts directly for information about campsites and reservation policies; we have listed phone numbers for specific campgrounds whenever possible throughout this book. Generally, most public campgrounds operate on a **first-come, first-served** basis. During the summer months, especially on holiday weekends, get there early.

Many US Forest Service campgrounds accept reservations through their national system by calling (800) 280-CAMP. Participating campgrounds are indicated in the text, but you can always call to double-check.

In Montana, Travel Montana's "Travel Planner" (see above) lists all campgrounds and their facilities, particularly useful for **RV campers.** Tourism divisions can often also provide campground information.

Prices

We have not given camping fees for most of the public campgrounds listed in this book, as they often fluctuate. Fees generally range, however, between $5 and $15 (US). Remember that Canadian dollars are quoted in the Canadian chapters.

Leave No Trace

In an effort to reduce the risk of loving the backcountry to death, be sure to use "Leave No Trace" skills, developed by the National Outdoor Leadership School (NOLS); call (800) 332-4100 for additional information. Briefly summarized, they are as follows:

- Know the regulations and concerns for the areas you visit.
- Head into the backcountry in small groups, and avoid overcrowding of popular areas.
- Out of respect for other visitors, choose subdued colors for equipment and clothing.
- Whenever possible, stay on designated trails. If traveling cross-country, choose the most durable surfaces, and use a map and compass to eliminate the need for rock cairns, tree scars, and ribbons.
- When encountering a pack stock, step to the downhill side of the trail.
- Camp at least 200 feet from streams or lakes at established sites, and restrict activities to areas where vegetation is already compacted or absent.
- Pack it in, pack it out. Don't leave any garbage—including toilet paper and wipe—or even biodegradable food scraps at camp. If you see garbage left by other campers, take that, too.
- Bury human waste 6 to 8 inches deep, at least 200 feet from water, camp, or trails. Then cover and disguise the hole.
- Even biodegradable soap can harm fish and other organisms. When washing stay at least 200 feet away from streams or lakes. Scatter strained dishwater.
- Minimize use of campfires, which cause lasting impact. If you must build a fire, use existing fire rings, fire pans, or mound fires. Don't use sticks larger than an adult's wrist, and don't snap branches off live, dead, or downed trees.
- Extinguish fires completely using water—don't just bury them. Remove all unburned trash from your fire ring, and scatter the cool ashes over a large area well away from camp.
- Leave flowers, rocks, and other natural formations in the wild, so others can enjoy them.

Hiking/Backpacking

Distances listed for hiking (and skiing) trails are one-way, unless otherwise noted.

Because **weather conditions** change quickly, be prepared for all types of weather, especially when hiking. Rain gear is advisable for activities in the parks, and it's good to bring mittens or gloves and a hat at all times, regardless of the season. Snowfall can occur in June and September in areas above 7,500 feet (2250 m), and throughout the summer on peaks and ridges above 9,000 feet (2700 m). Snow is generally gone from the lower elevations by mid-May.

Throughout the Rockies, most lower-elevation trails are passable by mid-June, although snowfields may still cover the trails in places. Trails that cross through higher elevations are often not passable until late July. Some trails cross permanent **snowfields,** and hikers should use extreme caution. Because of the daily melting and freezing cycle, the snowfields can be icy. Hikers should carry an ice ax, when appropriate, and be experienced in using it to arrest a slide down the snowfield. There is also **avalanche danger** well into the summer in high elevations, and melting snows often create streams and rivers under the snowfields; when a snow bridge over a river thins, falling through into the river presents an extreme danger to hikers. If the situation warrants, hikers should consider roping up or taking other precautions.

High winds often precede and follow violent storms, and hikers should take care to get down off narrow ridges until the storm passes. Winter chinook winds sweeping down the eastern slopes of the Rockies have reached more than 100 mph. Heavy rains can swell what was a trickle in an avalanche chute to a raging torrent in just a few hours, and hikers will need to take appropriate precautions to avoid getting knocked down the hillside by the gushing water. During summer lightning storms, stay off exposed ridges and away from tall trees.

Hypothermia is always a threat but is especially a concern in the mountains. Hikers should know the warning signs and be prepared to take appropriate action should a hiking companion become hypothermic.

Recommended Gear

Boots or shoes designed for hiking, with good ankle support, are recommended. Look for those that provide good traction on rocky slopes and some protection from sharp rocks that slide off the hillsides and can easily clip your ankles. Always take **drinking water** on your hikes; park officials recommend boiling any water, even from rushing streams, before drinking it. It's also a good idea to pack some **rain gear** such as a poncho, an **extra jacket** (even on the warmest days), and a lunch in your day pack before striking out.

The **10 Essentials** is a list of survival gear developed primarily by The Mountaineers, a Seattle-based mountaineering group. It's important to carry these items on all outings, regardless of whether you're planning a simple day hike or a more strenuous multi-night backpack. In fact, bikers, skiers, climbers, and other recreationalists should also have these supplies:

- Compass
- Extra clothing
- Extra food
- Fire starter
- First-aid kit
- Flashlight or headlamp
- Map
- Matches
- Pocket knife
- Sunglasses

Please Call First

We can't emphasize enough how important it is that you speak with US Forest Service and National Park Service rangers or Parks Canada officials before heading out. They know their districts, parks, and trails, and can advise you of trail closures, weather conditions, wildlife, scenery, and crowds. Use the phone numbers provided in the **Hiking** and **More Information** sections of each chapter.

Biking

One of the best resources for mountain bikers and cyclists is the Missoula, Montana-based **Adventure Cycling Association,** (406) 721-1776, a non-profit informational organization. Adventure Cycling has maps available of the Great Divide Mountain Bike Route, which follows the Continental Divide as it bisects North America. The association also publishes bicycle touring maps of the US and Canada and puts out a catalog of biking guidebooks and other biking products. In addition, it publishes the *Cyclists' Yellow Pages,* a directory for bicycle tour planning that lists useful contacts, maps, and books.

Remember: mountain bikes are not allowed in designated wildernesses.

Kayaking/Canoeing/Rafting

For most outdoor activities, we advise you to talk with local US Forest Service or park officials. When it comes to kayaking, canoeing, and rafting, however, you're best off heading to the local outdoor store or outfitter for advice; they keep track of river conditions and can give you an idea of what obstacles you might encounter. Where appropriate, we've listed some good resources in individual chapters. Rangers can sometimes provide lists of approved or operating outfitters in their area.

Fishing

Please practice good fishing etiquette throughout the Northern Rocky Mountain region. Stick to **catch-and-release** fishing when possible. Watch for and try to avoid trout spawning beds (or redds), which are circular, depressed areas of shallow gravel. Don't add to **streamside erosion,** and try to keep river and lake areas clean by taking all your garbage home with you, including cigarette butts.

For information about fishing in Montana, contact the Montana Department of Fish, Wildlife and Parks in Helena, (406) 444-4720; for northwestern Wyoming, contact the Wyoming Game and Fish Department in Jackson, (307) 733-2321; for Idaho, call Idaho Fish and Game, (800) 635-7820; and for Alberta, contact Alberta Wildlife Department, (403) 297-6423.

Whirling Disease

In the mid-1950s, a shipment of frozen, processed European trout arrived in Pennsylvania. Scientists now believe that these fish were infected with "whirling disease," which subsequently spread to fish within the United States. Since then, the disease has infected fish in 20 states, causing large declines in fish populations. And there is no end in sight.

Caused by a single-celled parasite, *Myxobolus cerebralis,* that attacks the cartilage in young fish, whirling disease results in serious deformities, including sunken skulls and other cranial malformations; "black tail," in which a third of the fish turns black; and a curved skeleton, causing the "whirling" behavior for which the disease is named. While the disease itself is not fatal, these deformities leave young fish extremely vulnerable to predation. If, however, a fish manages to reach four or five inches (about a year old) without being affected by the parasite, it apparently has a much greater chance for survival; once the fish's cartilage ossifies into bone, the parasite no longer has the same devastating effect on its growth.

First detected in **Montana** in December of 1994 in the Madison River, whirling disease has decimated the rainbows there, killing as much as 90 percent of the population. At press time, the disease has spread to 30 Montana streams and rivers, mostly in the state's western portion and, with no known treatment and no sure way to prevent its further spread, whirling disease threatens the entire state's fish populations—particularly rainbow trout, which appear to be most susceptible. While the parasite has been observed in most cold-water fish—including rainbow, brown, brook, and westslope cutthroat trout, as well as salmon and grayling—so far its major victim has been the rainbow population. (Brown trout in the Madison, for instance, so far remain largely unaffected.) Extremely hardy, the parasite lives in both live and dead fish, in water, and in riverbed mud—in short, everywhere the fish live.

To help prevent the spread of whirling disease, the Montana Department of Fish, Wildlife and Parks has created a set of **guidelines:**

■ Remove all mud and aquatic plants from your vehicle, boat, anchor, trailer and axles, waders, boots, and fishing gear before departing the fishing access site or boat dock.

■ Drain all water from your boat and equipment—including coolers, buckets, and live wells—also before departing the fishing access site or boat dock.

■ Dry your boat and equipment between trips.

■ Don't transport fish from one body of water to another.

■ Don't dispose of fish entrails, skeletal parts, or other byproducts in any body of water.

■ Don't collect sculpins (bullheads) or use sculpins as bait.

Wildlife

The Watchable Wildlife Series, a public-private venture coordinated by Defenders of Wildlife, includes the *Montana and Idaho Wildlife Viewing Guides* (Falcon Press), useful publications that are widely available at outdoor stores.

Bear Necessities

The Northern Rockies are prime bear habitat for both **black bears** and **grizzlies.** Bears, however, are less interested in an encounter with you than you are with them. Bear attacks are rare and generally occur when a bear is surprised. If you follow proper precautions, you should not have to deal with a bear encounter. You will find specific information about bears in various chapters of this book, particularly in the Glacier National Park and Yellowstone National Park chapters, where bear-viewing and encounters are more frequent. **Rangers** at these and other parks can provide additional information and publications on how to behave properly.

While bears are unpredictable, the following suggestions, provided by the Interagency Grizzly Bear Committee, the Wyoming Game and Fish Department, and the US Fish & Wildlife Service, should preserve your safety:

Food and **odors** attract bears. Avoid smelly foods, such as tuna fish and peanut butter, and gut and clean fish away from your campsite. Don't sleep in the same clothes in which you cooked. Don't wear perfumes, cosmetics or scented products. In much of the Northern Rockies backcountry, there are special food storage requirements in place. Even where there aren't, however, it's a good idea to store food in a bear-proof container, or hang your food at least 10 feet high and at least four feet out from a tree trunk. Sleep at least 100 yards from properly stored food.

When hiking, make a lot of **noise**: sing, wear bear bells, or talk loudly at all times. Hiking in groups is a good idea. Keep your **dogs** under control. Dogs may startle and anger a bear, then lead it back to you.

If you do **encounter** a bear, don't look it in the eye—a sign of aggressive behavior. Instead, look down at the ground, talk in a soft monotone and back away slowly. If the bear begins to charge, don't run (you'll never outrun a bear), and don't try to climb a tree unless you have time to get 10 feet or higher. If the bear charges, stand your ground—bears often "mock charge" several times, then simply leave an area. Shooting a bear that's charging is not recommended, as the bear almost always remains alive long enough to seriously maul the shooter. As a last resort, crouch into a cannonball position with your hands behind your neck to play dead. Leave your backpack on for greater protection.

In the rare event that a bear enters your camp, get to safety as quickly as possible by slowly backing out of the area and looking for a tree to climb. Climb as high as you can and stay there until you are sure the bear is gone. If the bear should attack, fight back—playing dead will not work, as the bear has made a conscious choice to approach a human or attack. Don't remain in a campsite that has been visited by a bear.

Report all bear encounters to the authorities. Your report may save someone else's life.

For more information, contact the US Forest Service Northern Region headquarters in Missoula, Montana, and ask for the public relations office, (406) 329-3511.

Skiing/Winter Sports

As you might expect, the region is chock-full of ski resorts, and we've tried to list them all, with honest assessments of their strengths and weaknesses. Resorts in the Northern Rockies run the gamut, from national destinations such as Jackson Hole to regional destinations like Schweitzer.

And a lot of smaller, less expensive, family-owned day resorts—often favored by locals—are also included.

Travel Montana's "Winter Guide" (see General Information, above) lists all of that state's ski resorts and stats, as well as cross-country trails and popular snowmobile routes. Other visitors centers and tourism bureaus will have good information on snowmobiling in the region, while your best bet for backcountry skiing is to inquire at local outdoor stores and ranger districts. We've listed useful names and phone numbers in individual chapters.

Border Crossings

Canada

For any questions or concerns about arriving in Canada, contact Canadian Customs' Alberta Regional Office at 720, 220 - 4th Ave SE, Calgary, AB T2G 4X3; or call (403) 292-8750.

To enter Canada, US citizens or permanent residents do not need a passport but must have some kind of **identification,** such as a passport, birth certificate, voter's registration card, social security card, or driver's license. Visitors from other countries must have a valid passport. Sporting goods and personal baggage may need to be declared on arrival, and it's a good idea to register serial numbers of equipment such as cameras, bicycles, and skis. Mace or pepper spray, including bear spray, must have a Canadian agriculture department inspection number on the label or it will be confiscated; it can be left at the border and retrieved within 40 days. Fishing tackle is allowed, but serial numbers and descriptions should be provided. Ports of entry hours vary.

Canada uses dollars and cents as a monetary system with the same ratios as US dollars. Canadian businesses accept US money, but visitors should exchange **currency** as soon as possible. The best rate of exchange can be found at banks and at airport and border crossing exchange booths. ATMs marked with the Plus or Interac symbols will accept banking cards from outside Canada.

A seven percent **Goods & Services Tax** (GST) is applied to most goods and services in Canada. Foreign visitors may obtain a rebate of the GST by presenting original receipts to a Canadian Duty Free shop when leaving the country, or by mailing a refund application (available at the border stations) to Revenue Canada, Customs & Excise, Visitor Rebate Program, Ottawa, Canada K1A 1J5; call (800) 668-4748 in Canada or (613) 991-3346 outside Canada for more information.

Visitors may want to obtain travelers' health insurance, unless their personal health insurance plan includes coverage outside the country of residence. Charges of adult hospital care can start at $900, and some provinces impose a surcharge of up to 30 percent on care for non-residents.

Posted **temperatures** are in Celsius with the freezing point 0 degrees. To convert Celsius to Fahrenheit, multiply Celsius temperature by 1.8 and add 32; to convert Fahrenheit to Celsius, subtract 32 from Fahrenheit temperature and divide by 1.8.

All **measurements** follow the metric system. Distances are noted in kilometers, where 1 kilometer (km) is equal to ⅝ mile. To convert kilometers to miles, multiply number of kilometers by 0.6; to convert miles to kilometers, multiply number of miles by 1.6. Speed limits are posted in kilometers per hour (100 km/hr on highway signs is equal to 60 miles per hour). Volume is usually measured in liters, where 1 liter is equal to 0.22 US gallons. To convert US gallons to liters, multiply gallons by 3.79; to convert liters to gallons, multiply liters by 0.22. (Note that a Canadian gallon is one-fifth larger than a US gallon, so 10 Canadian gallons equal 12 US gallons.)

United States

Canadian citizens or permanent residents do not need a passport to enter the US, but must show some type of valid identification, such as a passport, driver's license, or birth certificate. Proof of Canadian citizenship (a *certified* birth certificate or a passport) is recommended by US customs agents but is not mandatory.

For questions or concerns about returning to the US or customs regulations about bringing purchased goods or alcohol into the US, contact your local Customs office for a free brochure, "Know Before You Go." In Seattle call (206) 553-8274, and in Spokane call (509) 353-2833.

About Best Places® Guidebooks

The restaurant and lodging reviews in this book are written in the *Best Places* guidebook tradition. The *Best Places* series is unique in the sense that each guide is written by and for locals, and is therefore coveted by travelers. The best places in the region are the ones that denizens favor: establishments of good value, often independently owned, touched with local history, run by lively individuals, and graced with natural beauty. *Best Places* reviews are completely independent: no advertisers, no sponsors, no favors.

All evaluations are based on numerous reports from local and traveling inspectors. *Best Places* writers do not identify themselves when they review an establishment, and they accept no free meals, accommodations, or any other services. Every place featured in this book is recommended, even those with no stars.

Stars

Restaurants and lodgings are rated on a scale of zero to four stars, based on uniqueness, loyalty of local clientele, performance measured against goals, excellence of cooking, value, enjoyment level, and professionalism of service. Reviews are listed by star rating.

☆☆☆☆   The very best in the region
☆☆☆   Distinguished; many outstanding features
☆☆   Excellent; some wonderful qualities
☆   A good place
no stars   Worth knowing about, if nearby

Price Range

In Canadian chapters, prices are in Canadian dollars. All prices are subject to change. Contact the establishment directly to verify.

$$$ Expensive (more than $80 for dinner for two; more than $100 for lodgings for two)
$$ Moderate (between expensive and inexpensive)
$ Inexpensive (less than $30 for dinner for two; less than $60 for lodgings for two)

Directions

Basic directions are provided with each review; contact each business to confirm hours and location.

Checks and Credit Cards

Most establishments that accept checks require a major credit card for identification. American Express is abbreviated as AE, Diners Club as DC, Discover as DIS, MasterCard as MC, Visa as V.

Ranches and Resorts

The listings under Ranches and Resorts range from dude ranches to fly-fishing resorts, and are intended for active folks who have a week or more to spend exploring the outdoors. These listings tend to be more expensive than other lodgings, and often have week-long minimum stays. Call ahead for specific information about activities offered by each establishment.

Backcountry Cabins

Backcountry cabins are designated as such by their remoteness—many of these cabins are inaccessible by low-clearance vehicles and require a hike or ski in. In the US they are often run by National Forest Service rangers and some are old fire lookouts. Most US cabins cost between $15 and $30 per night; in Canada prices vary widely. Cabins are often primitive, with no heat or indoor plumbing. Call the ranger district in the specific area for more information and reservations.

Reader Reports

At the end of this book is a report form. Feedback from readers, either suggesting new places or agreeing or disagreeing with our assessments, greatly benefits our research and helps inform our evaluations. We encourage and appreciate your response.

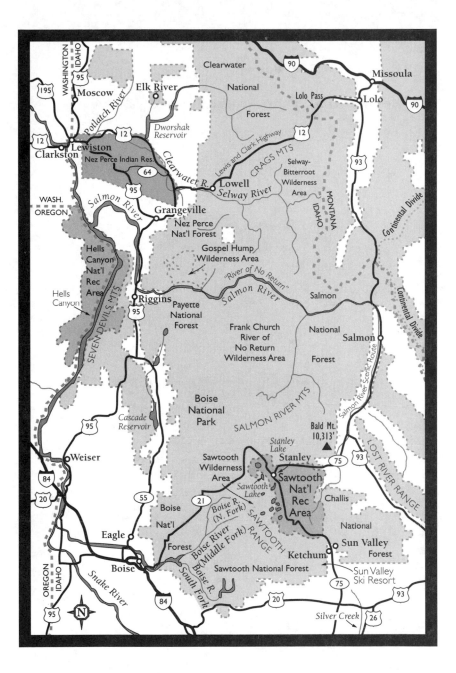

Central
Idaho

Central
Idaho

Boise and Sun Valley

Including Ketchum, Stanley, and the Sawtooth National Recreation Area.

Sun Valley is nearly synonymous with Idaho, almost to the exclusion of the rest of the state. For decades it's been the outdoor playground of the rich and famous who ski or fly-fish on nearby rivers. With Ketchum, as its base town, Sun Valley is at the doorstep of prime Rocky Mountain real estate—most of it virtually unknown and unspoiled, despite its fame. It has become one of the nation's premier downhill ski destinations, with 10,313-foot Bald Mountain towering over the communities and beckoning skiers to its slopes like a siren.

Once an area inhabited only by traveling bands of Shoshoni or Bannock Indians, in the 1930s, Union Pacific Railroad Chairman Averell Harriman contracted an Austrian surveyor, Count Felix Schaffgotsch, to scour the West in search of the perfect spot to build a destination ski resort. After visiting a number of areas— including Jackson Hole, Alta, Yosemite, Mount Rainier, and Mount Hood—the Count was still not satisfied. His long search ended with Ketchum, the last site he visited and from where he immediately wired Harriman: "Among the many attractive spots I have visited, this combines more delightful features of any place I have seen in the United States, Switzerland, or Austria for a winter sports resort." Sun Valley Resort opened with international fanfare on December 21, 1936. The guest list for the grand opening included millionaire socialites and Hollywood stars—a cross-section of society that still maintains residences in the famous area.

Count Schaffgotsch recognized the potential of the valley as a winter resort, but the area also offers a host of outdoor activities for summer visitors. Backcountry adventure awaits just outside the city limits for enthusiastic hikers or mountain bikers. Stanley, a small town just north of Sun Valley (the year-round population occasionally tops 70), is at the heart of the Sawtooth National Recreation Area, a paradise for outdoor adventurers. The town was named for explorer and gold prospector John Stanley, who led a group of miners into the area in July 1864. The miners soon became discouraged by the isolation, supply shortages, and tense relations with native Shoshoni Indians. The party left, but others returned. During the 1870s more than a half-million dollars in gold was taken from the Stanley Mining District. Like many mountain towns, Stanley turned from the mining industry to tourism, and it's well-situated to make this transformation. Each year, more than 1.5 million visitors from around the world find their way to this community, nestled comfortably at the foot of megalithic granite peaks that make for a breathtaking year-round setting.

The Sawtooth National Recreation Area, one of the largest and most scenic in the country, is easily the crown jewel of Idaho's treasury of natural beauty. Four mountain ranges—the Sawtooths, Smokies, White Clouds, and Boulders—provide magnificent landscapes in every direction. With 40 peaks reaching over 10,000 feet and thousands of high-mountain lakes, the 756,000-acre Sawtooth Recreation Area is an outdoor lover's dream come true.

Centrally located in the state, Boise is well out on the high-elevation sagebrush plains that stretch north from Utah and on west into eastern Oregon and Washington. Its terrain is more desert than mountain, and the snowfall is seldom enough to qualify the city as a winter destination, although summers provide hot, dry days and cool, pleasant evenings. Although Boise, itself, isn't exactly an outdoor destination, it does have its charms and is the gateway to Sun Valley and the Sawtooths.

Getting There

Sun Valley and the adjoining communities are at the foot of the Rockies, but Boise, the Idaho state capital, is the gateway through which most mountain visitors must pass. To reach Boise, take Interstate 15 from the south or northeast, then I-84; take I-90 from the north. Several major airlines offer daily service to Boise Municipal Airport, (208) 383-3110, which is 3 miles from downtown. The airport is a hub for those arriving on major airlines, from which you must transfer to commuter flights to Sun Valley. Amtrak offers daily service to Boise; call (800) 872-7245.

Ketchum/Sun Valley is north of I-84 from Twin Falls on Idaho Highway

75. *Stanley is just 64 miles north of Sun Valley on Hwy 75, at the junction with US Highway 21. Several commuter airlines (sometimes affiliated with the major carriers) offer daily flights to Hailey, (208) 788-4956, just south of Sun Valley.*

Adjoining Areas

NORTH: **Lewiston and the Snake River**

EAST: **Bitterroot Valley**

inside out

Fly-Fishing

From fast-moving waters to quietly flowing spring creeks, the Sun Valley-Ketchum area has it all. The area has become known as an angler's paradise, due in part to famous fisherman Ernest Hemingway, who spent his later years here.

Anglers snap their lines into the rivers and streams throughout the summer. But summers are short, so the fishing season comes and goes at a furious pace (there are only an average of 40 frost-free days a year in the region). Wading the streams can be refreshing and enjoyable in the heat of summer, but waders are a must outside the peak summer heat (July and August). An Idaho fishing license is required; changes in fishing regulations and possession limits warrant a check with local fish and game regulations prior to fishing.

The **Big Wood River** offers fishermen a classic freestone stream of medium size, with an abundance of available insect life to feed the numerous and surprisingly large population of trout. Overfishing in the past had greatly depleted the numbers of fish in the Big Wood River; however, a strict policy of catch-and-release for nearly 20 miles of river, as well as a slot limit of two fish under 12 inches for approximately 12 miles of river, has brought the population back. The river runs the length of the Wood River Valley. Accessibility is an easy matter from nearly anywhere in the area.

Fishable tributaries to the Big Wood River include **Trail Creek, Warm Springs,** and the **North Fork of the Lost River.** These small streams can be enjoyed by anglers of all abilities. The trout in these waters tend to be smaller than in other waterways, but they are active and, as a general rule, will readily take a well-presented fly.

Silver Creek is arguably one of the most famous waterways in the fly-fishing world. The summer mayfly hatches here are nearly as famous as the trout themselves. With the abundance of insect life to feed on, the Silver Creek trout grow to spectacular size, and will not tolerate a slouch at the end of the fly rod. Spider web-thin tippets and flies the size of baby gnats are required to fool the most selective and sophisticated of them. Silver Creek represents one of the last examples of a high-desert, cold-spring ecosystem; its waters flow entirely from springs emanating from an aquifer below the foot of the mountains to the north. Silver Creek is located within the boundaries of the Silver Creek Preserve, run by The Nature Conservancy (TNC), south of Ketchum and near the town of Picabo. Fishermen planning on testing their skills at Silver Creek must first sign in at the TNC Visitor Center.

Many fishing **guide services** are available for anglers looking to maximize their time on the water (see More Information, below). Silver Creek Outfitters, (507 N Main St, Ketchum, (208) 726-5282), and Bill Mason Outfitters in the Sun Valley Mall, (208) 622-9305, are widely recognized as the top fly-fishing guide services in the area.

Mountain Biking/Cycling

Hundreds of miles of biking, hiking, and skiing trails are accessible from the Ketchum/Sun Valley area. Trails for everyone from rank beginner to trail expert can be found in this amazing and scenic area. Mountain bike and cross-country or backcountry ski rentals can be found at the Elephants Perch, (208) 726-3497, on Sun Valley Road in Ketchum, or Backwoods Mountain Sports, (208) 726-8818, on Main Street. There is no shortage of outdoor sporting goods shops and guide services in and around Ketchum.

The **Adams Gulch Area Trail System** is considered the premier spot in the area to mountain bike (although hikers also use these trails). Breathtaking mountain views, the mixed terrain, and a well-maintained trail system make the area a must-visit. It's located just 1 ½ miles north of Ketchum on Hwy 75. Turn left on Adams Gulch Rd, veer right after crossing a bridge, and continue on to the trailhead.

The **Shadyside Trail,** on the southern side of Adams Gulch, is an easy 1 ½-mile one-way route kept cool by the shade of forest and valley walls. The **Adams Gulch Loop** offers bikers and hikers a more challenging 5 ½-mile loop. It incorporates magnificent vistas with exhilarating, moderately difficult riding. Bring plenty of water; a Forest Service sign at the trailhead diagrams other trail options.

A left turn at the Lake Creek Trailhead, 4 miles north of Ketchum on Hwy 75, brings you to the beginning of the **Fox Creek Loop.** This trail

(No. 149) is a 5-mile loop that parallels picturesque Fox Creek for approximately 2 1/4 miles. The trail turns to the left at the 1 3/4-mile point and continues up Fox Creek before making another left turn and heading back south toward the trailhead. This trail can be difficult but offers exceptional views of the Boulder Mountains. Watch for hikers, other bikers, and equestrians also looking for excellent mountain views.

Near Boise, off-road mountain bike trails are found mostly north of town, as the wide-open, high-desert flatlands south of town make for hot and tedious riding. The trails north of Boise see a fair amount of traffic from cyclists and hikers, as well as motorcyclists and ATV riders. Many trails can also be found through the sage-covered hills surrounding Boise.

The **Swan Falls Loop** is a scenic, fairly flat 17 1/2-mile ride that follows the Snake River on a road suitable only for vehicles with four-wheel drive. The trail is within the Snake River Birds of Prey National Wildlife Refuge Area (see Wildlife, below), home to dense populations of nesting raptors. To get to the Swan Falls Loop take I-84 west from Boise to the Meridian exit. Turn south and drive 10 miles to Kuna. On the east edge of Kuna watch for a sign indicating the way to the Snake River Birds of Prey area. Turn south and drive 17 miles to Swan Falls Dam. A steep switchback takes you to the bottom of the canyon. Park downstream from the dam; the road will have a wide variety of obstacles and riding terrain, depending on the time of year—from ruts, rocks, and spring creek crossings to sandy spots in the road and a braided trail system. Halverson Lake, a water-filled lava tube about 8 1/2 miles down the trail, makes a good lunch stop. A single-track trail up a small ridge at the western end of the lake winds through a brushy boulder field. The trail then descends back toward the river. The remains of an old stone cabin, built around the turn of the century by Chinese laborers, is located about 1 mile east. Proceed back the way you came to Swan Falls Dam. Although people frequently use this area, it is still a good idea to come prepared. Bring plenty of water and a patch kit for your tires.

The **Corral Loop** is a relatively strenuous 15-mile ride just north of Boise on Bogus Basin Rd. Riders can drive about 3 miles up Bogus Basin Rd to the Corral Loop turnout. This road is currently unmarked, so it can be a bit evasive. The dirt road takes off to the east, where a broken-down cattle gate and a cable across the road signify the beginning of the Corral Loop ride. Follow the dirt road through the foothills. The riding here is easy and offers a real taste of the high desert. Ride past the remnants of old stock corrals and a small cluster of satellite antennae on the north side of the trail. The trail loses elevation as it drops to a northern turn into a gulch. The trail then heads uphill to the crux of the ride. After a steep one-quarter-mile-long climb the trail tops out at an intersection. Take the center route headed downhill and east. This single track again loses elevation quickly as it winds through brushy, rolling terrain. Take a left turn where the trail comes to a road. A short ride up and over the cattle gate places you on a four-wheel-drive road. Follow this road just over a mile to a trailmarker on the left-hand side. This next portion of the trail is probably the best mountain biking in the Boise area. The trail breezes across open hillsides before plunging down into a foothill gulch, crossing a small stream several times during spring and early summer. Follow this trail downhill until it comes out at the end of a housing development. Follow the paved road, taking the first right turn, to a stop sign. Turn right again and coast downhill back to Bogus Basin Rd. Turn right and huff it 3 miles back to your vehicle.

The **Boise River Greenbelt** is a 29-mile paved pathway that parallels the Boise River and bisects Idaho's capital city. The multi-use pathway is quite popular with the city's cyclists, as well as its in-line skating and walking contingents. The Boise River Greenbelt extends from Discovery State Park, about 8 miles east of Boise, through eight major parks and the Warm Springs Golf Course to the town of Eagle. It can be accessed from any of the city parks adjacent to the Boise River. Ann Morrison Park, on the south side of the Boise River between Americana and Boise Avenue, and Julia Davis Park, on the north side of the river between Capital and Broadway Aves, are the most popular starting points for users of the Greenbelt.

Cyclists or in-line skaters looking to escape the sometimes congested conditions on the Greenbelt may want to begin at **Municipal Park.** To get there from Warm Springs Ave, turn south onto Walnut Ave and continue 2 1/2 blocks; Municipal Park will be on the east side of the road. From Municipal Park, follow the Boise River Greenbelt east (upstream) toward Discovery Park. The route leaves Municipal Park and quickly winds through the groomed and manicured vistas of the Warm Springs Golf Course. The path parallels the river for a short while, then leaves the riverbanks for several miles; this stretch has little shade, so it's quite hot during spring and summer. Be sure to carry water, since it's nearly 8 miles to the next water fountain. The pathway begins up a canyon as the Greenbelt reconnects with the Boise River. Cliffs of columnar basalt rise above the river to the left. The **Black Cliffs,** as they are called by locals, are frequented by rock climbers. It's a great place for cyclists to take a break beside the Greenbelt and watch the climbers practice their skills. Municipal Park to Discovery Park is an out-and-back ride of about 18 miles. Summer heat can be brutal, so consider a morning or evening ride from June to September.

Riding the Boise River Greenbelt downstream from **Ann Morrison**

Park is an enjoyable jaunt along the water. As the path leaves Ann Morrison Park, it travels through three underpasses; the last is the Main St underpass, but users of the Greenbelt will find it easy to forget they are in the middle of a capital city at this point. The Greenbelt winds between the Boise River and a number of **fishing ponds** that lie on the river's north side. Several dirt side trails wind around these ponds to provide fishing access. This area is home to muskrat and beavers, as well as ducks and geese. Great blue herons can also occasionally be seen plying the shallow sections of the river or ponds for a quick fish snack, while Bald eagles have been spotted in the tops of cottonwood snags that line this section of the river.

The Greenbelt passes Veterans Memorial Park and under Veterans Memorial Parkway as it approaches the Willow Lane Athletic Complex. A series of **outdoor work-out stations** with instructions line the Greenbelt to the right. **Softball** and **soccer** games continue almost any time of year at the Willow Lane complex. From Willow Lane, the Boise River Greenbelt passes the Idaho State Fairgrounds and the Les Bois Horse Racing Facility. The Greenbelt ends in Eagle.

Rent bicycles in Boise at Idaho Mountain Touring, 915 W Jefferson, (208) 336-3854. Action Sports, (15th and Front St, (208) 383-0073), also offers a good selection of rental equipment.

Hiking/Backpacking

Visitors planning to hike in the Sun Valley area should be well prepared. Along with rugged natural beauty comes potential hazards. Temperatures can drop to nighttime lows below freezing during any month of the year. Weather changes at high elevation can happen in a blink of an eye. Hiking boots with good ankle support are a must, as is appropriate clothing. Hikers should bring plenty of water, since dehydration can occur more rapidly at higher elevations. The hikes discussed in this chapter are all well-marked trail routes, but it is still a good idea to have a map and compass handy.

The **Trail Creek** area northeast of Sun Valley is one of the most popular destinations for hikers and those who want to see some of the varied terrain that is snow-covered in winter. Most of the Trail Creek routes afford outstanding views of Bald Mountain and the town of Sun Valley. (Hikers here should be aware that equestrians and bikers also use the trails.) To get to the Trail Creek area drive east from Ketchum on Sun Valley Rd for 3 miles. Turn right at the **Trail Creek Cabin** (see Cross-Country Skiing, below). Some of our favorites follow.

The **Aspen Loop Trail** (No. 119A on maps) offers a rolling hike through beautiful stands of mixed aspen and conifer. The Aspen Loop is an easy 1 ¾-mile walk.

The **Corral Creek Trail** (No. 119B) is a more difficult 7-mile out-and-back hike. The trail bypasses Boundary Campground, then follows Trail Creek upstream for approximately 1 mile. In another half mile the trail takes a slight right-hand tack where it begins to follow Corral Creek drainage to the trail's end—about 3 ½ miles. Corral Creek offers pleasant hiking through sweet-smelling sage and beautiful stands of aspen. The proximity to the water provides a good chance of viewing wildlife that take advantage of the cooler streamside temperatures.

More adventurous hikers can tackle the **Proctor Mountain Trail** (No. 119), a 6-mile round-trip hike that rewards with an excellent view of Bald Mountain. Near the peak of Proctor Mountain, note the remains of the world's first chairlift. The design for this relic was based on a conveyor system used by freighter ships to load bananas. Past this point, be careful as the trail branches and tends to become confusing.

Aspen Loop, Proctor Mountain, and Corral Creek Trails are all located behind the Trail Creek Cabin. If catered functions are going on at the cabin, the trails may also be accessed a quick half mile up the road from Boundary Campground. The trail is visible at several points along Trail Creek Rd and may be accessed easily from these points.

The Sawtooth Mountains just outside of Stanley have often been called Idaho's version of the Swiss Alps. These jagged granite peaks that thrust to more than 10,000 feet got their name from early explorers who felt the rugged skyline resembled the upturned teeth of a crosscut saw. Even day hikers can access breathtaking vistas rivaling (and some say exceeding) those found in the Tetons. And the Sawtooth National Recreation Area is this wilderness at its best—awe-inspiring natural beauty that most folks only see on picture postcards.

The **Fishhook Creek Trail** is an easy 4 ⅖-mile round-trip hike just south of Stanley. To get to the trailhead, drive south from Stanley approximately 4 miles on Hwy 75, turning west onto paved Redfish Lake Rd; continue 2 miles to the Fishhook Creek trailhead parking lot. The trail begins just across the road northwest of the parking lot. The marked trail follows an old road up the right side of Fishhook Creek, as it rollicks down its rocky course. The majority of the hike is along this old road, which is closed to motor vehicles. The hike gains 242 feet and tops out at about 6,800 feet. At about 2 miles, the trail enters a glaciated valley with a picturesque meadow where a beaver dam creates a quiet pond. Mountain peaks frame the valley on both sides. Horstmann Peak rises to 10,470 feet on the left, while 10,751-foot Thompson Peak reaches skyward on the right. A dazzling array of wildflowers awaits hikers who visit the Fishhook Creek area from late spring to midsummer.

Bridalveil Falls plunge hundreds of feet in a cascade of lacy water. This multi-leveled fall tumbles through lush foliage and clumps of brightly colored wildflowers, and its namesake trail offers hikers a moderate 8-mile round-trip trek through meadow and forest. The sandy trail meanders through high meadows and crosses crystal-clear Stanley Lake Creek at about 3 miles. Rugged McGown Peak, 9,860 feet high, overlooks the panoramic scenery. Deer and elk frequently graze in the meadows along the way. The falls can be seen to the right at 4 miles. To get to the Bridalveil Falls trailhead, drive northwest of Stanley on US 21 for 5 miles. Turn left onto Stanley Lake Rd and go 3 4/5 miles to the Inlet Campground. The trailhead is located at a marked gateway just west of the campground. In early spring, hikers should be aware that the meadows along the Bridalveil Falls Trail can be saturated with runoff; the trail may be closed until the area dries out. Early summer is the best time to hike this trail, when the fresh meadows are carpeted with wildflowers.

Flatrock Junction is an easy 7-mile round-trip route that rewards hikers with dramatic views capturing the essence of the Sawtooth Mountains. The trail through Redfish Canyon, a glacial trough framed by granite spires and hanging valleys, offers up incredible alpine views at each bend of the trail. At 1 1/2 miles, the trail winds through an area littered with huge boulders and towering rock formations called the Garden of the Giants. To reach the Flatrock Junction trailhead turn west on Redfish Lake Rd, about 4 miles south of Stanley on Hwy 75. Drive 2 3/10 miles to Redfish Lake Lodge, (208) 774-3536. The lodge operates a boat shuttle service to the trailhead on the opposite side of the lake. There the trail to Flatrock starts in the campground and proceeds northwest to a Forest Service registration box. Follow the trail up the canyon to Flatrock Junction where trails to **Alpine** and **Cramer Lakes** split off. The left branch of the trail continues for about 12 miles to Cramer Lakes. The right branch climbs nearly a thousand feet in 2 miles to scenic Alpine Lake.

Sawtooth Lake, the largest lake in the Sawtooth Wilderness area, sparkles emerald and sapphire as it reflects the 10,190-foot visage of Mount Regan. The hike to the lake winds a 9 1/2-mile round-trip course through forests of lodgepole pine. It fords tumbling Iron Creek, cuts through wildflower meadows, and zigzags up granite steps and benches as it gains 1,700 feet in elevation. The views are spectacular along this well-used trail. The route begins at the **Iron Creek Trailhead.** To reach it, drive 2 1/2 miles north of Stanley on US 21, then turn west on Iron Creek Rd and continue 3 miles to the transfer camp. The trailhead is well-marked and clearly visible. A trail junction at 1 1/5 miles splits off toward

Marshall Lake and the Stanley Ranger Station. The Iron Creek Trail continues up the side of a ridge where it makes several cutbacks as it gains elevation. A junction at 3 4/5 miles offers a 200-yard path to Alpine Lake. (Hikers examining topo maps of the Sawtooth National Recreation Area might note that with more than a thousand lakes, this is just one of several named "Alpine.") Continue on the main branch of the trail less than a mile to Sawtooth Lake.

The **Boise River Greenbelt** (see Mountain Biking/Cycling, above) is quite popular with city walkers.

Rafting

One of Stanley's most popular summertime tourist activities is floating the **Salmon River.** The river is typically floatable from April through September and offers adventure seekers a thrilling ride on Class II and III whitewater.

Migrating chinook salmon use the Salmon River during the fall as a spawning area. The decline in the number of returning chinook has sparked recovery measures, as well as controversy, in the Stanley area. In late summer and early fall parts of the Salmon River are completely closed to boaters in efforts to aid recovery of the river's chinook populations. Day floats on the upper Salmon generally take between 3 and 6 hours. Floaters will enjoy crystal-clear, smooth water stretches interspersed with exhilarating rapids as they drift through rugged country first explored in the early 1820s.

Several whitewater **guide services** operate out of Stanley and the surrounding area. Float trips can be chartered in Stanley through the highly recommended River Company, (208) 744-2244, in west Stanley on US 21, May through September. The guides are expert boat handlers who also have a working knowledge of local history and wildlife. Trips depart from Stanley twice a day; the most popular floats are those that include a tasty riverside meal prepared Dutch oven-style. Floaters with the River Company can pick their craft. Those who like to get involved can grab a paddle and dig in under the direction of the guide, while other rafts let passengers relax and take in the scenery while the guide rows. Inflatable kayaks allow confident floaters to cut the apron strings and test their skills alone, with the guide leading the way. Photographers from Sawtooth Photography, (208) 774-3332, are located at the larger whitewater sections of the float, where they shoot pictures of rafters as they brave the rapids. The film is then rushed to the studio in Stanley where it is developed that afternoon and awaits those who would like a memento of their Salmon River experience.

Floating the **Boise River** is perhaps the one activity that truly identi-fies the Boise lifestyle. Floaters on all manner of inflatable watercraft bob along on the river's cool waters. Hundreds of floaters make this trip each day during the hot summer. Floaters put in at Barber Park, east of Boise and just off Eckert Rd, on the south side of the river, where there is an air-filling station. The take-out at Municipal Park is about 4 miles down-stream. The Boise River flows along at a gentle clip but offers some exhilaration as it drops over a pair of 2-foot waterfalls.

Downhill Skiing

The **Sun Valley Ski Resort,** (800) 786-8259, built its popularity in the late '30s and early '40s on the merit of its skiing venues. Bald Mountain (also known as Baldy Mountain), rising 9,151 feet above sea level, is the centerpiece to Sun Valley's winter recreation scene. Fourteen chairlifts provide access to runs for skiers of all abilities. The most sophisticated and complete snow-making system in the world insures there is plenty of the white stuff even during low-snow years. Five lodges interspersed on the mountain provide first-class service to hungry skiers looking for a midday break, while a pair of heated outdoor pools are available for soak-ing after a day of skiing. Ice skating, shopping, and elegant dining top out the list of amenities at this premier resort.

Skiers taking off from the new River Run Plaza have a 4-minute ride on a high-speed quad to a junction where the skier has a choice of three lifts and destinations. The center lift, the Lookout Express, whisks skiers to the summit of Bald Mountain and incredible alpine views in a quick 5-minute ride. The Exhibition lift, to the left, provides access to the Seattle Ridge area, while the Sunnyside lift, to the right, accesses the Warm Springs area of the mountain. A nice mixture of intermediate to advanced runs awaits skiers who opt for the Warm Springs area. The Flying Squirrel and Picabo Street runs provide intermediate skiers with excellent and challenging terrain.

Sun Valley ski lifts operate daily, although access to the Seattle Ridge closes midafternoon. Lessons for beginners to expert are available through the Sun Valley Sports Center, (208) 622-2288.

Cross-Country Skiing

The **Sun Valley Nordic Center,** (800) SUN-VALY or (208) 622-2250, located just behind Sun Valley Resort, maintains about 25 miles of marked and beautifully groomed cross-country ski trails. Trail difficulty ranges from "easier" to "most difficult" at this world-class facility, where Nordic fans have access to all the same amenities as downhillers. The center offers rental equipment and instruction in cross-country and telemark skiing.

One of the most popular winter experiences in the Sun Valley-Ketchum area is a visit to the **Trail Creek Cabin**. This cabin, constructed of log and rock, was a favorite New Year's Eve hideaway of early movie stars, such as Gary Cooper and Clark Gable. Just a short 1 3/4-mile cross-country ski jaunt from the famed Sun Valley Nordic Center, today the Trail Creek Cabin offers hearty lunches and dinners in a rustic setting; meals range in price from $16 to $24, and reservations are required, (208) 622-2135. Tours to the cabin follow a groomed, designated trail over gentle terrain, winding through spectacular meadows that evoke a true winter wonderland. Sleigh rides to the restaurant are also available. Skiers may want to take a moment to visit the **Hemingway Memorial** located in a quiet grove alongside Trail Creek.

Wildlife

Birders with a passion for raptors will be well rewarded in the **Snake River Birds of Prey Natural Area**, (208) 362-8687, 482 acres of public land along 81 miles of the Snake River Canyon. Located about an hour's drive south of Boise, the region boasts the largest concentration of nesting raptors on the continent. In addition, many species that actually nest elsewhere spend winters here, making it a mecca for bird-watchers year-round. Fourteen species of **raptors** nest here, including American kestrels; northern harriers; red-tailed, Swainson's and ferruginous hawks; golden eagles; turkey vultures; and long- and short-eared owls. Wintering species include bald eagles, merlins, goshawks, osprey, and rough-legged and sharp-shinned hawks. The area is more desert than forest, so expect to see sagebrush **songbirds** as well. Best viewing times are between mid-March and July; after that the heat here can be intense. The area is managed by the Bureau of Land Management, Boise District, 3948 Development Ave, Boise, ID 83705; (208) 384-3300.

Nearly 115 miles of the Snake River banks are protected in the **Deer Flat National Wildlife Refuge**. Perhaps more important than the banks are the islands—107 of them—which are prime nesting grounds for birds and home to **beaver** and **mink**. Thousands of **waterfowl** can be seen in the refuge, including white pelicans, gulls, black-crowned night herons, avocets, goldeneyes, Canada geese, mergansers, widgeon, and teal. There are also **raptors** and **songbirds**, and **red foxes** den near the observation tower. The refuge surrounds Lake Lowell, which is ringed by roads. Boat traffic is allowed on the lake. From Nampa west of Boise, drive south on 12th Ave to Lake Lowell Ave and go 4 miles to the refuge sign. Deer Flat

National Wildlife Refuge, 13751 Upper Embankment Rd, Nampa, ID 83686; (208) 467-9678.

A trio of National Wildlife Refuges in the most southeastern portion of Idaho offer opportunities to see white-faced ibises, sandhill cranes, grebes, gadwalls, shovelers, trumpeter swans, and peregrine falcons. **Bear Lake National Wildlife Refuge** claims the largest nesting colonies of **white-faced ibis** anywhere, on Dingle Swamp. But there are plenty of other birds to watch on the refuge and on Bear Lake. White pelicans can be seen here, even though this isn't their breeding area, and diligent birders will see American bitterns. There's an auto tour and trails on dikes (closed until July 1 to minimize disturbance to nesting birds; canoeing is allowed only after July 1 also). About 7 miles west of Montpelier, take Hwy 89 about 2 miles, then go 5 miles on a gravel road (turn at the refuge sign). Bear Lake National Wildlife Refuge, 370 Webster, Box 9, Montpelier, ID 83254; (208) 847-1757.

A reintroduced population of **trumpeter swans** has successfully nested on **Grays Lake National Wildlife Refuge,** so refuge officials hope the rare swans will thrive here. Bring a spotting scope to see these shy birds. The other rare bird here is the **peregrine falcon,** transplanted here from the Idaho Birds of Prey Center and also visible via spotting scope. Other species are more abundant, such as **Franklin's gull,** which nests here in a colony of more than 10,000 birds. Eared and western **grebes** also nest here. Behind the refuge headquarters there is a viewing platform, but some of the best vantage points are from the roads outside the refuge. Take State Route 34 north from Soda Springs about 35 miles to the refuge turnoff. Grays Lake National Wildlife Refuge, 74 Grays Lake Rd, Wayan, ID 83285; (208) 574-2755.

Lake Walcott in the **Minidoka National Wildlife Refuge** supports the only breeding population of **white pelicans** in the state. Other birds include snowy egrets, great blue herons, western grebes, great horned owls, and, of course, mallards and Canada geese. **Songbirds** here are sagebrush desert varieties—sage thrashers, larks, sage sparrows, and kingbirds. **Pronghorn antelope** also live in this refuge, one of the oldest in the nation, set aside by President Theodore Roosevelt in 1909 after construction of a dam across the Snake River created Lake Walcott. The best way to see this refuge is from a canoe (bring your own, although sometimes boat rentals are available), April to September. The refuge terrain is rugged and cut by basalt ridges, so a four-wheel-drive vehicle is highly recommended, as are sturdy hiking boots. Take I-84 east from Burley to the Burley-Rupert exit, then go north on US 24 through Rupert to the refuge sign. Continue 6 miles northeast on US 24 to another refuge sign, then go 6 miles east on County Rd 400 to Minidoka Dam. Minidoka

National Wildlife Refuge, 961 E Minidoka Dam, Rupert, ID 83350; (208) 436-3589.

The **Morrison Knudson Nature Reserve** in Boise's Municipal Park recreates a **wild trout** habitat. We recommend a quick tour through the outdoor facility. Underwater viewing stations give an excellent view of the trout's life stages and habitat. Viewing 10-pound rainbow trout from beneath the water surface is well worth the free admission.

Other Activities

The Sawtooth National Recreation Area boasts some of the most stunning scenery Idaho has to offer. Those who prefer to see the mountains from a broader perspective can fly over the peaks. Stanley Air Taxi, (208) 744-2276, offers hour-long **scenic flights** over the high mountains and azure glacial lakes of the Sawtooths.

Because Boise is something of a mecca for those who like to play in the outdoors, the city's parks have been well-developed. Some are simply open spaces and traditional urban parks; others resemble natural areas. One such park is **Julia Davis Park,** on the Boise River between Capital and Broadway Aves, which features interesting attractions such as the **Boise City Zoo,** (208) 384-4260, a rose garden, tennis courts, an amusement park, and a miniature golf course. **Pedal boats** and **canoes** can be rented for use on the Julia Davis Park pond. Wheels R Fun, a bicycle and float tube rental shack, is located on the north side of the river in Ann Morrison Park, just off 13th St.

Horseback riders see the Hiking/Backpacking or Mountain Biking/Cycling sections above; many of the trails listed are also open to equestrians.

outside in

Attractions

Sun Valley has its share of shops and galleries, and adjacent Ketchum grew up around a core of shops, art galleries, and tony cafes. Visitors can find everything from designer clothes to diamond jewelry, as well as some of the finest art available in the country (much of which has taken a decided Native American and Southwest bent in the past decade) at the nearly two dozen galleries. For a current lineup of artists or genres being shown in Ketchum, contact the Sun Valley Gallery Association, (208) 726-2602. There's another concentration of shops and galleries at Sun

Valley Village in the Sun Valley Resort.

Those who want an overview of Boise can take a city tour on the **Boise Tour Train,** (800) 999-5993, a motorized locomotive replica that departs from Julia Davis Park (it doesn't run winters, though). Like most state capital cities, the capital campus in Boise is well-groomed and pleasant for visitors. The **Capitol Building** is a scale replica of the capitol in Washington, DC. An old warehouse building near the capitol campus at Capitol Blvd and Front St, **Eighth Street Market,** has been converted to a mall of small shops. The primary shopping district in Boise is on Eighth St between Grove and Broad. The **antique district** in Boise is just northwest of the capitol campus, at 13th and Eastman, in Hyde Park. The **Idaho Historical Museum,** (208) 334-2120, and the **Boise Art Museum,** (208) 345-8330, are located in Julia Davis Park.

Calendar of Events

The **McCall Winter Sports Carnival** dates to 1924; the 10-day festival, held the first week in February, includes snow sculpturing, parades and snowmobile racing. Call (800) 260-5130 or (208) 634-7631 for more information.

The **Idaho Shakespeare Festival** runs June through August under the stars in Boise. Call (208) 336-9221 for details.

Some of the nation's best country fiddlers compete in the annual **National Old-Time Fiddlers' Contest** in late June in Weiser; call (208) 549-0450 for registration or other information.

A nighttime parade, air show, and hot air balloon festival are part of the annual **Boise River Festival,** the last weekend in June, in Boise; call (208) 344-7777 or (208) 338-8887 for further information.

Restaurants

Christina's ☆☆ This is where the over-30 locals go for a civilized breakfast or a laid-back lunch. Sun Valley's best take-out food is carried out of Christina's doors. Picnics can be ordered to fuel you as you tackle the region's demanding outdoor activities. Pasta dishes and bread are particularly good. Sunday brunch is worth an entire morning. *Downtown; 2nd St E, Ketchum; (208) 726-4499; breakfast, lunch every day; MC, V; checks OK; $$.*

Cristina's Bakery and Coffee Bar ☆☆ Boise locals get their espresso, cinnamon rolls, and other hand-formed carbohydrates at Cristina's. And little wonder: Even the croissants are made from scratch on the premises. Breads are crusty chews in the best Italian country style. Two other departments join the bakery to make up the total Cristina's—lunches are served up in the front, and if you follow the aisle around to the right you'll find The Atomic Taco. From 11:30am until 2pm Monday through Saturday, you will find some of the best meat and meatless Mexican dishes in the Northern Rockies. With so much going on in such a small space, aromas and flavors sometimes migrate, but that's seldom more than a minor annoyance. *5th and Main St; 504 Main St, Boise; (208) 385-0133; breakfast, lunch every day; no credit cards; checks OK; $.*

The Kneadery ☆☆ Dress warm in the winter if you intend to eat at The Kneadery, because there is almost always a line waiting to be fed. This is the center of the meat-and-potato world in these parts. Scramble a few eggs, chug some industrial-strength coffee, and you're ready to herd dogies on your mountain bike all day. *Downtown, near intersection of Sun Valley Rd; 260 Leadville Ave, Ketchum; (208) 726-9462; breakfast, lunch every day; MC, V; checks OK; $.*

Flying Pie Pizzeria ☆ Consistently voted Boise's best, this is Connecticut-style pizza or as close to it as you'll find in Idaho. Crusts are hand-thrown discs of flavor covered up with everything from spinach to habanero peppers. No need to clean up after a day of rafting the Boise River, since the interior design is rustic flower-child quaint. Besides the Fairview location, there are branches on State St, (208) 345-8585, and Broadway (mostly take-out), (208) 384-0000. *About 4 miles west of downtown, corner of Fairview and Liberty; 6508 Fairview, Boise; (208) 376-3454; lunch, dinner every day; AE, DIS, MC, V; checks OK; $$.*

Globus ☆ Globus is a Paris-style bistro that serves Pacific Rim flavors. All entries are served up in what appear to be large, white porcelain woks without handles. The menu is sometimes too adventurous, but the things that don't quite click are still above average. Steamed Pearl Balls, vegetable shu mai, and hummus are the best starters. Crisp snapper is the most popular item on the menu, and green Thai curry carries real heat. *Near 13th and Eastman; 1520 N 13th, Boise; (208) 331-9855; lunch Mon–Fri, dinner every day; DIS, MC, V; checks OK; $$.*

Gretchen's ☆ This restaurant named for Olympic skier Gretchen Fraser has exceptionally good food for a resort cafe. As a bonus, you can watch the skaters on Sun Valley's ice rink. From July 4 to Labor Day, there is an excellent buffet served on the patio. *In the Sun Valley Lodge; 1 Sun Valley Rd, Sun Valley; (208) 622-2144; breakfast, lunch, dinner every day; AE, DC, DIS, MC, V; checks OK; $.*

Perry's ☆ Excellent fruit salad and the valley's best espresso are Perry's strengths. If it has any weaknesses, you won't find out from the crowds at the counter, which will tell you that everything is good here. Perry's has the best apple pie we have found in a restaurant. *1 block north of the post office, 4th St and 1st Ave; 131 W 4th St, Ketchum; (208) 726-7703; breakfast, lunch every day; MC, V; checks OK; $.*

Lodgings

Sun Valley Lodge and Inn ☆☆☆ The number one-rated ski resort in the United States has become one of the best destinations for summer hiking, golfing, fishing, and mountain biking. Rooms in the Sun Valley Lodge and Inn are surprisingly affordable. Most have been remodeled in the past five years. You will find comfy beds and bathrooms full of marble. Guests at the lodge are shuttled to the ski resort at Baldy Mountain or they can cross-country ski right on the grounds of the lodge, snow permitting. The ice rink is on the lodge grounds, and when the professional world-class skaters aren't staging a show, guests can take a turn or two around the ice year-round. Summer days, lodge guests have access to the four golf courses, including two 18-hole, par 72 courses designed by Robert Trent Jones Jr. The lodge also has tennis courts as well as the full complement of fitness rooms, massage, saunas, steam rooms, an outdoor swimming pool and hot tubs. The Sun Valley Nordic Center, with 30 miles of groomed cross-country ski trails used by hikers in summer, is adjacent to the lodge. *In Sun Valley; PO Box 10, Sun Valley, ID 83853; (800) 786-8259 or (208) 622-4111; AE, DC, DIS, MC, V; checks OK; $$.*

Boise Park Suite Hotel ☆☆ Park Center Boulevard parallels the Boise River, so you can bike, jog, or fish almost as you walk out the door of this hotel. Boise's Greenbelt (see Mountain Biking/Cycling, above) is a stone's throw away from the back door. A few of the 238 suites are equipped with Jacuzzis. Fitness enthusiasts can work out in the weight room and swimmers can do laps in the outdoor pool, then relax in the outdoor Jacuzzi, which is open year-round. There's also a business center with fax machine and copier on-site. An expansion in 1996 doubled the size of the hotel, so ask for one of the newer rooms for a view of the Greenbelt out your window. Downtown Boise is beyond walking distance, but the Boise State University campus is an easy stroll away. Special weekly and weekend rates. *Downtown, adjacent to the Boise River Greenbelt; 424 E Park Center Blvd, Boise, ID 83706; (800) 342-1044 or (208) 342-1044; AE, DIS, MC, V; checks OK; $$.*

Red Lion Riverside ☆☆ At the Red Lion, ask for a ground-floor riverfront room and walk 20 steps from some of Boise's quietest rooms to Boise's Greenbelt (see Mountain Biking/Cycling, above). A brisk walk around this city's convention center—and the Red Lion's 304 rooms—will take most people about 10 minutes. Both Boise's downtown district and

Boise State University are about a 10-minute drive away. Summers, guests can use the outdoor pool or rent a bicycle at a poolside shop for a ride on the Boise River Greenbelt. A fitness center at the hotel includes laundry facilities for guests. A few rooms include a Jacuzzi, only one boasts a fireplace. *Near I-84 connector; 2900 Chinden Blvd, Boise, ID 83714; (800) 547-8010 or (208) 343-1871; AE, DC, DIS, MC, V; $$-$$$.*

Tamarack Inn ☆☆   This is as close to the center of Ketchum as you can get. From the Tamarack Inn you can walk to just about any place in Ketchum but the ski runs, and a shuttle runs every 20 minutes to the downhill ski area. Relax in an outdoor Jacuzzi or heated year-round indoor pool. Or zone out in front of your fireplace—in 7 of the 26 rooms—or television while zapping popcorn in your microwave. There's no restaurant on-site, but the Tamarack is at the heart of the shopping, cafe and gallery district of Ketchum. While the decor doesn't exactly speak to the name of the inn, the Tamarack is newly remodeled with an interior that's more rustic than contemporary. *At Sun Valley Rd and Walnut Ave; PO Box 2000, Sun Valley, ID 83353; (800) 521-5379 or (208) 726-3344; AE, DC, DIS, MC, V; checks OK; $$.*

Elkhorn Village ☆   The main switchboard at Sun Valley Resort can reserve lodge rooms and condominiums at Elkhorn, somewhat removed from the hubbub of Sun Valley but just a 10-minute bike ride away. The amenities of the several dozen condos vary but all include kitchens and fireplaces. Size ranges from studio and loft condos to four bedrooms, scattered among the condominium complexes at Elkhorn. Skiers can catch the free shuttle that runs every 20 minutes to the downhill area from Elkhorn Village. Cross-country trails run right past the village. Clean and plain, the condos are a good value. *Elkhorn Village at Sun Valley; PO Box 6009, Sun Valley, ID 83354; (800) 355-4676 or (208) 622-4511; AE, DC, DIS, MC, V; checks OK; $$.*

More Information

For information on 360 licensed outfitters and guides for hiking, horsepacking, fishing, whitewater rafting, photo safaris, climbing, backpacking, bicycling, hunting, and backcountry skiing, contact Idaho Outfitters and Guides Association, PO Box 95, Boise, ID 83701, (208) 342-1919.

Boise medical facilities: St. Alphonsus Regional Medical Center, (208) 378-3221, or St. Luke's Regional Medical Center, (208) 386-2344.

Boise Visitors Bureau: (800) 635-5240 or (208) 344-7777.

Idaho Department of Fish and Game: (208) 334-3700.

Idaho Department of Parks: (208) 334-4199.

Idaho Outfitters and Guides Association: (208) 342-1919.

Idaho Tourism: (800) 847-4843.

Idaho Travel Council: (800) 635-7820.

Sawtooth National Forest Supervisor's Office, Twin Falls: (208) 737-3200.

Sawtooth National Recreation Area, Stanley Ranger District: (208) 774-3000 or (208) 774-3681.

Stanley-Sawtooth Chamber of Commerce: (208) 774-3411.

Sun Valley-Ketchum Chamber of Commerce: (800) 634-3347.

Sun Valley Resort: (800) 786-8259.

Lewiston
and the Snake
River

Including Clarkston, Moscow, Hells Canyon National Recreation Area,
the Selway–Bitterroot Wilderness, Elk River and the Clearwater
Mountains, and the Salmon River.

Lewiston and its twin city across the Snake River, Clarkston,
have longer histories than most inland Northwest communities and, given the names, it's not too difficult to guess why: the
famed Lewis and Clark expedition spent time here in 1805.
Crossing the Rocky Mountains, early snows had slowed the expedition. When the tired party finally reached the confluence of the
Snake and Clark Fork Rivers, the Nez Perce Indians gave them
food, and the explorers regrouped and were able to continue their
journey. Meriwether Lewis named the camp after himself
(Clarkston was settled later and the name was only natural).

Native Americans gathered here for centuries to fish for the
wild salmon that swam upriver to breed in streams deep in Idaho.
Now it's barge traffic that plies the waters of the Columbia and
Snake Rivers—even though it's hundreds of miles from the Pacific
Ocean, Lewiston is the most inland seaport in the West. An elaborate system of locks and dams along the rivers allows barges
loaded in Lewiston with potatoes or timber products to navigate
one of the largest river systems on the continent downstream to
Portland, Oregon, and return with consumer goods. One of the
best places to watch the barge traffic is from the paved path that
flanks the Snake River.

The economies of Lewiston and Clarkston were actually built

on fruit orchards. The apple and peach trees eventually gave way to wheat, peas, and lentils, and the economy grew up on the lumber milled in Lewiston from a thriving forest industry in the nearby mountains. Now, with the forest industries waning—although the Potlatch pulp mills are still the biggest employer in the city—and the future of the port threatened by the need to restore wild salmon runs, Lewiston has turned to tourism. It's well-positioned to play this role. The city is the jumping-off point for those who want to hop a jet boat for a ride up the Snake River into the famous Hells Canyon, or who seek a whitewater challenge on a portion of the Salmon known as the "River of No Return." Everywhere around Lewiston there are mountains and wilderness areas—the Blue Mountains to the west, just across the Oregon border; the Selway–Bitterroot and Mallard–Larkin wilderness areas to the east; and the Gospel Hump Wilderness Area to the southeast. And, because the city is deep in a canyon, it's in a northern banana belt, with moderate winter temperatures.

The Snake River originates at the Continental Divide in Yellowstone National Park and flows a thousand miles through mountain ranges, canyons, sagebrush desert, and lava plains to the confluence with the Columbia River near Tri-Cities, Washington. The Snake—one of the largest rivers in the United States—and its tributaries drain most of Idaho, western Wyoming, northern Utah, northern Nevada, eastern Oregon, and southeastern Washington, dumping 50,000 cubic feet of water a second into the Columbia River.

Hells Canyon, the deepest gorge in the country (7,900 feet deep), was preserved in 1975 as a National Recreation Area and is accessible by jet boat and raft. The canyon was dug with a big stick by Coyote, according to Nez Perce legend, to protect Indian ancestors in the nearby Oregon Blue Mountains from the "seven devils," a range of peaks across the gorge in Idaho, now called Seven Devils Mountains. Humans have used the area for at least 7,100 years and in some places there are still Indian pictographs on the canyon walls, although the age and origin of these is debated among experts. More than 1,500 cultural sites have been uncovered. Now the gorge is recognized for the treasure it is, and more than 67 miles of the Snake River plunge through the massive chasm, managed under the National Wild and Scenic River System.

Getting There

Lewiston is at the intersection of US Highways 195, 95 and 12, about 108 miles south of Spokane on US 195. Several commuter airlines service the Lewiston-Nez Perce County Airport, (208) 746-7962, with connections most frequently made in Boise or Spokane.

Adjoining Areas
    NORTH: **Idaho Panhandle**
    EAST: **Bitterroot Valley; Missoula and Environs**
    SOUTH: **Boise and Sun Valley**

Rafting

Whitewater enthusiasts flock to the **Salmon River**, which rages through the Frank Church River of No Return Wilderness Area, the largest wilderness area in the continental United States. The Salmon offers an awesome wilderness experience—stunning mountain scenery, rapids, and sandy beaches. Most rafters depart from near Riggins, 110 miles south of Lewiston on US 95, and float the lower section of the Salmon between Riggins and Lucile. Permits are required for floaters from the North Fork to Long Tom Bar from June 20 to September 7.

The Salmon—also known as the **"River of No Return"**—begins deep in the Sawtooth Mountains and, 450 miles later, joins the Snake River. Because of the caliber of its rapids, floaters should be very experienced or hire an experienced outfitter. A number of guides and outfitters work on the Salmon River, putting in at Riggins. Among the **outfitters** that come highly recommended is Brundage Mountain Adventures, which books its clients at the Mill Park Condominiums in McCall, (800) 888-7544 or (208) 634-4151; Brundage runs half-day and full-day trips in oar boats (the guide does all the work) or paddle rafts (each guest also paddles). Salmon River Experience, (800) 892-9223, guides whitewater rafting trips of one to five days on the Salmon, including eco-trips and theme trips in paddle or oar rafts or inflatable kayaks. Among the outfitters who operate their own lodging near the launch site is Salmon River Challenge, (800) 732-8574, which runs the Rapid River Guest Ranch. Lodging is in log buildings with meals served in the main lodge. In addition to whitewater raft trips on the Salmon River, the outfitters will guide fishing, hiking, horseback riding, mountain biking, and snowmobiling trips.

Additional information about licensed guides and outfitters in Hells Canyon National Recreation Area is available in Lewiston at the Chamber of Commerce, 2207 E Main St, (800) 473-3543; and in Clarkston at the Chamber of Commerce, 502 Bridge St, (800) 933-2128.

The 1.3-million-acre Selway–Bitterroot Wilderness flanks the Montana-Idaho state line. The **Selway River** pierces the Selway–Bitterroot

Wilderness for 47 miles in Idaho and is protected as a Wild and Scenic River. Although remote, the Selway River offers prime whitewater rafting; from the Paradise Guard Station at the mouth of White Gap Creek to Selway Falls, the river drops an average of 28 feet per mile. The rapid elevation loss and comparative low water volume means technical whitewater expertise is required to navigate the river. This section of river has many submerged rocks and unbroken white water with few recovery pools, and there are several Class III and Class IV rapids. Open canoes and paddle boats are not recommended, and those without extensive whitewater experience should not attempt to navigate the Selway without a guide. The put-in is on the Upper Selway, 47 miles from Darby, Montana. The takeout is at Race Creek (from Lowell, Idaho, the road parallels the Lower Selway for 20 miles to the takeout). Shuttle distance from Paradise to Selway Falls is 245 miles; the average float time for this trip is four days. A **permit** is required to float the Selway River between May 15 and July 31 with one launch per day and a maximum party size of 16 people. Four licensed guides are each awarded 4 launch dates a year, with the remaining 62 launch dates available through a random drawing. Apply between December 1 and January 31 for a launch date the following summer by contacting the District Ranger, West Fork Ranger Station, Darby, MT 59829; (406) 821-3269. The ranger station also has information about guides who have been awarded launch dates.

Boating

Tour boats take more than 20,000 people up the **Snake River** every year, with outfitted tours leaving from launch sites below Hells Canyon Dam, Pittsburg Landing, and the Lewiston–Clarkston Valley. On the 16 miles of upper canyon, floating is restricted to those with permits because of limited camp and launch sites. The upper canyon is part of the 214,000-acre Hells Canyon Wilderness, which is roadless and through which powerboats are not allowed. There is a network through Hells Canyon of more than 850 miles of trails, but even the trails cannot pierce the deepest parts of the canyon, accessible only by river. Information about private boating permits in the Hells Canyon National Recreation Area is available by calling (509) 758-0616.

Some people like to see the Snake River quickly, and that can be done from a jet boat. The most popular **jet boat tour** is the famous **Mail Run**, operated by Beamer's Hells Canyon Tours, (800) 522-6966, a licensed mail carrier as well as a guide service. The jet boat leaves Lewiston every Wednesday and takes mail to residents along the remote Snake River and returns Thursday afternoon. Visitors spend the night at Copper Creek

Lodge, 70 miles upriver. Other tours are available, ranging from full-day to fishing and rafting excursions and a dinner cruise. River Quest Excursions, (800) 589-1129, operates half- and full-day jet boat trips along 182 miles of **Hells Canyon,** with stops at historic pioneer ranches and Indian pictographs along the riverbanks.

We think a trip with Hells Canyon Lodge, (800) 727-6190, is something like heli-hiking—you get there fast and easy, but get to see it all—great for those short of time. With this outfitter you get to see two canyons and two rivers within 6 hours. A jet boat roars 50 miles up the Snake River, stopping at Indian pictographs, then continues 12 miles up Class III and IV rapids on the **Salmon River** to the outfitter's lodge, where a barbecue lunch is served. Tour participants are back in Lewiston by 4pm. Hells Canyon Lodge will accommodate those who want to stay overnight at the log lodge deep in the canyon. After a day of jetting about the river, guests can soak in a hot tub overlooking the water.

One-day tours by Snake Dancer Excursions, (800) 234-1941, travel 200 miles round trip through Hells Canyon, stopping at abandoned mines and historic sites. The boats follow the same route as the Mail Run but do not deliver mail. Hells Canyon Jet Boat Tours, (800) 422-3568, offers 2- and 3-hour as well as full-day and overnight tours on the Snake. This outfitter also guides one-day whitewater rafting in Hells Canyon.

Other types of boats also ply the waters of area rivers: Northwest Dories, (800) 877-3679, offers float trips aboard **dories**—small, flat-bottomed boats—down the Snake River through Hells Canyon, on the Salmon and Lower Salmon Rivers, and on the Owyhee River. See More Information, below, about boating restrictions on these rivers.

Fishing

Steelhead are the show around Lewiston. Hundreds of fishers head for the **Snake River**, usually in the winter, to catch these immense trout, ranging from 4 to 18 pounds. (Steelhead and chinook salmon reach the Snake via fish ladders, which are open to public viewing at four dams—Ice Harbor, Lower Monumental, Little Goose, and Lower Granite—and at the Lewiston Levees.) Fishing for steelhead is equipment-intense, so it's best to hire a guide. But bring your patience—these aren't fish that leap into your boat. At the height of the steelhead season, anglers are happy with one catch a day; and if it's a native trout or too small, you have to put it back in the river. A state fishing license is required (Idaho or Washington, depending on the portion of the river to be fished); your guide will know the regulations. Fishing guides abound, so before booking your trip, ask about the type of boat the guide uses (we've fished in blizzards in November, so be sure part of the boat is enclosed), what equipment is provided, and whether the guide is licensed. Among the **guides** that come recommended are Jig Masters, (509) 758-2310; Hells Canyon Lodge, (800) 727-6190; and Scenic River Charters, (208) 746-6808. Jig Masters is based in Clarkston, and Hells Canyon and Scenic River both run catch-and-release **sturgeon** fishing expeditions on the Snake River. The ancient giant white sturgeon grow to 12 feet in the river's depths.

An Idaho **fishing license** is available from the Idaho Department of Fish and Game, (208) 334-3717, and most outdoors equipment stores. The Idaho Department of Fish and Game schedules a couple of free fishing days in June, during which no license is required. The department also maintains an angling hotline, (800) ASK-FISH, with information about where to fish, rules, buying a license, boat launching ramps, access sites, and wheelchair-accessible sites. In Idaho, lakes, ponds, and reservoirs are open for fishing year-round; rivers and streams are open Memorial Day weekend through November. The season varies for steelhead longer than 20 inches in the Snake and Salmon River drainages. Native steelhead must be released; hatchery raised steelhead have the adipose fin removed, and those that meet the size requirement may be kept. Some streams in the state are catch-and-release only.

Mountain Biking

Mountain bike enthusiasts need go no further than Moscow for prime riding terrain. Several trails begin at the **Giant White Pine Campground**, north of Moscow about 17 miles on US 95, then east on Hwy 6 for 18 miles. One popular trail here follows the old **Sampson Trail**, a road built in the 1920s that stretched from the Canadian border into southern Idaho. Hikers also use this 15 1/5-mile loop trail, so be alert on downhills.

Bikers who want to climb mountains head for **Moscow Mountain** just north of the town. Trails crisscross the mountain, and not all are loop trails; be aware that you may not end up at the trailhead from which you started if you just head downhill. A 5-mile dirt road goes to the top of the mountain. To get there, drive 4 1/2 miles north from Moscow on US 95, turn right after the overpass, and take the gravel road to the mountain.

Those who want a full day of riding through the woods should head for the town of **Elk River**, on Hwy 8 from Moscow (through Troy). Old logging roads and trails lead deep into the forest; information about the trails and routes is available at Huckleberry Haven Lodge in Elk River. Most of the terrain is relatively flat and easy.

Hiking/Backpacking

An easy access to the Clearwater Mountains in central Idaho is the tiny community of **Elk River**, a 54-mile drive east of Moscow, Idaho, on Hwy 8. The region is rich with hiking trails, although hikers will need Forest Service trail maps to navigate since many of the trails are not maintained annually and may be poorly marked or grown over. One of the more popular hikes is to **Elk Butte**, elevation 5,824 feet, from which there's an impressive view of two national forests and the Selkirk–Bitterroot Range. (There's also a road to the top of Elk Butte, but we recommend getting to the top on your own power!) Elk River's biggest claim to fame can be found in a nearby **cedar grove**, where the largest known cedar tree in the Rocky Mountains—more than 3,000 years old and 18 feet in diameter— can be found. Hikers who want to spend a half-day on the trail can reach **Elk Creek Falls**, which has a freefall of 300 feet. Elk River is also on the doorstep of the Mallard–Larkin Wilderness Area.

Camping

Dworshak Reservoir, the lake created by Dworshak Dam from the Clearwater River, is another place people around here go for water sports. Prior to the building of the dam, 50 to 60 million board feet of timber was floated in a massive log drive down the Clearwater to mills every year. The last log drive was in 1971, but log-handling facilities were built at the dam, allowing a continued removal of 35 million board feet of timber every year. Power boaters should be aware there may be occasional logs floating in the reservoir that have escaped the booms. Camping on the 53-mile-long reservoir is allowed at 80 locations; each of 125 campsites has a fireplace grill, picnic table, and tent pad. There are also remote campsites accessible only by boat; for these a permit is required, available at the Dworshak Dam Visitor Center at the north end of the dam, (208) 476-1255.

Golfing

Public golf courses in the Lewiston–Clarkston area range from hilly and challenging to gentle with tree-lined fairways. **Bryden Canyon Golf Course** in Lewiston, (208) 746-0863, has rolling fairways from which the Snake and Clearwater Rivers and the Waha and Blue Mountains can be seen. Across the river in Clarkston, **Quail Ridge Golf Course**, (509) 758-8501, has the same vistas but the terrain is more forgiving of less-experienced golfers.

Scenic Drives

In the 1930s the **Lolo Motorway** (Forest Road 500) was built by the Civilian Conservation Corps along much of the original Lolo Trail. Those who are adventuresome and have a four-wheel-drive vehicle can still travel this 2-day route from Lolo, Montana, to Weippe, Idaho. Much of the route is on primitive dirt road, snow-covered from November through June, and there are only a few rustic campsites along the way. Travelers should carry supplies of fuel, fresh water, food, and warm clothing. Information about specific road conditions and a route map is available at the Powell Ranger District station in Lolo, (208) 942-3113; the Missoula Ranger District office in Missoula, (406) 329-3705; and the Clearwater National Forest Service office in Orofino, (208) 476-4541.

The lower 112 miles of the Salmon River can be seen from **US 95**— 59 miles of this road parallels this exceptionally scenic river, until the road climbs to higher ground at White Bird.

outside in

Attractions

Some of the trappings of Lewiston's pioneer history can be seen at the **Nez Perce County Historical Society Luna House Museum**, Third and C Streets, (208) 743-2535. The **Lewis-Clark Center for Arts & History,** 415 Main, (208) 799-2243, houses artifacts from the early Chinese miners in the area.

A small university town just north of Lewiston on US 195, **Moscow** is closer to the mountains and, at an elevation of 2,460 feet, more temperate than the cities in the Snake River Canyon (elevation only 750 feet). Moscow's in the heart of wheat and lentil farming country—the Palouse— and is the site of one of Idaho's two land-grant universities, the University of Idaho (the other is Idaho State in Pocatello). The town has a modest shopping district that caters to college students, and a couple of brewpubs and cafe-style eateries. Those who prefer Moscow's environment to that of more industrial Lewiston are still close to whitewater rafting, jet boating, and hiking opportunities. And equipment and gear for all activities— whitewater rafting, kayaking, climbing, skiing, backpacking, and camping—can be rented from the university outdoor center: ASUI Outdoor Rental Center, 709 Deakin Avenue, (208) 885-6170.

Calendar of Events

Some of the world's top jazz artists appear at the annual **Lionel Hampton Jazz Festival** in late February in Moscow. Call (208) 882-1800 for details.

The jet boats gather in mid-April for the **Salmon River Jet Boat Races,** the first leg of the US Championship Jet Boat Race, at Riggins. Call (208) 628-3440 for more information about this high-speed event.

Spring is celebrated with the annual **Dogwood Festival** the last two weeks of April in Lewiston. Call (208) 799-2243 for information.

The big rodeo event in the region, the **Lewiston Roundup,** (208) 743-3531, attracts world-class cowboys in early September.

Lodgings

Beau's Butte Bed and Breakfast ☆   For those who would rather forego Lewiston and instead stay nearer the mountains and out of the canyon there's Beau's Butte Bed and Breakfast near Moscow, a university town at the southern edge of the Palouse region. The B&B sits atop a hill that affords pleasant views of the rolling Palouse farmlands. The 4-acre grounds include some forested sections, all of which guests can explore. The decor of the two guest rooms is cute, perhaps to a fault, and we would recommend the room with private bath, albeit down the hall; the other room shares a bath with owner Joyce Parr. Guests can use the hot tub in the solarium, and in winters there's always a fire in the family room fireplace. Breakfast is generous and caloric. *From Hwy 95 downtown take a right onto Martin St, left onto Polk St, and right onto Public Ave; 702 Public Ave, Moscow, ID 83843; (208) 882-4061; MC, V; checks OK; $$.*

More Information

Travel in several wilderness areas is restricted to nonmotorized activities such as hiking, floating, or horsepacking. For recreation rules on the Middle Fork, Main, or Lower Salmon Rivers, contact the North Fork Ranger District, PO Box 180, North Fork, ID 83466, (208) 865-2383.

Clarkston Chamber of Commerce: (800) 933-2128 or (509) 758-7712.

Elk River City Hall: (208) 826-3209.

Forest Service Information Center: (208) 875-1131.

Hells Canyon National Recreation Area: (208) 628-3916.

Idaho State Fish and Game offices: Idaho Falls, (208) 525-7290; Jerome, (208) 324-4350; Lewiston, (208) 799-5010; McCall, (208) 634-8139; Nampa; (208) 465-8465; Pocatello, (208) 232-4703; Salmon, (208) 765-2271.

Lewiston Chamber of Commerce: (800) 473-3543 or (208) 743-3531.
Moscow Chamber of Commerce: (208) 882-1800.
Nez Perce National Forest: (208) 983-1950.
Salmon River Chamber of Commerce: (208) 628-3778.
Ski conditions, Idaho: (800) 243-2754.

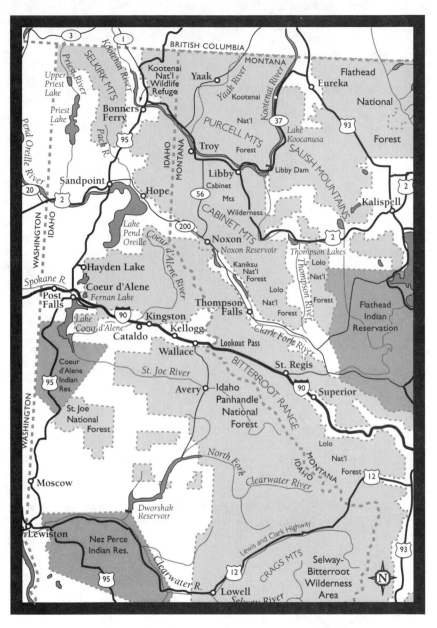

Idaho Panhandle and Northwest Montana

Idaho
Panhandle
and Northwest
Montana

Idaho
Panhandle

Including Wallace, Kellogg, the Interstate 90 corridor, Coeur d'Alene, Sandpoint, Coeur d'Alene and Priest Lakes, and Lake Pend Oreille.

Idaho is a state that always seems overlooked—it's not quite part of what is considered the Pacific Northwest and not quite mountainous enough to be thought of as a Rocky Mountain state. In fact, when the states were carved from the territories (Oregon in 1859, Washington and Montana in 1889), the misshapen leftovers became the state of Idaho in 1890. Still, the people of northern Idaho tend to identify more with Montana to the east and Washington to the west than with their fellow Idahoans to the south—maybe because, for a long time, the state lacked a passable route from its northern portion to its southern part.

The wild terrain that was impassable for so long is what divides and defines the two parts of Idaho. As the state narrows to what is known as the Panhandle, the mountains characterize the region, its economy, and its people. This is mining and logging country; extensive mining at the turn of the century built the city of Spokane just over the Washington border. Between 1884 and 1988, more than $5 billion worth of metals were mined in the district. Northern Idaho's economy was built on silver. A billion ounces have been extracted in just over a century, earning the area the designation "Silver Valley." Enormous amounts of silver, as well as nearly 9 million tons of zinc, 200,000 tons of copper, and a half-million ounces of gold, were extracted from deep underground tunnels at mega-mines such as Bunker Hill and the Sunshine Mine, as well as at thousands of smaller mining operations that pocket these mountains. Thousands of hardy workers were employed by smelters that extracted ore from rock and by railroads that carried the precious metals west to Spokane, which grew up as a shipping hub. The building of mine tunnels required timber and that, too, grew in abundance in the northern mountains. Logging operations clear-cut thousands of acres of forest. These early industries are, for the most part, gone. The small mining and logging towns are trying, like their neighbors to the south, to build new economies based on the tourist industry.

The main road through North Idaho is Interstate 90, which slices through the mountains over Lookout and Fourth of July passes. Deep in the mountains, Wallace and Kellogg boast ideal terrain for skiing, snowmobiling, fishing, hiking, and mountain biking. Coeur d'Alene has its namesake lake, a grand body of fresh water that's big enough to generate sturdy winds for windsurfing and sailing and deep enough to nurture big trout.

North of Coeur d'Alene, tucked in the Selkirk Mountains as they race north into British Columbia, is Sandpoint, a logging-turned-resort town perched on the shore of Lake Pend Oreille. There are many other lakes in the area, including Priest Lake, but Lake Pend Oreille's the granddaddy, with a depth of 1,200 feet that supports major-league trout for patient (and hardy) trollers, as well as Navy submarines.

The third of the three big lakes in North Idaho, Priest Lake, just south of Sandpoint, is the least-developed and smallest but still, at 19 miles long, hardly modest in size. Finding solitude is easier here. But be aware there are few shopping opportunities; this place is for those interested in serious time spent outdoors. The lake has attracted those interested in wilderness for decades. Among the notable people to have spent time on the shores of Priest Lake is Nell Shipman, a 1920s silent film star who gained notoriety as one of the first women directors in a male-dominated industry. She made her first movie on the tundra near Great Slave Lake in the Northwest Territories north of Edmonton, during which her leading man died from pneumonia after insisting on exercising outdoors in subzero temperatures. She filmed her next few movies—most notably *Girl From God's Country* (in which she scandalously appeared nude, prompting advertising to ask "Is the Nude Rude?") and *Lookout Mountain*—at the north end of Priest Lake. She transported nearly 100 animals including raccoons, skunks, and bears on barges to the site, 20 miles up the lake from Coolin, Idaho. She spent two long, snowbound winters at the lodge before her leading man, Burt Tyle, went crazy from frostbite, ran out onto the ice, and had to be rescued by dogsled. Shipman's silent films were rediscovered during a search for artforms created in Idaho to celebrate the state's centennial. Now a Nell Shipman Film

Festival is held irregularly at Lionshead State Park on Priest Lake.

Because North Idaho is less known than other mountainous regions flanking the Rockies, and its backcountry is relatively less accessible, it's also less crowded. Lift lines don't exist at the ski resorts near Sandpoint and Kellogg, while solitude is bliss on cross-country skiing and hiking trails. To this day, there are remote alpine lakes, glacial-carved valleys, and mountain slopes, all inaccessible even by trail.

Getting There

The main east-west highway through North Idaho is I-90, which runs through Kellogg, Wallace, and Coeur d'Alene. US Highway 95 goes north from Coeur d'Alene to Sandpoint or, from Spokane, Washington, take US 2.

Coeur d'Alene has a small commuter airport but most people fly to Spokane International Airport, 35 miles to the west, which is served by major airlines. There is no passenger train service to Coeur d'Alene, but Greyhound buses, (208) 667-3343, stop in there, en route east from Spokane.

Sandpoint is at the crossroads of US Hwys 2 and 95 and Hwy 200, about 48 miles north of Coeur d'Alene and about 70 miles from Spokane, or 200 miles west of Missoula. It's 390 miles south of Calgary. Priest Lake is 25 miles east of US 95 between Spokane and Sandpoint; take the turnoff at the small logging town of Priest River, a half-hour drive south of Sandpoint. Sandpoint has a small airstrip but is not served by commercial flights; the nearest airport served by major airlines is, again, in Spokane. Amtrak passenger trains stop here daily en route between Seattle and Chicago. The depot is within walking distance of downtown Sandpoint.

Adjoining Areas

EAST: **Northwest Montana**

SOUTH: **Lewiston and the Snake River**

inside out

Fishing

An Idaho fishing **license** is required, available from the Idaho Department of Fish and Game, (208) 769-1414, and most outdoor equipment stores. The Idaho Department of Fish and Game schedules a couple of free fishing days in June, during which no license is required. The department also maintains an angling hotline, (800) ASK-FISH, with information about where to fish, rules, buying a license, boat launching ramps, access sites and wheelchair-accessible sites. In Idaho, lakes, ponds, and reservoirs are open for fishing year-round; rivers and streams are open Memorial Day weekend through November. Some streams in the state are catch-and-release only.

River Fishing

There are cutthroat trout all over Idaho, but one of the favorite destinations for fly-fishermen based in the Silver Valley is the **St. Joe River,** which plunges out of the Bitterroot Mountains into Idaho. The river yields westslope cutthroat trout in a walk-and-wade experience. But the drive there from Coeur d'Alene is significant, so locals will often head for Montana and the **Clark Fork River,** which runs between the Bitterroot and Cabinet Mountains just across the state border. Here, fishing from a drift boat is recommended, and anglers reel in brown, rainbow, and cutthroat trout reaching 20 inches in length. Winters, the **North Fork of the Coeur d'Alene River** is the place to catch whitefish. A Silver Valley guide service that comes well-recommended is Don Johnson's Fishing Guide Service in Wallace, (208) 556-1007.

All the fly patterns you'll need and other fly-fishing equipment, as well as **guide service**, is available at Castaway Fly Fishing Shop, with two locations at 3620 N Fruitland Lane, Coeur d'Alene, (800) 410-3133 or (208) 765-3133, and at 210 Sherman Avenue, Coeur d'Alene (208) 667-5441. Equipment rental (rods, flies, waders, and fishing license) costs extra. The best time of year to reel in big trout is September and October, just before they run upstream to spawn.

Lake Fishing

Those satisfied with fishing from a dock will find plenty of room and probably free advice from other anglers at the Forest Service boat launch and dock at **Fernan Lake.** At one time this may have been a deep bay of Coeur d'Alene Lake, but now it's separated from the bigger lake by the freeway and a narrow section of city. To get to the day-use area, exit I-90 at Sherman Ave in Coeur d'Alene and drive east on Sherman, just past the Fernan Forest Service station, to Theis Drive, which dead-ends at the boat launch.

A string of small lakes called the **Chain Lakes** flank the Coeur d'Alene River through the Silver Valley. Locals say there are northern pike plying the waters that weigh in at more than 30 pounds. To try your luck, take the Rose Lake exit from I-90 and drive south on US 2 to Rose Lake. Other lakes in the chain are Bull Run, Kilarney, Cave, Medicine, Black, and Thompson. Take everything you need on this excursion, since stores and communities are scarce.

Ice fishermen frequent several lakes in the Silver Valley, catching bass, crappie, and perch.

Year-round, anglers drop lines into **Coeur d'Alene Lake** and pull up chinook salmon and northern pike. Some hardy anglers ice fish in the bays that freeze over every winter, but all safety guidelines should be observed before heading out onto the ice. Check with the Idaho Fish and Game Department Panhandle office, 2750 Kathleen Ave in Coeur d'Alene, (208) 769-1414, for ice conditions and restrictions. A state fishing license is required.

Coeur d'Alene locals in need of fishing equipment head for Fins & Feathers, 1816 Sherman Ave, (208) 667-9304. Guide service, both half- and full-day trips, can be arranged. Everything that's needed for trolling Coeur d'Alene Lake is provided, except lunch and a cooler for the catch. August through October is the best time to snag the big fish—14- to 16-pound salmon or 8- to 20-pound pike. As can be guessed from the name, Cast and Blast (9121 N Government Way in Hayden, just north of Coeur d'Alene, (800) 473-6551) has fishing and hunting equipment.

Lake Pend Oreille is one of the hot spots on the continent when it comes to fishing for trophy steelhead trout, at least according to a book titled *In Quest of Big Fish*, by Henry Waszczuk and Italo Labignan. Indeed, fishing is big business in these parts and guides are available in Sandpoint. The best season for catching the big fish, however, is autumn, especially October and November. Successful anglers report the key is to troll with large plugs that resemble the smaller rainbow trout in the lake (the favorite dinner of bigger fish). Among the guide services on Lake Pend Oreille are Pend Oreille Charters, (208) 265-6781, and Eagle Charters, (208) 264-5274, which run half- and full-day fishing trips year-round out of Sandpoint. (Pend Oreille Charters gives a 10-percent discount for catch-and-release fishing.) Diamond Charters, (208) 265-2565, operates out of Hope, on the northeast shore of Lake Pend Oreille. Guides can also be arranged through the Idaho Guides and Outfitters Association, Box 95, Boise, ID 83701. Regional anglers also pull kokanee from Lake Pend Oreille and consider 15-inchers a good catch.

Because much of the shoreline around **Priest Lake** is part of the Idaho Panhandle National Forest, few marinas and resorts are located here. And there are fewer guide services. Among the few is Priest Lake Outdoor Adventures, (208) 443-5601, which guides fishing excursions year-round on the lake (most folks fish for trophy-sized lake trout); all tackle is provided.

Hiking/Backpacking

Washington's Cascade and Olympic Mountains don't have all the nation's old-growth trees—there are still a few left in Idaho. The easiest way to see trees that are 500 to 600 years old is at the **Settlers Grove of Ancient Cedars.** A 1 ½-mile trail winds through a stand of old growth. To get there take the Kingston exit (Exit 43) from I-90 and turn north on Hwy 9 past Enaville. Continue through Prichard and Eagle, and at Eagle take Forest Route 805 (West Fork Eagle Creek) 7 miles to the grove.

Idaho's not known for waterfalls, but two worth the drive are **Fern** and **Shadow Falls,** requiring only a quarter-mile walk from the road. Take the Coeur d'Alene River Rd 14 miles north of Prichard to Yellow Dog Creek. Yellow Dog is a dirt road; go 3 miles to Fern Falls, then follow the trail to Shadow Falls. Call a Forest Service station before leaving for this excursion, since in some years the Yellow Dog road is closed through the summer because of spring flood damage.

The Forest Service has maps available for **45 hikes** along the north and south forks of the **Coeur d'Alene River.** The hikes range from less than one-quarter mile to Shadow and Centennial Falls to 22 miles to the St. Joe Divide. All of the trailheads are accessed from Forest Service roads, and the condition of those roads changes every year. Heavy snows and flooding keep some roads closed through the summer. The best plan for hiking the area is to contact the Wallace Ranger District, PO Box 14, Silverton ID 83867, (208) 752-1221, to request maps and inquire about access road conditions before choosing a route.

Hikers have plenty of open terrain to wander at the top of **Silver Mountain Resort,** (208) 783-1111. All the roads and trails open to mountain bikers are also open to hikers. The most popular is the **East Ridge Nature Trail,** a 2-mile route with clear views of Kellogg Peak and the South Fork of the Coeur d'Alene River.

The paved **Centennial Trail,** begun when Washington and Idaho celebrated their statehood centennials, runs 63 miles from Riverfront Park in Spokane to Coeur d'Alene Lake's Higgens Point. The section east of Coeur d'Alene is especially inviting, since it flanks the lake with many benches for sitting and watching the sailboats or the setting sun. A portion of the Idaho trail, which is 23 miles long, is still under construction and on those sections hikers (and bicyclists) may need to join the traffic on the streets until completion.

At all hours of the day and evening and even in inclement weather, walkers, joggers, in-line skaters, and those strolling with dogs or babies turn onto a paved path that runs from Coeur d'Alene Resort to North Idaho College and into the promenade along Coeur d'Alene Lake. The **City Park Path** follows the lakeshore. Its most popular section separates the City Park from City Beach, a broad, gentle piece of sandy beach that's public and crowded on hot days. Swimmers need to be thick-skinned, since the lake is on the chilly end of the temperature scale (we're talking lower than 40°F when swimming season opens in June). There seems to be an annual debate about the appropriateness of thong swimming suits on City Beach, so bring along more conventional swim attire just in case.

The gem of Coeur d'Alene has to be **Tubbs Hill**, a wooded peninsula that juts into Coeur d'Alene Lake and offers the city's best view of the sunset. An unpaved walking path around the peninsula qualifies as a hike in all seasons but is unpopular in winter because of mud and snow. Two small sandy beaches in coves are perfect for a picnic; no fires are allowed during summer because of high fire danger in the woods. Half the length of the trail affords great views of the lake, and the other half winds through sometimes-dense stands of pines and firs and crosses a canyon on a short suspension bridge. The trailhead is in the public parking lot just east of Coeur d'Alene Resort.

Mountain Biking

The 46-mile **Route of the Hiawatha Rail-Trail** from St. Regis, Montana, to the old townsite of Pearson, Idaho, north of Avery, links Idaho and Montana. The rail-trail crosses the Bitterroot Divide and is in the early stages of conversion from a railroad to a trail for mountain bikers and hikers. It uses the abandoned Milwaukee Railroad and includes a series of spectacular trestles, tunnels, and stunning mountain scenery, but the most spectacular section—11 miles that include the 1 $7/10$-mile Taft Tunnel—has been closed since 1993 for reconstruction. When the tunnel is repaired and guardrails have been installed on several high trestles, the route will be reopened. For now, mountain bikers can ride a 10-mile route on single-track and primitive roads, between Avery and the Route of the Hiawatha. Information on the status of the trails is available from the St. Joe Ranger District, HC Box 1, Avery, ID 38301, (208) 245-4517, or from the Superior Ranger District, 209 W Riverside, Superior, MT 59872, (406) 822-4233.

Mid-June to mid-October, mountain bikers can load their bikes on the **Silver Mountain Resort** gondolas and cruise the many trails and old logging roads that crisscross the peaks rising above the lodge. Most riders opt to bump and brake down the long routes back to the gondola parking lot, but after a day of play up top, riders can also load their bikes back on the gondola for a pleasant and more sedentary ride down. A **trail map** of more than a dozen trails is available from the mountain office at 610 Bunker Ave in Kellogg, (208) 783-1111. Mountain bikes can be rented at the gondola terminal. Pick up a map to the Silver Mountain trails and look carefully at the difficulty ratings so the route chosen doesn't exceed your abilities.

The Excelsior Bike Shop, 10 W Portland, (208) 786-3751, also rents mountain bikes and that's the place to head if you want to ride the miles of trails beyond Silver Mountain. No formal maps exist, but the avid cyclists at the Excelsior have hand-drawn a number of routes and will offer good directions to the trailheads, which are also unmarked and often difficult to find. Favorites include a trail that stretches from **Silver Mountain to Lookout Pass,** a 65-mile loop that utilizes several trails and a north-south trail that will eventually go clear to the Canada-US border. None of these routes is completed, and none has signage or maps at the trailhead. It's not unusual to join a group of bikers who hang out at the Excelsior for an excursion, and a shuttle service for bikers who don't want to do loop trails is available from Silver Service, (208) 786-8800.

The lift operators at **Schweitzer Mountain Resort,** 11 miles north of Sandpoint, (800) 831-8810, cheerfully load mountain bikes on the quad chairs. Bikers choose a variety of former logging roads and ski area service roads back to the bottom. The most direct route is 8 $^3/_5$ miles with a vertical descent of 2,574 feet. Hikers can ride both ways after spending the day hiking up and down the ridges at the top. Huckleberry season—usually early August—is the optimum time to go; take a bucket and pick these quintessential Rocky Mountain berries.

Although it's hardly a mecca for mountain bikers, **Priest Lake** offers about 75 miles of trails, mostly through the forest on Forest Service roads. The terrain offers hills, but most are modest when compared to the terrain at area ski resorts. A trail map is available at area Forest Service stations.

Boating/Canoeing/Kayaking

The most-accessible public boat launch on **Coeur d'Alene Lake** is located just east of the Coeur d'Alene Resort. At this lake, boating is a year-round activity, although in severe winters even the largest bays in the lake freeze over. The lake's size, and the fact that winds blow nearly constantly down from the mountains to the east, make it ideal for **windsurfing.** Other ways to play in the water range from **water skiing** and **Jet-skis** to **sailing.** Smaller craft such as kayaks and canoes should be aware sizable waves can form on the lake, even during the calmest days.

Summers only, daily **cruises** of Coeur d'Alene Lake and the **St. Joe River** are offered by Lake Coeur d'Alene Cruises, (800) 365-8338, ext. 7123, or (208) 765-4000. Sunset cruises, Sunday brunch, and Fourth of July fireworks cruises also run.

Summer cruises of the **Spokane River,** the outlet of Coeur d'Alene Lake near Post Falls, can be arranged on the *Spokane River Queen,* based at Templin's Resort in Post Falls, (208) 773-1611, ext. 571. The *Spokane River Queen* also runs **eagle-watching cruises,** (208) 765-2367, from late November through mid-January from Higgins Point Landing on Coeur d'Alene Lake to Wolf Lodge Bay, where a sizable population of bald eagles winters, feeding on kokanee salmon and ducks.

Because of its size, **Lake Pend Oreille** is an ideal lake for sailing but not for canoeing or kayaking. When the winds blow, the waves are of sufficient size to splash over a canoe. Sailboats can be rented at Windbag, by the jetty on City Beach in Sandpoint, (208) 263-7811. Those fortunate to be on the lake when it's calm can rent canoes here or at Pend Oreille Shores Resort in Hope, on the east side of the lake on US 200 between mile markers 47 and 48. Jet-skis are also available here, as are pedal boats.

An old river boat named the *Shawnodese* plies the waters of Lake Pend Oreille and will take passengers on half-day, full-day and **lunch and dinner cruises.** The yacht's available for charter, too, for those who might want to spend the night in one of Lake Pend Oreille's secluded bays. The boat has been renovated and is moored at Harbor Marina in Garfield Bay, 13 miles southeast of Sandpoint (take the Long Bridge toward Coeur d'Alene and look for the signs to Garfield Bay). Reservations can be made at Tamarack Knoll Enterprises, 303 Pine St, Sandpoint; call (800) 765-5539 or (208) 263-5539.

When motorized boat traffic was taken off the 5-mile-long **Upper Priest Lake,** it became a haven for canoers who paddled to remote campsites along the lakeshore. Upper Priest Lake is accessible through the 2-mile-long Priest Lake Thoroughfare, a relatively narrow channel between the two lakes in which motorized boats are not allowed.

The outlet of Priest Lake, **Priest River,** is open to kayakers and canoers who can handle Class II and III rapids. The put-in is at the Outlet Campground on Priest Lake, a 1-mile paddle from the river outlet dam that requires a portage around the dam. Past the dam there's a set of Class III rapids, the most difficult on this paddle. The route extends clear to the **Pend Oreille River,** a very long 1-day trip that's better done in 2 days. Canoers can camp at **Dickensheet Campground,** about a 5-hour paddle from the put-in. There are several other take-outs along the river where parking is available. A map is available from the Priest Lake Ranger District office in Priest Lake, (208) 443-2512.

Golfing

A golf vacation to the Panhandle area just wouldn't be complete without a round at the **Coeur d'Alene Resort Golf Course,** (800) 688-5253 or (208) 765-4000, which boasts the only floating green in the world and was selected by *Golf Digest* as America's most scenic golf course. Much of the course flanks Coeur d'Alene Lake, and the 14th green floats on pontoons out in the lake (the distance varies since the green is moved around). A motor boat takes golfers out to the green to putt out, regardless of whether they actually land a ball on the island. Since the course is new, few mature trees get in the way on the fairways, but water hazards (there are others besides the lake) and sandtraps qualify the course as challenging—not surprising since it was built with hopes of attracting professional tournaments.

For sheer beauty, **Hidden Lakes Golf Course** is one of the best in North Idaho. The fairways punch deep into the dense forest of cedar, birch, and firs, and, as the name indicates, there's plenty of water in the area. In fact, 15 of the 18 holes have water hazards—and we aren't talking puddles here—and water comes into play on 2 other holes in the form of the Lower Pack River. The course is at the north end of Lake Pend Oreille on the Lower Pack River, 7 miles east of Sandpoint. For a tee time call (208) 263-1642.

Horseback Riding

At the end of the gondola ride at **Silver Mountain Resort,** one option is to climb aboard a horse for a jaunt from the Mountain Haus to the top of Kellogg Peak. The 90-minute rides can be arranged by calling the mountain office, (208) 783-1111.

Cross-Country Skiing

Cross-country skiers using any of Idaho's 18 trail systems and 4 state park ski areas will need a **parking permit** from the Idaho Department of Parks and Recreation. Season and three-day permits are available at outdoor stores, state parks, Forest Service stations, and some chambers of commerce. For information on the Park N' Ski Program, call (208) 334-4199.

Cross-country skiers can ski free at the nine groomed trails near the **Lookout Pass Ski Area** lodge, (208) 744-1392. No cross-country ski trails in the Wallace area are groomed, but two near Mullan, a small community just west of Wallace, are signed and well-marked. A Lookout Pass Recreation Area trail map is available from the Lookout Pass Ski Shop, the Lolo National Forest Superior Ranger District in Montana, (406) 822-4233, and the Idaho Panhandle National Forest Wallace Ranger District, (208) 752-1221. Some favorites in the area are listed here.

The 3 1/2-mile **Lookout Pass Trail** follows the route of early-day explorer Captain John Mullan, who built the first road through the area. Take the Lookout Pass chairlift to the top of Runt Mountain (buy a one-ride ticket) and look for the trailhead sign to the right of the ski patrol hut. The trail leads to the St. Regis Basin Trail (No. 267) in the Lolo National Forest in Montana, which offers access to serious backcountry terrain (heed all avalanche warnings). Skiers can complete a 6-mile loop by skiing a slightly uphill grade back to the ski area parking lot on an abandoned railroad grade or old Hwy 10 (it's signed).

An easy route on an old mining road, **Beacon Light Trail** begins across the road from the Hale Fish Hatchery; take the East Mullan exit, Exit 69, from I-90, turn north to Hwy 10, then continue on Park Rd to the hatchery. The 2 1/2-mile trail ends at the Beacon Light Mine. Side trips on an abandoned railroad right-of-way are optional.

The relatively easy 5-mile **Cedar Creek-Cinnabar Trail** is on an old roadbed along the Coeur d'Alene River, with several short side trips. To get to the trailhead, take the Kingstone exit, Exit 43, from I-90 to Forest Rd 9, then drive east almost 17 miles to the junction with Character Ridge Rd. From Wallace drive north 15 1/2 miles over Dobson Pass to Cedar Creek bridge.

An easy marked and groomed 5-mile trail begins at the Idaho Park N' Ski area at **Fourth of July Pass,** 15 miles east of Coeur d'Alene. A few gentle hills offer beginners a challenge but can be handled easily by experienced skiers; there's a warming hut near the parking lot. A Washington Sno-Park Pass or Idaho Park N' Ski permit is required here, available at area sporting goods stores or Forest Service stations.

Aggressive cross-country skiers take to the 400 miles of snowmobile trails in the Priest Lake area, but they are not groomed for skiing and require that skiers watch for snowmobiles and get off the trail. Most cross-country skiers stick to the three main trails near Priest Lake's Luby Bay, which are groomed by a local ski association. The most popular trail begins at the Hill's Resort tennis courts and winds through a clear-cut, through woods, and onto the **Priest Lake Golf Course,** where skiers can ski the entire golf course. A second trail is the **Lake View Loop,** a short drive to the Luby Bay Campground and the trailhead. The third trail— **Hanna Flats**—is a more challenging route not suitable for beginning skiers; the trailhead is a 4-mile drive up Hwy 57.

Downhill Skiing

Drivers heading east from Washington cross two mountain passes in North Idaho before they drop into Montana; the first is Fourth of July Pass and the second is Lookout Pass, where a small ski area at its summit draws skiers from Wallace to the west and Missoula to the east, looking for deep snows at high elevation. **Lookout Pass Ski Area** opened in

1938. It's just off I-90 at Exit 0, 13 miles east of Wallace. There's one lift (a second is planned) and seven runs, and is only open on weekends. Nordic skiers and mountain bikers also flock to the pass because of access to high-elevation backcountry. There are no public overnight accommodations at the ski area, although a small condominium-style complex is planned. The ski area has rental equipment and ski lessons; call (208) 744-1301 or (208) 744-1392 in winter for information.

The gondola terminal of **Silver Mountain Resort** (610 Bunker Ave, (208) 783-1111) is in the heart of Kellogg (which made an ill-fated attempt to fashion itself as a Bavarian-themed village) and is flanked by expansive parking lots. The lodging and dining choices in Kellogg lag behind the resort development, and most skiers use the resort as a day area, choosing to stay in Coeur d'Alene, an hour's drive west.

The 3 1/10-mile gondola ride here takes 19 minutes and climbs 3,400 vertical feet to the Mountain Haus, at 5,700 feet elevation. From the top there are views of three states and portions of Canada. The lodge on the mountain offers the usual facilities for skiers—rentals, a cafeteria, a nicer restaurant in the loft, and an area for brown-baggers. The actual ski lifts—a quad, two triples, and two doubles—are right outside the door of the lodge and offer access to 50 runs. Ski rental, lessons, and day care are available. Unlike some ski resorts, the terrain at Silver Mountain is too vertical for cross-country skiers. To get to the gondola, take Exit 49 from I-90.

The backcountry near Silver Mountain Resort is accessible to downhill skiers, **snowboarders,** or **telemarkers** via snowcat. Day-long **snowcat tours,** offered daily December to April, can be arranged through Peak Adventures, (208) 682-3200.

Schweitzer Mountain Resort aspires to be a destination ski area, but so far it falls short. Even construction of a hotel and condos, installation of a quad chairlift (in addition to four double chairlifts), and development of a decent cross-country area with groomed trails haven't drawn the skiers in numbers needed to qualify it as a destination resort. What it has done, though, is make Schweitzer one of the best day-use areas in the region, given the diversity of activities. In addition to skiing and snowboarding on 55 runs, there's **snowmobiling, ice skating,** and **sleigh rides.** Holidays are celebrated with a torchlight parade of skiers down the runs leading to the lodge and fireworks after dark. The varied terrain and deep powder, after snow at other regional resorts has become hard-packed, draw experienced telemark skiers. Go 11 miles north of Sandpoint on US 95, and watch for the signed turnoff. Call (800) 831-8810 or (208) 263-9555 in Idaho for more information.

Snowmobiling

Idaho has more than 5,000 miles of snowmobile trails. Guided trips can be arranged through the Idaho Outfitters and Guides Association, (208) 342-1438 or (800) 847-4843. For trail information, contact the Idaho Department of Parks and Recreation, (208) 334-4199.

The Silver Valley can't afford to be a one-note tourist destination, so the 1,000-mile **Silver Country Trail System** was developed. It's used primarily by snowmobilers during winter, but the route's also used by mountain bikers and hikers in summer. Much of the trail is as yet unmarked, but in winter, when it's groomed for snowmobiles, it's still easy to follow. (When the snow melts and bushes grow in the route, bikers and hikers have difficulty finding some of the portions.) *SnoWest Magazine* and *SnoGoer Magazine* both named the Silver Valley one of the best full-service snowmobiling hot spots in the world, although West Yellowstone is still the acknowledged capital. Snowmobile tours, half-day and full-day, can be arranged through Orton's 2 Cycle, (208) 556-4402.

About 100 miles of snowmobile trails begin at or near the **Lookout Pass Ski Area** and connect with another 400 miles of groomed trails. Nearly a dozen trails are groomed from mid-December until early March, ranging from 12 to 67 miles. One popular trail begins at the ski area parking lot and goes to **Millan's Shoshone Park** (8 miles) or to the **St. Joe River** (30 miles). Snowmobiles can be rented in Wallace at Schaefer's Marine (60412 Silver Valley Rd, (208) 753-5271) with guided tours available, too. Rentals and guides are also available through Lookout Snowmobile Tours, (208) 556-7211, and through Gloria's Steak House and Lodge on the North Fork of the Coeur d'Alene River, (208) 682-3031. The Wallace Ranger Station, (208) 752-1221, has trail information.

There are more than 400 miles of groomed trails on Forest Service land near Priest Lake, labeled the **Priest Lake Snowplay Area.** Maps of the trails are available from the Priest Lake Ranger District office in Priest River, (208) 443-2512.

Wildlife

Part of the Old Mission State Park near Cataldo is **Old Mission Landing,** a primitive day-use area with a boat launch. The landing was the upstream terminal for ore-carrying steamships. The steamships are long gone and many of the mines are played out. Boating is allowed, but the more popular activities are canoeing and **bird-watching.** Because of contaminants in the river bottom, landing, and surrounding flats from mining waste discharged for decades upstream, warnings are posted to avoid handling the dirt or eating fish caught in the streams and rivers in this area. Birders, however, will be rewarded with frequent sightings of great blue **herons**, **osprey** which nest in the flats, and an occasional **bald eagle**, as well as grebes, wood ducks, red crossbills, yellow-rumped warblers, American pipits, and violet-green swallows. The best birding times are April to June and September to November.

The variety of habitats on the **Kootenai National Wildlife Refuge** ensure a similar variety of resident wildlife. Plenty of wetlands on the refuge support populations of **beaver, muskrat, moose**, and **waterfowl**. And since the refuge butts up against the Selkirk Mountains, there is abundant conifer forest and meadows for **deer, black bear,** and **songbirds.** In all, 225 species of birds have been spotted here. During spring migration—March to May—the population of mallards is impressive and pintails abound. Other migrant visitors have included **tundra swans,** red-necked grebes, wood ducks, and songbirds such as golden-crowned kinglets, black-capped chickadees, pygmy and red-breasted nuthatches, brown creepers, yellow warblers, and yellow-rumped warblers. Look for dippers along Myrtle Creek. Nesting birds include osprey and bald eagles. The best time on the refuge is May through July; in early spring wear boots you don't mind getting wet and muddy. One of the best trails for sighting a range of wildlife is the **Island Pond trail.** Fall migration brings about 40,000 waterfowl to the wetlands on the refuge; however, hunting is allowed here, so take appropriate precautions (wear plenty of hunter orange clothing in the autumn). It's on US 95 about 30 miles north of Sandpoint and 5 miles west of Bonners Ferry (turn off US 95 onto Riverside Rd on the south bank of the river); Kootenai National Wildlife Refuge, HCR 60, Box 283, Bonners Ferry, ID 83805, (208) 267-3888.

Other Activities

Hour-long, half-day, and full-day **dogsled rides** are available at Lookout Pass Ski Area, (208) 744-1392.

For an overhead view of Coeur d'Alene Lake, TMP Helicopters, (208) 765-9338 or (208) 683-3463, and Brook's Seaplane Service, (208) 664-2842 or (208) 772-5649, both offer **scenic flights** over the lake.

Anyone wanting to see Lake Pend Oreille from the air can take a **parasail ride** with Wind Walker Parasail, (888) PARA-SAIL or (208) 263-2136, located at the Sandpoint Marina. Parasailing goes on from morning to sunset, May to September; fliers are airborne for about 15 minutes, but the boat ride is 75 minutes. There's a weight minimum (80 pounds) and maximum (240 pounds); those with a combined weight of less than 220 pounds can take a tandem flight.

outside in

Attractions

For years, **Wallace** boasted the distinction of having the last stoplight on I-90 between Seattle and Boston. The interstate now bypasses Wallace, but it would be a mistake to fly right past this gem of a mountain town just because there's no stoplight to make you pause and look around. Hardly is there a town where the juxtaposition of old and new is more striking. Downtown, the saloons have names that hark to mining days. There's even a brokerage house that specializes in mining stocks. Turn-of-the-century downtown bordellos that catered to miners earned Wallace a regional reputation, and now one of these houses of ill-repute is a museum. But in between the jewelry stores that specialize in silver necklaces and earrings are signs of modern times—a cybercafe with pastries and coffee to munch on while grazing the Internet, a couple of espresso bars, a plethora of antique/mining artifacts shops, and several art galleries. The mountain town garnered at least 15 minutes of fame in the summer of 1996 when the Hollywood movie *Dante's Peak,* starring Pierce Brosnan as a geologist, was filmed on location here.

Wallace is the kind of town where everyone wears a couple of hats. Locals agree the place to buy the best hand-tied fishing flies is at the photography studio, **Shauna Hillman's Indelible Tidbits,** 604 Bank St, (208) 753-0591, where Shauna spends idle time in the shop tying an impressive array of flies. Mining memorabilia can be seen at the **Wallace District Mining Museum,** 509 Bank St, (208) 556-1592. A pleasant way to spend a couple of hours is simply taking your own informal **walking tour** through the residential district adjacent to downtown, which is loaded with fine Victorian-style homes.

Wallace is most proud of its **Northern Pacific Depot Railroad Museum,** Sixth and Pine, (208) 752-0111, which, after extensive community effort, was moved 200 feet rather than razed to make way for the new section of I-90. The chateau-style depot houses a fine collection of railroad memorabilia and is the focus of an annual community celebration, Depot Days, held in early May.

For a real look at the mining history of the area, head for the **Sierra Silver Mine Tour** office, 420 Fifth, Wallace, (208) 752-5151, and sign up for a tour of the Sierra Mine, a short motorized trolley ride from Wallace. The hour-long tour goes 200 yards deep into a nonworking mine where the miners' tools and working conditions remain as they were when it was a productive shaft. Wear a jacket, since the temperatures underground remain a constant 42°F, even on the hottest and coldest days; you'll be required to don a hardhat.

In the heart of the Silver Valley, **Kellogg** was once home to some of the richest silver mines in the world—and to one of the biggest smelters in the region. In 1981 the mines closed. The smokestacks at the Bunker Hill Mining and Smelter Complex were razed in 1996, and what's left are enough mine tailings and slag heaps to qualify the valley as an EPA Superfund site. While the EPA cleanup efforts continue to fuel the economy here, so does Silver Mountain Resort, a year-round resort with world-class powder skiing during winters and mountain biking and a concert series (see Calendar of Events, below) in summers. What sets this resort apart is the world's longest single-stage gondola to the mountaintop. To help Kellogg establish a new industry, federal funds were obtained to build the gondola to carry skiers from the valley floor to Kellogg Peak and a ski resort then named Jackass Ski Bowl. Built in the late '60s by Bunker Hill, Jackass Ski Bowl boasted extreme terrain and legendary powder skiing, but a narrow, winding 7-mile road with sheer drop-offs discouraged heavy skier traffic. With the new gondola, funded with a $6.4 million grant from Congress, Jackass got a new name and a future. Locals hope that it will become a destination area, but for now it attracts hundreds of regional skiers and snowboarders.

The Silver Valley is steeped in mining history. A memorial was erected at **Big Creek** just west of Kellogg to honor 92 men who died when a fire swept through the nearby Sunshine Mine in 1972. Mining artifacts can be seen at the **Staff House Museum,** 820 McKinley Ave in Kellogg, (208) 786-4141, open Memorial Day weekend through September.

As the Coeur d'Alene River flows west from the mountains near Kellogg, it opens into a broad valley that is the site of one of Idaho's earliest settlements. The floodplain flanking the Coeur d'Alene River at what is now **Cataldo** supported a thriving community of Native Americans when the first Jesuit missionaries arrived in the mid-19th century. Indian legend said the Black Robes would come someday to offer wisdom to the natives, and, indeed, the priests did come. The Jesuits founded the **Old Mission of the Sacred Heart** in 1842 on the St. Joe River, and many natives converted to Catholicism. Four years later the priests moved the mission to Cataldo, 24 miles east of present-day Coeur d'Alene. Under their guidance, the Indians built the church, which still stands. Erected between 1850 and 1853 by weaving willow saplings and grass and plastering it with mud and clay, the mission is the oldest structure in the state. The church was used regularly until 1872 when the mission was moved to Desmet, but Mass is still celebrated several times a year at Cataldo. The Old Mission building at Cataldo is the centerpiece of **Old Mission State**

Park, (208) 682-3814, although other historic sites such as the mission cemetery, bakery, and orchard still remain. The visitor center has excellent displays and an interpretive slide show.

Coeur d'Alene, a town that named itself the Lake City, grew up in the '80s as a mecca for Californians wanting to move to an affordable and pristine part of the Northwest. Indeed, the city has attributes of which many former mining towns can only dream. For starters, there's Coeur d'Alene Lake with 135 miles of shoreline. The lake stretches 25 miles south, with deep bays, deep water (averaging 120 feet) for fishing, and plenty of wind for sailboats. Breezes blow down from the Selkirk Mountains that hem the lake's eastern edge, and rivers flowing from the Selkirks feed it.

Of towns that have renewed their lagging resource-based economies, Coeur d'Alene is one of the success stories. People come here to play and all the amenities are in place to help them. As the hub of life for those in North Idaho, there's enough of a permanent community to keep the town lively even in winter. A small college has a venue for concerts and a local symphony orchestra; there's also a professional summer theater at which local notables such as actors Patty Duke, Ellen Travolta, and Jack Bannon have performed. The main street boasts all the boutiques, espresso bars, and art galleries expected at a resort town. There are even a couple of microbreweries—one, T. W. Fischers, doubles as the local sports bar. Serious shoppers head 8 miles west on I-90 to the Post Falls Outlet Mall, (208) 773-4555.

For a quick adrenaline rush, head for **Silverwood Theme Park** just north of Coeur d'Alene on US 95, (208) 683-3400, open summers only. Rides include Thunder Canyon, a whitewater rafting ride, and a rebuilt wooden roller coaster—The Grizzly—that reaches 55 mph. An airplane hangar was converted to an indoor ice rink, which hosts ice shows; at the adjacent airfield biplanes put on air shows. The **Museum of North Idaho,** 115 NW Blvd, Coeur d'Alene, (208) 664-3448, specializes in artifacts and tools from the areas early mining days.

For two physically similar resort towns located within a hundred miles of each other, **Sandpoint** and Coeur d'Alene couldn't be more different. Both turned from resource-based economies (Sandpoint from logging, Coeur d'Alene from mining) into tourist destinations; they both sit on the shores of large lakes with recreational fishing and watersports opportunities; and both have good day ski areas nearby (Sandpoint has Schweitzer Mountain Resort, Coeur d'Alene has Silver Mountain Resort). But where Coeur d'Alene has the loud glitz of a major destination resort and is the summer playground for the region, Sandpoint just quietly goes about its tourism business—but with no less seriousness. The city at the edge of Lake Pend Oreille with mountains as its backdrop has seen more than a few tourists fall in love with the town and pick up and move here. Those who already live here guard Sandpoint's ambience as though it were a resource. Visitors are welcome, but for some they're just as welcome to remain visitors only. That doesn't mean the people of Sandpoint are unfriendly; they're just serious about preserving their high quality of life.

Those browsing the main street through Sandpoint will find boutiques, art galleries, and shops sporting Northwest souvenirs (many with a bear or huckleberry theme). But where the shops in Coeur d'Alene have Southwest leanings, those in Sandpoint are all lodge-flavored. For a sample of the wares, don't miss Cabin Fever, (208) 263-7179, or Coldwater Creek, (208) 263-2265, which anchors the downtown at one end and spans the Cedar Street Bridge market. Coldwater Creek sells wilderness-themed goods primarily through catalogs and is among the fastest growing companies in the country.

Sandpoint, too, has its museum, the **Bonner County Historical Museum,** in Lakeview Park at 609 S Ella St, (208) 263-2344. It includes exhibits of Native American artifacts from the Kalispel and Kootenai tribes, and from early-day fur trader and explorer David Thompson.

Calendar of Events

The **Sandpoint Winter Carnival,** which includes a torchlight parade down the ski slopes of Schweitzer Mountain Resort, is the last two weeks of January; call (208) 263-2161 for details.

The **summer concert series** at Silver Mountain Resort runs from early July until Labor Day and focuses on country acts and regional musicians. Seating is, for the most part, on grass in an open-air amphitheater, and the ticket price includes the gondola ride. Experienced concert-goers bring a sand chair (full-sized lawn chairs block the view of those behind). Blankets (and hats and mittens) are in order; this is a mountaintop. But during a starry night in late July, you'll think music never sounded this good, regardless of the act. Tickets for the concert series are available at the mountain office, 610 Bunker Ave in Kellogg, and through G&B Select-a-Seat, (800) 325-SEAT. (Reserved seat tickets only get you a first-come spot on grass terraces up front; the sound is just as good from the general admission area.)

Depot Days, with the historic Northern Pacific Depot Railroad Museum as the focus, is held in early May in Wallace. For more information, call (208) 752-0111.

Traditional skills such as spinning, quilting and black powder shooting are demonstrated at the one-day **Historic Skills Fair** at Old Mission State Park, (208) 682-3814, in Cataldo.

The **Festival at Sandpoint** concerts are held outdoors at Memorial Field in Sandpoint mid-July through mid-August; call (208) 263-2161 for tickets and information.

The **Coeur d'Alene Indian Pilgrimage** is held mid-August and includes the Coming of the Black Robes Ceremony of the Coeur d'Alene Indians, at Old Mission State Park in Cataldo; call (208) 682-3814 for details.

The annual **Idaho Draft Horse International** focuses on the big horses, but the event also includes exhibits and food, held the first weekend in October in Sandpoint; call (208) 263-2117 for more information.

Restaurants

Beverly's ☆☆☆ The showcase restaurant at the Coeur d'Alene Resort, Beverly's is long on atmosphere and is regarded by locals as one of the best special-occasion places to eat in the region. The restaurant is on the top floor of the resort, where wall-to-wall windows afford impressive views of the lake and the mountains. The menu tries hard to satisfy a broad range of dining desires and in most cases it's successful. If you're undecided, we recommend one of the entrees that nods to local fare such as trout or salmon. *Within the Coeur d'Alene Resort, on the lake; PO Box 7200, Coeur d'Alene; (800) 688-4142; lunch, dinner every day; AE, DC, DIS, MC, V; local checks only; $$$.*

Swan's Landing ☆☆☆ This lodge-style eatery isn't easy to find, especially for those confining their search to Sandpoint proper. It's found across the long bridge toward Coeur d'Alene at the site of an old boat landing. Once there, however, you'll find this restaurant is just about perfect. Summers, lunch and dinner are served on the patio. Diversions include watching the boats come and go from the restaurant's private marina (you can arrive here by boat—moorings are available for diners). But any diversions from the fare here are a shame, because the eclectic cuisine is innovative and delicious. The menu ranges from pizzas from a wood-fired oven topped with a mix of Northwest- and Southwest-influenced toppings to salads, which might have a mango dressing. Desserts focus on fresh berries in season, but are nevertheless sinful. Ale from the local microbrewery, Pend Oreille Brewing, is included on the menu. Inside, the decor is pure 1990s with a wall-sized stone fireplace dominating the dining room and separating diners from the lounge. Floors are poured concrete, the roof is corrugated aluminum, beams are exposed wood, and it all works. *At the south end of Sandpoint's Long Bridge; 1480 Lakeshore Dr, Sagle; (208) 265-2000; lunch, dinner every day, brunch Sun; AE, MC, V; checks OK; $$-$$$.*

Enaville Resort (The Snakepit) ☆ Let's get one thing straight: there are no snakes on the menu, and this isn't a resort. The name dates to the days before the turn of the century when this resort housed women of ill repute and was frequented by the miners (the snakepit reference we leave to your imagination). More than a century later—100 years of atmosphere, boasts the restaurant—the reputation of the patrons here is top-notch. Most come for steaks served up around the big central stone fireplace where a fire blazes most of the year. You won't find any froufrou entrees here; the menu's built around meat—beef, buffalo burgers, chicken, prime rib. Dinners come with soup or salad and potatoes served in several styles. Real men order up the Rocky Mountain oysters and don't wince when they think about eating them (they're beef testicles; the menu says to ask if they're available, since sometimes the bulls don't cooperate). There's no trout on the menu, but if you fly-fish, ask about the supply of locally tied fly patterns at the cashier's counter. We've had some fishing success using flies made from skunk hair we got at the Snakepit. *30 miles east of Coeur d'Alene—from Exit 43, 1¹/₂ miles upriver on Coeur d'Alene River Rd; 1480 Coeur d'Alene River Rd, Kingston; (208) 682-3453; breakfast, lunch, dinner every day; MC, V; local checks only; $-$$.*

Ivano's ☆ Year in and year out Ivano's has served some of the best Northern Italian fare in the region. Perhaps it's because the menu hasn't strayed into other regions. Or maybe it's because the food isn't sacrificed for ambience; this eatery's in a renovated house and diners sit in what were the living room and bedrooms. It's downright cozy. *Downtown; 124 S Second, Sandpoint; (208) 263-0211; lunch Mon–Fri, dinner every day; AE, DC, DIS, MC, V; checks OK; $$.*

Jimmy D's ☆ For years the menu at this downtown Coeur d'Alene eatery leaned toward California cuisine—heavy in avocados and tropical seafood. Slowly it's found its way to a more Northwest flavor; now there's rainbow trout on the menu as well. Perhaps the wine list is most telling, in that a broad selection of Idaho and Washington wines overwhelm California-produced vino. Like nearly everything in Coeur d'Alene, Jimmy D's is overshadowed by the Coeur d'Alene Resort and its upscale restaurant, Beverly's. (The gourmet eateries all compete for the same crowd.) But Jimmy D's holds its own in the food department. Where it falls short is in ambience; tables are on the cozy side for intimate dining, and the front window looks out on Sherman Ave, the city's busiest street. *Downtown; 320 Sherman Ave, Coeur d'Alene; (208) 664-9774; lunch, dinner every day, brunch Sun; DIS, MC, V; checks OK; $$.*

Third Street Cantina ☆ Many restaurants that try to cross too many cuisine styles don't do any of them well. That's not the case at this

Mexican restaurant, which could also be described as a seafood eatery. Order from the Mexican side of the menu or the seafood portion and the entrees arrive equally well prepared. But for the most interesting fare try one of the entrees that combines the two, often found on the fresh sheet, such as fresh halibut served with lime and salsa and a Spanish-style rice, or fish tacos. *2 blocks north of Sherman Ave; 201 N 3rd, Coeur d'Alene; (208) 664-0581; lunch, dinner every day; AE, DC, DIS, MC, V; checks OK; $$.*

Lodgings

Clark House ☆☆☆ A 15,000-square-foot mansion, Clark House presides over Hayden Lake just as it did when it was built in 1910. Beautifully restored, the mansion has five guest rooms with private baths and bathtubs you can sink down into. The rooms also have cozy feather beds, and some have fireplaces. Staying here is sampling life in the lap of Victorian luxury. Wintry evenings can be spent in the library reading or playing board games. Continental breakfast is set out for early risers in the second-floor sitting area; otherwise there's a gourmet breakfast served in the mansion's dining room. True to the era, the rooms have no phones or TVs, and we would be disappointed if it were otherwise. Guests can also make reservations for a six-course dinner at the mansion; the dining room is open to non-guests as well, with reservations. The dinner menu changes nightly. *On Hayden Lake north of Coeur d'Alene; 4550 E South Hayden Rd, Hayden Lake, ID 83835; (800) 765-4593 or (208) 772-3470; AE, DC, MC, V; checks OK; $$$.*

Coeur d'Alene Resort ☆☆☆ The center of life in Coeur d'Alene is the Coeur d'Alene Resort, a $60 million mega-complex with hotel rooms, suites, restaurants, shops, bowling alley, swimming pool, convention rooms, and a penthouse suite with a per-night price tag that can run into four digits, all within an 18-story tower at the water's edge. The resort was built in the 1980s by millionaire Duane Hagadone, who owns the town's newspaper as well as a vast array of other properties. The Coeur d'Alene Resort was picked in 1990 by readers of *Condé Nast Traveler* magazine as the top mainland US resort. It doesn't fall short of this honor. The resort includes 338 lakeside rooms, 3 restaurants, 3 lounges, indoor and outdoor pools, and a marina. And it's all surrounded by the world's longest floating boardwalk. *Downtown, 2nd and Front St; PO Box 7200, Coeur d'Alene, ID 83816; (800) 688-5253 or (208) 765-4000; AE, DC, DIS, MC, V; checks OK; $$$.*

Beale House Bed and Breakfast ☆☆ The mining boom in the late 1800s created a building boom in Wallace as the newly rich erected what were in their day beautiful Victorian-style mansions. Certainly one of the finest that has been restored true to the period is the Beale House, built in 1904 by mining attorney Charles W. Beale. Owners Jim and Linda See say extensive restoration wasn't required since they are only the fourth owners and the home's always been a private residence. The oak woodwork, intricate parquet floors (laid by a teenager the Beales brought over from Europe for just such a task), fireplace mantels, bathroom fixtures, and tile all are original. It's easy to relax in the parlor and imagine a grand life here in the early 1900s, or to add a bit of 1990s lifestyle by sitting in the backyard spa. Four guest rooms share two baths; a fifth has a private bath. We recommend foregoing the private bath and staying in either the Fireplace Room or what the owners call the Window Room, which is smaller but bright with broad windows that afford views of the backyard and mountainside behind the house. These two share a truly generously sized Victorian-era clawfoot tub. Otherwise, opt for the Balcony Room, which has private access to a balcony through French doors (summers only, of course). *4 blocks west of downtown; 107 Cedar St, Wallace, ID 83873; (208) 752-7151; no credit cards; checks OK; $$.*

Berry Patch Inn ☆☆ There's nothing Victorian about the Berry Patch Inn; it's pure Northwest chalet-style. The home is on 2 acres—all landscaped—on a mountainside, and guests can wander trails that extend beyond the grounds. The landscaping includes a waterfall. Winters, guests can cozy up to a fire in the stone fireplace and watch a video. The main-floor guest room has a private entrance through French doors to the back deck. Two second-floor rooms offer forest and mountain views. Nice touches include the cushy robe and slippers provided guests, to keep them warm as they sip a nightcap of berry liqueur. Innkeeper Lee Ray specializes in cozy, so in winters the beds have flannel sheets and down comforters. Breakfast takes a low-fat bent, but the fare doesn't suffer. *3 miles southwest of Coeur d'Alene; 1150 N Four Winds Rd, Coeur d'Alene, ID 83814; (208) 765-4994; MC, V; checks OK; $$.*

Edgewater Resort ☆☆ The Edgewater's literally on the beach of Lake Pend Oreille. There's no need to ask for a room with a view here; all face the lake and have patios or balconies. Some have fireplaces, a nice amenity after a day of playing in the snow. The resort includes a restaurant, but we recommend heading for one of the other dining options within walking distance in downtown Sandpoint. *Downtown, 1 block north of main drag; 56 Bridge St, Sandpoint, ID 83864; (800) 635-2534 or (208) 263-3194; AE, DC, DIS, MC, V; checks OK; $$-$$$.*

Serendipity Country Inn ☆☆ True to its name, the Serendipity Country Inn is really in the country and guests here get maximum privacy. The 5,700-square-foot house sits at the edge of a fruit orchard on 12 acres, much of it forested, and the innkeepers live in another building. But civilization—meaning noise, nightlife, shopping—isn't all that far away. It's just 12 miles to Sandpoint. The Serendipity, which caters to adults (those traveling with children under 16 are discouraged), has two guest rooms and a spacious suite; decor is Southwest lodge. The suite has a four-poster king-size bed, a couch, a fireplace, a wet bar, a dressing room, a whirlpool tub, and a separate room with a Murphy bed. Both of the other guest rooms, while not as spacious, are still generously sized. Guests can use the great room for relaxing or the library/game room with a TV and fireplace. Outside, there's a hot tub near the orchard and walking paths through the woods. Breakfast incorporates fresh fruit and berries in season; guests can also book a dinner package. *12 miles northeast of Sandpoint at the northern end of Lake Pend Oreille; 2400 Selkirk Rd, Sandpoint, ID 83864; (800) 988-9284 or (208) 265-9049; AE, MC, V; checks OK; $$ $$$.*

Connie's Motor Inn ☆ For a location central to Sandpoint's downtown, Connie's can't be beat. The motel's a favorite with area skiers. It's not the best place in town, but the rooms are clean and nicely furnished in a basic motel way, and the food at the on-site restaurant is good, albeit basic. During winter the fire's always lighted in the lounge fireplace. In nice weather, the garden deck is pleasant. *Downtown; 323 Cedar St, Sandpoint, ID 83864; (800) 828-0660 or (208) 263-9581; AE, DIS, MC, V; checks OK; $$.*

Jameson Restaurant, Saloon, and Old-Time Boarding House ☆ Rumors say some of the rooms at the Jameson are haunted, and if that's the case, the ghosts are probably the women who worked at this early-day version of the no-tell motel. Before the turn of the century, Wallace was best known for its bordellos, and the Jameson, which opened in 1889 as the Theodore Steak and Billiard Hall, was the upscale version of a house of ill-repute. The rooms have been restored to their glory days, sans the working women. The third-floor guest rooms are small but cozy and well-appointed with antiques. On weekends, ask for a room that's not located above the saloon. For the best breakfast in town, this bar's the place to be. The fare's basic and definitely not low-cal, with eggs and bacon and all the fixings. At lunch or dinner, save room for a piece of apple or cherry pie, some of the best in the region. Lunch and dinner are what you might expect in a small town deep in the mountains—burgers, sandwiches, and soup for lunch, and chicken and beef for dinner. We recommend the charbroiled rainbow trout. Sit back and enjoy late-1800s saloon atmosphere; it's the showcase of the restored hotel. Diners are served in the saloon until it's full, then seated in the adjacent dining room, which is more formal but a lot less fun. The boarding house is open summers only. *Downtown at 304 Sixth St; PO Box 469, Wallace, ID 83873; (208) 556-1554; AE, MC, V; checks OK; $$.*

Old Northern Inn ☆   Early in the century, the Old Northern was a hotel on the shore of Priest Lake, a modest building clad in split logs that served as a summer residence for the well-heeled who spent hot days at lakeside. Now it's that again, except the stays are shorter. The Great Northern inn is located in Coolin, Idaho, a community that extends along the main road with a small church that doubles as a community hall, a new motel, a marina, restaurant, and a string of private cabins. The two-story building boasts broad decks, one with a firepit at the center, with cheery pots of geraniums and petunias, and an interior restored to its early 1900s charm. The inn has a private beach and dock, so guests can boat right up to the inn if that's how they want to arrive. Priest Lake can be downright chilly until late August, when it's finally comfortable for extended swims. Because it's not winterized, the Great Northern is open Memorial Day to mid-October. Guests wanting maximum privacy and space should request the Kalispel Room, a suite with a small sitting room, spacious private bath, and a modest deck outside the door of the private entrance. Breakfast is hearty fare, including Priest Lake huckleberries, served in the dining room . *At the south end of Priest Lake at Coolin, 5 miles from turnoff from Hwy 57; PO Box 177, Coolin, ID 83821; (208) 443-2426; MC, V; checks OK; $$-$$$.*

Pinewoods B&B ☆   There are advantages to staying outside a resort town, especially in summer when the streets are noisy and you seek quiet. Pinewoods is well off the beaten highway, but only 5 miles from Sandpoint, and there's a bicycle trail to town. The contemporary log home is tucked in a forest of pine and offers cross-country skiing right out the door. Avid skiers will want to head for the trails at Schweitzer Mountain Resort, however, a 30-minute drive from Pinewoods. The house is pleasant and bird-watchers will be in good company since innkeepers Fran and Bob Walkley are avid birders and surround the home with bird-feeders and birdhouses. Only one of the two guest rooms has a private bath. There are bicycles on-site for guest use. *Across the Long Bridge from Sandpoint in Sagle; 1065 Lignite Rd, Sagle, ID 83860; (800) 366-5851 or (208) 263-5851; cash and checks only; $-$$.*

Templin's Resort Hotel ☆   For those wanting a little distance from the tourist crush of peak season in Coeur d'Alene, Templin's Resort Hotel is a good choice. The hotel is actually in Post Falls, a smaller lumber mill town that's a 10-minute drive on I-90 west of Coeur d'Alene, and is situated on the Spokane River, the outlet of Coeur d'Alene Lake. Its rooms are standard-issue motel, although most have views of the river and the hotel's marina. The on-site restaurant, Mallards, has a menu that delivers competently prepared meals that cover the poultry, beef, and pasta selections found at most high-end family eateries. The relaxing views of the Spokane River will overwhelm any minor disappointments in the cautious menu. The 167-room hotel includes an indoor pool and sauna; river cruises board from the marina and can be arranged through the hotel. *On the banks of the Spokane River; 414 E 1st Ave, Post Falls, ID 83854; (800) 283-6754 or (208) 773-1611; AE, DC, DIS, MC, V; checks OK; $$-$$$.*

Wallace Inn ☆   Almost simultaneous with the installation of the Silver Mountain Resort gondola in Kellogg was the construction of this motel located on what used to be the I-90 route through town. Now that the interstate's been elevated and relocated to the edge of Wallace, the street out front is decidedly more quiet. With a dearth of quality lodging in Kellogg, this motel is the closest stop for skiers not wanting to make the drive west over Fourth of July Pass to Coeur d'Alene after a stimulating day on the slopes, or who want to make it a weekend at Silver Mountain. Facilities include a modest work-out room, swimming pool, Jacuzzi, and two saunas. Those seeking maximum privacy should ask for a room in the wing opposite O'Rourke's Bar, which is part of the restaurant and gift shop complex on the ground floor of the west wing. *At the west end of Wallace just off I-90; 100 Front St, Wallace, ID 83873; (800) 643-2386 or (208) 752-1252, fax (208) 753-0981; AE, DC, DIS, MC, V; checks OK; $$.*

Ranches and Resorts

Hill's Resort   The original Hill—George—bought the property in 1919; now, eight decades later, Hill's Resort is a rambling collection of cabins and lodges lining the shore of Luby Bay. It's earned regional, if not national, attention. The dining room and lounge in the main lodge have commanding views of the Selkirk Mountain Crest, a ridge of granite on the eastern boundary of Priest Lake. The rest of the year-round resort is tucked among a dense forest of cedar and fir trees, affording visitors a semblance of privacy even during the busiest weeks of summer. A fine sandy beach runs the length of the resort, with firepits ringed by chairs. Water traffic can be fierce when the temperatures rise in July and August, so the swimming area must be roped off from the Jet-skis and ski boats. We prefer Hill's during the quiet autumn months when the larch trees have turned golden and quiet walks down forest roads are the order of the day. In winter, the place is downright delightful because of the miles of cross-country ski trails in the area and the coziness of a cabin at lakeside with a fire in the fireplace.

In summer, the lodge dining room is open daily for lunch and dinner; be sure to try the baby back ribs, a bit messy but delicious. During winter the dining room is open for dinner only Friday through Sunday; otherwise guests must cook in their own cabins. A week's stay in summer (the maximum rental)—especially for those lucky enough to catch the few sunny weeks—may not be long enough. There are tennis courts on-site and a nine-hole golf course nearby; the resort rents boats, canoes, mountain bikes, and cross-country skis. For privacy and less traffic we recommend cabins 104–109 (at lakeside). Condo units are adjacent to the lodge and on the beach as well, but look out on the marina. In late July and early August, the area's a veritable mecca for huckleberry pickers; the lounge and restaurant at Hill's have numerous huckleberry concoctions on the menu. In the fall, those searching for morel and chanterelle mushrooms come here and seldom go away empty-handed. *On Priest Lake at Luby Bay—take the Luby Bay turnoff from Hwy 57; HCR 5, Box 162A, Priest Lake, ID 83856; (208) 443-2551; DIS, MC, V; checks OK.*

More Information

Bonners Ferry Visitors Center: (208) 267-5922.

Clearwater National Forest: (208) 882-3557.

Coeur d'Alene Visitors Center: (208) 664-0587.

Forest Service Camping Reservations: (800) 280-2267.

Idaho Dept. of Parks & Recreation, Northern Region Headquarters: (208) 667-1511.

Idaho Panhandle National Forest, headquarters: (208) 765-7223.

IPNF, Avery Ranger District: (208) 245-4517.

IPNF, Bonners Ferry Ranger District: (208) 267-5561.

IPNF, Fernan Ranger District: (208) 769-3000.

IPNF, Priest Lake Ranger District: (208) 443-2512.

IPNF, Sandpoint Ranger District: (208) 265-6600.

IPNF, St. Maries Ranger District: (208) 245-2531.

IPNF, Wallace Ranger District: (208) 752-1221.

Kellogg Visitors Center: (208) 784-0821.

Kootenai County Sheriff: (208) 664-1511.

Kootenai Medical Center: (208) 666-2000.

Old Mission State Park: (208) 682-3814.

Post Falls Tourism: (800) 292-2553 or (208) 773-4080.

Priest Lake State Park: (208) 443-2200.

Priest Lake Visitors Center: (208) 448-2721.

Sandpoint Visitors Center: (800) 800-2106 or (208) 263-2161.

Wallace Visitors Center: (208) 753-7151.

Northwest Montana

Including Libby, Eureka, the Upper Clark Fork River, the Cabinet Mountains Wilderness, and Kootenai National Forest.

The remote, sparsely populated northwestern corner of Montana distinguishes itself from the rest of the state with its markedly wetter climate—residents call it modified coastal—and its heavy dependence on the timber industry. Lincoln County, of which Libby (city pop: 2,800; county pop: 18,700) is the seat, ranks first in the state in the number of board feet logged annually, traditionally right around 100 million. Libby's high school teams are the "Libby Loggers," and one of the town's largest celebrations is Logger Days. But you don't have to read the statistics to figure it out: clear-cuts on surrounding mountainsides give stark testimony to the principal industry.

The area's isolation and vast tracts of public lands (74 percent of the county is federally owned) make it attractive to extremists on both ends of the political spectrum. Pockets of hippies and back-to-the-landers include folks who've fled the upscale development of the Flathead and other trendy areas. Among their neighbors you'll find a few reactionary right-wingers, such as those who draw attention to the town of Noxon, home of the Montana Militia. The area's most noted resident, however, is environmental writer Rick Bass, whose book *The Book of Yaak* details a season in the Yaak River valley. Read the book for a better understanding of the region, but don't sing Bass's praises too loudly in any of the local taverns.

Though the area claims vast recreational opportunities, its communities have been slow to cater to tourism, making outdoor activity largely a do-it-yourself proposition. Where else can you volunteer at the local downhill ski resort and earn yourself a free ticket? Montana's Northwest corner is one of the last refuges for folks who eschew espresso stands and upscale fly-fishing shops in favor of primitive campgrounds and the chance to explore somewhat uncharted territory. The Cabinet Mountains Wilderness and the Ten Lakes Scenic Area offer spectacular scenery and rugged hiking; the Kootenai River, despite the Libby Dam, claims blue-ribbon fishing status. Hunting is a primary fall sport, and not just for show: with unemployment regularly figuring in the double digits, people in these parts often live off what they shoot.

The Kootenai (meaning "Deer Robe") Indians, known for their hunting and hide-tanning skills, were the original human inhabitants of this part of the state. They lived primarily in the Tobacco Plains near present-day Eureka until they were removed to the Flathead Reservation in the late 19th century. In 1807 David Thompson—a British explorer, geographer, and astronomer whom the Native Americans called KooKooSint, or "he who looks at the stars"—became the first white person to explore the region. He set up trading posts along the Kootenai and Clark Fork Rivers, including one near what later became the town of Thompson Falls, today the Sanders County seat.

Northwestern Montana's stunning scenery and wild lands beckon to anyone with a passion for the outdoors. Enjoy yourself. But allow us to offer a survival tip: Peel environmentally sensitive bumper stickers off your car before heading this way.

Getting There

Libby is located at the crossroads of US Highway 2 and State Highway 37, 89 miles east of Kalispell. The closest airport is Glacier International Airport near Kalispell. Libby is served by Rimrock Trailways bus lines.

Adjoining Areas

EAST: **Kalispell and the Flathead Valley**
WEST: **Idaho Panhandle**
SOUTH: **Missoula and Environs**

inside out

Fishing

For information or a copy of Montana State fishing regulations, contact the Montana Department of Fish, Wildlife and Parks in Libby, (406) 293-4161, or Kalispell, (406) 752-5501.

Dave Blackburn's Kootenai Angler in Libby (115 W Second St, (406) 293-7578) offers full- and half-day guided fly-fishing trips on the Kootenai River. The store also rents out a recently built 1,500-square-foot log home on the river that sleeps six. Orvis-endorsed Linehan Outfitting, (406) 295-4872, and Kootenai River Outfitters, (800) 537-8288 or (406) 295-4615, both of Troy, come highly recommended for guided trips as well.

Rent aluminum fishing boats on Lake Koocanusa at Koocanusa Resort and Marina, 7 miles north of the Libby Dam on Hwy 37, (406) 293-7548.

Lake Fishing

The big draw here is **Lake Koocanusa,** a 90-mile-long backup of water behind Libby Dam, which straddles the US-Canadian border. Named for the Kootenai River plus the two countries in which it lies, Lake Koo-Can-USA—get it?—is renowned for its kokanee salmon, generally 10 to 14 inches long, which make great eating. Also found in Koocanusa is the kamloops trout, a type of rainbow that feeds on other fish including kokanee; kamloops may weigh up to 20 pounds. You can fish all year, but kokanee fishing is best May through August. **Ice fishing** is terrific in the rare event that the lake freezes—about once every five years. Fishing for kamloops is best March through May and September through November. December through March there's good fishing for ling (with a six-week closure mid-January through February). You can fish for westslope cutthroats and rainbows near any of the Kootenai River tributaries, but you'll want a boat for trolling or jigging for salmon and kamloops trout. Spawning salmon move from south to north as the season progresses; by August the best fishing is in the Rexford area.

The 17-lake **Thompson Chain of Lakes** along US 2 between Libby and Kalispell offers just about every conceivable type of lake fishing, from warm water to cold water and bass to rainbows. Thirteen-hundred-acre **McGregor Lake** is the biggest of the chain, boasting tremendous trolling opportunities for orange-fleshed lake trout, from 14 to 26 inches, with a liberal limit. When it freezes, usually mid-January, McGregor is also popular for ice fishing. Just 10 miles west, catch largemouth bass in the three Thompson Lakes. There's good shore fishing in many of the chain's small lakes, stocked annually with rainbow and/or cutthroat; try **Cad, Cibid,** or **Banana Lakes.** The Montana Department of Fish, Wildlife and Parks in Libby has general information, but you'll get the up-to-date skinny from Happy's Inn on US 2, 5 miles west of the Thompson Lakes, (406) 293-7810.

Noxon Reservoir has been called one of the state's five best bass fisheries, since it's home to both smallmouth and largemouth bass. You can fish the reservoir year-round, but a catch-and-release regulation is in effect during spring spawning. Typically the smallmouths stay in the upper half of the reservoir between the town of Thompson Falls and Vermilion Bay; the largemouths spend their time in the reservoir's more lakelike lower half. Most people either jig or cast lures for bass, with the best luck just after spring runoff has cleared, in mid-June. In July, the Clark Fork Bass Anglers host a tri-state bass fishing tournament.

Fishing for brown trout is good in spring and fall, and best at the mouths of the tributaries. Locals like to bait fish for the reservoir's large population of perch. Boat ramps are located all around the reservoir; two good launch sites are **Flat Iron Ridge** on the south end of the reservoir and **Trout Creek Park** in the middle. Nearly the entire shoreline offers public access. For more information, contact the Department of Fish and Wildlife in Thompson Falls, (406) 827-9320.

River Fishing

You can pull some good-sized rainbows and a few westslope cutthroats out of the **Kootenai River** between Libby Dam and Kootenai Falls. The fish tend to be bigger just below the dam, but don't let that keep you from checking out the entire 28-mile stretch. Depending on the dam discharge, this blue-ribbon trout stream may offer good fishing early in the season when other rivers haven't cleared yet. Check with the dam before you go; you can do well at high or low flows, but you want to make sure the flows are stable. Contact the Libby Dam river discharge recording at (406) 293-3421.

You also can try to catch cutts, rainbows, and brookies in the **Yaak River.** Start at the Yaak Falls and work your way up; there's good spin- or fly-fishing from the falls upstream to the Dirty Shame Saloon. Much of the river is accessible from Hwy 508, but be sure not to trespass on private land. There's good shore access from just above Red Top Campground to Pete Creek Campground. You'll find pretty Forest Service campgrounds all along the river.

Hiking/Backpacking

The remote northwestern corner of Montana holds many of the state's most beautiful and least crowded hiking trails. These are particularly scenic in fall, when the larches turn yellow. In the very western part of the state near the Idaho border the weather is notably wetter (vegetation includes subalpine fir, spruce, cedar, and hemlock) and often very foggy. Come prepared for all conditions. This is bear country, with both black bears and grizzlies; take all the necessary precautions. The Fortine Ranger District, (406) 882-4451, loans out food storage containers and panniers.

Maps of the Kootenai National Forest and the Cabinet Mountains Wilderness are available at district offices. Consult the guidebooks *Hiking Montana* by Bill Schneider or *Wild Montana* by Bill Cunningham for additional hiking suggestions and more detailed information. We also highly recommend consulting with district rangers before setting out on any of the hikes below; rangers know the trail conditions and can help tailor a trip to your needs. Distance hikers might consider staying in one of the area's backcountry cabins (see Lodgings, below).

Nestled against the Canadian border just northeast of Eureka, the small but spectacular **Ten Lakes Scenic Area** is currently being proposed for designation as wilderness, and once you see it you'll know why. You can day hike or backpack in from either **Little** or **Big Therriault Lakes** to **Bluebird** and **Wolverine Lakes.** This moderate to moderately difficult hike cuts through high alpine forest to two cirque-enclosed lakes. A nice 11-mile loop trip from Little Therriault Lake goes north to Wolverine Lake and back past Bluebird and Paradise Lakes. Bighorn sheep live here, and you'll likely see horses on the trails. From the lookout atop Stahl Peak, you get a panoramic view of the Ten Lakes area, the nearby Canadian Rockies, and even Glacier National Park. The Ten Lakes Scenic Area lies 36 miles from Eureka; to get there, take US 93 south 10 miles to Grave Creek Rd, then turn left (east) and follow the signs. Fortine Ranger District, (406) 882-4451.

The 94,000-acre **Cabinet Mountains Wilderness** lies west and southwest of Libby, boasting more than 80 spectacular glacial lakes, craggy peaks, great huckleberry picking, and 100 inches of precipitation annually—which means a lot of lush old growth. Trails open by mid-June but creek crossings can be dangerous; check with district rangers. Again, this is bear country, so take all necessary precautions. Trail use in the Cabinets is on the increase, and the routes suggested below are well known; for more obscure, less crowded hiking possibilities in the Cabinets, talk to those rangers.

The quintessential—and therefore most popular—day hike from Libby is the short but fairly steep 1 1/2-miler to **Leigh Lake,** the largest lake in the wilderness set at the base of 8,712-foot Snowshoe Peak. On this, the highest mountain between Glacier National Park and the Cascades, you'll often see mountain goats. You can climb the peak, if you're game, by working your way up the ridgelines. The trailhead is located off the Bear Creek turnoff, 7 miles south of Libby. With its proximity to town and its relatively easy access, Leigh Lake is predictably crowded, especially on weekends when you may see dozens of other hikers. Camping is prohibited within 300 feet of the lake.

A similarly popular and accessible trail is the one leading to **Upper** and **Lower Geiger Lakes,** which lie 2 and 3 ½ miles respectively from the trailhead. From Lost Buck Pass, a mile past the upper lake, you'll be able to see Noxon Reservoir and Wanless Lake. The trailhead is located off US 2, 26 miles south of Libby.

A good 2- or 3-day, 20-mile loop trip to **Upper** and **Lower Cedar Lakes** begins on the Cedar Creek Trail, just outside Libby off US 2. The route meets up with Cabinet Divide Trail #360 and circles back on the Flower Creek Trail. It's best done with a shuttle. (To do the trip without one, head out instead on the Parmenter Trail, on the outskirts of Libby.) For more information, call the Libby Ranger District, (406) 293-7773.

A good overnight or day hike on the south end of the Cabinets is the moderately difficult, 4 ½-mile trail to lovely **St. Paul Lake.** You'll pass through stands of old-growth cedar, then slog over a ridge to burst upon the lake, where you'll find yourself surrounded by jagged peaks. Bring bug dope and take proper bear precautions. Take Hwy 200 to Hwy 56, then drive north 8 miles to East Fork Rd #407. Turn right and follow the signs to the trailhead. Contact the Cabinet Ranger District in Trout Creek, (406) 827-3533.

The 6-mile (one-way) **National Recreation Trail** through Fish Lakes Canyon north of Libby passes by a spectacular 50-foot waterfall and a chain of five lakes. Some people make this fairly level hike a day trip, but you can slow things down by camping overnight at any of the lakes. This low-elevation hike is clear of snow early in the season, usually mid-May, but mosquitoes can be fierce. Look for pileated woodpeckers, barred owls, goshawks, and other birds in the enormous red cedars and larch at the creek crossing, 2 miles in. You may spot moose and black bear, too. The trailhead is off Vinal Lake Rd #746 or Pipe Creek Rd, 30 miles north of Libby. Three Rivers Ranger District, Troy, (406) 295-4693.

One of the most remote hiking spots in Montana is in the small, rugged **Northwest Peak Scenic Area,** comprising 60,000 acres in the Yaak River region, simply known here as "the Yaak." Part of the Purcell Mountain range, the scenic area is about 65 miles northwest of Libby. You can hike 2 ½ tough miles to the historic **Northwest Peak lookout,** elevation 7,700 feet, which the Forest Service currently is restoring. This is windy and rocky terrain best used for day hikes only. Due to the high elevation, hiking season here lasts only from mid-July to mid-September. The trailhead is off Pete Creek Rd #338, which is paved to Pete Creek Meadows. Plan on a 2-hour drive from Libby. Three Rivers Ranger District, Troy, (406) 295-4693.

Trails in the Cabinet Ranger District see most of their use during hunting season, so if it's summer solitude you seek, look no further. You can drive right to the **State Line Trail** on the Montana-Idaho divide west of Trout Creek (best done with a high-clearance vehicle). This high alpine route is part of the **Trout Creek National Recreation Trail,** and lends views into both states (Idaho's the one with the clear-cuts; the Montana side is largely roadless). The area is rife with huckleberries. From Trout Creek, take the road that runs along the west side of Noxon Reservoir. Turn left (west) on Tuscor Creek Rd #322 and follow it about 20 miles to the state line and 93 Mile Lake. Cabinet Ranger District, Trout Creek, (406) 827-3533.

Ancient western red cedars as tall as 175 feet and up to 8 feet in diameter are the centerpiece of the **Ross Creek Cedars Scenic Area** off Hwy 56 southwest of Libby. A mile-long, wheelchair-accessible interpretive trail winds through part of the 100-acre grove. In winter, this trail makes a nice cross-country ski, though the road isn't plowed all the way to the trailhead. On the west side of Bull Lake, 4 miles off Hwy 56 in the Three Rivers Ranger District, (406) 295-4693.

Kayaking/Rafting

Since there are no commercial maps of the rivers in this area to date, kayakers should talk with local experts. Rent canoes and kayaks and get instruction from Kootenai Canoe and Kayak in Libby (804 California Ave, (406) 293-8419). Part-time logger/part-time boater Charlie Lawrence runs the business and dispenses advice out of his house; ask for his informative brochure about boating the Kootenai River. Cabinet Mountain Adventures of Troy, (800) 201-7238 or (406) 295-1302, offers commercial raft trips down the Kootenai River. These are flatwater scenic trips. Contact Glacier Sea Kayaking, (406) 862-9010, for kayaking on Lake Koocanusa.

You can boat various stretches of the **Kootenai River** as it runs alongside Hwy 37 and US 2 from below Libby Dam to Kootenai Falls, a total of 28 miles. This is mostly Class I and II water, with only one Class III rapid—Chinamen's, 6 miles below Libby, was named for an ill-fated party of Chinese miners who capsized there in the 1860s, losing all their gold. Keep in mind that the river fluctuates with the dam output; call (406) 293-3421 for recorded information about river discharge. Put in at **Dunn Creek** or **Blackwell Flats** just below the dam and float to town (take out at the Hwy 37 bridge) for an all-day trip, or cut off several miles and avoid Jennings Rapids by putting in near mile marker 12 (you'll see cars in the parking lot), several miles north of the Libby Ranger District. There's 6 miles of flatwater past Libby before you arrive at the Class III Chinamen's

Rapids, a good play spot. Two miles past Chinamen's you'll have to take out at **Williams Creek** or kiss your boating days goodbye—the river pours over Kootenai Falls shortly thereafter. Even during the dog days of summer, the Kootenai runs very cold, 54°F to 62°F.

The remote, little-used **Fisher River** offers strong intermediate boaters a chance to paddle Class II and III water during spring runoff. Put in at the so-called Nine-Mile Bridge at the 9-mile marker on Fisher River Rd (off Hwy 37 about 13 miles east of Libby) and take out at the confluence of the Kootenai, a total of 9 miles.

During spring runoff, expert boaters can test their skills against the lower **Yaak River.** Starting below Yaak Falls, this section of river passes through a beautiful canyon to the highway. Don't mess with this unless you know what you're doing: this is Class IV and V water, with boiling hydraulics.

Camping

There's no shortage of public or private campgrounds in the northwestern corner of Montana. The Kootenai National Forest map indicates public campsites, many of them located along waterways; the ones along the **Yaak River** are particularly scenic. Below are our favorites; for a complete listing, refer to the *Montana Travel Planner,* available through Travel Montana, (800) 847-4868 out-of-state or (406) 444-2654 in-state, and at local motels and chambers of commerce; look under "Glacier Country."

Sites fill up early summer weekends at the small (10-site and 6-site, respectively), isolated Forest Service campgrounds at **Big** and **Little Therriault Lakes** northeast of Eureka. No wonder—they offer great views of the Ten Lakes Scenic Area peaks and up the Wigwam Basin into Canada. This is big bear country—so take all necessary precautions—and part of the Fortine Ranger District, (406) 882-4451.

Bad Medicine Campground has 16 sites in the trees just above Bull Lake and within 3 miles of the ancient Ross Creek Cedars (see Hiking/Backpacking, above). There's a good swimming beach with great views of the Cabinet Mountains and a boat launch below the campground. Although you can see the highway from the lake, it's far enough away that noise isn't an issue. Eighteen miles south of US 2 on Hwy 56, then 2 miles on a Forest Service road just south of Bull Lake; in the Three Rivers Ranger District, (406) 295-4693.

Of six Forest Service campgrounds on **Lake Koocanusa,** probably the nicest is **McGillivray Campground,** on the west side of the reservoir, with paved picnic pavilions and a good, sandy swimming beach. For a bit more quiet, try the small, 15-site **Barron Creek Campground,** just north of McGillivray. Ask about the lake's water level—camping here is not much fun when it's low. Libby Ranger District, (406) 293-7773; sites at McGillivray can also be reserved by calling (800) 280-CAMP.

Locals come to the pretty, 10-site **Howard Lake Campground** for the scenery, the fishing, and the nearby gold panning (see Attractions, below). Twelve miles south of Libby off US 2, then 14 miles southwest on Libby Creek Rd (Forest Rd 231). Also in the Libby Ranger District, (406) 293-7773.

Logan State Park Campground on Middle Thompson Lake, 45 miles west of Kalispell, attracts fishermen, boaters, and swimmers. Forty-four sites are surrounded by a 17-acre forest of western larch and ponderosa pine. The area is popular on summer weekends and, of course, during fishing season. Contact the Montana Department of Fish, Wildlife and Parks in Kalispell, (406) 752-5501.

Mountain Biking

Even beginners can manage the mostly level **Bighorn Trail,** which runs for 4 ½ miles along the Kootenai River north of Libby. This scenic out-and-back trail offers opportunities to see birdlife and bighorn sheep in the **Kootenai Falls Wildlife Management Area.** It's popular with hikers and dog walkers, too. Park at the end of Kootenai River Rd, 1 mile north of Libby off Hwy 37.

Advanced mountain bikers can make a loop trip by following the jeep trail up **Turner Mountain** and then bump down the backside of the mountain on a single-track trail. This is tough, steep biking, not for beginners or bikers with out-of-shape quads. Park at the turnoff to Turner Mountain on Pipe Creek Rd, 20 miles north of Libby.

Only experienced riders with helmets and good shocks should attempt the challenging, 6 ½-mile **Bobtail Ridge Trail** outside Libby. It's best to do this steep, rocky ride north to south, to avoid much uphill riding. Arrange for a shuttle back to your starting point. Request a point-to-point informational brochure about all of these rides from the Libby Ranger District, (406) 293-7333.

Climbing

Stone Hill at Lake Koocanusa is one of the state's premiere climbing areas, with both bolted and unbolted climbs rated 5.4 to 5.13. The wall is located along Hwy 37 on the lake's east shore, 3 miles south of the Lake Koocanusa bridge—look for climbers dangling from ropes. Rocky Mountain Outfitters in Kalispell, (406) 752-2446, can provide more information, while Glacier Sea Kayaking, (406) 862-9010, offers guided rock climbing/kayaking trips to Stone Hill and the lake. First-timers are welcome.

Horseback Riding

Clients rave about trail rides organized by Lazy JR Outfitting of Libby, (406) 293-9494.

Cross-Country Skiing

From December through mid-March, the Forest Service, the Department of Natural Resources, and the town of Libby maintain three cross-country ski areas in the Libby Valley, all suitable for beginners. The **Bear Creek Trails,** 7 miles south of Libby off US 2, offer 3 1/2 miles of rolling hills. The **South Flower Creek Trails,** 4 miles south of town on Flower Creek Rd, have 4 1/2 miles of groomed trails and generally better snow conditions. There are an additional 2 miles of trails starting from the **Timberlane Campground,** 8 1/2 miles north of Libby on Pipe Creek Rd. All three areas are groomed on a regular basis. Libby Ranger District, (406) 293-7773.

Access terrific backcountry skiing from either the **Flatiron Summit** or the **Rainbow Ridge Trails** on Flatiron Mountain. Each area offers 1 1/2 miles of groomed trails that lead to nice glade skiing. Snow conditions are generally excellent into April. The Rainbow Ridge parking lot is 22 miles north of Libby on Pipe Creek Rd, 2 miles past the turnoff to Turner Mountain; Flatiron Summit is 2 miles beyond that. Be familiar with avalanche safety; current conditions are available from the Glacier Country Avalanche Center, (800) 526-5329 or (406) 257-8402. Libby Ranger District, (406) 293-7773.

The Forest Service intermittently grooms the 5-mile-long **Therriault Cross-Country Ski Trail,** which starts 10 miles east of Eureka on Forest Rd 7077, just northeast of Glen Lake. The trail follows old logging roads and is of moderate difficulty; more advanced backcountry skiers with avalanche skills can follow an ungroomed trail to Therriault Pass. Fortine Ranger District, (406) 882-4451.

See Backcountry Cabins, below, for additional skiing options.

Snowmobiling

Travel Montana's *Winter Guide* provides an overview of snowmobiling in the state, with specific trails listed by region and with reference phone numbers; it's available through Travel Montana, (800) 847-4868 out-of-state or (406) 444-2654 in-state, local chambers of commerce, and many businesses. The Northern Region of the Forest Service also puts out a trail inventory, available through individual ranger districts. The Montana

Snowmobile Association (PO Box 4714, Missoula, MT 59806) can also provide more information. Guided tours are available through John Church of Troy, (406) 295-5858, or Kurt Briethaupt in the Yaak, (406) 295-5493.

The **Keeler-Rattler area** south of Troy provides 34 miles of trails leading to Clarkfork, Idaho. The highlight of the 12-mile **Buckhorn Ridge Trail** in the Yaak is 5 miles of riding on the crest of the Purcells. The **Pete Creek Trail** is periodically groomed and offers access to the Hawkins Lakes in the stunning Northwest Peaks Scenic Area. Maps and information are available through any ranger district in the Kootenai National Forest or through the Lincoln County Sno-Kats Snowmobile Club, (406) 295-5858.

Downhill Skiing

Started in 1961 by a group of local skiers who decided to install their own rope tow, and still run by a volunteer board of directors, Libby's **Turner Mountain** is, by any standards, rustic—the "Fred Flintstone of ski areas," as one board member puts it. There's no lodge, no running water, no chairlift (though plans are in the works to install a used one), no espresso stand. And no lift lines. What's there is this: a 2,150-foot vertical drop, 24 intermediate and advanced runs (40 percent of them groomed), 200 inches of snowfall annually, a warming hut heated by a barrel stove, and North America's longest T-bar—5,600 feet, more than a mile long. Lift tickets are a measly $16, $12 for students. You may be able to volunteer 2 hours of labor in exchange for a free lift ticket, since Turner only has one full-time employee. Rental skis are available. The season generally runs from Christmas through mid-March; the area is open weekends and holidays, and the entire week between Christmas and New Year's Day. Or, live it up and rent the entire mountain for $1,000! Twenty-two miles north of Libby in the Purcell Mountains, Turner Mountain often boasts clear weather when its larger competitors, Schweitzer Mountain and the Big Mountain, are plagued by fog. From Libby, take Pipe Creek Rd north 22 miles, then drive 2 miles on an access road (it's signed). Snow tires are recommended. The Turner Mountain message phone is at the home of board member Dave Anderson: (406) 293-4317.

Wildlife

In morning or late evening stop at the **Kootenai Falls Wildlife Management Area** along the Kootenai River just north of Libby, where **bighorn sheep** are found year-round. Turn left (west) on Kootenai River Rd, the first paved road north of the Hwy 37 bridge, then drive to the parking area. The 4 ½-mile Bighorn Trail is also a popular mountain biking spot (see Mountain Biking, above). Libby Ranger District, (406) 293-7773.

Mid-November to mid-December (and sometimes earlier in the fall) and March through May, bighorn sheep often hang out on the rocky outcroppings at the **KooKooSint Sheep Viewing Area** and vicinity, 8 miles east of Thompson Falls on Hwy 200. There are informational signs posted at the turnout. Plains Ranger District, Lolo National Forest, (406) 826-3821.

October through mid-December, **bald eagles,** sometimes numbering over 100, congregate below Libby Dam on the Kootenai River to catch spawning kokanee salmon. Aside from floating the river (see Kayaking/Rafting, above), the best viewing is from the **Alexander Creek Picnic Area** on the west side of the river just below the dam; access it by driving 13 ½ miles north of Libby on Hwy 37, then taking Forest Rd 228 across the river to the picnic area. Libby Dam Visitors Center, (406) 293-5577.

outside in

Attractions

Gold was discovered on Libby Creek in 1867, and though you probably shouldn't give up your day job to look for it, it's still possible to pan for the precious metal at the **Libby Creek Gold Panning Area,** 25 miles south of Libby. This Forest Service-owned area lies 1 mile north of the Howard Lake Campground in the Libby Ranger District, (406) 293-7773.

In 1972, nearly 20 years after Congress authorized construction, the US Army Corps of Engineers completed **Libby Dam,** creating Lake Koocanusa. Memorial Day through Labor Day, you can take a free 1 ½-hour tour (beginning on the hour, 10am through 5pm) or a half-hour mini-tour (available on demand) of the dam and its powerhouse for an up-close look at the generator. The Libby Dam Visitors Center, (406) 293-5577, is 17 miles north of Libby on Hwy 37.

Calendar of Events

Libby Logger Days, held the third weekend in July, celebrate the town's logging heritage with a parade, machinery demonstrations, and contests such as the double bucksaw, grapple skidder, and "Bull of the Woods"—a kind of King-of-the-Hill game for loggers—which offer a couple hundred dollars in prize money. Held on the south end of town on US 2, Logger Days is Libby's excuse to party.

So what if the majority of Libby residents don't have a drop of Norwegian blood in them? They still turn out for the **Libby Nordicfest,** the town's largest public event, held in venues all over town the second weekend in September. There's a parade, a Fjord horse show, a bowling tournament, a golf tourney, a fine arts show, and a quilting exhibition— and, of course, ubiquitous food booths. Contact the Libby Chamber of Commerce, (406) 293-4167, for more information on either of the above events.

In June, the **West Kootenai Amish** community holds its annual one-day auction of handmade quilts, furniture, and crafts. Proceeds benefit the local school. Contact Kootenai Log Homes, (406) 889-3250, for more information.

Restaurants

The **Libby Cafe** (411 Mineral Ave, (406) 293-3523) in downtown Libby has the region's best huckleberry pancakes; for dinner and a little mingling with the locals try the homemade pizza at the **Red Dog Saloon,** (406) 293-8347, 7 miles north of Libby on Pipe Creek Rd. For a taste of the real Montana, attend the Cajun Crawfish Festival at the **Dirty Shame Saloon,** (29453 Yaak River Rd, (406) 295-5439) in Yaak, held the third weekend in April. You have to be 21 to enter; free camping is allowed for the festival only.

Mornings through afternoons, the hip, upbeat **Sunflower Bakery and Coffeehouse** in Eureka (312 ½ Dewey Ave, (406) 296-2896) serves good sandwiches, salads, and unusual, ethnic-type specials, as well as enormous scones and espresso.

West Kootenai's Amish community offers all-you-can-eat Friday night buffet dinners at **Kootenai Craft and Grocery** (5253 W Kootenai Rd, (406) 889-3588). Seatings are at 5:30pm and 7pm. In winter, the dinners are offered the first Friday of the month only. On the west side of Lake Koocanusa, 15 miles north of the Lake Koocanusa Bridge.

Lodgings

Bighorn Lodge ☆ You'll see plenty of wildlife at this secluded log lodge located along the remote Bull River, 50 miles southwest of Libby. Inside, the enormous living area is decorated with taxidermy; from the outside deck you might see bighorn sheep, elk, bear, eagles, moose, and white-tailed and mule deer, as well as a tremendous view of the Cabinet Mountains. Four large bedrooms with private baths overlook the living area and picture windows opening onto stunning views. Owner Inez Wates can arrange fishing, canoeing, riding; her son Rus Willis uses the lodge as a base for his big-game guiding in the fall. Rates include a full breakfast, and you can make special arrangements for additional meals. Closed mid-October through mid-December for hunting season, with other occasional off-season closures. Reservations necessary at other times; no children under eight. *50 miles southwest of Libby on Hwy 56, 7 1/4 miles north of the junction of Hwys 200 and 56; 710 Bull River Rd, Noxon, MT 59853; (406) 847-5597; MC, V; checks OK; $$$.*

Huckleberry Hannah's Montana Bed & Breakfast ☆   Named for the main character in owner Deanna Doying's cookbook, *Huckleberry Hannah's Montana Country Sampler,* this log B&B claims a beautiful location on Tetrault Lake west of Eureka. Doubles start at $55 for either of two very small but nice rooms; three larger suites and a separate cabin go for slightly more. All accommodations come with private bath. As you might expect from a cookbook author, breakfast is both delicious and ample; weather permitting, it's served buffet-style on the lovely deck overlooking the lake. Open May through New Year's weekend. *From Eureka, take Hwy 37 west 1 mile, turn right on Airport Rd, left on Tetrault Lake Rd, then, at the T-intersection, turn left on Sophie Lake Rd; 3100 Sophie Lake Rd, Eureka, MT 59917; (406) 889-3381; MC, V; checks OK; $$.*

Backcountry Cabins

For a complete list of available Forest Service cabins and lookouts, request the *Northern Region Recreational Cabin and Lookout Directory.* Rental rates generally run between $15 and $30 a night.

The modern four-bedroom **Bend Guard Station,** 32 miles north of Thompson Falls, sits off by itself on the flats close to the Thompson River and the Thompson Chain of Lakes. It has two fully furnished kitchens and hot showers. It can sleep up to 16—a perfect excuse for a family reunion. There's good mountain biking and cross-country skiing on surrounding logging roads. In summer, you can drive right to the cabin; in winter the road is generally plowed within about 500 feet of the cabin. Bring sleeping bags and food. Reservations are taken a maximum of 90 days in advance. Plains Ranger District, Lolo National Forest, (406) 827-3589.

May through September, rent the **Big Creek Baldy Lookout,** 25 miles north of Libby. You can drive right to the 5,768-foot fire lookout after mid-June, but you'll have to climb the stairs to the 41-foot tower. The lookout has one twin and one double bed with mattresses, a propane cooking stove, propane lights, and a wood stove for heat; you'll have to bring sleeping bags, cooking utensils, food, and water (the district can provide containers). Make reservations beginning April 1; available times go quickly, especially weekends. Libby Ranger District, (406) 293-7773.

Although the **Sex Peak Lookout Cabin,** 8 miles south of Trout Creek in the Bitterroot Range, is technically open year-round, the road in is only plowed within 20 miles, greatly reducing its off-season popularity. If the name doesn't intrigue you, the scenery will: the lookout sits at 5,798 feet with views of the Clark Fork River valley and the Beaver Creek drainage. Cabin furnishings are more spartan than usual: there's one single bed and mattress. There is a wood stove, though thieves sometimes pilfer the wood. You'll have to bring pretty much everything, including bedding, a cook stove, utensils, and water. And you'll want a high-clearance vehicle to get there. Reservations accepted year-round. Cabinet Ranger District, Trout Creek, (406) 827-3533.

At press time, the Forest Service was in the process of renovating **McGuire Lookout Cabin** (elevation 6,991 feet), 14 miles south of Eureka, with plans to get it listed on the National Historic Register. The cabin's available year-round. It's a moderately difficult 2 ½ mile hike in summer; a tough 8-mile ski or snowshoe in winter. The cabin sleeps two to four (there are no mattresses) and has a wood stove for heat and cooking. Bring sleeping bags and pads, food, water, and utensils. Reservations accepted in the same calendar year. Rexford Ranger District, (406) 296-2536.

On a clear day you can see Glacier National Park from the **Webb Mountain Lookout Cabin** (elevation 5,988 feet), 15 miles southwest of Rexford. It's possible to drive there in summer with a low-clearance vehicle, but the last half-mile can be nasty. Old logging roads up here are perfect for mountain biking. The cabin is available all year, but the road's only plowed within 15 miles. It sleeps six on four mattresses and has a wood stove for heat. Bring food, water, sleeping bags, extra sleeping pads, a cook stove, and kitchen utensils. Reservations accepted in the same calendar year. Rexford Ranger District, (406) 296-2536.

More Information

Glacier Country (a regional arm of Travel Montana): (800) 338-5072 or (406) 756-7128.

Glacier Country Avalanche Center: (800) 526-5329 or in-state (406) 257-8402.

Kootenai Canoe and Kayak: (406) 293-8419.

Kootenai National Forest Supervisor's Office: (406) 293-6211.

KNF, Cabinet Ranger District: (406) 827-3533.

KNF, Fortine Ranger District: (406) 882-4451.
KNF, Libby Ranger District: (406) 293-7773.
KNF, Rexford Ranger District: (406) 296-2536.
KNF, Three Rivers Ranger District: (406) 295-4693.
Libby Chamber of Commerce: (406) 293-4167.
Libby Dam River Discharge Recording: (406) 293-3421.
Libby Dam Visitors Center: (406) 293-5577.
Lolo National Forest, Plains Ranger District: (406) 826-3821.
Montana Department of Fish, Wildlife and Parks, Libby: (406) 293-4161.
Travel Montana: (800) 847-4868 out-of-state, (406) 444-2654 in-state.

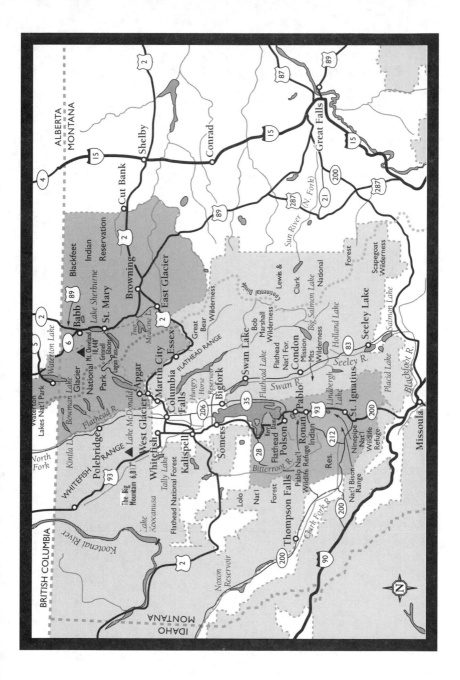

Glacier and the Flathead

Glacier
and the Flathead

Glacier National Park

Including Waterton Lakes National Park in Alberta, Canada.

Mountains are what adjoining national parks Glacier and Waterton have to offer. Sure, there are lakes—200 of them in Glacier alone—and rivers and many miles of forested trails. But people come to Glacier National Park and its northern neighbor to get up above the tree line near the peaks and more than 50 glaciers. Here, where the Rocky Mountains race from the United States into Canada, the mountains seem to rise up in concert and announce their presence.

To Native Americans the area we now call Glacier National Park was sacred, a place they came to for power and inspiration. Straddling the Rocky Mountains and the Continental Divide at the US-Canada border, Glacier National Park in Montana and adjacent Waterton Lakes National Park in Alberta offer breathtaking vistas of jagged mountains sharply carved by glaciers. The US Congress and Canadian Parliament established Waterton-Glacier International Peace Park in 1932 to symbolize the bonds of peace and friendship between the two countries.

In July the creamy globes of flowering beargrass ornament hillsides and hanging valleys scoured by ice. The area is home to grizzly bear, mountain goats, pikas, beaver, golden-mantled ground squirrels, and soaring bald eagles. Although nearly two million visitors a year travel to these high-mountain parks, hikers can find solitude beside stunning alpine lakes cradled in glacial cirques. These are hikers' parks, and those who walk on the more than 900 miles

(1,500 km) of trails are well-rewarded. Both are so diverse in terrain, views, flora and fauna, and wildlife viewing opportunities that you could spend many summers here exploring the backcountry.

It should be pointed out that, because of extremes in elevation in both Glacier and Waterton, weather can vary from valley to valley throughout the year. Elevations range from 3,100 feet (930 m) above sea level at Lake McDonald to more than 10,000 feet (3,000 m) on many of the higher peaks. In some of the glacial cirques in the west-facing mountain regions, precipitation can average more than 30 feet (9 m) a year, most of it falling as snow. At Marias Pass near East Glacier, for instance, the annual snowfall averages 21 feet (6 m). Inclement weather, including snow and freezing temperatures, is possible even in July and August. Generally, summer afternoon temperatures reach the 65°-85°F (18°-29°C) range. After sunset, mountain temperatures drop quickly—campers in the valley bottoms may see frost in midsummer.

Getting There

Glacier National Park is north of Kalispell, Montana, on US Highway 2. To reach Glacier from the west by car, take Interstate 90 past Frenchtown, Montana, to US 93 and turn north. At the south end of Flathead Lake at Polson, continue on US 93 toward Kalispell. Alternately, turn onto Highway 35, which goes around the east side of Flathead Lake through Bigfork. From Bigfork continue north on Hwys 35 and 206 to the junction with US 2, then turn east to West Glacier. From Sandpoint, Idaho, take US 200 east through Thompson Falls, Montana, and turn north on US 28 at Plains, Montana. US 28 becomes US 93 when it flanks the west side of Flathead Lake. At Kalispell, turn east on US 2, which continues through Columbia Falls to West Glacier.

To reach Glacier Park from the east, take US 2 west from Shelby, Montana, and at Browning turn south on US 21 to reach East Glacier. Drivers can also stay on US 20 and turn north on US 89 to reach St. Mary and continue north to Waterton. From Great Falls, take I-15/Hwy 91 north to Shelby and turn west for the park, or take the US 89 exit from I-15 to Choteau and continue northwest to Browning.

Waterton Lakes National Park is 159 miles (264 km) south of Calgary, Alberta, on US 2, about a 3-hour drive; it's 78 miles (130 km) southwest of Lethbridge (a 1 1/4-hour drive).

The nearest airports to Glacier-Waterton are at Kalispell, Missoula, or Great Falls in Montana; and Lethbridge or Calgary in Alberta. There is no public transportation from these cities to the park, but rental cars are available at all five cities.

Amtrak, (800) 872-7245 (ask for Essex, MT), offers passenger rail service to West Glacier, Essex, and East Glacier. Rental cars are available at the

Izaak Walton Inn at Essex and at Whitefish, Montana, a resort town west of the park where the train also stops (see Kalispell and the Flathead Valley chapter).

Both parks are open year-round; in winter, however, the highways are plowed only to the north end of Lake McDonald in Glacier and to Waterton Townsite in Waterton. From there cross-country skiers can travel the roads and traverse low-elevation meadows. In-park transportation is available via scenic coach in summer. The Glacier Park Inc. vintage red tour buses depart from Glacier Park Lodge, St. Mary Visitors Center, Many Glacier Hotel, Lake McDonald Lodge, Logan Pass, the Prince of Wales Hotel, Belton, and Rising Sun Campground. One-way trips are available; fees vary. Call (406) 226-9311. For a schedule, check at visitors centers or lodges (see Lodgings, below). Note: These buses do not stop at all trailheads or scenic pullouts to let hikers on or off.

Visitors traveling between Glacier and Waterton Lakes National Parks must cross the US-Canada international border and clear customs. The Chief Mountain Port of Entry is open mid-May to mid-September only, from 7am to 10pm. The Carway, Alberta–Peigan, Montana Port of Entry is open year-round, 7am to 11pm.

Adjoining Areas

WEST: **Kalispell and the Flathead Valley**

NORTH: **Lethbridge and the Border**

SOUTH: **Mission Valley; Seeley–Swan and Blackfoot Valleys**

inside out

Visitors Centers

The visitors center at **Apgar** near the West Glacier entrance to Glacier National Park is open from late April through mid-November, and weekends only through the winter months. The visitors center at **St. Mary** on the east side of Glacier is open from late May to mid-October and has a natural history exhibit; 10-minute slide programs are offered in the auditorium every half-hour. Evening programs are at 7:30pm and 9pm. The **Logan Pass Visitors Center** opens in mid-June, or whenever the Going-to-the-Sun Hwy is plowed, and closes in mid-September. Those chilled from a walk at the high elevation of Logan Pass can warm up in front of the fire that burns almost continually in the fireplace here. It's a great place to pause for the striking scenery, too. Get information about guided walks and interpretive programs at all the visitors centers by contacting Glacier National Park, West Glacier, MT 59936; (406) 888-5441. Information on Waterton is available from Waterton Lakes National Park (Waterton Townsite, AB T0K 2M0; (403) 859-2224) or the Waterton Park Visitors Association (PO Box 5596, Waterton Lakes National Park, AB T0K 2M0; (403) 859-2224). The Waterton information center is open daily 8am–10pm, May to September.

Scenic Drives

Most visitors see Glacier National Park by driving between West Glacier and East Glacier over the historic 50-mile **Going-to-the-Sun Highway,** which crosses the Continental Divide at 6,664-foot-high Logan Pass. Views of jagged peaks, pristine glaciers, and lush valleys are outstanding.

The highway is closed from the time snow falls in October until late May (or, in some years, late June) when snowdrifts up to 70 feet deep are dynamited, bulldozed, and plowed off the highway in a production that takes about a month. **RVers** should note that vehicles exceeding 21 feet long or 8 feet wide are not allowed over the Going-to-the-Sun Hwy; RVs can't make the sharp turns on the west side of Logan Pass—the two-lane road was completed in 1932, long before such vehicles hit the road. Those who want to leave the driving to others can ride the vintage 1936 **red tour buses** that link all of the lodges and hotels in Glacier National Park. The buses seat 18, and their rollback canvas tops allow a full view of the dramatic vistas. The round-trip fare varies depending on the destinations; there are narrated full-day and half-day sightseeing tours that include stops for photography, sightseeing, and lunch. Reservations for the tour buses can be made at any of the hotels or lodges, or after May 15 and through the summer by calling (406) 226-9311. (Credit cards and travelers checks are accepted, but personal or business checks are not.)

In Waterton Lakes National Park the **Red Rock Parkway** is a 9-mile (15 km) drive from the township to **Red Rock Canyon** where creeks cascade over the canyon's colored rocks. The park's highest peak, at 9,646 feet (2,940 m), **Mount Blakiston** is visible from the parkway.

Hiking/Backpacking

Hikers flock to Glacier, a park rich in trails that wind through a variety of habitats ranging from thick cedar forests to alpine desert. You don't need to be an experienced backpacker, though, to hike the trails in these parks. The 730 miles of trails in Glacier range from short strolls to vistas to rigorous hikes that cross the international border. Waterton has 191 miles (255 km) of trails. Both parks offer guided walks and hikes ranging from

1 to 8 hours; check with the park information centers for a schedule. Although **dogs** are allowed in the parks, they must be on-leash at all times and are not allowed on any trails.

To **camp overnight** in the backcountry in either park, a backcountry permit is required and available at any park information center. The competition is sometimes stiff for the best backcountry sites since permits are issued a maximum of 24 hours in advance on a first-come basis. Camping and fires are permitted only in designated areas in Waterton, which has just 13 designated backcountry campgrounds, all of which have dry toilets and a surface water supply. Backcountry campers in Glacier are required to use self-contained stoves.

Among the outfitters that run **guided backpacking trips,** one of the best is Glacier Wilderness Guides (Box 535, West Glacier, MT 59936; (800) 521-7238 or (406) 387-5555). Guide services for Waterton Lakes National Park, which can include combination fishing and hiking excursions, can be arranged at the Tamarack Mall in Waterton Townsite, or through Canadian Wilderness Tours (504 Cameron Falls Drive, Waterton, AB T0K 2M0; (403) 859-2058 or fax (403) 859-2342).

The lodges in Glacier Park will all pack a **trail lunch** for hikers. Leave your lunch order at the lodge dining room the night before and the sack lunch will be waiting early the next morning. In Waterton, you can find everything you need at Tamarack Mall where there are fresh sandwiches and baked goods.

Topographic maps of Glacier–Waterton, Yellowstone, Banff, and Jasper National Parks are available from the Trail of the Great Bear Travel Store in Waterton village (Box 142, Waterton Park, AB T0K 2M0; (800) 215-2395 or fax (403) 859-2621).

Hiking **distances** listed are one-way (the full distance for loop hikes) unless otherwise noted.

Glacier National Park

Because sections of the Going-to-the-Sun Hwy are under construction almost constantly during the few weather-friendly months, hikers should pick up a Glacier road construction information pamphlet at one of the visitors centers before planning hikes. Parking areas at trailheads along the highway could be closed for the season if near a construction zone. Two other transportation options are available for hikers not using loop trails, or not wanting to backtrack. Glacier Park Inc. provides vintage **red tour buses** for shuttling hikers to Siyeh Bend, Logan Pass, and The Loop; call (406) 226-9311 for reservations and departure times (all in early morning), and pick-up times in the afternoon. (See also Scenic Drives, above, for more information.) A relatively new hiker shuttle service,

Rocky Mountains Transportation, (406) 881-4311, provides a more extensive hiker shuttle service, but operates only in July and August. Its three vans provide drop-off and pick-up service at trailheads along the Going-to-the-Sun Hwy.

The best-developed trail that's accessible to wheelchair-users is **Trail of the Cedars,** located just north of Lake McDonald at Avalanche Creek. The boardwalk trail is less than a mile long and winds through a mature forest of cedar trees, many as old as 700 years. Another popular hike (not wheelchair-accessible) leaves from the same parking area: the 4-mile jaunt with a modest elevation gain ends at **Avalanche Lake,** which is ringed with waterfalls splashing down surrounding cliffs.

Perhaps the single most-used hiking trail is the short walk to the **Hidden Lake Overlook.** You can't miss the boardwalk that climbs the slope above the Logan Pass Visitors Center. The elevation gain is about 2,000 feet, and it's a good sampling of what the park has to offer: wild-flowers, wildlife, snowfields, meltwater trickling everywhere and forming pools atop tarns, and, on top, mountain views that stretch out across the landscape.

A short walk with more visual reward is at **Baring Falls,** 8 miles east of Logan Pass on the Going-to-the Sun Hwy, with a view from the bottom of the 80-foot waterfall. The turnout for this walk is well-marked from the road.

A favorite route for day hikers is the trail along the Garden Wall, also known as the **Highline Trail.** The trailhead is across the highway from the visitors center parking lot at Logan Pass, and the trail is visible just below the ridgeline clear to a large outcropping named Bear Hat Mountain, about 5 miles away. Granite Park Chalet (see Backcountry Cabins, below) is located about 7 miles along this relatively flat trail. Those who can handle a short but rigorous elevation gain should watch for the switchback trail to the **Grinnell Glacier Overlook,** well worth the climb since it ends on the ridge right on top of the glacier.

Backpackers not planning to stay at Granite Park Chalet can camp just down the slope from the lodge buildings in an approved camping area. You'll need a backcountry camping permit. Be aware that this area is frequented by grizzlies—it's the campground written about in Jack Olsen's book *Night of the Grizzlies,* an account of the fatal bear maulings that happened one night in the mid-'60s. Many backpackers spend their second day hiking to Many Glacier Hotel (see Lodgings, below) over **Swiftcurrent Pass,** a walk that's downhill most of the way.

To see icebergs in August, head for **Iceberg Lake.** The trailhead is at the end of the Many Glacier Campground past Swiftcurrent Lake. The trail itself is a moderately difficult day hike up a canyon to the lake. One way is not quite 5 miles with a 1,000-foot elevation gain; take the trail to the left at Ptarmigan Falls. Those who reach the lake too early in the summer will find it still frozen over; crossing snowfields near the lake at that time may require crampons and ice axes, to be on the safe side. Once the ice sheet on the lake melts, large chunks of ice begin calving off overhanging snowfields.

If you take a right instead at Ptarmigan Falls and make a 1,000-foot elevation gain, in just 1.7 miles you'll find yourself at **Ptarmigan Lake,** a quintessentially pristine glacial-fed alpine lake. Ambitious hikers don't stop at the lake—they add an additional mile and 500-foot climb to reach **Ptarmigan Tunnel.** This trail is not for those nervous about heights: it crosses narrow ledges and requires hikers to crawl through the tunnel in places.

Hikers don't get quite so personal with **Grinnell Glacier,** but they do get a clear view of the ice, the moraines, and the many waterfalls along the 5.4-mile trail. The trailhead is south of Many Glacier Hotel. At **Josephine Lake,** take the trail that heads left and begins to climb—1,500 feet in just 3 miles, in fact. But the climb's worth it. To cut 2 miles off the distance, take the boat trip across Josephine Lake.

Another popular destination for day hikers is **Sperry Glacier,** accessible via an extension of the hike to Sperry Chalet (see Backcountry Cabins, below). When the trail to Sperry Glacier was built some 60 years ago, the glacier spilled over the ledge of the cirque. Workers installed a metal ladder up the rock wall so hikers could climb to the actual edge of the ice. Now, the ice has receded more than 3 miles. Hikers still climb the ladder, but then cross several tarns and a series of glacial moraines to reach ice. Some summers, the entrances to ice tunnels in the glacier open. The tunnels are created when melt water runs underneath the glacier. Entering these tunnels is extremely dangerous; a fall can mean a long slide into a river underneath the glacier.

Only ambitious and experienced hikers attempt the full-day **Siyeh Pass** hike, because of the elevation gain—3,180 feet—the need to cross broad snowfields even in late summer, talus slopes with uncertain footing, and the length of the hike (about 10 miles). Among the rewards, however, are near-constant in-your-face views of mountains and glaciers. The trailhead is just east of Logan Pass at Siyeh Bend and ends at Sunrift Gorge, so you must arrange for a shuttle.

Waterton Lakes National Park

In Waterton Lakes National Park, recreationalists engaging in a potentially hazardous activity (such as mountain climbing, rock climbing, or hiking alone) can voluntarily register their trip at the park warden's office in Waterton Townsite. Those registering to go out must also register when they get back in, since wardens will investigate all overdue permits.

The popular **tour boats** that ferry visitors on scenic cruises around Upper Waterton Lake also offer drop-off and pick-up services for hikers at two trailheads on the lake shore, **Crypt Landing** and **Goat Haunt.** For a tour boat schedule, call (403) 859-2362. (Also see Boating/Canoeing/Rafting, below.) Crypt Landing has a dock and primitive **campsite** on the lakeshore. Overnight camping is allowed only in approved campsites such as this one.

The boat docks briefly at Crypt Landing—just long enough for hikers to get off or on the boat. At Goat Haunt, it docks for about a half-hour, during which a parks naturalist gives a brief lecture about the area, and visitors are free to view displays, maps, photos, and books at the dockside nature center and adjacent ranger station. **Guided nature walks** are conducted daily at the nature center during summer. Hikers can stay at Goat Haunt and make arrangements to catch a later boat, or head to the primitive **Waterton River campsite,** 1.2 miles (1.9 km) from the ranger station on the Waterton Lakeshore Trail; camping on the beach is not allowed. Hikers can return to Waterton Townsite via a lakeshore trail (see below) along the west side of Upper Waterton Lake. (Or you can do the circuit in the opposite direction—walk from the Townsite to Goat Haunt and return via water taxi.) Since Goat Haunt is in the United States, visitors arriving from Canada and planning to stay overnight must report to the US-Canada Customs official at the ranger station near the dock. The same law applies to hikers crossing the international border on foot.

The trails at Goat Haunt connect with several trails in Glacier National Park, the most notable of which is the **Highline Trail** (see also above), ending at Logan Pass on the Going-to-the-Sun Hwy. Most hikers require 3 days to do the Highline route from Logan Pass to Goat Haunt. (Because of the location of the backcountry campsites, it's most often hiked from south to north.) Backpackers going in from Goat Haunt will need backcountry camping permits for Glacier National Park and will need to drop a vehicle at Logan Pass since hitchhiking is not permitted in either park. Most hikers begin at Logan Pass and take the Highline Trail 7 miles (11.6 km) to Granite Park Chalet (see Backcountry Cabins, below) or its backcountry campground. It is vital that campers use the on-site bins to protect food from bears. The usual second night's campsite is about an equal distance north; the third day hikers arrive at Goat Haunt and can catch the scenic tour boat to Waterton (bring cash for the ticket fee), or camp and walk the 9.3-mile (14 km) trail along the west shoreline of Upper Waterton Lake to the Townsite.

The **Crypt Lake Trail** is the quintessential day hike of the northern

Rocky Mountains. This trail has it all—views of waterfalls plunging over towering cliffs into a glacier-carved valley, icy streams tumbling down the boulder-strewn canyon floor, wildflowers, a tunnel, and a stunning glacial lake tucked into a cirque from which vertical walls rise into snowfields. Mountain goats often frolic on cliff walls around the lake, and cutthroat trout swim the frigid waters. A Canadian hikers' magazine once rated Crypt Lake as the best hike in the country.

Take the water taxi from Waterton Townsite (see Boating/Canoeing/Rafting, below) to **Crypt Landing** on the east side of Upper Waterton Lake. Hikers should arrange for an afternoon or evening pick-up if they are not staying overnight. In addition to the campsite at the landing, backpackers can camp at a designated primitive site near the Crypt Lake tunnel. The 5.4 mile (8.6 km) trail begins at the south end of the Crypt Landing campsite and climbs to the campsite and kitchen shelter at 6,400 feet (1,920 m). Hikers who have trouble with heights should stop here. In order to reach Crypt Lake, you must climb a steel ladder bolted to the cliff wall. At the top, you'll have to crawl through a 65-foot (200-meter) **natural tunnel**. A flashlight is in order. The narrow trail on the far side of the tunnel wraps around the wall of the cirque; there's a safety cable attached to the rock wall, which drops several hundred feet to the canyon floor here. Hikers crest the cirque rim at Crypt Lake. The lake is usually strewn with small icebergs that have broken off the snowfields flanking the lakeshore. The lake's outlet stream, adjacent to the trail, plunges over the lip of the cirque as a waterfall. Footing is precarious at the top of the waterfall, so be cautious; this is not a place to allow children to venture. The US-Canada border runs along the southern tip of the lake.

Hikers searching for straight, flat trails or who are happy to spend the day strolling through forest with occasional lake vistas will find the 9.3-mile (14.8 km) **Waterton Lakeshore Trail** exactly to their liking. Hikers can get to the lakeshore easily in only four places along the trail. And although there are vistas at other high points along the way (the elevation gain is only 350 feet (105 m), this is predominately a forest walk. There's a dock for boaters at the US-Canada border (you'll recognize it as the wide swath cut through the woods on both sides of the lake), an ideal place to stop for lunch, sit on the dock, and hang your feet into the water. The best beach on the trail is at **Bertha Bay,** about 2 miles (3.2 km) south of Waterton Townsite. The water is cold, so only those with hardy constitutions will do more than wade. Even if you aren't going to go the distance to Waterton Townsite, the walk from Goat Haunt to **Rainbow Falls,** not quite a mile (1.4 km) along the lakeshore trail is worth the time. The series of short falls cascade prettily over boulders.

One of the more popular all-day hikes in Waterton Lakes National

Park, the **Carthew-Alderson Trail,** begins at Cameron Lake, climbs 2,500 feet (750 m) to Summit Lake, then crosses 7,900-foot (2,370-m) Carthew Pass and the Continental Divide to end at Waterton Townsite. Take time to walk south on the wind-swept ridge for a panoramic view of glacial lakes and cirques, Glacier National Park, and east to the Alberta prairies. Most hikers begin at Cameron Lake because the climb to the pass can be done in less than a half-day and from there it's all downhill—the trail falls 3,700 feet (1,110 m) over 8 miles (13.3 km) before it reaches Waterton Townsite. Rather than take a vehicle to Cameron Lake and have to retrieve it later, make arrangements a day ahead at **Park Transport Co.** (at the outdoor store in Tamarack Mall, (403) 859-2378) in Waterton Townsite to be driven (for a modest fee) the 9 miles (15 km) to Cameron Lake. Plan to be on the trail by 9am so you reach the avalanche chutes with huckleberries (and the highest probability of browsing bears) before late afternoon.

The best overview of Waterton Townsite is from the top of **Bear's Hump,** just west of town. The short climb is rigorous and not for the faint of heart, but no special equipment other than good walking shoes is needed. The trailhead is at the Park Information Center, across the road from the Prince of Wales Hotel.

Camping

Campgrounds in Glacier National Park do not take reservations and a morning arrival is recommended. Major campgrounds within the park often fill up by noon during the busiest weeks of summer. Signs at the park entrances list which campgrounds are full when you enter the park, and they are updated regularly. Backpackers need a **permit** to stay overnight in the backcountry, available at visitors centers. Camping information is also available at visitors centers or by calling Glacier National Park, (406) 888-5441. Information about camping and backcountry permits in Waterton is available from Waterton Lakes National Park, (403) 859-2224.

Glacier National Park

Glacier Park has eight campgrounds accessible by paved road—Apgar, Fish Creek, Avalanche Creek, Sprague Creek, Rising Sun, St. Mary, Two Medicine, and Many Glacier. All sites will accommodate trailers except Sprague Creek, which is closed to towed vehicles. Facilities include fireplaces, tables, rest rooms, and cold running water; utility connections are not provided at any of the campgrounds. Park naturalists present nightly programs on some aspect of the park's history, geology, or wildlife at each of the campgrounds in outdoor amphitheaters or around a firepit. The time varies according to the time of nightfall.

Five campgrounds are accessible by graveled road—Bowman Lake, Cut Bank, Kintla Lake, Logging Creek, and Quartz Creek. The roads to these campgrounds are narrow, rough, and sometimes not maintained, however, so campers towing trailers or driving RVs should ask about current road conditions at a nearby ranger station. Facilities at these more remote sites include only fireplaces, tables, and pit toilets.

All of the following campgrounds are along or accessible from the Going-to-the-Sun Hwy:

Apgar Campground, which surrounds Apgar Village at the south end of Lake McDonald, is the largest and most popular campground. Nearby you can get burgers and fries or ice cream and browse in several large shops with all the requisite tourist items, including bear bells. The Apgar Campground is traditionally the first to open in spring and the last to close in fall. It tends to fill up first and have more people spend multiple nights because of its proximity to the park entrance, the lake, and tourist facilities.

Even if Apgar's not filled to capacity, we prefer **Fish Creek Campground.** It's only a couple of miles up the road (look for the sign at the intersection with the Going-to-the-Sun Hwy) on the southwest end of Lake McDonald. It's not unusual for Fish Creek to be one of the last major campgrounds in the park to fill up. Fish Creek doesn't have the casual traffic of Apgar, and its dense woods offer more privacy. There also are more sites that accommodate tents better than RVs—and it's only a few minutes' drive back to Apgar for a snack. There is access to Lake McDonald for foot traffic only, and a couple of beaches, but playing in the frigid water is only for the most hardy.

One of the park's smaller campgrounds, **Sprague Creek,** is situated on the east shore of Lake McDonald. Because the highway borders the campground, it's one of the noisiest places to stay. It opens early in the summer and, because it does not accommodate towed vehicles, is more tent-friendly. Those who want to play in cold Lake McDonald would be happy here, but if there are other camping options available, others should move on.

North of Sprague Creek Campground, on the east side of the road, is **Avalanche Creek Campground.** It's smaller still and dark well into the morning since it's tucked right against the mountain to the east. Avalanche Creek offers a deep-woods experience. If you have a couple of hours after your tent's pitched here, you can dash up to Avalanche Lake, a pleasant 2-hour hike (2.5 miles one way) with a modest elevation rise of 440 feet. Waterfalls that look like ribbons decorate the mountain slopes surrounding the lake.

East of Logan Pass on the drier Montana-plains side of the park is **Rising Sun Campground.** It's big and a favorite with RVers. Although

Rising Sun is alongside St. Mary's Lake, it doesn't have easy lake access. But, like Lake McDonald, this lake is fed by glacial runoff and thus bearable to only the hardiest of swimmers. Since Rising Sun Campground is located on a floodplain, the streams flowing out of St. Mary's Lake sometimes flood the campground during spring and early summer runoff.

Perhaps because it's not on the Going-to-the-Sun Hwy, **Many Glacier Campground** often has space when other, more popular campgrounds such as Apgar or Rising Sun are full. But we think Many Glacier is the best campground in the park. Lucky campers can snap up a site alongside a creek that borders the campground, but none of the area's sites are ill-situated. Because it's at the end of the road, Many Glacier is quiet and has enough prime trails to keep hikers busy for several days. Evenings can be spent on nearby Swiftcurrent and Josephine Lakes, or dining in style at Many Glacier Lodge. Take the turnoff just south of Babb, Montana, to Many Glacier from US 89 on the east side of Glacier National Park.

Waterton Lakes National Park

Three campgrounds—Belly River, Crandell Mountain, and Waterton Townsite—are accessible by paved road and accommodate tents and trailers. But **Waterton Townsite** is the best, primarily because of proximity to the town's eateries and attractions, and also because it's on the lakeshore. All three campgrounds have kitchen shelters, firewood, tables, bathrooms (with hot shower, sinks, and toilets), and running water (be prepared in late summer to boil all water used for consumption, however). And this is the only campground, located at the south edge of town and open mid-May to October, has sewer, water, and electrical connections for trailers and RVs, in 227 spaces. There is also a small walk-in area with 10 tent-only spots, which are nearest the lakeshore. The campground is right on Waterton Lake's rocky beaches, and Cameron Creek flows through it.

Maximum stay at the Waterton Townsite Campground is 14 days. Firewood is supplied for the firepits. Garbage is to be disposed of in the bear-proof containers provided. Pets are allowed but must be on a leash at all times. Laundry facilities are available in town.

The campgrounds at **Crandell Mountain** (open mid-May to Labor Day) and Waterton Townsite have waste disposal sites; the **Belly River Campground** (open mid-May to mid-September) has no facilities for trailers but the campsites are large enough to accommodate self-contained units.

Boating/Canoeing/Rafting

Five large lakes in the parks—McDonald, Sherburne, St. Mary, Two Medicine, and Upper Waterton—offer opportunities for canoeing or seeing the lakes via scenic tour boats. In summers only, of course.

Glacier National Park

From Memorial Day to Labor Day, tour boats regularly cruise the waters of **Lake McDonald, Swiftcurrent Lake,** and adjacent **Josephine, St. Mary,** and **Two Medicine Lakes.** All offer **sunset cruises** and all but the Lake McDonald cruise offer hikers pick-up and drop-off service. The boat schedules vary with the season and the lake, and some cruises include short hikes with a naturalist for an additional charge. Contact the Glacier Park Boat Co. at (406) 257-2426.

If tour boats aren't your style, canoes and boats can be rented by the hour for paddling or motoring. Canoes are available at Swiftcurrent, Josephine, and Two Medicine Lakes; rowboats can be rented at Lake McDonald, Swiftcurrent, and Two Medicine Lakes; boats with electric motors are available at Two Medicine or with 5 1/2-hp gas motors at Lake McDonald. Those with their own boats or canoes can launch at all of these lakes, as well as at Kintla and Bowman Lakes (limit of 10 hp on both) in northwest Glacier National Park.

One of the most popular places among canoers is on **Josephine Lake,** just a 5-minute portage from Swiftcurrent Lake. The waters of Josephine Lake lap deep into glacial-carved valleys, including the one from which Grinnell Glacier spills.

Join **whitewater rafting** expeditions—and combination rafting and horseback riding tours—through Great Northern Whitewater, PO Box 278, West Glacier, MT 59936, (800) 735-7897; Glacier Wilderness Guides, Box 535, West Glacier, MT 59936, (800) 521-7238 or (406) 387-5555; and Glacier Raft Co., No. 6, Going-to-the-Sun Hwy, MT 59936, (800) 332-9995.

Waterton Lakes National Park

Cruises on **Upper Waterton Lake** double as water taxis, offering hikers rides to and from trailheads. The water taxis depart the marina mid-May to mid-September in Waterton Townsite nearly every hour between 9am and 7pm daily. The cruise around Upper Waterton Lake takes about 2 hours. (The 7pm boat will not drop off hikers, but will pick them up at trailheads.) Some weekend cruises do not land at Goat Haunt at the southern tip of the lake, which is in Montana. Early morning and evening cruises are best for wildlife viewing and photography. Hikers and sightseers should arrive at the marina in Emerald Bay about 20 minutes prior to departure time to purchase tickets. Contact Waterton Inter-Nation Shoreline Cruise Co., (403) 859-2362, for more information.

Boats can be rented at **Cameron Lake,** 11 miles west of Waterton Townsite, and at Waterton Townsite itself.

Fishing

Glacier National Park

Every fall, freshwater kokanee salmon swim up **McDonald Creek** from Lake McDonald to spawn. In turn, bald eagles flock to the area to feed on the fish. Hundreds of tourists watched the big birds catch and eat the fish until the early '80s, when a crash in the kokanee population brought that late September ritual almost to a halt. The kokanee population is rebounding, though, and bringing eagles back to the park for fall feeding. Salmon-watchers can look for brilliant displays of fall color along the creek and up the west side of the Going-to-the-Sun Hwy. People with plenty of patience can catch kokanee in **Lake McDonald,** but these deep-water fish aren't easy to hook. Most who really want to catch fish ply the waters of **Flathead Lake,** to the south (see Kalispell and the Flathead Valley chapter).

Fishing from boats is allowed on **Lake McDonald** and on **St. Mary, Swiftcurrent, Sherburne,** and **Two Medicine Lakes.** Boat motor size is restricted to 10 hp. No fishing license is required to dip a line into a stream or lake in Glacier, but a catch-and-release policy is encouraged. A few of the park's alpine lakes are planted or have resident fish in modest numbers. Some unlucky anglers believe the existence of fish in Glacier's high-mountain lakes is only a legend. Backcountry lakes reputed to support fish are **Lake Ellen Wilson,** west of Gunsight Pass in Glacier, and **Crypt Lake,** east of Upper Waterton Lake in Waterton. Both require ambitious hikes to get there, and you won't be able to build a fire to fry fresh trout since no fires are allowed in the backcountry of either park.

Waterton Lakes National Park

Unlike Glacier anglers, fishermen over the age of 16 must have a fishing permit (available in Waterton Townsite) to fish in Waterton Lakes National Park, as well as other Canadian national parks. (A fishing license that is good in all of Canada's national parks is available.) Fish in Waterton lakes and streams include pike, whitefish, and trout—lake, rainbow, eastern brook, and cutthroat varieties. The most popular fishing spots are any of the lakes in the **Waterton Valley,** and **Cameron Lake, Crandell Lake,** and the **Waterton River.**

Upper Waterton Lake, at an average depth of 200 feet (60 m) is the deepest lake in the Canadian Rockies. It supports populations of lake, rainbow, and cutthroat trout. A record 52-pound, 12-ounce (23.7 kg) lake trout caught in 1921 has yet to be bested.

Guide services for Waterton Lakes National Park, which may include combination fishing and hiking excursions, can be arranged at the Tamarack Mall in Waterton Townsite, or through Canadian Wilderness Tours, 504 Cameron Falls Drive, Waterton, AB T0K 2M0, (403) 859-2058 or fax (403) 859-2342.

Wildlife

Mountain goats scamper across the narrow ledges throughout Glacier and Waterton. Although mangy-looking when they shed winter coats in June, by August the goats have grown new long, white coats and are ready for postcard photos. It's almost a sure bet to see mountain goats near the visitors center at Logan Pass but, tame as they seem, keep your distance when taking photos. The goats have been known to charge when annoyed. **Hoary marmots** and **golden-mantled ground squirrels** thrive in alpine zones. Midsummer, the shrill call of **pikas** can be heard across the moraines. Above the tree line, there are few **birds,** although hikers may see white-tailed ptarmigan, rosy finches, rock wrens, hermit thrushes, Townsend's solitaires, bald and golden eagles, and Clark's nut-crackers. In the forested zones, nuthatches and black-capped and boreal chickadees flit about the tree canopy, and you may spot pileated and three-toed woodpeckers, Hammond's flycatchers, and a cross-section of warblers and finches that are summer residents only. **Osprey** hunt the waters of the large lakes in the parks and occasional harlequin ducks can be spotted in Glacier's McDonald Creek, where University of Montana students conduct research on this normally shy waterfowl.

In the continental United States, Glacier and Yellowstone National Parks offer the only good opportunity to see **grizzly bears,** which at one time roamed the mountain regions of the West well into California and the Southwest. (There are also grizzlies in some wilderness areas, such as the Bob Marshall and Mission Mountains in Montana and the Selkirk Mountains in Idaho, but they are seldom seen.) Up until the early 1960s, visitors fed the bears from their car windows, and tourists gathered around open-air garbage dumps near the lodges and backcountry chalets in the evenings to watch the bears dine. Park biologists, however, found this not only encouraged the bears to congregate near tourist lodgings, but also made the bears dependent on handouts from humans. When the hand-outs stopped, the bears became testy. Over the last couple of decades, the grizzlies have returned to a more natural lifestyle and most often graze on vegetation in the avalanche chutes and on grubs and huckleberries. They will, on occasion, kill small mountain goats and young deer and elk or ferret out marmots.

Be aware that bears are highly protective of their food and their young. For this reason, there are **hikers' guidelines.** Hiking in a group is always a good idea. Make some noise or use bear bells while walking in bear country to let the animals know you are in the area, especially when rounding outcroppings or approaching thickets. Be aware of your surroundings and pause before you head into a valley to look for browsing bears. If you see a young bear, leave the immediate area. Some hikers carry pepper spray, which can be effective but only works at close range. If you encounter a bear on the trail, move off the trail slowly. Should the bear charge, don't run—the theory is that anything running away is considered prey to be chased. If attacked, lie on the ground and curl up in the fetal position with your hands behind your neck; protect your vital organs. In some cases, hikers have survived an attack by playing dead. There is no one sure way to avoid a grizzly attack since the bears are wild animals, and hence unpredictable. But bears tend to be nocturnal feeders that browse evenings and early mornings. Common advice for hikers is to get on the trail after 8am and complete your hike by late afternoon. When packing lunch, avoid highly odorous foods such as peanut butter and tuna fish. And never leave food or food scraps on the trail; pack everything out with you.

Guidelines for camping in bear country, especially outside popular campgrounds, are available at park offices. Park rangers track grizzly movements closely throughout both parks and in Waterton. Before heading out, hikers can check any park office for the latest report of trails from which bears have been spotted. If the bears are feeding on wildlife, or have young, it's not unusual for park rangers to close nearby trails until the bears have moved out of the area. **Trail closings** are posted at park offices and at major trailheads. (The policy for bears in Waterton Lakes National Park is similar, but trails are rarely closed, regardless of bear activity. Hikers should take extra care when bears have been observed nearby or choose another hike that day.)

The **Bison Paddock** near the north entrance to Waterton Lakes National Park (off Hwy 6) has a small herd of **plains bison;** viewing is from vehicles only on a narrow road through the paddock. The road is not suitable for vehicles with trailers.

Wildflowers

Because both Glacier and Waterton Lakes National Parks flow off the eastern slopes of the Rockies onto the rolling prairies, they hold a rich variety of flowers. Waterton's 203 square miles (525 square km) boast more than half of Alberta's total wildflower species. Glacier, the fourth-largest park in the United States, claims 1,034 species of flowering plants, including 22 species of native orchids. **Beargrass** is perhaps the most famous flower in the parks, although it's actually a mountain lily and not a grass at all. And while the grizzlies certainly include the white globes of blooming beargrass among their cuisine, it's not their favorite fare. Blame members of the Lewis and Clark expedition for this misnaming.

The display of beargrass, glacier lilies, paintbrush, and penstemon paints the avalanche chutes in brilliant hues by late July. The wildflower season begins in June at the lower elevations but really peaks at the high elevations in early August. Above the tree line, the alpine zone has long winters, short summers, and is buffeted by winds, creating a dry, desert-like climate in which few plants can survive. On the drier east side of the Continental Divide, red and white geraniums, asters, shooting stars, pasqueflowers, and paintbrush abound. The most accessible place to see meadows of wildflowers is above Glacier's Logan Pass Visitor Center on the path to the **Hidden Lakes Overlook.** For a close-up view of the tiny alpine flowers, bring a magnifying glass. It's not unusual to see avid photographers hunched closed to the ground capturing the tiny blooms with macro lenses.

Horseback Riding

Some park trails allow horseback riding, and visitors can rent horses by the hour or sign up for a guided trip into the backcountry. **Guided trips** are available summers in both Glacier and Waterton parks. You will need reservations for either horse rentals or guided trips. Visitors with their own horses should request brochures listing the regulations and trail restrictions from the visitors centers in either park. A relatively small number of trails are open to equestrian traffic.

In Glacier, sign up for a trip at **Many Glacier Lodge, Lake McDonald Lodge,** or **Apgar.** Early spring reservations for summer horse-packing trips can be arranged through Glacier Park Outfitters (8320 Hazel Avenue, Orangevale, CA 95662; (916) 988-3765), which runs guided backcountry horse-packing trips. Combination rafting and horseback riding tours are also available (see Boating/Canoeing/Rafting, above).

Private guides also operate in Waterton, and information on those trips is available at the park information center in Waterton Townsite. Pack trips in Waterton can also be arranged at Alpine Stables, (403) 859-2462, just north of the Prince of Wales Hotel. Hourly and daily rentals are available, too.

Biking

In Glacier National Park, bicycles are allowed only on established roads and parking areas or on designated routes. No trails are open to mountain bikes. The park has become popular among **cyclists** who want to experience Glacier's **Going-to-the-Sun Highway** in a more intimate way than from a vehicle. The elevation gain is challenging, but more daunting is the narrow and winding road with little shoulder much of the way—no shoulder in some stretches. From June 15 to Labor Day, bicycling is restricted in the most hazardous sections of the highway during peak traffic periods, which means cyclists must cross Logan Pass early in the morning (before 11am) or in the evening (after 4pm). Signs are posted at both ends of the road listing the restricted time periods. Because of the extreme elevation gain from Lake McDonald to Logan Pass, the preferred bicycle route is from east to west.

In Waterton Park, three trails are designated for **mountain bike** use—the **Snowshoe Trail,** from Red Rock Canyon to the Showshoe Warden Cabin; the **Akamina Pass Trail,** off the Akamina Hwy to Akamina Pass; and the **Park Line Trail,** from the bison paddock (see Wildlife, above) to the Oil Basin Warden Cabin. Because the condition of trails in the park changes due to melting snow and weather, it's best to stop at the park information center for details about bicycle use. Bicycles are allowed on roads in Waterton but, like roads in Glacier, these have narrow or nonexistent shoulders and seem even more narrow because of the preponderance of RVs.

Swimming

Those who can brave the clear, cold waters of the parks' lakes, which warm to only about 47°F (8°C) in summer, can windsurf or swim. Waterskiing is allowed only on Upper and Middle Waterton Lakes. Those determined to swim, but not hardy enough for any of the glacial-fed lakes, can take a dip in an outdoor heated **swimming pool** in the Waterton Townsite city park adjacent to the campground, open daily from 11am to 7pm from mid-June to Labor Day (a modest fee is charged). The town park also contains four **tennis courts,** open to the public.

Photography

The unobstructed vistas and abundance of wildlife make Glacier and Waterton meccas for photographers. In Glacier early risers can watch the sun rise over St. Mary Lake from **Logan Pass** or, in the evening, watch the sun set on the riffles and cascades of **McDonald Creek.** Wildflowers also make for a great subject here. The moonrise over **Upper Waterton Lake** in Waterton park qualifies as a peak shutterbug experience.

Golfing

Those who brought their clubs will find plenty of courses south of Glacier National Park, especially in the Kalispell area. Waterton boasts an 18-hole course right in the park—with plenty of water hazards, of course. The **Waterton Lakes Golf Course,** (403) 859-2114, just a mile north of the Townsite, is open daily from mid-May through September.

Climbing

The naked rock faces, cliffs, and jagged peaks of Glacier-Waterton mountains here offer a plethora of climbing opportunities for climbers with appropriate equipment and expertise. For information, contact Glacier National Park, (406) 888-5441.

Cross-Country Skiing

The ski season lasts from November through April in Glacier National Park. As in all areas, skiers heading into the backcountry should be well-versed in avalanche safety—it's advisable to carry a transponder. Storms blow in quickly and unexpectedly, so be prepared for severe wind and quickly changing conditions.

The **Going-to-the-Sun Highway** is plowed only to the north end of Lake McDonald. There, cross-country skiers can park and ski the roadway as far as they want (or their abilities will safely allow). The road parallels McDonald Creek for several miles; once the road leaves the canyon bottom, however, skiers will find themselves in vertical terrain with high avalanche danger and should take appropriate precautions.

While cross-country skiers use the Going-to-the-Sun Hwy as a winter ski trail, a more popular destination for skiers is the **Izaak Walton Inn,** (406) 888-5700, at Essex, on US 2 between East Glacier and West Glacier (see Lodgings, below), which receives an average snowfall of 244 inches. The 19 miles (30 km) of trails around the inn are maintained and groomed regularly and a small section (less than a mile) is lighted for **night skiing.** The innkeepers post a map of the trails they groom. The easy 2-mile **Upper Essex/Middle Essex** beginner trail gently climbs a Forest Service road. The rewards for skiers going the distance are vistas and an avalanche chute at the upper end. A more challenging trail for intermediate-level skiers is the **Middle Essex** loop trail off Upper Essex. After a sharp downhill curve at the upper end it slopes gently downhill back to Upper Essex.

Another beginner trail is **Lower Essex,** which offers a gentle, out-of-the-way scenic route through the woods. For skiers who are also railroad buffs, the **Essex to Dickey Creek Trail** follows the train tracks on a Forest Service road rated for beginners.

Other trails for beginners are **Middle Fork River Trail** and **Dickey Creek Road.** The Middle Fork River Trail starts at the inn but heads through a schoolyard (follow the signs). It crosses US 2 at the Essex turnoff—you'll have to cross US 2 again to return (usually requiring removal of skis). The trail covers rolling terrain with side trails leading to the Middle Fork River. Much of the trail is on private property, so stay on marked routes. The Dickey Creek Rd trail follows Essex Creek Rd north to a junction with Dickey Creek Rd. About 4 miles up a gentle grade, the trail forks; those taking the south fork will find an open meadow and numerous avalanche chutes about 2 miles (3.3 km) down the trail.

Advanced skiers can tackle **Upper Dickey,** a challenging one-way trail with steep downhill curves that begins at the lower Dickey Loop. To stay off the downhill slopes, stay on the intermediate-level **Dickey Loop,** a wooded trail with a moderate slope.

Some who come here to ski want to see Glacier Park even if they aren't going to ski into it. For a magnificent view of the park, take a trail appropriately named **Park View.** It's rated intermediate. When you leave the woods, you break out into a clear-cut overlooking Dickey Creek and the park.

A few guide services have been licensed to operate **ski tours** in Glacier National Park. Glacier Park Ski Tours (728 Kalispell Ave, Whitefish, MT 59937; (800) 646-6043 ext. 3724 or (406) 862-2790) offers day-long ski trips and **overnight igloo tours** (they promise igloos are warmer than they sound but, if you prefer, tents can be pitched). When there's a full moon, skiers can sign up for an 8pm to midnight ski trip.

There is plenty of terrain in and near **Waterton Townsite** for cross-country skiing, and snow's not a problem. But avid cross-country skiers usually head elsewhere in the Rockies. Few facilities are open in winter and, because the mountains rise directly from the Townsite, backcountry skiing is the activity of choice. The road to the Townsite is plowed so skiers can ski other closed roadways, such as the road to **Cameron Lake,** but the downhills coming back to the Townsite can be daunting.

outside in

Attractions

The largest community in Glacier National Park is **Apgar,** at the south end of Lake McDonald just a few miles beyond the West Glacier entrance to the park. It's more a large campground than a town. There's a **park information center;** a couple of **shops** stocked with bear bells, souvenir sweatshirts, and Indian jewelry; a small family **restaurant;** a modest **marina;** and a **motel.** The huckleberry ice-cream cones available at the **ice cream shop** draw raves from campers on hot summer nights!

Daily guided tours with a naturalist, including the history of the **Native American** presence in the Glacier National Park area, can be arranged June to September through Sun Tours, (406) 226-9220. The tours depart from East Glacier, Browning, and St. Mary.

For those who want an overview of Glacier National Park, **helicopter tours** can be arranged through Glacier Heli Tours, (800) 926-7481 or (406) 728-9363, mid-May to mid-October. The flights begin a half-mile south of West Glacier on US 2. One-day **field trips** that focus on the history of the region can be arranged through the Glacier National History Association (Box 428, West Glacier, MT 59936; (406) 888-5756) or Waterton Natural History Association (PO Box 145, Waterton Park, AB T0K 2M0; (403) 859-2624).

Whereas Apgar is a summer-only community, **Waterton Townsite** in Waterton Lakes National Park is a full-blown town where some hardy Canadians live year-round. At times, though, the deer and mountain goats outnumber the residents—the official population is 90. Take an evening stroll along the sidewalk that separates the Waterton Lake beach from the town, dash into the Big Scoop Ice Cream Parlour on Waterton Ave for a huckleberry ice cream cone, and sit on one of the many lakeside benches to watch the waves roll in as the sunlight fades on the peaks.

Restaurants

See hotel cafes and restaurants in listings under Lodgings, below.

Lodgings

For **information and reservations** in hotels within Glacier National Park contact Glacier Park Inc., Viad Corporate Center, Phoenix, AZ 85077-0928; (602) 207-6000. Reservations are taken year-round by phone only. The company will also book scenic coach tours of the park. One-way trips and full-day tours are available. For information about backcountry chalets, call Glacier National Park information at (406) 888-5441.

Lodging in and near Glacier ranges from camping to staying in historic lodges inside the park boundaries to motels and inns in Bigfork, Whitefish, and Kalispell, a short drive out of the park. Visitors to Waterton Lakes National Park usually stay at Waterton Townsite, a year-round community located in the heart of the park on the shores of Upper Waterton Lake or in Lethbridge, Alberta, an hour's drive northeast. Aside from camping, the places to stay in the parks, especially Glacier, are limited. Those wanting to stay in one of Glacier's lodges (open for 100 days in summer only) or backcountry chalets, or in Waterton at the elegant Prince of Wales Hotel or one of several motels, should consider reservations a must.

Prince of Wales Hotel ☆☆☆   The photos of Waterton Lakes National Park often include a stunning view of the Prince of Wales Hotel (circa 1927) with Upper Waterton Lake and the Rockies as a backdrop. In person, it's every bit as impressive. The magnificent gabled hotel perches atop a hill near Emerald Bay at Waterton Townsite. Its three-story-high lobby windows afford clear views all the way into Montana. The lobby of the hotel, really the only common area for guests, is turned over to tables for diners during mealtimes (there's a buffet breakfast and lunch). Those wanting to simply enjoy the view can sit outside on the bluff, although the sturdy winds that blow off the lake can be daunting. Indeed, one of the stories about the construction of the building holds that the first winter after the building was erected, a wind blew up the lake so fiercely it shifted the six-story building 8 inches on its foundation. By reputation, it's the only hotel with whitecaps in the toilets. True or not, the winds are ever-present. Like other lodges built in the early part of the century, the Prince of Wales boasts a grand lobby and tiny rooms. When making reservations, ask for rooms on the south side of the hotel, which have the best views of Upper Waterton Lake. The elevator in the hotel only goes to the fourth floor, so those who want the same view of the lake but don't mind carrying their luggage upstairs should ask if there are any value rooms available higher up.

The Prince of Wales has a full-service restaurant with regional fare such as trout on the menu. The food is competently prepared, but there are no surprises. Expect to pay for the elegant ambience. English high tea is served afternoons at the hotel. The hotel and restaurant are open early June to early September. *On the north side of Emerald Bay at the entrance to the town of Waterton, AB; mail: Glacier Park Inc., Viad Corporate Center, Phoenix, AZ 85077-0928; (403) 859-2231 or (602) 207-6000 for reservations year-round; MC, V; no checks; $$$.*

Glacier Park Lodge ☆☆   Glacier Park Lodge was built about 75 years ago using sixty 500- to 800-year-old trees. The 155-room lodge is located just outside the eastern boundary of Glacier National Park at East Glacier. The 40-foot-long timbers used as support beams in the lobby are Douglas fir; others in the lodge are cedar. At the time the lodge was built, the timbers were installed with the bark intact. Area Indians named the lodge Oom-Coo-La-Mush-Taw, meaning The Big Tree Lodge. Glacier Park Lodge has car rentals available, a heated pool, and a nine-hole pitch-'n-putt golf course on the front lawn. Scenic launch cruises are available at

Two Medicine Lake (a 30-minute drive), and transportation to the dock can be arranged. Open early June to early September. *At the southeast edge of the park along US 2; mail: Glacier Park Inc., Viad Corporate Center, Phoenix, AZ 85077-0928; (406) 226-9311 or (602) 207-6000 for reservations year-round; DIS, MC, V; no checks; $$-$$$.*

Izaak Walton Inn ☆☆ The Izaak Walton Inn, outside Glacier National Park at Essex, Montana, may draw summer visitors who want to hike in nearby Glacier, but winters are when this historic inn really hums. The inn at the southern tip of Glacier caters to cross-country skiers—each winter a couple of thousand of them stay in the hotel's 30 rooms or in one of four refurbished cabooses permanently located across the railroad tracks. The most popular way to get here is still by car, but some do ride the rails into Essex, which is natural since the historic Izaak Walton Inn was built in 1939 to accommodate crews servicing the Great Northern Railway. The Izaak Walton Inn is listed on the National Register of Historic Places and boasts a Finnish sauna, laundry facilities, and mountain bike and ski rentals. Outside it's a three-story English Tudor-style with broad chaletlike overhangs. Inside it's on the simple side, but steeped in historical touches. Meals in the dining room are served on reproductions of Great Northern Railway china. Evenings can be spent in the game room, a saloon-style lounge, or in the lobby in front of a fire. Pets are not allowed at the Izaak Walton Inn. Light sleepers should be aware that train tracks run about 200 yards from the inn. December 1 to April 1, weekend reservations must be made for 2 nights; President's Day weekend guests must stay at least 3 nights. *Off US 2 midway between East Glacier and West Glacier, or on the Amtrak route, (800) 872-7245 (the train drops travelers at the door of the inn); PO Box 653, Essex, MT 59916; (406) 888-5700; MC, V; checks OK; $$-$$$.*

Kilmorey Lodge ☆☆ More modest in scale, Kilmorey Lodge nevertheless offers everything a historic parks lodge should. Built in 1915 on the shoreline homesite of the founding warden of the park, Kootenai Brown, it's rustic with a couple of common rooms for conversing after a day of hiking or cross-country skiing. It's one of the few lodging options that remains open year-round in Waterton. There's wood paneling throughout, including wainscoting in the rooms, which, with floral curtains and comforters, are more country in decor than lodgelike. Some rooms even have sitting areas. The dining room menu offers standard fare, but if it's interesting choose the special of the day. The lodge is on Emerald Bay, within easy walking distance of Waterton Townsite and the marina from which sightseeing cruises depart. When weather permits, there's a cafe in a gazebo on the lawn beside the lodge, called Gazebo Cafe on the Bay, (403)

859-2334. It's all a very pleasant and old-fashioned lodge experience. *On Emerald Bay at the entrance to Waterton Townsite; PO Box 100, Waterton Park, AB T0K 2M0; (403) 859-2334, fax (403) 859-2342; AE, DC, DIS, MC, V; checks for deposit only; $$.*

Lake McDonald Lodge ☆☆   Like most of the decades-old lodges in national parks, Lake McDonald Lodge—established in 1895, though the present structure was built in 1913—boasts a grand lobby. But its rooms are meager in comparison. What sets this old hotel on the east shore of Lake McDonald apart, however, is that its lobby really does function as a huge common room for the guests. Couches, chairs, and coffee tables are placed in conversation groupings and around a fireplace that's large enough to walk into and still stand upright (the logs burned in it are 4 feet long). Balconies on the second floor overlook the lobby and evenings guests sit on both levels reading, playing cards, talking, or having a post-hike beer. The decor is pure hunting lodge—more than two dozen mounted heads of mountain goats, deer, antelope, and other native animals hang from the massive timbers that support the building. Ask for a lakeside room, since rooms above the second floor tend to get less noise from the lobby. In addition to 30 rooms in the main lodge, there are 17 rooms in adjacent cottage buildings, 21 rooms in small cottage buildings in the forested area between the lodge and the highway, and 30 motel-style rooms in a newer building near a camp store and cafe. Amenities include a full-service dining room and a lounge, and natural history talks are given by a park ranger at 9pm nightly in the auditorium adjacent to the hotel. Open early June to late September. *On the east shore of Lake McDonald, 10 miles from Glacier's west entrance on the Going-to-the Sun Hwy; mail: Glacier Park Inc., Viad Corporate Center, Phoenix, AZ 85077-0928; (406) 888-5431 or (602) 207-6000 for reservations year-round; DIS, MC, V; no checks; $$-$$$.*

Many Glacier Hotel ☆☆   The five-story structure was built on the shore of Swiftcurrent Lake in 1914–1915 by 400 men working day and night from May until September. The annex was finished in 1917. With more than 200 rooms, Many Glacier Hotel is the largest inn in the park. Evenings are best spent in the lobby reading (try to snap up a spot alongside the fireplace), playing a board game at tables that flank windows overlooking the lake, or eating an ice-cream cone (available at a snack shop in the hotel's lower level) on the lawn out front. The lobby at Many Glacier is a receiving area and gathering place for tour groups, which makes it seem chaotic rather than a place for guests to retreat and relax. The massive lobby is flanked by couches, but there's also a large gift shop, a waiting area for the dining room, and a lot of tourists just wandering in for a look-see. The rooms are tiny and older than those at Lake McDonald Lodge by a couple of decades, so be prepared to tolerate clanking pipes and squeaky floorboards. Ask for a room on the upper floors and the lake side. (Because the lodge is on a hillside the lobby's on the second floor; the rooms on the first level have the feel of being in the basement and for some reason are numbered in the 500s—avoid those if possible.) Many Glacier boasts the best location in Glacier National Park, close to the trailheads of several of the most popular hiking trails, among them routes to Grinnell Glacier and Iceberg Lake (see Hiking/Backpacking, above). The kitchen will pack a hiker's lunch (as will kitchens at all the lodges); order it at the front desk the night before. Other amenities include boat tours, box lunches, and canoe and fishing boat rentals. Guided tours are conducted daily from the riding stables adjacent to the hotel. Open early June to early September. *11 miles west of Babb, Montana, in the northeast corner of Glacier National Park; mail: Glacier Park Inc., Viad Corporate Center, Phoenix, AZ 85077-0928; (406) 732-4411 or (602) 207-6000 for reserva tions year-round; DIS, MC, V; no checks; $$-$$$.*

The Village Inn ☆   The Village Inn is a 36-room motor-inn facility at Apgar, on the south shore of Lake McDonald and just inside the west entrance to the park. The inn is within easy walking distance of shops and restaurants, the ranger station, and the campground at Apgar. Homesteaders Milo B. Apgar and Charles Howe, having settled at this site at the south end of Lake McDonald, found farming to be impossible. Instead they began building cabins for visitors and local miners; these later became Apgar Village Lodge. Cabin 21 was Milo Apgar's first home. The present inn was built in 1956 and sold to the National Park Service three years later. Canoe, rowboat, and motor boat rentals are available at the dock near the inn. *At Apgar village near the West Glacier entrance to Glacier Park; mail: Glacier Park Inc., Viad Corporate Center, Phoenix, AZ 85077-0928; (406) 888-5632 or (602) 207-6000 for reservations year-round; DIS, MC, V; no checks; $$-$$$.*

North Fork Hostel and Cabins   The privately run North Fork Hostel and Cabins in Polebridge offer rustic accommodations and a step back in time for those looking for the ultimate hippie experience and/or a cheap place to stay near Glacier. The hostel doesn't have electricity, but then again neither does anyplace else in Polebridge. Dorm-type facilities with kitchen, shower, and clawfoot bathtub (but no indoor toilets) run $12 per night; there's also one private room for couples. Three- to four-person cabins go for $25 per night; larger six-person cabins with kitchen cost $40 per night. You can borrow skis or mountain bikes, but you'll need to bring your own sleeping bag, flashlight, and food. Make winter reservations in advance to ensure someone's there; the cabins and hostel also may be closed in March and April. The hostel offers shuttle service to and from the West Glacier Amtrak station for an additional fee. *On the western edge of Glacier National Park, a quarter-mile southeast of the Polebridge Mercantile at the end of Beaver Dr; PO Box 1, Polebridge, MT 59928; (800) 775-2938 or (406) 888-5241; AE; checks OK; $.*

Rising Sun Motor Inn This 72-room motel and cabin facility located at Rising Sun Campground near St. Mary Lake on the east side of Glacier Park is one of the few lodging options inside the park other than the historic lodges. The area has a view of the lake but is not on the lakeshore. At the turn of the last century, the area near this inn was mined for copper, silver, and gold. This was the only lodging facility in the park not closed during World War II. Open early June to early September. *Just inside Glacier Park at the St. Mary entrance; mail: Glacier Park Inc., Viad Corporate Center, Phoenix, AZ 85077-0928; (406) 732-5523 or (602) 207-6000 for reservations year-round; DIS, MC, V; no checks; $$.*

Backcountry Cabins

The two **backcountry chalets** in Glacier National Park, Sperry and Granite Park, are the only ones remaining of the string of chalets built in 1913–1914 by railroader Louis W. Hill. One of the owners of the Great Northern Railway, Hill was the primary developer of the hotel system in the park. The facilities were bought by the National Park Service in the early 1950s and operated by private concessionaires until they were closed for renovation in the early 1990s. Following an ambitious private fund-raising effort and appropriations from Congress, Granite Park Chalet has reopened as a backpackers' hut. Renovations to Sperry Chalet, which include new water and sewer systems and changes for fire safety, should be completed for the 1997 season.

The chalets, both located almost on top of the Continental Divide, are reached only by trail. Reservations (required) are sometimes difficult to secure because the season is so short—the chalets open July 1 and close Labor Day. Because the chalets have been closed for several years, the reservations system has not been well-established. For information, contact Glacier National Park, (406) 888-5441. You may not be able to make actual reservations through the park staff, but they will know how the reservation system will operate for the coming season. Hikers without reservations who want to stay at the chalets should check at the Glacier Park visitors centers for cancellations.

Granite Park Chalet, at an elevation of 6,690 feet, perches on a promontory along the Garden Wall northwest of Logan Pass. It's accessible via the Highline Trail (see Hiking/Backpacking, above). The chalet has 11 rooms. Visitors sleep in the second story of the main lodge or in an annex building. Rooms have bunk beds and, for now, hikers must bring bedding, food, and water. Composting toilets have been installed on-site. There is no electricity at the chalet, and propane is used for lighting in the main lodge. Bring a flashlight for your room.

Most hikers park at the visitors center parking lot at Logan Pass and hike the Highline Trail along the Garden Wall 7.4 miles to the chalet. Allow 4 hours, one-way, for this relatively flat hike along a well-maintained trail. The other trail to Granite Park is via Swiftcurrent Pass. The trail begins at the Many Glacier Campground and rises steadily to the pass. This route is an 8-mile hike, one-way; allow about 5 hours. Hikers can also park at the Loop Trail parking lot on the Going-to-the-Sun Hwy and hike the 4.5 miles up to the chalet. There is a 2,300-foot elevation gain on this trail, used primarily for early season access and by day hikers. Allow 3 hours for the hike. Be aware that this trail is frequented by grizzly bears, more so perhaps than other trails in the park.

Sperry Chalet, at an elevation of 6,500 feet, sits on the edge of a glacial cirque with views of Lake McDonald and the mountains to the west. While Granite Park Chalet is known as the place to see grizzlies, Sperry is famous for the many mountain goats that frequent the area, often lounging on rocks or grazing just outside the doors of the chalet buildings. Sperry Chalet has 16 rooms, all in a lodge building separate from the main lodge/dining room. As at Granite Park, there is no electricity. Bedding, towels, and soap are provided but, again, bring a flashlight.

Most hikers reach Sperry Chalet via a 6.7-mile hike from the Lake McDonald Hotel. Hikers can park in the hotel parking lot; the trailhead is across the road. This trail is challenging in that it has a 3,300-foot elevation gain. Allow about 5 hours.

Hikers can also reach Sperry Chalet via Gunsight Pass, a 12.1-mile hike. The trailhead for this route is at the Jackson Glacier Viewpoint, 5 miles east of Logan Pass. Allow at least 9 hours for this hike, more if you want to stop to fish in Gunsight Lake or Lake Ellen Wilson along the way. Those who want a longer hike can park at the Sunrift Gorge parking lot and take the trail to the gorge and on to Gunsight Pass. The first section of this hike is through dense forest in a hanging valley, but once the trail begins climbing to Gunsight Pass, the vistas are worth the effort. There's an old stone shelter on the pass, as well as plenty of mountain goats.

More Information

Canadian Wilderness Tours: (403) 859-2058.

Chinook Country Tourist Association: (800) 661-1222.

Glacier Country Regional Tourism: (406) 756-7128.

Glacier National History Association: (406) 888-5756.

Glacier National Park: (406) 888-5441.

Glacier Park Inc.: (602) 248-6000.

Glacier Park Outfitters: (916) 988-3765.

Glacier Raft Co.: (800) 332-9995.

Great Northern Whitewater: (800) 735-7897.

Royal Canadian Mounted Police: (403) 859-2244 (May to Oct); (403) 653-4932 (Cardston); (403) 624-4425 (Pincher Creek).

Sun Tours: (406) 226-9220.

Trail of the Great Bear Travel Store: (800) 215-2395.

Travel Montana: (800) 847-4868.

Waterton Lakes National Park: (403) 859-2224.

Waterton Natural History Association: (403) 859-2624.

Waterton Park Visitors Association: (403) 859-2224.

Kalispell
and the Flathead
Valley

Including Whitefish, The Big Mountain, Columbia Falls, Flathead Lake, Polson, and Bigfork, with portions of the Flathead National Forest.

The Flathead Valley (pop: 67,000) or simply "The Flathead," as it's called, is one of Montana's most popular recreational getaways. That's partly due to its location bordering Glacier National Park, and partly due to its own stupendous outdoor opportunities.

In winter, the major draw is The Big Mountain, north of Whitefish, an emerging destination ski resort. But the ski area isn't the only thing big about the Flathead: slightly larger than the state of Connecticut, the valley claims Flathead Lake, the largest natural freshwater lake west of the Mississippi, as its centerpiece—plus more than 250 smaller lakes dotting the valley floor and surrounding mountains. The enormous peaks of Glacier National Park form the valley's northeast border; and the Canadian Rockies rise to the north.

Many tourists never leave: the Flathead is perennially among the three fastest growing counties in the state. Timber still plays a major role in the region's economy, but increasingly tourist dollars, service industries, and retirees are sustaining its population. The valley boasts five towns of note, each with its own distinct personality.

Traditionally, the county seat of Kalispell (pop: 13,000), just north of Flathead Lake, has served as the area's commercial center. Retailing aside, Kalispell is the prettiest city in the Flathead, and its east side boasts some of the county's grandest homes. Among these is the Conrad Mansion, built for Kalispell's founding father, who believed that the railroad would come through town—it went through Whitefish instead, leaving Kalispell with only a spur line. Although not a tourist destination itself, centrally located Kalispell often serves as the jumping-off point for the Flathead Valley's many attractions.

Once known as "Stumptown" for the tree stumps that littered its streets, Whitefish (pop: 4,500) is the closest thing to a tony resort community west of Bozeman. Its raison d'être is The Big Mountain, which looms 8 miles north. Occasional sightings of Hollywood stars lend Whitefish a certain mystique, but as ski towns go it's pretty low-key. Many tourists arrive in Whitefish via Amtrak; the old Great Northern Depot (later the Burlington Northern Depot) is a beauty, a two-story Tudor-style station worth a visit. Just west of Glacier National Park, Columbia Falls and the Bad Rock Canyon area claim Flathead's largest concentration of man-made amusement: this is kitschy kid heaven, with everything from an enormous maze to a black bear park.

Little more than a main street and a marina, the quaint village of Bigfork, on the northeast corner of Flathead Lake, seems an unlikely spot for a dose of culture, but it's where you'll find the valley's largest concentration of good restaurants, art galleries, and live entertainment. It's touristy, sure, with espresso carts and shopping opportunities galore, but Bigfork's appeal is undeniable. No wonder one of our friends refers to Bigfork as "Carmel on the Flathead." The Flathead Indian Reservation includes the southern half of Flathead Lake, and that's where you'll find Polson, the reservation's largest town. Since it anchors that end of the lake, Polson centers its recreation offerings around water activities.

With such varied options, it's quite possible you could visit the Flathead and skip Glacier National Park altogether. Many people do.

Getting There

Kalispell sits at the junction of US Highways 93 and 2. Glacier Park International Airport lies 8 miles north of Kalispell. Kalispell and Whitefish are served by Rimrock Trailways bus lines; Whitefish also is served by Amtrak's Empire Builder. Both Whitefish and Columbia Falls are approximately 14 miles north of Kalispell on US Hwys 93 and 2, respectively. The Big Mountain is 18 miles farther north on US 93. Polson is at the south end of Flathead Lake at the junction of US 93 and Hwy 35. Bigfork is on the northeast corner of the lake on Hwy 35, just below its junction with Hwy 83.

Adjoining Areas

EAST: **Glacier National Park**

WEST: **Northwest Montana**

SOUTH: **Mission Valley**

Kayaking/Rafting

Most of the kayaking, canoeing, and rafting in the Flathead takes place on the North and Middle Forks and the main Flathead River; the North Fork is noted for fishing and scenery, while the Middle Fork boasts the best whitewater. Local kayak fanatic Brian Sullivan, (406) 862-5775, offers **kayak lessons and guiding.**

Beginning boaters should stick to the **main Flathead River** west of Columbia Falls, or alternatively, head for the flatwater of the **Whitefish River** from Whitefish Lake to the Hwy 40 bridge (good for canoeists and beginning kayakers). There is Class I through III water on the **North Fork,** but also lots of logjams and braiding. Make sure you call for current conditions and, when in doubt, scout. From Ford Creek to Polebridge is generally the safest stretch, with Class II and sometimes Class III water (very scenic; watch for wildlife on the edge of Glacier National Park), but do check—conditions may have changed.

Another scenery-filled Class II–III trip starts at **West Glacier** and runs to Blankenship Bridge on the **Middle Fork.** A good Class II float on the main Flathead River starts at **Pressentine Bar** (a fishing access site) midway between Kalispell and Columbia Falls and ends at the Old Steel Bridge just east of Kalispell.

More challenging boating is on the Middle Fork's Class II, III, and IV water east of West Glacier. The most popular kayak run for experienced boaters starts at **Moccasin Creek** on the Middle Fork of the Flathead and ends at West Glacier; you can cut a mile or so of flatwater off the trip by putting in at Kootenai Creek, but there's limited parking.

The Flathead Whitewater Association (Brian Sullivan, (406) 862-5775) can provide further information and help connect kayak partners. Hungry Horse Ranger District, (406) 387-5243, has water levels and conditions.

Sea kayaking is a great way to explore the shores and islands of **Flathead Lake.** Mornings or evenings are best to avoid boat wakes. Rent sea kayaks from Snowfrog in Whitefish, (406) 862-7547. Glacier Sea

Kayaking, (406) 862-9010, owner and veteran outdoorswoman Bobbie Gilmore knows what's most important when it comes to adventure travel: food! Whether you choose a day trip, dinner cruise, or full moon adventure, you'll be treated to some of the best fixin's in the Flathead—the guides even take along a portable espresso maker so you can sit back and sip your latte. Trips leave from **Rollins,** on the west side of the lake. This is pillow-soft adventure and trips are suitable for beginners. Gilmore also teaches group sea-kayaking lessons; there's a four person minimum.

Glacier Raft Company, (800) 332-9995 or (406) 888-5454, has self-guided canoe and raft trips, with a brief lesson and evaluation. In Columbia Falls, Rising Sun Outdoor Adventures, (406) 892-2602 or (406) 862-5934, rents rafts, kayaks, canoes, inflatable kayaks, and all the necessary gear, including a trailer if need be. Northwest Voyageurs, (800) 826-2724 or (406) 387-9453, rents paddle and oar rafts, or hard-shell and inflatable kayaks; rates include shuttle service. Glacier Raft Company, Montana Raft Company, (800) 521-RAFT or (406) 387-5555, and Northwest Voyageurs all offer half- and full-day whitewater trips on the Middle Fork of the Flathead River. Glacier Raft Company is Montana's oldest rafting company (used to shoot the movie *The River Wild*) and offers multi-day combination rafting/fishing trips on the North or Middle Forks, and a 4- to 6-day float in the **Great Bear Wilderness.**

Montana Raft Company's sister company, Glacier Wilderness Guides, (800) 521-RAFT or (406) 387-5555, has the exclusive backpacking contract with the National Park Service, so they specialize in combination rafting/hiking trips within **Glacier National Park.** Northwest Voyageurs offers multi-day whitewater trips and dinner floats on the Middle Fork. Both Montana Raft Company and Northwest Voyageurs also offer one-day and multi-day rafting/horseback riding trips with Flying Eagle Ranch. All three raft companies will customize trips. Call for brochures and schedules.

Boating/Sailing

About 28 miles long and 15 miles wide at its widest point, **Flathead Lake** is big enough to handle an awful lot of activity and never seem crowded. Views are best from the west side, but to really appreciate the lake, get on it. In Bigfork, Marina Cay rents ski boats, pleasure boats, pontoon boats, fishing boats, pedal boats, canoes, rafts, and Jet-skis—all available by the hour or half-day. The marina also rents water skis and knee boards. Call (800) 433-6516 or (406) 837-5861 for details.

Flathead Surf-N-Ski, which operates out of KwaTaqNuk Resort in Polson, (406) 883-3900, rents ski and fishing boats, sit-down Jet-skis, canoes, pedal boats, water skis, and fishing equipment. Wet suits come free with boat rental, and there's free delivery within a limited area.

June through September, the 40-passenger *Princess* tour boat offers **motorized cruises** on Flathead Lake; morning and afternoon cruises last 1 ½ hours, and a longer afternoon tour around **Wild Horse Island** is also available. The *Princess* operates out of KwaTaqNuk Resort in Polson, (406) 883-2448. Spring and fall schedules vary.

The *Far West*, (406) 857-3203), books 1 ½-hour lunch, afternoon, and evening cruises; it's a 200-passenger boat that leaves from the northwest corner of the lake. It's best to call in advance since a charter may cause cancellation. On the Fourth of July, they offer an **evening fireworks cruise** to Lakeside with a picnic dinner and cash bar; reservations required. The *Far West* is docked 1 mile south of Somers or 9 miles south of Kalispell on US 93.

You'll find western Montana's best **sailing** opportunities also on Flathead Lake, where a northerly wind generally blows in the mornings. Two-hour Flathead Lake sailing trips on the 51-foot *Questa* and her sister ship *Nor'Easter,* both champion racing sloops, leave four times a day from Flathead Lake Lodge south of Bigfork, (406) 837-5569. The 7pm **sunset cruise** is reserved for adults only and includes wine and beverages. Rising Sun Outdoor Adventures, (406) 862-5934 or (406) 892-2602, offers 3-hour or day-long sailing trips on a 24-footer; there's a two-person minimum. Trips leave from Somers.

Do-it-yourselfers can rent 21- or 23-foot sailboats from Quiet World Marina, (406) 849-5423, in Dayton, on the lake's west side.

Camping

The *Montana Travel Planner,* published by Travel Montana, (800) 847-4868 out-of-state or (406) 444-2654 in-state, is available at chambers of commerce and many motels and lists the state's public and private campgrounds; look under "Glacier Country" for Flathead Valley sites. RV travelers should check to make sure campgrounds can accommodate their vehicles. The *Flathead Valley Road Map* published by Montana Map Co., (800) 676-5160 or (406) 892-3884, keys campgrounds; it's available at local outdoor stores and chambers of commerce.

If you want to camp on **Flathead Lake,** the Montana Department of Fish, Wildlife and Parks operates five lakeshore campgrounds. Very popular is the lovely **Wayfarers Unit,** half a mile south of Bigfork, where you can sit on huge rocks and watch the sunset. For reservations and information call (406) 837-4196 in summer, or (406) 752-5501 in winter.

For great views, consider the **West Shore Unit,** 20 miles south of Kalispell on US 93, (406) 844-3901 summer or (406) 752-5501 winter.

Campsites here are located in thick coniferous forest; head down to the picnic areas at the shore to see the Mission and Swan Ranges. Shoreline campsites at the **Big Arm Unit,** (406) 849-5255 summer or (406) 752-5501 winter, are primitive, but the shared facilities are modern, with showers and flush toilets. Big Arm also has one of the closest boat launches to Wild Horse Island (see Wildlife, below).

The **Yellow Bay Unit,** 15 miles north of Polson on Hwy 35, offers a wide, graveled beach for swimming, but it's generally considered a day-use area: there are only four tent sites (you'll have to walk the last 20–50 yards) amid much traffic noise. Additionally, there have been water problems and at press time there is no water available; call (406) 752-5501 for current information. The **Finley Point Unit,** (406) 887-2715 summer or (406) 752-5501 winter, was designed with **RVs** in mind and is the most developed campground in the state. Tents are only allowed on four tent pads. To get to Finley Point, drive 11 miles north of Polson on Hwy 35, then 4 miles west on the signed county road.

You can make advance reservations at the Confederated Salish and Kootenai Tribes-operated **Blue Bay Campground,** (406) 982-3077. With 50 sites, a swimming beach, a fishing pier, and the lake's best boat ramp, Blue Bay is understandably popular. Find it on the lake's southeast corner, 20 miles from Polson. Blue Bay is open May through September, with day-use year-round.

You can also reserve sites at **Big Creek Campground,** (800) 416-6992, on the North Fork of the Flathead near the Camas entrance to Glacier National Park; but more spontaneous travelers don't panic—half the 22 sites are saved for walk-ins. This is a popular boating and fishing access as well. Contact the Glacier View/Hungry Horse Ranger District, (406) 387-5243.

It doesn't have the spectacular mountain views that many other Flathead campgrounds claim, but **Lake Mary Ronan State Park,** with 26 campsites about 7 miles west of Dayton, is very peaceful. It's located in a thick forest of Douglas fir. During kokanee season, from the end of May through June, the campground is likely to be very crowded, but at other times it's a nice break from the always popular Flathead Lake campgrounds. Contact the Department of Fish, Wildlife and Parks in Kalispell, (406) 752-5501.

Half of all the Forest Service campgrounds in the Flathead National Forest (nearly a dozen) are on **Hungry Horse Reservoir,** Glacier View/Hungry Horse Ranger District, (406) 387-5243. **Emery Bay Campground,** 7 miles off US 2 on Forest Road 38, on the east side of the reservoir (South Fork Rd), has nice views of the Swan Range. Rebuilt in 1994, the 24 sites see light use.

Located 55 miles (about 2 hours) south of US 2 at the confluence of the wild and scenic South Fork of the Flathead and Spotted Bear Rivers, **Spotted Bear Campground** has 13 wooded sites, coveted for their good fishing access (cutthroats) and lovely views. If the campground is full (often the case on summer weekends) there is nearby dispersed camping (no facilities) at roadside pullouts. Call the Spotted Bear Ranger District, (406) 758-5376 in summer or (406) 387-5243 in winter.

Tally Lake Campground sits on the shore of the deepest lake in Montana (just under 500 feet). Of 39 nicely spaced, wooded sites, those on the north shore have the best views of the lake. Hot summer weekends you'll see water-skiers and plenty of day-use activity at the picnic area and swimming beach, but weekdays are still only about half-full. Turn off US 93 on Twin Bridges Rd 20 miles north of Whitefish, and follow the signs, or call the Tally Lake Ranger District, (406) 862-2508.

Biking

Plenty of backroads in the area mean plenty of good **road cycling.** Rails to Trails of Northwest Montana puts out a map indicating gravel and paved routes. It's available at Bikology in Kalispell, (406) 755-6748, and other area outdoor stores.

A legacy of old logging roads ensure good **mountain biking** as well. Weather permitting, Glacier Cyclery in Whitefish (336 E Second St, (406) 862-6446) offers guided mountain bike rides on Monday nights; bikers split up into three groups according to ability. Meet at Glacier Cyclery at 6pm. All Seasons Cycling in Columbia Falls (615 Nucleus Ave, (406) 892-2755) leads similarly organized group rides on Wednesday nights in summer; meet at 6pm at the shop. Snowfrog, (406) 862-7547, in Whitefish and All Seasons Cycling also rent bicycles.

There are 8 miles of mountain bike trails (intermediate level) beginning at the base of **The Big Mountain,** (800) 858-5439 or (406) 862-2900; an additional 7-mile trail leads to the summit. Alternately, you can take the gondola up and cruise down. There's no fee for use of the trails, but the gondola ride will cost. Bike rentals are available.

The Glacier View/Hungry Horse Ranger District, (406) 387-5243, north of Columbia Falls has plenty of old logging roads to explore, with great views into Glacier National Park. You can ride 12 miles (one way) to **Hay Lake;** turn off on Forest Rd 376 a mile south of Polebridge. Or make a 25-mile loop ride up into **Wedge Canyon** and past **Hornet Mountain Lookout;** lock your bikes and hike up the last 1 ½ miles to the 6,744-foot lookout. One paved option: simply follow the **North Fork Road** out of Columbia Falls—it's best in fall when the larch are turning and traffic has dropped off. The pavement ends after 11 ½ miles; after that it's all gravel and dust and a mess you may want to avoid. This is big grizzly country, so take proper precautions.

You'll find the good (old growth), the bad (tough biking), and the ugly (clear-cuts) at the **Tally Lake** area about 15 miles west of Whitefish, where there's plenty of territory to explore. You will want a map and can get by with a Flathead National Forest map, but a better one is put out by Glacier Cyclery in conjunction with the Tally Lake Ranger District. It lists 10 recommended loop rides combining road and single-track trails. Some are suitable for novice riders, but most are at a solid intermediate level. The map includes the **Beaver Lake area** east of US 93, where you'll find more casual, short loop rides on gravel roads. Weather permitting, take a dip at Little Beaver Lake. To get to Tally Lake, take US 93 north about 4 miles, following the signs to Tally Lake Campground. To get to the Beaver Lake area, take US 93 to mile marker 135 (no sign) and turn right on Beaver Lake Rd. Follow this road to the Beaver Lake area sign (there's a map on the sign). Contact the Tally Lake Ranger District, (406) 862-2508, for more information.

The **Strawberry Lake area** has plenty of good intermediate to advanced trails. The most famous is the **Alpine Trail** up to Strawberry Lake just south of Glacier National Park. It's received a lot of attention since several national magazines highlighted it, but this is an extremely difficult and technical trail that you shouldn't attempt unless you know what you're doing. You'll need monster quads, a good map (it's not well-signed), and a shuttle to do the entire 20-mile ride from the Strawberry Lake Trail to Columbia Mountain and down to Columbia Falls. The good news is that it's only 3 uphill miles to the lake itself (plan on a good hour of riding in the lowest gear). Intermediate trails stay lower but are a lot of fun. You'll find the Strawberry Lake Trail at the end of Krause Basin Rd (Forest Rd 5390) off Foothills Rd south of Lake Blaine. All Seasons Cycling in Columbia Falls sells highlighted maps of the area showing you where to ride. It's located in the Swan Lake Ranger District, (406) 837-5081.

Fishing

The Flathead is a region of lakes—more than 250 of them including Flathead itself—and it's there that you'll find the biggest fish: lake trout, whitefish, perch, and pike. The three forks of the **Flathead River** are not nearly as prolific as their more southern brethren, but do offer good late summer fishing because of consistently cold water temperatures. The runoff generally doesn't clear until mid- to late July. The Montana

Department of Fish, Wildlife and Parks in Kalispell, (406) 752-5501, has regulations and information; most useful is the *Region One Monthly Fishing Guide,* a calendar of fishing options.

Outfitter Jim Landwehr's Glacier Fishing Charters runs four **charter boats on Flathead Lake;** he says 90 percent of his clients catch the biggest trout they've ever caught. Half- and full-day trips include all necessary equipment. Landwehr operates out of Woods Bay, 4 miles south of Bigfork. Call (800) 735-9244 or (406) 892-2377 for details. Another outfitter, Jim Crumal, (406) 862-5313, offers **Whitefish Lake** fishing trips on his beautifully restored 24-foot wooden boat. These are highly recommended.

Lakestream Fly Fishing Shop in Whitefish (15 Central Ave, (406) 862-1298) can help with fly-fishing advice and guide services. Lots of fishermen like to stop in at Lakestream just to admire its decor. Lakestream also offers private **fly-fishing instruction** as well as 2-hour summer clinics at The Big Mountain, (800) 858-5439 or (406) 862-2900, June through September. For spin-casting or fly-fishing information in Kalispell, try Sportsman & Ski Haus (40 E Idaho St, (406) 755-6484) or Snappy Sports Senter (1400 US 2 E, (406) 257-7525).

We hear good things about Glacier Raft Company's fishing guide Rick Schmidt. Glacier Raft Company, (800) 332-9995 or (406) 888-5454, Montana Raft Company, (800) 521-RAFT or (406) 387-5555, and Northwest Voyageurs, (800) 826-2724 or (406) 387-9453, offer half-day, full-day and multi-day fishing trips on the **North and Middle Forks of the Flathead.** Customized extended trips are also available. (See Kayaking/Rafting, above, for additional information.)

Lake Fishing

Flathead Lake holds the state record for lake trout: a 42-pounder was caught there in 1979, and every year one or two exceed 40 pounds. The state is also trying to restore the kokanee salmon population, which crashed in 1986; millions of fish have been planted in recent years, but the jury's still out about the program's success. In the meantime, you're likely to catch a lot of lake trout, particularly in the 3- to 5-pound range. **Ice fishing** for yellow perch and whitefish, as well as lake trout, is popular in **Polson Bay,** which freezes on a regular basis. Twenty other species of fish live in the lake. You might see westslope cutthroats and bull trout (which you can't keep). Fishing is open on the lake year-round, and the state maintains six free fishing access sites and boat launches, in addition to the facilities at the state parks.

Note: The southern half of Flathead Lake is owned by the Confederated Salish and Kootenai Tribes. To fish these waters, you will need a **Tribal Recreation Permit** and fishing stamp, available at local outdoor stores.

May through September, fish **Whitefish Lake** for cutthroat trout and good-sized pike, while in July there's a giant yellow mayfly hatch on the lake that moves from the south end to the north. During January and February you can ice fish for lake trout or the Lake Superior whitefish from which the lake takes its name.

Nearly 500 feet deep, **Tally Lake,** north of Whitefish, has a reputation for numerous northern pike. There's also kokanee salmon and some lake and rainbow trout. The lake is 5 miles north of Whitefish; follow the signs to the Tally Lake Campground.

Wheelchair-accessible **Lion Lake** is open year-round for rainbow trout and westslope cutthroat. There's good shore access, which makes it an appealing choice for children or novice anglers. It's 3 miles southeast of Hungry Horse on Hungry Horse Dam Rd.

Echo Lake, northeast of Bigfork, is renowned for largemouth bass and pike fishing, but you'll want a boat as shore access is poor. May and June are the best months, before the lake gets too warm.

Kokanee fishing is very good at **Lake Mary Ronan,** and best during spring, fall, and winter. You'll need a boat as, again, shore access is limited. Fishing for largemouth bass or rainbows is good anytime. Unfortunately, illegally planted perch may threaten this fishery.

When the hot summer sun kills off most of the good fishing, stick with **Lake Mary Ronan** or **Smith, Swan, Ashley,** and **Little Bitterroot Lakes.** Or hike into the high mountain lakes for westslope cutthroat trout: try **Crater, Cliff,** or **Birch Lakes** in the **Jewel Basin Hiking Area** (see Hiking/Backpacking, below).

River Fishing

The North Fork of the Flathead forms the western border to Glacier National Park, while the Middle Fork defines its southern boundary. The South Fork of the Flathead begins in the Scapegoat Mountains and meets the main river at Bad Rock Canyon. All three forks of the **Flathead River,** plus the main river itself, stay cold enough to maintain good fishing in the heat of summer. You're likely to catch westslope cutthroat trout, whitefish, and the occasional rainbow trout in the main river. You'll find good shore access on the North Fork from Big Creek to Polebridge. Runoff generally doesn't clear until mid- to late July.

You'll have to drive 55 miles on a gravel road to access the good cutthroat trout fishing on the **South Fork** of the Flathead. Try floating from Harrison Creek to Spotted Bear—but be aware of special catch-and-release regulations here. Wilderness fishing limits apply to the rest of the South

Fork and to **Hungry Horse Reservoir.** There's good shore access from Spotted Bear to the Reservoir. For more information contact the Montana Department of Fish, Wildlife and Parks listed above or the Spotted Bear Ranger District, (406) 758-5376 or (406) 387-5243 in winter.

Fish the **Whitefish River** in early spring for pike, sometimes as heavy as 15 or 20 pounds. There's good access in town or at the Hwy 40 bridge.

Hiking/Backpacking

With Glacier National Park so close, many local hikers simply figure, why settle for anything less (see Glacier National Park chapter)? Glacier's appeal is undeniable, but there are plenty of other hiking opportunities in the Flathead—and you'll encounter a lot less traffic getting there.

In most of the **Flathead National Forest,** there are special restrictions for storing food when your camp is unoccupied: you must keep it in a bear-resistant container, hanging from a tree, or continually guarded. For a small donation, the ranger districts will loan you a container or rope. Call the Flathead National Forest Supervisor's Office in Kalispell, (406) 755-5401, or specific ranger districts listed at the end of the chapter for information. Roads in the Flathead National Forest often are closed due to wildlife and watershed concerns; ask the appropriate district for a current *Open Road* map (free). In addition to the hikes listed here, see Backcountry Cabins, below.

The **Danny On Memorial Trail** on The Big Mountain opens sometime after mid-June, with lower-elevation portions open by the first of June. This is a gorgeous day hike, particularly in July when beargrass and other wildflowers cover the meadows. The entire trail is 5 ³/₅ miles one way, but you can take a shortcut and make it to the top in 3 ⁴/₅ miles, or take the chair lift to the top and walk down. If you hike up, you can then take the chairlift or gondola down at no charge. In August, this is good huckleberry picking territory, but the bears think so too—be sure to take proper precautions. The trailhead begins just above the main parking lot; ask at any of the village motels for a trail map.

Comprising 15,000 acres of high mountain country, the **Jewel Basin Hiking Area** holds 35 miles of trails and 27 easily accessed alpine lakes set aside specifically for hikers (mountain bikes and pack animals prohibited). Three of the lakes—Birch, Clayton, and Lower Pilgrim—are 100 feet or more deep; most are stocked with fish and draw plenty of local traffic. About half of the lakes are 8 miles or less from the trailhead—good destinations for short day hikes or easy overnights. The 2-mile **Noisy Creek Notch Trail** goes up a side hill from the parking lot, offering great views of the Flathead Valley, then drops over a ridge into two lovely alpine lakes. Lots of folks climb **Mount Aeneas** (7,528 feet), a 9-mile round-trip hike with views of the Flathead Range and Glacier National Park. Jewel Basin makes a fine alternative to Glacier: it's just as spectacular, with well-maintained trails and huge wildflower-filled meadows, but less hassle and cost. On summer weekends the trailhead parking lot is often full, but the area is still fairly quiet on weekdays or any time after Labor Day. The vast majority of people come from the west, where trailheads are about 13 miles northeast of Bigfork. To avoid the crowds, try any of four trailheads accessed from the South Fork Rd on the west side of Hungry Horse Reservoir. Jewel Basin maps are available at Bermel's Conoco, (406) 837-4727, at the intersection of Hwy 83 and the Swan River Rd, or at the Swan Lake, (406) 387-5081, or Glacier View/Hungry Horse, (406) 837-4727, Ranger Districts.

Beautiful **Alpine Trail #7** runs north-south along the Swan Divide for 60 miles from just outside Columbia Falls through the Jewel Basin Hiking Area. The Alpine Trail sees a lot of pack, motorcycle, and mountain bike use: avoid it by taking **Strawberry Lake Trail #5** for 3 miles then turning south on the Alpine Trail and dropping into Jewel Basin, where hikers only are permitted. Access the Strawberry Lake Trail from Krause Basin Rd (Forest Rd 5390) off Foothills Rd south of Lake Blaine. Glacier View/Hungry Horse Ranger District, (406) 387-5243.

The 1 1/2-mile hike to **Hornet Mountain Lookout** is all uphill, but it's not as bad as many climbs, and the views from the top are just as spectacular as you would imagine. To get there, take the North Fork Rd to Whale Creek Rd, then turn west and drive 5 miles to the trailhead. The Hornet Mountain Lookout is rented year-round, so you're not likely to have the place to yourself. Glacier View/Hungry Horse Ranger District, (406) 387-5243.

Avoid congestion by hiking the **Whitefish Divide Trail #26,** which runs north of The Big Mountain and divides the North Fork and Stillwater drainages. The recently reconstructed high alpine trail passes through timbered ridges and meadows and over Werner and Diamond Peaks, offering good views and solitude (though access is limited and the roads are rough). Watch for mule deer and grizzlies. Access the trail by driving on Forest Rd 1658 east of Olney. You can do a point-to-point 2- or 3-day overnight hike by leaving a shuttle at Red Meadows (about 20 miles north), but leave plenty of time as the road in is rough. There's a little lake and campground at Red Meadows, and the trail continues north of there, but it hasn't been maintained and is difficult to follow (it's slated for reconstruction soon; check with the Glacier View/Hungry Horse Ranger District, (406) 387-5243, about its status).

Swimming

Try any of the state park units on **Flathead Lake** or the newly refurbished city beach or state park at **Whitefish Lake. Tally Lake** also has a swimming beach; there's a fee for day use. Be prepared for swimmer's itch at the latter two places. It's caused by a barely visible water-borne parasite that strikes in warmer temperatures and shallow waters. You'll feel a slight sting as they attempt to burrow into your skin, followed by an itching sensation. Don't panic—they can't actually get into your skin—just dry yourself thoroughly to avoid further discomfort. Some people successfully avoid swimmer's itch by slathering baby oil on their bodies before entering the water.

Golfing

Talk about *A River Runs Through It:* the Flathead River flows alongside the 18-hole, Nicklaus-designed **Eagle Bend** golf course, (800) 255-5641 or (406) 837-7300. The course has garnered national attention for its scenic and well-maintained layout—among its recent honors was being named the state's premiere golf course by *Golf Digest* magazine. Eagle Bend has an additional nine-hole course as well. You can book tee times at Eagle Bend or any of seven other Flathead courses (the **Whitefish Lake Golf Course** is also recommended) by calling the Flathead Valley Golf Association, (800) 392-9795 or (406) 257-6402.

Climbing

In Kalispell, Turn to Stone (1 mile south of the courthouse on US 93, (406) 755-6322) has an indoor climbing and bouldering gym; it's also a good place to collect climbing information. So is Rocky Mountain Outfitters in Kalispell (135 Main St, (406) 752-2446). You'll find good climbing at **Stone Hill** west of Eureka, about 60 miles north of Whitefish (see Climbing in the Northwest Montana chapter).

Wildlife

One of the largest islands in the inland United States (2,160 acres), the part private, part public **Wild Horse Island** on Flathead Lake is a spectacular setting in which to view **bighorn sheep, bald eagles,** and **waterfowl.** The wild horses for which the island is named are long gone (legend has it that the Flathead Indians swam out to the island to keep them safe from the enemy Blackfeet), but the state has planted a small herd of **wild geldings.** The state is currently working on a designated loop trail; until it's completed you can utilize game trails. Head up to the higher knolls and grasslands to see bighorn sheep (there are about 100). The horses tend to hang out on the western side of the island. You'll have to arrange your own transportation out to Wild Horse, as organized tours circle the island but are not allowed to land there. The best public access points are at the Walstad Fishing Access Site, 2 miles east of Big Arm, and at the Big Arm Unit of Flathead Lake State Park, 3 miles southwest of Wild Horse Island. The most convenient boat rental is at Dillon's Resort and Marina, (406) 849-5838, in Big Arm. The state puts out a brochure and map of the island with five recommended landing areas, but you can land anywhere that's not privately owned or posted. Be sure to secure your boats, since sudden windstorms can cause conditions to change radically. The island is for day use only; you can picnic but no fires or pets are allowed. Maximum group size is 15.

Horseback Riding

Old West Adventures offers dinner **wagon rides** and short **trail rides** on The Big Mountain, (800) 858-5439 or (406) 862-2900.

Cross-Country Skiing

Aside from trails at The Big Mountain (see Downhill Skiing, below), the Flathead Valley has several other reliable cross-country destinations, as well as several more that receive inconsistent snowfall. Generally you have to head away from Flathead Lake, which warms up area temperatures, for decent conditions. Backcountry skiers can obtain **avalanche** condition updates from the Glacier Country Avalanche Center, (800) 526-5329 or locally (406) 257-8402.

Rent **touring and telemark equipment** at Snowfrog in Whitefish (903 Wisconsin Ave, (406) 862-7547), the Outback Ski Shack (across from Grouse Mountain Lodge, (406) 862-3000 ext. 418), or Rocky Mountain Outfitters in Kalispell (135 Main St, (406) 752-2446). Touring and telemarking lessons are offered at The Big Mountain.

The Big Mountain, (800) 858-5439 or (406) 862-2900, offers 10 kilometers of groomed cross-country trails, with spectacular views of the Flathead Valley and Glacier National Park. The Outpost Lodge on the mountain rents Nordic equipment.

On the Whitefish Lake Golf Course, the **Glacier Nordic Center** keeps 10 kilometers of groomed tracks suitable for beginner through advanced skiers, including skate-skiers. Part of the course is lit for **night skiing.** Laura Nugent, who runs the Outback Ski Shack there, is a long-time Whitefish resident, veteran outdoorswoman, and fountain of information. Ski rentals are available and there's a fee for use of the trails.

Located on US 93 just north of Whitefish across from Grouse Mountain Lodge, (406) 862-3000 ext. 418.

With more than 7 kilometers of intermittently groomed trails suitable for beginners, plus 24 additional kilometers of tougher, ungroomed trails, **Round Meadows** offers five loop trails and a nice break from the crowds. Grooming is done on Fridays, when it's done at all. To get there, take US 93 north 10 miles to Farm Market Rd, turn left, and then turn right in 2 miles on Star Meadows Rd. Maps are available from the Tally Lake Ranger District, (406) 862-2508.

At **Blacktail Cross-Country Ski Trails,** 20 kilometers of groomed trails follow logging roads and tough descents high above the west side of Flathead Lake. The altitude of 5,500 feet nearly guarantees good snow conditions. With impressive views of the Mission Mountains, the Swan Range, and Flathead Lake, Blacktail is a great place to get away from the crowds. It's also a good place for a possible moose sighting. There are two parking lots; leave a shuttle at the lower one, then ski down from the upper lot along the 13.3-kilometer **Power Line Trail**. The Flathead County Department of Parks and Recreation grooms tracks every Friday, and sometimes more often, December through March. Turn west on Blacktail Rd just south of Lakeside (you'll see the sign), then drive 7 miles to the parking lot. Maps are available through the Flathead County Department of Parks and Recreation, (406) 758-5800.

The 15,000-acre **Jewel Basin Hiking Area** offers exceptional backcountry skiing. The only catch: you have to slog about 5 miles up the steep, unplowed road leading there. The road is a good option for novice skiers, though it's too steep for real beginners to descend. Once at the entrance, you can access some stunning high alpine country, with terrific views of the Flathead Valley as well as the Bob Marshall and Great Bear Wilderness Areas. Snowmobilers can use the road but are not allowed into the Jewel Basin area itself. Go 13 miles northeast of Bigfork, off Echo Lake Rd. You'll want to get avalanche information first (see above). Glacier View/Hungry Horse Ranger District, (406) 387-5243.

For additional cross-country options, see Backcountry Cabins, below.

Downhill Skiing

With 63 marked runs, 9 lifts, and a vertical drop of 2,300 feet, **The Big Mountain,** (800) 858-5439 or (406) 862-2900, is big by anyone's standards. General lift-ticket prices are competitive with other high-end western resorts, but beginners ski free on the platter lift and Chair 6. Kids under six ski free no matter what level they can handle. The backside, served by Chair 7, usually has the best snow conditions and is less crowded. Experts like The Big Mountain's it's-your-life stance on out-of-bounds skiing. Snowcat skiing is another way to get to otherwise inaccessible territory. When skiing here is good, it's very, very good—and when it's bad, it's horrid (the mountain is often socked in). Because of its proximity to the Amtrak station in Whitefish, The Big Mountain offers good deals on train/ski packages. Preseason voucher tickets (available through the mountain and local outdoor stores) are terrific values, too. The Big Mountain is about 30 miles north of Kalispell on US 93.

Snowmobiling

There are more than 200 miles of groomed snowmobile trails in Flathead National Forest, concentrated in the Glacier View/Hungry Horse Ranger District and the Stillwater State Forest. The beautiful **Canyon Creek** trail is a good choice; it begins north of Columbia Falls and connects to Werner Peak, Olney, and Red Meadow. Get trail maps and advice from the Glacier View/Hungry Horse Ranger District, (406) 387-5243, the Flathead Convention and Visitors Association, (800) 543-3105 or (406) 756-9091, or local chambers of commerce. Guided tours and rentals are available through Adventure Motor Sports in Columbia Falls, (800) 531-3511 or (406) 892-2752.

Other Activities

See the Flathead Valley from on high in a **hot-air balloon** with Big Sky Balloon Adventures, (406) 862-3432, or Let's Go Ballooning!, (406) 387-4646. Offered seasonally only.

With a refrigeration unit and a Zamboni, the open-air **Mountain Trails Ice Skating Center,** (406) 862-8244, is Montana's best skating facility on the west side of the Divide. It's open from late fall to early spring.

Half of Dog Sled Adventure's 65 dogs come from unwanted homes or animal shelters. Thanksgiving through mid-April you can see them go from the back of a **dogsled** in the Stillwater State Forest, 20 miles north of Whitefish. You'll be wrapped in elk fur and a sleeping bag for the wild 12-mile, 1 1/2-hour ride while a musher steers the dogs. Cost is $50 per adult, $25 per child. Contact Jeff Ulsamer, (406) 881-BARK, for more information.

Old West Adventures offers Clydesdale-pulled **sleigh rides.** The half-hour ride culminates in a huge barbecue dinner, complete with live, western-style entertainment; call (406) 862-2434 for information or (406) 862-2900 for reservations.

outside in

Attractions

Memorial Day through September, you can take a **gondola or chairlift ride** to the 7,000-foot summit of The Big Mountain, which, in addition to offering tremendous 360-degree views into Glacier National Park and Canada, houses the **Forest Service Environmental Education Center.** The center offers free wildflower walks, a slide show, and other educational activities. The center is open daily from Memorial Day through September and weekends and holidays in winter, and offers avalanche awareness education and snow ecology; call (406) 862-1972.

When you or your kids tire of Mother Nature's subtleties, it's time to head for Columbia Falls and the surrounding Bad Rock Canyon area. There's nothing remotely subtle about the **Big Sky Water Slide,** (406) 892-5025, actually four slides of varying degrees. Even adults will blanch at the sight of the 70-foot glide! A cruise up US 2 towards Glacier National Park leads first past the gravity-defying **House of Mystery** (where marbles roll "up") and then to Coram and the **Amazing Fun Center** with its gigantic Glacier Maze, mini-golf, and bumper boats. In Coram, also visit the **Great Bear Adventure** drive-through black bear park, (406) 387-4290. Don't fret—the bears were raised in captivity.

When trader Charles Conrad moved from Fort Benton to Western Montana in the 1890s to expand his business interests and found the city of Kalispell, he built what is still one of the city's most beautiful homes. Designed by Spokane architect Kirkland Cutter, the stunning **Conrad Mansion** is in impeccable condition and features Tiffany stained glass and priceless antiques. Thanks to Conrad's daughter Alicia, who recognized the historical importance of her family home, 90 percent of the original furnishings remain. A tour of the mansion is an excellent opportunity to learn about early Montana life. Tours are available every day mid-May through mid-October. The mansion is in Kalispell, on Woodland Ave between Third and Fourth Sts E, (406) 755-2166.

Bob Gatiss spent most of his long life planting and tending his flower gardens, which he loved to share with the public. Gatiss died in April 1996, but Paul and Elizabeth Siblerud continue to maintain the lovely 5-acre **Gatiss Gardens** with the same generous spirit. There's no entrance charge, though donations are accepted. Guests are encouraged to picnic among the thousands of flowers (all identified) and to mull over the inspirational quotations that Bob Gatiss posted around the grounds. It's 6 miles north of Bigfork on Hwy 35 and is open 9am to dusk; call (406) 755-2418.

For nearly 40 years, Don and Judy Thomson have been importing some of the nation's best young performers for the summer-stock productions at the **Bigfork Summer Playhouse**. The season kicks off in late May with a comedy, the first musical opens in June, and by July four shows rotate nightly (except Sunday), so you can see more than one even if you're only in town for a weekend. The Bigfork Summer Playhouse has a deservedly fine reputation, and tickets go fast; call (406) 837-4886 for information and reservations.

When you're in a toe-tapping, hip-swiveling kind of mood, head for the Bigfork Inn (at the north end of Electric Ave in Bigfork, (406) 837-6680), where a **swing band** entertains on weekends. Sunday afternoons, stop by Electric Avenue Books (490 Electric Ave, (406) 837-6072) to hear octogenarian Nina Russell bang out some **jazz** on the grand piano.

Calendar of Events

In an attempt to shake off the winter blahs, Whitefish holds its **Winter Carnival** on the first full weekend in February. Friday night there's a torchlight parade at The Big Mountain, and on Saturday at noon, the carnival royalty leads a downtown procession. Street games are fun for younger kids, and sidewalk sales make adults happy, but the big deal is the Saturday parade. Call Kris Fuehrer, (406) 862-2597, for information.

Each May, the **Bigfork Whitewater Festival** challenges the region's best kayakers on the Mad Mile, a Class V stretch of the Swan River where it empties into Bigfork Bay. Bigfork Chamber of Commerce, (406) 837-5888.

Mother Nature's best annual Flathead event is the **blossoming of the Flathead cherry trees** every May. Drive the east side of the lake from top to bottom for stunning scenery.

From mid-July through the beginning of August, the **Flathead Festival** schedules a series of concerts ranging from classical to country and jazz to R&B. Concerts take place at indoor and outdoor venues throughout the Flathead Valley. Flathead Music Festival office, (406) 257-0787.

The **Christmas season in Bigfork** might make you forget about all the crass commercialism the holiday seems to generate. In late November (generally the Saturday before Thanksgiving) volunteer elves dress up the town in fresh garlands and lights. At the beginning of December, the town turns out for the procession to light the public tree; afterwards there's caroling and hot chocolate and all the spirit of the season. Take part in sleigh rides, caroling, and Santa's workshop every Saturday evening during December. Bigfork Chamber of Commerce, (406) 837-5888.

Restaurants

Summers, the Hellroaring Saloon on The Big Mountain transforms into the **Hellroaring Cantina,** (800) 858-5439 or (406) 862-6364, and serves very good southwestern cuisine amid great views. Big Mountain's much-ballyhooed **Cafe Kandahar,** (406) 862-6247, a European-style bistro, offers such elaborate—and expensive—fare as shrimp risotto and pork loin au Provence. The food doesn't always live up to expectations, but it's definitely the mountain's most romantic place to eat.

In Whitefish you can get the morning skinny over a generous plate of huevos at the **Buffalo Cafe** (516 Third St, (406) 862-2833) or hobo potatoes at **Swift Creek Cafe** (307 E Second St, (406) 862-8186). Rehash the day's powder over burgers and beer at the **Great Northern Bar** (27 Central Ave, (406) 862-2816). You'll find good sandwiches at **Trail's Head Deli and Coffeehouse** (234 E Second St, (406) 862-9599).

In Kalispell, get a cup of java and fresh baked goods at **The Knead Bakery and Cafe,** (328 W Center St, (406) 756-2326) which shares a building with the Montana Coffee Traders near the Kalispell Center mall.

We're not exactly sure what Bigfork did to deserve such a rich selection of fine dining, but whatever it did, it did right: despite lonely off-seasons, gourmet restaurants continue to flourish here. Summer pretheater crowds keep these places packed; you'll need reservations. For a more leisurely experience, consider coming after 8pm when the crowds have thinned. The town's best breakfasts are at the **Swan River Inn Cafe,** 360 Grand St, (406) 837-2220; diner-type breakfasts with terrific views are at the **North Shore Bowling Alley,** (406) 837-5381, just north of town off Hwy 35 at Holt Drive. In addition to weekend swing dancing, the **Bigfork Inn,** (406) 837-6680, at the north end of Electric Ave features terrific black-and-white beef tournedos. The prettiest restaurant in town, and probably in the entire Flathead Valley, is **Bridge Street Gallery**, at the south end of Electric Ave, (406) 837-5825. Its cherished longtime chef has left, however, and at press time the new chef was just getting settled. Stop by for a glass of wine and admire the stunning artwork and lovely interior, then decide for yourself whether to stay.

For good organic baked goods and light lunches, try the **Sunflower Bakery** on Main St in Polson, (406) 883-2450.

Coyote Riverhouse ☆☆☆ Located in a converted pig sty (honest!), Gary Hastings's unassuming riverside restaurant has become a Western Montana legend, and deservedly so. We've never heard of anyone having a bad meal here. The seven-page menu is an inexplicable mix of Cajun, Italian, Mexican, and Southwestern cooking—it's got everything from chargrilled Mayan pork tenderloin to cioppino to scampi étouffée and blackened aged sirloin, plus nearly a dozen specials in the heart of summer. Coyote Riverhouse covers its ethnic bases with considerable flair. Owner Hastings trained with Paul Prudhomme and has earned his own reputation as a demanding perfectionist, and even though he doesn't cook here anymore—chef T. J. Bladholm is in charge of the Riverhouse kitchen—the quest for perfection is evident in the manicured grounds, the handmade wood tables, the extensive wine list, and, most importantly, the exquisite food. Fish and seafood are flown in fresh every 2 days, and Hastings means it when he says spicy. Portions are superhuman. The New Orleans combo plate, for instance, a mix of Hastings's renowned jambalaya, shrimp étouffée, bayou chicken, and red beans and rice, is served in a cast-iron skillet—and it's full. The key lime pie is the real thing. In summer, the place is always packed; there's a 1 1/2-hour dining limit before you'll be asked to move to an outside table. Reservations are imperative in summer and recommended in spring and fall. At press time, Hastings was talking about closing the Coyote to concentrate on his neighboring B&B; be sure to call ahead. Closed winters. *6 miles east of Bigfork—take US 209 to Ferndale, turn north at the Ferndale Fire Department, then follow signs 1 1/2 miles; 600 Three Eagle Lane, Ferndale; (406) 837-1233; dinner Tues–Sun in summer, Wed–Sun in spring and fall; MC, V; checks OK; $$-$$$.*

Quincy's ☆☆☆   Under the skilled tutelage of chef Douglas Day, Quincy's has become that rarest of culinary finds: a superb hotel restaurant. Start with an appetizer of delicately smoked Flathead Lake whitefish, or handmade ravioli stuffed with roasted duck, walnuts, and Gorgonzola. Don't miss the light and delicate Dungeness crab cakes, sautéed with a pine nut crust—they're a four-star find. The standard menu also includes a renowned Kentucky bourbon steak and a breast of chicken stuffed with foie gras. Fish and seafood items change daily, depending on availability. Desserts range from a killer raspberry swirl cheesecake to homemade French-style ice creams. With its recent remodel, artful presentations, and top-notch service, Quincy's ranks among Montana's best restaurants. Reservations, especially in summer, are a good idea; you can eat in the small dining room or outside on the deck overlooking the marina. The clientele tend to be slightly older and more conservative than average; to fit in, you may want to put on a skirt or tie. *At Marina Cay Resort, on the north end of Bigfork on Grand Ave, one block east of Hwy 35; PO Box 663, Bigfork; (800) 433-6516 or (406) 837-5861; dinner every day May to Sept, Tues–Sat rest of year; DIS, MC, V; checks OK; $$$.*

Showthyme! ☆☆   Bigfork locals are passionate about what's affectionately referred to as Blu Food, after Showthyme! chef/owner Blu Funk (he legally changed his name years ago; don't ask). Blu Food is difficult to define, but it's always innovative and well-seasoned, so good that the staff eats it on days off. Standard menu items run from roasted pork loin in molasses, rye whiskey, and pecan sauce to roasted king salmon served with lemon-caper-dill aioli. Specials include a delicious yellowfin tuna fillet grilled and topped with a slightly spicy wasabi aioli and a very good rack of lamb with a sun-dried cherry and rosemary port demiglace. Stay away from the overly tough surf clam appetizer and instead order salad. Chocoholics shouldn't miss the Chocolate Paradise, a flourless chocolate soufflé. Located in the 1907 bank building next door to the playhouse, Showthyme! is predictably packed during the theater season, so leave plenty of time in order to get to a show. Call 48 hours in advance for an "ABC" meal—a four- or five-course prix-fixe dinner, chef's choice, for $25. There's outdoor dining in summer; indoors, you can sit in the airy, red brick upstairs room, or the more austere, rock-walled downstairs area. The lunch menu offers good value. Extensive wine list. *Downtown Bigfork, next door to the playhouse; 548 Electric Ave, Bigfork; (406) 837-0707; lunch, dinner Mon–Sat in summers, Tues–Sat rest of year (subject to change); AE, DIS, MC, V; checks OK; $$-$$$.*

Whitefish Lake Restaurant ☆☆   Built in the '30s as part of the Work Projects Administration, this conservative log restaurant on the grounds of the public golf course (not to be confused with Grouse Mountain Lodge across the highway) is "the" place to go for a special dinner in Whitefish. Chef Dan Crumbaker has emboldened the menu: You can still get prime rib on Fridays and Saturdays, but there's also a roasted rack of lamb finished with a pinot noir and dried cherry demiglace, and a steak au poivre with a Madeira cream sauce. Fish (including, oddly enough, Atlantic salmon) is flown in fresh. The smoked trout appetizer with blackberry horseradish is superb. In summer months, light lunches are served in the bar and on the outside patio; dress runs the gamut from ties to madras shorts. *On US 93 1 mile north (west) of Whitefish on the north side of the highway; PO Box 1540, Whitefish; (406) 862-5285; lunch every day in summer, dinner Fri–Tues in summer, every day rest of year; AE, MC, V; checks OK; $$.*

Alley Connection ☆   There's almost always a wait at this casual spot inside the old Kalispell Hotel, and once you've eaten here you'll know why. The Lam family, originally from Viet Nam, runs one of Montana's best Chinese restaurants. Superb wonton soup features a bounty of both fresh and deep-fried wontons in a delicately flavored broth garnished with barbecued pork and greens; it may just be the best wonton soup we've ever had. Sichuan entrees are perfectly spiced, with vegetables just this side of crispy and shrimp that's not overcooked (hallelujah!); tender ginger beef is chock-full of flavor. The only sign that you're still in land-locked Montana is that the Alley Connection defines prawns as shrimp that are breaded and deep-fried. There's also a smattering of American entrees, among them a terrific glazed Cornish game hen. The restaurant boasts a decent wine list, including sake; beer and cocktails are available from the hotel bar. Reservations are suggested for dinner; but you'll have to wait it out at lunch (or take out). Alley Connection is closed in November. *Downtown Kalispell in the Kalispell Grand Hotel; 22 1st St W, Kalispell; (406) 752-7077; lunch, dinner Tues–Sat; AE, DIS, MC, V; local checks only; $.*

Loon's Echo Resort ☆   Brochures declare that the Loon's Echo is "conveniently located in the middle of nowhere," and few people would argue. It claims a spectacular setting on a private pond at the base of Stryker Peak. The resort—a bizarre combination of Tudor and western styles with added luxuries such as an indoor lap pool and hot tub (ask nicely and you may be allowed to take an after-dinner soak)—nearly defies description. The menu, too, is an unusual blend of styles, from Cajun to Italian to your basic prime rib. Amazingly, the food works, thanks to the expertise of chef Neil Carloss. Folks brave the 30 miles from Whitefish and the nasty gravel road (call for conditions before you sacrifice your low-clearance vehicle) to sample elk tournedos with huckleberry demiglace or crawfish étouffée. We recently swooned over heavenly pesto ravioli in a basil-oregano cream sauce and a jambalaya fettucini, Carloss's very tasty twist on the old creole classic. Desserts are ample, and include praline bananas Foster and bread pudding in whiskey sauce. If you recognize some of the entrees from the Tupelo Grille in Whitefish (see below), you're not dreaming: the chefs are brothers. *30 miles north of Whitefish on US 93, then 4 miles east on Forest Rd 900 (there'll be a sign to Mount Marston Lookout); 1 Fish Lake Rd, Stryker; (406) 882-4791 or (800) 956-6632; dinner every day in summer (varies off-season); AE, V; checks OK; $$.*

Tupelo Grille ☆   A tupelo is a type of tree prevalent in swampy areas, especially in the South, which is where Tupelo Grille chef/owner Patrick Carloss hails from—and, no, he's not related to Elvis. Since opening in the summer of 1995, the Tupelo Grille has developed an enthusiastic local following; diners come not only for the modestly priced Cajun dinners (try the smooth and rich crawfish étouffée, or the seafood gumbo with snow-crab, halibut, and shrimp), but also for inexpensive lunches. More than once we've heard people swear that "Tupelo's" makes the best Poor Boy sandwiches in the world. Skip the overcheesy artichoke-mozzarella appetizer spread, but definitely save room for the exquisite bread pudding, laced with a whiskey-cinnamon glaze. Tupelo's doesn't serve liquor but it's conveniently located next door to the Great Northern tavern, so you can BYOB and not worry about returning your glass (the waitress will do it for you). *Between 1st and Railway; 17 Central Ave, Whitefish; (406) 862-6136; lunch Mon–Sat, dinner Tues–Sat (subject to change); no credit cards; checks OK; $.*

The Watusi Cafe ☆ Don't be put off by the cutesy menu at this simple storefront cafe; the food is delicious. Everything's homemade here, from corned beef to cranberry chutney and unusual salad dressings. Try the Caribbean chicken and field greens salad, featuring large slices of Jamaican jerk-spiced chicken and orange slices on fresh greens, served with your choice of homemade dressing (we love the garlicky Gorgonzola). Reubens are real; the East of the Sun pasta, an oriental vegetarian dish, is perfectly spiced; and pasta specials are always a good bet. Chef/owner Peg Schaefer learned her trade under chef Blu Funk of Bigfork's Showthyme!, so it's no wonder she knows her stuff. Appealing desserts disappoint. *3 blocks west of US 93; 318 Main, Polson; (406) 883-6200; breakfast, lunch Mon–Sat; no credit cards; local checks only; $.*

Rocco's You'll have to drive 7 miles north of downtown Kalispell on US 2 to get to Rocco's (unless you've been shopping at Costco, across the street), but the homemade pastas (try the raviolis) and tasty sauces are worth the trip. The minestrone soup is quite good. The restaurant's decor is informal, but despite a story printed on the back of the menu, we still don't understand the two model airplanes hanging from the ceiling (and neither did our waiter). No matter—the food's good, the staff is pleasant, and there doesn't have to be a reason for everything. *4 miles north of the Kalispell K-Mart or 1 mile south of the airport across from Costco—look for the blue building; 3796 US 2 E, Kalispell; (406) 756-5834; dinner every day; AE, DIS, MC, V; checks OK; $$-$$$.*

Lodgings

The sizable village at the base of The Big Mountain offers a variety of shops and services as well as condos, lodges, and vacation homes; the all-purpose reservation line is (800) 858-5439 or (406) 862-1960. With eight restaurants, four bars, and a grocery store on-site, The Big Mountain is self-contained. The **Hibernation House** is the mountain's economy hotel; rooms come sans phone or TV; but the full breakfast included in the room rate reportedly is so big you can ski all day and never worry about lunch.

The Garden Wall Inn ☆☆☆ From the turn-down service and Godiva chocolate on the bedstand to plush, monogrammed towels and Crabtree & Evelyn toiletries, the Garden Wall boasts a professionalism and attention to detail we rarely find in this neck of the woods. Innkeeper Rhonda Fitzgerald has decorated all five bedrooms (including a two-room suite) of this 1920s house with period antiques; the lovely decor makes up for the slightly small rooms. In the afternoon, guests congregate around the living room fireplace for sherry and hors d'oeuvres; in the morning, you'll find coffee outside your room on a silver tray. A three-course breakfast follows in the dining room, beginning with fresh-squeezed orange juice and building to a sumptuous gourmet entree like scrambled eggs and shrimp in puff pastry. Innkeeper Fitzgerald coaches the local cross-country ski team and her husband's an avid kayaker, so they possess a wealth of knowledge about recreational opportunities. Although the Garden Wall is located on the main drag entering Whitefish, you won't have to worry about noise: the house is very well insulated. Ski season package deals available. *At the corner of 5th and Spokane (US 93); 504 Spokane Ave, Whitefish, MT 59937; (406) 862-3440; AE, DIS, MC, V; checks OK; $$$.*

Grouse Mountain Lodge ☆☆   Set on the grounds of the 36-hole Whitefish Lake public golf course just west of downtown Whitefish, the modern, 144-room Grouse Mountain Lodge is the Flathead's premiere hotel, with all the amenities: an indoor pool, indoor and outdoor Jacuzzis, beautiful views, and stunning landscaping. Rooms are quite nice, with high-end decor; of Grouse Mountain's standard accommodations the third-floor rooms, which have the nicest furnishings, vaulted ceilings, and better views (of mountains or golf course, your choice) are best. (There are extra large corner rooms and two-story apartmentlike suites as well.) Avoid first-floor "mountain-view" rooms, from which you'll only get an eyeful of the parking lot. The hotel has free loaner racquets for the neighboring public tennis courts and rents bicycles as well; the concierge can arrange outdoor activities ranging from dogsledding to guided fly-fishing. The lodge offers good ski packages for The Big Mountain. Kids 12 and under stay free. Off-season rates drop substantially. *1 mile west of town, 1205 US 93 W, Whitefish, MT 59937; (800) 321-8822 or (406) 862-3000; AE, DIS, MC, V; no checks; $$$.*

Good Medicine Lodge ☆   Designed specifically as a bed and breakfast, this enormous 6,500 square-foot log home comes with western and native American art on the walls, lodgepole furniture in the rooms, and a huge, cathedral-ceilinged common area with fireplace. Owners Susan Moffitt and Christopher Ridder quit the Seattle rat race in the early '90s (she was a manager at the Sheraton; he ran a travel agency) and traded it in for a quieter lifestyle. Now they're busier than ever renting out nine rooms, all with phone and private bath. There's an emphasis on health here, with hearty breakfasts and fresh-squeezed orange juice served buffet-style. The owners also follow a "green" program: they're big on recycling, sheets are unbleached, and guests may choose to reuse their towels. Room 1, with an optional attached sitting room (costs extra) is best; rooms 6 and 7 also have good views and a balcony. In summer, request one of three air-conditioned rooms in the old building, or one of four with ceiling fans in the new building. Skiers appreciate the hot tub on the back porch and the storage area; parents like the fact that kids under 10 share their room free of charge. *On the way to The Big Mountain; 537 Wisconsin Ave, Whitefish, MT 59937; (800) 860-5488 or (406) 862-5488; AE, DIS, MC, V; checks OK; $$-$$$.*

Kandahar Lodge ☆   The upscale choice of Big Mountain lodgings, this comfy 48-room cedar lodge offers spacious rooms (including some with lofts and/or kitchenettes), all with down comforters and televisions. Spend an extra $10 for a charming studio with kitchenette and sleigh bed. Rooms are fine, but the real appeal of the Kandahar Lodge is downstairs, where there's a common area with couches, over-stuffed chairs, and a river-rock fireplace; a tiny, homey bar; and a Jacuzzi, steam room, and sauna. The on-site Cafe Kandahar, a European-style bistro, has great atmosphere if somewhat inconsistent food. *At The Big Mountain, 7 miles north of Whitefish—first hotel on The Big Mountain Rd; PO Box 1659, Whitefish, MT 59937; (800) 862-6094 or (406) 862-6098; AE, DIS, MC, V; checks OK; $$$.*

Abbott Valley Cabins   Montana residents since the '40s, the Foley family recently remodeled some of the original buildings on their 360-acre spread west of Glacier National Park. Located on two different creeks, these homes make convenient, scenic, and private bases from which to explore Glacier. There's nothing fancy here, and no extras save the splendid scenery, but all the homes are clean and comfortable, with kitchen facilities, full baths, and live plants. Managers Marion Foley and Brian Sparks are very hospitable, ready to help at every turn, but these are definitely rentals for low-maintenance guests; don't come expecting daily maid service or designer sheets. One note: the Apikuni Rose Cabin is fine as long as you like kids; it's right next door to the home of Marion and Brian, who have four. Summer rates run from $85 to $150, three-day minimum preferred; off-season rates drop by half. *2 miles south of Martin City, on the Southfork/Hungry Horse Reservoir Rd. Follow the signs to Apikuni Rose; PO Box 98, Martin City, MT 59926; (406) 387-5774 or (406) 387-5330; MC, V; checks OK; $$-$$$.*

Best Western KwaTaqNuk Resort   Owned and operated by the Confederated Salish and Kootenai Tribes, and affiliated with Best Western, KwaTaqNuk proves the old adage of "location, location, location" to be true. At the south end of the lake, where it drains into the Flathead River (KwaTaqNuk is Kootenai for "where the water leaves the lake"), the 112-room resort commands a sweeping view of the lake and the Mission Mountains beyond. The hotel restaurant and lovely bar also offer spectacular views, though we hear the food disappoints. The resort has an indoor pool and hot tub, and an outdoor pool and deck. Spend the extra $10 to $15 and get yourself a lakeside room; the view and private balcony make all the difference. Kids under 12 stay free, though there is a charge for extra beds. Rent boats through Surf-N-Ski at the attached marina; the *Princess* cruise boat leaves from the marina three times daily in summer. *3 blocks south of downtown; 303 US 93 E, Polson, MT 59860; (800) 882-6363 or (406) 883-3636; AE, DIS, MC, V; checks OK; $$$.*

Cavanaugh's at Kalispell Center With 132 rooms, the centrally located Cavanaugh's largely caters to conventions, conferences, and tour groups. Despite a few attempts at intimacy—there's a fireplace and couches in the main lobby, and a sky-lit lobby restaurant—it feels pretty much like any large hotel: clean and comfortable, but nothing to get excited about. Besides the indoor pool and hot tub (also a hot tub outside) and ground floor restaurant and bar, there's the Kalispell Center mall—and you don't even have to step outside to get there! To avoid traffic noise and gain a view of the Whitefish Range, ask for second floor rooms on the north side—but make sure no tour groups have been booked there. Kids under 18 stay free, but there's a charge for extra beds. *Downtown, next door to the Kalispell Center mall; 20 N Main, Kalispell, MT 59901; (800) 843-4667 for reservations or (406) 752-6660; AE, DIS, MC, V; checks OK; $$$.*

Kalispell Grand Hotel Completely remodeled since its days as a run-down Main St hotel, the Kalispell Grand is very pleasant, with a convenient downtown location and nice staff. Rooms are tastefully decorated but small (if you can afford it, ask for the more spacious third floor Jacuzzi suite). Because it's located on Main St, the Kalispell Grand can be noisy; Thursday through Saturday, bands play at the bar next door. Rates include a very basic continental breakfast. Wheelchair-users and elderly persons note: There are no ground floor rooms and no elevators. *On Main and 1st downtown; 100 Main St, PO Box 986, Kalispell, MT 59903; (800) 858-7422 or (406) 755-8100; AE, DIS, MC, V; checks OK; $$$.*

Marina Cay Resort As Bigfork's largest resort complex, with 125 rooms and condos, Marina Cay offers the town's most complete range of accommodations and amenities: it's got an outdoor swimming pool and hot tubs, boat and equipment rentals, one of Montana's best restaurants (Quincy's), and a casino/piano bar and restaurant. And it is conveniently located at the water's edge. Unfortunately, service is not always up to snuff, and some of the rooms are beginning to wear in places. Waterfront rooms are really only marina front with a limited view (unappealing in spring when the water level has dropped), so you may want to opt for less-expensive courtyard mini-suites, which offer two spacious rooms (each with its own television), and are gathered around a courtyard and hot tub. The only accommodations with a full lake view are the one-bedroom condos, from which you can see the lake and the mountains beyond. *On Grand Ave, 1 block east of Hwy 35 at the north end of Bigfork; PO Box 663, Bigfork, MT 59911; (800) 433-6516 or (406) 837-5861; AE, DIS, MC, V; checks OK; $$$.*

Ranches and Resorts

Averill's Flathead Lake Lodge   If you think the place looks familiar, you may be right: *Good Morning America* broadcast from here a few years ago, adding to the Flathead Lake Lodge's already well-established reputation as an upscale ranch resort. Started in 1945 by Les Averill and now run by his son, Doug, Flathead Lake Lodge bills itself as a dude ranch, but it's got one thing most dude ranches don't—a waterfront location on Flathead Lake. Guests can take a trail ride and sailing trip, or witness a roping exhibition and water-ski, all in the same day. They can also play tennis or lounge around the outdoor swimming pool. Weekly rates ($1,582/week) include all horse and water activities, except for rafting trips and extended fishing trips. Gourmet meals are served family-style in the main lodge (kids eat separately). The 2,000-acre ranch can accommodate 120 guests; lodging choices range from rooms in the main lodge (potentially noisy) or in the south lodge (better), to older cabins and newer quad and triplex units. Decor is nice, if a tad spartan, but the grounds are perfectly manicured. With a setting like this, who wants to stay inside? Some 80 percent of Flathead Lake Lodge's are repeat clients; reservations can—and should—be booked a year in advance for the lodge's very short season (mid-June through Labor Day). *1 mile south of Bigfork on Hwy 35; 150 Flathead Lake Lodge Rd, PO Box 248, Bigfork, MT 59911; (406) 837-4391; AE, MC, V; checks OK.*

Backcountry Cabins

The Forest Service lists all available cabins in its *Recreational Cabin and Lookout Directory,* available through the Flathead National Forest Supervisor's Office in Kalispell, (406) 755-5401, or any district office. Rates generally run from $15 to $30 per night.

On benchland half a mile back from the North Fork of the Flathead, with tremendous views of Glacier National Park, the modern, wheelchair-accessible **Schnaus Cabin** is the most popular of the Flathead National

Forest's cabins. With two bedrooms and a sleeping loft, the cabin can hold up to 12 campers. It's wood stove heated, and there's a propane cook stove and kitchen utensils. You have to haul water from a spring 150 feet over the bench. Bring a sleeping bag and food. You can drive to the cabin year-round, but reservations go very quickly. The Forest Service takes reservations up through the end of the calendar year; on the first of November they begin accepting reservations for the following year. Go 42 miles north of Columbia Falls on North Fork Rd. Glacier View/Hungry Horse Ranger District, (406) 387-5243.

You can drive within 1 ½ miles of the historic **Hornet Lookout Cabin,** a cupola-style log cabin that claims great views of Glacier. From the road, you climb a moderately steep trail (kids can do this one) to reach the summit. The lookout is available year-round but the road's not plowed, which adds 5 or so miles to the uphill journey. The lookout has two cots, a wood stove, and some cooking utensils; it's best to bring your own cookware. You also need to bring water. Glacier View/Hungry Horse Ranger District, (406) 387-5243.

One of the newest cabins to join the Forest Service rental program, **Rover Cabin** sits on the river between Polebridge and the entrance to Glacier National Park. This modern frame home has three bedrooms and accommodates eight persons; there's a wood stove and a propane cook stove, lights, and fridge. Utensils are provided; bring a sleeping bag and food. Due to its location near Glacier, this one's very popular. Glacier View/Hungry Horse Ranger District, (406) 387-5243.

Backed up against the Great Bear Wilderness off US 2 along the Middle Fork, **Zip's Place Cabin** has good views into Glacier National Park as well as hiking trails from its back porch. The one-bedroom cabin sleeps eight; it's available June through March with water and indoor plumbing until about October. (After that you'll have to get water from the creek.) When snow comes you'll have to ski or walk the last 2 (fairly level) miles. The cabin has electricity and propane heat. Cooking utensils are provided, but bring your own sleeping bag and food. About 48 miles east of Hungry Horse on US 2, then 2 miles on a county road. Glacier View/Hungry Horse Ranger District, (406) 387-5243.

More Information

The Big Mountain: (800) 858-5439 or (406) 862-2900.
Bigfork Chamber of Commerce: (406) 837-5888.
Columbia Falls Chamber of Commerce: (406) 892-2072.
Flathead Convention and Visitors Association: (800) 543-3105 or (406) 756-9091.

Flathead County Parks: (406) 758-5800.

Flathead National Forest Supervisor's Office: (406) 755-5401.

FNF, Glacier View/Hungry Horse Ranger District: (406) 387-5243.

FNF, Spotted Bear Ranger District: (406) 758-5376 or winter (406) 387-5243.

FNF, Swan Lake Ranger District: (406) 837-5081.

FNF, Tally Lake Ranger District: (406) 862-2508.

Glacier Nordic Center: (406) 862-3000 ext. 418.

Kalispell Chamber of Commerce: (406) 758-2800.

Montana Department of Fish, Wildlife and Parks, Kalispell: (406) 752-5501.

Polson Chamber of Commerce: (406) 883-5969.

Whitefish Chamber of Commerce: (406) 862-3501.

Mission Valley

Including the Flathead Indian Reservation, the Mission Mountains Tribal Wilderness, Ninepipe and Pablo National Wildlife Refuges, and the National Bison Range.

The high, arid Mission Valley, bounded to the east by the towering Mission Mountains and on the north by Flathead Lake, is home to the Flathead Indian Reservation of the Confederated Salish and Kootenai Tribes. Originally, these tribes shared an enormous chunk of territory that straddled parts of present-day western Montana, southern British Columbia, eastern Washington, and northern Idaho. In 1855, the Treaty of Hell's Gate snatched most of those lands, leaving the tribes with a relatively measly 1.3 million acres, much of it not suitable for farming and therefore not desirable for settlers. The St. Ignatius Mission, for which the valley is named, worked to convert the Indians to the Catholic religion and white customs.

Flathead is a misnomer, indeed, though no one seems certain how the name came about. One legend has it that fur traders mistakenly confused the inland Salish people with the coastal Salish, whose infants got flattened foreheads from a unique style of cradleboard. Another version is that the Salish identified themselves in sign language by pressing down upon their heads.

Most people pass through the Mission Valley en route to Glacier National Park or Flathead Lake. Although the reservation doesn't announce itself the way other destinations do (there's no "Welcome to the Flathead Reservation" sign), the tribes have distinguished themselves and their home in several ways. For one thing, gambling is currently not permitted on the reservation. For another there's the 89,500-acre Mission Mountains Tribal Wilderness. Established in 1979, it was the first wilderness in the nation to be so designated by a tribe on its own and is carefully managed; much of the area is closed seasonally to provide grizzly bear habitat. Outdoor recreation is encouraged but carefully regulated with tribal permits, and the tribes put a big emphasis on properly educating users of the outdoors. The reservation is also home to the National Bison Range, so eerily beautiful it will send chills down your spine, and to the Ninepipe National Wildlife Refuge, a wetland haven for birds.

The Kootenai-Salish Tribes own only 51 percent of Flathead reservation land, but they generate income through timber, hydroelectric power, and tourism. The recently built People's Cultural Center in Pablo is aimed not only at teaching non-Indians about Kootenai-Salish culture, with historical exhibits and native-led tours, but also at preserving Indian language and culture for the 6,700 tribal members and their future generations. We encourage you to take the time to stop in the Mission Valley and learn a little about these tribes, instead of steaming through on US Highway 93.

Getting There

US 93 runs north-south through the Flathead Indian Reservation, which is located just north of Missoula. The closest airport is in Missoula. Rimrock Trailways bus line serves Polson at the south end of Flathead Lake.

Adjoining Areas

EAST: **Seeley–Swan and Blackfoot Valleys**

WEST: **Northwest Montana**

NORTH: **Kalispell and the Flathead Valley**

SOUTH: **Missoula and Environs**

inside out

Kayaking/Rafting

Every individual (except those on a guided trip) needs a **tribal recreation permit** to boat the Flathead River below Polson, available from local outdoor stores and the Wildlands Recreation Program of the Confederated Salish and Kootenai Tribes, (406) 675-2700. There are no commercial river maps of the Flathead River, so be sure to scout anything that looks tricky. The river changes depending on flows from Kerr Dam near Polson;

call the Montana Power Company Hydro Hotline, (800) 247-9131, for current water flows. One nice thing about the lower Flathead is that, since the water comes off the top of Flathead Lake, it tends to be warmer than that of surrounding rivers.

You can camp along the river in established **campsites,** but camping is not permitted on any islands—and of course you'll need a camping stamp, too. There's a 15 hp limit on the river and a complete ban on motors between March 15 and June 30. Be sure to read tribal regulations carefully.

The only company allowed to offer commercial rafting trips on tribal waters is Glacier Raft Company, (800) 654-4359 or (406) 883-5838, which runs half-day whitewater trips down the lower Flathead. The **Flathead River below Kerr Dam** is a good whitewater stretch for kayakers and rafters, with Class II and Class III water for the first 4 miles, including the formidable **Buffalo Rapids.** Put in below the powerhouse and take out at Buffalo Bridge for a 7-mile trip, but watch out for the wind, which can make the last 2 miles pretty darn slow. This stretch can be tricky with rapidly changing flows. Spring flows tend to be more stable. Advanced kayakers like to play when the water is flowing at 8,000 CFS; novice boaters prefer flows at 10,000 to 13,000 CFS.

From below Buffalo Rapids to the confluence of the **Clark Fork River,** the Flathead River is all Class I water. A very beautiful, quiet full-day flatwater float through uninhabited grasslands begins at Buffalo Bridge and ends at Sloan's Bridge, due west of Ronan. Again, beware of winds—you could end up paddling much of the way.

Wildlife

There aren't many places left in Montana where the buffalo roam, but the **National Bison Range** at Moiese, 40 miles northwest of Missoula, is one of them. Established in 1908, the 18,500-acre refuge is one of the oldest big game areas in the United States and protects one of the few remaining wild herds of **buffalo**. About 400 bison graze the natural grasslands in this "land of shining mountains." In addition to the bison, there's also the occasional **bighorn sheep, mountain goats, elk, pronghorn antelope, white-tailed deer,** and **mule deer**. There are 50 wildlife species and 200 bird species in all. But it's the views that really make the place memorable: when you see the craggy, snow-covered Mission Mountains rising behind the refuge's grasslands and coniferous forests, you can just about imagine Montana before the need for wildlife refuges had crossed anyone's mind. The 19-mile, 2-hour scenic **Red Sleep Mountain Loop Drive** (open mid-May to October) is well worth the time; the shorter, 5-mile **Prairie Drive** tour will give you the basic idea. Visitors aren't allowed out of their vehicles except near the visitors center, but there are two short walking trails off the Red Sleep loop; in May and June, look for blue grouse doing their mating display on the **Bitterroot Trail.** You can sometimes catch elk bugling in September, and look for newborn bison calves mid-April through May. Trailers and other towed units are not allowed on the loop route.

Every October (usually the first weekend), refuge personnel round up the buffalo to check the health of the animals and cull the herd so it won't overgraze the area. The excess animals are auctioned, and the buyers load up the wild animals. It's an event that's fun to watch; the bison aren't as docile as they look. The visitors center, with its excellent wildlife exhibits, is well-equipped for people with disabilities. It is open year-round, with limited hours in winter. For information about the roundup or visitors center hours contact the Refuge Manager, National Bison Range, 132 Bison Range Road, Moiese, MT 59824; (406) 644-2211. To get there from Missoula, take US 93 north 35 miles to Ravalli. Turn west on Hwy 200 to Dixon, then go north on Hwy 212 for 4 miles to the refuge entrance.

Birding

Just north of the National Bison Range, the Flathead Valley widens. Wetlands form here from the spring runoff of the Mission Mountains to the east. The water—in marshes and reservoirs—and the grassy uplands attract both birds and the people who want to see them. At **Ninepipe** and **Pablo National Wildlife Refuges,** birders will have to be satisfied driving around the perimeter of the refuges or walking a few dikes that jut into the wetlands—but there's still plenty of great bird-watching. The 4,500 acres in the two refuges provide a stopover for spring migration; as soon as the water on the glacial potholes in the area is ice-free, **waterfowl** arrive. Birdlife ranges from the horned grebe to the American bittern, a plethora of ducks, spotted sandpipers, phalaropes, and avocets; in late spring the **songbirds**—warblers, meadowlarks, sparrows, and bluebirds—perch in the shrubs and cattails to belt out territorial songs. Spring migration peaks from late March to early May when as many as 100,000 birds can be observed. Fall migration peaks from early October to November, when bird numbers have reached 200,000. Nesting season for waterfowl is April until July. Birders may also soon be able to see **trumpeter swans** at Pablo; a 1996 project attempted to reintroduce the rare big birds to the site.

Boats or flotation devices are not allowed on either refuge, but there are still good access points for birders. At Ninepipe, about 5 miles south of Ronan, Hwy 212 cuts west through the refuge; watch for an unmarked pullout and a dike that runs about a quarter-mile into the water. There's also a parking lot, interpretive material, and a quarter-mile paved trail to a viewing area just off US 93 north of St. Ignatius.

The access road to Pablo Refuge is from US 93, about 15 miles north of Ninepipe. Three good access points are located along the north and east shorelines from a dike (the area is well-marked).

Those inclined to fish can try their skills at catching yellow perch and largemouth bass at Ninepipe or rainbow trout at Pablo. **Fishing** is from shore except during winters, when ice fishing is allowed. (A state license is required.) Both refuges are closed during migratory waterfowl hunting season. A refuge bird list and specific regulations are available from the Refuge Manager, National Bison Range, Moiese, MT 59824, (406) 644-2211.

Hiking/Backpacking

US 93 offers access to the **Mission Mountains Tribal Wilderness,** though it is generally steeper here than trails accessed from the east side. About 12,000 acres in the southern half of the wilderness are closed seasonally for bear habitat, and much of the rest of the area is purposely kept unmarked and not maintained. You'll need a **tribal recreation use permit** to hike tribal lands; additionally, overnighters or anglers will need a **camping stamp** or **fishing stamp,** available at local outdoor stores. The regulations reflect the tribes' priority to maintain the wilderness as a wild place. In fact, the Mission Mountains Tribal Wilderness has the most stringent regulations of any wilderness in the nation, including a 3-day limit on same-site camping. Be sure to familiarize yourself with the regulations, available wherever permits are sold and also printed on the joint Forest Service/Tribal Mission Mountain Wilderness map. Tribal officials prefer to talk with hikers before they set out; they can help select an appropriate trail. Contact the Fish, Wildlife, Recreation and Conservation Division of the Confederated Salish and Kootenai Tribes, (406) 675-2700, and ask for the Wildlands Recreation Program.

The steep, 2-mile trail to **Mission Falls,** a series of beautiful cascades from the mountains, is the area's most accessible day hike. To get to the trailhead, take Airport Rd just north of St. Ignatius and turn right after 3 miles, then left on Mission Dam Rd, which dead-ends at the trailhead at the east end of Mission Reservoir.

Camping

The Confederated Salish and Kootenai Tribes maintain eight campgrounds at the base of the Mission Mountains Tribal Wilderness, all marked on the joint Forest Service/Tribal Mission Mountain Wilderness map. These are small (one- to seven-site), primitive campgrounds, with fire pits and sometimes picnic tables but no water. The tribes also put out a brochure describing these campgrounds. The **Lower Mission Falls Campground,** for instance, is at the east end of Mission Reservoir at the trailhead for the Mission Falls Trail. You'll need a tribal recreation permit and a **camping stamp,** available at local outdoors stores and through the Wildlands Recreation Program of the Confederated Salish and Kootenai Tribes, (406) 675-2700.

It's not exactly camping, but at **Biking Bunks Hostel** you can sleep in the so-called Earthship, an underground tire- and tin can-insulated dormitory just outside St. Ignatius. The unusual, environmentally friendly accommodations also include indoor bicycle storage, showers, and laundromat. Nonbicyclists are welcome, too: there's space to pitch a tent or park an RV. Just off US 93 north of St. Ignatius, (406) 745-3959.

Fishing

You'll need a tribal recreation permit and a **fishing stamp** to cast into tribal waters. Stop at Ronan Sports & Western, (406) 676-3701, for the latest fishing information, but be sure to read the regulations yourself, available through the Wildlands Recreation Program of the Confederated Salish and Kootenai Tribes, (406) 675-2700.

Fish the lower **Flathead River** year-round for northern pike anywhere from 1 to 15 pounds. Fall is best, with more consistent water flows. There's decent shore access from Buffalo Bridge to Sloan's Bridge between Polson and Ronan.

outside in

Attractions

Take a **Native Ed-Ventures tour** from a tribal member. Half-day and day tours focus on heritage and history, the arts, or natural resources. Special tours to area powwows can be arranged, with a family-stay option. We've heard only good things about this unusual opportunity to learn about the world from an Indian perspective. Contact the People's Cultural Center in Pablo (see below) for more information.

Sqelix'u/Aqlsamknik (People's) Cultural Center, (800) 883-5344 or (406) 883-5344, is on US 93, about 1 mile north of Pablo or 60 miles north of Missoula, and represents the Confederated Salish and Kootenai

Tribes' efforts to preserve their history. The displays of Salish, Kootenai, and Pend d'Oreille artifacts are greatly enhanced by an audio tour (it's free and available at the front desk), which features Native elders telling stories in their own language.

The clean but slightly run-down private soaking pools at **Wild Horse Hot Springs,** (800) 204-1677 or (406) 741-3777, 30 miles west of Flathead Lake off Hwy 28, are lots of fun—as long as you don't expect The Ritz. Five dollars per person will get you an hour in a private room with a spring-fed plunge pool, private steam room/sauna, shower, and toilet. Room 5 has been repaneled with real wood; the owners plan to redo the others, too. Wild Horse has two guest rooms with attached private soaking rooms; they go for $55 and $65 per night.

During daylight hours, you can also visit the natural, **outdoor soaking pools** in the nearby town of Hot Springs. There's no admission, but you take your chances since no one maintains them on a regular basis; the once renowned Camas Bathhouse is now nothing more than a dilapidated shack. Although the springs no longer attract hordes, they remain internationally known among a subset of people who swear the minerals cure everything from cancer to arthritis, and even drink the water from an outdoor pump. The Corn Hole pool farthest from the road used to be devoted solely to mud baths, but so many people scooped out the mud and took it home that you have to reach 5 feet down to find it. At press time, the future of the springs was uncertain—there have been efforts to clean them up or close them down. To get to the pools, drive through Hot Springs and turn right on Spring Street, then go two blocks. You'll see the bowling alley on your left and the springs on your right. About 75 miles northwest of Missoula on Hwy 28. Hot Springs Chamber of Commerce, (406) 741-2662.

Built in 1854, the **St. Ignatius Mission** served as a Jesuit base from which to convert members of the Salish and Kootenai tribes. It's famous for its 58 Bible-based murals and frescoes, but of perhaps greater interest is a small, moving photographic exhibit about the tribes' conversion and removal from their historic homelands in the Bitterroot. The photo exhibit is housed in one of the original log cabins behind the church. About 45 miles north of Missoula off US 93. St. Ignatius Chamber of Commerce, (406) 745-2190.

Calendar of Events

Skip the fireworks (they're prohibited on the dry powwow grounds) and celebrate the Fourth of July in Indian fashion at the **Arlee Fourth of July Celebration.** The celebration has been held for nearly 100 years and includes western Montana's biggest powwow, traditional games, arts and crafts, and food concessions. Confederated Salish and Kootenai Tribal Headquarters, (406) 675-2700.

Restaurants and Lodgings

See Kalispell and the Flathead Valley or Missoula and Environs chapters for nearby restaurants and lodgings. For a cheaper sleep, see Biking Bunks Hostel, listed under Camping, above, or Wild Horse Hot Springs under Attractions, above.

More Information

Confederated Salish and Kootenai Tribes Wildlands Recreation Program: (406) 675-2700.

Hot Springs Chamber of Commerce: (406) 741-2662.

Sqelix'u/Aqlsamknik (People's) Cultural Center: (800) 883-5344 or (406) 883-5344.

St. Ignatius Chamber of Commerce: (406) 745-2190.

US Fish and Wildlife Service, National Bison Range: (406) 644-2211.

Seeley–Swan
and Blackfoot
Valleys

Including Seeley, Holland, and Swan Lakes, the Bob Marshall and Scapegoat Wilderness Areas, and the Mission Mountain Wilderness Area.

The stunning Seeley–Swan Valley actually comprises two drainages bordered to the west by the craggy peaks of the Mission Mountains and to the east by the equally dramatic Swan Range. Driving north on Highway 83, you technically go *up* the Seeley Valley and *down* the Swan Valley, since their waters flow south and north, respectively. (The valley divide lies just north of Summit Lake.) Residents may get a little huffy at the term Seeley–Swan (they like their separate identities), but for practical purposes it makes sense. Seeley Lake (pop: 2,500) is the largest community in the valley, though it's not incorporated—a clear sign of the independent nature of its residents. This is still a very rural area; what passes for towns on the map—Condon, Swan Lake—are in fact little more than a post office, bar, gas station, and restaurant.

Lots of Missoulians weekend at Seeley Lake and the other lakes in the Clearwater chain, while Swan Lake's visitor base comes largely from the Flathead. Recreation is an economic mainstay, along with timber. A Forest Service map of the area reveals a checkerboard pattern of public and private ownership, with much of the latter belonging to Plum Creek Timber Company. Wildlife, including grizzly and black bears, is abundant, and the seemingly omnipresent white-tailed deer makes driving notoriously dangerous here, particularly at dusk. Seeley Lake and the connecting

Clearwater Chain of Lakes also claim one of the largest populations of nesting loons in the western states.

Even with all the clear-cuts, the Seeley–Swan area remains one of the most appealing places in Montana—and it's got tough competition. The lovely Clearwater Chain of Lakes in the Seeley Valley and Holland and Swan Lakes farther north are a legacy left over from the Ice Age. Today they draw fishermen, water sports enthusiasts, and families looking for lakeside camping. The Seeley–Swan also has the unusual distinction of offering access to two separate wilderness complexes—the Bob Marshall and the Mission Mountains Tribal Wilderness Areas.

South of where the Seeley–Swan is hemmed in by two huge mountain ranges lies the Blackfoot River Valley, comprised of wide-open pasture and lush, irrigated crops. The Blackfoot River begins at the Continental Divide east of Lincoln and meanders through scenic canyons and ranch country before it meets up with the Clearwater River. Whether the Blackfoot will remain pristine is questionable: at press time, a debate was raging over a proposal to put one of the world's largest gold mines at the head of the river near Lincoln.

For now, though, it's no surprise that entertainment in the Seeley–Swan and Blackfoot River valleys is pretty much limited to outdoor recreation—the closest movie theater is 50 or more miles away in Missoula—which is to say, it's virtually limitless.

Getting There

Hwy 83 runs through the Seeley and Swan Valleys. Hwy 200 follows the Blackfoot River from Interstate 90 just east of Missoula to Ovando, Lincoln, and beyond the Continental Divide. The closest airport is in Missoula, 50 miles southwest of the town of Seeley Lake.

Adjoining Areas

WEST: **Missoula and Environs; Mission Valley**

NORTH: **Kalispell and the Flathead Valley; Glacier National Park**

SOUTH: **Helena and Environs**

inside out

Hiking/Backpacking

The Seeley–Swan and Blackfoot River valleys boast proximity to some of the wildest terrain left in the Lower 48. From the Seeley and Swan Valleys you can access the Mission Mountains to the west (best for shorter day hikes and overnights) and the Swan Range to the east, which leads into the Bob Marshall Wilderness (suitable for multi-day trips). From the Blackfoot River valley you can access the Scapegoat Wilderness, which makes up the southern portion of the Bob Marshall Wilderness Complex. All together the Bob Marshall, Scapegoat, and Great Bear Wilderness Areas comprise 1.5 million acres, named for Bob Marshall, a famed New Yorker who became an advocate for Montana's wildlands.

This is **grizzly country,** so act appropriately to minimize human-bear encounters. On these wildlands the Forest Service has issued special restrictions for storing food when your camp is unoccupied: you must keep food in a bear-resistant container, hanging from a tree, or guarded. For a small donation, the districts will loan you a container or rope. Ranger districts have copies of these regulations.

A great family hike is the 2-mile trail to 90-foot **Morrell Falls** just north of Seeley Lake. The falls are most spectacular during spring runoff (usually late May and early June), though the road may be soft then. Come armed with bug dope. From the lower falls an unmaintained trail leads straight up to the upper falls; it's worth the short grunt. Turn east on Cottonwood Lakes Road, just north of the town of Seeley Lake, and drive 10 more miles to the trailhead. Seeley Lake Ranger District, (406) 677-2233, can provide more information.

What is commonly referred to as "The Missions" actually is comprised of two adjoining wilderness areas running north and south for 40 miles: the federally administered **Mission Mountains Wilderness** of 73,000 acres and the 92,000-acre **Mission Mountains Tribal Wilderness,** owned and administered by the Confederated Salish and Kootenai tribes. The latter is the only private wilderness in the nation and has many restrictions (for instance, you need a tribal recreation permit to hike here). The tribes maintain 44 miles of trails but, recognizing that the purpose of wilderness is not necessarily simply to serve man, they put special emphasis on trail-less areas. Please see the Mission Valley chapter for more information on the tribes' recreation office and regulations.

The Forest Service also maintains 44 miles of trails on its portion of the Mission wilderness, which is managed by the Swan Lake Ranger District, (406) 837-5081. Many of the trails here dead-end in lake basins. (There are a few trails that cross the 10-mile-wide wilderness, but because of the logistical difficulties of leaving shuttles at one end most people come out the same side they entered.) Two popular day hikes are the trails to **Glacier Lake,** a good 1 1/2-mile family hike up Kraft Creek Rd, and **Cold Lakes,** a tougher 2-mile trail up Cold Creek Rd, with a couple of tricky log creek-crossings. These trails see so much use, however, that the Forest Service has closed them to overnight camping. A popular overnighter, that is also a tough slog, is the 9-mile hike to **Gray Wolf Lake,** off Beaver Creek Rd; you'll need a tribal recreation permit since the trail meanders onto the tribal wilderness.

The **Bob Marshall Wilderness Complex,** or simply known as "The Bob," encompasses 1.5 million acres of wilderness and an additional 1 million acres of surrounding roadless land. It's some of the wildest and most remote terrain left in the Lower 48, and one of the last bastions of the grizzly bear. Its immense distances and long access routes mean The Bob is not well-suited to day hikers, but backpackers love it because they can hike for a week or 10 days without ever doubling back on their tracks. Its size and good grazing opportunities means it's big horse country as well; usage is nearly split between hikers and horses. Dozens of outfitters take clients into The Bob on horseback (see Horseback Riding, below). Hikers may want to avoid The Bob in the fall—not only does snowfall come early to the high country, but it's also popular with hunters.

The entire complex straddles six Forest Service districts in four different national forests. The Spotted Bear Ranger District, Flathead National Forest, (406) 758-5376, handles 60 percent of the wilderness, all west of the Continental Divide; 25 percent, or the entire Eastern Front, is administered by the Rocky Mountain Ranger District, Lewis and Clark National Forest, (406) 466-5341. For information about access from the west side through the Swan Range, contact the Swan Lake Ranger District, Flathead National Forest, (406) 837-5081. For information about access from the north into the Great Bear Wilderness, contact the Glacier View/Hungry Horse Ranger District, (406) 387-5243, or the Spotted Bear Ranger District, (406) 758-5376, both part of the Flathead National Forest. The Lincoln Ranger District, Helena National Forest, (406) 362-4265, and the Seeley Lake Ranger District, Lolo National Forest, (406) 677-2233, handle most access into the Scapegoat Wilderness from the south. Any of these ranger districts and local outdoor stores sell maps; ask for the Bob Marshall, Great Bear, and Scapegoat Wilderness Complex map. Talk to individual rangers for advice geared to your needs, and find more detailed trail information in *The Trail Guide to Bob Marshall Country* by Erik Molvar.

The Bob's most famous feature is the **Chinese Wall,** a 13-mile-long stretch of sheer limestone cliff rising 1,000 feet along the Continental Divide. The Chinese Wall is most easily accessed from the Eastern Front, near Choteau or Augusta. It's only about 16 to 20 miles in from the east side to reach the Chinese Wall but a long drive to the trailhead from the Seeley–Swan or Blackfoot Valleys. The easiest and most popular trail leading there runs along the South Fork of the Sun River, which begins west of Augusta at Benchmark. One caveat: if your idea of wilderness is solitude, skip the Chinese Wall in favor of other less-traveled destinations. In peak season (mid-July through August) you may see as many as 10 other parties in a day along the Sun River route. The Rocky Mountain Ranger District in Choteau keeps itineraries of outfitter trips, so you can schedule yours accordingly. Good alternatives to the Chinese Wall include the **North Wall,** similar in size and shape though not of the same formation as its more famous cousin to the south; the **Bob Marshall Addition** in the northeast corner; or the **Scapegoat Wilderness.**

About half a dozen trails lead from the Seeley–Swan into The Bob. The most popular west-side hiker access (big with horse packers, too) is via the **Holland Lake Connector Trail #415,** which leaves from Holland Lake Lodge and gradually climbs 6 ½ miles to **Upper Holland Lake.** The lake sits in an alpine basin just west of the wilderness boundary. For an overnighter, you can circle back around via Sapphire Lake, in which case you'd never actually enter The Bob, or bear right just past Sapphire Lake and continue into the wilderness over Necklace Pass and the Necklace Lakes.

An easy 3 ½-mile round-trip hike suitable for families leads from the Holland Lake trailhead to **Holland Falls** at the head of the lake. Start at the Holland Lake Connector Trail and follow the trail that hugs the shoreline. Holland Lake trails fall under the jurisdiction of the Swan Lake Ranger District, (406) 837-5081.

One suggestion for an overnight trip in The Bob is the 9-mile hike to **Falls Point Lookout,** which begins at the North Fork Trailhead northeast of Ovando, in the Blackfoot River Valley on the south edge of the wilderness. The trail follows the gradual river grade until the last 2 steep miles, winding up at the 7,561-foot summit with good views into the Scapegoat Wilderness and the Blackfoot. This trail is susceptible to blowdowns; call the Seeley Lake Ranger District, (406) 677-2233, in advance for conditions.

Fishing

The rivers and lakes in the Seeley, Swan, and Blackfoot River valleys are not the blue-ribbon trout streams and giant fisheries that you'll see downstream. But the scenery is quite lovely, and you can pick up some midsized fish here. Lakes are fishable year-round. The folks at High Basin Sports in downtown Seeley Lake, (406) 677-3605, can tell you about fishing in the immediate Seeley Lake area. The Swan Village Market, (406) 886-2303, can keep you up to date on Swan Lake area fishing.

Fishing regulations are available through the Montana Department of Fish, Wildlife and Parks in Missoula, (406) 542-5500, or in Kalispell, (406) 752-5501, and through licensing agents.

Lake Fishing

Historically, the **Clearwater Chain of Lakes** have been known for small (up to 12 inches) kokanee, yellow perch, and largemouth bass, though the populations have diminished significantly within the past decade due to illegally introduced northern pike. The chain of six lakes, which begins with Clearwater Lake and runs along the west side of Hwy 83 south to Salmon Lake, also contains good-sized westslope cutthroat and the only significant numbers of lake-dwelling bull trout in the Upper Clark Fork basin. There are also a few rainbows and brown trout, the latter sometimes as big as 10 to 12 pounds.

Fish for salmon in all but Clearwater and Rainy Lakes with spoons during summer; during fall spawning, you can snag them downstream from Lake Inez to Seeley Lake. The illegally planted northern pike have transformed **Salmon Lake** and **Lake Inez** into a pike fishery, with lower densities of pike in adjoining lakes. You'll find the pike all year—lots of people **ice fish** for them—though fisheries experts say they're rapidly depleting their food supply and probably won't remain so large for long.

You can still fish the other four lakes in the chain—**Clearwater, Rainy, Alva, and Seeley**—for westslope cutthroat trout (up to 2 pounds) and bull trout as large as 20 pounds, though the latter are catch-and-release only. Seeley, Alva, Inez, and Salmon also have limited numbers of rainbow and brown trout, and Seeley and Placid have largemouth bass, though once again the pike are taking a large toll on these populations. While not technically part of the Clearwater chain, **Placid Lake** lies on a tributary of the Clearwater River and also has westslope cutthroat and bull trout, limited numbers of rainbows and browns, and is the only one of these lakes with a significant population of yellow perch.

Seeley Lake, at 1,300 acres, is the biggest of the chain, and the busiest (it draws a lot of water-skiers). The other lakes range from 100 to 650 acres. You can drive to any of them, but you'll have to carry boats 50 yards to put in at Rainy Lake and hike half a mile to reach Clearwater Lake (and an additional half-mile in winter when the road is closed). Most people fish here with boats, especially later in the season when the weeds along the shore take over. Look for the access signs along Hwy 83.

Fish for kokanee salmon and cutthroat trout in **Holland Lake**. Bull trout are there, too, but it's illegal to keep them. This, too, is boat fishing territory.

Swan Lake is the only place in the state where it's still legal to keep bull trout: they grow to 15 pounds here. The lake also has a good population of kokanee salmon in the 12-inch range and yellow perch, northern pike, westslope cutthroat, rainbows, and eastern brook trout.

The state plants retired brood stocks of rainbows in **Van Lake**, about

10 miles south of Swan Lake. Fish this lake as soon as the ice breaks up (through June) and again beginning in October. There's good shore access, but it's better with a boat—even a small float tube will do. Van Lake is located off Hwy 83 on Van Lake Rd; it's poorly maintained, so you should not attempt the drive without a high-clearance vehicle.

Most high mountain lakes of the **Mission Mountains Wilderness, Swan Range,** and **Bob Marshall Wilderness Complex** have fish.

River Fishing

Fish the **Blackfoot River** above Clearwater Junction for rainbow, brown, cutthroat, and bull trout (the last as catch-and-release only). The first 13 miles above the junction are an extension of the 26-mile Blackfoot River Corridor, a cooperative public-private venture; please respect private landowners. Regulations here are restrictive; make sure you read the current version. There are five state-run fishing access points along the river.

Fish the **Clearwater River** for pike and all species of trout during spring runoff or in the fall; the Chain of Lakes ensures that its water really does stay clear when other rivers are muddied. But in summer the warm water draining from the lakes heats up the river and fishing tends to be poor.

The **Swan River** boasts big rainbows (up to 5 pounds) but it's catch-and-release only from Piper Creek Bridge down to Swan Lake.

The Bob is also known for blue-ribbon fishing on the **North Fork of the Sun River,** east of the Continental Divide. West of the Divide, there's good fishing on the Wild and Scenic **South Fork of the Flathead River,** which bisects the wilderness north to south, and on the smaller Wild and Scenic **Middle Fork of the Flathead.** Access the Sun River from the Eastern Front (Rocky Mountain Ranger District); reach the South Fork of the Flathead from the south or west (Lincoln Ranger District, Seeley Lake Ranger District, Swan Lake Ranger District, or Spotted Bear Ranger District); and get to the Middle Fork from the north (Spotted Bear Ranger District). There's better fishing on the South Fork, but the Middle Fork is less crowded. **Outfitters** operate combination pack and fishing or floating trips to the South Fork; you ride or hike in and raft out. The Spotted Bear Ranger District keeps a list of all outfitters who fish the South Fork and the Middle Fork. The Rocky Mountain Ranger District can point you to outfitters who fish the North Fork of the Sun River.

Camping

Travel Montana's *Montana Travel Planner* brochure lists all public and private campgrounds; look under "Glacier Country." It's available through Travel Montana, (800) 847-4868 out-of-state or (406) 444-2654 in-state, and at chambers of commerce and many motels. If you're an RV traveler, be sure to check whether a particular campground can accommodate your vehicle. In addition to the fee areas, the Forest Service often has free "dispersed" campsites with no facilities but fewer crowds. Check with the individual ranger districts; if you're unsure which district to call, phone the forest supervisor's office: south of Summit Lake, phone the Lolo National Forest Supervisor's Office, (406) 329-3814; north of Summit, phone the Flathead National Forest Supervisor's Office, (406) 758-5204. You can also call the Montana Department of Fish, Wildlife and Parks in Missoula, (406) 542-5500.

Both **Salmon Lake State Park** and **Placid Lake State Park** have wheelchair-accessible campsites, the only ones in the area. Placid Lake also has 16 slip docks for boats. Both campgrounds are located in forested areas and are very pretty. Placid Lake has some lakeside campsites, while Salmon's are all on a hill overlooking the lake. Both draw crowds on weekends, but weekdays are considerably slower.

The Forest Service operates three campgrounds on Seeley Lake. The 29-site **Seeley Lake Campground** has flush toilets and a nice swimming beach; **River Point Campground** has 27 sites, a volleyball sand court, and horseshoe pits (bring your own net and horseshoes); and the 50-site **Big Larch Campground** has a nice swimming beach. All are very crowded on weekends. Campsites are set back from the water in stands of Douglas fir, spruce, lodgepole, and some old-growth larch. Quieter is the **Lake Alva Campground**, 10 miles north, with 41 camping units and an adequate swimming beach. Tent campers may want to skip these fee areas altogether and head for the three nonfee campgrounds on the Clearwater Chain: there's one each at Lake Inez, Lake Alva, and Rainy Lake. In general these are quieter, with less RV traffic, though sometimes they turn into major party sites. Please be sure to follow no-trace policies, especially in the more primitive sites. For more information, contact the Seeley Lake Ranger District, (406) 677-2233.

The Swan Lake Ranger District, (406) 837-5081, has several camping options. Stunning views and a nice, sandy swimming beach add to the **Holland Lake Campground.** The 41-site campground often fills up on summer weekends, but you shouldn't have a problem securing a spot during the week.

Just off Hwy 83, across the road from Swan Lake, the **Swan Lake Campground** has been refurbished specifically with RVs in mind—each of the 36 camping sites has a double-wide parking area. The parklike day-use area across the highway has a boat launch, picnic tables, and a nice gravel swimming beach. It's just north of the Swan River National Wildlife Refuge (see Wildlife, below).

There's an informal camping area with room for 8 to 12 parties at **Lindbergh Lake** at the base of the Mission Mountains. Even though there are no views of the peaks, it's still pretty and usually less busy than more developed campsites. There are picnic tables, toilets, and a boat ramp, but you'll have to bring your own water. Off Hwy 83 on Lindbergh Lake Rd; the road dead-ends 5 miles in at the campground.

Canoeing/Kayaking

Rent canoes and pedal boats at **Holland Lake Lodge,** (800) 648-8859 or (406) 754-2282. Pick up river maps at outdoor stores or through the Montana Department of Fish, Wildlife and Parks in Missoula, (406) 542-5500, or in Kalispell, (406) 752-5501. Rent canoes at Seeley Lake Fun Center, (406) 677-2287, in downtown Seeley Lake.

You don't even need a shuttle to canoe the **Clearwater Nature Trail.** The slow-moving Clearwater River meanders 3 ½ miles through prime bird habitat; a 1 ½-mile hiking path leads back to the trailhead. In addition to bald eagles, osprey, great blue herons, and other waterfowl, watch for American redstarts, loons, and the rare wood duck. You can complete the whole circuit within 2 to 3 hours. Lolo National Forest publishes a brochure specifically about the Clearwater Nature Trail; ask at ranger stations. About 4 ½ miles north of the town of Seeley Lake; the trailhead is clearly marked.

There's mainly Class I and Class II water on the **Blackfoot River** above Clearwater Junction near Ovando. The river winds through spectacular canyons and ranching country. Floaters and kayakers can put in at the Russell Gates access point and take out at Clearwater Bridge for an easy half-day 6-mile float or continue on to Roundup, 5 ½ miles farther. Beware the rock garden 2 miles above the Clearwater Bridge. A good flatwater trip starts at River Junction and ends at Russell Gates after a 12-mile float that goes through beautiful Box Canyon. It can seem a lot longer in low water.

Wildlife

You'll find the largest concentration of **common loons** in the western United States nesting on Seeley and Salmon Lakes and Lake Alva in the Clearwater Chain of Lakes. These red-eyed birds are best known for their eerie calls; they have a total of four in their repertoire. During nesting season (May through mid-June), please stay 200 to 300 yards away from any nests. The Lolo National Forest publishes an informative brochure about loons, or contact the Seeley Lake Ranger District, (406) 677-2233.

As many as 171 species of birds and big game such as **black bear,**

moose, and **elk** have been identified in the **Swan River National Wildlife Refuge.** Technically, the refuge is closed from March 1 to July 15, but you can walk the so-called "Bog Road" that intersects Hwy 83 (look for the sign) all year; you can also canoe the Swan River where it borders the 1,568-acre refuge anytime. Look for **tundra swans** and nesting **bald eagles** in the spring, and for **wood ducks** anytime but winter. Put in at the county bridge on Porcupine Rd at the southern end of the lake, then take out at Swan Lake Campground, about 1 ½ miles downriver on the lake's eastern shore. Bird lists are available at the Bog Rd parking lot in summer, or through the US Fish and Wildlife Service, (406) 758-6868 in Kalispell, or the Swan Lake Ranger District in Bigfork, (406) 837-5081.

Directly adjacent to the national refuge to the south, the Nature Conservancy operates the 400-acre **Swan River Oxbow Preserve.** The 1 ½-mile-long Sally Tollefson Memorial Trail winds through the preserve, with interpretive signs along the way. This is prime **grizzly** and **black bear** habitat, though—do not hike here between April and mid-June and never hike alone. In addition to bear, **moose,** and **waterfowl,** the preserve is home to half a dozen rare plant species, including the threatened water howellia. Bring bug dope and expect to get your feet muddy in spring and early summer. Off Hwy 83 on Porcupine Rd; watch for the sign on your right. The Nature Conservancy Crown of the Continent office, (406) 837-0909, is in Bigfork and can provide more information.

Nine miles southeast of Ovando, **Brown's Lake** is home to plenty of **waterfowl:** look in the lake's northeast corner for American coots, grebes, and herons. During spring migration, you'll also see sandhill cranes, loons, white pelicans, and upland sandpipers. You can cross the fence and walk in the 1,000-acre Blackfoot Waterfowl Production Area to the east of Brown's Lake, where small ponds and wetlands provide additional birding habitat. About 7 miles past Ovando turn south on the signed road, then drive 4 miles to the fishing access site. Montana Department of Fish, Wildlife and Parks, Missoula, (406) 542-5500.

During winter, stop at the **Blackfoot–Clearwater Wildlife Management Area** turnout on Hwy 83 (three-tenths of a mile north of Clearwater Junction) to view **elk.** You can also drive through the 50,000-acre area by continuing north to the first road on your right. The 6-mile road will take you past ponds and wetlands that are home to **sandhill cranes, bald eagles,** and other waterfowl, including occasional **snow geese** during migration. The Wildlife Management Area is closed to traffic between December and mid-May. Montana Department of Fish, Wildlife and Parks, Missoula, (406) 542-5500.

Horseback Riding

There are somewhere between 60 and 70 **outfitters** who pack into **The Bob**, with a variety of itineraries. Forest Service rangers keep lists of outfitters who operate within their districts. District rangers can't recommend one outfitter over another, but they can help you narrow your choices based on your needs.

Smoke Elser's Wilderness Outfitters of Missoula leads no-trace horsepack trips into The Bob from the east and south. The 6- to 10-day trips are geared for scenery, fishing, and wildlife, the latter of which is particularly emphasized during two September trips into the **Sun River Game Preserve.** No riding experience necessary; call (406) 549-2820.

We also hear good things about the following outfitters who go into The Bob from the west side: Cheff Guest Ranch in Charlo, (406) 644-2557, which runs trips into the Mission Mountains Wilderness as well; Holland Lake Lodge, (800) 648-8859 or (406) 754-2282, which also offers half-day and day trips; and the Bob Marshall Wilderness Ranch in St. Ignatius, (406) 745-4466.

Mountain Biking

Summers, you can bike the **Seeley Creek Nordic Ski Trails** (see Cross-Country Skiing, below). For the most part these are wide, forested trails, not too steep but sometimes very rough. Maps are available at the trailhead a quarter-mile north of the town of Seeley Lake. Turn east on Cottonwood Lakes Rd and drive 1 mile; the trailhead will be on your left. Seeley Lake Ranger District, (406) 677-2233.

You can also bike up the wide, relatively level trail to **Morrell Falls** nearby (see Hiking/Backpacking, above). Seeley Lake Fun Center, (406) 677-2287, in downtown Seeley Lake rents mountain bikes.

Boating/Water Sports

Motorboats and Jet-skis are prevalent on the larger lakes in the Clearwater Chain of Lakes, especially **Seeley, Holland,** and **Swan Lakes.** Rent pontoon boats, fishing boats, canoes, sit-down Jet-skis, water skis, knee boards, and wet suits at Seeley Lake Fun Center, (406) 677-2287, which offers free shuttle service to Seeley Lake. Kurt's Polaris, at the south end of the lake, rents waverunners and a fishing boat; call (406) 677-2833.

Cross-Country Skiing

The Forest Service maintains the **Seeley Creek Nordic Ski Trails,** about 11 miles of novice- to intermediate-level terrain at the north end of Seeley

Lake. For the most part, this is skiing on wide roads in a heavily forested area. There's a warming shelter across from the trailhead with toilets and barbecue pits. Trails are groomed once a week, and maps are available at the trailhead. To get there, head north of the town of Seeley Lake and turn east on Cottonwood Lakes Rd. After 1 mile, the trailhead will be on your left.

Before **backcountry skiing** in either the Missions or the Swan Range, be sure to check with the Swan Lake Ranger District, (406) 677-2233, about current conditions and avalanche danger.

Snowmobiling

Rent snowmobiles from Kurt's Polaris in Seeley Lake, which also offers snowmobile deliveries; call (406) 677-2833. **Seeley Lake** is the hub of the snowmobile activity, with 300 miles of trails radiating out in every direction. Get trail maps from Kurt's Polaris or the Seeley Lake Ranger District, (406) 677-2233.

outside in

Calendar of Events

Seeley Lake Loon and Fish Festival offers interpretive nature walks, loon viewing tours, and a wildlife art festival Memorial Day weekend. It's hosted by Alpine Artisans. Call Seeley Lake Ranger District, (406) 677-2233, for complete information.

Seeley Lake's annual **Fourth of July Celebration** features an afternoon parade, bed races, dog pulls, a pig roast, and of course, fireworks on the lake. View the fireworks from the parking lot at Lindey's Steak House, or from any of three Forest Service campgrounds. The Seeley Lake Chamber of Commerce, (406) 677-2880, has more information.

The **Swan Lake Huckleberry Festival** is held the second Saturday in August. You'll find huckleberry pie and other baked goods, as well as games and locally made arts and crafts at the Swan Lake Recreation Site on the southeast end of the lake. Contact the Swan Lake Chamber of Commerce at Swan Village Market, (406) 886-2303.

Restaurants

Lindey's Prime Steak House, on Hwy 83 in Seeley Lake, (406) 677-9229, is the place to go for steaks and nothing else; one of Lindey's Specials will feed two easily. The **Hungry Bear Steak House**, (406) 754-2240, a big log cabin on Hwy 83 in Condon, has good steaks and pizzas. The **Swan Bar and Grill**, (406) 886-2170, on the south end of Swan Lake lake, serves terrific broasted chicken; weather permitting, you can dine al fresco.

Seasons Restaurant Tucked inside the main log lodge at the Double Arrow Lodge, this small dining room offers some of the valley's best fare: a blend of steaks, seafood, and chicken dressed up in demiglace and cream sauces. Fish is fine but, predictably, meat entrees are better. It's a cozy, woodsy setting for a meal, though service can be inconsistent. Request one of the window tables. The elaborate Sunday brunch looks better than it tastes. Reservations recommended. *At the Double Arrow Lodge, 2 miles south of Seeley Lake off Hwy 83; PO Box 747, Seeley Lake; (800) 468-0777 or (406) 677-2777; dinner every day in summer (with a Sunday barbecue), dinner Wed–Sat rest of the year; MC, V; checks OK; $$.*

Lodgings

Double Arrow Lodge ☆   Just south of the town of Seeley Lake, the 200-acre Double Arrow Resort maintains a comfortable, old-timey quality, even with its modern indoor pool and spa, outdoor tennis courts, golf course, volleyball nets, and horseshoe pits. Built in 1929 as one of the area's first dude ranches, the main log lodge features the fieldstone fireplace and taxidermy you'd expect. The three main lodge rooms are simply but tastefully decorated, with private baths (though the upstairs loft room is very dark). There are also small cabin apartments (four units per cabin) scattered among the tamaracks; they're self-contained but most don't have kitchens. Some units have a Jacuzzi, too, and four new small cabins are single units only. Rates include use of the facilities (except for the golf course) and, except for Sundays, when there's a lavish-looking brunch, a simple buffet breakfast of cold cereal, juice, fruit, and coffee. In summer, the lodge operates guided horseback riding trips. There's a 3-night minimum on holiday weekends and a 2-night minimum on summer and winter weekends. Friendly staff and an unpretentious feel make the Double Arrow a very pleasant getaway. *2 miles south of Seeley Lake off Hwy 83; PO Box 747, Seeley Lake, MT 59868; (800) 468-0777 or (406) 677-2777; MC, V; checks OK; $$-$$$.*

Holland Lake Lodge ☆   The only thing fancy about the Holland Lake Lodge, besides its French chef, is its location. What a location it is! On the shores of Holland Lake, backed up against the Swan Range with a view of the Mission Mountains, Holland Lake Lodge is actually on Flathead National Forest land. Despite a revolving door of owners and managers, only a few things have changed since the lodge was home to a girls summer camp in the '40s. Management recently redecorated four of the five cabins and the main lodge rooms, adding a reception desk—you don't check in at the bar anymore. And, yeah, prices have gone up a bit, but what hasn't? Lodge rooms share two baths down the hall; they're pleasant but may be noisy if people are playing pool downstairs. Shorefront cabins are a better bet, though reservations for these go very early. Either way, you won't be spending much time in your quarters: it's too beautiful outside. The lodge rents pedal boats and canoes for use on the 3-mile-long lake; and an outfitter based at the lodge leads horseback trips ranging from a couple of hours to overnights in the neighboring Bob Marshall Wilderness. Or you can just sit on the lawn with a beer and soak up the glorious outdoors. Holland Lake Lodge may be closed seasonally, so call ahead. One note: At press time, the lodge was once again up for sale. We can only hope any new owners maintain the integrity of the place. *On Holland Lake, 75 miles north of Missoula, 4 miles off Hwy 83; Hwy Box 2083, Condon, MT 59826; (800) 648-8859 or (406) 754-2282; AE, DIS, MC, V; checks OK; $$ (rooms), $$-$$$ (cabins).*

More Information

Flathead National Forest Supervisor's Office, Kalispell: (406) 758-5204.

FNF, Glacier View/Hungry Horse Ranger District: (406) 387-5243.

FNF, Spotted Bear Ranger District: (406) 758-5376.

FNF, Swan Lake Ranger District: (406) 837-5081.

Helena National Forest, Lincoln Ranger District: (406) 362-4265.

Lewis and Clark National Forest, Rocky Mountain Ranger District: (406) 466-5341.

Lolo National Forest Supervisor's Office, Missoula: (406) 329-3814.

LNF, Seeley Lake Ranger District: (406) 677-2233.

Montana Department of Fish, Wildlife and Parks, Kalispell: (406) 752-5501.

Montana Department of Fish, Wildlife and Parks, Missoula: (406) 542-5500.

Seeley Lake Chamber of Commerce: (406) 677-2880.

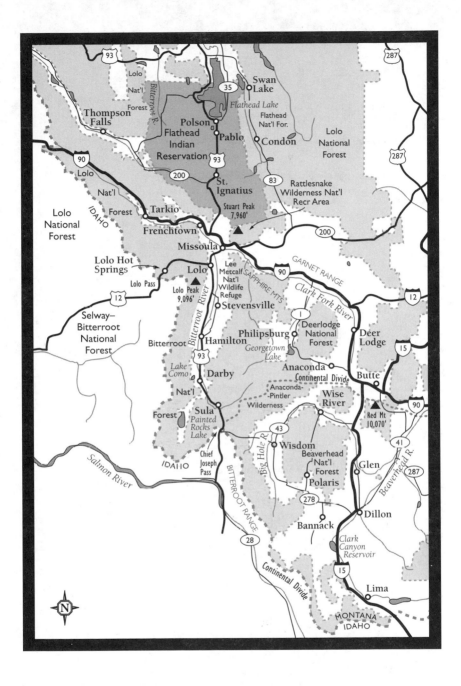

Southwestern Montana

Southwestern Montana

Missoula
and Environs

Including Lolo, the Interstate 90 corridor west to Idaho, the Rattlesnake Wilderness National Recreation Area, and portions of the Lolo National Forest.

The cultural capital of Montana, Missoula (city pop: 45,000; county pop: 87,000) has a longstanding reputation as the state's most progressive city. Located along the banks of the Clark Fork River, at the base of Mount Sentinel and at the hub of five valleys, Missoula is a typical university town, serving as home to the University of Montana and boasting more than its fair share of writers, artists, and Ph.Ds. Even recently retired Mayor Daniel Kemmis has published two books, *Community and the Politics of Place* and *The Good City and the Good Life,* which have made him something of a national media darling when it comes to community issues. Beyond a literate politician, what really makes the city unique, though, is its eclectic population mix: intellectuals, East Coast transplants, and blue-collar workers plus international students and Laotian Hmong, Russian, and Tibetan immigrants all make Missoula their home. Old hippies and young hippie wannabes congregate at Missoula's coffeehouses, and movie buffs get their foreign-film fix at the Crystal Theater. Just down Higgins Avenue at the 24-hour Oxford Pub, old-timers—and anyone else who dares—can order up a plate of cow brains and eggs. And just about everyone takes advantage of the immense outdoor recreation possibilities by fishing the Clark Fork River or hiking and skiing in the nearby mountains.

About 15,000 years ago, the only recreation around here

would have been swimming. During the Ice Age, what is now the Missoula valley was completely submerged beneath Glacial Lake Missoula, which stretched west to Lake Pend Oreille in Idaho. The lake level rose and fell dozens of times during the greatest floods in geological history, etching giant "stairsteps" into Mount Sentinel and Mount Jumbo. These "steps" are still visible today.

Thousands of years later, the Salish Indians named the area Ne-Missoula-Takoo, or "Place of Fear by the Water," because their enemies, the Blackfeet, often ambushed them at the mouth of Hellgate Canyon (just east of the present-day city). The city of Missoula was founded in the 1860s as a regional trading center for nearby timber communities and nicknamed the Garden City—with a moderate elevation of 3,500 feet, produce matured earlier here. Today Missoula's raison d'être is the university, which serves 11,000 students and is the cultural lifeblood of the area. Missoula is also headquarters for the Forest Service's Northern Region and home to numerous environmental groups.

Often compared to Boulder, Colorado, before the BMW invasion, Missoula has managed to remain refreshingly unpretentious in the face of tremendous growth pressure over the past decade. Telecommuters, retirees, and urban refugees are flocking to Missoula, and the results can be seen in the subdivisions surrounding the city, the increasingly high housing costs, and the heavier traffic—not to mention the terrible air quality in winter, courtesy of thermal inversions that lock in pollutants. Still, these problems remain relatively small, and most Missoulians feel their city offers such an unusual balance of cultural and recreational opportunities that they're willing to give up high wages to live here. Where else can you hike in prime black bear and elk habitat by day, then catch a ballet or jazz concert by night? Missoulians know a good thing when they see it. With any luck, they'll figure out how to keep it that way.

Getting There

Missoula is located on I-90 and US Highway 93 south. It's 40 miles west of the Idaho border as the crow flies and 90 miles by the freeway. Missoula is served by Johnson Bell International Airport (though Canadian air traffic has since been canceled), and by Greyhound and Rimrock Trailways bus lines. The city of Lolo is just south of Missoula on US 93 at the junction with US 12.

Adjoining Areas

EAST: **Seeley–Swan and Blackfoot Valleys**
WEST: **Northwest Montana; Lewiston and the Snake River**
NORTH: **Mission Valley**
SOUTH: **Bitterroot Valley**

Hiking/Backpacking

Look in any direction from Missoula and your gaze will be met with mountains, so it goes without saying that hiking is a predominant activity here. The Forest Service Region 1 Headquarters office is in downtown Missoula (behind the post office, 200 E Broadway, (406) 329-3511), and can provide **maps;** so can the Missoula Area Visitor Information Services located in the Lolo National Forest Supervisor's Office at Fort Missoula, (406) 329-3814. This National Forest office also manages most of the areas described below. The Missoula Area Chamber of Commerce (on Front Street between Goldsmith's Ice Cream Parlor and the footbridge, (406) 543-6623) also keeps some information. Ask for the **"Trails Missoula"** brochure, a useful, 23-page newsprint flyer that covers nearly two dozen area trails in detail, including nearly all of those listed here.

David and Amy Harmon's Ecollama company offers **guided wilderness trips** west of Missoula; you hike and the **llamas** pack in your stuff. Day trips and multi-day trips available; specialty trips include women only, children only, and one with an emphasis on fishing. The Harmons have a very good reputation for their eco-friendly, no-trace camping policies; call (406) 542-1625 for details.

Listed below are some of our favorite area hikes; for additional ideas see Backcountry Cabins listed under Lodgings, below.

A quintessential Missoula experience is hiking the **"M" Trail** up Mount Sentinel to the white stone letter emblazoned on the mountain. It's a half-hour of switchbacking, but the view of the Missoula valley is worth it. Alternatively, you can walk up to the "L" on neighboring **Mount Jumbo.** Notice the "stairsteps" etched into the mountains, a result of the ebb and flow of Glacial Lake Missoula, which covered the entire valley during the Ice Age. You'll often see paragliders hovering above Jumbo; there's also a hang glider launch site on the top of Mount Sentinel.

A rails-to-trails project has converted the old Milwaukee Railroad route along the Clark Fork River into a downtown pedestrian walkway and bicycle path. At the university, this 1 ½-mile **Southside Trail** links up to the **Kim Williams Trail,** namesake of the late National Public Radio naturalist and commentator, and continues another 2 ½ miles along the river. This is great bird-watching territory. Sorry, in-line skaters: the trail's not paved.

About 5 miles northeast of downtown is the beloved **Rattlesnake Wilderness National Recreation Area,** 61,000 acres open to hikers, horseback riders, and cross-country skiers. The Rattlesnake is home to frequently sighted black bear, elk, and deer but few or no rattlesnakes. Most people just follow the main trail, an old road, but others veer off the beaten path. A popular but strenuous trail leads 12 miles to **Stuart Peak,** at 7,960 feet one of the highest points in the area. The trail doesn't actually lead to the peak, but you can scale it by traveling cross-country about a mile. Bring plenty of water.

Dog owners beware: there's a strict leash law in effect in the Rattlesnake for the first 1 ⁷/₁₀ miles and a prohibition on dogs throughout the area during winter months and year-round in Sawmill and Curry gulches. Violators are slapped with a $50 fine. One restriction-free option is to take the **Wood's Gulch Trail** east of the main area, a less popular (and more strenuous) trail where liberated dogs are welcome. To get there, drive about 50 yards past the turnoff to the main area and hang a right, then follow the road uphill, bearing right. The trailhead begins where the road makes a U-turn.

The **Blue Mountain Recreation Area** south of the city along the Bitterroot River is another of Missoula's beloved open spaces. Watch out for flying plastic discs: Blue Mountain features Missoula's only **folf** (Frisbee-golf) course. It's also a place for great sledding in the winter and huckleberry picking in summer. There's a wheelchair-accessible interpretive trail at **Maclay Flat,** where you're likely to see bald eagles, osprey, and blue herons. You can also fish there. In fire season (generally July and August), you can tour the fire lookout at the top of Blue Mountain (take Forest Road 365 to Forest Rd 2137 and follow it to the peak). The University of Montana owns the **Blue Mountain Observatory** near the fire lookout; it's open to the public twice a month, June through September, weather permitting; call (406) 243-5283 for more information.

High above the city to the southeast is the **Pattee Canyon Recreation Area,** with several trails. The 3-mile **Crazy Canyon Trail** leads to the top of Mount Sentinel, offering tremendous views of the Missoula valley and the occasional glimpse of a mountain lion.

A tough but spectacular hike is the one to **North Summit** (8,694 feet) or **Lolo Peak** (9,096 feet), both of which loom to Missoula's southwest. To get to the trailhead, take US 12 west from Lolo about 4 miles, then turn left onto Mormon Peak Rd and follow it 8 miles. The trail leads through stands of lodgepole pine and alpine fir, then climbs through alpine larch. From Carlton Lake, about 4 miles in, you'll have to scramble another 1 ½ miles to North Summit, 2 ½ to Lolo Peak. Snow usually covers the trail until mid-July.

Once known as Squaw Tit but changed for obvious reasons, **Squaw**

Peak (7,994 feet), west of Missoula, is easily recognized by its conical breast shape. As mountains go, it's relatively easy to climb, which makes the route to its summit a popular day hike. On a clear day you can see all the way to Glacier National Park from the top. The easiest route, 3 ½ miles long, is the **Reservation Divide Trail.** To get there, take I-90 west of Missoula to the Ninemile exit, then follow the signs to the **Ninemile Remount Station**. From there drive 10 miles up Edith Peak Rd until you reach the trailhead. The trail doesn't lead all the way to the summit, but you can scramble the last bit. Take plenty of water. Find more information in the "Trails Missoula" brochure or the *Reservation Divide Trails* map put out by Lolo National Forest, or call the Ninemile Ranger District at (406) 626-5201.

West along the I-90 corridor toward Idaho, the **State-Line Trail** follows the ridgetop that forms the Idaho-Montana border, offering spectacular views of Montana's Clark Fork River valley on one side and Idaho on the other. At higher elevations, timber is sparse or nonexistent. The trail's relatively open, level course once drew Native Americans, miners, trappers, and forest rangers looking for an easy way to cross this rugged country. Glacial lakes are located in cirques all along the Montana side. Getting to **Heart Lake,** at 60 acres one of the largest in the area, is a relatively easy 8-mile round-trip day hike, as is the even easier trail to **Hoodoo Lake,** a 3-mile round-trip distance. Both are very popular. But there are a myriad of other choices: the trail passes above a different lake every 5 to 9 miles, so backpackers staying out more than one night can progress from one to the next. Because of the open nature of the country, trails are sometimes obscured; bring a topographical map and a compass. The trail isn't usually snow-free until after Fourth of July. Contact the Superior Ranger District, (406) 822-4233, for more information.

Camping

A few private, RV-type campgrounds dot the Missoula area, but there aren't many public campgrounds close to the city. The *Montana Travel Planner,* published by Travel Montana—(800) 847-4868 out-of-state or (406) 444-2654 in-state, and available at chambers of commerce and many motels—lists the state's public and private campgrounds; look under "Glacier Country." RV travelers should be sure to check whether campgrounds can accommodate their vehicles.

Below are some recommended sites; contact the Montana Department of Fish, Wildlife and Parks in Missoula, (406) 542-5500, for more information. State parks do not accept reservations and sites are taken on first-come, first-served basis.

Beavertail Hill State Park, 26 miles east of Missoula off I-90, was named for the historic shape of the hill where it's located, but when they built the freeway they cut away the "tail." Nevertheless, you might see live beaver from these Clark Fork River campsites, as well as great blue herons (there's a rookery about a mile downriver). Though the 26 campsites are only a quarter-mile from I-90, the ponderosa pines and cottonwoods keep noise pollution to a minimum. At Beavertail Hill Pond just up the road, you can fish for warm-water species such as bass and sunfish. The park's proximity to the freeway ensures its popularity; try to arrive early in the day.

There are 18 sites at the state-run **Chief Looking Glass Campground,** just north of Florence and 20 miles southwest of Missoula. Right on the Bitterroot River with good views of the Sapphire Range, it's far enough off the highway that the traffic won't keep you awake at night. But you're not likely to have the place to yourself; it's a popular fishing access.

Another nice riverside getaway is the Blackfoot River Corridor, beginning with **Johnsrud Park,** 20 miles east of Missoula off Hwy 200. Johnsrud is a busy put-in and takeout site for boaters, as well as a campground. There's a little beach here and calm eddies to swim in. But be forewarned: summer weekend nights attract boisterous campers and teenage partygoers, and the sound travels from campsite to campsite. If you're looking for quiet, continue up the rough gravel road to encounter six more designated campsites before you meet up with Hwy 200 again. **Riverbend Campground,** 10 miles upriver from Johnsrud, is a personal favorite. At press time, there was no fee for camping there, but the possibility of fees was being discussed.

Kreis Pond, a 5-acre, man-made reservoir 20 miles west of Missoula, has two primitive campsites on its shores. No drinking water or garbage services are available, and there is a 2-night maximum stay. It's a pleasant place for a dip and a picnic. The pond is stocked with trout and large-mouth bass. To get there, continue north from the Ninemile Remount Station (see Hiking/Backpacking, above) on Remount Rd to Forest Rd 476. Follow this to Forest Rd 456, where you hang a left and then take another left on Forest Rd 2176. Call the Ninemile Ranger District, (406) 626-5201, for information.

About 80 miles northwest of Missoula and 10 miles west of St. Regis, **Cabin City Campground** offers 24 forested, creekside sites, a pleasant and secluded stopover for anyone traveling I-90. Take the Henderson exit off I-90, then follow the signs. Superior Ranger District, (406) 822-4233.

Camping is also allowed in the **Rattlesnake Wilderness National Recreation Area** (see Hiking/Backpacking, above), but not within 3 miles of the trailhead.

Biking

Missoula is not a great road-cycling area, because its roads tend to be busy (getting busier all the time), narrow, and shoulderless. That's not to say people don't ride them—but at the very least wear a helmet. Highway 200 east towards Lincoln has a wide shoulder but a lot of traffic; less busy is the route southeast to Clinton.

Much preferable here is off-road mountain biking; even beginners can find plenty of suitable trails. The best source of information for both off-road and road rides is Missoula-based Adventure Cycling (formerly Bikecentennial), (406) 721-1776, a sort of AAA for cyclists. In addition to being an information clearinghouse, Adventure Cycling organizes the annual **Cycle Montana,** a two-week cross-state ride. The company is also advocating a **Great Divide Mountain Bike Route** that will run the length of the Continental Divide. The Montana portion is already completed; get maps at Adventure Cycling.

Rent bikes from Open Road Bicycles, (406) 549-2453; New Era Bicycles, (406) 728-2080; or Shamrock Sports, (406) 721-5456. May through October, a **women's ride** leaves from Open Road (517 S Orange) every Wednesday at 6pm; riders of all levels are welcome. May through September, Missoulians On Bicycles (MOB) schedules **group rides** Thursdays at 6pm; check *The Missoulian's* About Town section on Thursday for departure point and length. Rides get more difficult as the season progresses. Wild Rockies Tours, (406) 728-0566, offers **guided day trips,** some with van support, to nearby destinations.

The best in-city ride is along the **Southside Trail** near the Clark Fork River, which links up to the **Kim Williams Trail** (see Hiking/Backpacking, above). This is a flat trail, but about a mile beyond the university it gets pretty gravelly. More ambitious bikers can follow the Kim Williams Trail to Deer Creek Rd, a steep gravel route that winds up **Mount Sentinel** to **Pattee Canyon,** then zips down Pattee Canyon Rd and circles downtown and back to the river for a 16-mile loop.

The **Rattlesnake Wilderness National Recreation Area** northeast of town (see Hiking/Backpacking, above) is a wonderful choice for off-road rides. The main trail, a defunct road, follows Rattlesnake Creek 8 miles to **Franklin Bridge**; it's a nice, gradual ascent, and the ride back is a piece of cake—all downhill! There are plenty of offshoot trails as well. Even when the parking lot is full, it's possible to enjoy some solitude in the Rattlesnake. Bicycles are not permitted beyond the wilderness area boundary, 12 miles past the trailhead or 17 miles in on the main trail.

During weekends from the end of June through mid-September, you can mountain bike at **Montana Snowbowl** ski area, (406) 549-9777, where a lift ticket for you and your bike runs $7.50. You'll get great views of the Missoula valley and the Mission Mountains. Helmets are required.

There are 35 miles of marked mountain bike trails originating from **Kreis Pond,** 20 miles west of Missoula near the Ninemile Remount Station (see Hiking/Backpacking, above). The 2 3/10 mile **Yellow Loop** is a good choice for families, while the steep and narrow 14 3/5-mile **Red Trail** can satisfy even the most hard-core mountain biker. Pick up trail maps at the Ninemile Ranger Station, (406) 626-5201.

The **River Trail** follows the south side of the Clark Fork River from St. Regis, some 70 miles northwest of Missoula, to the 14 Mile fishing access. This is an advanced trail; it's 10 challenging miles one way (though you can turn around wherever you like, or leave a shuttle at one end). The highway also follows the river here (it's a National Scenic Byway), but the cars are on the opposite side and not too distracting. For directions and more information, call the Superior Ranger District, (406) 822-4233.

Fishing

Located near the confluence of three rivers—the **Clark Fork, Bitterroot,** and **Blackfoot**—Missoula is blessed with plenty of water. Fishing for brown, cutthroat, and rainbow trout is good throughout the area; some people fish right in town. You may want to stick to catch-and-release in the Clark Fork, though, due to high concentrations of heavy metals from upstream mining operations. In any case, we recommend releasing native cutthroats. Fishing is good before and after spring runoff, which generally spans the month of June.

Many local fishing stores offer **guided fishing tours** and more detailed information. Recommended shops include: Grizzly Hackle, (406) 721-8996 or (800) 297-8996; Miller Barber's Streamside Anglers, (406) 728-1085; and the Missoulian Angler, (406) 728-7766. Based out of Helena, the Orvis-endorsed Paul Roos Outfitters, (800) 858-3497 or (406) 449-2292, has lodges on the Blackfoot River and Rock Creek.

Montana Afloat makes maps of the Clark Fork, Blackfoot, and Rock Creek Rivers, available at any outdoor store. For general fishing and licensing information, contact the Montana Department of Fish, Wildlife and Parks Missoula office, (406) 542-5500.

Fly-fishermen swarm **Rock Creek,** a blue-ribbon trout stream in the Sapphire Mountains 20 miles east, and well-known for its salmonfly hatch in late June and early July. At the beginning of August, just when you're about to throw in your pole, there's an emergence of spruce moths. You can float Rock Creek part of the season (check the current regulations), but you don't need a boat, as there's plenty of shore access. Take the Rock Creek exit off I-90 20 miles southeast of Missoula. The road turns to gravel and follows Rock Creek for 40 miles. Important note: Whirling disease has recently been detected in Rock Creek. At this writing, however, the impact is uncertain. See the Northern Rockies Outdoor Primer at the beginning of this book for information on the disease.

Browns, rainbows, and cutthroats live in the **Clark Fork River.** You can fish right in town near the university, and there is shore access off Mullan Rd west of Missoula, but really it's best to float this one. The flat-water ends at Cyr Bridge near Alberton, 30 miles northwest of Missoula.

Author Norman Maclean's (*A River Runs Through It*) old haunts lie along what is now the 26-mile **Blackfoot Recreation Corridor** above Johnsrud Park and about 20 miles east of Missoula off Hwy 200. Some say the fishing was not there for a while, but the Blackfoot is back! Fish for browns, rainbows, and cutthroats (the latter catch-and-release only). There are more than a dozen state-run access sites along the corridor, some limited to day-use only. Due to a cooperative agreement between Montana Department of Fish, Wildlife and Parks and private landowners, many of these access sites are located on private land; please be respectful.

You can also fish **Rattlesnake Creek** in the Rattlesnake Wilderness National Recreation Area beyond Beeskove Creek (6 miles past the trail-head; see Hiking/Backpacking, above), but you'll have to walk or bike in. This creek is catch-and-release only. In July and August bring a good golden stonefly imitation. Please don't throw fish entrails into Rattlesnake Creek, which is Missoula's alternate water supply.

Kayaking/Rafting

Few people spend much time in the Missoula area without getting on one of its three major waterways—the **Blackfoot, Bitterroot,** and **Clark Fork Rivers.** Spring runoff usually starts in April; by August all but the lower sections of the Bitterroot and Blackfoot are unrunnable, but the levels rise again in mid-September after farmers stop irrigating. Call the Montana Department of Fish, Wildlife and Parks in Missoula, (406) 542-5500, for information and river maps. (Maps are also available at local sporting goods stores.) Contact the United States Geological Survey office in Helena, (406) 441-1319, or The Trail Head outdoor store in Missoula, (406) 543-6966, for current river conditions. Shamrock Sports, (406) 721-5456, rents rafts and inner tubes. The Trail Head rents kayaks and rafts. **Kayak lessons** are available through 10,000 Waves, (406) 549-6670, and Headwaters Canoe and Kayak School, (406) 549-4524.

Beginning kayakers, canoeists, and rafters prefer the Class I and

Class II water of the Bitterroot and Blackfoot Rivers; more experienced boaters head for spectacular **Alberton Gorge,** 30 miles west of Missoula on the Clark Fork River, which features Class III and IV rapids. Panagea Expeditions, Lewis and Clark Trail Adventures, and 10,000 Waves all offer competitively priced raft trips in the area, including one-day excursions down "the Gorge," as it's known locally. We highly recommend 10,000 Waves, which offers sit-on-top kayaks as well as wonderful gourmet lunches. Panagea Expeditions, (406) 721-7719, offers **women-only trips;** Lewis and Clark Trail Adventures, (800) 366-6246 or (406) 728-7609, also runs Idaho's **Lochsa River.**

In Alberton Gorge, rafters put in at Cyr Bridge (there's a launch ramp) and take out at Tarkio (10 miles down); for a longer float continue through the spectacular **Tarkio Canyon** to Forest Grove, another 7 miles downstream (but don't try this section in late summer; you'll end up paddling most of the way). Although this float begins and ends by the freeway, it soon meanders into a remote area where you will feel wonderfully removed from civilization. The reddish rocks glinting in the sun on the side of the Gorge are rarely exposed pre-Cambrian rock, more than 800 million years old.

Wild Rockies Tours, (406) 728-0566, offers day- and multi-day canoe trips on the Bitterroot, Blackfoot, and Clark Fork Rivers. Most floats on the Blackfoot either begin or end in the vicinity of **Johnsrud Park,** 20 miles east of Missoula on Hwy 200. A popular and pleasant day trip runs 10 miles from Johnsrud to the Bonner Weigh Station, calm enough for beginners and tubers. The only bummer about this stretch is that the river never gets away from the highway. Alternatively, you can put in at any of the fishing access sites above Johnsrud north to Clearwater Junction; try Whitaker Bridge to Johnsrud, but beware the Class III rapids at Thibodeau Falls. This stretch gets very low in late summer.

Climbing

The closest spot for climbing is in the **Bitterroot Mountains,** about a 45-minute drive southwest of Missoula (see the Bitterroot Valley chapter). Pipestone Mountaineering, (406) 721-1670, is the best source for climbing information. Or try the folks at the Hold On **indoor climbing gym** (235 W Main, (406) 728-9157).

Swimming

Missoula Parks and Recreation, (406) 721-7275, operates two outdoor swimming pools in summer, with scheduled lap and open swim times. The **McCormick pool** is lovely, 164 feet (50 m) long with a view of the mountains.

Frenchtown Pond, (406) 542-5500, is small enough to warm up during the summer months. It's not very secluded (right off the freeway), but kids love it. At the Frenchtown exit off I-90, 15 miles west of Missoula.

The small swimming hole at Johnsrud Park, 20 miles north of Missoula on the Blackfoot River, is a popular hangout on hot summer days. River currents make this unsuitable for beginners, however.

Cross-Country Skiing

The groomed trails at Lolo Pass, 45 miles southwest of Missoula on the Montana-Idaho border, are among the most popular cross-country ski trails for Missoulians, especially families. They're easily accessible (on US 12), the snow is reliable, and the trails are easy. Buy a parking pass for your car from local outdoor stores or at the pass itself. Call the Powell Ranger District, Clearwater National Forest, (208) 942-3113. Afterwards many skiers stop for a soak at Lolo Hot Springs, (406) 273-2290, down the road. It's pretty basic—just one indoor and one outdoor pool and a forgettable bar and restaurant. The water can be tepid, too, but who are we to argue with tradition?

The ghost town of Garnet east of Missoula is a popular destination for cross-country skiers and snowmobilers, who cherish the 110-mile network of multiple-use trails in the Garnet Range. Skate skiers love the Garnet Range Rd up from Hwy 200. It's a grueling 12-mile workout rewarded with astounding views (you can see five mountain ranges). Plan it right and you can stay overnight: from late November through the end of April you can rent two fully equipped cabins in Garnet (see Backcountry Cabins, below). Call the BLM Garnet Resource Area, (406) 329-3914.

In winter, the bike trails at Kreis Pond near the Ninemile Remount Station convert to cross-country ski trails, but they are not groomed. Access is limited because the roads aren't plowed either. In periods of heavy snow, try the nature trails at the Menard Picnic Area, about a mile up Forest Rd 476 from the Ninemile Ranger Station, (406) 626-5201.

Downhill Skiing

From downtown Missoula, you can see the trails of Montana Snowbowl, (406) 549-9777, 12 miles north of town. With only two chairlifts and a very basic day lodge, Snowbowl isn't fancy. But it has a deserved reputation as one of the most challenging mountains in the west, with plenty of tree skiing. It's also one of the last remaining ski areas of any caliber to price lift tickets under $30. (Note: At press time, Snowbowl was building a new hostel tentatively scheduled to open in 1997. Call to inquire.) Take I-90 west to Reserve St. exit; turn right on Grant Creek Rd and follow signs.

Marshall Mountain, (406) 258-6000, a small area 7 miles northeast of Missoula, caters to beginners and families. Though Marshall is considerably lower than Snowbowl, its snow-making capacity and night-skiing make it viable.

Snowmobiling

There are 250 miles of groomed snowmobile trails in the **Lolo Pass** area, 45 miles west of Missoula. You can begin either at the hot springs (7 miles east of the pass on US 12) or at the pass itself. There are about 110 miles of trails around **Garnet ghost town,** 40 miles northeast of Missoula—a fun overnight destination (see Backcountry Cabins, below). Information and trail maps are available through the Missoula Area Visitor Information Services at the Lolo National Forest Supervisor's Office, (406) 329-3814; for Garnet, call the BLM Garnet Resource Area, (406) 329-3914.

Wildlife

Bighorn sheep often populate the cliffs in the Petty Creek drainage, just south of the Ninemile Valley. Take Exit 77 off I-90 (west), then drive south about 5 miles, keeping your eyes on the cliffs to either side of the road. Ninemile Ranger District, (406) 626-5201.

outside in

Attractions

Thanks in large part to the University of Montana's renowned graduate writing program, Missoula boasts a disproportionately large number of published and soon-to-be published writers. For a taste of the Missoula literary scene, check out the **Second Wind Reading Series,** which showcases two different writers every Sunday night from September through May at the Old Post Pub, (406) 721-7399. Missoula also prides itself on its vast selection of **bookstores,** including Freddy's Feed & Read, (406) 549-2127, a bookstore-cum-deli, and Second Thought, (406) 549-2790, a cozy coffeehouse that offers a good selection of remaindered books, as well as great desserts (try the chocolate-zucchini cake).

Broadway it ain't, but Missoula's **theater** scene is alive and well. Besides the university productions, which range from fair to good, there are two independent companies, Montana Players and the Montana Repertory Theater. Several times a year the Associated Students of the University of Montana (ASUM) also bring in touring shows of high caliber, (406) 243-2451. Missoula is home to the innovative **Missoula Children's Theater (MCT),** (406) 728-1911, which sends out teams of adults to schools and communities all over the nation to produce hour-long musicals starring the kids themselves. MCT's community theater also produces popular musicals for adults.

The **Missoula Museum of the Arts,** (406) 728-0447, tends to high-light regional artists but not always: recently the museum showcased Kenyan artwork and Jacob Lawrence prints. The first Friday evening of every month in Missoula is **GAGA night,** a downtown gallery walk patterned after Seattle's First Thursday.

The **Missoula Symphony,** (406) 721-3194, now in its fifth decade, performs five concerts each year at the stately Wilma Theater; the **String Orchestra of the Rockies,** (406) 243-5371, offers concerts at the university. A real world-class music event comes every third summer, when Missoula hosts the **International Choral Festival,** (406) 251-4226 (see Calendar of Events, below). ASUM manages to book an impressive and eclectic lineup of **concerts,** (406) 243-2451. Tickets are reasonably priced and generally plentiful; big shows are scheduled at the UM Field House but better is the smaller, acoustically superior University Theater.

As for the bar scene, the **Top Hat,** one of Robert Cray's old stomping grounds, snags a fair number of bands passing through on their way to or from bigger cities. The **Iron Horse,** Missoula's closest thing to a brew pub, features local bands in its beer garden on summer Saturday nights. Belly up to the bar at the **Missoula Club,** a.k.a. the MO Club, a tiny hole-in-the-wall on Main, for Missoula's best late-night burgers and handmade shakes.

Smokejumping, a risky technique of fighting wildfires by parachuting into them, was developed in Missoula, and immortalized by Missoula native Norman Maclean in his book *Young Men and Fire.* Summers you can tour the **Smokejumpers Base and Aerial Fire Depot,** still in operation near Missoula, (406) 329-4934. The **Historical Museum at Fort Missoula,** (406) 728-3476, located on the site of a World War II internment camp for Italian seamen and relocated West Coast Japanese, concentrates on more local history.

Just before the turn of the century, the mining town of **Garnet** boasted a population of several thousand. The miners searched not for the worthless garnets found in the area but for gold. Today this **ghost town** 40 miles northeast of Missoula, still claims two dozen old cabins, saloons, and stores, thanks to the Bureau of Land Management and the Garnet

Preservation Association. In summer, you can drive up the Garnet Range Rd from Hwy 200 (look for the signs between mileposts 22 and 23) or get there via the heart-stopping steep and narrow Bear Gulch Rd from I-90 (head east and take the Bearmouth exit, then take the frontage road east 5 1/2 miles to Bear Gulch Rd). A minimal entrance fee will get you a self-guided tour map of the town, and volunteers are on hand seven days a week in summer to answer questions. If you've got the time, venture 1 mile out of "town" to Warren Park, where you'll find a century-old swing set. BLM Garnet Resource Area, (406) 329-3914; guided tours and area hikes available through 10,000 Waves, (406) 549-4524.

Since the 1930s, the **Ninemile Remount Station,** 25 miles west of Missoula, has served as a breeding and training ground for mules and horses used to supply equipment to firefighters. Built largely with the labor of the Civilian Conservation Corps, the Remount Station complex was designed to look like a Kentucky horse farm, which explains the all-white, Cape Cod-style buildings. During summer you can take a self-guided tour of the Remount visitors center. The Ninemile Ranger District still operates out of the complex, which is listed on the National Historic Register. Ninemile, by the way, is not 9 miles from Missoula but 9 miles west of Frenchtown. To get there, take I-90 west of Missoula to the Ninemile exit, then follow the signs. Ninemile Ranger District, (406) 626-5201.

The Farmer's Market practically defines summer in Missoula. Missoulians turn out in droves for the veggies, fruit, herbs, bedding plants, flowers, home-baked goods, and handmade crafts. But to be honest, the real attraction is social: the Farmer's Market is less a shopping excursion than a weekly community celebration. You'll see everyone you know—and if you don't know anyone, you will by the time you leave. It runs mid-May through mid-October at the north end of Higgins Ave on Saturday mornings, and, in the heart of the season, on Tuesday evenings too.

A Carousel For Missoula has become one of downtown Missoula's must-see attractions. Hand-carved by volunteer artisans, it's a real beauty and the first completely hand-carved carousel built since the Depression. The carousel is located in Caras Park and open year-round; call (406) 549-8382. Every Wednesday at noon from June through mid-September, Caras Park also hosts **Out To Lunch,** featuring free entertainment.

Montana claims few professional sports teams; instead, Montanans rally behind the state's university teams. In Missoula, the **University of Montana Grizzlies** inspire fanaticism. The city went nuts in 1995 when the UM football team won the NCAA Division I-AA championship. UM also boasts a better-than-average men's basketball team and a near-great women's basketball team, known as "the Lady Griz," who, more often than not, advance to the NCAA tournament. For schedules and ticket information, call the University of Montana at (406) 243-4051.

Calendar of Events

The Snowbowl Cup Gelande Championship, an alpine-ski jumping event, sends skiers soaring as much as 200 feet over a knoll. Generally held the last weekend in February, the Gelande (pronounced gul-ón-day) draws competitors from all over the United States as well as hundreds of spectators. Call (406) 549-9777 for dates and information.

Each April, Missoula hosts the **International Wildlife Film Festival,** a weeklong juried show of the world's best wildlife films; call (406) 728-9380 for details.

The annual 200-plus mile bicycle **Tour of the Swan River Valley (TOSRV)** originates in Missoula each May. Contact the Missoula Bicycle Club (PO Box 8903, Missoula, MT 59807) for details.

The **International Choral Festival** turns whitebread Missoula into a singing United Nations, with performances by 800 singers representing a dozen different countries. The free, four-day songfest is held every third July; the next festival is scheduled for 1999. Call (406) 251-4226 for more information.

The **Western Montana Fair,** (406) 721-3247, takes place the second week of August at the Missoula fairgrounds; besides the usual carnival rides, pig races, and displays of local culinary and artistic talent, the fair sports a professional rodeo, horse racing, and decent headliner musicians.

For a comprehensive community calendar, tap into the computerized Community Resource Bank through the Missoula Public Library, (406) 543-5418 or (406) 549-1611.

Restaurants

In a city overflowing with fine bakeries, **Bernice's Bakery** (190 S Third W, (406) 728-1358) is a tiny but mighty institution, with pound cake that should be patented and the best croissants this side of the Atlantic. Call ahead to reserve one in your favorite flavor. A popular little bar, the **Missoula Club** (139 W Main, (406) 728-3740), serves up Missoula's best burgers and handmade milkshakes. Get late-night espresso drinks and great pie at **Break Espresso** (432 N Higgins, (406) 728-7300).

The historic **Nine Mile House,** (406) 626-5668, an old stage stop 20 miles west of Missoula, serves a terrific prime rib. Stray to other items at your own risk.

Red Bird ☆☆☆ It didn't take long for Missoula's discriminating diners to discover this quiet downtown hideaway. At press time Red Bird has been open only two months, and, despite the lack of a liquor license—or an advertising campaign—already reservations are advisable not only for weekend dinners but also for weekday lunches as well. Red Bird is owned by the mother-daughter team of Margo Sturgis and Christine Staggs, who serve up an inexpensive, adventurous, yet gracious lunch: tablecloths add a touch of class, and presentation is artful. Meals begin with a small basket of homemade foccacia (bread lovers will be forced to ask for more) served with a delicious smoked eggplant spread. The innovative lunch menu changes daily; sandwiches are served on foccacia and come with roasted potatoes (alsatian cheese or salami, basil, tomatoes, and marinated red onions is one such offering), and the unusual soups are standouts. The lobster and clam chowders, especially, are first-rate, and are served in rotation with a red-based Harbor Stew. We haven't yet had the opportunity to sample the more extensive (and considerably pricier) à la carte dinner menu, which sounds just as intriguing: a salad of grilled radicchio rolled around herbed goat cheese, or pennini pasta with grilled chicken breast and artichoke hearts in a lemon cream sauce. For dessert, don't miss the terrific homemade tiramisu—heaven on a plate. Don't bother to search for the namesake red bird in the nature mural on the restaurant's back wall; unable to agree on what type of bird it should be, the principals left it up to their customers' imaginations. *In the back of the Florence Hotel—entrance is in the alley a half-block north of Front St, between Higgins and Ryman; 120 W Front St, Missoula; (406) 549-2906; lunch, dinner Mon–Fri, dinner only Sat; MC, V; checks OK; $ (lunch); $$-$$$ (dinner).*

Hob Nob ☆☆ You wouldn't expect to find a hip little restaurant tucked in the back of the Union Club bar behind pool tables and men in plaid workshirts, but that's where Marianne Forrest serves up some of Missoula's best meals. Everything's good here: you can stick with a basic burger and fries, try a tender grilled salmon sandwich, or sample something new: a super-spicy quesadilla with chipotle cream sauce or a meatless Planet Burger with chutney, so good carnivores swear by it. Regular favorites include Forrest's signature sweet-potato fries and rich, garlicky roasted tomato soup. Desserts often include a terrific chocolate cake. More elaborate dinner entrees change nightly. It's best to order before 7:30pm; specials disappear quickly. There's live jazz on Thursdays and Sundays, and the house R&B band plays Fridays from 9pm on. Be prepared to wait for a table; the Hob Nob doesn't take reservations. *In the Union Club, 1 1/2 blocks east of Higgins; 208 E Main, Missoula; (406) 542-3188; lunch Mon–Fri, dinner every day (Mon–Sat in summer); no credit cards; checks OK; $-$$.*

Perugia ☆☆ After a long hiatus from the restaurant business, the talented and much-missed Ray Risho opened Perugia as a showcase for what he calls Old World Cooking, referring to his cuisine's Middle Eastern and European roots. The highly unusual menu covers a wide range of territory, from the Greek *psari se ambelofilla* (salmon wrapped in grape leaves) to Risho's renowned wiener schnitzel to traditional Moroccan chicken or lamb tagines, broiled and served inside an earthenware bowl. Some dishes work better than others—the melanzane appetizer is bland and Risho tends to go heavy on the olive oil—but when things work they really work. The cannelloni alla Piedmontese is terrific. And we like the fact that there's not one demiglace on the menu. Ray and his wife, Susie, an artist, have done much to spruce up the somewhat funky, dark interior: painted fabric adorns the back of the booths, and Susie's stunning pottery is on display in the front gallery. *At Broadway and Hawthorne, 1 block west of Scott St; 1106 W Broadway, Missoula; (406) 543-3757; dinner Tues–Thurs; AE, MC, V; checks OK; $$$.*

The Buck Snort ☆ Owners Gary and Kathi Stone have transformed this former workingman's cafe on Hwy 93 into one of the area's gourmet restaurants. We especially like the seafood and chicken dishes. Try the Scallops Tuaca, an innovative preparation teaming scallops, sun-dried tomatoes, and liqueur in a cream sauce. As far as we know The Buck Snort serves the only paella in Missoula. The menu's heavy on sauces, but there's a smattering of Cajun dishes as well. If the management would pay a bit more attention to bread and salads, and get rid of the electronic gambling machines in the bar, they'd have a real class act. *14 miles north of Missoula; 16995 Hwy 93 N, Evaro; (406) 726-4190; dinner Tues–Sun, brunch Sat–Sun; AE, MC, V; checks OK; $$.*

Guy's Lolo Creek Steakhouse ☆ Guy boasts about serving steaks western-style, which as far as we can figure means big and good. Most nights he'll greet you at the door of this homey, cathedral-ceilinged log building on the edge of the Bitterroot Mountains. Once seated, you can watch your steak sizzle on the open-pit grill, or admire the many examples of taxidermy hanging on the walls. Dinners come with the standard baked potato and iceberg lettuce salad. You can get chicken and seafood here, too, but no one does. Guy's is about steak, and he does it near to perfection. Be prepared to take home leftovers. *10 miles southwest of Missoula at the intersection of Hwy 93 and Hwy 12; 6600 Hwy 12 W, Lolo; (406) 273-2622; dinner Tues–Sun; AE, DIS, MC, V; checks OK; $$.*

Black Dog Cafe Located across from the county courthouse, Missoula's only completely vegetarian restaurant draws a mixed crowd of veggies and nonveggies with unusual homemade soups, healthy sandwiches, and fresh, organic salads. There's always a bean of the day, often served with an innovative salsa. A spicy Sichuan stir-fry with tofu (available dinner only) serves as a fine antidote for anyone craving good Chinese food. Garlic lovers shouldn't miss the skordalia appetizer, a no-holds-barred combination of potatoes and garlic and garlic and garlic. Just make sure your dining companion indulges, too. Save room for dessert, especially the mocha mousse. *At the corner of Broadway and Ryman; 138 W Broadway, Missoula; (406) 542-1138; lunch, dinner Mon–Fri, dinner only Sat; no credit cards; local checks only; $.*

The Bridge Formerly a hushed gourmet restaurant known as The Lily, this intimate bistro upstairs from the Crystal Theatre has quickly become one of Missoula's favorite eateries and now exudes a certain urban energy. It's also one of Missoula's only late-night restaurants, remaining open weekends until 11pm. Gourmet California-style pizza, topped with inventive combinations (spinach/ricotta/sun-dried tomato; roasted pork with homemade apple chutney) is available whole or by the slice; caesar salads are also very good. More elaborate and rich Italian-style entrees (chicken piccata, vegetarian lasagna filled with duxelle and vegetables, fettucine with smoked salmon, mushrooms, and Gorgonzola) range from adequate to excellent. Expect to wait for a table. *Above the Crystal Theatre, between 3rd and 4th; 515 S Higgins Ave, Missoula; (406) 542-0002; dinner every day; AE, DIS, MC, V; local checks only; $-$$.*

The Depot Every decent-sized city has a reliable steakhouse; the Depot is Missoula's. The decor is conservative, the steaks and prime rib are good, and the service is accommodating. In summer, the back deck is an informal setting for cocktails and appetizers; when the temperature drops, we like a glass of sherry on the couch by the fireplace. Don't bother with chicken— it's a steakhouse. Trust us. *2 blocks west of Higgins; 201 W Railroad Ave, Missoula; (406) 728-7007; dinner every day; AE, DIS, MC, V; checks OK; $$.*

Food For Thought A popular hangout for UM students and staff (conveniently located across from campus), Food For Thought is our favorite choice for inexpensive, good food and friendly, on-the-ball service. The sandwiches are enormous, the soups tasty, the baked goods homemade, and, yes, there's good coffee and espresso. But it's the ample breakfasts we adore: thick cinnamon-raisin french toast, enormous breakfast burritos. We're addicted to the veggie taters, FFT's version of homefries with vegetables and melted cheese. With a side of salsa, it's breakfast heaven. In good weather, the outdoor patio adds to FFT's appeal. *On the corner of Arthur and University, across from UM; 540 Daly, Missoula; (406) 721-6033; breakfast, lunch, dinner every day; no credit cards; local checks only; $.*

Zimorino's Red Pies Over Montana In the late 1970s, the Zimorino brothers were the first to bring real pizza to Missoula's crust-deprived population. Success was immediate and, despite competition, lasting. Zim's, as it's known locally, has since branched out to include pasta and Italian entrees such as chicken or veal piccata and lasagna. But it's the pizza—with a thick chewy crust and fresh toppings—that keeps us coming back. Our favorite is the Jalapeño Holiday, a spicy combo not for the faint of heart. *Downtown, just south of Spruce; 424 N Higgins Ave, Missoula; (406) 549-7434; dinner every day; MC, V; checks OK; $-$$.*

Lodgings

Goldsmith's Bed and Breakfast Inn ☆   Home for a brief time to the University of Montana's second president, this 1911 brick mansion was scheduled to be razed when restauranteur Dick Goldsmith bought it for a dollar. He subsequently cut it in half and had it moved across the Clark Fork River, where it sits today with a full shot of the university and the Bitterroot Mountains to the west. Rooms 4 and 7 upstairs have river views; best is the honeymoon suite, with its own riverfront porch and 75-gallon Japanese soaking tub. Rates include complimentary espresso drinks, juice, and tea from Goldsmith's Restaurant and Ice Cream Parlor next door. That's also where you'll eat breakfast, a particularly appealing arrangement for those who eschew obligatory B&B socializing. Guests order off the menu; try the unusual pancakes made with ice cream batter. *Half a block west of the Eastgate Shopping Center; 809 E Front, Missoula, MT 59802; (406) 721-6732; AE, MC, V; checks OK; $$$.*

Greenough Bed and Breakfast ☆   Built to house the college-age children of Thomas Greenough, a wealthy Missoula businessman, and later owned by one of Missoula's founding families, this Victorian home is exactly what you hope for in a B&B: elegant and spacious, with high ceilings, hardwood floors, an inviting fireplace, and period antiques. Owners Jerome and Elaine Gregory serve a full breakfast in the formal dining room. Of the three rooms available, the Master Bedroom is the nicest, with a clawfoot tub; the Green Room is located in the front of the house and may get too much street noise. You'll have to hurry to catch the Gregorys, though: Montana natives, they're a little unnerved by Missoula's newfound popularity, and are talking about heading for remote eastern Montana. *Just south of 6th St; 631 Stephens Ave, Missoula, MT 59801; (406) 728-3626; MC, V; checks OK; $$.*

The Albert Hotel   In 1911, the year after the Great Burn decimated the logging town of DeBorgia, the Albert family built this little six-room hotel to house railroad workers and others who passed by on the old Mullan Trail. There's not much left of DeBorgia, but the Albert has been restored to a pleasant B&B; at night, floodlights show off its false front and you feel like you're in an old Hollywood Western. Inside, owner Pam Motta keeps up four small bedrooms, all with shared bath. There's no hot tub but the claw-footed bath tub serves the same purpose (bubble bath provided). Motta cheerfully welcomes guests and their small, well-behaved dogs; she's also equipped with information about nearby outdoor recreation. Ask about seeing one of DeBorgia native Don Cooper's hilarious travel videos; this logger-turned-videographer has earned quite a national following—sometimes tour buses actually stop at his house. Breakfasts are hearty. *At Exit 18 off I-90, 18 miles east of Lookout Pass, 88 miles west of Missoula; 2 Yellowstone Trail, PO Box 300186, DeBorgia, MT 59830; (800) 678-4303 or (406) 678-4303; AE, MC, V; local checks only; $-$$.*

The Schoolhouse and Teacherage Bed and Breakfast Owners Les and Hanneke Ippisch live in the old schoolhouse; guests stay in four small rooms (all with shared baths) in the former teacherage. The rural setting is lovely, the grounds charming, and the hosts fascinating company (*Sky,* Hanneke's autobiography, details her experiences in the Dutch Resistance). The Schoolhouse is a peaceful getaway for out-of-towners as well as Missoulians except during Christmas and Easter, when the Ippisches, master wood-carvers, sell their wares. Their seasonal markets have become a real Missoula tradition: thousands of people pass through the wrought-iron gates, some waiting up to 1 ½ hours to gain entrance. A less frenetic (though also less festive) shopping method is to visit the B&B's store on summer weekends or by appointment. Discounts are available for children and senior citizens. *27 miles west of Missoula, take the Ninemile Rd exit off I-90 and follow signs to the Remount Station—the B&B is on your left, 1 mile shy of the station; Ninemile, Huson, MT 59846; (406) 626-5879; no credit cards; checks OK; $.*

Village Red Lion Missoula's nicest hotel also has one of the best locations—along the Clark Fork River across from the University of Montana. Of 172 rooms, those in the newly remodeled River Wing are the most pleasant (and quietest); river view rooms there are worth the extra $10. Ask for third-floor rooms to ensure quiet. Amenities include a small outdoor pool (open seasonally) and hot tub (open year-round). *On the north side of the Clark Fork River at the corner of Front and Madison; 101 Madison, Missoula, MT 59802; (800) 541-1111 or (406) 728-3100; AE, DIS, MC, V; checks OK; $$$.*

Backcountry Cabins

For a complete listing of Forest Service cabins and lookouts available in Montana, ask for the *Northern Region Recreational Cabin and Lookout Directory* from the Lolo National Forest Supervisor's Office, (406) 329-

3814, or any ranger district.

The **West Fork Butte Lookout Cabin,** 35 miles southwest of Missoula in the Lolo National Forest, is available October through May. In summer you can drive there; in winter you have to ski or snowmobile up the 7 ½-mile road (with a 2,300-foot elevation gain) It's an all-day ski; don't believe anyone who tells you otherwise. The cabin sleeps four and has cooking utensils and a wood stove; you need to bring a sleeping bag and food. Don't expect privacy; this area's no secret to snowmobilers. Reservations are booked well in advance. Lolo National Forest Supervisor's Office, (406) 329-3814.

The **Hogback Homestead Cabin** up Rock Creek is top of the line as far as Forest Service accommodations go. This newly restored, two-story, three-bedroom house 29 miles up Rock Creek Road even has a wheelchair-accessible toilet. Hogback sleeps a maximum of eight. It's available for rent year-round, but the road is not maintained in winter. Bring sleeping gear and food. Book reservations well in advance. Lolo National Forest Supervisor's Office, Missoula, (406) 329-3814.

From the end of November through April, there are two cabins available for rent at **Garnet** ghost town. The Dahl cabin is two rooms and sleeps 8–10; the smaller Willis cabin sleeps four. You'll need a sleeping bag and food. No pets. Prices are slightly higher than Forest Service cabins. Garnet Preservation Association, (406) 329-1031.

More Information

Adventure Cycling: (406) 721-1776.

Glacier Country (a regional arm of Travel Montana): (800) 338-5072 or (406) 756-7128.

Lolo National Forest Supervisor's Office, Missoula (also Missoula Area Visitor Information Services): (406) 626-5201.

LNF, Ninemile Ranger District: (406) 626-5201.

LNF, Plains Ranger District: (406) 826-3821.

LNF, Superior Ranger District: (406) 822-4233.

Missoula Convention & Visitors Bureau (an arm of the Missoula Chamber of Commerce): (800) 526-3465 out-of-state or (406) 543-6623 in-state.

Missoula Regional Avalanche Advisory (mid-December to mid-March): (800) 281-1030 or (406) 549-4488.

Montana Department of Fish, Wildlife and Parks, Missoula region: (406) 542-5500.

Travel Montana: (800) 847-4868 out-of-state or (406) 444-2654 in-state.

USDA Forest Service, Region 1 Headquarters: (406) 329-3511.

Bitterroot Valley

Including Stevensville, Hamilton, Darby, the Bitterroot River, the Lee Metcalf National Wildlife Refuge, and the Bitterroot National Forest.

Bordered by the craggy peaks and steep canyons of the Bitterroot Mountains to the west and the lower-lying Sapphire Mountains to the east, the fertile Bitterroot Valley stretches for 60 miles, paralleling the Montana-Idaho border as the Bitterroot River wends its way north. Historically, cattle ranching, farming, and logging have been the Bitterroot's economic mainstays, with the small settlements of Stevensville, Hamilton, and Darby serving as centers of commerce or as watering holes—the two often synonymous.

Its spectacular scenery, moderate climate (it's Montana's "banana belt," though the term is relative), and abundant recreational opportunities have made the Bitterroot a favorite getaway for those in the know. But the Bitterroot is no secret anymore: retirees, telecommuters, and trust-funders have flooded into the area, with a resulting population increase of more than 25 percent between 1990 and 1995. The Bitterroot also is home to vocal members of extreme right-wing groups, drawn by the solitude this wide valley once promised.

In 1841, Catholic missionaries arrived in what later became Stevensville and opened the first church in Montana, at the behest of the Salish Indians who lived there. But the US government soon forced the Indians to move to a reservation farther north, in what is now the Flathead Valley. In 1866, John Owen, a licensed sutler who came west with the US Mounted Riflemen, converted the original St. Mary's Mission into a trading post; today a few of the original buildings have been preserved at Fort Owen State Park, outside Stevensville.

Hamilton (city pop: 3,410, county pop: 32,230) is the largest town in Ravalli County and serves as the county seat. It also claims an unusual history: like Athena, who sprang from the head of Zeus, Hamilton was born fully formed, or nearly so, thanks to the imagination and money of Butte "Copper King" Marcus Daly. After buying up lumber mills and 22,000 acres in the valley, Daly imported two planners to layout a commercial center. Today Hamilton serves as hipster central for the Bitterroot, with a fine bookstore, a decent local theater company, and a reading series to boot.

The northern end of the Bitterroot—including the towns of Florence and Stevensville—is becoming a bedroom community for Missoula. Darby, at the south end, struggles to maintain an equilibrium between timber and the tourist industry. You'll see the valley's growth evidenced in suburban-type subdivisions, in "For Sale" signs lining the roadsides, and in heavy traffic on US Highway 93 ("I drive 93; pray for me," read popular bumper stickers). Even with all these changes, many Bitterrooters vigorously oppose development efforts, fearful of any laws that might affect their individual rights.

Still, the pull of the Bitterroot is hard to resist. Hundreds of miles of trails offer tremendous hiking up steep-walled canyons and onto the peaks of the Bitterroot National Forest and the Selway–Bitterroot Wilderness. The Bitterroot River lures fishermen and rafters looking for a gentle ride and a big catch. And from its wetlands to its peaks, the Bitterroot is prime wildlife-watching territory: moose, deer, elk, black bear, and, if a current proposal to reestablish them is approved, grizzlies all make their home in the Bitterroots. With two wildlife refuges bordering the river, the Bitterroot also offers great bird-watching opportunities.

Understandably, the influx of newcomers and tourist traffic is making Bitterroot residents a little, well, *bitter,* or at least edgy. Tread lightly in the Bitterroot. You won't be sorry you came; make sure the folks who call it home aren't either.

Getting There

US 93 runs north-south through the Bitterroot Valley, from Missoula to Lost Trail Pass on the Montana-Idaho border. The closest airport is in Missoula.

Adjoining Areas

NORTH: **Missoula and Environs**

EAST: **Butte and Environs; Beaverhead and Big Hole Valleys**

WEST: **Lewiston and the Snake River**

inside out

Hiking/Backpacking

Ahhh . . . the Bitterroots. They get steeper and more spectacular as you travel south, but even the more innocent-looking drainages on the north end aren't too shabby. Everyone's got their favorite access point: Bass, Blodgett, Kootenai, and Sweeney Creeks are all popular. Early in the season, head for any of the canyons. These are particularly appealing for beginner hikers, since grades are low. After mid-July, you can bag a number of peaks. Bitterroot rangers have become very concerned about high usage, particularly up the more popular canyons, so please employ no-trace policies. You will want a Bitterroot National Forest or Selway–Bitterroot Wilderness map (the latter is nice because it also provides topographic information). For maps, advice, and conditions, call the **Bitterroot National Forest Supervisor's Office** in Hamilton, (406) 363-7117, or any of the district offices listed at the end of this chapter. For more hikes in the Bitterroots, consult *Hiking the Bitterroots* by Mort Arkava, available at area bookstores, and see Backcountry Cabins (under Lodgings, below) for an additional suggestion.

Blodgett Canyon is the quintessential Bitterroot hike: the trail follows Blodgett Creek up a jagged, steep-sided canyon, with spectacular views west into the Selway–Bitterroot Wilderness. Because of its relatively low elevation (the trail begins at 4,300 feet), the trail is passable early in the season and stays that way through late fall. The trail continues 20 miles before it peters out; most people just stop whenever they're tired. There are five campsites at the trailhead and others scattered along the trail. Unfortunately, Blodgett has received so much traffic in the past five years that rangers have talked about limiting access. So far that's just talk; act responsibly to keep it that way. It's about 5 miles northwest of Hamilton; follow the signs with the hiker symbol until the road divides, approximately 3 miles out of town. The left fork goes to Canyon Creek (see below); keep straight for Blodgett Canyon.

The 1 ½-mile **Blodgett Canyon Overlook Trail** begins at the Canyon Creek trailhead west of Hamilton, then climbs up the north ridge to a viewpoint over Blodgett Canyon. This is a good beginner's hike—lots of bang for the buck, with great views of the Bitterroot Valley and up the canyon. Begin at the Canyon Creek trailhead, then almost immediately veer off on the path to the right as it switchbacks up the ridge. The start point is about 7 miles west of Hamilton; follow the directions above to Blodgett Canyon, but at the fork turn left to Canyon Creek. It's one drainage south of Blodgett.

Kootenai Canyon is one of the most popular hikes in the Bitterroots, and with good reason: it has easy access and offers a fairly level path into a lush, steep-walled canyon. You'll see lots of day hikers and climbers in Kootenai, but if you continue up the trail 3 or 4 miles (or spend the night) the crowds drop off. There are a couple of nice creekside campsites just a mile or so up the trail, but it's a long, 10-mile haul to the Kootenai Lakes. The trailhead is located outside of Stevensville up North Kootenai Road. Call the Stevensville Ranger District, (406) 777-5461.

Glen Lake offers instant gratification (or nearly instant), because the trailhead starts high up. From there you climb 3 more steep miles up and into the wilderness, gaining good views of the Bitterroot Valley to the east and glimpses of higher mountain peaks to the west, until finally you drop to a small, cirque-enclosed lake. Bring plenty of water. The trailhead is just north of Victor, along a rough road to the Big Creek trailhead.

The Lake Como National Recreation Loop Trail is 6-plus easy miles around this man-made lake. The north shore trail is open only to hikers and mountain bikers, but once you hit the south side you'll likely be sharing the trail with plenty of pack horses. This is a very popular entrance into the Selway–Bitterroot Wilderness. At the west end of the lake the trail links up to the **Rock Creek Trail,** which leads west into the wilderness area. Lake Como is between Hamilton and Darby off Lake Como Rd. The Darby Ranger District, (406) 821-3913, has additional information.

The trail to **St. Mary Peak** (9,335 feet) climbs 3,000 feet in 4 miles, with the last mile completely above tree line. Because the trail has south and east exposure, it opens relatively early, often by July. This is a good choice for peak hunters who don't want to face the grueling climb to Trapper Peak (see below). Take plenty of water. The trailhead is located midway between Victor and Stevensville off Indian Prairie Loop Rd.

The 6-mile trail to **Trapper Peak** (10,157 feet) is steep, rocky, and in some places difficult to follow, but for in-shape hikers the effort is worthwhile—you'll get a view of the entire Bitterroot Range. Bring plenty of water, and be prepared to maneuver around rocks the last quarter-mile to the summit. Just below timberline, take the time to meander off trail into wildflower-filled meadows, which generally bloom in August. This trail is not passable until late July. It's southwest of Darby, off Hwy 473 (West Fork Rd). For details call the West Fork Ranger District, (406) 821-3269.

Camping

There are a whopping two-dozen plus Forest Service campgrounds and two state-run campgrounds in the Bitterroot Valley. Many of the entrances to the Bitterroot drainages offer campsites, and there are scattered sites along many of the trails. There are also riverside campsites and plenty of privately owned campgrounds along the highway for travelers passing through. Travel Montana's *Montana Travel Planner* lists all private and public campgrounds alphabetically—call (800) 847-4868 out-of-state or (406) 444-2654 in-state; it's also available at chambers of commerce and local motels—look under "Glacier Country." The Bitterroot Valley Chamber of Commerce, (406) 363-2400, puts out an area map that indicates campgrounds. The Bitterroot National Forest Supervisor's Office in Hamilton, (406) 363-7117, or the Montana Department of Fish, Wildlife and Parks in Missoula, (406) 542-5500, can assist with specifics. RV travelers should double-check with authorities to see whether campgrounds can accommodate their vehicles.

The state-run **Chief Looking Glass Campground,** along the Bitterroot River and just north of Florence, offers 18 sites with good views of the Sapphires and is far enough off the highway that the traffic won't keep you awake at night. You're not likely to have the place to yourself, though; it's a popular fishing access.

Located at the Bass Creek trailhead, the **Charles Waters Campground** is very pretty, with 18 sites, a nature trail, and a fitness trail. It goes without saying (but we'll say it anyway) that this campground is a natural jumping-off point for fishing and hiking Bass Creek. Call the Stevensville Ranger District, (406) 777-5461.

There are two Forest Service campgrounds at **Lake Como;** the new, lower one is more developed, with two wheelchair-accessible sites, RV hookups, electricity, and water. Neither campground sits right on the lake, but both are close enough and the views of Trapper Peak are spectacular. The Forest Service also has established a small, rocky beach at the lake, but chilly water temperatures scare off all who aren't hard-core. Darby Ranger District, (406) 821-3913.

It's best to arrive at **Painted Rocks State Park Campground,** 20 miles south of Hamilton, early in the season: once irrigation drawdowns begin in mid-July, you'll wake next to a lake bed instead of Painted Rocks Lake. Montana Department of Fish, Wildlife and Parks, (406) 542-5500. The Forest Service operates the forested creekside **Slate Creek Campground** nearby, not on the lake but within spitting distance. The golden hues of the cliffs are terrific any time of year. West Fork Ranger District, (406) 821-3269.

Fishing

Numerous streams and lakes in the Bitterroot Range have fast-running water that doesn't encourage nutrient buildup, so the fish generally are small. There's no shortage, however, of outdoor stores and outfitting services. For guiding and fishing information call: Fishaus Flyfishing, (406) 363-6158; Grizzly Hackle, (406) 363-4290; or Bob Ward & Sons, (406) 363-6204. The Fishaus also rents equipment. Andy Carlson of Bitterroot Anglers, (406) 777-2341, has a dedicated high-end clientele. Lazy T-4's Spence Trogdon, (406) 642-3586; Riffles & Runs, (406) 961-4950; and John Perry's West Slope Outfitters out of Missoula, (406) 258-2997, also come highly recommended. Most Missoula fishing stores and outfitters, in fact, run guide trips in the Bitterroot (see the Missoula and Environs chapter for specifics). Fishing regulations are available through the Montana Department of Fish, Wildlife and Parks in Missoula, (406) 542-5500, or any licensing outlet. Improve your fishing IQ with a visit to the **Ravalli County Museum** in Hamilton (205 Bedford, (406) 363-3338), which boasts a fine exhibit on the history of fly-fishing.

The main attraction is the **Bitterroot River,** with rainbow, brown, cutthroat, and occasionally bull trout, and brook trout in some of its smaller tributaries. The river is easily accessible from shore: the state maintains nine public access sites, and there are many more unofficial ones. In Hamilton, try the Main Street bridge, Kiwanis Park, or the end of Desta St. In general, it's best to fish the lower reaches of the river early in the season, then move upstream (south) as the season progresses, since irrigation drains off much of the water. The Bitterroot has a large skwala hatch from mid-March through April.

A 1,000-acre reservoir southwest of Hamilton, **Lake Como,** is stocked annually with rainbow trout. Shore access is possible but poor; you'll have much better luck with a boat.

Climbing

The Bitterroot offers the best climbing in the area, with the most stable rock and established routes. For specifics, consult the *Bitterroot Climber's Guide* by Rick Torre, available at area bookstores. Or consult Torre in person at Canyon Critters (175 S Second St, Hamilton, (406) 363-5270), which also has the Bitterroot's only indoor climbing wall. The Trail Head (320 N First Ave, Hamilton, (406) 375-0330) has climbing information, too.

Kootenai Canyon is the best beginner's choice, with some low-grade climbs (starting at 5.6) and top-roping. Climbs get as difficult as 5.12. The majority of climbs are bolted. They begin a quarter-mile up the trail. **Blodgett Canyon** has longer approaches and more difficult climbs on multi-pitch spires, ranging from 5.9 to 5.12. Routes are both traditional and bolted. See Hiking/Backpacking, above, for directions to either canyon.

Lolo Domes, near Lolo Pass on US 12, are just what they sound like: huge domed rocks, with intermediate to difficult slabby climbs ranging from 5.6 to 5.12. It's a good area for bouldering. Three separate turnoffs—East Fork Lolo Creek Rd, Fish Creek Rd or Crooked Fork Rd—from Hwy 12 just west of Lolo Hot Springs will take you there.

Rafting

The Class I water and easy access of the **Bitterroot River** make it a perfect family or beginner float, especially from Stevensville to Missoula. South of there, looks can be deceiving: make sure you watch for occasional logjams and diversion dams from the West Fork to Hamilton. You'll want to portage the diversion dam at Sleeping Child, and possibly the one at Lost Horse Creek. Bird-watching opportunities abound, especially while you're floating past the Teller or Lee Metcalf Wildlife Refuges (see Wildlife, below). In Hamilton, Fishaus Flyfishing, (406) 363-6158, and The Trail Head, (406) 375-0330, rent rafts; from Missoula try Shamrock Sports, (406) 721-5456, or The Trail Head's other branch, (406) 543-6966.

Horseback Riding

Trail rides are available through Camp Creek Inn, (406) 821-3508, 4 miles south of the Sula store on US 93.

Cross-Country Skiing

In the heart of winter cross-country skiers can venture up just about any of the **Bitterroot drainages,** but blowdowns and avalanche dangers can make conditions difficult. Snow conditions vary greatly within each canyon, too. In any case, you'll need a good vehicle to make it to the trailhead. Check on conditions before venturing out by calling the Bitterroot National Forest Supervisor's Office, (406) 363-7117. Rent touring or telemark skis from The Trail Head (320 N First Ave, Hamilton, (406) 375-0330).

Chief Joseph and a band of 750 Nez Perce fleeing US government troops in 1877 crossed over the Continental Divide on their way to the Big Hole Valley and, ultimately, a tragic defeat (see Big Hole Battlefield National Park in the Beaverhead and Big Hole Valleys chapter). The Bitterroot Cross-Country Ski Club maintains an extensive series of loop trails at **Chief Joseph Pass,** which straddles the Continental Divide and defines the southern end of the valley near where the Indians passed. With an elevation of 7,264 feet, snow is abundant here through May. Trails are well marked, and maps are available at the entrance. Dogs are prohibited, but there's no use fee. The Sula Ranger District, (406) 821-3201, has more information.

The same map that covers the Chief Joseph trails also includes the more advanced touring and telemark trails (ungroomed) of **Saddle Mountain,** which radiate out from Lost Trail Powder Mountain on the east side of US 93. These trails are for experts only—the snow is often deep with advanced conditions. There is also a series of ungroomed trails southeast of the pass, known as the **North Big Hole Mountain Touring Trails;** they lead into the Big Hole Valley. Beginners need not apply. Two very popular forest service cabins are located in this area; see Backcountry Cabins in the Beaverhead and Big Hole Valleys chapter.

Downhill Skiing

There's no après-ski action and, incredibly, they don't take credit cards, but **Lost Trail Powder Mountain,** (406) 821-3211 or (406) 821-3508, at the top of Lost Trail pass, offers some of the most reliably good snow conditions in the region. With only 2 chairs and 18 runs, Lost Trail can't compete with larger resorts in terms of variety. But it's a fine place for intermediate skiers, and expansion plans are on the horizon. Thankfully, owner Bill Grasser is sensitive to local budgetary constraints and is hoping to keep lift tickets a bargain at under $20. Lost Trail has the added advantage of being located just off US 93, which means no nasty mountain roads to negotiate (though the pass itself can be tricky in poor weather). By the way, no one actually got *lost* at this pass (that we know of), but Lewis and Clark crossed here trying to find a better way west; they eventually went over Lolo Pass.

Snowmobiling

In winter the **Skalkaho Highway** (Hwy 38) that links Hamilton to Georgetown Lake becomes a beautiful and little-used groomed snowmobile route. The 25-mile highway accesses 25 miles of groomed trails at the Skalkaho Pass Area, and plenty more backcountry. More information is available through the Bitterroot National Forest Supervisor's Office, (406) 363-7117, or the Bitterroot Ridge Runners Snowmobile Club, (406) 363-4689. Bitterroot Snowmobile Adventure, (406) 961-3392, rents snowmobiles and gives guided tours.

Wildlife

The 2,800-acre **Lee Metcalf National Wildlife Refuge** is the no-muss, no-fuss approach to bird-watching—you don't even have to get out of your car. Wildfowl Lane, a county road, travels through the southern part of the refuge past ponds, wetlands, and river bottomlands. March through April is the best time to see **tundra swans** and other waterfowl. **Bald eagles** are also common during winter and spring. In April you can watch **osprey** reclaiming their nests from **Canada geese** who've taken them over during winter. There are 2 miles of trail open year-round, including a half-mile paved trail leading to a riverside picnic site. In mid-April, there's a "Welcome Back Wildlife" day with scopes and volunteers to identify species. Mid-July through September an additional 2-mile track is open, accessing four ponds in the refuge's southeast corner. Several blinds allow closeup observation of birds. Hunting is allowed on the refuge. To get there, take the Eastside Hwy south 1 ½ miles until you see the sign for the refuge. Call the US Fish and Wildlife Service, (406) 777-5552, for details.

The **Teller Wildlife Refuge** encompasses 1,300 acres of prime river bottomland, riparian zones, and croplands just north of Corvallis. It mainly serves as a refuge for birds and animals rather than people, but there is a 1 ½-mile trail that follows the Bitterroot River north from Woodside Bridge (from Corvallis, take the cutoff road toward US 93). The refuge staff happily gives tours by appointment, explaining the Teller Refuge's innovative restoration efforts, an attempt to bring the land back to pre-European conditions. The refuge is notable for bird-watching opportunities; more than 200 species, including **blue herons, bald eagles, osprey,** and plenty of waterfowl have been sighted there. The refuge also hosts the Environmental Writing Institute each May; participants must pay for the workshops but a free reading by the institute's featured author is open to the public. Call the Teller Wildlife Refuge at (800) 343-3707 or (406) 961-3707.

Talk about a prime location. The Broad Axe Lodge and Restaurant, a steak and seafood house 6 miles east of US 93 on the East Fork of the Bitterroot River, overlooks a steep hillside populated year-round by **bighorn sheep.** The area also serves as winter range for **white-tailed deer** and **elk. Golden eagles** are also frequently sighted. The restaurant provides binoculars for restaurant patrons and gives sighting tips free of charge, and if you just want to view from the parking lot that's okay, too. Broad Axe Lodge and Restaurant, (406) 821-3878.

outside in

Attractions

Mid-April through mid-October, you can tour the 24,000 square-foot **Daly Mansion,** which served as a summer home for Copper King Marcus Daly and his family. Known as Riverside, the 24-bedroom, 15-bath

Georgian Revival-style mansion was actually constructed around one of the original Bitterroot homesteads, though you can't tell by looking at it. Most of the original furnishings were sold at auction, but many items have come back to the house. Photographs taken when Margaret Daly still lived there help visitors put together the whole luxurious picture. The exquisitely landscaped grounds once included an Olympic-sized swimming pool, tennis court, trout pond, and children's playhouse. It's just south of Hamilton on the Eastside Hwy, (406) 363-6004.

Calendar of Events

In mid-July, musicians and fans come from all over the region for the **Bitterroot Bluegrass Festival** at the Ravalli County Fairgrounds in Hamilton. Call the Bitterroot Chamber of Commerce for details, (406) 363-2400.

Hamilton hosts the **Ravalli County Fair and Rodeo** the last weekend of August. In addition to the competition and exhibits, it features country western entertainment and carnival rides. The Bitterroot Chamber of Commerce can provide more information, (406) 363-2400.

Restaurants

For gourmet breakfasts head to the **Soft Rock Cafe** in Corvallis (1025 Main, (406) 961-5678). **Nap's Grille** in downtown Hamilton (220 N Second St, (406) 363-0136) has the best lunch deal—12-ounce burger, fries, and a coke for $5.50. When you drive the 7 ½ miles from downtown Hamilton into the Bitterroots to **The Grubstake**, (406) 363-3068, you'll see why it's only open seasonally; take Main St west and follow the signs. From its perch 5,500 feet up, you can see Lost Trail ski resort to the south and the Mission Mountains to the north. Especially popular are the barbecue ribs and chicken, served Sunday through Tuesday.

Marie's Italian Restaurant ☆☆   From the outside Marie's looks like a large, well-kept garage alongside US 93. But every weekend this family-run operation just north of Stevensville serves up authentic Italian food that inspires reverence among locals. There's no menu, per se. Even before they're seated, diners are steered to the steam table behind which chef/owner Michael Molle has displayed the night's selections, described in brief on notecards propped on top of the counter. Instead of a wine list, you consult the display of bottles by the door, and your waitress is likely to be one of the Molles' adolescent daughters. Whatever Marie's lacks in sophisticated service (it's often rushed) or elegant interior design, the restaurant more than makes up for with its food. Its eggplant parmesan is some of the best we've tasted; we also have good memories of scallops in a red clam sauce over linguini and roast pork loin served with cheese-stuffed shells. The menu varies: you might find salmon and crab-stuffed canneloni, seafood lasagna with layers of cod and white sauce, handmade meatballs, or lamb-filled tortellini. Dinners come with your choice of several varieties of bread (we recommend the unusual rosemary-grape), and soup or salad (the latter served family-style). Portions are so big we hesitate to recommend appetizers; on the other hand don't pass up the spinach gnocchi. Desserts are just as good as they sound. Because of its family-run nature, Marie's is sometimes closed for "vacation"; in any case, reservations are a good idea. *On the east side of the road just north of Stevensville; 4040 US 93 S, Stevensville; (406) 777-3681; dinner Fri–Sun; no credit cards; checks OK; $$.*

The Hamilton You've got to admire John Hamilton for opening a bar in downtown Victor and naming it after himself, never mind that the town of Hamilton is only a stone's throw away. We applaud Hamilton (the man, not the town) for having the chutzpah to open a Scottish-style pub in the Bitterroot at all, substituting live bagpipe music for a jukebox and dartboards for gambling machines. Customers regularly make the trek from Missoula for the bar's excellent beer-battered fish and chips; we also recommend the calamari, served with a zesty cocktail sauce. The Hamilton offers a good selection of beers on tap and a smattering of British-style beer drinks as well. Thursday through Saturday, a kilted Hamilton usually can be found demonstrating his bagpiping skills; Wednesday nights he teaches beginner classes. The place is small, and crowded weekends; dinner reservations are a good idea. *Just off US 93 in downtown Victor; 104 Main St, Victor; (406) 642-6644; lunch, dinner Mon–Sat; no credit cards; checks OK; $.*

Wild Oats Cafe With handpainted tables, local artwork, abundant reading material, good coffee drinks, and a huge tea selection, plus a waitstaff that knows most of the clientele, Wild Oats is Hamilton's hippest spot—exactly what a coffeehouse should be. You can get breakfast—good omelets, huevos rancheros, or veggie spuds—until 2pm when the cafe closes. Lunch fare runs from a roast-beef baguette sandwich to quesadillas and veggie burgers. Unusual soups, such as curried lima bean, are standouts; they vary daily. On Fridays and Saturdays, Wild Oats serves dinner: homemade gourmet pizza, burritos, salads, and pastas. There's live music on weekends, and during the school year the Triggering Town Reading Series takes place the third Thursday night of the month. *Upstairs near the corner of Main and 2nd, downtown; 217 Main St, Hamilton; (406) 363-4567; breakfast, lunch every day, dinner Fri–Sat; no credit cards; checks OK; $.*

Lodgings

Camp Creek Inn ☆ Braided rugs and broken-in furniture are the order of the day in this 1920s farmhouse. It's clean and well-kept, and claims a spectacular meadow setting. Of the three upstairs bedrooms (two with private bath), the blue Nez Perce Room has a private porch; the lavender Selway Room has the best south-facing view. Elk are frequent visitors in winter and spring. Rates include a "western-style" breakfast, which means anything from scrambled eggs, bacon, and pancakes to French toast and sausage—whatever the menu, there'll be plenty, pardner. Owner Bill Grasser also owns Lost Trail Powder Mountain, 9 miles south, which explains the great $40 per person winter stay and ski deal; in summer an outfitter runs trail rides in the mountains behind the inn. Camp Creek Inn also rents two cabins on the grounds next to the house. *On US 93, 4 miles south of the Sula store; 7674 US 93 S, Sula, MT 59871; (406) 821-3508; no credit cards; checks OK; $.*

Best Western Hamilton Inn Efficiently run by a local couple named, ironically, the Hiltons, this little horseshoe-shaped motel is the Bitterroot's best, with standard, clean, comfortable rooms. Unfortunately, the motel is located on US 93; request a room in back to avoid traffic noise. For a few extra dollars you can stay in the motel's one "suite," really a larger room, which has the quietest location and a limited view of the mountains; otherwise, you'll be staring at the parking lot. Amenities are limited to an enclosed hot tub and a little landscaped courtyard. Summer reservations, especially for the suite, go early. *On the corner of US 93 and Madison; 409 S First St, Hamilton, MT 59840; (800) 426-4586 or (406) 363-2142; AE, DIS, MC, V; no checks; $$.*

Broad Axe Cabins Set on 28 remote acres along the East Fork of the Bitterroot River, these four simple cabins, all with fully equipped kitchens and bathrooms, make a reasonably priced, quiet getaway. Owners Tom and Barbara Anderson haven't done any fancy landscaping, but there's plenty of natural beauty to recommend the place. Cutthroats and brookies live in the river, and bighorn sheep haunt the rocky cliffs along the road (the on-site restaurant has binoculars for better viewing). You're on your own for breakfast and lunch, but Wednesday through Sunday (weekends only off season), the Broad Axe Restaurant serves an upscale dinner menu; reservations are recommended. The cabins are closed for part of December every year. *17 miles south of Darby off US 93, then 5 1/2 miles east on East Fork Rd; 1237 East Fork Rd, Sula, MT 59871; (406) 821-3878; MC, V; checks OK; $$.*

Ranches and Resorts

Bear Creek Lodge Former New Mexico schoolteachers Roland and Elizabeth Turney traded in the healers of Santa Fe for a Montana-style cure: they took over a creekside log lodge nestled against the Bitterroot Mountains west of Victor. Of eight moderate-sized bedrooms (all with private baths), three are upstairs and probably less noisy; five are on the ground floor with more light. The rooms themselves are nothing special—you're much more likely to gather in front of the fireplace in the comfortable, cathedral-ceilinged living room, or in the hot tub on the enormous deck. Rates ($250/day double occupancy, three night minimum in summer) include three gourmet meals a day, served family-style (wine included), and afternoon appetizers and cocktails. For an additional fee, you can horseback ride or take a guided fly-fishing trip. This is an informal place, designed for people who like to relax and socialize and can amuse themselves hiking, fishing, or reading. Rates drop in the off season, or you can opt to skip lunch and dinner and treat Bear Creek as a (pricey) B&B. *6 miles southwest of Victor, 1/2 mile east of the Bear Creek trailhead; 1184 Bear Creek Trail, Victor, MT 59875; (800) 270-5550 or (406) 642-3750; AE, DIS, MC, V; checks OK.*

Teller Wildlife Refuge Guest Homes In order to fund and publicize its preservation and restoration efforts, the nonprofit corporation that runs the 1,300-acre Teller Wildlife Refuge rents out two lovely and tastefully decorated 1860s homesteads on the property, providing an unusual opportunity to share your vacation with nothing and no one but wildlife. The Slack House is the larger of the two homes, with four bedrooms and two baths, a wraparound porch upstairs, and two screened-in porches on the ground floor. Because the Slack House relies on wood-stove heat, it's open seasonally only. Just down the road, the Teller Lodge has three bedrooms and 2 1/2 baths, with a view of the Bitterroots out the front door. Rates ($180 day/person) guarantee the entire house is yours, and include daily maid service and all meals, cooked to your specifications and time schedule. Homegrown, homemade fare is the rule here, with an emphasis on fresh, organic foods, many of which are harvested from the refuge's own garden. The 3-day minimum stay is flexible, and group rates are available.

   Depending on the time of year, you're likely to see osprey, eagles, blue heron, deer, fox, beavers, and occasional elk and moose, along with more than 200 other bird species. Guests are welcome to try their hand at fishing the creek that meanders through the north end of the property; it yields rainbow and brown trout averaging 20 inches, but only to experienced fishermen. The Teller Wildlife Refuge also rents out fishing cabins (they're really more like vacation homes) by the week. Meal service is not included; these are booked up to a year in advance. *From the Eastside Hwy, turn west on Quast Rd, then right on Chaffin Rd (1 mile north of Corvallis); 1292 Chaffin Rd, Corvallis, MT 59828; (800) 343-3707 or (406) 961-3707; no credit cards; checks OK.*

Triple Creek Ranch Located on 250 acres up the West Fork of the Bitterroot River, and bordered on three sides by National Forest, the exclusive Triple Creek Ranch caters to an adult clientele for whom rustic holds absolutely no appeal. Eighteen plush log cabins, some with private hot tubs, are conservatively decorated with fireplaces, fully stocked wet bars, refrigerators, and televisions. The steep rates ($475-$765 per night, double occupancy) are all inclusive: there's no charge for use of the tennis court and small outdoor pool, on-ranch trail rides, fly-casting lessons (there's a stocked trout pond on the property), or alcohol. Gourmet meals are served in the cathedral-ceilinged restaurant in the central lodge or by room service. An upstairs bar is decorated in a western theme, complete with saddle-shaped bar stools. This is a grown-up getaway only; children under 16 are not allowed. Open year-round. *12 miles southwest of Darby, and 7 miles west of US 93; 5551 West Fork Stage Rte, Darby, MT 59829; (800) 654-2943 or (406) 821-4664; AE, DIS, MC, V; checks OK.*

West Fork Meadows Ranch Run by a German/Swiss couple, the family-oriented West Fork Meadows Ranch caters to an international clientele (about half of guests are European) looking for a real "western experience," and you can see why. This ranch is quintessential Montana, boasting a beautiful and remote location 30 miles up the West Fork of the Bitterroot River, in a 160-acre meadow property surrounded by the Bitterroot peaks. Guests stay in seven simple cabins (we like the four streamside) and eat in the main log lodge. After a hiatus, the renowned cuisine of West Fork's famed Black Horse Restaurant will be back in 1997, serving both western-style (elk loin) and European-style (wiener schnitzel) entrees. Rates ($999-$1,299 per person/weekly July and August, $129 per person/night June and September, flexible 3-night minimum) include three meals, use of the swimming pond, hot tub, game room, mountain bikes, canoes (Painted Rocks Lake is 1 mile away, but by the end of August there's not much water left), fishing equipment, and, for weekly guests, horses—plus guns for target practice (quintessential Montana, remember?). October through May the ranch rents out cabins but doesn't provide any meals or services; snowmobile packages are available. *28 miles southwest of Darby, 6 miles past Painted Rocks Lake Dam; 52 Coal Creek Rd, Darby, MT 59829; (800) 800-1437 or (406) 349-2468; AE, MC, V; checks OK.*

Backcountry Cabins

The Forest Service lists all available cabins in its *Recreational Cabin and Lookout Directory*, available through the Bitterroot National Forest Supervisor's Office in Hamilton, (406) 363-7117, or any district office. Rates generally run between $15 and $30 per night.

You can drive year-round to the **East Fork Guard Station,** 16 miles east of Sula along the East Fork of the Bitterroot River. The 16- by 24-foot cabin is well equipped with two sets of large bunkbeds, electric lights, water, cooler, outhouse, wood stove, propane stove, cooking utensils, and outdoor fire pit. You bring mattresses and ice. Sula Ranger District, (406) 821-3201.

McCart Lookout Tower sits atop Johnson Peak on the edge of the Anaconda–Pintler Wilderness, at the end of an easy 1 1/2-mile trail. Firewood, wood stove, and cooking utensils are provided, and there's one bed and an outhouse. You'll need your own mattress, sleeping bag, water, and toilet paper. Because the lookout is above ground with only a single railing around its catwalk, don't bring small children. Open May through October, weather permitting. It's 20 miles east of Sula, off the East Fork Hwy. Sula Ranger District, (406) 821-3201.

More Information

Bitterroot National Forest Supervisor's Office, Hamilton: (406) 363-7117.

BNF, Darby Ranger District: (406) 821-3913.

BNF, Stevensville Ranger District: (406) 777-5461.

BNF, Sula Ranger District: (406) 821-3201.

BNF, West Fork Ranger District: (406) 821-3269.

Bitterroot Valley Chamber of Commerce, Hamilton: (406) 363-2400.

Montana Department of Fish, Wildlife and Parks, Missoula: (406) 542-5500.

Butte
and Environs

Including Deer Lodge, Anaconda, Georgetown Lake, Philipsburg, and the Anaconda–Pintler Wilderness.

The old mining city of Butte (joint city-county jurisdiction, pop: 35,000) gets a bad rap in terms of modern-day aesthetics, but it dominates the early history of the state and is a fascinating stopover for anyone even vaguely interested in Montana's past. Located a mile high just west of the Continental Divide, on what became known as "the richest hill on earth," for many years Butte was among the wealthiest and most cosmopolitan cities in the state, with residents representing dozens of different ethnicities. Distinct neighborhoods bore names testifying to Butte's diversity, such as Dublin Gulch, Finntown, Meaderville, and Chinatown. Tales of the 19th-century business and political rivalry between mining magnates Marcus Daly and William A. Clark make up some of Montana's most colorful and infamous stories.

For more than a century Butte was a union stronghold, the birthplace of Local Miners Union Number 1 of the Western Federation of Miners. Butte and the neighboring smelter town Anaconda offered sure and steady employment. Their prosperity bestowed the towns with some of the finest architecture in the state, as well as one of the nicest public parks, the lovely Columbia Gardens, that featured botanical gardens, amusement rides, and a dance pavilion sponsored by Copper King William Clark. Alas, in 1973 Columbia Gardens, like so much of Butte, was swallowed up in an expansion of the open pit mines.

Butte's fortunes took a nosedive in the late 1980s after the

Atlantic Richfield Co. (ARCO) closed the Anaconda mines. In 1986, Missoula businessman Dennis Washington bought out the company and reopened the Continental Pit with nonunion labor. It's a profitable business once again, though the mine employs a lot fewer people than it once did.

Butte has a reputation as one of Montana's ugliest cities and as having some of the ugliest weather—throughout the state it's referred to as "butt." Don't mention this while in Butte, though; Butte people are very proud of their mining heritage, and rightfully so. Residents enjoy a deserved reputation for being hard-drinking, hard-living folks with an almost unrivaled loyalty to their hometown. "I'd rather put on a steel beak and eat shit with the chickens than leave Butte," one woman quoted her grandmother as saying, in a fine example of the flamboyant and passionate speech you'll hear. You can see evidence of Butte's former glory in its stunning turn-of-the-century architecture—the Uptown area is one of the largest National Historic Districts in the country—and in the mining headframes that still dot the city's neighborhoods. Butte sits on the nation's largest Superfund cleanup site, including the now-defunct Berkeley Pit, once the largest open-pit mine in the nation that is currently filling with toxic water.

Although Butte and neighboring burgs have a ways to go before winning any beauty contests, the surrounding scenery doesn't need any facelifts. The area is rife with recreational possibilities. From Butte, it's less than an hour to Georgetown Lake or the rock-climbing and hiking possibilities of the Highlands, Humbug Spires, and the Anaconda–Pintler Wilderness, and an equal distance to the famous fly-fishing on the Big Hole and Jefferson Rivers.

Getting There

Butte is just west of the Continental Divide at the junction of Interstates 90 and 15. It is served by Bert Mooney Airport and by Greyhound and Rimrock Trailways bus lines. Anaconda is about 20 miles west of Butte off I-90 on the Highway 1 spur. Philipsburg is another 30 miles or so along Hwy 1, while Deer Lodge is northwest on I-90.

Adjoining Areas

NORTH: **Helena and Environs**

SOUTH: **Beaverhead and Big Hole Valleys; West Yellowstone and the Madison Valley**

EAST: **Bozeman and Environs**

WEST: **Bitterroot Valley**

inside out

Mountain Biking

Butte's mining heritage left behind several unintended legacies, among them an extensive series of old mining roads connected by game trails. They're great to ride, but you'll have to know what you're doing. The folks at Great Divide Cyclery in Butte (827 S Montana Street, (406) 782-4726) can provide **route advice.** They can also provide a written narrative of eight area rides, put together by a local graduate student. Every Sunday, Great Divide Cyclery owner Pete Smith or one of his employees leads an all-day, intermediate-oriented **group ride;** it's a sure thing April through October and sporadic in winter. Meet at 10am at Great Divide Cyclery.

The Butte Ranger District/Supervisor's Office Annex in Butte, (406) 494-2147, can also provide information on any of the following rides.

A 13-mile, moderate to difficult route leads up **Toll Canyon** to the Continental Divide, providing good views of Butte and Red Mountain. The loop route begins southwest of Butte on Roosevelt Road near Pipestone Pass, following a dirt road up and a steep single track down.

In a rain shadow on the east side of the Continental Divide, **Spire Rock** is a good place for early season, intermediate-level riding. There are no maps, but a four-wheel club flags the trails there, and as long as you remember that the freeway is east you'll be able to keep your bearings. In late summer the sandy soil dries out and makes riding more difficult. Take the Pipestone exit off I-90, 16 miles east of Butte, then turn north on the road to Delmoe Lake (it's signed). Park at the railroad tracks 2 miles up the road and look for the flagged trails.

More advanced cyclists should check out the **beaver ponds** area near Pipestone Pass. A 6-mile, single-track loop ride begins on Hwy 2, a little more than 1 mile west of the Continental Divide. It leads up the pass and veers off into a wide drainage pockmarked with beaver ponds, then descends steeply back to Hwy 2. You can extend the ride by exploring 12 miles of interconnected single-track loops radiating from the beaver ponds, known locally as the **Krueger Memorial Trails** after the man who cleared them. You'll want written information for this ride, since it's not all well-marked and there are many cow paths to lead you astray.

The Philipsburg Ranger District, (406) 859-3211, has jurisdiction over some good biking areas and provides trail maps.

The first is 13 to 16 moderate miles around **Georgetown Lake,** depending on which route you take; either road has great views of the lake and the Pintler Range. Start at the dam on Georgetown Lake Rd;

when the road forks at Piney Campground you can take either the upper or lower road—the lower one will cut 3 miles off your total trip, but the upper one is mostly paved. Avoid this ride on summer weekends (too much traffic).

The cross-country ski trails around **Ski Discovery** and **Georgetown Lake** offer various loop rides; start at either Lodgepole Campground off Hwy 1 or Cable Mountain Campground off the Ski Discovery Rd on North Fork Flint Creek Rd. When you get to the parking lot at the ski area, take the gated logging road to Echo Lake, where there's a nice picnic area and good (but chilly) swimming. Watch for moose; they've been known to get aggressive there.

There are many old logging roads behind the town of **Philipsburg.** For a real grunt of a workout try the 5-mile, 2,000-foot climb to the remains of the old ghost town of Granite. Unfortunately, some of the land near the old townsite is private, so you might want to watch your step or get a map from the ranger.

Hiking/Backpacking

You'll want either a Deerlodge National Forest map or an Anaconda–Pintler Wilderness map (the latter is nice because it includes topographical information). The Anaconda–Pintler Wilderness Coordinator, Bitterroot National Forest, Sula Ranger District, (406) 821-3201, can provide **maps** and more detailed **information**, as can the Butte Ranger District/Supervisor's Office Annex, (406) 494-2147, for trails not in the Anaconda–Pintlers.

Undoubtedly the best overnight hiking in the area is in the 158,000-acre **Anaconda–Pintler Wilderness,** which straddles the Continental Divide southwest of Butte and contains the headwaters to Rock Creek and branches of the Bitterroot and Big Hole Rivers. For years, the "AP" has been a favorite local alternative to better publicized areas such as Glacier National Park, but now it, too, is gaining fame with use increasing dramatically in the past five years. And no wonder. Pockmarked with glacial lakes, distinguished by 10,000-plus foot peaks, home to mountain goats, black bear, elk, moose, and deer, the AP doesn't have any trouble competing with the big boys. It's especially popular with horse packers and hunters, and fishermen and hikers who don't want to deal with tourist traffic. You can access the AP from all sides, but trails generally don't open until July.

Few people hike the AP without heading to one of its many lakes, most of which sport cutthroat and rainbow trout. **Johnson and Rainbow Lakes** are both popular because of easy access; from either you can easily day hike to other surrounding lakes. The **Hi-Line Trail #111** crisscrosses the Continental Divide, with offshoot trails leading to cirques and lakes; need we tell you that the views are great? To get away from people, try some of the longer drainages that don't lead to lakes: the **East Fork Trail #38** or **Page Creek Trail #39** are good bets. Alternatively, go in from the less popular southeast side of the range; you'll have to hike farther to get to a lake, but you'll get more solitude.

The **Haystack Mountain National Recreation Trail** in the Boulder Mountains north of Butte is a good choice for a moderate to difficult day hike, with terrific 360-degree views that include Elk Park and the Helena valley (watch for elk in the fall). Theoretically this is a 6-mile round-trip hike to an old lookout (only the stairs remain), but low-clearance vehicles will have to park at the horse ramp, about 1 ½ miles below the trailhead. It's about 20 miles north of Butte; take the Elk Park Rd exit off I-15, then Forest Rd 1538 from the Frontage Rd.

High-clearance vehicles can drive within 2 miles of the 10,070-foot **Red Mountain** lookout, 15 miles south of Butte in the Highlands; others might want to leave their car farther down the Forest Service road, adding as many as 3 miles to their round-trip excursion. The moderate to difficult hike up an old road above tree line is very popular with day hikers, since it leads to panoramic views of Humbug Spires, the Tobacco Root Mountains, and the Jefferson River Valley. The road is actually passable (hard-core mountain bikers, listen up!), but concerned about steep dropoffs, the Forest Service has denied access to vehicles.

There are not a lot of options when it comes to hiking the 11,000-acre **Humbug Spires Wilderness Study Area,** located 26 miles south of Butte, but the unusual, enormous granite formations and very old Douglas firs are enough to recommend it. A 4 ½-mile trail leads from the parking lot up Moose Creek to The Wedge, an enormous spire popular with climbers. From there, you can follow game trails in numerous directions, or scramble to the top of one of the ridges. Due to its relatively low elevation, this is a good spot for an early-season day hike; kids and adults love climbing on the huge boulder formations that rise along the creek. To get there, take I-15 south and exit at Moose Creek, then drive east on Moose Creek Rd 3 miles to the parking lot. This area is administered by the Bureau of Land Management in Butte, (406) 494-5059.

Camping

The Forest Service puts out a "Guide to Recreational Opportunities" that highlights recreation and lists all public campgrounds. Call the Beaverhead/Deerlodge National Forest Supervisor's Office in Dillon, (406) 683-3900, or the

Butte Ranger District/Supervisor's Office Annex in Butte, (406) 494-2147, for a copy; the district office can also provide more specific information on the sites listed below. Travel Montana's *Montana Travel Planner,* (800) 847-4868 out-of-state or (406) 444-2654 in-state, lists all public and private campgrounds alphabetically; look under "Gold West Country." RV travelers should check to see that the campgrounds can accommodate their vehicles. The Montana Department of Fish, Wildlife and Parks in Missoula, (406) 542-5500, can provide information on state parks.

You can camp for free at spectacular **Lost Creek State Park,** located in a deep, narrow canyon outside Anaconda. Campsites line the creekside; the best ones are farther up the road, where the limestone cliffs are more dramatic. Look for bighorn sheep and mountain goats on the cliffs; there's a pullout at the entrance that offers good views. Keep your eyes open for moose in the creek bottom, too. The road ends at a short pathway to a scenic, 50-foot waterfall. Lost Creek is 10 miles northeast of Anaconda; turn off Hwy 1 just east of town and follow the signs.

Creekside campsites at **Beaverdam Campground,** 20 miles south of Butte off I-15, offer a quiet respite in thick stands of lodgepole pine. An on-site host can direct you to the nearby Starlight Mountain Trail or the Rocky Ridge Trail, both of which lead to the Continental Divide Trail in the Fleecer Range. Take the Feeley exit off I-15 and drive west 8 miles on Divide Creek Rd.

Located 18 miles northwest of Butte and 2 miles from **Sheepshead Mountain Recreation Area** (day-use only), the **Lowland Campground** has 11 sites with wheelchair-accessible facilities. Lowland itself doesn't have much in the way of amenities, but at Sheepshead, which was developed specifically for barrier-free access, you can fish 15-acre Maney Lake or stroll the short paved nature trail. Popular with groups, Sheepshead has softball fields, volleyball courts, and horseshoe pits as well as picnic facilities. The 16-mile **Hail Columbia Gulch Road** from Sheepshead to Rocker is a good bet for wildlife viewing. The unmarked Sheepshead Overlook trail, an old Forest Service road that adjoins the paved trail, leads 2 miles to a nice viewpoint. Ask the campground host for directions.

Of three Forest Service campgrounds at Georgetown Lake, **Piney Campground** (48 units) is the nicest. Both Piney and **Philipsburg Bay Campground** (69 units) fill up quickly, since they're off the highway and on the water. Both have small, sandy beaches, but swimming isn't recommended: the lake's too shallow and weedy, and there are leeches. Your third choice is the smaller, 31-unit **Lodgepole Campground,** on the north side of the highway across from the lake. All three sites are managed by the Philipsburg Ranger District, (406) 859-3211.

Fishing

In addition to the fisheries listed below, Butte offers easy access to the Big Hole, Beaverhead, and Jefferson Rivers (see the Fishing section in the Beaverhead and Big Hole Valleys chapter). Stop at Fran Johnson's Sport Shop (1957 Harrison Ave, Butte, (406) 782-3322) for **regulations** and the latest fishing information. The Montana Department of Fish, Wildlife and Parks in Missoula, (406) 542-5500, can also help.

Dammed around the turn of the century to generate electricity for surrounding mining communities, and later used to power the smelting operations in Anaconda, **Georgetown Lake** is heavily fished for rainbow and brook trout and kokanee salmon. Shore fishing is allowed; however, it is shallow and very weedy, so it's a good idea to have a boat. You can rent boats at Stewart's Georgetown Landing along Hwy 1, (406) 563-5900, or at Georgetown Lake Lodge at Denton's Point on the west side of the lake, (406) 563-7020. In winter, lots of folks like to **ice fish** here. Much of the southern and eastern sides of the lake are closed until July 1 for rainbow spawning. Be sure to read the regulations.

You also can access the upper reaches of **Rock Creek** from Hwy 1. This blue-ribbon trout stream is enormously popular with fly-fishermen (see Fishing in the Missoula and Environs chapter). Watch for big salmonfly hatches in late May and early June.

Most of the lakes in the **Anaconda–Pintler Wilderness** have cut-throat and rainbow trout, and some of the lower-elevation streams have brookies, too. **Johnson** and **Rainbow Lakes** are popular destinations. But come to the AP for the scenery first and the fishing second. Call the Anaconda–Pintler Wilderness Coordinator at the Sula Ranger District, (406) 821-3201; she'll have more information or refer you to the appropriate district.

Climbing

You can find climbing advice, equipment, and an **indoor climbing wall** at Pipestone Mountaineering in Butte (829 S Montana St, (406) 782-4994). Additionally, all the employees next door at Great Divide Cyclery (827 S Montana St, (406) 782-4726) are fanatic climbers and good sources of information.

On weekends you'll find plenty of climbers at **Spire Rock,** 20 miles east of Butte on the east side of the Continental Divide. There are both sport routes and traditional routes ranging from 5.6 to 5.12. Take I-90, 16 miles east of Butte to the Pipestone exit, then drive north 4 miles on Delmoe Lake Rd; when you come to the 150-foot spire, you'll see a dirt road forking off that leads to the back side.

You'll have to work a little harder to get to **Humbug Spires,** south of Butte. A 4 1/2-mile trail leads from the parking lot to The Wedge, a 550-foot spire with bolted and traditional climbs, most ranging from 5.8 to 5.10. Take I-15, 26 miles south of Butte to the Moose Creek exit, then drive east 3 miles on Moose Creek Rd to the Bureau of Land Management Parking Lot.

Golf

Located on part of the nation's largest Superfund site, the Jack Nicklaus-designed **Old Works Golf Course** is part of a plan to transform Anaconda from a depressed former smelting town into a tourist destination. Officials in charge of the project tell us not to worry: they've capped the entire 21-hole course with 2 inches of limestone and 16 inches of new soil, a barrier against arsenic and other heavy metals beneath. Still, you're not likely to forget where you are. The sand traps are filled with black slag, refuse rock left over from the smelting process. The course is scheduled to open in spring 1997. It's at the north end of Anaconda at the junction of Cedar and Pizinni Memorial Way; call (406) 563-5670 for details.

Swimming

Peaceful it's not, nor inexpensive, but kids dig **Fairmont Hot Springs Resort.** It features indoor and outdoor Olympic-sized swimming pools, hot soaking pools, and a 350-foot enclosed water slide (lots of fun, but it costs extra). The full-service resort complex includes a massive, characterless hotel with lounge and restaurant, tennis courts, and an 18-hole golf course. Weekends are mobbed. Bring your own towel and save two bucks. About 12 miles west of Butte; take Exit 211 off I-90. Call (800) 332-3272 or (406) 797-3241.

Cross-Country Skiing

Rent touring and telemark skis at Pipestone Mountaineering in Butte (829 S Montana, (406) 782-4994). Pipestone also rents snowshoes.

The Mile High Nordic Club grooms about 15 miles of marked cross-country tracks at **Mount Haggin Wildlife Management Area** north of Anaconda, which offers tremendous views of the Pintlers. About 10 of those miles are groomed specifically for skate skiers. There's also plenty of telemark skiing here or at nearby Grassy Mountain, over the Continental Divide. Maps of Mount Haggin are available at the area, but they don't indicate difficulty factors: beginning skiers should stick to the loop trails closest to the parking lot. Keep an eye out for moose on the way to the ski area. Road conditions can be very bad. Even if the parking lot is windy, though, the trails often are not. There's no fee, but donations are requested; trails are groomed on Saturday mornings and often midweek as well. The club also offers occasional ski lessons. To get to the tracks, take Hwy 1 east of Anaconda 3 miles to County Rd 274. You'll see skier and snowmobiler signs near the Continental Divide. For more information call Joe Griffin, (406) 782-0316.

A series of loop trails lead from the **Ski Discovery** parking lot near **Georgetown Lake.** The beginner trail to Echo Lake is groomed regularly. You can also ski a marked loop trail taking off from the Lodgepole Campground on Hwy 1; it's very scenic and follows a ridge above the lake, but call the Forest Service for conditions since it's not groomed regularly. Maps are available at the ski area, (406) 563-2184, and through the Philipsburg Ranger District, (406) 859-3211.

See Backcountry Cabins, below, for additional options.

Downhill Skiing

Ski Discovery's front side caters to beginners and intermediates, while its backside boasts all double diamond runs with plenty of tree skiing. There are 36 runs in all, with four chairlifts and a vertical drop of 1,200 feet. The friendly, family-run ski area is developing a large regional following, especially when snow conditions at lower elevations aren't good (Discovery's base is at 6,850 feet). The food at Discovery's cafeteria goes way beyond normal ski-bum fare—another plus. Off Hwy 1 at Georgetown Lake, 18 miles west of Anaconda, (406) 563-2184.

Snowmobiling

Four major snowmobile trail systems crisscross the **Georgetown Lake** area: Carp Ridge, Peterson Meadows, Red Lion Racetrack Lake, and Echo Lake. Together they make a total of 90-plus miles of groomed trails. Get snowmobile maps and more information from the Philipsburg Ranger District, (406) 859-2311.

Wildlife

With 54,000 acres of rolling hills, bottomlands, and forested mountains, Mount Haggin Wildlife Management Area boasts great opportunities to see **moose, elk,** and **deer**—plus a lot of birdlife, including nesting **sandhill cranes.** There are plenty of unmarked trails and nothing is off-limits, so you can walk where you please. It's 10 miles southeast of Anaconda off Hwy 1 and County Rd 274. Call (406) 821-3201 for information.

Other Activities

About 10 miles west of Anaconda, in the foothills of the Anaconda–Pintler Wilderness, Pintler Sled Adventures, (406) 563-2675, will transform you from a no-nothing into a rookie musher in 2 short hours. Owner Bob Davis teaches you how to harness and drive his **dogsled** teams, then you're on your own while Davis rides ahead on his Snowcat. A basic 2-hour orientation and ride costs $60 for two, with discounts for kids ages 6–11; children 5 and under ride free. Davis also owns a primitive cabin on nearby Twin Lakes Creek; for $220 (provisions included), he'll drop you there by dogsled and pick you up the next day.

The month of November is the best time to catch the US National Speed Skating Team practicing at the US High Altitude Sports Center, (406) 494-7570 or (406) 494-3406. Weekend afternoons in December and January there's public **ice skating** on the 400-meter oval. Some skate rentals are available, mostly speed skates. Admission is $2 for adults, $1 for children. The center is in Butte, at the Continental Drive exit off I-90.

outside in

Attractions

To truly understand this community's vital spirit, visit **Our Lady of the Rockies,** a 90-foot statue looking down on Butte from atop the Continental Divide. Back in 1979, Anaconda worker and devout Catholic Bob O'Bill made a pact with God: save his ill wife, and he would build a statue dedicated to the Virgin Mary. The timing of the project was fortuitous in an odd sort of way, because ARCO was downscaling, leaving hundreds of employees out of work. The idea of building an enormous statue on the Divide seized the workers' imaginations, distracting them from their economic woes. Soon a large volunteer force was working to weld the 51-ton iron statue and blast the steep, 6-mile road to the top. Six years later, with the help of the National Guard and a Ch-54 Sikorsky Sky Crane helicopter, the last piece of the statue was erected. Local legend has it that the day Our Lady of the Rockies went up was the day Butte's fortunes changed. By the way, O'Bill's wife lives on. You can see a 20-minute video about the construction of Our Lady of the Rockies at the visitors center; it goes a long way towards explaining the present-day community of Butte, too. Plans are in the works for a tram leading to the statue, but currently the only way to get there is via a $10, 2 1/2 hour tour. June through September, tours leave several times a day, weather permitting, from the

Our Lady of the Rockies Gift Shop in the Butte Plaza Mall at 3100 Harrison. The Uptown Visitors Center is at 434 N Main and is open Monday through Friday; the mall store is open every day but does not show the video. Call (800) 800-5239 or (406) 782-1221 for details.

Climb aboard the **Old Number 1,** a trolley replica, for an overview of Butte's history and architecture. The 1 ½-hour tour covers all of Butte's must-sees, including historic Uptown and brief stops at the Berkeley Pit and the World Museum of Mining. The open-air ride gets chilly, so bring a sweater. The quality of the trip varies with the guides; best is 20-year veteran driver Hollis Coon. Tours run June through September and leave four times a day from the Chamber of Commerce, 2950 Harrison Ave, (800) 735-6814 or (406) 494-5595.

A reconstructed 1899 mining town sits on the site of the now-defunct Orphan Girl mine; the **World Museum of Mining** is much more interesting than it sounds. There's not a dull rock exhibit in sight. Instead, visitors wander up and down the "streets" and into the "businesses" of Hell Roarin' Gulch, taking a look at a mining headframe up close. It's a big, fascinating place, so plan on staying at least an hour. Open seasonally; near Montana Tech at the end of West Park and Granite St, (406) 723-7211.

More than a mile long and 1,800 feet deep, the **Berkeley Pit** was once the largest open-pit mine in the country. Now filling up with toxic water, it's at the heart of the nation's largest Superfund cleanup site. You can view The Pit from an observation deck, where a recorded informational tape plays continuously. There's also a gift shop at the site on Continental Drive, (406) 494-5595.

For a glimpse into the opulent world of Butte mining magnate William A. Clark, don't miss a tour of the 32-room **Copper King Mansion** (219 W Granite, (406) 782-7580). From the stained glass to the elaborate woodwork and hand-painted ceilings, Clark spared no expense in building his magnificent 1884 home. The three-story mansion is privately owned and operated; tours are daily on the hour April through October; off season is only by appointment (also see Lodgings, below).

In 1898, William Clark's oldest son Charles Clark, a Butte lawyer, built what is now the **Arts Chateau** (321 W Broadway, (406) 723-7600). Clark's furnishings have been sold, but using period pieces, the house has been decorated as closely as possible to its original splendor. Two galleries house changing regional and national art exhibits. Tours are available as needed; just stop by. Open Tuesday to Saturday year-round.

Even non-baseball fans might want to catch a **Copper Kings baseball** game, just to see what antics owners Mike Veeck and Bill Murray (the comedian) have cooked up. Veeck, son of legendary Chicago White Sox owner Bill Veeck, is the man responsible for the infamous 1979 Disco Demolition at Chicago's Comiskey Park, when he blew 10,000 records sky high and got himself drummed out of the major leagues. Murray's reputation (*Saturday Night Live, Caddyshack, Groundhog Day*) precedes him. But one thing's for sure: with a donkey carrying out the first ball and a St. Patrick's Day celebration in August, these guys know how to get an audience going. The Copper Kings are a farm team for the Anaheim Angels and play on the Montana Tech campus; call (406) 723-8206 for tickets and information.

Outside Butte, it's well worth taking time to detour off I-90 and drive the **Pintler Scenic Loop** (Hwy 1) past the old smelting town of Anaconda, Georgetown Lake, and the picturesque Philipsburg. A few examples of beautiful architecture remain in **Anaconda,** which, if Copper King Marcus Daly had had his way, would have been named state capital. Despite sinking millions into his bid, though, Anaconda lost out to Helena, rival William Clark's choice. You can't miss Anaconda—its 585-foot smelter smokestack still stands as a tribute to better days. So does the Washoe Theater, an art deco beauty (305 Main). Management often lets visitors tour the place—just knock. Have a drink at the Club Moderne at Park and Ash, another art deco gem; don't miss the back lounge, with its naugahyde booths, individual jukeboxes, and pink mood lighting.

The **Granite County Museum & Cultural Center** in **Philipsburg** boasts a terrific historical photographic exhibit in its Ghost Town Hall of Fame. The museum's basement, meanwhile, houses a very good Historical Mining Display, with old equipment, mining maps, and a replica of a mine and an assay office. The museum is located at 155 Sansome St, just south of Broadway, and is open every day in summer; call for off-season hours, (406) 859-3020.

They call it **sapphire mining** when it's actually more like sapphire tweezing—gadget in hand, you search through a bucket of gravel provided by Philipsburg's Sapphire Gallery. Still, it's fun when you spot a gem, even if, as so often happens, it's not worth much. Some people do manage to find valuable stones; in any case, no one comes out empty-handed. The gallery will be more than happy to cut and polish the ones worth keeping, for a fee. Contact the Sapphire Gallery, 115 E Broadway, Philipsburg, (406) 525-0169.

Plan to take at least an hour to look around the buildings and exhibits of the **Grant-Kohrs Ranch National Historic Site** in Deer Lodge, a tribute to the early days of cowboys and ranching. This property once served as headquarters for the Kohrs' vast cattle empire; they controlled a million acres in four states and parts of Canada. The Kohrs family preserved their valuables and records so well, it's almost as if they planned on having the place opened to the public someday. You need to join a half-hour tour to gain entrance to the ranch house, a veritable mansion in the middle of nowhere. The bunkhouse holds an impressive collection of old wagons and buggies; in summer, a blacksmith demonstrates smithing techniques, and a chuckwagon serves up authentic cowboy cuisine. The ranch also has very good bird habitat; ask for the Park Service brochure listing species you're likely to see. Tours and admission are free. The ranch is open year-round every day but Thanksgiving, Christmas, and New Year's and is administered by the National Park Service, (406) 846-2070.

Who would expect to find more than 100 antique cars in Deer Lodge, Montana—in an old prison, no less? That's where Edward Towe's collection of antique cars wound up, in the **Towe Ford Museum,** an adjunct display for visitors touring the **Old Montana Prison.** The Towe Ford Museum is located at 1106 Main, Deer Lodge, and is open February through November; call (406) 846-3111 for details.

Calendar of Events

People come from all over the state, and sometimes farther, for Butte's **St. Patrick's Day** celebration, which includes a large parade and the 3-mile Blarney Stone Fun Run (you have to kiss the "stone" halfway through). With 45,000 people, more than the city's entire population, lining the parade route, it's crazy and chaotic—and definitely not for teetotallers. The parade winds through Uptown; stay away from the intersections of Park and Main or Broadway and Main, which get so ridiculously crowded that the parade barely makes it though. Celebrations generally start the night before and continue through St. Patrick's Day and sometimes beyond. Call Butte Celebrations, (406) 782-0742, for more information.

Restaurants

You can get a taste of the real Butte with a boneless pork chop sandwich from **Pork Chop John's,** (406) 782-0812, and a beer at the **M & M,** a 24-hour bar/cafe/casino that reputedly has been open nonstop since before 1900, (406) 782-0812. Despite its wild reputation, however, Butte has a more genteel side. Witness the advent of several hip coffeehouses (try the **Blue Venus** on Main for good lattes and desserts, (406) 782-1137). Two doors up, at the corner of Main and Galena, the **Irish Times Pub** is a pleasant, gambling-free tavern that sometimes features live music, (406) 782-8142. You'll find good takeout at the **Front Street Market** (8 W Front St, (406) 782-2614), a tiny family-run grocery chock-full of imported goodies, deli salads, and terrific raviolis. **Ski Discovery,** (406)

563-2184, claims the outlying area's best offerings, thanks to Italian chef Dora Goodman, who makes the pastas, chili, soups, famed chocolate chip cookies, and cinnamon rolls. Unfortunately, the cafeteria is only open for lunch, and only during ski season.

The Uptown Cafe ☆ Depending on whom you talk to, the Uptown is either Butte's most sophisticated or most pretentious restaurant. Call it what you will, the austere Uptown serves what is definitely not typical Butte fare, and that's earned the restaurant several favorable mentions in national publications. Fish and seafood, flown in fresh from Seattle and served in decidedly un-Butte-like presentations, are best bets; on a recent visit we sampled a delicious seared salmon fillet in black bean sauce. Regular menu selections include beef Wellington and an unusual cioppino with scallops, shrimp, and sausage. Entrees, high-priced by Butte standards, are very good, but the rest of the meal could use some attention: our caesar salad, for instance, wasn't tossed, and the Clams Maison that comes with every entree seems thrown in largely for effect. Popular cafeteria-style lunches with rotating entrees, on the other hand, are an excellent value, as is an $8.95 early-bird dinner special. The waitstaff is young and casual, eager to please if not always well-informed. *Uptown, 1/2 block east of Main; 47 E Broadway, Butte; (406) 723-4735; lunch Mon–Fri, dinner Tues–Sat; AE, DIS, MC, V; checks OK; $$.*

Matt's Place They call it a drive-in, and it's true that you can get curbside service if you just honk. But most people go inside and sit at the counter, where Butte natives have been enjoying burgers and fries since the Depression. It's not often you find a drive-in that's been run by the same woman (octogenarian Mabel "Mae" Laurence) for more than half a century—or, for that matter, a drive-in that peels, cuts, and cooks french fries to order, shapes burger patties from 100 percent ground round, and makes malts from ice cream that packs a whopping 17 percent butterfat content. Sure, it's Cholesterol City, but it hasn't seemed to bother owner Laurence any. Most locals stick with a burger, fries, and a malt, but you can push the envelope and try a nutburger (topped with mayo and chopped nuts) or a fried egg sandwich. *At Montana St and Rowe Rd, next to the gas station; 2339 Placer, Butte; (406) 782-8049; lunch, dinner Tues–Sun; no credit cards; checks OK; $.*

Lodgings

Copper King Mansion ☆☆ A gem. You can't help but feel pampered when you spend a night at the Copper King, William A. Clark's elaborate three-story mansion. Sure, the floor's beginning to wear and the plaster's cracking in a few spots, but for the most part the place is absolutely stunning, lovingly maintained by owner Erin Sigl. Though many of Clark's possessions were sold before Sigl's grandmother bought the house in 1953, she's retained the flavor with her family's period antiques, glassware collections, and china; staying here is like staying in a museum. Of four bedrooms, the master suite with its hand-carved bed, fireplace, separate sitting area, and enormous bathroom is the nicest (and most expensive), but the family room, with its hand-painted ceiling, runs a close second. Two pretty back bedrooms share a bath, but that's part of the fun—it contains the mansion's original bird-cage shower, an elaborate contraption that sprays you from all sides (and nearly drowns most guests). At $55 a night, these back bedrooms are some of the best lodging bargains in the region. From May to October, guests are required to breakfast at 7:30am in order to check out before the first public tour at 9am. Off-season you can linger as long as you like. Breakfasts are not the production the setting might lead you to expect, but you'll be too busy soaking up the atmosphere to notice. A full house tour is free to guests. *Uptown, at the corner of Granite and Idaho; 219 W Granite, Butte, MT 59701; (406) 782-7580; AE, MC, V; checks OK; $-$$$.*

Best Western Copper King Park Hotel In most cases, we avoid airport hotels, but the Butte airport isn't busy enough to be a problem. This 150-room hotel is Butte's best, with a nice indoor swimming pool and exercise room, and accommodating service. For an additional fee, hotel guests can use the indoor tennis courts at the adjacent Copper Dome Racquet Club. Poolside rooms may be noisy; the pool stays open until 11pm. The quietest rooms are in the back, but views are best from the front. *2 miles south of I-90, near Bert Mooney Airport; 4655 Harrison Ave S, Butte, MT 59701; (800) 332-8600 or (406) 494-6666; AE, DIS, MC, V; checks OK; $$.*

Blue Heron On the second floor of an unassuming downtown building in Philipsburg, the tasteful interior of the Blue Heron bed and breakfast comes as a welcome surprise. Owners Myrlin Rasmussen and John Ohrmann left their ranch in Drummond to remodel this former boardinghouse, decorating it with their antiques and artwork. Of five available rooms, by far the best is the front suite, which comes with private bathroom. The remaining four rooms are very small and share a bath, but the common area is spacious, and prices are good value, particularly off season. Breakfast is guest's choice. *Downtown, upstairs; 138 W Broadway, PO Box 821, Philipsburg, MT 59858; (406) 859-3856; no credit cards; checks OK; $-$$.*

Scott Bed and Breakfast Located next door to William Clark's original mine site high above the city, this three-story brick served as a miners' boarding house before it fell into disrepair. California transplants (and absentee owners) Everett and Donna Sheffield have completely renovated the Scott into a spiffy B&B that would surely make those miners green with envy. Seven rooms, each with private bath, are small but comfortable, and there's a lovely sitting/dining area on the second floor as well as a TV room on the ground floor. (For that reason, third-floor rooms are apt to be more quiet.) Breakfasts, prepared by the innkeeper, are special, four-course affairs. *1 block north of the Silver Bow County courthouse, just east of Montana St; 15 W Copper, Butte, MT 59701; (406) 723-7030; DIS, MC, V; checks OK; $$.*

Backcountry Cabins

The Forest Service's *Recreational Cabin and Lookout Directory* lists all back-country options. Rental rates generally fall between $15 and $30/night. To request a copy, contact the Beaverhead/Deerlodge National Forests Supervisor's Office in Dillon, (406) 683-3900, or any district office.

Originally built to house miners, **Doney Lake Cabin** sits 11 miles northwest of Deer Lodge in the Flint Creek Range with good access to alpine hiking trails. Don't be fooled by the name, though; Doney Lake is more like a swamp, and the water is not potable so you'll have to bring your own. The cabin sleeps six; there's a wood stove and some kitchen utensils, but after problems with vandalism no one's guaranteeing what you'll find there. The cabin's available year-round. In summer you can drive right to the door; in winter, depending on snow depth, you'll be able to drive within about 5 miles of the cabin. Deerlodge Ranger District, (406) 846-1770.

The more modern **Douglas Creek Cabin** is located in a creekside clearing about 10 miles northeast of Philipsburg. Generally you can drive to the door year-round, where you should find plenty of privacy, except during hunting season. You can boil and drink creek water, but in sum-mer the water level may be unreliable. The wood-stove heated cabin sleeps six; some utensils are available, but many are missing. Deerlodge Ranger District, (406) 846-1770.

On Stony Creek across from Squaw Creek Campground, which pro-vides water, **Stony Cabin** is open year-round—though in winter you may have to walk or ski the last quarter-mile. The cabin sleeps four. Bring propane and utensils. From the cabin you can walk the quarter-mile to Rock Creek or hike to Stony Lake. It's 19 miles northwest of Philipsburg in the Sapphire Mountains. Philipsburg Ranger District, (406) 859-3211.

The road to **Moose Lake Guard Station** is open year-round though, again, in winter you may have to walk or ski the last quarter-mile. The cabin sleeps four; bring your own cooking utensils and propane. It's in a timbered valley 24 miles southwest of Philipsburg, close to good fishing on the middle fork of Rock Creek. Philipsburg Ranger District, (406) 859-3211.

More Information

Anaconda–Pintler Wilderness Coordinator, Bitterroot National Forest, Sula Ranger District: (406) 821-3201.

Beaverhead/Deerlodge National Forest Supervisor's Office, Dillon: (406) 683-3900.

Beaverhead/Deerlodge NF, Butte Ranger District: (406) 494-2147.

Beaverhead/Deerlodge NF, Deerlodge Ranger District: (406) 846-1770.

Beaverhead/Deerlodge NF, Jefferson Ranger District: (800) 433-9206 or (406) 287-3223.

Beaverhead/Deerlodge NF, Philipsburg Ranger District: (406) 859-3211.

Butte-Silver Bow Chamber of Commerce: (800) 735-6814 or (406) 494-5595.

Great Divide Cyclery: (406) 782-4726.

Montana Department of Fish, Wildlife and Parks, Butte: (406) 821-3201.

Montana Department of Fish, Wildlife and Parks, Missoula: (406) 542-5500.

Ski Discovery: (406) 563-2184.

Beaverhead and Big Hole Valleys

Including Dillon, Bannack, the Beaverhead and Big Hole Rivers, and the Pioneer Mountains.

In August of 1805, the explorers Lewis and Clark camped near what is now the town of Dillon at Beaverhead Rock. Nearly six decades later, this southwestern corner of the region became one of the first areas to be settled: in 1862, gold was discovered on Grasshopper Creek 20 miles west of Dillon—the first major gold strike in what was to become the Montana territory. Flooded with fortune seekers, the strike town of Bannack quickly swelled to a population of 3,000 and became the first territorial capital.

Dillon (city pop: 4,000, county pop: 9,200) sprung up where it is—in the arid sagebrush-covered Beaverhead Valley—because of the stubbornness of one rancher and the business savvy of a few others. In 1880, construction of the Utah and Northern Railroad was halted here by a rancher who refused to sell an easement. Headed by Lambert Eliel, a group of local businessmen who had a stake in the area's development bought out the rancher, and not only granted the right-of-way to the railroad, but also founded Dillon to boot. Dillon later became the Beaverhead County seat because the gold-mining town Bannack was considered too isolated. The railroad tracks remain the defining feature of Dillon (they parallel the main street and run past the historic Hotel Metlen); freight trains still pull right past the Beaverhead Chamber of Commerce, housed in the old depot.

These days Dillon serves as a trading center for cattle and

sheep ranchers spread out overmiles of open range. For a college town (Western Montana College, an arm of the University of Montana, is located here), it's sleepier than you might expect. Aside from the Labor Day rodeo, when open-container laws are suspended, the biggest draws are the legendary salmonfly hatch each June along the nearby Big Hole River and the fall big-game hunting season. Many people also trek to Dillon to shop at the Patagonia clothing manufacturer's outlet. And Dillon is the unlikely national headquarters for the ever-expanding Great Harvest Bread Company, although you can't buy even a single loaf of the stuff there (it's simply an administrative center and training ground for new franchisees).

The Beaverhead and Big Hole Valleys are extraordinarily rural; what are marked on maps as towns often turn out to be little more than a tavern and a couple of fly-fishing outfitters. Drive through during haying season and you'll see how the Big Hole Valley got the nickname, "Valley of 10,000 Haystacks." Rather than bale their crops, local farmers use beaverslides to stack their hay into what appear to be giant loaves of bread. Despite fishing and hunting, agriculture remains the economic mainstay of the area.

Newcomers to the Big Hole and Beaverhead Valleys generally have already found their fortunes elsewhere; take, for instance, the powerhouse couple Ted Turner and Jane Fonda, who've recently purchased a large spread along the Beaverhead River south of Dillon to add to their already sizable land holdings near Bozeman. Like other areas of western Montana, the southwestern part of the state is experiencing an influx of outsiders, though the growth is decidedly smaller here. Tourists are welcome, but so far the tourism industry has not been very well developed, making the Big Hole and Beaverhead Valleys a haven for people looking for "the real Montana"—as long as you realize that that means foregoing luxury in favor of authenticity.

Getting There

Dillon can be reached from Interstate 15, 65 miles south of Butte, which is where the closest airport (Bert Mooney) lies. It is also served by Greyhound Bus Lines.

Adjoining Areas

NORTH: **Butte and Environs**

EAST: **West Yellowstone and the Madison Valley**

WEST: **Bitterroot Valley**

inside out

Fishing

The Big Hole and Beaverhead Rivers are two of the state's most popular fishing destinations, so there is no shortage of capable, licensed guides to float them. Most guides will also address Clark Canyon Reservoir, too. Get **licenses, regulations,** and more information through the Montana Department of Fish, Wildlife and Parks in Bozeman, (406) 994-4042, or any of the outfitters below. Montana Afloat makes **maps** of the Beaverhead, the Big Hole, and other rivers, which are available at outdoor stores.

For a complete list of **outfitters,** write the Fishing Outfitters Association of Montana (FOAM), Box 67, Gallatin Gateway, MT 59730. Among those we recommend are Tony Schoonen, Butte, (406) 782-1560; Frank Stanchfield's Troutfitters, just north of Wise River, (406) 832-3212; Dave Decker's Complete Fly Fishing Company, Wise River, (406) 832-3175; Lyle Reynolds' Sundown Outfitters, Melrose, (406) 835-2751; Dick Sharon of Fishing Headquarters, Dillon, (406) 683-6660; Tim Tollett of Frontier Anglers, Dillon, (406) 683-5276; Monty Hankinson of M & M Outfitters, Dillon, (406) 683-4579; and Bill T. Kemph of Red Rock Outfitters, Dillon, (406) 683-5651.

The **Big Hole River** offers exceptional fishing for rainbows and browns, with the occasional grayling, cutthroat, brookie, and whitefish. Mid-June through the Fourth of July there's a renowned salmonfly hatch; all summer and through September there are daily caddis fly hatches. There's good shore access for 50-plus miles from Squaw Creek east of Wisdom all the way to Glen, but it's best to float the Big Hole, especially through the canyon between Dewey and Divide and through Maiden Rock Canyon south of Divide to Melrose. Maps and more information are also available from Fran Johnson's Sport Store in Butte, (406) 782-3322.

Fish the **Beaverhead River** below Clark Canyon Dam to its confluence with the Jefferson for big (2- to 5-pound) browns and rainbows; the fishing tends to be best in the upper section, between the dam and Dillon. Though the Beaverhead doesn't have a salmonfly hatch like its renowned neighbor, it does boast daily caddis hatches and late summer or early fall brings a cranefly hatch. There are plenty of access points all along the river. Get current information through the Buffalo Lodge on Clark Canyon Reservoir, (406) 683-5535.

You can fish **Clark Canyon Reservoir** year-round for 3- to 6-pound rainbows and browns (they can get up to 10 pounds). Trollers and bank fishermen do well in spring, fly-fishermen score in summer, and everyone does well in the fall. **Ice fishing** for rainbows, browns, and ling (burbot) is exceptional. Obtain current information from the Buffalo Lodge, (406) 683-5535.

Most of the high mountain lakes in the Pioneer Mountains have fish. You can drive to **Brownes Lake,** about 30 miles northwest of Dillon, and from there hike 2 steep miles to **Agnes Lake,** a good grayling fishery. Take I-15 north 22 miles to the Glen exit and follow the signs west 8 miles up Rock Creek. Or try any of the lakes in the Birch Creek area, also about 30 miles northwest of Dillon (take the Apex exit off I-15); **Deerhead Lake** is well-known for its cutts. In addition to the above sources, try the Dillon Ranger District, (406) 683-3900 for fishing information.

Hiking/Backpacking

The Beaverhead and Deerlodge National Forests have been combined, but for the meantime the **maps** remain separate. Get a Beaverhead National Forest Service Map (west half), or an Interagency Visitor Map for Southwestern Montana. We prefer the former, which is more readable, though the latter covers a wider territory and indicates road closures and trail restrictions. Maps are available through the Beaverhead/Deerlodge National Forest Supervisor's Office in Dillon, (406) 683-3900, or at any district office and area outdoor stores. The Dillon Ranger District, (406) 683-3900, has a printed packet with **descriptions** of popular hikes; the Beaverhead Chamber of Commerce, (406) 683-5511, also has written descriptions of many area trails.

This is very remote and rugged hiking. You will want to be in good shape and check with the local ranger station about trail conditions, but here are a few suggestions to get you started. (See also Backcountry Cabins, below, for other options.)

Several agencies maintain the 237-mile Beaverhead National Forest segment of the **Continental Divide National Scenic Trail,** (or "CD trail") as it traverses the rugged and remote Montana-Idaho border from the Anaconda–Pintler Wilderness to the Gallatin National Forest. Of particular note is the high, mostly treeless country around the Italian Peaks, in the very southwest corner of the state. Some of the segments in the Beaverhead are on roads, some on trails. Segments of the trail are heavily used by fall hunters, but in the summer this is little-traveled. Day hikes are possible, but it's best to spend at least a night or two because trailheads are remote; generally it's a 4- to 5-mile hike to access the CD trail. The trails are not snow-free until early to mid-July. The main trail passes by numerous stocked lakes, though you may have to bushwack to get to them. The Dillon Ranger District, (406) 683-3900, can provide a map on which the CD trail is highlighted; for the southernmost section of the trail in Montana's Centennial Mountains, contact the Bureau of Land Management in Dillon, (406) 683-2337.

You can access several lakes in the Birch Creek area 30 miles northwest of Dillon. **Rainbow Lake** is an easy 1-miler, from which you can continue on another couple of miles to **Agnes Lake** (where there's good fishing for grayling). Other easy day hikes in the same area include **Tendoy** and **Long Lakes.** From Dillon, drive 12 miles north on I-15 to the Apex/Birch Creek exit. Take Birch Creek Road west 9 miles to Willow Creek Rd, then take Willow Creek Rd another 10 ½ miles to the trailhead.

The 3-mile trail to **Sawtooth Lake** near Polaris climbs steadily, gaining 1,600 feet before topping out at the 8,511-foot lake, which sits in a forested basin between Sawtooth and Goat Mountains. Sawtooth Lake contains brook and golden trout, and is popular with local hikers. Motorcycles also are permitted in summer but aren't too common. When you come out you can soak in the nearby Elkhorn Hot Springs. The trailhead is about 37 miles northwest of Dillon, off the gravel road leading to Elkhorn Hot Springs and the Pioneer Mountains Scenic Byway (see Attractions, below). From Highway 278, drive 9 ½ miles north and turn right on Clark Creek Rd. The trailhead is 2 miles up Clark Creek Rd, past the subdivision.

Camping

Public campgrounds are marked and listed on Forest Service maps; for the area around Dillon and the Big Hole and Beaverhead Valleys, you'll want a Beaverhead National Forest (west half) map or an Interagency Visitor Map of Southwestern Montana. For a complete list of all private and public campgrounds, refer to Travel Montana's *Montana Travel Planner,* widely available at chambers of commerce and many local hotels and motels (or call (800) 847-4868 out-of-state, (406) 444-2654 in-state). Look under "Gold West Country."

The Forest Service maintains eight campgrounds along the Pioneer Mountains Scenic Byway, which links Hwy 278, about 25 miles northwest of Dillon, to Hwy 43 at Wise River. The nicest are **Fourth of July, Willow, Lodgepole,** and **Boulder Campgrounds;** you can also camp for free at **Grasshopper Campground** near Elkhorn Hot Springs (spend your money for a soak instead). Wise River Ranger District, (406) 689-3243.

The **Twin Lakes Campground** offers an opportunity to drive to a high alpine lake (it sits at 7,200 feet) in the formidable shadow of the Continental Divide, but you'll need a high-clearance vehicle to get there. Most of the 21 campsites at Twin Lakes offer views of the lakes, which are closed to motorized boats, while a nearby trailhead offers access to the Continental Divide Trail. The campground doesn't usually open until mid- to late June. It's about 25 miles southwest of Wisdom; from Wisdom, drive south 7 miles on Hwy 278, then turn west on Briston Lane and follow the signs. Wisdom Ranger District, (406) 689-3243.

The recently upgraded **Divide Recreation Area** offers camping on the Big Hole River. It's very scenic but also very busy, especially during the salmonfly hatch in late June. Call the Bureau of Land Management in Dillon, (406) 683-2337, for more information.

Mountain Biking

The Dillon Ranger District, (406) 683-3900, publishes a mountain bike guide with **descriptions** of area trails. Rent bikes or get maps at Bad Beaver Bikes, Skis & Tours, in Dillon (25 E Helena, (406) 683-9292). Owner Ed Renfro runs day and multi-day trips in the Beaverhead National Forest and on private land; meals are included. The store is a good source of biking information, even if you don't plan on signing up for a guided tour.

The best riding in the Dillon area is in the little-used Pioneer Mountains north of town. The **Birch Creek** area offers a number of trails suitable for intermediate to advanced riders. From Dillon, take I-15 north 12 miles to the Apex/Birch Creek exit. Drive 9 miles on Birch Creek Rd, then lean right on Willow Creek Rd and drive another 6 miles to the trailhead sign and map. There are plenty of lakes in this area; try the tough but beautiful 6-mile loop to **Rainbow Lake,** returning along Willow Creek Rd. Or park at the Dinner Station Campground at the end of Birch Creek Rd and ride up to **Pear Lake** (5 1/2 miles one way, mostly moderate with a mile of tough climbing), surrounded by the 10,000-foot peaks of the Tent and Sawtooth Mountains. It's a good idea to get either a Beaverhead National Forest (west half) map or an Interagency Visitor Map of Southwest Montana (see Camping, above).

Horseback Riding

The wide open range land and miles and miles of rugged alpine country in southwestern Montana lend themselves to horse packing. Dillon-based Claris Yuhas's, hour, 2-hour and half-day rides come recommended; call (406) 683-2593 for information. Diamond Hitch Outfitters, also in Dillon, (800) 368-5494 or (406) 683-5494, takes guests into the Pioneer Mountains north of Dillon for all-day pack and fish rides. Diamond Hitch also offers multi-day horse pack trips; riders may base themselves at Sand Lake or move camp daily through more rugged country. Shorter rides are also available. Montana High Country Tours, (406) 834-3469, offers half-day and day rides, plus cattle drives and pack trips in the Elkhorn Mountains near Elkhorn Hot Springs.

Based in the far southwestern corner of the state, in Lima, Mel and Chris Montgomery of Centennial Outfitters, (406) 276-3463, offer day and multi-day trips in the remote Centennial Mountains along the Continental Divide Trail and in the Lima Peaks area. They can set up cattle drives, and they are flexible and will work with you to design a trip specified to your needs.

Snowmobiling

Hundreds of miles of snowmobile trails link the communities of southwestern Montana via both open meadows and river drainages. Snowmobilers tend to congregate on the 23-mile **Wise River-Elkhorn Hot Springs National Snowmobile Trail** along the Pioneer Mountains Scenic Byway; it's groomed once a week and provides access to powder parks and hill climbs. It also links to trails that lead all the way to Wisdom and Wise River, as well as to Salmon, Idaho, with the right snow conditions. Sledders also drive through the Centennial Valley, which connects West Yellowstone, the self-described "snowmobile capital of the world," with Lima.

Get a **map** of the Pioneer Mountains snowmobile trails through the Beaverhead/Deerlodge National Forest Supervisor's Office in Dillon, at the Wise River or Wisdom Ranger Districts, or at Elkhorn Hot Springs. Montana High Country Tours, (406) 834-3469, also provides maps, rents snowmobiles, and gives guided tours. (Also see Backcountry Cabins, below.)

Cross-Country Skiing

Bad Beaver Bikes, Skis & Tours, in Dillon (25 E Helena, (406) 683-9292) rents skis. Owner Ed Renfro also leads guided day and multi-day ski tours.

The best cross-country skiing around Dillon is at the **Mount Haggin Wildlife Recreation Area,** 80 miles north (see the Butte and Environs chapter).

The ungroomed cross-country ski trails originating at **Elkhorn Hot Springs** are beautiful but steep. Some of them share track with snowmobilers. You'll find a brochure and map at the base of the trails, which start at the Elkhorn Hot Springs Resort, (800) 722-8978 or (406) 834-3434, due east of Jackson; take Hwy 278 another 10 miles, then turn north on the Pioneer Mountains Scenic Byway (it's marked) and drive 14 miles.

Additional cross-country skiing can be found at Big Hole National Battlefield (see Attractions, below).

Downhill Skiing

Like most ski resorts in western Montana, **Maverick Mountain** can be very, very good—but when it's bad, it's horrid. This isolated, family-oriented ski hill in the Pioneers has 18 runs on a 2,120 foot vertical; it's served by a double chair and rope tow. Two-thirds of the terrain is suitable for intermediate skiers, with the remaining slopes equally split between beginner and advanced runs. Snow conditions vary greatly; you would do well to call before making the trip. Generally the season runs from mid-December until April. This is a day-use facility only, open Thursday through Sunday, and patronized mostly by locals. Ski and snowboard rentals are available, as is day care with reservations. Maverick Mountain is 35 miles northwest of Dillon, 13 miles off Hwy 278 on the Pioneer Mountains Scenic Byway, (406) 834-3454.

outside in

Attractions

Retired Forest Service ranger Dan Pence and his wife, Lois, offer one-day **historical tours** of the Big Hole Battlefield, the Lewis and Clark Trail, Bannack, and other sites of interest through his Great Divide Wildlands Institute in Dillon, (406) 683-4669. They also offer in-depth five-day tours concentrating on natural history, local industry, and wildlife.

Stop at the visitors center and walk the trails at the hauntingly beautiful **Big Hole National Battlefield,** the site of one of the more shameful and tragic chapters of American history. In 1877, five "non-treaty" bands of Nez Perce Indians fled their ancestral homelands in northeastern Oregon and central Idaho in an attempt to escape the US military, with whom they'd been in conflict over a new treaty that reduced the Nez Perce reservation to one-tenth its original size. Thinking they had outrun their pursuers, 800 Indians with 2,000 horses were camped in the Big Hole Valley the night of August 9, 1877. Unbeknownst to the Indians, a second Montana-based infantry had joined the chase, and on the morning of August 10, the Indians were awakened by a surprise attack. Upwards of 60 Nez Perce, many of them women and children, died in the battle; the US Army lost 29 soldiers. The so-called Nez Perce War didn't end until after an arduous journey of 1,300 miles. On September 30, 1877, just 40 miles from the Canadian border and freedom, Chief Joseph surrendered in his famous "I will fight no more forever" speech. Some 200 Nez Perce did make it to Canada, and a few hid in the mountains, but Chief Joseph and 431 remaining Nez Perce were moved to reservations. The rest had died in battles en route. Seven enlisted men who had fought on the army's side in the Battle of the Big Hole received Congressional Medals of Honor.

The visitors center has a small exhibit room and plays a video that explains the significance of the battle; two short, self-guided interpretive trails lead to the Indian camp and the area where the US soldiers lay under siege for nearly 24 hours. It's well worth the time to visit these eerie sites; in winter, you can cross-country ski the trails, though temperatures and wind conditions may be extreme. On the weekend closest to the anniversary of the Battle of the Big Hole, the National Park Service holds commemorative activities. The battleground is 10 miles west of Wisdom on Hwy 43, (406) 689-3155.

Montana's first territorial capital, **Bannack,** was also the site of the territory's first major gold strike (in 1862), first jail, first hotel, first school, first chartered Masonic lodge, first hard rock mining, and first commercial sawmill. Once home to a population of 3,000, Bannack is now a ghost town, preserved as a state park. Some buildings are in better shape than others: the Masonic Temple has its original furniture and symbolic rugs; the Apex Mill still claims its original ore-milling equipment. There are few interpretive signs, but a self-guided walking tour is available at the entrance for a quarter (called the *Bannack Free Press*, it looks like a reproduction of an old newspaper). You can camp along Grasshopper Creek; the upper sites have more shade. The third weekend in July the state puts on Bannack Days, a recreation of 19th-century life. Bannack is reached by paved road 4 miles south of Hwy 278, 25 miles west of Dillon. The park is open during daylight hours, November through March (weather permitting). Bannack State Park, (406) 834-3413.

May 15 through September, you can rockhound for quartz crystals at **Crystal Park** north of Elkhorn Hot Springs. Even neophytes won't have any trouble finding the crystals, which are abundantly scattered through the decomposed granite. Bring a shovel, hand trowel, and gloves; you may also want a screen with quarter-inch mesh. Administered by the Forest Service and the Butte Mineral and Gem Club, Crystal Park is a free facility, though donations are gratefully accepted. There's often a host present to answer questions. A wheelchair-accessible trail leads to the crystal digging area. Call the Dillon Ranger District, (406) 683-3900, for details.

Two commercial **hot springs** operate in the area, and while both leave something to be desired, we know we'd be taken to task for leaving them out. Jackson Hot Springs, 48 miles west of Dillon, (406) 834-3151, has one enclosed outdoor soaking pool, a large lodge with video games and gambling machines, and several overpriced cabins. Past management has shown a lack of hospitality, but things may have changed. Elkhorn Hot Springs Resort, (800) 722-8978 or (406) 834-3434, has two outdoor soaking pools and a very hot indoor one as well; the setting is stunning but the overnight facilities are unacceptable: lodge rooms are dilapidated and cabins are furnished with cheap, ripped furniture and bare light bulbs (and the cabins don't have indoor plumbing). If we had to pick, we'd soak at Elkhorn, then camp at nearby Grasshopper Campground or any of several other campgrounds along the **Pioneer Mountains Scenic Byway**. Jackson Hot Springs is located in Jackson on Hwy 278, 18 miles south of Wisdom. Elkhorn Hot Springs is located due east of Jackson; take Hwy 278 another 10 miles, then turn north on the Pioneer Mountains Scenic Byway (it's marked) and drive 14 miles.

Calendar of Events

Held the third weekend in July in Montana's first territorial capital, **Bannack Days** recreates the gold-mining era with frontier crafts, music, drama, and food. Bannack State Park, (406) 834-3413.

The **Dillon Jaycees Rodeo** takes place Labor Day weekend at the Beaverhead County Fairgrounds. Patty Loveless was a recent headliner—not too shabby for a small town. Caveat emptor, however: open-container laws are suspended for the weekend. Call the Beaverhead Chamber of Commerce, (406) 683-5511, for details.

Restaurants

Despite some inconsistencies in the kitchen, and entrees that may be a little too "dressed-up" for locals, the **Centennial Inn** (122 S Washington, (800) 483-4454 or (406) 683-4454), a lovely renovated Victorian home, is the most pleasant place to eat in Dillon. The **Buffalo Lodge** on Clark Canyon Reservoir (19 miles south of Dillon, (406) 683-5535), has good steaks and prime rib and, hands-down, the best sunset views.

Yesterday's Calf-A Touristy as it looks from the outside—the grounds are littered with old ranching paraphernalia and a little "museum" is out back—this former schoolhouse-turned-cafe serves as the local meeting place for Beaverhead Valley residents, which makes it a lot of fun. While the menu is standard cafe fare, pretty much everything—including hashbrowns, hamburger buns, salad dressings, pies, and doughnuts—is made from scratch, a rare find these days. So what if the coffee is Folger's and not some fancy, locally roasted brew? The roast beef is renowned, and where else are you going to find buttermilk on the menu? In deference to tourists, breakfast is served until 11:30am. *At the Dell exit off I-15, 35 miles south of Dillon; Dell; (406) 276-3308; breakfast, lunch, dinner every day; no credit cards; local checks only; $.*

Lodgings

Beaverhead Rock Ranch Guest Houses ☆ Located along a private stretch of the Beaverhead River just south of Dillon, these two private homes are some of the nicest and most reasonably priced, self-contained accommodations we've seen, perfect for independent travelers. Stay in either a recently renovated, comfortably furnished two-bedroom farm-house or, even better, in a beautifully restored century-old cabin (closed during winter months). There's nothing fancy here, but the places are spotless and tastefully furnished—very homey. Both places have fully fur-nished kitchens, washing machines, and weekly housekeeping, as well as stunning views of the rocky cliffs along the river. Owners Gary and Sonja Williams tend to let guests alone, but as former director of the Beaverhead County Museum, Sonja is a fine source of information about the area; she can recommend outfitters and activities. The only drawback about these guest houses is that freeway traffic noise intrudes on their idyllic setting. All considered, that's a minor complaint. There's a 2-night minimum, and Beaverhead is closed from December to February. *6 miles south of Dillon—from Exit 56, drive south on the frontage road and cross the railroad tracks into the campground, then follow the private drive leading over a bridge from the parking lot; 4325 Old Stage Rd, Dillon, MT 59725; (800) 338-0061 or (406) 683-2126; no credit cards; checks OK; $$.*

Centennial Inn ☆ Cattle ranchers Jean and Sandy James came in off the range to lovingly restore the Centennial, a fine example of Dillon's old Queen Anne-style Victorian homes. Breakfast is served downstairs, where the Jameses run a restaurant by the same name. Upstairs, four spacious rooms, all with private baths (and claw-footed tubs) are tastefully deco-rated with antiques. Best, and no more expensive than the others, is the gracious Tilton Room, in the front of the house, with a fainting couch and attached sitting room. As artistic director of the Dillon Junior Fiddlers, Jean welcomes piano playing in the restaurant; ask nicely and Sandy might even accompany you on the fiddle, or perform a few of his hilari-ous cowboy songs. The restaurant continues the Victorian theme, with waitstaff in period costumes, and a Saturday afternoon high tea. The Jameses can also arrange archaeological and horseback tours near their ranch, 45 miles south on the remote Horse Prairie. *2 blocks south of the Beaverhead County Museum; 122 S Washington, Dillon, MT 59725; (800) 483-4454 or (406) 683-4454; MC, V; checks OK; $$.*

Best Western Paradise Inn "Paradise" may be stretching it a little, but Dillon's Best Western, located on the main drag a stone's throw from downtown, does have the town's best motel digs, with a small, indoor heated pool and hot tub. To avoid traffic noise, you'll want to be in the curve of the 65-room, U-shaped layout; ask for rooms 122 through 125 or, even better, 225 through 228, or 230 through 235. Live a little and get a suite ($70/night), with a huge bathtub and extra living space. Winters are slow, but during fishing season things get hopping; reservations are a good idea. *Near Exit 63 off I-15; 650 N Montana St, Dillon, MT 59725; (406) 683-4214; AE, DIS, MC, V; no checks; $.*

Backcountry Cabins

The Forest Service rents backcountry cabins and lookouts that are no longer in use; rates run from $15 to $30 per night. For a complete list of all available cabins and lookouts, request the *Northern Region Recreational Cabin and Lookout Directory* from any ranger district.

Available December through March only, the **Hogan Cabin** sits in a high mountain meadow with a creek running through it. You'll need a sleeping bag, food, and something to boil your water in. There are three trails to the cabin: easiest is from Shoofly Trailhead, 4 miles east of Chief Joseph Pass on Hwy 43. The 3 ½-mile trail, known as the "Shoofly Alternate," because it veers off from the more difficult Shoofly trail, is suitable for intermediate skiers. You won't see snowmobiles—they're not allowed—but expect to hear plenty of them. The Forest Service begins taking reservations October 15 (or the closest Monday); you've got to be quick to get weekend reservations—they fill up within 2 hours. Wisdom Ranger District, (406) 689-3243.

An easy 2 ½-mile trail follows the drainage from May Creek Campground to the **May Creek Cabin,** 8 miles east of Chief Joseph Pass on Hwy 43. You'll need a sleeping bag and food. The area is open to snowmobilers but tends to be less popular with them than the trails around the Hogan Cabin. Winter weekend reservations open October 15 (or the closest Monday) and are snapped up within a couple of hours; May Creek Cabin is also open July through Labor Day. Wisdom Ranger District, (406) 689-3243.

In summer, it's a 2 ½-mile hike to the **Foolhen Cabin,** 12 miles west of Wise River at the north end of the Pioneers. Winter and spring access is pretty much limited to snowmobiles (and very hardy skiers), since the road is only plowed within 12 miles of the cabin. Available December through August. Wise River Ranger District, (406) 832-3178.

More Information

Bannack State Park: (406) 834-3413.

Beaverhead Chamber of Commerce: (406) 683-5511.

Beaverhead/Deerlodge National Forest, Supervisor's Office, Dillon: (406) 683-3900.

Beaverhead/Deerlodge NF, Dillon Ranger District: (406) 683-3900.

Beaverhead/Deerlodge NF, Wisdom Ranger District: (406) 689-3243.

Beaverhead/Deerlodge NF, Wise River Ranger District: (406) 689-3243.

Bureau of Land Management: (406) 683-2337.

Gold West Country (an arm of Travel Montana): (800) 879-1159 or (406) 846-1943.

Montana Department of Fish, Wildlife and Parks: (406) 994-4042.

Travel Montana: (800) 847-4868 out-of-state or (406) 444-2654 in-state.

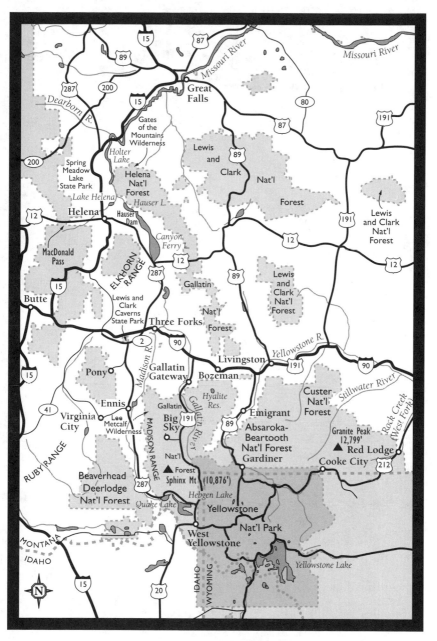

South Central Montana

South
Central
Montana

West Yellowstone and the Madison Valley

Including Ennis, Virginia City, Nevada City, and the Madison River.

The Madison River valley is a picture-perfect Hollywood rendition of Montana. You half expect to see the Lone Ranger galloping across the sagebrush-covered flats, triumphantly waving his white cowboy hat against the relief of mountains behind him. And, in fact, there was a time when the Lone Ranger could have been useful to the people who first settled here. Virginia City was founded in 1863 in the mountains between the Madison and Ruby Rivers, after gold was discovered in nearby Alder Gulch. Within a year, 10,000 people swarmed to the area; within 3 years, they would find more than $30 million worth of gold in them thar hills. Inevitably, along with the gold and the population increase came crime, from notorious road agents to vigilantes and the attendant murders and hangings.

Virginia City served as capital of the Territory of Montana from 1865 until 1875, when Helena obtained the honor. Though its permanent population has dwindled to a sparse 150, Virginia City still serves as the Madison County seat. In the 1940s, Charles Bovey and his wife, Sue, bought a substantial amount of the downtown area and restored it. Bovey also purchased what was left of nearby Nevada City and added to it, making a complete and accurate replica of a mining town. It was so convincing that it was used as the backdrop for the movies *Little Big Man* and *Return to Lonesome Dove,* among other Hollywood ventures.

Today the gold comes to the Madison Valley area in the form of Visa, MasterCard, and American Express—credit cards signed by tourists anxious to fish the renowned Madison River. One of the most beautiful rivers in Montana, the Madison is also one of Montana's most famous fisheries, with rainbow and brown trout and grayling. Anglers come from all over the world to cast into the waters of the Madison as it flows out of Yellowstone National Park through West Yellowstone and then north, between the Madison Range to the east and the Gravelly and Tobacco Root Mountains to the west, and finally winds up at Three Forks, where it joins the Gallatin and Jefferson Rivers to form the big Missouri.

West Yellowstone is best known as a gateway to the national park (the park entrance is a few blocks from downtown), but, in fact, it has its own attractions, one of which is its claim to be the "snowmobile capital of the world." In winter, you'll see—and hear—motorized sleds on the streets, and snowmobile tours and rentals are big business.

Many visitors wind up in the Madison Valley en route to Yellowstone National Park; others skip the park and its crowds entirely to concentrate on the valley's charms. You just might want to stop and see what it is they know.

Getting There

US Highway 287 parallels the Madison River from West Yellowstone to Ennis. Montana State Hwy 287 veers west from Ennis to Virginia and Nevada Cities and north to Twin Bridges. The closest year-round airport is Gallatin Field in Bozeman; the West Yellowstone Airport is open summers only. Greyhound Bus Lines also serve West Yellowstone.

Adjoining Areas

NORTH: **Bozeman and Environs**

EAST: **Yellowstone National Park**

WEST: **Beaverhead and Big Hole Valleys**

inside out

Fishing

One of the most famous waterways in Montana, the **Madison River** has historically been among the top three fisheries in the state, with rainbow and brown trout and occasional grayling. But **whirling disease,** a parasitic infection that attacks the cartilage of young rainbow trout, was discovered in the Madison in December 1994, and since then has decimated the huge population of rainbows between Hebgen Dam and Ennis Dam, killing off as much as 90 percent of the fish. That's the bad news. The good news is, so far the massive population of brown trout in the Madison has remained unaffected, and some large adult rainbows have escaped unscathed as well. Though its future (and the future of other Montana rivers and streams) remains uncertain, the Madison still ranks among the state's top trout streams.

The Montana Department of Fish, Wildlife and Parks has produced a set of **guidelines** to slow the spread of whirling disease, which so far has been detected in 30 streams and rivers in Montana, as well as waterways in 20 other states. The basic rules of thumb are to thoroughly clean and dry all gear before moving from one waterway to the next, and to never transplant a fish from one body of water to another. For more information, see the Northern Rockies Outdoor Primer in the front of this book or contact the Montana Department of Fish, Wildlife and Parks in Helena, (406) 444-4720.

The tiny town of Ennis claims four fishing stores, all with their own **guides, outfitters,** and other services. The Madison River Fishing Company, (800) 227-7127 or (406) 682-4293, hands out free maps of the Madison River, detailing when and where to fish. Their guiding services are well regarded, and they're also happy to dispense advice. Bob Walker of the T Lazy B Ranch, (406) 682-7288 (see Ranches and Resorts, below), also claims a fine reputation as an experienced outfitter. For nearly 20 years, he's been guiding trips on the Smith and Madison Rivers. The Tackle Shop, (800) 808-2832 or (406) 682-4263, is Orvis-endorsed and one of only two commercial outfitters with permits to fish and float Bear Trap Canyon, which runs through the spectacular Lee Metcalf Wilderness. These trips are severely limited in number, and reservations fill as much as a year in advance, so call ahead. In West Yellowstone, try Madison River Outfitters, (800) 646-9644 or (406) 646-96440; Arrick's Fishing Flies, (406) 646-7290; or Jacklin's, (406) 646-7336.

Most local fishing stores offer their own brochures with **maps and hatch charts** of the Madison River. Montana Afloat publishes commercial river maps, including one of the Madison, available at most stores. For **regulations** and information, contact the Montana Department of Fish, Wildlife and Parks in Bozeman, (406) 994-4042, or any of the shops listed above.

The best **wade fishing** on the Madison River is from just below Quake Lake to the West Fork Bridge, and from Varney Bridge to Ennis (but beware of the washboard road to Varney Bridge). You'll want to **float** between Lyons Bridge and the Ennis Campground. Spring runoff on the Madison generally clears in late June. Sometime between the end of June and July 4 the renowned salmonfly hatch begins; from mid-July through mid-August look for caddis, mayflies, and little stoneflies. Hopper fishing is very good from mid-August through mid-September; use streamers in mid-September for 2- to 3-pound spawning brown trout. The 35-mile stretch of the Madison from Quake Lake to Ennis is catch-and-release only for rainbows and grayling; from Varney Bridge to Ennis Lake you can hang onto a limited number of browns.

Sometime in mid-July to August, large schools of rainbow and brown trout begin cruising just beneath the surface of **Hebgen Lake,** gulping down the tricos and calibaetis mayflies that lie on the water, and offering internationally known "gulper" fishing opportunities. You'll want a float tube or boat; just cast your fly in the path of oncoming fish and wait for one of them to gulp.

Hiking/Backpacking

Hiking anywhere in the Greater Yellowstone ecosystem entails dealing with the possibility of bears, both black and grizzly: know proper **bear precautions.** Ranger districts can supply further information. Restrictions in place in the Greater Yellowstone area, including the Madison Range, specify keeping food in bear-proof containers or hanging it while not in camp. Both the Gardiner and Hebgen Lake Ranger Districts have loan programs for bear-proof storage gear.

Yellowstone Alpen Guides, (800) 858-3502 or (406) 646-9591, leads day trips in the Greater Yellowstone region; owner Scott Carsley is a former Yellowstone Park naturalist who knows his stuff. Following are some of our favorite day hikes; also see Backcountry Cabins, below.

The short, beautiful hike up **Red Canyon** switchbacks steadily as it follows Red Creek, until it opens up into a huge meadow near the top of the ridge, offering tremendous views of the Madison Valley and, if you climb high enough, the Lee Metcalf Wilderness. It's about 3 miles to the very top; from the ridge you can pick up the Cabin Creek or Tepee Creek trail. Do this one in August, when wildflowers are out in force. The trailhead is located 3 miles off US 287, about 4 miles west of the junction of US 287 and US 191. You'll see the sign for Red Canyon. Hebgen Lake Ranger District, (406) 646-7369.

The **Taylor-Hilgard Unit** of the **Lee Metcalf Wilderness** gets a great deal of hunting traffic in fall, which makes it a good place to explore during summer. The western portion is handled by the Madison Ranger District of the Beaverhead/Deerlodge National Forest; the eastern side is administered by the Hebgen Lake Ranger District of the Gallatin National Forest. To get to **Avalanche** and **Blue Danube Lakes,** follow the west fork of Beaver Creek; you'll hit Avalanche in 3 ½ miles; Blue Danube is another 1 ½ miles. A strong hiker can do this one in a day. The trailhead is about 3 ½ miles off US 287 up Beaver Creek Road, just east of the Quake Lake Visitors Center.

In-shape hikers can grunt up 10,876-foot **Sphinx Mountain,** a brutal 4,000-foot elevation gain over 5 miles, which is made up of unusual conglomerate rock. Watch for mountain goats and Old Ephraim (the mountain-man term for grizzly bears). The trailhead is 9 miles up Bear Creek Rd, which takes off from US 287 about 12 miles south of Ennis. Madison Ranger District, (406) 682-4253.

You may see mountain goats, mule deer, or elk as you hike into the **Coffin Lakes** on the west side of Hebgen Lake. The 4 ½-mile hike follows an old road bed for the first 2 miles, then continues to climb gradually along Watkins and Coffin creeks until about the last half-mile, when you grind up into the high alpine basin where the lakes sit. From West Yellowstone, take US 20 west 7 miles, then turn right on Hebgen Lake Rd; the trailhead is 9 ½ miles off US 20, about a mile past the Spring Creek Campground. Hebgen Lake Ranger District, (406) 646-7369.

There's no set trail to the top of **Black Butte,** at 10,546 feet the highest point in the Gravelly Range, but you can easily make the scramble over the shale and open country—it takes most people about 40 minutes. Black Butte is actually the core of an extinct volcano that's been eroded over eons. A good place to start is along the Gravelly Range Rd, 2 miles south of the junction of Standard Creek and Cottonwood Rds, just past the sign identifying Black Butte. Madison Ranger District, (406) 682-4253.

The challenging 6-mile hike to **Hollowtop Lake** out of Pony is steep and rocky, with a river crossing that may be deep in spring. But once you've arrived at this scenic cirque-enclosed lake you won't regret the effort. The trailhead is 2 miles outside Pony off US 287. Follow the drainage through town and continue upstream; when the road splits, go left. This trail is also open to motorcycles, so you might want to hike it during the week. Madison Ranger District, (406) 682-4253.

Camping

Public campgrounds are marked and listed on Forest Service maps. For the areas around West Yellowstone and Ennis, you will need a map of the western half of the Gallatin National Forest; for sites farther north in the Tobacco Roots, you'll want one covering the Deerlodge National Forest. For a complete list of all private and public campgrounds, refer to Travel Montana's *Montana Travel Planner,* widely available at chambers of com-

merce and many local hotels and motels (or call (800) 847-4868 out-of-
state, (406) 444-2654 in-state); look under "Gold West Country" or
"Yellowstone Country."

You can make advance **reservations** at five Forest Service campgrounds in the West Yellowstone/Hebgen Lake area through the national
system; call (800) 280-CAMP. You can also obtain information from the
Hebgen Lake Ranger District, (406) 646-7369. Two of these camp-
grounds—**Bakers Hole,** on the Madison River at the border of
Yellowstone National Park, and **Rainbow Point,** on the Grayling Arm of
Hebgen Lake—are limited to hard-sided camping vehicles for bear protection. The other three include the 26-site **Lonesomehurst
Campground,** which sits on the west shore of Hebgen Lake; the 65-unit
Beaver Creek Campground overlooking the Madison River; and the 16-
unit **Cabin Creek Campground,** located on the north end of Hebgen
Lake at the trailhead to the Cabin Creek Trail, which leads into the Cabin
Creek Wildlife Management Area. Only a portion of the sites are reserv-
able, but there is plenty of room for walk-ins. You'll find fewer people—
and fewer developed sites—on Hebgen Lake at **Cherry Creek** and **Spring
Creek Campgrounds,** both located on the lake's west shore. No reservations here, but call the Hebgen Lake Ranger District for information.

Get away from the crowds at the very pretty **Wade Lake
Campground,** which sits above isolated Wade Lake, part of the chain of
lakes southwest of Quake Lake. Surrounded by forested, low-lying hills,
the lakeshore is completely undeveloped except for the 30-site campground and Wade Lake Resort, a five-cabin resort where you can rent
canoes. There's decent fishing for browns and rainbows and a swimming
dock, too—but the water's spring-fed and quite cold. This is also a good
spot for bird-watching, especially for eagles, osprey, and mergansers. It's
27 miles west of the junction of US 287 and US 191, and 6 miles off US
287 on Forest Rd 5721 (you'll see the signs). Madison Ranger District,
(406) 682-4253.

The **Potosi Campground** is located along South Willow Creek in the
Tobacco Root Mountains north of Ennis, at the end of what can be horrific
road conditions driving from Pony. But there are a couple of incentives:
good hiking trails into the mountains and a trail to the natural **hot springs**
along South Willow Creek begin at the campground. Plus you're within a
couple of miles of the Lodge at Potosi Hot Springs, which serves some of
the best dinners in the state (see Restaurants, below). The campground is
3 miles southeast of Pony on County Rd 1601, 5 miles southwest on Forest
Rd 1501; it's well-signed. Madison Ranger District, (406) 682-4253.

The 6-site campground at **Upper Branham Lake,** 14 miles outside
Sheridan (north of Virginia City) in rugged alpine territory, often isn't

snow-free until late in the season. Once it opens, though, it provides an unusual opportunity to car camp at a high-elevation lake (and fish for brook trout). You may need a high-clearance vehicle to get there; towing a trailer is a poor idea. Call the Madison Ranger District's Sheridan Work Center, (406) 842-5432, for road and weather conditions.

Mountain Biking

The *Mountain Biker's Guide to West Yellowstone Area Trails* by Kurt Westenbarger (Chewy Press) is a slim little booklet chock-full of interesting rides in the West Yellowstone area. Pick up a copy at Free Heel and Wheel (40 Yellowstone Ave, West Yellowstone, (406) 646-7744) and other book and outdoor stores in town. Free Heel and Wheel also rents bikes.

The obvious place to mountain bike is on the **Rendezvous Ski Trails** cross-country trail system, a series of 20 miles of well-marked loop trails that begins at the corner of Geyser and Obsidian (you'll see the archway). Close to town, the trails are easy; they get tougher as you ride farther from town. You might see moose, elk, or ruffed grouse, and maybe grizzly bear tracks. One word of caution: please don't ride in wet or soft conditions, as these trails are maintained for cross-country skiers at considerable expense and effort. There's no charge, but donations are gratefully accepted in the box at the trailhead. The West Yellowstone Chamber of Commerce, (406) 646-7701, or the Hebgen Lake Ranger District, (406) 646-7369, can provide additional information.

Horseback Riding

Based near Virginia City, Vision Quest Horseback Rides of Alder offers 2-hour or all-day rides (the latter with a gourmet lunch) in the rugged **Ruby Mountains.** Groups are limited to five riders, who must be at least eight years old. Owners Dave and Julie Maddison come highly recommended; call (406) 842-5952 for more information.

Tim Beardsley Outfitting of Ennis, (406) 682-7292, does day rides and multi-day pack trips (some with fishing). Beardsley's is the only company permitted to do summer overnight trips in the stunning **Lee Metcalf Wilderness;** he also leads rides in Yellowstone National Park.

Parade Rest Ranch, 9 miles outside West Yellowstone, (800) 753-5934 or (406) 646-7217, offers 1-, 2-, and 4-hour rides, as well as full-day trips, into the Gallatin Range. On Mondays and Fridays, the ranch puts on a western cookout. Maximum rider weight is 210 pounds; children must be nine years or older, with younger children restricted to the corral. Sundays are a day of rest.

Kayaking/Rafting

North of Ennis, the Madison River gets wild and woolly as it flows through the famed **Bear Trap Canyon** in the Lee Metcalf Wilderness. Most of the rapids are Class III; the notorious Kitchen Sink rates a Class IV, but it's easily portaged. Put in below Ennis Dam; take out 10 miles downriver at Warm Springs off Hwy 84. Call the US Geological Survey for water flows at (406) 441-1319.

The Yellowstone Raft Company, (800) 348-4376 or (406) 995-4613, runs day trips through the whitewater of Bear Trap Canyon. Do-it-your-selfers can rent rafts and kayaks in Bozeman (see Rafting/Kayaking in the Bozeman chapter). Scott Darby at Rapid Discoveries in Bozeman, (406) 582-8110, provides good information and kayak lessons.

Scenic Drives

For expansive views and a feeling of remoteness, drive the spectacular **Gravelly Range Road,** which follows the 8,500-foot crest of the Gravelly Range for about 35 miles. A good 70-mile, 4-hour loop tour starts just south of Ennis on Varney Rd, then heads southwest on Call Rd to Gravelly Range Rd. Follow Gravelly Range Rd south for about 8 miles, then take Johnny Ridge Rd 12 miles to US 287, and circle back around. Considering its elevation, this road is in remarkably good shape.

Cross-Country Skiing

In West Yellowstone, rent touring and skate skis at Free Heel and Wheel (40 Yellowstone Ave, (406) 646-7744) or Yellowstone Alpen Guides (555 Yellowstone Ave, (800) 858-3502 or (406) 646-9591). The latter also leads ski tours in the area with a strong naturalist bent; owner Scott Carsley is a former Yellowstone National Park naturalist. For an overnight ski experience, see Backcountry Cabins, below.

Snowmobiles are not allowed on the **Rendezvous Ski Trails,** which are an official training site for the US Nordic and Biathlon teams. The trails begin just south of town at the corner of Obsidian and Geyser. During the November training camps, all 30-plus kilometers are groomed for diagonal stride and skate skiing; the rest of the season only about 12 kilometers are. In general, the trails closer to town are easiest. In November there's a charge of $45 per month or $7 per day; at other times the trails are free, though donations are welcome in a box at the trailhead. On Thanksgiving weekend there are 3- and 5-day and women's and junior race clinics. (See Calendar of Events, below.) Trails are well marked, and you can purchase passes at the Three Bear Lodge, Stagecoach Inn, or West

Yellowstone Chamber of Commerce, (406) 646-7701.

When the new snow is not too deep, beginner to intermediate back-country skiers practice their turns at **Telemark Meadows,** 18 miles north of West Yellowstone just inside the western border of Yellowstone National Park. It's an easy half-mile to get to the slopes, which are visible from the road. Take US 191 north to mile marker 18, look for the cars and ski tracks on the west side of the road.

Snowmobiling

You'll be right at home in West Yellowstone if you've got a motorized sled, and even if you don't, since just about every motel in town offers rental packages. The 32-mile **Two Top Loop,** the 32-mile **Horse Butte Loop,** and the 20-mile **Madison Arm Loop** are all groomed 6 days a week. Trails depart from the old airport in West Yellowstone. The Hebgen Lake Ranger District, (406) 646-7369, or West Yellowstone Chamber of Commerce, (406) 646-7701, can provide more details.

Many West Yellowstone-based companies also run **snowcoach tours** through Yellowstone National Park in oversized, covered snowmobiles (See the Yellowstone National Park chapter).

Wildlife

Located in the remote Centennial Valley, **Red Rock Lakes National Wildlife Refuge** was established in 1935 to protect the rare and lovely **trumpeter swan.** Today, the refuge is a significant breeding area for them, with about 100 swans in the vicinity. Red Rock Lakes is also renowned as one of the most beautiful wildlife refuges in the nation, though you really have to want to get there—the gravel roads leading to the 44,000-acre refuge are not very well maintained (check with refuge headquarters before attempting the notoriously poor Elk Lake Road, which accesses the refuge from the north). In addition to trumpeter swans you'll find thousands of birds living in the wetlands here, including **sandhill cranes.** Look for **moose** in the willows along the streambeds. You can camp on either the upper or lower lakes, and in the morning you'll be treated to a raucous symphony of bird calls. You can also canoe on the upper lake after July 15, while a terrific paddling trip between the two lakes opens after September 1. The lakes are 33 miles west of West Yellowstone, or 45 miles east of Lima. Refuge headquarters are at Lakeview, but several sign-boards stock informational flyers. Call Red Rock Lakes National Wildlife Refuge, (406) 276-3536.

Visitors are welcome at the **Ennis National Fish Hatchery,** one of three rainbow trout brood stock hatcheries in the nation. It provides 25 million eggs annually to hatcheries, universities, and fish technology centers in more than two dozen states. Once a week, usually Wednesdays, you can watch hatchery staff simulate the spawning process, fertilizing eggs and setting them in incubators. The hatchery is open daily year-round. It's 12 miles outside Ennis. From Ennis, take Hwy 287 west 2 miles, then drive south on Varney Rd 10 miles to the hatchery. Call (406) 682-4847 for details.

Other Activities

In winter, try **dogsledding** with Northern Lights Dog Sled Adventures. This outfit runs 1-hour ($30/person), half-day ($90/person), full-day ($150/person) and, weather permitting, moonlight trips in the Tobacco Root Mountains south of Pony. Brothers Clark and Rod Young own two strings of Alaskan and Canadian huskies. The eager dogs are straight off the race circuit, so be prepared to clip along at 12 to 14 mph. Two-person maximum. Call (800) 484-3870 and use access code 5682, or (406) 685-3237.

outside in

Attractions

West Yellowstone's main distinction is its location, but other attractions exist. Children will love the **Grizzly Discovery Center,** essentially a glorified zoo in town, which houses wolves as well as grizzly bears, and a rudimentary educational exhibit about them. There's also an IMAX theater with a film about Yellowstone (but, honestly, why go for the simulacra when you can have the real thing?).

The **Earthquake Lake Visitors Center,** on US 287 about 27 miles northwest of West Yellowstone, has a good vantage point from which to view the devastating effects of the 1959 earthquake. Measuring 7.5 on the Richter scale, the quake killed 28 campers and caused an entire mountainside to slide into the Madison River, damming the water to create Quake Lake. The visitors center also has a small exhibit on the causes and effects of earthquakes worldwide. Open daily, Memorial Day through mid-September; call the Hebgen Lake Ranger Station, (406) 646-7369.

The old gold mining towns turned open-air museums of **Virginia City** and **Nevada City** historically have been among the state's most prized tourist attractions, with their boardwalks and false fronts, well-regarded theater productions, and, if you believe in them, ghosts. Unlike so many 19th-century towns, Virginia City never suffered a major fire, so its original wooden structures remain; many of them house displays of period goods and clothes. Virginia City is still home to about 150 residents, and you can walk down the main street and peek into the storefronts for no charge; pick up a self-guided walking tour brochure at area businesses. Less than a mile west, uninhabited Nevada City was recreated by owner Charles Bovey, who restored 12 original buildings, then moved numerous cabins and historical structures (including Montana's first schoolhouse) to the site. From the road, Nevada City doesn't look like much, but there's a whole ghost town behind the worn facade, worth the price of admission even though it's not in tip-top shape. The Alder Gulch Short Line, an open-air, gas-powered narrow gauge railroad, runs between the two locations. Unfortunately, both towns are looking a little shabby these days, and at press time, their future was unclear: Charles Bovey's son Ford Bovey wants to sell, but he and the state (the most likely buyer) had reached a standoff. In any case, the tourist season traditionally is short, running from Memorial Day to Labor Day. Check with Bovey Restorations, (800) 648-7588 or (406) 843-5377, or with the Virginia City Chamber of Commerce, (800) 829-2969 or (406) 843-5555, about the status.

Assuming the best for Virginia City, don't miss the terrific theatrical productions offered there from mid-June through Labor Day. The **Brewery Follies Players** perform an adult-oriented musical variety show at the old Gilbert Brewery; their political satire is very, very funny. The state's longest running summer-stock troupe, the locally acclaimed **Virginia City Players** perform melodrama and comedy at the old livery (now called the Opera House). Again, at press time the future of these troupes was uncertain; check with Bovey Restorations or the chamber of commerce.

Twin Bridges' claim to fame is the **R. L. Winston Rod Company,** which produces some of the world's finest quality fly rods. Monday through Friday, free 20-minute tours of the factory begin daily at 2pm; visitors arriving at other times can watch a video and see the factory goings-on from a viewing window. The factory is located at 500 S Main, at the south end of Twin Bridges; call (406) 684-5674.

Explorers Meriwether Lewis and William Clark never visited their namesake caverns (and in fact never knew they existed), but no matter: **Lewis and Clark Caverns State Park** is fascinating enough in its own right. Discovered by two ranchers in the winter of 1892 and first explored in 1898, the caverns became Montana's first state park in the 1930s. May through September (and April and October weekends, weather permitting), you can take a 2-hour tour of the **limestone caverns,** which boast

2 miles of underground passageways lying as deep as 326 feet below Cave Mountain. Obviously, this tour is not for claustrophobics or those afraid of bats (western big-eared bats live in the caves). The tour covers a total of 2 miles; three-quarters of a mile of that is underground. Bring a sweater, since even in the heat of summer the caves stay at 50°F. There are small, three-person cabins available for rent; bring your own bedding, food, and kitchen utensils (there's no stove but a barbecue pit out front); there's also a 50-site state-run campground that's nice off season (summers can be brutally hot, and there's little shade). Tours of the caverns leave on demand, beginning at 9:30am and finishing at 4:30pm; from June 15 through Labor Day the last tour leaves at 6:30pm. Two miles off Hwy 2, 55 miles west of Bozeman or 45 miles east of Butte, (406) 287-3541.

Calendar of Events

Each March, hundreds of cross-country skiers participate in the **Yellowstone Rendezvous Nordic Ski Race,** which features a series of races ranging from 2 kilometers (kids only) to 50 kilometers. The races take place on the Rendezvous trail system in West Yellowstone. On Thanksgiving weekend, specialized race clinics are offered by the US Ski Team and Biathlon Fall Camp. For more information, contact Drew Barney, (406) 646-9379, in the evenings.

Each July, Twin Bridges holds its **Floating Flotillas and Fish Fantasies,** a 2-day river celebration along the Beaverhead River. The fish-centered events include a river parade, a fly-casting competition, and wader and canoe races at the Madison County Fairgrounds. Call Twin Bridges Chamber of Commerce President Frank Colwell, (406) 684-5686, for details.

Restaurants

You'll find good chicken teriyaki and an old-fashioned soda fountain at Virginia City's **Copper Palace** (126 W Wallace, (406) 843-5234), a recently renovated building that boasts real copper plating and the town's best food. West Yellowstone's local bookstore, The Book Peddler, has a small cafe in back called **Cappy's Bistro,** where you'll find sandwiches, soups, daily specials, and the best latte in town (112 Canyon St, (406) 646-9537). **The Old Hotel** in Twin Bridges (101 E Fifth Ave, (406) 684-5959) recently has been restored and made into an art gallery and restaurant; meals can be uneven, but the lemonade is fresh and the desserts are good. Set off by itself 6 miles north of Ennis on US 287, the **Bear Claw,** (406) 682-4619, is a locally renowned bar-cum-steakhouse with a few surprises. Steaks and burgers are the raison d'être, but the homemade vegetarian egg rolls are good if greasy, served with a hot mustard sauce, and the brat and sauerkraut lunch is a welcome relief for road-weary, burger-exhausted travelers.

The Continental Divide ☆☆☆ An oasis in the vast culinary wasteland of the Madison Valley, the "CD," as it's known locally, is a godsend for aficionados of fine dining, and as such has developed a devoted following who all but weep when the restaurant closes off season. Eat in the lovely peach-colored dining room or outside on the deck; either way, don't miss the spicy salmon cake appetizer, served with a chipotle glaze, or the frequent appetizer special of polenta with red sauce. Of a wide variety of meat, chicken, seafood, and vegetarian selections, the pork chop entree with chutney is a standout. Owners Jay and Karen Bentley know the details that count: fresh bread is served with extra virgin, organic olive oil, and entrees come with your choice of three different salads (not just salad dressings). The crème brûlée dessert is justifiably coveted; be sure to reserve one at the beginning of your meal, or, for larger groups, when you make table reservations. Open mid-May to mid-October. *In downtown Ennis; 307 E Main, Ennis; (406) 682-7600; dinner Tues–Sat; DIS, MC, V; checks OK; $$$.*

The Lodge at Potosi Hot Springs ☆☆☆ It's not a restaurant per se, but non-guests can partake of the Lodge at Potosi Hot Springs' exquisite $50, four-course, prix-fixe dinners (wine included), providing space is available. Don't let the casual setting (guests share the dining room table, in full view of the kitchen) or the isolated location in the remote Tobacco Root Mountains near Pony fool you. Trained at Seattle's Northwest Culinary Academy and the Académie Cordon Bleu in Paris, Patti Trapp and her stepson Eric, also a professional chef, regularly make the 1 ½-hour drive to Bozeman to purchase the freshest ingredients, from which they create masterful meals—quite possibly the best in Montana. We're still savoring the memories: appetizers of grilled shrimp dressed in a roasted red pepper vinaigrette on a bed of sautéed cabbage; an extraordinary fennel, corn, and coconut chowder; a marinated grilled chicken breast served on soba noodles with a soy ginger sauce and wasabi cream, and a fresh apple crisp à la mode. Dinner was accompanied by two kinds of wine and coffee. Not exactly backcountry fare. Our advice: get to The Lodge at Potosi Hot Springs ASAP, before Patti and Eric Trapp tire of entertaining dinner guests every night. Reservations are required at least 48 hours in advance; off-season dining available Friday and Saturday nights only. Call about seasonal closures. *7 miles southwest of Pony—follow Willow Creek Rd toward Potosi Campground; PO Box 651, Pony; (800) 770-0088 or (406) 685-3594; dinner every day in summer, Fri–Sat off season; MC, V; checks OK; $$$.*

Lodgings

The Stonehouse Inn ☆   Built from locally quarried stone 2 feet thick, this 1884 gothic-revival home is the nicest place to stay in Virginia City. The inn sits on a hill overlooking the squat wooden buildings of the town spread out below and is surrounded by rugged sagebrush country, the Tobacco Root Mountains, and the Ruby Range beyond. Owner Linda Hamilton, a fourth-generation Montanan and former mayor of Virginia City, knows how to make guests feel at home. She serves terrific breakfasts in the casual dining room or on the wraparound porch (request the cream-cheese stuffed French toast with strawberries). During breakfast Linda and her husband, John, can fill you in on both historical facts and more recent goings-on in their town. All five bedrooms come with brass beds, antique furnishings, and a shared bathroom. *2 blocks east of St. Paul's Episcopal Church; 306 E Idaho, Virginia City, MT 59755; (406) 843-5504; DIS, MC, V; checks OK; $$.*

West Yellowstone Conference Hotel ☆   This new 123-room Holiday Inn is a cut above most tourist motels (certainly a cut above those in West Yellowstone), distinguishing itself with its spacious rooms and modern amenities: all rooms are equipped with hair dryers, microwaves, mini refrigerators, coffee-makers, phones, and TVs, and there are several rooms designed specifically for wheelchair users. Third-floor front rooms come with the best views; bargain hunters should ask about several slightly smaller, less expensive rooms on the ground floor. The hotel also has Jacuzzi and two-room family suites, a very nice gift shop, and one of West Yellowstone's better restaurants, the Oregon Shortline. The hotel houses the beautifully restored 1903 Executive Car, an old railroad car that once transported railroad executives—it's worth a look even if you're not staying there. *Between Electric and Faithful Sts in West Yellowstone; 315 Yellowstone Ave, West Yellowstone, MT 59758; (800) 646-7365 or (406) 646-7365; AE, DIS, MC, V; checks OK; $$$.*

Rainbow Valley Motel   This small, independently owned motel just south of Ennis distinguishes itself from the others in the area with its spacious rooms (some with full kitchens), comfortable decor, lodgepole furniture, and colorful flowerpots and landscaping. Owners Ed and Jeanne Williams run a tight ship—and it shows. The Rainbow Valley also has a heated, outdoor pool. *1 mile south of Ennis on Hwy 287; PO Box 26, Ennis, MT 59729; (800) 452-8254 or (406) 682-4264; AE, DIS, MC, V; checks OK; $$.*

Ranches and Resorts

This is big fishing country, so there are a lot of mid- to high-end resorts catering to the angling crowd. Watch for the new **Healing Waters Resort** to open outside of Sheridan. Owners Greg and Janet Lilly (famed fisherman Bud Lilly's son and daughter-in-law), have been managing the exclusive and well-regarded Montana Trout Club; now they've got plans to open their own place. At press time, the Lillys had just purchased property and were planning to open in summer 1997, with gourmet food and guiding services included in the rates; for current status of Healing Waters Resort, call (406) 842-5027. Some other standout establishments follow:

Diamond J Ranch   For seven decades, urban cowboys and their families have been vacationing at the Diamond J Ranch as (for the last 40 years) guests of owners Pete and Jinny Combs, deep in spectacular Jack Creek Canyon outside Ennis. No wonder: the Orvis-endorsed Diamond J has plenty of activities to keep even the most neurotic city slicker occupied. All-inclusive rates of $1,150/week (less for kids) cover fishing on a privately owned stretch of Jack Creek as well as on the nearby Madison River; two horseback rides daily; skeet and trap shooting (shells extra); a heated pool; an indoor tennis court; and a pond for fly-fishing practice. Top that off with three gourmet meals daily (kids eat separately), plus barbecues and barn dances, and you can see that packing a daybook might not be a bad idea. Guided fly-fishing trips on the nearby Madison River can be arranged at an additional cost.

On paper, the Diamond J sounds pretty glitzy, but actually it's one of the more casual ranches we've seen; 11 cabins (maximum occupancy: 35) are modestly furnished, and the main lodge is comfortable, not opulent. The Diamond J is kid-friendly and designed for people who like to make the most of their time and money in one of the state's most spectacular settings. June to September or October is reserved for bird-hunting packages. *12 miles east of Ennis on Jack Creek Rd; PO Box 577, Ennis, MT 59729; (406) 682-4867; MC, V; checks OK.*

Firehole Ranch   About 18 miles west of West Yellowstone at the end of Hebgen Lake Road, with a view of the lake and the Madison Range beyond, the Orvis-endorsed Firehole Ranch sets the standard for luxurious, adult-oriented fly-fishing ranches. Built in the 1940s but recently refurnished, the ranch's 10 spacious cabins (maximum ranch occupancy: 20) are luxuriously appointed, with native-stone fireplaces and covered verandas. Gourmet meals and an open bar are served in the main lodge (Wednesdays there's a barbecue and live music), which boasts antiques, oriental rugs, and a sunshine-filled dining area. It caters to fly-fishermen (weeklong packages run from $2,000 to $2,400/person) who are shuttled across the lake in the morning to meet their guides and journey forth to the area's blue-ribbon streams, but the Firehole also has enough activities to keep non-anglers busy: daily non-angling rates of $215 to $265/person include guided horseback rides and use of canoes and mountain bikes. Children under 12 must have prior permission to partake of the Firehole's hospitality. For $50 a head non-guests may indulge in the multi-course dinners, space permitting; a week's notice is requested. Open June to September with a 4 day minimum stay. *From West Yellowstone, take Hwy 20 7 miles south, turn right on Hebgen Lake Rd, and drive 11 1/2 miles to the ranch; 11500 Hebgen Lake Rd, PO Box 686, West Yellowstone, MT 59758 (summer only); (406) 646-7294; no credit cards; checks OK.*

The Lodge at Potosi Hot Springs If the Lodge at Potosi Hot Springs offered only the private soaking pools (one outdoor, one indoor) at the base of the Tobacco Root Mountains, it would have been enough. But add to that four custom, western-themed cabins (maximum occupancy: 24), with their isolated creekside location along little-used South Willow Creek Rd, fishing in South Willow Creek, summer horseback riding and hiking into the adjacent mountains, and gourmet meals, and the Lodge at Potosi Hot Springs becomes a highly luxurious experience, one you'll talk about for years to come. In summer, the lodge functions as a small guest ranch, with daily rates of $200/person covering lodging and three meals; there's a 3-day minimum stay. Owners Dale and Patti Trapp can arrange additional activities, including horseback riding in the Tobacco Roots on their 16 resident horses, or guided fly-fishing trips on the famed Madison River. In the off-season, cabins rent for $175/night and include breakfast for two (request the Grand Marnier french toast). All four cabins include a fully equipped kitchen, but who wants to cook when the best food in Montana is a 3-minute walk up the road? Non-guests can make arrangements to eat dinner at the lodge, providing there's space available (see Restaurants, above).

It's a sign of the times that the once-public Potosi Hot Springs is now the centerpiece of some of the most exclusive accommodations in southwestern Montana. But for those who can afford it, the Lodge at Potosi Hot Springs remains a real find. One note of caution: The road leading to the lodge can be brutal; be sure to ask about conditions before you subject your low-clearance vehicle to its indignities. There is a 3-night minimum stay in summer, and possible seasonal closures. *7 miles southwest of Pony—follow S Willow Creek Rd toward Potosi Campground; PO Box 651, Pony, MT 59747; (800) 770-0088 or (406) 685-3594; MC; V; checks OK.*

Parade Rest Ranch Named by the retired US Cavalry colonel who founded it, the Parade Rest Ranch is a good, basic, moderately priced family getaway. Daily rates of $99/person (less for children) include three meals and all the horseback riding you can handle; guided fishing trips with a West Yellowstone outfitter run extra. Owner Shirley Butcher runs the Parade Rest with a good heart and a firm hand. Fifteen homey, spacious cabins (maximum occupancy: 48), all with private baths, are clustered along Grayling Creek 8 miles north of West Yellowstone, with beautiful views of the Madison Range and Hebgen Lake (unfortunately, you can still hear the highway traffic). Hearty meat-and-potatoes buffet meals are served in the dining room, with its checkerboard tablecloths and friendly staff. Horseback rides—walking speed only—head into the neighboring hills; on Mondays and Fridays there's a western cookout. Unless you want to be near the hot tub, request the cabins on the far side of the creek, away from the hubbub. Open mid-May through September; 3-night minimum stay. *8 miles north of West Yellowstone on Hwy 191, then 1 mile west on Hwy 287; 7979 Grayling Creek Rd, West Yellowstone, MT 59758; (800) 753-5934 or (406) 646-7217; MC, V; checks OK.*

Ruby Springs Lodge This luxurious new fly-fishing lodge takes full advantage of Montanans' legendary aversion to zoning: six cabins, all with river rock fireplace and private bath, sit along the banks of the Ruby River in what would surely be subject to floodplain restrictions anywhere else. You can cast from the back porch. A boardwalk leads to the stunning main lodge, where a maximum of 12 guests enjoy gourmet meals and views of the Tobacco Root Mountains. But the real attraction of Ruby Springs Lodge is the fishing: either on 5 privately owned miles of the Ruby River, a coveted brown trout fishery which has no public access, or on guided float trips along the nearby Madison, Big Hole, Beaverhead, or Jefferson Rivers. Double occupancy rates for the five standard, one-room cabins run $385/night per person including meals and fishing, $225/night per non-angler. Rates for the larger Tobacco Root Cabin, which includes a living area, run $435/night per person including fishing, $270/night per non-angler. Open May to mid-October. *On Hwy 287 south of Twin Bridges, between Alder and Laurin; PO Box 119, Alder, MT 59710; (800) 278-7829 or (406) 842-5250; MC, V; checks OK.*

T Lazy B Ranch It's not a ranch so much as a paradisiacal, private fishing retreat, a home base for owner Bob Walker's highly regarded outfitting business (he runs trips on the Madison and the Smith Rivers). That's not to say that non-fishermen can't enjoy any of three small, nicely furnished, 1930s cabins, which sit alongside Jack Creek some 13 miles outside Ennis. Bob's wife Theo cooks the meals, which are served in the original main log lodge, but the T Lazy B is so small (there's an eight-person maximum) that there are no real rules: guests are welcome to help themselves to cookies or snacks at will. Rates of $120/night don't include any child-centered amenities (or, for that matter, adult amenities, save the outdoor hot tub), but the Walkers' young daughter is always happy to have new playmates. And the Walkers can make anyone instantly feel at home; as one local put it, "If you don't like Bob or Theo Walker, well, you can't get along with anyone." One important note: Because none of the cabins have indoor plumbing (guests share a remarkably modern bathhouse next door), the Walkers prefer group bookings. But they will rent a cabin separately if space permits. They can also arrange guided horseback riding trips with a nearby outfitter. Open late May to October. *9 miles east of Ennis; 532 Jack Creek Rd, Ennis, MT 59729-0002; (406) 682-7288; no credit cards; checks OK.*

Backcountry Cabins

Forest Service cabins and lookouts generally rent for between $15 and $30 a night. For a complete list, request a copy of the *Forest Service Northern Region Cabin and Lookout Directory,* available through any ranger district. Our recommendations follow.

From May to mid-October, you can drive to the **Beaver Creek Cabin,** 21 miles northwest of West Yellowstone. The rest of the year, you'll have to ski (moderate) or snowmobile the last 3 miles. The cabin sits in a timbered canyon; there's a bunk bed downstairs and a loft area upstairs that can fit four more people. Bring your own mattresses, sleeping bags, and kitchen utensils; the cabin has a wood stove for heat and cooking. It's easiest to bring your own water, but the cabin is within walking distance of Beaver Creek. Reservations accepted a maximum of 60 days in advance. Hebgen Lake Ranger District, (406) 646-7369.

From mid-May through mid-October, you'll have to hike 5 miles to the remote **Cabin Creek Cabin,** 22 miles northwest of West Yellowstone, but the effort is worthwhile: the cabin sits in the Madison Range and the southern portion of the beautiful Lee Metcalf Wilderness. The cabin is available year-round, but the road is only plowed within 12 miles, and it's easy to get lost in the area—don't take this one in winter unless you know the area well. The cabin has a set of bunk beds and a wood stove for heat and cooking; bring your own mattresses, sleeping bags, and kitchen utensils. Should you decide to use the cabin in winter, the Forest Service suggests you bring wood as well. The creek is within walking distance. Reservations are taken a maximum of 60 days in advance. Hebgen Lake Ranger District, (406) 646-7369.

About 6 miles west of West Yellowstone, the **Basin Station Cabin** is accessible by car May through mid-October, and via an easy 1- or 2-mile ski the rest of the year. Completely surrounded by mountains, the cabin is particularly lovely in winter, when the traffic has died down. Bring your own mattresses, sleeping bags, water, and utensils. Make reservations a maximum of 60 days in advance. Hebgen Lake Ranger District, (406) 646-7369.

The modern **Bear Creek Cabin and Bunkhouse,** 21 miles south of Ennis in the Madison Range next to the Lee Metcalf Wilderness, are available December through April (the road is plowed regularly), offering a quiet winter getaway and fair cross-country skiing along the creek. Located next to each other, they are rented as separate units. The cabin is the nicer facility of the two; it sleeps six (two in the loft area), and has electricity, a modern stove, kitchen utensils, and a sitting area. The smaller bunkhouse sleeps two and also has electricity, a stove, and kitchen utensils. Bring sleeping bags and water. Reservations are accepted after August 1. Madison Ranger District, (406) 682-4253.

You'll get a good view of the Gravelly Range from the very popular **Black Butte Cabin,** which sits at 9,161 feet in the Gravelly Range 50 miles southwest of Ennis. The one-room cabin sleeps four; it has a wood-burning stove and kitchen utensils. You can rent it July through March, but generally it's only driveable until November, and road conditions may necessitate a high clearance vehicle; the road is only plowed within 20 miles. Bring sleeping bags, food, and water. Make reservations for July and August starting May 15; make reservations for September through March on or after August 1. Madison Ranger District, (406) 682-4253.

More Information

Beaverhead/Deerlodge National Forest, Madison Ranger District: (406) 682-4253.

Ennis Chamber of Commerce: (406) 682-4388.

Gallatin National Forest Supervisor's Office: (406) 587-6701.

GNF, Hebgen Lake Ranger District: (406) 646-7369.

GNF, Madison Ranger District: (406) 682-4253.

Gold West Country (an arm of Travel Montana): (800) 879-1159 or (406) 846-1943.

Montana Department of Fish, Wildlife and Parks: (406) 994-4042.

Travel Montana: (800) 847-4868 out-of-state; (406) 444-2654 in-state.

US Geological Survey (stream flows): (406) 441-1319 or through the Internet at http://www.dmthln.cr.usgs.gov/.

Virginia City Chamber of Commerce: (800) 829-2969 or (406) 843-5555.

West Yellowstone Chamber of Commerce: (406) 646-7701.

Yellowstone Country (an arm of Travel Montana): (800) 736-5276 or (406) 446-1005.

Bozeman
and Environs

Including the Gallatin and Paradise Valleys, Big Sky, Three Forks, Livingston, and Gardiner.

Ever since 1864, when Georgia native and entrepreneur John Bozeman staked out a city in the midst of fertile soil, Bozeman has been markedly different from other Montana settlements. It wasn't founded on boom-and-bust cycles of mining, like Butte and Helena; logging, like Missoula; cattle, like Great Falls; or railroads, like Billings. Bozeman's earliest pioneers followed the so-called Bozeman Trail through the heart of hostile Indian country. Many decided to stay and plant roots when they saw the agricultural potential of the Gallatin Valley, known to Native Americans as "the valley of flowers."

Today, grain farming retains a hold on the outskirts of Bozeman (city pop: 30,000; county pop: 65,000), but the valley's modern-day economy is largely driven by small companies: computer firms, backpack manufacturers, and an expanding corps of modem-linked entrepreneurs. Bozeman is also home to Montana State University, a land-grant institution sometimes referred to as "Cow College" that serves 12,000 students. The bulk of the town's population is highly educated—more than half of Bozeman's adult residents hold at least a bachelor's degree, and the number of residents with Ph.D.s is downright embarrassing.

Increasing numbers of newcomers are drawn to the incredible scenery and fantastic outdoor recreational opportunities that have made Bozeman, the surrounding Gallatin Valley, and nearby Paradise Valley among the fastest-growing areas in the Northern

Rockies—with some of the highest real estate prices. Driving the growth, in part, is the area's reputation as Hollywood North: celebrities Ted Turner and Jane Fonda, Dennis Quaid and Meg Ryan, Margot Kidder, Michael Keaton, and Peter Fonda are among those who own local retreats. Some vestige of Bozeman's comfortable old character remains (you can, for instance, still watch ranchers bringing their cattle to town every Monday), but it increasingly feels like a poor (or at least poorer) Santa Fe, with boutiques, coffeehouses, and art galleries lining its historic Main Street.

Less than 30 miles east of Bozeman, the old railroad town of Livingston is legendary, not only for its proximity to the Yellowstone River (which flows through town), but also as a magnet for novelists, poets, and painters. More recently, tourists have been coming to admire its quaint western architecture and experience the feel of the real West. Among the cast of colorful characters who have lived in or near Livingston are gunslinger Calamity Jane and the late writer Richard Brautigan. Today the Paradise Valley's most eccentric residents are members of the controversial Church Universal and Triumphant, a doom-and-gloom religious order often described as a cult. Fifty-three miles south of Livingston lies the tiny town of Gardiner, the northern gateway to Yellowstone National Park.

Six distinct mountain ranges, millions of acres of public lands, and hundreds of miles of hiking trails are found within an hour's drive of Bozeman—and Yellowstone National Park is only 1 ½ hours away. Standing on Peet's Hill in the middle of town on a clear day, you can see the commanding profile of the Bridger Mountains due north, the Bangtails to the northeast, the Absarokas to the east, the Hyalite–Gallatins to the south, the Spanish Peaks–Madison Range to the southwest, and the Tobacco Roots barely visible on the western horizon. Add to that the renowned fly-fishing on the nearby Gallatin, Yellowstone, and Madison Rivers, the ski slopes at Bridger Bowl and world-class Big Sky, and the Nordic trails at Lone Mountain Ranch, and you can see why *Outside* magazine recently rated Bozeman as one of the 15 best sporting cities in the United States.

Getting There

Bozeman is situated along Interstate 90, approximately 95 miles southeast of Helena and 80 miles north of Gardiner and Yellowstone National Park. It is served by Gallatin Field, 9 miles north of town at Belgrade. Greyhound Bus lines provide ground transportation. Livingston is another 26 miles east on I-90.

Adjoining Areas

EAST: **Red Lodge**

WEST: **Butte and Environs**

NORTH: **Helena and Environs**

SOUTH: **Yellowstone National Park; West Yellowstone and the Madison Valley**

inside out

Hiking/Backpacking

The **Gallatin National Forest** is covered in two separate maps. The western section includes the Hyalite drainage and the Lee Metcalf Wilderness; the eastern section covers the Absaroka–Beartooth Wilderness. Both **maps** are available through the Gallatin Visitors Center, which also serves as headquarters for the Bozeman Ranger District, (406) 587-6920. Maps and advice also are available through Northern Lights Trading Co. in Bozeman (1716 W Babcock, (406) 586-2225). This is big bear country, with both black **bears** and grizzlies; be sure to take the proper precautions. There are special food-storage restrictions in parts of Gallatin National Forest, specifying that food must either be stored in a bear-proof container, hung from a tree, or guarded. Be sure to check if your destination falls within the restriction boundaries.

There are millions of acres of wildlands and thousands of miles of trails in the Bozeman area, and obviously we can't cover them all. Gallatin National Forest's "Recreation Opportunities in the Hyalite Drainage" brochure details options within that area, or contact the Bozeman office of the **Montana Wilderness Association,** (406) 582-8600, to obtain a list of free, guided hikes included in its "Walk in the Wild" program. We also recommend Bill Schneider's guide *Hiking Montana*. Here are a few suggestions, though, to get you started. You'll also want to check out Backcountry Cabins under Lodgings, below, for additional ideas.

Part of the national rails-to-trails program, Bozeman's **Galligator Trail** stretches more than a mile between South Church Avenue and South Third past creeks and duck ponds. Popular with both walkers and joggers, it's also wheelchair-accessible. The Galligator is part of a broad plan laid out by the Gallatin Valley Land Trust for a network of public trails connecting with surrounding mountains. For a map of existing routes, contact the Gallatin Valley Land Trust, 321 E Main, (406) 587-8404.

Newcomers to Bozeman often acclimate themselves by ascending the popular **"M" Trail,** which leads to the giant "M" emblazoned on the Bridger Mountains outside town. (Not to be confused with the "M" trail outside Missoula, which also leads to a large letter.) The trail itself consists of less than a mile of vertical hiking, but you can continue another dozen miles along the entire mountain ridgeline, clear up to the Bridger Bowl ski area and Sacajawea Peak, the highest peak in the Bridgers. Once the bottom of a great sea and graced, at another time, by dinosaurs, these mountains are fertile fossil-hunting ground. The trailhead is located in the **Bridger Foothills National Recreation Area,** 2 miles northeast of Bozeman on the left (north) of Bridger Canyon Road (Hwy 86).

The 250,000-acre **Lee Metcalf Wilderness** sprawls across both the Madison and Gallatin Ranges southwest of Bozeman. Most of the wilderness trails are accessible from the Gallatin Canyon south and west of Bozeman along US Highway 191. Many trails heading east of the highway lead to Yellowstone National Park. The trail following the **south fork of Spanish Creek** is a gateway to magnificent lakes and pine forests at the foot of the Spanish Peaks. It's also a good excuse to try your hand at spotting celebrities—or at least celebrity-owned buffalo. To get to the trailhead, you have to drive through part of Ted Turner's and Jane Fonda's Flying D Ranch. A word to the wise: this power couple doesn't take kindly to trespassers; be sure to stay on the public road. From the trailhead, you can hike 3 miles one way to the river's confluence with **Falls Creek** (a terrific place to fish) or continue several miles more to the trout-filled tarns of Lake Solitude, Mirror Lake, and the Spanish Lakes. Most people take 2 or 3 days to allow for plenty of hiking, camping, and fishing. The trailhead is 30 miles south of Bozeman; from Four Corners drive 16 miles south on US 191, then turn right (west) on Spanish Creek Rd and drive another 14 miles.

About 20 miles south of Bozeman and anchored by **Hyalite Reservoir,** the Hyalite area holds a web of well-maintained hiking trails and campgrounds, including several that are part of the **Hyalite Challenge,** a federal outdoor program aimed at people with disabilities. Several interpretive trails can accommodate wheelchair-bound visitors, and there are interpretive signs in braille. By hiking just a couple of miles in from the Hyalite Reservoir, you can reach pristine lakes, gorgeous peaks, and remote places to camp. (You can also, by taking a wrong turn, reach clear-cuts and logging roads; make sure you know where you're headed.) Among the more popular trails from the reservoir shores are the half-mile hike to **Palisade Falls,** and the 6-mile hike up the **East Fork Hyalite Creek Trail** past Horseshoe Falls to Heather and Emerald Lakes. Watch for wildlife, including mountain goats.

One other splendid option here is the 5 ½-mile hike to upper **Hyalite Lake,** which will take you past nearly a dozen small waterfalls and to the Hyalite–Porcupine–Buffalo Horn area. After ascending more than 1,800 feet through timber and meadows you'll reach a wide, open basin with a panoramic view of the Gallatins. To reach the Hyalite trailheads from Bozeman, take South 19th (County Hwy 345 on the Montana state map) south about 7 miles, then turn left at the sign for Hyalite Reservoir. Follow the road 12 miles to the reservoir, then turn left so you're driving on the reservoir's north side. Turn left again when the road forks and travel past Window Rock Ranger Station to the end of the road. This is grizzly country; take all proper precautions. Many people use the upper Hyalite Lake route as a day hike, but some camp at the lake then scale Hyalite or Fridley Peaks in the morning. You can also make this a multi-day trip by continuing along the **Gallatin Crest Trail** another 36 miles into Yellowstone National Park.

From Paradise Valley you can access the Absaroka Mountains on the west side of the gargantuan 930,000-acre **Absaroka–Beartooth Wilderness.** Among the summits in the Absaroka Range that rise above Paradise Valley are Emigrant Peak (elevation 10,960 feet), Monument Peak, Elephanthead Peak, Mount McKnight, Mount Delano (10,200 feet), and Mount Cowan (11,206 feet), all of which can be climbed from either the Paradise or Boulder River valleys.

The 5-mile trail to **Pine Creek Lake** starts out gradually enough, leading past Pine Creek Falls (a nice destination itself) before climbing more than 3,000 feet in 4 steep miles. You can make this a day hike, but it's great to stay overnight at the lake, where you may be able to see alpenglow on the surrounding peaks. Don't try this one before mid-July, however. To reach the trailhead, drive south from Livingston 5 miles on US 89, then turn left on East River Rd (County Rd 540) and continue south another 8 miles. Just past the tiny enclave of Pine Creek turn left (east) onto a paved road that leads to the Pine Creek Campground and the trailhead. Livingston Ranger District, (406) 222-1892.

The **Gallatin Petrified Forest** contains the remains of dozens of tree species 55 million years old. It sits astride the Gallatin crest just north of Gardiner. Thousands of petrified stumps can be seen in the hills; a 6-mile round-trip hike into **Tom Miner Basin** will take you to the heart of the forest and back. Note: It's illegal to take the fossilized wood without a permit. This is grizzly country; take proper precautions. To get there, take US 89 to the turnoff for Tom Miner Rd, 18 miles north of Gardiner, and follow it to the Tom Miner Campground and interpretive trail. Take the interpretive trail and continue up to the crest of the Gallatin Range for a spectacular view of Gallatin Canyon. Gardiner Ranger District, (406) 848-7375.

Camping

The Bozeman and Livingston areas have several private campgrounds, as well as an abundance of public options. Travel Montana's *Montana Travel Planner,* (800) 847-4868 out-of-state and (406) 444-2654 in-state, lists all private and public campgrounds alphabetically (look under "Yellowstone Country") and is also available at area motels and chambers of commerce. Travelers with RVs should check that campsites can accommodate their vehicles. For additional ideas, check out Backcountry Cabins under Lodgings, below.

The Forest Service contracts with a private concessionaire to provide camping sites in **Gallatin Canyon** south of Bozeman along US 191. Three campgrounds lie along the Gallatin River in close proximity to each other: the 14-site **Greek Creek Campground,** 31 miles south of Bozeman; the 11-site **Swan Creek Campground** another mile farther south; and the 14-site **Moose Flat Campground,** yet another mile south. In addition to terrific fishing opportunities, all three offer excellent hiking up side drainages. Make advance reservations, (406) 587-9054, or obtain information through the Bozeman Ranger District, (406) 587-6920.

Campgrounds on and near **Hyalite Reservoir** south of Bozeman are popular weekend getaways for local families and are also part of the reservation system above. The 12-site **Langohr Campground,** 11 miles up the Hyalite Canyon Rd, sits on Hyalite Creek and claims decent fishing; 7 miles farther, the 10-site **Chisholm Campground** boasts a lakeside location; and the 18-site **Hood Creek Campground,** across the dam on the east side of the reservoir, has a boat launch. The reservoir is nicest early in the season, before the drawdown begins. To get there, drive 8 miles south on South 19th St and turn on Hyalite Canyon Rd (it's well-signed).

Southeast of Livingston off US 89 are two very nice Forest Service campgrounds, again managed by private concessionaires. The 24-site **Pine Creek Campground** (11 miles south of Livingston, then 6 miles east on Pine Creek Rd), serves as a great base camp for hiking to nearby Pine Creek Falls and Pine Creek Lake (see Hiking/Backpacking, above). Farther south, the 12-site **Snow Bank Campground** (16 miles south of Livingston, then 12 miles southeast on Mill Creek Rd) sits at the end of the breathtaking Mill Creek drainage. These are very popular, especially on summer weekends. Call the Livingston Ranger District, (406) 222-1892, for information.

About 27 miles northeast of Bozeman on the east face of the Bridger Mountains, the peaceful **Fairy Lake Campground** is a favorite of Bozemanites. None of the 9 campsites are actually on the lake, but they're close enough to be pleasant. Motorboats are prohibited on the lake. Fairy

Lake is a great staging area for climbing up to the saddle of the Bridgers. No reservations here, but check with the Bozeman Ranger District, (406) 587-6920.

If you're getting into town late and need a quick and easy place to pitch the tent or park the trailer, consider **Bozeman Hot Springs KOA,** 8 miles west of town on US 191, (406) 587-3030. In addition to the usual KOA amenities (hot showers, laundry facilities, and a general store), this facility offers on-site hot springs, though, granted, they're a little funky.

Fishing

Fishermen who come to Bozeman have access to two venerable rivers—the Gallatin and the Yellowstone, as well as the Madison to the west and south (see West Yellowstone and the Madison Valley chapter). All three rivers have headwaters in the high country of Yellowstone National Park, and each is filled with brown, rainbow, and cutthroat trout. The current main attraction is **fly-fishing,** but the rivers are revered equally by spin-casters. Spring runoff generally begins in late May and lasts through June. Note: Certain stretches are catch-and-release only. Licenses, regulations, and river maps are available through the Montana Department of Fish, Wildlife and Parks in Bozeman, (406) 994-4042, and outdoor stores.

In Bozeman, rent **equipment** and hire **guides** from Montana Troutfitters Orvis Shop, 1716 W Main, (406) 587-4707; the River's Edge, run by fly-fishing guru Bud Lilly's son, at 2012 N Seventh Ave, (406) 586-5373; or R. J. Cain and Co., 24 E Main, (406) 587-9111.

In Livingston, stop at Dan Bailey's, 209 W Park, (800) 356-4052 or (406) 222-1673, one of the oldest and most respected fly-fishing stores in the West; or try the newer but equally hospitable Anderson's Yellowstone Angler, 2½ miles south of downtown on US 89, (406) 222-7130. In downtown Gardiner, you can't miss Park's Fly Shop along US 89, (406) 848-7314. Proprietor Richard Parks is always willing to part with at least one or two secrets about area fisheries. For another guiding option, see Bud Lilly's Anglers Retreat under Lodgings, below.

The **Gallatin River** flows west of Bozeman, taking a northerly course toward its eventual terminus with the Missouri River near the town of Three Forks. There's plenty of shore access on the Gallatin along US 191; in fact, it is illegal to fish from a boat on the Gallatin from Yellowstone National Park to its confluence with the East Gallatin River at Manhattan. Every summer the annual stonefly and salmonfly hatches put trout into a feeding frenzy.

The nation's last major free-flowing (i.e., undammed) river, the **Yellowstone River** attracts nearly twice as many fishermen as the

Gallatin, most of whom float it with drift boats. A good all-day float runs from Loch Leven to Carter's Bridge, a span of more than 15 miles through generally gentle water with plenty of side channels and riffles. In May, the caddisfly hatch inaugurates the fishing season.

Fish **Hyalite Reservoir** south of Bozeman for cutthroat and rainbow trout and arctic grayling. Shore and boat fishing both prove rewarding.

Rafting/Kayaking

At the peak of spring runoff in late May and June, stretches of the **Gallatin** and **Yellowstone Rivers** are churned into raging Class III and Class IV whitewater. **Guided group floats** are offered through the Yellowstone Raft Co., (406) 848-7777, and Wild West Rafting, (406) 848-7110, both based out of Gardiner, and from Geyser Whitewater Expeditions, (406) 995-4989, and the Yellowstone Raft Co.'s second branch, (406) 995-4613, in Big Sky.

Obtain river flow information and rent rafts and kayaks at Northern Lights Trading Co. (1716 W Babcock, Bozeman, (406) 586-2225). Northern Lights also has an outlet in Big Sky at the Meadow Center, (406) 995-2220. Scott Darby of Rapid Discoveries' kayak school, (406) 582-8110, is another good source for kayaking information.

The most popular stretch of Class III and Class IV whitewater on the Gallatin lies between **Moose Creek Campground** and **Squaw Creek Bridge,** just above House Rock rapids. You'll see many commercial rafters on this portion of the river.

In the spring and early summer, experienced kayakers play in Class III and IV rapids in the Yellowstone River's **Yankee Jim Canyon**; put in at Gardiner and take out at Carbella Fishing Access.

Mountain Biking

Rent bikes and get advice from Bozeman's Bangtail Bicycle Shop (508 E Main, (406) 587-4905) or Summit Bike & Ski (26 South Grand Ave, (406) 587-5401). Ask about **guided rides.** Two handy guidebooks are *Bozeman Trails* by Andrew Gerlach and *Fat Trax: Bozeman* by Will Harmon, available at bookstores and bike shops. The Bozeman Ranger District, (406) 587-6920, will also have information and maps.

The **Hyalite drainage** south of Bozeman has quietly cultivated a much-deserved reputation in the Northern Rockies as a mountain biking hub. Even beginners can find plenty of suitable trails in the extensive maze of old logging roads snaking through the Hyalite Mountains. One popular and pretty out-and-back option is the **Bozeman Creek Trail,** an old logging road that follows Bozeman Creek 14 miles to Mystic Lake (you can turn around anywhere along the way). To get to the trailhead from Bozeman, follow 19th St south to Nash Rd, about 5 miles out of town. Turn left (east) on Nash and follow the road another 2 miles to Bozeman Creek Rd, where you turn right (south) and drive another mile to the parking lot.

Another vast network of trails is located in the **Big Sky** area. The easiest option is to take your bike up the aerial tram at Big Sky Ski and Summer Resort to the top of 11,166-foot **Lone Mountain** and then cruise down the switchback road on your own wheels. Rent bikes at Big Sky. A cheaper option is to access the **Buck Creek Ridge Trail,** 3 miles south of Big Sky, and bike 8 miles one way to Yellow Mule Cabin. This moderately difficult ride provides fantastic views of the Spanish Peaks and Taylor–Hilgards. The trailhead is 6 miles off US 191 on Buck Creek Ridge Rd.

Climbing

Most of the mountains around Bozeman require more scrambling and bouldering than technical climbing, but there are several natural headwalls around town that even veteran alpinists consider challenging. Barrell Mountaineering (240 E Main, (406) 582-1335) and Northern Lights Trading Co. (1716 W Babcock, (406) 586-2225) can provide gear and advice. Or stop by the Bozeman Climbing Center (1408 Gold Ave, (406) 582-0756) to pick up some tips.

About 6 miles west of Bozeman along I-90, you'll find **Bozeman Pass–Rocky Canyon,** an unofficial training area that has good vertical challenges ranging in difficulty from 5.5 to 5.8.

During winter, **ice climbers** assemble at the base of the waterfalls in the **Hyalite drainage** south of Bozeman, scaling frozen cataracts with crampons and ice axes.

Parks

The 19th-century explorers Lewis and Clark had to journey upriver to reach the headwaters of the Missouri in 1805; today visitors can drive there easily enough and see for themselves where the Gallatin, the Madison, and the Jefferson Rivers converge. Interpretive signs at scenic **Missouri Headwaters State Park,** (406) 994-4042, tell the story of the explorers and explain much of Montana's early history. Facilities include a nice camping and picnic area, a boat launch, hiking trails, and fishing access. Take the Three Forks exit off I-90, driving east on County Rd 205, and north 3 miles on County Rd 286.

Horseback Riding

In Bozeman, Tom and Joan Heintz operate Medicine Lake Outfitters, (406) 388-6942, offering guided trail rides and wilderness pack trips. Operating out of Big Sky, Jake's Horses, (406) 995-4630, offers trail rides and pack trips. In Livingston, try the highly recommended Flying Diamond Guide Service, (406) 222-1748. Chico Hot Springs Lodge, (800) HOT-WADA or (406) 333-4933, runs trail rides into the foothills of the Absarokas (see Lodgings, below). For additional riding options, see Ranches and Resorts, below.

Swimming

Known locally as Bozeman Beach, the East Gallatin Recreation Area's **Glen Lake** is the place families go for a quick swim and a sunbath—there's about 300 feet of beachfront. With only 7 acres of water, it's really more like a pond, but it's pretty, set at the base of the Bridger Mountains, and very convenient. The lake is stocked with small rainbow, golden, and cutthroat trout. From Bozeman, drive north on North Seventh, take a right on Griffin, cross the railroad tracks, then take a left on Manley Rd to the park entrance, about a half-mile. Bozeman Parks Division, (406) 585-5571, has more information.

Beloved by locals and tourists alike, the two outdoor pools (an Olympic-sized swimming pool and a very hot soaking pool) at **Chico Hot Springs**, (800) HOT-WADA or (406) 333-4694, offer a chance to sit in natural mineral waters while soaking up glorious views. Some swimsuits (not in every size) are available for use. See Lodgings, below, for directions.

Boating

A primary source of Bozeman's drinking water, **Hyalite Reservoir** attracts canoeists and motor boaters, and lots and lots of families. It's best early in the season, before drawdown. A no-wake restriction keeps noise pollution to a minimum. (See Hiking/Backpacking, above.)

Golfing

The lower fork of the Gallatin River actually flows through the 18-hole, par 72, Arnold Palmer-designed **Big Sky Golf Course.** Views of Lone Mountain and the Spanish Peaks are terrific, and the high altitude (6,500 feet above sea level) gives you higher drives! Open to the public from June to September; call (800) 548-4486 or (406) 995-5000 for more information.

Downhill Skiing

Forty-three miles south of Bozeman, **Big Sky Ski & Summer Resort** is Montana's premiere destination ski resort, with the longest vertical drop (4,180 feet) in the United States—and high-end lift-ticket prices. Founded in the early 1970s by former NBC newscaster (and Montana native) Chet Huntley, Big Sky has 75 runs served by 10 chairlifts, a tram, a gondola, and three surface lifts on 3,500 acres. It's also got a world-class Nordic resort nearby (Lone Mountain Ranch; see Cross-Country Skiing, below). There's a full-service village, including more than 1,000 rooms on-mountain, plus 15 restaurants, 11 night spots, and various other amenities. With a base elevation of 6,970 feet and a summit elevation of 11,150 feet, Big Sky rarely has to worry about conditions: the average annual snowfall here is 400 inches. Only 10 percent of the mountain is suitable for beginners; the rest of the terrain is evenly split between intermediate and expert (the recently added Lone Peak Tram opened up 1,200 additional acres of advanced to extreme territory). Children 10 and under ski free with a paying adult (limit two per adult), and the resort offers a children's day camp for kids ages 6 to 14. Ski season generally runs from mid-November through mid-April. Call (800) 548-4486 or (406) 995-5000 for information and reservations; for snow conditions, call (406) 995-5900.

Only 16 miles northwest of Bozeman, **Bridger Bowl** attracts locals and families who eschew the glitz and costly lift tickets at Big Sky—lift tickets are nearly half what they cost up canyon. This community-owned, nonprofit resort claims 60 runs and 6 chairlifts spread out over 2,000 acres, with a vertical drop of 2,000 feet. One-quarter of the runs are rated beginner, 35 percent rank as intermediate, and 40 percent are for advanced skiers only. Serious experts can access an additional 500 vertical feet of terrain on Bridger's Ridge (avalanche transceiver, shovel, and skiing partner required). Day care and programs for kids ages 4 to 6 are available. Here's an insider's tip: whenever you see a blinking blue light above Bozeman's Baxter Hotel, it means at least an inch of fresh snow has fallen at Bridger Bowl. Ski season usually runs from mid-December through the beginning of April. For information, call (800) 223-9609; for the ski report, call (406) 586-1518.

Cross-Country Skiing

Rent touring and telemark skis in Bozeman at Chalet Sports (corner of Willson and Main, (406) 587-4595) or Northern Lights Trading Co. (1716 W Babcock, (406) 586-2225). The Gallatin National Forest publishes several snow trail brochures detailing backcountry options, which are available through the Bozeman Ranger District, (406) 587-6920. For additional ideas, check out Backcountry Cabins, below.

One of the nation's premier cross-country ski centers, **Lone Mountain Ranch** at Big Sky claims more than 75 kilometers of groomed trails for both diagonal stride and skate skiers. Those who can afford to stay overnight at this luxurious resort should (see Ranches and Resorts, below), but Lone Mountain also welcomes day-users. The superb restaurant holds even more appeal after a long day on the trails. Rentals, lessons, guided ski tours, and meals are available. For information, call (406) 994-4644.

The day-use only **Bohart Ranch Cross-Country Ski Center** recently has also been used as a training site for Olympic cross-country skiers and biathletes. With 25 kilometers of groomed trails, rentals, lessons, and a warming hut, Bohart is the locals' pick. It's located at 16621 Bridger Canyon Rd (Hwy 86); from Bozeman, take Hwy 86 (Bridger Canyon Rd) 16 miles northeast, just past the turnoff to Bridger Bowl. Call (406) 586-9070 for more information.

Nice backcountry options just beyond Bohart Ranch are found at the **South and Middle Brackett Creek Trails.** Snowmobiles are prohibited on South Brackett Creek, which dead-ends at Bohart Ranch. These trails seem fine for novices but get progressively harder as they work up the east slope of the Bridgers. Middle Brackett Creek winds up on Ross Pass; make sure you have avalanche skills. The trails begin about 50 feet from each other roughly 2 miles past Bohart Ranch where the road forks; to get to the parking lot, bear right.

More convenient, if less reliable, are the city-groomed tracks for cross-country skiers at **Lindley Park** in Bozeman. These rolling meadows are a nice place to practice if your time is limited. It's particularly pleasant by moonlight, with views overlooking town. Trails are free. Lindley Park is on the east side of Bozeman just off East Main—look for the signs to Sunset Hills Cemetery; the park is adjacent to it. Season buttons cost $10 and are available at Bozeman Department of Parks and Recreation (Bozeman Swim Center, 1211 W Main, (406) 587-4724) and at local outdoor stores.

For backcountry options close to Bozeman, try the **Bear Canyon–New World Gulch** trails about 10 miles east of Bozeman. These trails aren't groomed but are typically tracked. Beginners should stick to the Bear Canyon Trail; more advanced skiers will enjoy the New World Gulch Trail. Take the Bear Canyon exit 7 miles east of Bozeman off I-90; turn right at the end of the ramp then make an immediate left onto Bear Canyon Rd. Follow this road south to the end, where you'll see the trailhead.

Snowmobiling/Other Activities

For **snowmobiling** try the 120-mile **Big Sky Snowmobile Trail,** which links Bozeman and West Yellowstone. **Buck Creek Ridge,** south of Big Sky off US 191, offers good play areas. The Bozeman Ranger District, (406) 587-6920, and the Bozeman Area Chamber of Commerce, (406) 586-5421, can provide more information.

Lone Mountain Ranch at Big Sky offers **sleigh-ride dinners** to non-guests, as well as their overnight clientele. You'll take a horse-drawn sleigh to a log cabin, where you'll enjoy a prime-rib dinner and after-dinner entertainment from Walkin' Jim Stoltz, a local folk singer. The whole evening is lots of fun. Book well in advance, particularly over the holidays; call (800) 514-4644 or (406) 995-4644.

Four parks in Bozeman boast outdoor **ice skating** rinks; for information, call the Bozeman Department of Parks and Recreation, (406) 587-4724.

Wildlife

In Bozeman, Ken Sinay's Northern Rockies Natural History, (406) 586-1155, provides wildlife-watching day trips around the Bozeman area, including visits to Yellowstone National Park and Red Rock Lakes National Wildlife Refuge. Watch for all the usual suspects: **black bear, grizzly, elk, mule deer,** and **white-tailed deer.**

You can also sign up for a naturalist-led tour at Lone Mountain Ranch in Big Sky, (406) 994-4644. In Livingston, renowned wildlife photographer Tom Murphy leads both group and individual trips afield in search of wildlife around the Yellowstone region. You can reach Murphy at (406) 222-2302.

One of the oldest **fish hatcheries** in the west, the US Fish and Wildlife Service's Bozeman Fish Technology Center raises half a dozen species of trout and endangered fish for release in Rocky Mountain waters. Visitors are welcome year-round for free, self-guided tours. In spring, the center hosts an annual kids fishing derby. Located 2 miles northeast of Bozeman across from the "M" at the foot of the Bridger Range, at 4050 Bridger Canyon Rd (Hwy 86), (406) 587-9265.

outside in

Attractions

The **Museum of the Rockies** is world-renowned for its collection of dinosaur bones as well as its curator of paleontology, Jack Horner, who fostered a whole new approach to his subject when he insisted that the behavior of dinosaurs was related more closely to birds than to lizards. (He served as the inspiration for the main character in *Jurassic Park*.) In addition to its well-designed interactive exhibits about prehistoric Earth, the museum also is home to the impressive Taylor Planetarium, with rotating shows. Leave plenty of time to explore this excellent museum; admission fees allow you to come back a second day, and you may very well want to. Located near Montana State University at 600 W Kagy Boulevard; call (406) 994-2251 for hours and admission prices.

Located in the old county jail, the **Gallatin County Pioneer Museum and Historical Society** has a terrific collection of local relics, including historic photographs, cavalry artifacts from Fort Ellis, a homesteader's cabin, and the gallows where an outlaw faced his maker. It's a great place to learn about frontier life in Montana. Admission is free, but a donation is recommended. The museum is located at 317 W Main, (406) 582-3195.

An offbeat way to appreciate Bozeman's past is to pick up a copy of *Who's Who In the Bozeman Cemetery*, available for $2 at the Gallatin County Pioneer Museum and at local bookstores. **Sunset Hills Cemetery** is 4 blocks east of downtown on East Main in Lindley Park. Not only does it claim the graves of city founder John Bozeman, television broadcaster Chet Huntley, and the Story family (marked by the arch from their glorious mansion, Bozeman's first), but the cemetery also offers gorgeous views. For $4, you can also pick up a copy of the 24-page booklet, *Bozeman Women's Heritage Trail*, describing a route that strolls through the historic South Side past older homes, boarding houses, and onto the campus of Montana State University.

Bozeman's cultural claim to fame is Montana's **Shakespeare in the Parks**, (406) 994-5881. Every summer, in various venues throughout the city and state, this Bozeman-based troupe gives free performances of two separate works, one by Shakespeare and one by another playwright. The troupe celebrates its 25th anniversary in 1997.

When it comes to spectator sports, **Montana State University's Bobcats** are the most popular game in town. In recent years, the university's track, volleyball, rodeo, and basketball teams have fared well in intercollegiate play. The university's Ask Us Information Desk, (406) 994-4636, knows the current schedule. In 1996, Bozeman won a franchise for a junior league hockey team; the **Bozeman Icedogs** are tentatively scheduled to play at the new Bozeman Ice Center, which was under construction at press time. Call information for the Bozeman Ice Center's phone number.

Calendar of Events

In Livingston, take a step back to Happy Days at **Mark's In & Out Rod Run and Car Show** held the third week of June. The whole town turns out for a gander at dozens of mint-condition vehicles and the best milk shakes in town. Livingston Chamber of Commerce, (406) 222-0850.

Livingston's annual Roundup rodeo is held July 2, 3, and 4 (whether or not it falls on a weekend). In addition to the usual bronco- and bull-riding, calf-roping, and barrel racing, this is a good opportunity for celebrity spotting—plus fireworks, country-western dancing, and a huge opening parade. Livingston Chamber of Commerce, (406) 222-0850.

The third week of July is synonymous with the **Gallatin County Fair.** Livestock, arts and crafts, carnival rides, and country-western music are in abundance. It's all held at the Gallatin County Fairgrounds on the north side of Bozeman. Call (406) 582-3270 for more information.

Nearly a century old, Bozeman's **Sweet Pea Festival** is now so popular, it's no longer widely advertised. Held the first weekend in August, the festival includes a parade and fun run, restaurant vendors, theater and dance performances, outdoor concerts, and art exhibitions. Most activities fill Lindley Park on the east edge of Bozeman; call (406) 583-4003 for details.

In early December, the locals turn out en masse for **Bozeman's Christmas Stroll.** Downtown streets are blocked off for pedestrians and carolers, and kids can take hay rides and visit with Santa. Bozeman Chamber of Commerce, (406) 586-5421.

Restaurants

Like every college town, Bozeman's got plenty of coffeehouses: the **Rocky Mountain Roasting Co.** (one block north of Main St at 111 E Mendenhall, (406) 586-2428) is a favorite of java snobs. The **Western Cafe** (443 E Main, (406) 587-0436) has Bozeman's best caramel rolls. **Columbo's Pizza** (1003 W College, (406) 587-5544) makes the best vegetarian pizza in town. For a true dive, head for **The Haufbrau,** (22 S Eighth Ave, (406) 587-4931) a student hangout; actor Rob Lowe and other celebs come here when they're in town.

Lone Mountain Restaurant ☆☆☆   The moment you walk into the restaurant at Big Sky's Lone Mountain Ranch, you know you've stumbled upon someplace special—an American culinary legend in the making. From the copper-clad bar top to the rustic pine furnishings, elk antler chandeliers, and fireplace crackling with freshly chopped wood, your eyes are treated to one feast while your belly waits for another. Chef Kim Mitchell's menu has attracted raves in leading magazines (*Bon Appétit, Travel & Leisure*). Among our favorite dishes are the bison tenderloin with Montana huckleberry and sage sauce, venison rosettes with forest mushrooms, sun-dried cherries and chasseur sauce, and Rocky Mountain trout stuffed with crab meat, spinach, and basil. They are complemented by an exceptional wine list and classic desserts. There's a fixed dinner price for five courses. The atmosphere is unhurried since on most nights only a single seating of guests is planned; make reservations as far in advance as possible. An interesting and enjoyable Nordic offshoot of the restaurant is the sleigh-ride dinner (see Snowmobiling/Other Activities, above). This is sold out months in advance during the holidays but usually has space later in the season. Note: Visitors are welcome to the dining room and sleigh ride even if they are not staying at the guest ranch (call ahead— there are some exceptions). The ranch is closed in October and November. *From the Big Sky turnoff on US 191, drive 4 miles on the main road and look for the sign to Lone Mountain Ranch on the right—ranch is another half-mile; PO Box 160069, Big Sky; (406) 995-4644; breakfast, lunch, dinner every day; DIS, MC, V; local checks only; $$$.*

Buck's T-4 Lodge ☆☆   It's the Best Western sign that throws travelers off, but inside Buck's T-4 Lodge is one of the best-kept secrets for dining in Montana. Buck's T-4 turned 50 years old in 1996 and the restaurant's hunting lodge motif (stuffed animal heads, lodgepole furniture, river rock fireplace) will make you believe you have entered the Old West. Both *Gourmet* magazine and *Wine Spectator* have bestowed stamps of excellence upon the menu. Noteworthy entrees are the eight different wild game dishes, from New Zealand red deer in port wine and shallots to South Dakota buffalo or Texas antelope bathed in a sauce of Madeira wine, mustard, and juniper. Buck's T-4 has more than 100 premium wine listings and a dessert tray that includes freshly made ice cream. The hot apple dumpling with cinnamon ice cream is divine. Reservations are strongly recommended, and Buck's T-4 is closed for a couple of weeks each spring and fall. *Roughly 1 mile south of the turnoff to Big Sky on US 191, on the west side of the road; PO Box 160279, Big Sky; (406) 995-4111; breakfast, dinner every day; DIS, MC, V; local checks only; $$.*

Chico Inn ☆☆   Renowned as one of the best restaurants in the state, this unpretentious restaurant (diners are often in jeans) at rustic Chico Hot Springs draws Hollywood celebrities, vacationing government officials, and locals ready to splurge on a festive evening. Start with the artichoke hearts, smoked trout, or baked brie, then move on to tenderloin medallions or rack of lamb. Presentations are artful. Top off the evening with the famous Chico Oránge, a hollowed-out orange coated with chocolate and filled with vanilla ice cream, orange juice, and orange liqueur. It is served tableside, flaming. Be forewarned, though: dinner plus a late-night soak in the hot springs are lethal cures for insomnia; you may need to stay overnight here. *23 miles south of Livingston off US 89, turn left (east) at Emigrant and follow the signs to Chico Hot Springs Lodge, another 3 miles; PO Drawer D, Pray; (800) HOT-WADA or (406) 333-4933; dinner every day; AE, DIS, MC, V; checks OK; $$.*

Gallatin Gateway Inn ☆☆ By far the most elegant dining in the Bozeman area, the restaurant at the Gallatin Gateway Inn is *the* place for a special occasion. It was recently voted the most romantic restaurant in Montana, and strolling into it you discover why. Chef Erik Carr describes the atmosphere as casual fine dining, but it has a flair for mood. Candlelit, white-clothed tables are spaced across a hardwood floor, and you can feel warmth lightly radiating from the hearth. Carr, trained at the Culinary Institute of America, has designed menus in Nantucket, Aspen, and the Napa Valley. Here, he assembles delectable feasts using foods native to the region. Try the Sherry-grilled duck breast with portobello mushrooms, spinach, and goat cheese canelloni. Or try the peppercorn-seared beef tenderloin with cream garlic potatoes, Cabernet sauce, cranberry-orchard relish, and toasted pine nut wontons. Another delicacy is the bison osso bucco—a tender braised bison shank with sweet onions, basil, house-dried tomatoes, polenta, and flavorful broth. For dessert the house specialties are a flourless chocolate torte with fresh berry sauce or Bailey's-espresso cheesecake. Reservations are a good idea. *About 14 miles southwest of Bozeman on US 191 just north of Gallatin Gateway; Box 376, Gallatin Gateway; (406) 763-4672 or (800) 676-3522; dinner every day; AE, DIS, MC, V; checks OK; $$.*

The Mint Bar & Cafe ☆☆ Owned by Jay Bentley of the famed Continental Divide in Ennis (see West Yellowstone and the Madison Valley chapter), the new Mint Bar & Cafe in Belgrade has quickly developed a devoted meat-loving clientele. Though the atmosphere is casual western (no tablecloths), the steaks are of high quality—eight different cuts are seared on cast-iron plates. The Mint's extensive menu also features pork, veal, and, when available, excellent bison. Two fish specials (flown in fresh) change nightly; unlike many other steak houses, the Mint's fish dishes rank among its best. Desserts include apple crisp and New York-style cheesecake. *From Bozeman, follow N 7th 10 miles north to Belgrade; 27 E Main St, Belgrade; (406) 388-1100; dinner every day; AE, DIS, MC, V; checks OK; $$.*

O'Brien's ☆☆   A couple of doors down from John Bozeman's Bistro on Main Street (see below) is a quiet, unassuming eatery, a fine-dining counterpart to the frenetic pace of the Bistro. O'Brien's has long been known for its international-style food, culinary presentation, and consistency in service. It's one of those establishments that locals, particularly those aged 30 and above, covet. The restaurant decor is reminiscent of a place you might have found in the 1940s—the best seats in the house are the elevated booths. The ambience is formal but includes soft lighting and a romantic air. Best of all, the price is right. Owners John Adcock and John Stelmack have assembled an impressive menu. Try the veal with artichoke hearts and shiitake mushrooms, slathered in a tarragon beurre blanc sauce. If you're worried about the fat, fresh scallops and shrimp coated in jalapeño pepper, garlic, cilantro, and lime make a wonderful alternative. The in-house pastry chef contributes fresh fruit tarts in season, and in winter a flourless bittersweet chocolate cake. Call for reservations. *Downtown at E Main St and Rouse; 312 E Main St, Bozeman; (406) 587-3973; dinner every day; DIS, MC, V; local checks only; $$.*

Sacajawea Inn ☆☆   Englishwoman Jane Roedel has bestowed the same simple elegance upon her in-house restaurant as she has on the rest of the historic Sacajawea Inn. House specialties include baked huckleberry-pine nut halibut, French pepper steak, prime rib, and pesto chicken. Request a table at Charbonneau's courtyard window. Despite the antique furniture and dimly lit dining room, you're just as likely to run into casually clad anglers as young lovers on the cusp of a marriage proposal. *30 miles west of Bozeman—take I-90 to Exit 278; 5 Main St, Three Forks; (800) 821-7326 or (406) 285-6515; dinner every day; AE, DIS, MC, V; local checks only; $$.*

Sir Scott's Oasis ☆☆   You won't find better, beefier steaks in Montana than the ones served at Sir Scott's, which is why real cowboys frequent the place. Throwbacks to the supper clubs of the 1960s, meals at Sir Scott's come with relish tray, salad, main entree, potato, and ice cream. In addition to numerous cuts of beef, the menu includes fish and seafood—but don't bother. This is a classic steak house. The atmosphere is so authentically western that the Beef Council used Sir Scott's as a backdrop for a national television ad. Authenticity has its price, however, and Sir Scott's can be very smoky. *From Bozeman take I-90 25 miles northwest to the Manhattan exit on Manhattan's main street; 204 W Railroad Ave S, Manhattan; (406) 284-6929; dinner every day; DIS, MC, V; checks OK; $$.*

Uncle Looie's Ristorante ☆☆   A respectable Northern Italian restaurant in the heart of cattle country? Formerly of the Chico Inn at Chico Hot Springs, Chef Marvin Garrett has carefully assembled an authentic Italian menu, including such unlikely Montana fare as hot antipasto, calamari, and mussels marinara—and those are just appetizers. Entrees include chicken scarpaiello, steak Milanese, eggplant manicotti, and veal specials that change daily. Individual pizzas with various toppings (try the Florentine) are terrific. When the dessert tray comes around, sink your teeth into their torte. Make reservations. *In downtown Livingston, a few doors from the Murray Hotel; 119 W Park, Livingston; (406) 222-7177; dinner every day; AE, DIS, MC, V; checks OK; $$.*

The Winchester Cafe ☆☆ Despite inconsistencies in the kitchen, this lovely and reasonably priced Continental restaurant in the historic Murray Hotel is one of our favorites. Tucked into its own quaint wing, it harkens back to the early part of this century when the hotel attracted visitors arriving at the depot across the street. As you sit in its cozy confines and look out the windows, there is a sense that this was a venue for watching the changing West. Great care is put into the dining experience, but the ambience isn't ostentatious; you'll feel at home among antiques on the walls and wooden decor. It's a great place for watching famous people entering the hotel or stopping by for dinner and a late-night drink. Try the porterhouse steak, Hutterite chicken, or spicy Mediterranean pasta. Save room for rich flan or chocolate-chocolate cake. Early bird specials are available before 6pm. *In the Murray Hotel in downtown Livingston, kitty-corner to the old railroad depot; 201 W Park, Livingston; (406) 222-2078; dinner every day; AE, DIS, MC, V; checks OK; $$.*

John Bozeman's Bistro ☆ Bozeman's town founder never set foot in this eclectic eatery, but his portrait presides over the hippest dining room in town. The impressive menu at the Bistro ranges from pasta to Cajun-style fish and even sushi. The baked brie is terrific. The Bistro also claims Bozeman's best waiter, the handlebar-mustachioed Monte. *Downtown, E Main and Rouse; 242 E Main St, Bozeman; (406) 587-4100; lunch, dinner Tues–Sun; AE, DIS, MC, V; local checks only; $$.*

Rocky Mountain Pasta Company ☆ A cousin to the Bacchus Pub (also located in the lobby of the Baxter Hotel; see below), the Rocky Mountain Pasta Company is everything you'd expect from an Italian restaurant for working-class Joes, right down to the soft light, classical guitar music, and grass-coated bottles of Chianti. The homemade ravioli, tortellini, and canelloni are terrific, especially in sinfully rich white sauce. *In the back of the Baxter Hotel, corner of Main and Willson; 105 W Main, Bozeman; (406) 586-1314; lunch, dinner every day; AE, MC, V; local checks only; $.*

Spanish Peaks Brewing Pub ☆ Birthplace of the nationally distributed and award-winning Black Dog Ale, Spanish Peaks is the closest thing that

Bozeman has to a real microbrewery. The beer is actually brewed next door, as well as in a major facility in Minnesota; the Spanish Peaks Sampler allows you to try five small glasses of the current brews. Don't be put off by the austere interior; we often stop in for minestrone soup and an order of Toscano bread spread with garlic and olive oil and sprinkled with fresh Parmesan. Personal pizzas and Florentine ravioli are also noteworthy. Be mindful: the beer is strong. *200 yards north of the intersection of Main and 19th; 120 N 19th Ave, Bozeman; (406) 585-2296; lunch Mon–Sat, dinner every day; AE, DIS, MC, V; local checks only; $.*

The Bacchus Pub A typical college-town burger joint (in the venerated Baxter Hotel), the Bacchus is a Bozeman mainstay. The recently upgraded menu includes burgers and grilled chicken sandwiches; don't miss the spiced french fries. Eat on the alley porch during summer. *In the Baxter Hotel, corner of Main and Willson; 105 W Main St, Bozeman; (406) 586-1314; breakfast, lunch, dinner every day; AE, DIS, MC, V; checks OK; $.*

The Pickle Barrel A take-out sandwich joint beloved for its huge creations, the Pickle Barrel is a traditional lunchtime stop for students from Montana State University. This ain't Philadelphia or Chicago, but the Pickle Barrel's hot cheese-steak sandwiches may convince you otherwise. *Just west of 8th; 809 W College, Bozeman; (406) 587-2411; lunch, dinner every day; no credit cards; checks OK; $.*

The Livingston Bar and Grille Recently purchased by landscape painter, writer, and sportsman Russell Chatham (a longtime Livingston resident), the Livingston Bar and Grille is on the rebound. The handcrafted back bar won a Craftsman design contest at the turn of the century. At press time, the Bar and Grille hadn't opened yet, but if a preview party and Chatham's reputation as a gourmand are any indication, it's worth a visit. *In downtown Livingston on Park and Main, kitty-corner from the old depot; 130 N Main, Livingston; (406) 222-7909; dinner every day; AE, DIS, MC, V; local checks only; $$.*

Lodgings

Big Sky's two villages offer a huge range of accommodations—more than 1,000 rooms and condos in all. Among the top choices are the 29-room **River Rock Lodge,** (800) 995-9966 or (406) 995-2295, the mountain's newest and fanciest resort; the 200-room **Huntley Lodge** and the 94-unit **Shoshone Condominium Hotel** remain comfortable alternatives, both reached at (800) 548-4486 or (406) 995-5000. Condominiums are also available through property-management companies: **Big Sky Condominium Management,** (800) 831-3509 or (406) 995-4560; **Golden Eagle**

Management, (800) 548-4488 or (406) 995-4800; and **Triple Creek Realty & Management,** (800) 548-4632 or (406) 995-4848. For general information, contact **Big Sky Central Reservations,** (800) 548-4486 or (406) 995-5000.

Chico Hot Springs Lodge ☆☆   Over the years this Montana classic has gone through several incarnations, including a period of notoriety as a place of ill repute. Today the rustic, 80-room hotel is on the National Register of Historic Places and is a favorite for locals entertaining out-of-town guests. Rooms in the main lodge have the most charm, but noise from the hallway tends to drift through the thin walls. Quieter, though lacking the same character, are the modern rooms in the new, 18-room lower lodge. But most people don't spend much time in their rooms—they'd rather lounge in the hot pools or the funky saloon. Trail rides leave from the lodge (see Horseback Riding, above) and the on-site restaurant is among the best in Montana (see Restaurants, above). *23 miles south of Livingston off US 89; turn left (east) at Emigrant and drive another 3 miles—it's well-signed; PO Drawer D, Pray, MT 59065; (800) HOT-WADA or (406) 333-4933; AE, DIS, MC, V; checks OK; $$.*

Gallatin Gateway Inn ☆☆   Opened on June 17, 1927, to serve as a stopover for tourists traveling by railroad to Yellowstone on the Chicago, Milwaukee, St. Paul & Pacific Railroad, the 35-room Gallatin Gateway Inn offers one of the finest hotel-restaurant combinations in Montana (see Restaurants, above). The Spanish Mission-style decor is punctuated by high ceilings, a stylish sunlit common room with fireplace, and stunning Polynesian mahogany woodwork. Request rooms away from the restaurant. Out back is a trout pond where anglers can practice casting before setting out for the Gallatin River. The rooms themselves are comfortable and nicely done, with queen-sized beds and authentic furniture, but they're not the reason you stay here. Rather, it's all part of a package that comes with staying in a railroad hotel built for well-to-do tourists able to explore a rustic (but not too rough) West. Hotel personnel will gladly help you arrange horseback rides, fly-fishing trips, or naturalist tours of Yellowstone. *12 miles southwest of Bozeman on US 191; Box 376, Gallatin Gateway, MT 59730; (800) 676-3522 or (406) 763-4672; AE, MC, V; local checks only; $$.*

Lindley House ☆☆   Built in 1889 by one of Bozeman's early pioneers, Joseph M. Lindley, this Victorian manor house recently underwent a complete restoration. Owner Stephanie Volz has furnished the house with French period decor, including vintage wall coverings and antique beds to complement original stained-glass windows. The whistling parrot who greets guests in the foyer adds a touch of informality. Of five rooms, best is the Marie Antoinette Suite, with its king-sized bed and antique brass headboard, hand-carved oak fireplace with French tile, linen-covered padded walls, and an attached sitting room with balcony. Breakfast is included. *2 blocks south of Main, corner of Olive and Lindley; 202 Lindley Pl, Bozeman, MT 59715; (800) 787-8404 or (406) 587-8403; AE, DIS, MC, V; checks OK; $$.*

Sacajawea Inn ☆☆ Built in 1910 by the Milwaukee Road railroad to house railroad workers and travelers, the Sacajawea Inn had fallen into serious disrepair before it was rescued by a million-dollar renovation in the early 1990s. Owner Jane Roedel modernized all 33 small rooms, adding phones, televisions, and private baths, but managed to retain the original flavor of the place—the beamed ceilings, wood floors, and enormous front porch remain. Third-floor rooms have the best views. At night, a player on the foyer's grand piano may treat you to a rendition of "As Time Goes By." The on-site restaurant is very good (see Restaurants, above). *30 miles west of Bozeman—take I-90 to Exit 278; 5 Main St, Three Forks, MT 59752; (800) 821-7326 or (406) 285-6515; AE, MC, V; local checks only; $$.*

The Voss Inn Bed and Breakfast ☆☆ A classic 1883 brick mansion, the Voss Inn rates as one of Bozeman's oldest homes and nicest B&Bs. Certainly few inn owners can rival Frankee and Bruce Muller for romantic histories: the two met on photographic safari in Botswana (he's from Zimbabwe; she's American). Of six rooms, the Chisholm Room is a standout, with its 9-foot high antique brass headboard, claw-footed bathtub, and private breakfast nook (breakfast served here on request). *4 blocks south of Main St at Willson and Koch; 319 S Willson, Bozeman, MT 59715; (406) 587-0982; AE, DIS, MC, V; checks OK; $$.*

Bud Lilly's Anglers Retreat ☆ One of the most famous fly-fishermen in America, septuagenarian Bud Lilly runs a homey, white clapboard hotel specifically designed for those interested in pursuing piscatorial pastimes. Room rates include a personalized, Lilly-designed fishing itinerary, as well as use of his extensive fishing library. Once owned by Bud Lilly's mother, this rustic but comfortable old hotel is a step back into the 1930s. Of five small guest rooms, three share a bath. Reservations go quickly. *1 block off Main in Three Forks; 16 W Birch, Three Forks, MT 59752; (406) 285-6690 or (406) 586-5140; MC, V; local checks only; $.*

Murray Hotel ☆ This Livingston landmark has an impressive history: Calamity Jane, Whoopie Goldberg, Jack Palance, and the Queen of Denmark are among the names that grace its guest list. Of 32 spacious, renovated rooms, the Peckinpah Suite has the most character; you can still see where movie director Sam Peckinpah shot bullets into the ceiling. Located across from the old railroad station, this 1905 brick building still boasts original woodwork in its lobby. Request a south-facing room with a view of the Absaroka Mountains. *In downtown Livingston across from the old railroad depot; 201 W Park, Livingston, MT 59047; (406) 222-1350; AE, DIS, MC, V; checks OK; $.*

Paradise Gateway Bed and Breakfast ☆ Veteran travelers, Paradise Gateway owners Carol and Pete Reed decided to emphasize relaxation for their B&B guests, even going so far as to build a bonfire along the Yellowstone River in the evenings. Located roughly halfway between Livingston and the northern entrance to Yellowstone Park, this custom-built cedar home and separate cabin sit on 50 acres fronting the Yellowstone River, with Emigrant Peak as a backdrop (guests receive a complimentary photograph of the mountain). Of four bedrooms, the Wildflower and Burpatch Rooms offer the best views of the Absarokas. Full breakfasts include organically grown fruit. *4 1/2 miles south of Emigrant along US 89; PO Box 84, Emigrant, MT 59027; (406) 333-4063; AE, DIS, MC, V; checks OK; $$.*

Remember When Bed and Breakfast ☆ Filled with antiques (thus the name), this 1908 Victorian offers some of Livingston's nicest and most reasonably priced accommodations. All four rooms come with private bath and full breakfast. Request the spacious Fireside Room, with its fireplace and view, or the Victorian Room, with its walnut-spool bed and 1850s French day bed. Owners Dave and Chris Kinslow are very friendly. *At Yellowstone and 3rd, 4 blocks south of downtown Livingston; 320 S Yellowstone, Livingston, MT 59047; (406) 222-8367; AE, DIS, MC, V; checks OK; $.*

The River Inn Bed and Breakfast ☆ Few bed and breakfast inns can claim a setting as stunning as the River Inn's beneath the rugged Absaroka Mountains. It's also within casting distance of the Yellowstone River. Set on 5 acres at the mouth of Paradise Valley, Ursula Neese's and DeeDee Van Zyle's beautiful 19th-century farmhouse boasts 500 feet of river access with pools that attract big trout (and, in summer, guests enjoying a dip). All three bedrooms come with private baths and views of either the river or the mountains; guests may also choose to sleep in either a nearby cabin or sheepherder's wagon. Ursula and DeeDee also guide canoeing and hiking trips. *6 miles south of downtown; 4950 S US 89, Livingston, MT 59047; (406) 222-2429; AE, DIS, MC, V; checks OK; $$.*

Yellowstone Inn Bed and Breakfast These two beautifully landscaped turn-of-the-century stone cottages sit just a stone's throw from the entrance to Yellowstone National Park. All the rooms are bright and cheery. The smaller cottage (the one that houses the office) sits a bit farther from the highway; the three rooms there are naturally quieter. The two-bedroom Yellowstone Suite is a good choice for families. None of the rooms are air-conditioned, though all have fans; visitors coming in the heat of summer might prefer downstairs rooms. Rates are reasonable, and hosts Shelli Liddell and Terri Eddington can arrange rafting, fly-fishing, and horseback riding trips at an additional cost. *In Gardiner, at the corner of Main St and US 89; Box 515, Gardiner, MT 59030; (406) 848-7000; MC, V; checks OK; $$.*

Ranches and Resorts

Lone Mountain Guest Ranch   A year-round retreat, the revered Lone Mountain Ranch is perhaps best known for its 75 kilometers of Nordic trails, open to the public as well as guests. When the snow melts, Lone Mountain transforms into a dude ranch and Orvis-endorsed fly-fishing resort. All-inclusive winter weekly rates ($2,000/couple for a Sunday-to-Sunday stay) include accommodations in spacious, luxurious cabins with private baths and wood-burning stoves or fireplaces; all meals, including a sleigh-ride dinner and gourmet buffet lunch, served on-trail; and use of the outdoor hot tub. Ski lessons, rentals, and naturalist-guided trips into Yellowstone's backcountry cost extra, as do appointments with the on-site masseuse. Summer rates of $2,500/couple include accommodations in either the cabins or the newer Ridgetop Lodge; guided fly-fishing programs are available for an additional cost. Lone Mountain is family-friendly, offering various child-centered activities. The gourmet restaurant in the stunning log lodge is terrific any time of year (see Restaurants, above). Closed October and November, and again mid-April through the first week of June. *At Big Sky, 40 miles south of Bozeman; PO Box 160069, Big Sky, MT 59716; (800) 514-4644 or (406) 995-4644; DIS, MC, V; checks OK.*

Mountain Sky Guest Ranch   This upscale fly-fishing resort/dude ranch offers just about every activity you can think of (and with weekly rates at $2,000-plus/person it should). Horseback riding, guided fishing and hiking, tennis, swimming, and gourmet meals are included. There's a sauna, pool, and hot tub. Gourmet meals are served in the main lodge, with its vaulted ceilings and river rock fireplace. Guests stay in modern, western-themed cabins; kids are welcome—the ranch has a children's program. Open May through October. *12 miles southeast of Livingston; Box 1128, Bozeman, MT 59715; (800) 548-3392 or (406) 587-1244; AE, DIS, MC, V; checks OK.*

Nine Quarter-Circle Ranch   For more than half a century, Kelly and Kim Kelsey have been running this family-oriented dude ranch 17 miles south of Big Sky along the Taylor Fork River. That's some staying power. Guests sleep in basic cabins, some with private bath; eat simple, filling ranch-style meals, and—here's why they come back year after year—ride to their heart's content. Weekly rates of $850–$950/person also include square dancing, movies, hayrides, child supervision, a private trout pond, and pack trips. Open mid-June through mid-September. *17 miles south of Big Sky; 5000 Taylor Fork Rd, Gallatin Gateway, MT 59730; (406) 995-4276 or (406) 995-4876; AE, DIS, MC, V; checks OK.*

Sixty-Three Ranch   Founded in 1929 beneath the slopes of the spectacular Absaroka Mountains just east of Livingston, the Sixty-Three Ranch ranks as one of the oldest—and most hospitable—dude ranches in the West. It is also one of the best values; weekly rates of $900/person include accommodations in rustic cabins (with bath), family-style meals, and unlimited horseback riding. The family-oriented Sixty-Three also offers fishing and pack trips for an additional cost. Owners Bud and Sandra Cahill run their outfit with just the right amount of emphasis on leisure; celebrities choose the Sixty-Three because it is secluded and low-key. Make reservations well in advance. Open mid-June through mid-September. *40 miles east of Bozeman or 12 miles east of Livingston; Box MA979, Livingston, MT 59047; (406) 222-0570; AE, DIS, MC, V; checks OK.*

Backcountry Cabins

The Forest Service rents out backcountry cabins and lookouts that are no longer in use. Rates generally run $15 to $30 per night. For a complete list of available cabins and lookouts, request a copy of the *Northern Region Recreational Cabin and Lookout Directory,* available from the Gallatin National Forest Supervisor's Office, (406) 587-6701, or any ranger district. The Gallatin National Forest has a whopping 24 cabins, most of which date back to the 1920s and 1930s. The cabins are very popular; reservations are accepted up to six months in advance.

About 18 miles northeast of Bozeman at the foot of the Bridger Mountains (about 6 miles from Bridger Bowl), the two-room **Battle Ridge** cabin is open year-round, though you may have to ski or snowshoe the last quarter-mile in winter. Set at the edge of a meadow, the cabin is particularly lovely in spring and early summer, when wildflowers are out. Nearby meadows offer great cross-country skiing opportunities; it's also a rustic lodging alternative for those interested in skiing nearby Bridger Bowl. The cabin sleeps four; utensils and firewood are provided. Bring your own sleeping bag and food. Bozeman Ranger District, (406) 587-6920.

Used as the setting for Robert Pirsig's cult novel *Zen and the Art of Motorcycle Maintenance*, the **Fox Creek Cabin** requires a 2 1/2-mile hike or ski in. The cabin itself is nothing special, but the location, 14 miles south of Bozeman in the Gallatin Range, certainly is. You can access the cabin via two trails: the beautiful 6-mile hike along South Cottonwood Creek drainage, or the shorter downhill hike from the end of Langohr Rd (but then you have to hike out). Numerous other trails surround the cabin, which is open December through mid-October. Fox Creek is among the newest cabins to become available, and as such is often easier to reserve. It sleeps two; cooking utensils, firewood, and stove are provided. Bring sleeping bag and food. Bozeman Ranger District, (406) 587-6920.

Open year-round, the **Window Rock Cabin** beyond Hyalite Reservoir boasts a stunning location and access to a network of hiking trails. The cabin has one bedroom and loft, plus four beds with mattresses, a cookstove, and utensils. A small creek runs next to the cabin. In summer, you can drive right to the cabin; in winter it's a 3- or 4-mile ski. Bozeman Ranger District, (406) 587-6920.

About 29 miles south of Bozeman along the Gallatin Divide, the **Windy Pass Cabin** offers terrific views of the Taylor–Hilgards, and, in season, stunning wildflowers. You'll have to earn the views with a steep 2 1/2-mile hike in. There are only two mattresses on four beds. A stove and kitchen utensils are provided, but you'll have to cut your own firewood. Available June through mid-October. Bozeman Ranger District, (406) 587-6920.

The popular five-room **Big Creek Cabin**, 40 miles southwest of Livingston, sleeps 10, making it a good family option. (You can access it by car in season; in winter it's a half-mile ski). There's good hiking and mountain biking nearby (you can access the Gallatin Divide). Inside are two wood stoves and some kitchen utensils. Bring sleeping bag and food. The cabin is open year-round with the exception of a brief closure during fall hunting season. Livingston Ranger District, (406) 222-1892.

The modern (with electricity and even a phone!) **Mill Creek Guard Station,** 40 miles south of Livingston, is located in a premier recreation area. Hiking trails lead to the Absaroka–Beartooth Wilderness; in winter there's plenty of good backcountry skiing. The cabin sleeps three; it's open November through May and sometimes during summer. Livingston Ranger District (406) 222-1892.

You'll want a high-clearance vehicle to get to the **Porcupine Cabin** in the Crazy Mountains 45 miles north of Livingston (a 1 1/2-mile ski in during winter). This relatively isolated three-room cabin offers gorgeous views of the Bridgers and the Crazies. There are eight cots and mattresses, a wood stove, firewood, and kitchen utensils. Bring lantern fuel, sleeping bags, and food. Livingston Ranger District, (406) 222-1892.

More Information

Big Sky Chamber of Commerce: (406) 995-3000.

Big Sky Ski and Summer Resort: (800) 548-4486 or (406) 995-5000.

Bozeman Chamber of Commerce: (406) 586-5421.

Bridger Bowl: (800) 223-9609 or (406) 586-1518.

Gallatin National Forest Supervisor's Office: (406) 587-6701.

GNF Avalanche Advisory: (406) 587-6981.

GNF, Bozeman Ranger District: (406) 587-6920.

GNF, Gardiner Ranger District: (406) 848-7375.

GNF, Livingston Ranger District: (406) 222-1892.

Gardiner Chamber of Commerce: (406) 848-7971.

Livingston Chamber of Commerce: (406) 222-0850.

Montana Department of Fish, Wildlife and Parks: (406) 994-4042.

Montana Wilderness Association, Bozeman: (406) 582-8600.

Travel Montana: (800) 847-4868 out-of-state or (406) 444-2654 in-state.

Yellowstone Country (a regional arm of Travel Montana): (800) 736-5276 or (406) 446-1005.

Helena
and **Environs**

Including Canyon Ferry, Hauser, and Holter Lakes, Helena National Forest, and the Gates of the Mountains Wilderness.

Despite a history of independent-thinking politicians (US Representative Jeannette Rankin was the only member of Congress to vote against entry into both world wars) and a few radical residents, Montana has a rather conservative capital. Part small town, part political center, Helena is one of the state's most attractive cities, with a distinctly laid-back, friendly atmosphere.

In 1805, the Lewis and Clark expedition passed through the area just east of today's Helena, as the party paddled up the Missouri River through a canyon Lewis named the Gates of the Mountains. The city of Helena (city pop: 27,000, county pop: 52,785) was founded in 1864 after four hopeful miners panning for gold struck pay dirt on the east side of the Continental Divide, along what is now Last Chance Gulch. According to legend, these "Four Georgians" decided to take one "last chance" before calling it quits. Word of their find spread quickly, and soon Helena was a thriving miners' camp. In 1875, it was named territorial capital—some said its influence was so dominant that Montana was sometimes referred to as the "Territory of Helena."

By the 1890s, Helena claimed more than 50 millionaires—reputedly more per capita than anywhere else in the nation. In 1894, after an expensive and passionate battle between two Butte Copper Kings, Helena, backed by mining magnate William A. Clark, beat out Marcus Daly's company town of Anaconda to become the state capital. Government is still the biggest employer in present-day Helena, but the city is far less wealthy and less exciting than the Helena of yesteryear. Helena's mining legacy lives on, however, in its stunning architecture—it's not called the Queen City of the Rockies for nothing. You can see evidence of the former wealth in its lovely mansions, churches, and historic brick and stone buildings downtown.

Situated at 4,100 feet above sea level and surrounded by Helena National Forest, Helena has the dry, arid climate that characterizes the Rockies' eastern front, which means that recreational opportunities open up earlier here than in other parts of western Montana. The city overlooks the Helena Valley, with views of the Big Belt Mountains to the east. Mount Helena, an enormous city park well-used by hikers and mountain bikers, flanks its southwest corner. The mighty Missouri River lies to its north and east; controlled by a succession of three dams, it's no longer the free-flowing river Lewis and Clark floated nearly 200 years ago. But the river's reservoirs offer great fishing and boating opportunities that draw anglers from throughout the region.

Helena doesn't offer the glitz of Bozeman or the hipness of Missoula, and that's just fine with most Helenans. They're well-situated to visit other Montana locales and they like their moderate, low-key lifestyle, thank you very much. They also like the fact that Montana's capital city still feels like Montana as it used to be.

Getting There

Helena is located on the eastern side of the Rockies, at the junction of US Highway 12 and Interstate 15. It's served by the Helena Regional Airport and Rimrock Trailways bus line.

Adjoining Areas

WEST: **Missoula and Environs**

NORTH: **Seeley–Swan and Blackfoot Valleys**

SOUTH: **Butte and Environs; Bozeman and Environs**

inside out

Fishing

The large, man-made Canyon Ferry, Hauser, and Holter Lakes are among the most heavily fished bodies of water in the state. The Missouri River below Holter Lake is also very popular. Local **regulations** change yearly; for a current copy, or information and maps, contact the Montana Department of Fish, Wildlife and Parks in Helena, (406) 444-4720, or any licensing outlet.

Rent fly rods, waders, and other **gear** at Cross Currents fly-fishing shop (326 N Jackson, (406) 449-2292); the store offers free fly-casting clinics every Wednesday night in summer at 6:30pm at Spring Meadow Lake State Park. Based out of the Cross Currents store, Paul Roos Outfitters, (800) 858-3497 or (406) 442-5489, takes guided day and overnight trips on the Missouri River, where they have a base camp. Kim's Marina, (406) 475-3723, 2 miles south of the Canyon Ferry Dam on the east side of Canyon Ferry Lake, rents pontoon boats, fishing boats, canoes, and pedal boats. The Boat Loft, (406) 235-4435, on the northeast end of Holter Lake, rents pontoon boats and wave runners.

Lake Fishing

Hauser Lake has long been famous for its large (12- to 16-inch) kokanee salmon, though the take fluctuates (1996, for instance, was not a good year). Check with Montana Department of Fish, Wildlife and Parks for current status. You can fish the lake year-round, but salmon fishing is best from March through mid-summer; after that they begin to get soft as they prepare to spawn. You'll want to move up the reservoir (south) as the season progresses. You can fish for rainbows here, too; it's best in April and May. There's an occasional walleye caught in the Lake Helena arm. **Ice fish** for either rainbows or salmon.

Fish for rainbow trout in 25-mile-long **Canyon Ferry Lake.** March through May you can do well from shore; when the weather heats up, though, you'll want a boat for trolling. You can also **ice fish** Canyon Ferry for rainbow and burbot.

Holter Lake has rainbow trout, kokanee salmon, perch, and big walleye, when you can catch them. Early or late in the season you can fish from shore, but in the heat of summer you'll want a boat since the fish go deeper. **Ice fish** along Beartooth Road on the east shore. Find public launch sites at the Holter Lake Recreation Area on the north end of the lake, or at Log Gulch Campground on the east shore. Montana Department of Fish, Wildlife and Parks in Great Falls, (406) 454-5840, will have up-to-date information on Holter.

When the ice melts in late April, fish for arctic grayling and a few cutthroats at **Park Lake,** a very pretty alpine lake southwest of Helena (see Camping, below). Park Lake gets very busy during summer weekends.

Little kids like to bait fish for largemouth bass, yellow perch, sunfish, and rainbows at **Spring Meadow Lake State Park** on the northwest edge of Helena. There's a day-use fee. Take US 12 west to Joslyn, then turn right (north) and follow the signs.

River Fishing

There are a whopping 3,500 to 4,000 fish per mile on the **Missouri River** below (north) **Holter Dam.** It's mostly rainbows and browns up to 20 inches, so if you can't catch one here you might as well get a new hobby. There's a large caddis hatch mid-June through August; the trico hatch starts in July and runs through August. There's plenty of shore access and good floating, too. Avoid this stretch of the river between mid-May and mid-June, when spring runoff is highest.

Closer to Helena, fish the Missouri River year-round below **Hauser Dam** to Beaver Creek for huge rainbow and brown trout. The best time for lunker browns is September through November, when they make their way upstream to spawn. There's good shore access on the east side of the river across Hauser Dam.

The **Little Blackfoot River** along US 12 has good rainbow and brown trout fishing in early spring and stays clear from mid-June through mid-summer; it's low in August. Good shore access can be found at bridges and railroad right-of-ways from Elliston west to Garrison.

Access **Little Prickly Pear Creek** from the recreation road in Wolf Creek Canyon, 30 miles north of Helena. You'll have best luck there in late spring and late August for rainbows and browns ranging from 12 to 18 inches. There's a good caddis hatch here. Read regulations carefully, though—the stream closes after Labor Day. Drive north on I-15 to the Wolf Creek exit, then drive south along the recreation road.

Hiking/Backpacking

The Helena National Forest Supervisor's Office (2880 Skyway Drive, (406) 449-5201) and The Base Camp outdoor store (333 N Last Chance Gulch, (406) 443-5360) can provide area **trail maps** (you'll want a Helena National Forest map or a Gates of the Mountains Wilderness map) and advice. Most of the following hikes are described in greater detail in Bill Schneider's *Hiking Montana*. For additional ideas, see Backcountry Cabins, below.

Blessed with half a dozen trails at the 628-acre **Mount Helena City Park,** Helena residents don't even have to leave city limits to get to some great hiking. The mountain offers good views of the city and a chance to see deer and elk. The popular **1906 Trail** (1 3/5 miles one-way) leads past the hillside "H" and climbs gradually to the 5,465-foot summit. The 6-mile **Ridge Trail** begins at the west end of the park and follows a ridge-line southwest to the head of Grizzly Gulch. The Mount Helena Trail Users, volunteers who maintain the trails, publishes a small map available at the Adams Street trailhead. At the southwest corner of the city, take

Benton Avenue to Adams St and follow it to the parking lot. Call Helena Department of Parks and Recreation, (406) 447-8463, for more information.

The 2-mile trail along the Missouri River from **Hauser Dam to Beaver Creek** is an easy, level day hike through a spectacular river canyon. You'll see lots of birdlife—and anglers, since there's good shore access here. The trailhead is on the east shore; park at Hauser Dam and walk across, then follow the signs to the recreation trail.

A trail from **Refrigerator Canyon** leads 18 miles east-to-west across the 28,000-acre **Gates of the Mountains Wilderness.** It's a small but stunning area of jagged peaks and deep canyons, home to mountain goats and bighorn sheep. You'll want a shuttle for this point-to-point hike so you can take the Gates of the Mountains tour boat from the Meriwether picnic area, rather than hiking back the way you came. Aptly named, Refrigerator Canyon is usually 10 to 20 degrees cooler than the surrounding area. It makes a good early season hike; normally the refrigerator's snow has melted by May. The full route to Meriwether is either a grueling day hike or an overnight; either way, you'll have to pack your own water. The trailhead is about 20 miles northeast of Helena, near the small community of York.

It's 4 moderately steep miles and a 3,400-foot elevation gain one-way to hike through Casey Meadows to the top of **Casey Peak** in the **Elkhorn Range,** southeast of Helena. Burned in a 1988 wildfire, the area provides a good look at nature's reforestation process. Most people take **Trail #343** to **Trail #301**, then follow the trail signs to Casey Peak, where there are the remains of an old lookout. You can hike back a different route, looping around on Trail #301 to Trail #302, though these trails fade in places. The route to Casey Peak is generally open by the end of May; it's a popular family day hike, but nothing in this area gets too crowded. The trailhead is 10 miles southeast of Helena; take I-15 south to the Montana City exit. Take a right at the school and follow the road until the T. Turn left onto a Forest Service road and follow it just past Jackson Creek, where you'll bear left into a parking lot. You'll find the trailhead in the woods there.

Six steep miles lead to the spectacular **Hanging Valley,** a dry waterfall several hundred feet above Trout Creek Canyon. This is very unusual geography for Montana: you cross over a high ridge, then drop into a deep, narrow canyon lined with limestone pinnacles. It's not easy, but the unique scenery is well worth the trip. Bring water. The trailhead is located at the Vigilante Campground, 20 miles northeast of Helena and 6 miles past the community of York.

At press time, the Forest Service planned to construct a 2-mile, wheelchair-accessible interpretive trail at **Willard Creek,** south of

Helena, in addition to a variety of existing trails. To get there, take I-15 south to the Clancy exit. Cross under the highway and drive to Alhambra (site of a nursing home), then go 8 miles up Warm Springs Creek Rd to the parking lot.

Camping

Travel Montana's *Montana Travel Planner* lists all area public and private campgrounds alphabetically; look under "Gold West Country" for those near Helena. Call (800) 847-4868 out-of-state or (406) 444-2654 in-state to receive your copy. If traveling with an RV, be sure to check if the campgrounds can accommodate your vehicle. Your other source of information is the Montana Department of Fish, Wildlife and Parks in Helena, (406) 444-4720.

A lot of people camp on one of the three reservoirs northeast of Helena—Holter, Hauser, or Canyon Ferry—but the draws are fishing and water sports more than scenery. These campsites are fine if you just want a place to crash lakeside, but they're nothing out of the ordinary—and the lakes get lots of traffic. This is big RV country, and shade is at a premium.

The Bureau of Land Management, in conjunction with the Bureau of Reclamation, operates 11 campgrounds on **Canyon Ferry Lake.** Tent campers should head for the tents-only **Fish Hawk Campground,** with six sites, toilets, shade, and a good view of the lake (but no water). The quietest of the campgrounds, Fish Hawk is on the west shore of Canyon Ferry Lake, 1 mile south of the Yacht Basin Marina. **Jo Bonner Campground,** on the northeast end of the lake, 2 ½ miles from Canyon Ferry Village on County Rd 284 at the mouth of Magpie Creek, is your other best bet for shade and relative quiet. Summer weekends, these sites are very popular, so come early. Call the joint office of the Bureau of Reclamation and Bureau of Land Management, (406) 475-3319, for information.

Black Sandy is the only public campground on **Hauser Lake.** It tends to be crowded and there's not much shade—but at least there are showers and toilets.

The prettiest of the three man-made lakes, **Holter Lake** is bordered by the Beartooth Wildlife Management Area to the east and the Sleeping Giant Wilderness Study Area to the west. The Bureau of Land Management operates three campgrounds on Holter Lake; **Log Gulch Campground** is best for tent campers, though you shouldn't expect solitude, as there are 90 sites. About half of the sites are shaded, and there's a nice sand and pebble beach and a swimming area. Immediately south of the campground is the Beartooth Wildlife Management Area, where you can hike and bike along the roads. To reach the east side of the lake, go 8 miles south of the Wolf Creek exit off I-15; take the Bear Gulch Rd. Contact the Bureau of Land Management, Butte, (406) 494-5059.

You can camp for free at **Vigilante Campground** in the Big Belts, north of York, and never worry about seeing an RV. Twenty-two tent-only sites are located in a heavily wooded and bouldered area; some have creekside locations. The trailhead to Hanging Valley is located here (see Hiking/Backpacking, above). Managed by the Helena National Forest Supervisor's Office, (406) 449-5201.

Open from Memorial Day to Labor Day and gated the rest of the year, **Park Lake Campground** is very pretty. It's situated next to an alpine lake popular with fishermen. Bring your bug spray, though, since the horse-flies and other insects can get particularly nasty. Only nonmotorized boats are allowed on the lake; there's a hiking trail that leads around the lake as well. Take I-15 to the Clancy exit and turn right (west) on Lump Gulch Rd. Look for the signs. Helena National Forest Supervisor's Office, (406) 449-5201.

About 15 miles east of Lincoln off Hwy 200, **Copper Creek Campground** is in a thick stand of lodgepole pines and Douglas firs next to Copper Creek and man-made Snowbank Lake. Motorized boats are prohibited, so no one can wreck your serenity. You can swim in the lake, too, but it's cold. There are 21 sites suitable for tents or RVs. Go 7 miles east of Lincoln, then turn up Copper Creek Rd and follow it 8 miles (look for the signs). Lincoln Ranger District, (406) 362-4265.

At **Aspen Grove Campground,** 7 1/2 miles east of Lincoln, you'll sleep right next to the Blackfoot River in a stand of cottonwoods (there are no aspen). You can fish the Blackfoot River here for rainbow and brown trout, but the water's been tainted by nearby mines; local wisdom says catch-and-release. The 20-site campground is only a half-mile off Hwy 200 but the river obliterates traffic noise. Lincoln Ranger District, (406) 362-4265.

Mountain Biking

Great Divide Cyclery (336 N Jackson, (406) 443-5188) hands out high-lighted **maps** of a series of loop trails on the south edge of Helena. Beginning when daylight savings time does and ending when the time changes back again in the fall, a bike group departs from the store at 5:30pm on Fridays. The rides are suitable for intermediate through advanced cyclists. Great Divide also rents bicycles.

Many mountain bikers head for **Mount Helena City Park,** but it's heavily used by hikers as well. We recommend that bicyclists stay away during peak hours and stay off the 1906 Trail. Instead, ride the **Prairie Trail,** a single-track, intermediate-plus level trail, which is easier going anyway (although you may have to get off and walk in a few places). Helena Department of Parks and Recreation, (406) 447-8463.

A 10-mile intermediate to advanced loop ride begins in **Grizzly Gulch,** at the south end of Last Chance Gulch, and climbs onto the **Mount Helena Ridge Trail.** Begin by riding south on Park St, then bearing right onto a gravel road when it forks (there are signs to Grizzly Gulch). After 4 miles, bear right again at a group of mailboxes. About three-quarters of a mile farther up, you'll pass an address sign (2050 Grizzly Gulch Dr); keep going and take the very next right, about 50 yards past the sign. Pass through the parking area and continue onto the double track trail; after a quarter-mile you'll see a well-worn single track to your right. It will take you to the Mount Helena City Park, and you can loop back to town. Get a map from Great Divide Cyclery.

An easier one-way ride in the same vicinity is the trail up **Squaw Gulch.** Begin at the south end of Last Chance Gulch. Take Park St to Grizzly Gulch, and turn right. After about a half-mile watch for a gate on your left—toss your bike over and enjoy the double track trail. After 3 miles you wind up in a park meadow, a good picnic spot.

The 17-mile **Cave Gulch** ride, for advanced riders only, begins at the northeast corner of **Canyon Ferry Lake.** The descent's the appeal here, a really fun roller-coaster ride that you earn. Start at Kim's Marina on the lake's northeast side and ride southeast on the pavement. Bear left onto Magpie Creek Rd (marked). After 5 miles, you'll see a sign for Bar Gulch. Turn left onto Bar Gulch Rd and ride another 1 1/2 miles. You'll see a reclaimed logging road on your right; follow it another half-mile. Next you'll see a trail veering steeply off to your left for about 100 yards. Take it to the top where you'll hit a four-wheeler trail; turn left and follow this trail along the ridge. When it bisects a Forest Service road, turn right; when it descends, stay left. At the bottom of Cave Gulch, about 3 miles down, there's a private mining claim, the site of some unpleasant disputes. To avoid trespassing, take a left when the trail splits and head back uphill for about a mile, then descend the rest of the way to the pavement.

Cycling

The **Birdseye Loop** is a 28-mile paved circuit northwest of Helena. A series of rolling hills, it's suitable for intermediate road riders. Begin at **Spring Meadow Lake State Park** and follow Country Club Rd out of town. When the road comes to a T at Fort Harrison, bear right on Birdseye. Follow it for about 10 miles until it dead-ends at the Lincoln

Hwy. Turn right and after about 6 miles take another right on Green Meadow Dr, and follow it to another T near the high school. Turn right, then take a left onto Henderson. Ride under the train tracks up the hill, and turn right onto Euclid (US 12). At Joslyn, bear right again and ride back on Country Club Rd to the state park.

US 12 has a wide, smooth shoulder, so it's good for a work-out ride that starts in Helena and follows US 12 west to **MacDonald Pass.** It's 9 miles to the base of the mountains and 6 more tough miles to the top.

You can ride for 17 relatively flat miles through a pretty farming area out to the bar at Lakeside Marina on **Hauser Lake.** Take Custer Ave east of town, then bear left onto York Rd where the road forks. Avoid this ride on summer weekends.

Canoeing/Kayaking

There's flatwater canoeing and kayaking on the **Missouri River,** north of Helena below Hauser Dam, and on the three reservoirs. River maps are available through local outdoor stores. Rent canoes and kayaks at The Base Camp (333 N Last Chance Gulch, (406) 443-5360).

Naturalist and photographer Tom McBride, (406) 443-5286, offers **photography and interpretive floats** on the Missouri, Dearborn, and Blackfoot Rivers. Day trips and overnights are available May through mid-October; the best wildlife viewing times are in spring and fall.

The ideal Helena-area scenic float is on the Missouri through the **Gates of the Mountains,** 20 miles north of Helena. Begin at Gates of the Mountains Boat Club, where the tour boat departs (see Boating, below). There's a $3 launch fee. Don't worry about a shuttle: the river's so slow you can easily paddle back upstream. Beat the winds and the powerboats (especially bad on weekends) by doing this stretch in the morning; that's also when wildlife watching is best. You can camp at the Forest Service-run Coulter Campground, about 3 miles from the marina, or continue down river—the BLM manages 45 undeveloped westside campsites in the river channel past the Gates, beginning about 5 miles from the marina. Bureau of Land Management, Butte, (406) 494-5059.

Boating

Paddleboat tours of the Missouri River through the spectacular Gates of the Mountains area north of Helena began about a century ago, and the (now motorized) **Gates of the Mountains boat tour** still tops any list of things to do near Helena June through September. The 1,200-foot limestone cliffs that rise just north of present-day Helena were named in 1805 by explorer Meriwether Lewis. Mountain goats, bighorn sheep, and even the occasional mountain lion are among the wildlife you can expect to see. Improve your chances by taking the 10am tour, before the animals lie down in the heat of the day. You'll get closeup views of Indian pictographs, too, but mostly it's the scenery that will blow your mind. When the boat docks at Meriwether Picnic Area, you can hike 45 minutes or so up the trail to Vista Point and catch a later boat for the return trip. A much more strenuous hike takes you to Mann Gulch, the site of Montana's most famous forest fire, which killed 13 smokejumpers. (The 1949 conflagration was immortalized in Norman Maclean's book *Young Men and Fire.*) The 1 ¾-hour boat tours run Memorial Day through September from the Gates of the Mountains marina. Take the marked exit off I-15, about 20 miles north of Helena. It's well-signed. Call (406) 458-5241 for information.

Climbing

The Base Camp (333 N Last Chance Gulch, (406) 443-5360) has climbing gear and printed route information. Or consult *The Climber's Guide to Montana,* by Randall Green.

About 15 miles southeast of Helena, **Sheep Mountain** has a series of large granite domes; Right Rock has the most and the best climbs. There are some traditional crack climbs and some bolted face climbs, and several of the routes have both. For the most part, climbs are rated 5.10 and 5.11. To get there, take I-15 south to the Clancy exit, then drive 3 ⅕ miles west on Lump Gulch Rd. Take a right on the unmarked gravel road and drive one-tenth of a mile further, then bear left at the Y. You'll need a high-clearance vehicle to get to the parking area at Right Rock, and you'll have to walk about two-tenths of a mile from there.

The climbs at **Hellgate Gulch,** a steep limestone canyon, are mostly hard 5.10s, 5.11s or 5.12s, though there is one 5.6 route—all bolted. Find it on the east side of Canyon Ferry Lake about 6 miles south of the dam and 1 ½ miles up Hellgate Gulch Rd (signed). This one's not in *The Climber's Guide;* talk to The Base Camp, (406) 443-5360.

Swimming

Very popular is **Spring Meadow Lake** at the state park in Helena. There's a minimal day-use fee and a wheelchair-accessible trail around the lake.

Summers, Helena Department of Parks and Recreation operates the 164-foot (50 m) **Memorial Park swimming pool** for lap swims and open swims. It's one block north of the intersection of US 12 (Lyndale Ave) and North Main (Last Chance Gulch). Helena Department of Parks and Recreation, (406) 447-8463.

Cross-Country Skiing

The Base Camp outdoor store (333 N Last Chance Gulch, (406) 443-5360) posts current **conditions** for the following cross-country areas. The store also has copies of local **trail maps** and rents touring and telemark equipment. The Helena National Forest Supervisor's Office, (406) 449-5201, or the Lincoln Ranger District, (406) 362-4265, can also provide maps and helpful information. For additional ideas, see Backcountry Cabins, below.

Consistently, the best snow conditions in the area are at 6,736-foot **Stemple Pass**, very close to the former cabin site of the alleged Unabomber. (The cabin has been removed as potential evidence, and to limit gawkers.) There are four marked loop trails totaling 12 miles, suitable for beginner and intermediate skiers; none are groomed, but they get enough traffic that they're usually well-established. There's also lots of tough terrain here for advanced backcountry skiers to explore. Maps are normally available at the trailhead, or from the sources noted above.

The Helena Nordic Club has taken over responsibility for grooming the marked trails at **MacDonald Pass**; call The Base Camp for current conditions. Due to its proximity to Helena, this is a very popular area, and especially nice during the full moon. There's a good chance you'll see moose. Trails are suitable for intermediate skiers. Park at the Frontier Town site at the top of the pass on US 12 west of Helena.

It takes a little longer to get to the **Willard Creek Trails** in the Elkhorn Mountains, some 18 miles south of Helena (see Hiking/Backpacking, above), but there you'll find trails suitable for beginners, intermediates, and skate skiers. There are plans to groom from 3 to 10 miles of marked trails.

Downhill Skiing

Twenty miles northwest of Helena, **Great Divide** ski area above the old mining town of Marysville has a small vertical drop (1,330 feet), but 60 runs served by three double chairs. Most of the runs are suitable for intermediate to advanced skiers; there's not much here for real experts, but it's a fun family place.

There's snow-making on the lower part of the mountain and **night-skiing** Thursday through Saturday on one lift. Friday and Saturday nights there is also a ski-and-dine deal with the Continental Club restaurant at the base of the mountain: for $15 you get an all-you-can-eat barbecue buffet, including dessert, and a lift ticket good from 4pm to 9pm. Call (406) 449-3746 for more information.

Ice Skating

Open year-round, the **Queen City Ice Palace** is a full-size indoor skating rink 2 miles east of Helena on US 12. (It's just behind the Sleeping Giant Bowling Alley.) The Helena Ice Pirates play Junior A hockey there. Public skating is available during certain hours; call for times, (406) 443-4559.

Wildlife

You're likely to see **bald eagles, mountain goats,** and **bighorn sheep,** as well as a variety of waterfowl (**white pelicans** for sure) during the Gates of the Mountains boat tour, (406) 458-5241, about 20 miles north of Helena. Guides are well-informed. See Boating, above, for full details.

The wetlands and river bottoms of the 5,000-acre **Canyon Ferry Wildlife Management Area,** just north of Townsend, are a good place to see pintail ducks and **tundra swans** in March. Head for Pond Three on the east side of the area to see shorebirds and waterfowl. (Drive east of Townsend on US 12, then north on Harrison.) But Canyon Ferry is most famous for the large concentration—sometimes as many as 200—of **migrating bald eagles** that feed off spawning kokanee salmon below Canyon Ferry Dam each November. Call Montana Department of Fish, Wildlife and Parks, Townsend, (406) 266-3367.

outside in

Attractions

From mid-May through September, the **Last Chance Tour Train** offers a historical overview of the city. The tour hits all the major attractions, including the capitol, St. Helena Cathedral, and **Last Chance Gulch,** a winding downtown route that's now a pedestrian mall. Tours depart six times a day during summer and four in the spring and fall from the Montana Historical Society Building at Sixth and Roberts, across from the capitol. For details call (406) 442-1023.

The **Montana Historical Society Museum** (225 N Roberts, (406) 444-2694) boasts a good exhibit tracing Montana's history, and an extensive collection of Charles M. Russell paintings, sculptures, and sketches. It also has an interesting exhibit detailing the life of photographer F. Jay Haynes, the first commercial photographer of Yellowstone National Park. Traveling exhibits make up the rest of the museum's offerings.

The **Holter Museum of Art** features regional and national exhibitions, along with its permanent collection of work by Northwest artists. It's located near Last Chance Gulch at 12 E Lawrence, (406) 442-6400.

Helena's **architecture** ranks as the state's best. Pick up self-guided walking tour maps of the city at the Chamber of Commerce, 225 Cruse Ave, (406) 447-1530. Take the time, also, to stroll down **Ewing,** one of Helena's mansion rows, and visit the **St. Helena Cathedral,** a gothic-style gem modeled after the cathedral in Cologne, Germany.

The Montana Historical Society offers free tours of the **capitol,** well worth the 45-minute investment. They're held on the hour, 10am-4pm every day, Memorial Day through mid-September; off-season by appointment. Call (406) 444-4789. Constructed at the turn of the century, the capitol houses a great deal of artwork, including an enormous Charles M. Russell painting in the Senate chamber, depicting the meeting of Lewis and Clark and the Flathead Indians near Sula, Montana. Notice how the explorers fade away in the right-hand corner, while the Indians dominate the canvas—an indication of Russell's own bias.

The Montana Historical Society also offers free tours of the **Original Governor's Mansion** at Ewing and Sixth (Tuesday through Saturday, noon to 5pm from April through December; Sundays as well, Memorial Day through Labor Day). Home to a total of nine governors and their families, it's been renovated and furnished with donated period pieces, including some actual belongings of former governors.

The Archie Bray Foundation, (406) 443-3502, has earned a worldwide reputation as a ceramists' school and studio, enticing artists from around the world for residencies of varying lengths. You can tour the grounds and, with permission, the studios, located on the former site of the Western Clay Manufacturing Company. The Potter's Shrine, an outdoor melange of broken wares, is wonderful. Located 3 miles west of Helena, past Spring Meadow Lake State Park on Joslyn/Country Club Ave off US 12.

The **Myrna Loy Center,** named for the Radersburg, Montana-born film star and home to **Helena Presents,** draws world-class theatrical and musical performances to Montana. Jazz bookings are particularly strong, thanks in large part to the Myrna Loy's original executive director, Arnie Malina, who spearheaded the volunteer effort to renovate the old Romanesque-style Lewis and County Jail into a theater; today the auditorium sits where the old jail cells used to be. There's a small movie theater in the back where foreign films are screened nightly. It's worth a look even if you're not taking in a show; located at 15 N Ewing, (406) 443-0287, open daily.

The **Grandstreet Theatre,** Helena's community theater, produces musicals, dramas, and comedies. It's housed in a renovated turn-of-the-century Unitarian church that boasts a Tiffany stained-glass window (325 N Park, at the corner of Park and Lawrence, (406) 443-3311).

The **Helena Brewers** baseball team, a farm team for the Milwaukee Brewers, plays Pioneer League ball. Mid-June through Labor Day the team plays at Kindrick Legion Field at Memorial Park, (406) 449-7616.

The grand old **Boulder Hot Springs Resort,** south of Helena, has weathered a lot of hard times since it was built more than a century ago by a wealthy Anaconda miner. New owners have renovated parts of the enormous wood and stucco, California Mission-style building, cleaning up the facilities and imposing strict anti-alcohol rules to make this one of the nicest, most secluded commercial hot springs we know of. (Unfortunately, due to a lack of funds, the grand old lobby and ballroom remain closed to the public.) There's one outdoor pool, hot enough to swim in year-round, and two even hotter separate-sex plunge pools with locker rooms. Sorry, guys: women get what used to be the men's cold plunge pool, too, thanks to the fact that the new owners are of the female persuasion. Management is very serious about hygiene; guests are required to shower with anti-bacterial soap before soaking. Seven clean but rather spartan rooms are let out as part of a bed and breakfast operation. Sunday afternoons Boulder Hot Springs offers an all-you-can-eat brunch that has garnered a good reputation; snacks only are available the rest of the week. It's 5 miles south of Boulder on Hwy 69, 33 miles south of Helena; call (406) 225-4339 for details.

Suffering ailments ranging from arthritis to asthma, psoriasis to migraines, folks from around the world gather at the **radon health mines** in Boulder and Basin, south of Helena. It's known to be dangerous in large doses, but some people swear by the curative properties of this mineral in moderate amounts. They charge by the hour (about $2.50), but most of the mines allow curious visitors to have a quick peek for free; deep inside the mineshaft you'll find believers playing cards and reading, soaking their feet and sipping water. Don't be shy with questions: everyone loves to share a healthful tale or two. Try the Merry Widow Mine on the frontage road near the Basin exit off I-15; (406) 225-3220.

Calendar of Events

Montana's only marathon, the **Governor's Cup** brings more than 6,000 participants from 30 states to Helena on the first Saturday in June. In addition to the full marathon, there's a marathon relay and three shorter road races. The races are sponsored by Blue Cross and Blue Shield of Montana. Call Trish Bloom, (406) 447-3414, for details.

Mid-June to month's end, the annual **Montana Traditional Jazz**

Festival features Dixieland, ragtime, swing, and New Orleans-style jazz. The five-day festival takes place at the Best Western Colonial Inn and five sites along Last Chance Gulch. There are sporadic outdoor concerts as well. Montana Traditional Jazz Festival, (406) 449-7969.

The last weekend in July, Helena hosts the **Last Chance Stampede and Fair,** a rodeo and fair serving a three-county area. There's all the usual stuff: rides and exhibits, a demolition derby, and one night of country western entertainment. Lewis and Clark County Fairgrounds, (406) 442-1098, has more information.

Restaurants

Helena has many things to recommend it; great cuisine, alas, is not among them. At press time, the lovely Queen City Grill was closing, and its management was poised to take over the Montana Club. If that's come to pass, then the Montana Club (open to the public on certain weekends) will no doubt be the best restaurant in town.

The **No Sweat Cafe** (427 N Last Chance Gulch, (406) 442-6954) is Helena's vegetarian breakfast spot; **Morning Light Coffee Roasters** (503 Fuller, (406) 442-5180) is a favorite midmorning meeting place. **The Windbag Saloon** (19 S Last Chance Gulch, (406) 443-9669), which was a brothel known as Big Dorothy's until 1973, serves good burgers, huge salads, thick-cut steak fries, and homemade onion rings; it's where all the politicians meet (which may have something to do with the name). There's good Greek pizza at both **Bert and Ernie's** (361 N Last Chance Gulch, (406) 443-5680), a lively eatery, and in the attached (nonsmoking) **Bleacher's Sports Pub** next door, (406) 442-9311. The beloved **Parrot Confectionery** (42 N Last Chance Gulch, (406) 442-1470) has hand-dipped chocolates and an old-fashioned soda fountain, as well as very good chili.

The somewhat dingy but fun **Marysville House,** a renovated mining-era building, serves good steaks and seafood in a neighborhood bar atmosphere. You'll know someone before you leave—whether you want to or not. Service is leisurely; bring your patience. There's no phone; to get there drive 20 miles northwest of Helena to the old mining town of Marysville; take Lincoln Rd west and watch for the signs.

Holter Lake Lodge, (406) 235-4331, 32 miles north of Helena on the north end of Holter Lake, serves good steaks and burgers and a top-notch twice-baked potato, along with a nice view of the water from the patio or window tables.

Carriage House Bistro   Located in a converted house off US 12 in town, the Carriage House Bistro offers a limited Continental menu—appropriate for its tiny space. Chef Jeff Spurlin does best with chicken and beef; lamb and pasta dishes are not so reliable. Try the brie chicken, a frequent special. The restaurant's an odd mix of elegant and informal (white table-cloths but vinyl chairs; candlelight but paper menus; lamb served with demiglace but salads served family style). Still, the food's the best you'll see in Helena, which means it ranges from adequate to very good. Try the excellent homemade ice cream or tiramisu when available. Bring your own booze. *1 block north of Lyndale Ave (US 12) at Ewing; 234 1/2 Lyndale Ave, Helena; (406) 449-6949; dinner Mon–Sat; DIS, MC, V; checks OK; $.*

Toi's Thai Cuisine   Who could have predicted that conservative Helena wouldn't be able to get enough of coconut milk, lemon grass, and peanut sauces? For nearly 20 years, Toi Areya worked as a checker in a Helena grocery store, dreaming of bringing authentic Thai cuisine to her adopted homeland. Now reservations for the nine tables in this tiny, casual store-front are the hottest ticket in town, and for good reason. Toi has toned down the spices to please Montana palates (request hotter if need be), but this is real Thai food, not Chinese masquerading as such. Nothing radical here: the menu includes everyone's favorite noodle dish, pad thai; the classic hot and sour soup, tom yom goong; and green and red curries. Order à la carte or go for a four-course, $14 combination dinner. Service is not as knowledgeable as we might hope, but why look a gift horse in the mouth? *Next to Aunt Bonnie's Books; 423 N Last Chance Gulch, Helena; (406) 443-6656; dinner Tues–Sat; MC, V; checks OK; $.*

Lodgings

The Sanders ☆☆   The Sanders is what you think of when you imagine an old Victorian mansion: three-story brick, hardwood floors, bay win-dows, beveled glass, and high ceilings. No wonder it's considered Helena's premiere B&B, often hosting official guests and international visitors. Built for Montana's first US senator, Wilbur Sanders (that's his rock col-lection in the front entranceway), the house offers seven spacious guest rooms, all with phones, modems, televisions, and private baths. Our favorites are The Colonel's Room at the front of the house, with bay win-dows and a huge hand-carved bed, and Uncle Bob's Room, which claims a fireplace. Couples like the canopied bed and enormous two-headed shower in Teddy's Buckaroo, but it lacks the natural light of the other rooms. Best bargain is Althea's Room, which goes for less because you have to walk down the hall to get to the private bath. Owners Bobbi Uecker, a former attorney, and Rock Ringling, a staffer with the Montana Land Reliance, know the way to a customer's heart: in the afternoon there's a plate of homemade cookies in the parlor; you can help yourself anytime to the fresh fruit and brandy upstairs. *Downtown, between 7th and 8th; 328 N Ewing, Helena, MT 59601; (406) 442-3309; AE, DIS, MC, V; checks OK; $$$.*

Appleton Inn Bed and Breakfast Built by George Appleton to house one of Helena's first dentists, this 1890 Victorian on the western outskirts of town has been lovingly restored by owners Cheryl Bold and Tom Woodall. It's not nearly as large or elaborate as many other Victorian-era homes, but it's plenty comfortable, and chock-full of period antiques and Tom's handmade furniture (the couple runs the Appleton Heirloom Furniture Company on-site). Prices reflect the modest-sized rooms. Each of four second-floor rooms comes with phone and small private bath; the third floor houses a two-room family suite, complete with child's room and kitchen unit (but children under 12 need prior approval from the innkeepers). The Appleton's location on Hwy 12 looks noisy but the house is well insulated; traffic doesn't seem to be a problem. You'll need transportation, though; the Appleton is not within walking distance of downtown. *On Helena's west end at the intersection of Euclid (US 12) and Joslyn; 1999 Euclid Ave, Helena, MT 59601; (800) 956-1999 or (406) 449-7492; AE, DIS, MC, V; checks OK; $$.*

Best Western Colonial Inn The Colonial Inn is Helena's best full-service hotel, with large, comfortable rooms, a restaurant, small outdoor and indoor pools, and a Jacuzzi. The staff is eager to please. From the second-floor highway side you'll get a view of the Big Belt Mountains; ask for second floor backside for a view of the Elkhorns. Unfortunately, the Colonial Inn is not within walking distance of downtown Helena; you'll need your car. The 1pm checkout time is a nice touch. *Near the intersection of I-15 and US 12—take Exit 192B; 2301 Colonial Dr, Helena, MT 59601; (800) 422-1002 or (406) 443-2100; AE, DIS, MC, V; checks OK; $$.*

Backcountry Cabins

The Forest Service rents out backcountry cabins and lookouts; prices generally run from $15 to $30 per night. For a complete list of all available Forest Service cabins and lookouts, request the *Recreational Cabin and Lookout Directory* from the **Helena National Forest Supervisor's Office** (2880 Skyway Dr, (406) 449-5201) or any ranger district. Reservations for those in the Helena National Forest are accepted up to six months in advance.

The recently remodeled **Bar Gulch Cabin**—and its new outhouse!— are nestled in wooded foothills of the Big Belt Mountains close to Canyon Ferry Lake. It sleeps six, utensils provided. You can normally drive all the way to the cabin. Bring sleeping bag, food, water, and propane. Available year-round from the Townsend Ranger District, (406) 266-3425.

The two-room **Cummings Cabin** in the Blackfoot River Valley 10 miles east of Lincoln has a fireplace, an outdoor barbecue, and a creek running through the property. It sleeps five. Utensils are provided, but you have to bring your own cook stove. Bring water, food, and sleeping bags. It's available year-round except for fall hunting season (generally November). You may have to ski in the last hundred yards or so during winter. Lincoln Ranger District, (406) 362-4265.

Hiking trails leave practically from the doorstep of tiny **Kading Cabin,** across the road from Kading Campground and the Little Blackfoot River. This is a popular horse users' access. The cabin sleeps four; water is available. Bring your own sleeping bag. It's open for rentals year-round with the exception of mid-April to June 1. (The road is only plowed within 7 miles, though, and there may be restrictions during spring breakup.) The cabin is on the west side of MacDonald Pass near Elliston. Helena Ranger District, (406) 449-5490.

The recently built **Indian Flats Cabin,** 40 miles northeast of Helena in the Big Belt Mountains, is available year-round, but access may be restricted during spring melts. It's a tough 7-mile ski during winter. The wood stove-heated cabin sleeps four; bring sleeping bag, food, and utensils. Water is available in season. Helena Ranger District, (406) 449-5490.

More Information

The Base Camp: (406) 443-5360.

Bureau of Reclamation/Bureau of Land Management, Helena: (406) 475-3319.

Cross Currents: (406) 449-2292.

Gates of the Mountains Inc.: (406) 458-5241.

Great Divide Cyclery: (406) 443-5188.

Helena Area Chamber of Commerce: (800) 743-5362 or (406) 447-1530.

Helena National Forest Supervisor's Office: (406) 449-5201.

HNF, Helena Ranger District: (406) 449-5490.

HNF, Lincoln Ranger District: (406) 362-4265.

HNF, Townsend Ranger District: (406) 266-3425.

Montana Department of Fish, Wildlife and Parks, Helena: (406) 444-4720.

Travel Montana: (800) 847-4868 out-of-state or (406) 444-2654 in-state.

Red Lodge

Including the Beartooth National Scenic Byway (US Highway 212) to Yellowstone National Park, Cooke City, and the eastern portion of the Absaroka–Beartooth Wilderness.

Named for the red clay-coated tepees Native Americans once built along the banks of nearby Rock Creek, Red Lodge (pop: 1,900, county pop: 9,000) was founded in 1884 as a coal-mining community. It's no surprise, then, that it's the seat of Carbon County. Red Lodge history is littered with the names of colorful characters: before the turn of the last century, Buffalo Bill Cody met train passengers here and took them by stagecoach to his namesake community in Wyoming, and the town's first sheriff, Liver Eatin' Johnston, was so tough he supposedly once ate the innards of an enemy.

The mines drew more than half a dozen different ethnicities to the area, and, as in many larger cities, each one—Finnish or Italian or Cornish—had its own neighborhood. Ironically, it was the mining industry that anchored these communities and provided a bond for the diverse residents. An explosion in the Smith Mine just south of town on February 27, 1943, resulted in 74 deaths—everyone in Red Lodge had a relative or friend who was a victim, and everyone was joined in grief. The town's ethnic groups have since assimilated and its neighborhoods have blended, but Red Lodge still celebrates its heritage during an annual Festival of Nations.

Until the 1930s, Red Lodge was pretty much the end of the line—US Highway 212 ended here at the 5,555-foot base of the daunting Beartooth Range. But in 1932, under the Park Approach Act, which allotted for scenic routes to national parks through federal lands, construction began on the Beartooth National Scenic Byway (a continuation of US 212). This infrastructural feat switchbacks up and over the Continental Divide, peaking at nearly 11,000 feet on the Beartooth Plateau before dropping into the community of Cooke City and the northeast entrance to Yellowstone National Park. Today, Red Lodge is best known for its location at the beginning (or end, depending on which direction you're coming from) of this famed drive.

Considering its location and charm, it's no surprise that Red Lodge is quickly moving from hick to chic. Not only does it draw tourists on their way to and from Yellowstone, but it also has surrounding attractions of its own. There's not a more beautiful area to hike in summer than the Absaroka–Beartooth Wilderness Complex, at 1.2 million acres the second largest contiguous roadless area in Montana (and the fourth most heavily used wilderness in the nation), which includes 12,799-foot Granite Peak, the state's highest. Winters at Red Lodge Mountain Resort bring skiers— and hopes of even more after a massive expansion now in the works. "Red Lodge," according to *Snow Country* magazine, "is the next generation of ski towns." The growing abundance of gift and outdoor stores testifies to that fact.

Red Lodge faces the usual hurdles of economic survival as a tourist community. A tremendous amount of visitors—a million tourist-days annually—are discovering the surrounding forests and especially the Absaroka–Beartooth Wilderness but, in the process, are loving these wildlands to death. Please—tread lightly and leave no trace of your presence in this spectacular country.

Getting There

Red Lodge lies at the junction of US 212 (the Beartooth National Scenic Byway) and Hwy 78, 64 miles from the northeast entrance to Yellowstone National Park. Note: The Beartooth National Scenic Byway is only open seasonally. Red Lodge is equidistant—67 miles—from Logan International Airport in Billings to the northeast and Yellowstone Regional Airport in Cody, Wyoming, to the south. Cooke City sits at the northeast corner of the park; keep in mind that in winter, you can only reach the town via the park roads, as US 212 is closed.

Adjoining Areas

WEST: **Yellowstone National Park; Bozeman and Environs**

inside out

Scenic Drives

Even the most scenery-hardened veteran will gape at the **Beartooth National Scenic Byway** (US 212), which switchbacks up from 5,555-foot Red Lodge to 10,947-foot Beartooth Pass, before diving back down to Colter Pass (8,066 feet), Cooke City, and the northeast entrance of Yellowstone National Park. Well-traveled Charles Kuralt is one of many people who describe this as the most beautiful drive in the country. Leave plenty of time—3 hours is about average—for this incredible 64-mile journey to the top of the world and back again. It took four years to engineer and construct this astounding road, the only highway ever built under the Depression-era Parks Approach Act.

The Beartooth is a must-do for anyone in the area between mid-May until the first big snow, generally in October. (It's closed the rest of the year due to enormous snowfall and drifts.) The season may be shortened even further, since the National Park Service is under serious budget constraints and has expressed reluctance to help foot the enormous plowing bill.

Hiking/Backpacking

Red Lodge lies within spitting distance of the 943,000-acre **Absaroka–Beartooth Wilderness**, the heart of a 1.2 million-acre roadless triangle extending from Red Lodge to Livingston through the northeast portion of Yellowstone National Park. Composed of two mountain ranges, the Absaroka–Beartooth Wilderness is an astonishingly beautiful place, full of canyons, lakes, streams, meadows, million-dollar vistas—and plenty of hikers. The Beartooth Mountains to the east feature high tundra and 29 jagged peaks above 12,000 feet—the nation's largest contiguous landmass over 10,000 feet—plus some of the world's oldest exposed rock. To the west is the more heavily eroded, rounded Absaroka Range. **Human waste** is becoming a concern in this high country, where there's little soil to absorb it. The problem is exacerbated by the very short, perhaps six weeks, summer season, when most visitation is concentrated. To get away from people, you'll have to hike off-trail, which means you need good **orienteering skills.** Be sure to come prepared for extreme **weather:** violent thunderstorms are common during summer, and radical drops in temperatures occur throughout the year. Camping is banned within 200 feet of lakes and 100 feet of streams.

This chapter covers hiking in the Beartooths; for hiking in the Absarokas, see the Hiking/Backpacking section of the Bozeman and Environs chapter.

The Montana portion of the Absaroka–Beartooth Wilderness is administered by the Beartooth Ranger District of the Custer National Forest on the east, and the Gardiner Ranger District of the Gallatin National Forest to the west. The Wyoming portion is handled by the Clark Fork Ranger District of the Shoshone National Forest. To hike the Beartooths, you'll want either a Custer National Forest/Beartooth District **map,** or a map of the Absaroka–Beartooth Wilderness (and the appropriate topographical maps), available at the Beartooth Ranger District just south of Red Lodge on US 212, (406) 446-2103; maps are also available from Outdoor Adventures, (406) 446-3818, or Sylvan Peak, (406) 446-1770, both in downtown Red Lodge. Folks at both these stores are very knowledgeable about area trails. Outdoor Adventures leads **guided day trips** on nearby trails. Consult *The Trail Guide to the Beartooths* by Bill Schneider for lots more specifics; we also recommend *Wild Montana,* by Bill Cunningham, and *Hiking Montana,* by Bill Schneider.

Until the fire of 1996, one of the most scenic—and therefore most popular—areas was the **East Rosebud drainage**, which meanders by cascading waterfalls and numerous lakes. A great day hike begins at East Rosebud Lake and gradually climbs 500 feet in 4 miles to **Elk Lake**. A stunning 3-day, point-to-point overnighter begins just north of Chief Joseph Campground east of Cooke City and travels north to East Rosebud. The weather can be brutal, especially by Fossil Lake (as in all areas of the Beartooths), but come prepared and you won't be sorry. There are good fishing opportunities all along the way. To get to East Rosebud Lake, take Hwy 78 about 19 miles north to Roscoe, then turn south on Forest Road 2177—it's a bad road, and slow-going for the remaining 14 miles to the lake. Call the Beartooth Ranger District for updates on the burned areas, (406) 446-2103.

Day hike 4 miles (one-way) to **Quinnebaugh Meadows** off the West Fork Rd southwest of Red Lodge. These high meadows display beautiful wildflowers in August. Watch for harlequin ducks near Calamity Falls. This trail is also the beginning of a popular—and tough—19-mile point-to-point backpack over **Sundance Pass**, though it's actually easier to begin at Lion's Camp along the Lake Fork of Rock Creek and walk the trail clockwise. Views are great, and you'll pass by or near numerous fishable lakes. To get to the West Fork Rd trailhead (Camp Senia), take the West Fork Rd southwest out of Red Lodge about 12 miles; the trailhead is approximately 2 miles past the Cascade Campground. The Lake Fork of Rock Creek is off US 212 about 10 miles south of Red Lodge.

You can take a regular car but it's preferable to drive the road with a high-clearance vehicle (they actually filmed a recent Jeep commercial up here) to get to the treeless, lunar-looking landscape of the **Hellroaring Plateau.** From there you can walk down into **Slide Rock, Snowbank, Hairpin,** or **Crescent Lakes.** To get there, take US 212 about 12 miles south of Red Lodge and turn right (west) as if you were going to the Rock Creek Forest Service campgrounds (it's signed). At the fork bear right for the Hellroaring Plateau, or left to get to the trailhead for the strenuous 1 ½-mile hike to **Glacier Lake,** where there's some good bouldering action off to the side.

It's a 1 ½-mile easy hike to the relatively secluded **Kersey Lake Cabin,** 4 miles east of Cooke City. See Backcountry Cabins, below.

Biking

Trail guides with good descriptions of five local rides are free when you rent mountain bikes at Outdoor Adventures in Red Lodge, (406) 446-3818, two bucks if you're a nonrenter. The store can arrange shuttles to area trails. Rentals and other riding suggestions also available through Granite Cyclery at the south end of Red Lodge, (406) 446-2291, the town's most complete bike repair and sales shop, which leads **guided mountain-bike tours** in the area. In **Cooke City,** the very helpful Cooke City Bike Shack, (406) 838-2412, rents bikes and provides free advice and brochures about area mountain biking. Bicycles are not allowed in the Absaroka–Beartooth Wilderness or in certain areas of the national forest. The Beartooth Ranger District, (406) 446-2103, just south of Red Lodge has a travel plan that indicates where bicycles are allowed.

The historic **Meteetsee Trail,** part of the old stagecoach route from Red Lodge to Cody, runs 16 miles southeast of Red Lodge to Belfry. You can ride in either direction; easiest is to start just south of Red Lodge and ride east, meeting up with a shuttle at Chance Bridge, 9 miles south of Belfry on Hwy 72. The Meteetsee Trail begins about a half-mile south of Red Lodge on the east side of US 212; you'll see the sign. This is a moderate ride best in June and early July, when the area is knee-high in wildflowers.

The 4 ½-mile **Silver Run Trail Loop** southwest of Red Lodge is actually a series of three loops, two relatively easy and the third more challenging, with a steep, winding descent (going counter-clockwise). To get there, take West Fork Rock Creek Rd west 4 ⅖ miles from just south of Red Lodge; you'll see the signs. Transport to the Silver Run Trail Loop is free with half- or full-day rentals from Outdoor Adventures.

Follow the 16-mile steep, rugged **Morrison Jeep Trail** off the

Beartooth National Scenic Byway near Long Lake. It's mostly downhill to the Clark Hwy out of Clark, Wyoming. This challenging trail begins above timberline then drops all the way to the Clark Fork of the Yellowstone River; many bikers choose to walk its rocky switchbacks. This is for serious mountain bikers only, shocks recommended. Don't solo this one, and bring sunscreen. Granite Cyclery leads guided tours of this and other hard-core trips.

You want demanding? We'll give you demanding. The 18-mile point-to-point **Line Creek Plateau Trail** begins at 10,500 feet and descends 4,500 feet across trailless tundra; orienteering skills, superb brakes, shocks, helmets, and rain gear are essential to finding your way safely. So, for that matter, is sunblock—you're up awfully high here. That said, this is an extraordinary all-day adventure for the serious mountain biker. You'll need a Mount Maurice topographical quad map. The trail begins on the east side of the Beartooth National Scenic Byway (US 212), about 23 ½ miles southwest of Red Lodge, half a mile before you cross into Wyoming (you'll see the parking lot for the trailhead). The trail emerges at **Maurice Creek Trail # 6** across the creek from Piney Dell. Don't do this one alone. Granite Cyclery leads tours. Outdoor Adventures has a written description of the trail.

A tough and beautiful 15-mile loop ride just outside Cooke City leads straight up **Henderson Mountain,** the site of the failed proposal to build the controversial New World Mine. From Cooke City, ride north on US 212 half a mile, then turn left (north) on Daisy Pass Rd. Follow it all the way to the top of 9,700-foot Daisy Pass, which provides astounding views of Lake Abundance, the Beartooth Plateau, Yellowstone National Park, and Pilot and Index Peaks. There's a map on the pass. Loop around to the right and hook up with Lulu Pass Rd, which follows the Fisher Creek drainage back to US 212. Get maps and advice at the Cooke City Bike Shack.

For a serious road rush, cruise down the **Beartooth National Scenic Byway** (see Scenic Drives, above), from the top of Beartooth Pass into Red Lodge. For $22, Outdoor Adventures will shuttle you to the top and follow behind you for safety. Don't forget your helmet.

Camping

There are more than a dozen Forest Service campgrounds along the **Beartooth National Scenic Byway** (US 212) from Cooke City to Red Lodge, and numerous others up the drainages leading out of the Absaroka–Beartooth Wilderness. These are well-marked on Beartooth Division maps of the Custer National Forest. Beware of late seasonal openings and early closings due to extreme weather. Call the Beartooth Ranger District for more information, (406) 446-2103. Some of the campgrounds have reservation sites set aside; call (800) 280-CAMP to reserve yours. The *Montana Travel Planner* published by Travel Montana, (800) 847-4868 out-of-state or (406) 444-2654 in-state, lists all public and private campgrounds alphabetically; look under "Yellowstone Country."

Island Lake Campground offers a rare opportunity to car camp at 9,600 feet above sea level. All 20 sites have views of the lake and granite peaks beyond. The season is short (July through Labor Day, weather permitting), and sites fill up quick, so get there early—and bring your longjohns. It's about 6 miles west of Beartooth Pass on US 212. If Island Lake is full, try **Beartooth Lake Campground,** just 3 miles west. Both campgrounds have access to the wilderness hiking trails. At press time, there was talk of putting either or both of these campgrounds on the reservation system.

The 14-unit **East Rosebud Campground**, located on East Rosebud Lake, is a good choice for out-of-town camping. Boating is allowed here, but the lake is only 20 feet deep so you shouldn't see—or hear—anything too disruptive. Lots of people camp here before taking off on hiking trips; the lake sits at the gateway to the Absaroka–Beartooth Wilderness. To get to East Rosebud Lake, take Hwy 78 about 19 miles north to Roscoe, then turn south on Forest Rd 2177—it's a bad road, and slow-going for the remaining 14 miles to the lake. Note: A forest fire burned this area in the summer of 1996. While the campground has remained open, the aesthetic quality and facilities may have been affected. Call the ranger district for an update.

There are plenty of choices for camping near Red Lodge. **Greenough Lake Campground** is nice because it sits waterside (actually, the lake is more like a pond, but kids like to fish there). You can make advance reservations for many of the 18 sites at Greenough, a good idea on summer weekends. From Red Lodge, drive 12 miles south on US 212, turn right at the campground sign, and drive another 1 ½ miles.

Climbing

Beartooth Mountain Guides offers climbing classes and guided 4-day climbs up 12,799-foot Granite Peak, Montana's highest point. They also rent climbing shoes; call (406) 446-1952) for details and more information on climbs throughout the area.

The climbing pitches in **East and West Rosebud Canyons** range from 5.2 to 5.11, both traditional and bolted on stable granite. The road's better to West Rosebud, but the climbs are easier to find in East Rosebud.

To get to East Rosebud Canyon, take Hwy 78 north to Roscoe and turn south on East Rosebud Rd (it's a rough gravel road that turns into pavement) and drive about 13 miles; you'll see the parking area next to East Rosebud Creek where the pavement ends. To get to West Rosebud Canyon take Hwy 78 north to Fishtail, then turn west and follow the signs to the Mystic Lake trailhead. The climbing area is about a half-mile up the **Mystic Lake Trail.**

It takes 4 days total to reach the summit of 12,799-foot **Granite Peak**: 2 days to pack in, 1 day to ascend, and 1 day to hike out. The most popular route is over Froze to Death Plateau, but the Huckleberry Creek drainage from the end of Mystic Lake to Princess Lake is easier to follow. Camp overnight at Princess, then hike to Avalanche Lake following the Snowball Lakes drainage on the southeast side of Princess Lake (there's no established trail, but you'll see where other climbers and anglers have gone before you). Stay at Avalanche Lake the second night, then go for the ascent. Pitches range from 5.2 to 5.4; you'll want a rope and climbing gear.

Fishing

Get **licensing and regulation information** through local outdoor stores or the Montana Department of Fish, Wildlife and Parks, Billings, (406) 247-2940.

Rent **equipment** and get advice at Yellowstone Troutfitters Fly & Tackle Shop in Red Lodge, (406) 446-3819, which also offers **guided day trips** on the Stillwater River and Rock Creek. Black Butte Outfitters, (406) 446-3097, owned by fourth-generation outfitter J. O. Hash, offers multi-day fishing trips from a base camp on the West Rosebud River. Also try Ernie Strum of Rocky Fork Outfitters, (406) 446-2514, and Columbus-based River Quest Angler, (800) 356-2850 or (406) 322-4838, for trips on the Yellowstone and Stillwater Rivers.

Orvis-endorsed Beartooth Plateau Outfitters of Cooke City offers day and week-long pack and fishing trips on lakes in the Absaroka–Beartooth Wilderness. Call (800) 253-8545 or (406) 445-2293 from November to May and (406) 838-2328, June to October. Owner Ronnie Wright also offers guided fishing trips into Yellowstone National Park.

The best fishing near Red Lodge is on the **Stillwater River,** where rainbows and browns average 10-plus inches. Look for caddis, mayfly, and stonefly hatches. Fishing with grasshoppers is also very productive. You'll find the bigger fish below Absarokee—reach them via three public access sites between Absarokee and Columbus. The river can be waded after mid-July.

Fish **Rock Creek** early to mid-June for small (8- to 12-inch) rainbows and browns, and a few brookies upstream. In general, the fishing gets better as you head toward Billings, but you'll find good shore access from Red Lodge to Water Birch, about 11 miles downstream. There are good caddis and mayfly hatches, and good grasshopper fishing, too— we're told that these fish aren't picky.

If it's just a little scenery and a few bites you're looking for, the **West Fork of Rock Creek** along the road to Red Lodge Mountain Resort offers good stream fishing for 8-inch brookies and rainbows.

There are nearly 1,000 lakes on the **Beartooth Plateau**. About half of them are fishable for rainbow, brook, cutthroat and golden trout and arctic grayling. Until a 1996 fire, the East Rosebud drainage was the most scenic, but also the most heavily used, water in the area. You'll find the lakes in Lake Plateau or Hellroaring Plateau are less heavily fished.

Kayaking/Rafting

Outfitter Adventure Whitewater, (800) 897-3161 or (406) 446-3061, gets good press (the company's been featured on ESPN, and doesn't want you to forget it), but we've also heard very good things about Absaroka River Adventures, (800) 334-7238 or (406) 328-4606. Both run half- and full-day **whitewater trips** down the misnamed Stillwater River (it's anything but still). Inflatable kayaks and sit-on-top kayaks also may be available. Raft trips generally run Memorial Day through mid-August, while the inflatable and sit-on-top trips run through Labor Day. For the most excitement, run this stretch early in the season. Absaroka River Adventures also rents wet suits and booties.

The main stretch of kayaking whitewater is on the **Stillwater River** above Absarokee from Moraine to Cliff Swallow. It's a stretch of about 8 miles, with continuous Class III water and lots of play holes. But beware of low bridges—at peak flow you may actually have to roll to get under them. This is not novice water, so it's tough to recover.

Raft or, later in the season, kayak the Stillwater River from the Absaroka fishing access, just outside of Absarokee, to Fireman's Point, just outside of Columbus. It's Class II and, when the river's high, Class III water with good surfing waves at Swinging Bridge. The National Weather Service in Billings, (406) 652-1916, can provide river stages; safe novice flow is when the river is running 2 to 3 ½ feet. There are no river maps of the Stillwater.

Horseback Riding

The Stoney Lonesome Ranch, 15 miles northwest of Absarokee, is a working ranch that offers hour-long and day rides. Although it's a bit of a drive (about 40 miles) northwest of Red Lodge, they come recommended. You'll need reservations; call (406) 932-4452.

Golfing

The 18-hole public **Red Lodge Mountain Golf Course** is not only extraordinarily beautiful but also difficult, with a lot of water. It's below the ski resort. The season generally runs mid-May through mid-October, weather permitting. Call (800) 514-3088 or (406) 446-3344 for more information.

Cross-Country Skiing/Snowshoeing

Rent touring and telemark skis and get information at Outdoor Adventures, (406) 446-3818, or at Sylvan Peak, (406) 446-1770, both in downtown Red Lodge.

When snow conditions permit, **Red Lodge Nordic,** (406) 425-1070, grooms 10 kilometers of beginner to intermediate loop trails. You can rent skate and touring skis and take lessons, too. The trails are 2 miles west of Red Lodge on Hwy 78.

Nearly 8 miles of trail make up four different loops at the **Silver Run Cross-Country Ski Trails**. They're numbered by increasing difficulty. These are ungroomed trails, but they get enough use that you should have some tracks to follow. Get maps from the Beartooth Ranger District, (406) 446-2103. Take the West Fork Rd out of Red Lodge about 4 miles; you'll see the sign.

The Cooke City area is prime backcountry skiing territory. Just out of town, **Henderson Mountain** provides fresh powder almost daily, with something for everyone, from mellow trails to steep descents. You're skiing on top of several million dollars' worth of gold (Henderson Mountain was the proposed site for the now defunct New World Mine). This is avalanche territory, so you will need the proper skills, along with a transceiver and a shovel. Mid-November through April, the Cooke City Bike Shack, (406) 838-2412, runs **snowcat shuttles** to the mountain. The folks there are a great resource. Remember—in winter, you can only access Cooke City through Yellowstone National Park.

It's an easy 1 ½-mile ski to the relatively secluded **Kersey Lake Cabin,** 4 miles east of Cooke City. See Backcountry Cabins, below.

Trails in the high-elevation wilderness often aren't clear of snow before mid-July, so a pair of **snowshoes** comes in handy. You can rent them at Outdoor Adventures, and the folks there can advise you regarding trails.

Downhill Skiing

Until recently, the best skiing at **Red Lodge Mountain Resort** was to be had in February and March, after the snow base and the temperatures increased. But a massive $21 million expansion has given Red Lodge Mountain the state's largest snow-making capacity, so skiing should be as good at Christmas as at Valentine's Day. The expansion also doubled the number of trails to 60-plus, brought the number of lifts to 7 and 1 surface tow, and increased the vertical drop to 2,400 feet. For now, Red Lodge Mountain is still a family-oriented, day-use area, with 70 percent of trails geared to beginners and intermediate skiers, but in the next 10 years look for on-site accommodations, another 20 trails, and 3 new lifts to make it competitive with the top regional resorts. Among its many package deals, Red Lodge Mountain Resort offers a combination downhill skiing and Yellowstone National Park snowmobiling trip. The ski hill is 7 miles west of Red Lodge. Take the West Fork Rd about 3 miles and turn right at the sign to the mountain. Call (800) 444-8977 or (406) 446-2610 for more information and snow conditions.

Snowmobiling

Both Yamaha and Arctic Cat snowmobile manufacturers have used the **Cooke City** area as a test and a promotional film location. There are about 60 miles of groomed trails surrounding Cooke City; at press time, the Upper Yellowstone Snowmobile Club, (406) 838-2212, was in the process of developing a trail map. Although Cooke City sits at the northeast entrance to Yellowstone National Park, you cannot drive snowmobiles into the park—they're prohibited on the plowed Cooke City-Mammoth Rd. If you want to snowmobile in Yellowstone, you'll have to take your snowmobile to Mammoth. (See the Yellowstone National Park chapter for more details.) Snowmobiling also is prohibited in any designated wilderness. Get more information through the Upper Yellowstone Snowmobile Club, the Gardiner Ranger District of the Gallatin National Forest, (406) 848-7375, or the Cooke City Chamber of Commerce, (406) 838-2495.

outside in

Attractions

They're silly and touristy, but the **weekend pig races** at Bearcreek Saloon are great fun. The races last all of 5 seconds, and there's food for the pigs at the finish line. From the end of May through the beginning of September, the races take place outside; off-season, baby piglets race on an even smaller indoor track. The saloon serves Mexican food, but save your money to bet on the pigs. It's $2 a pop; winners take home $25. The saloon is 7 miles east of Red Lodge on County Rd 308; call (406) 446-3481.

Calendar of Events

June's **Red Lodge Music Festival** draws classical music students from all over the nation for a week of instruction and performances. There are several free concerts during the week by both faculty and students. It's held at the Red Lodge Veterans Memorial Civic Center. Red Lodge Area Chamber of Commerce, (406) 446-1718.

Since 1951, Red Lodge's **Festival of Nations** has celebrated the town's diverse ethnic roots. Held the first two weekends of August, the festival honors different ethnic groups each night, with representative food and dances at various venues throughout town. Red Lodge Area Chamber of Commerce, (406) 446-1718.

American history buffs gather in Red Lodge the last weekend in July and the first weekend in August to recreate 1840s Montana at the annual **Mountain Man Rendezvous.** That means seminars and demonstrations, old time melodrama, Native American dancers, and muzzle-loading shooting matches—all just west of Red Lodge behind the Rodeo Fairgrounds. Red Lodge Area Chamber of Commerce, (406) 446-1718.

Restaurants

The **Grizzly Bar** in Roscoe is the local favorite for red meat and cold beer. The steaks hang over the plate, and it's not because the plates are small. It's 19 miles north of Red Lodge on Hwy 78; turn left at the sign to Roscoe and the bar's about 50 yards across the bridge, (406) 328-6789.

Greenlee's at the Pollard ☆ Greenlee's is *the* place to go for a night out. Located in the historic and well-renovated Pollard Hotel, Greenlee's presents itself unabashedly as a place of fine dining, and the high prices on its small à la carte menu reflect its confidence in chef Scott Greenlee's elegant creations. (The menu changes weekly; there's also a $29 four-course, prix-fixe meal.) The atmosphere and the service are certainly gracious, but that confidence in the food is sometimes misplaced. Our dinners were not the mouth-watering experience we'd been led to expect: vegetables were seriously undercooked, but the duck with fresh elderberry sauce was overly well-done. The spinach and goat cheese salad and salmon in champagne and dill cream sauce were much tastier. The award-winning wine list is impressive, especially since this is Red Lodge, not Manhattan. We'd find it easier to lighten up if the restaurant did, too. *At the Pollard Hotel downtown, corner of 11th and Broadway; 2 N Broadway, Red Lodge; (800) 765-5273 or (406) 446-0001; dinner every day; AE, DIS, MC, V; checks OK; $$$.*

Lodgings

The Pollard ☆☆   Built in 1893, this landmark hotel hosted the likes of Buffalo Bill, Calamity Jane, and William Jennings Bryan before it fell into disrepair. In 1994, after a massive renovation and much fanfare, the 38-room Pollard reopened as the premiere accommodation in Red Lodge (indeed, in all of Carbon County). Standard queen rooms decorated with artwork and antique reproductions are very small (a sign of the old days), but come with thick towels and fancy soaps (a sign of the new). Guests staying more than 1 night should consider the larger suites, which come with either steam bath or hot tub and a balcony overlooking the hotel's pretty sitting area. Rates include use of a small fitness facility, racquetball courts (racquets provided), and hot tub, as well as a pleasant sit-down breakfast. Off-season rates are discounted $20 to $40 per night. *Downtown at Broadway and 11th; 2 N Broadway, Red Lodge, MT 59068; (800) 765-5273 or (406) 446-0001; AE, DIS, MC, V; checks OK; $$$.*

Rock Creek Resort ☆☆   Located along Rock Creek, 7 miles south of Red Lodge, this full-service, 85-unit resort offers Red Lodge's largest variety of accommodations, ranging from standard hotel rooms to one-bedroom condos, three-bedroom townhouses, and even a deluxe cabin off by itself. The older Beartooth Lodge sits creekside (request a creekside room with balcony, no more expensive than the others); rooms in the new Twin Elk building are smaller without the view, but come with prettier decor. Our favorites are the Grizzly Condos; you can get a spacious studio condo with bath for very nearly the same price you pay for a simple room in the Beartooth Lodge. Again, request a creekside location. Rock Creek Resort also has a small indoor pool and fitness center, tennis and volleyball courts, horseshoe pits, and a small fishing pond in front of the lodge. We've heard the Old Piney Dell Restaurant on-site is quite good, if rather pricey. *5 miles south of Red Lodge on US 212; Rte 2, Box 3500, Red Lodge, MT 59068; (406) 446-1111; AE, DIS, MC, V; checks OK; $$-$$$.*

Backcountry Cabins

It's an easy 1 ½-mile hike or ski to the relatively secluded **Kersey Lake Cabin**, 4 miles east of Cooke City. The cabin has a living and kitchen area, a loft, a double bed, and enough cots and benches to sleep 10. The Forest

Service provides wood for the wood stove, cooking utensils, and even a rowboat (from the middle of Kersey Lake you can see Index and Pilot Peaks). Available mid-June through mid-September (summer reservations accepted beginning April 15); and again mid-December through mid-March (winter reservations accepted beginning October 15). Bring sleeping bag, food, and lantern fuel. Gardiner Ranger District, (406) 848-7375.

More Information

Cooke City Chamber of Commerce: (406) 838-2495.

Custer National Forest Supervisor's Office, Billings: (406) 657-6361.

CNF, Beartooth Ranger District: (406) 446-2103.

Gallatin National Forest Avalanche Advisory: (406) 587-6984.

GNF, Gardiner Ranger District: (406) 848-7375.

Montana Department of Fish, Wildlife and Parks, Billings: (406) 247-2940.

Red Lodge Area Chamber of Commerce: (406) 446-1718.

Shoshone National Forest, Clarks Fork Ranger District: (307) 754-2407.

Travel Montana: (800) 847-4868 out-of-state or (406) 444-2654 in-state.

Yellowstone Country (a regional arm of Travel Montana): (800) 736-5276 or (406) 446-1005.

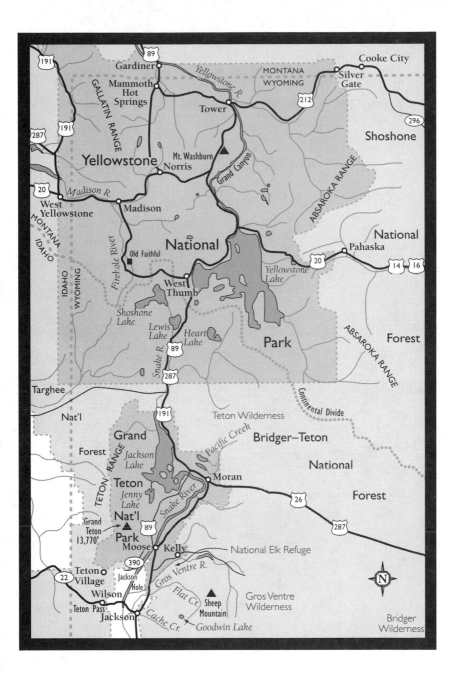

Northwestern Wyoming

Northwestern **Wyoming**

Yellowstone National Park

Including Mammoth Hot Springs, Old Faithful, Grand Canyon, and Yellowstone Lake.

Yellowstone National Park claims a special place in the consciousness of most Americans, even of those who've never been here. So what if they can't pinpoint it on a map (it's in northwestern Wyoming, with edges of wilderness bleeding into Montana and Idaho) or say what makes it unique (the park claims the world's largest concentration of thermal features, more than all others put together)? Everyone knows that Yellowstone's Old Faithful ranks up there with baseball, apple pie, and Mount Rushmore as a symbol of democracy, and many consider it downright un-American to die without seeing the world's first national park.

Some three million people—both Americans and foreign visitors—annually travel to Yellowstone, the nation's fourth busiest park, ensuring that its highways and major attractions often look like mall parking lots on post-Christmas sale days. On more than one occasion, cynics have compared Yellowstone to Disneyland, observing that Mother Nature's spectacles are easily accessible—the 142-mile Grand Loop Road passes every major feature—safely roped off, marked, and explained, with wildlife posing for photographs, just as obligingly as Mickey Mouse and Donald Duck. There may be some truth in that, but Yellowstone is still pretty darn incredible and, like Disneyland, everyone should go there at least once. Repeat visits are rewarding, too, because you can see how this stunning, dynamic landscape changes over time.

Wildlife—particularly bison, elk, and mule deer and occasional coyotes, wolves, moose, and black and grizzly bears—is abundant; Yellowstone and the surrounding national forests boast the greatest concentration of small and large mammals in the Lower 48. This includes a whopping 250 grizzlies, more than anywhere in the United States except for Alaska. Wildlife is largely to blame for the park's slow-moving traffic; "bison jams" are common, as the enormous beasts often meander nonchalantly onto roadways. (Bison gorings are an annual occurrence; keep your distance.) At frenzied roadside scenes, lines beget more lines as wildlife-seeking drivers swerve off the road whenever they notice other cars doing the same.

The infrastructure built to house tourists—including the historic Old Faithful Inn and the Lake Yellowstone Hotel—is now almost as famous as the natural features that brought the crowds there to begin with, and certainly worth a visit. As you drive around, you will also see plenty of signs of the wildfires that raged through more than a third of the park in 1988, the result of decades of well-intentioned but misguided fire suppression. Officials now agree that the fires actually improved the health of Yellowstone's ecosystem, allowing nature to clear out dead and diseased trees and release seeds for new growth; look closely and you'll see young lodgepoles sprouting among their charred kin.

Located over a hot spot in the earth, Yellowstone is the site of three cataclysmic volcanic eruptions that occurred in 600,000-year intervals. During the last one, the volcano spewed out 240 cubic miles of ash and debris, enough to cover Texas with a layer of ash 12 feet deep. After the eruption, the volcano collapsed like a cake on top of itself, creating an enormous caldera roughly the size of Rhode Island. This high-altitude basin is the heart of Yellowstone, the reason its geysers and mud pots and fumaroles exist. (The map you receive on entrance to the park notes the caldera boundary.) And here's a fair warning: scientists say we're due for another eruption within 100,000 years, give or take a few thousand.

Native Americans occasionally passed through Yellowstone, though only one band—the Sheepeaters, an offshoot of the Shoshone—made a permanent home there, on what are now the park's north and northeast fringes. In the winter of 1807, Yellowstone's thermal features caught the attention of mountain man John Colter, a former scout for the Lewis and Clark expedition. When he described "the hidden fires, smoking pits, noxious steams, and smell of brimstone," to those who hadn't been there, no one believed him. "Colter's Hell," skeptics dubbed the place. It wasn't until 1870 that the Washburn expedition documented Yellowstone's wonders for the government. Two years later, swayed by the photographs of

William Henry Jackson and the paintings of Thomas Moran, Congress created Yellowstone National Park, the world's first national park. Ironically, the Sheepeaters were removed and placed on the Wind River Reservation in Wyoming.

By the 1880s, tourists were arriving via stagecoach and train—and they've been coming ever since for an opportunity to see Nature strut her stuff. Visitors centers have brochures on just about every conceivable outdoor activity, from bird-watching to bicycling, climbing to backcountry camping. Not long ago, the way to avoid the crowds here was to visit the park off-season. In winter, wildlife is more visible, the scenery is gloriously pristine, and the thermal features are more dramatic in the cold air—plus you don't have to worry about bears. But now the secret of Yellowstone's winter beauty is out: winter visitors total 140,000, and park officials are scrambling to come up with a long-term winter-use management plan. Of particular concern are the snowmobiles, which generate significant amounts of noise and air pollution. In the meantime, tread lightly; winter is tough enough on wildlife without any extra stress.

Winter or summer, crowds or solitude, remember that with 2.2 million acres Yellowstone is larger than Delaware and Rhode Island combined. Try not to get caught up in the "must-see-everything" road rally. With time and patience, you will see why Yellowstone offers sublime and intimate rewards.

Getting There

Roads access the park from five entrances—West Yellowstone is the west entrance; Gardiner (Mammoth Hot Springs), north; Cooke City (Silver Gate), northeast; Cody, Wyoming (Pahaska), east; and Grand Teton National Park, south. The 142-mile Grand Loop Rd makes a figure-eight through the middle of the park, passing most of Yellowstone's major features. In season, there is almost always road construction somewhere in the park. Check with the entrance stations or see Yellowstone Today, *the park's newspaper, for more information. Call the general park information number, (307) 344-7381, with questions.*

Yellowstone is served by the West Yellowstone Airport (summers only), adjacent to the west entrance; by Gallatin Field in Bozeman, 87 miles from the north entrance; and by Jackson Hole Airport, 50 miles from the south entrance. A shuttle service called 4 x 4 Stage, (800) 517-8243 or (406) 388-6404, offers shuttles from Gallatin Field and Big Sky to West Yellowstone; in winter, it runs from Gallatin Field to Mammoth Hot Springs. The service requires 24-hour advance reservations year-round. Aside from organized tours, there is no bus service into the park.

Most of Yellowstone is open from May through October and again, with limited facilities, from mid-December through mid-March. The Mammoth Visitors Center and the Hamilton Store at Mammoth are the only facilities that remain open year-round. In winter, all in-park roads are closed except the northern road from Mammoth to Cooke City. Winter travel anywhere else within the park is done by snowmobile (see Snowmobiling, below) or by hired snowcoach, a sort of overgrown, enclosed, and heated snowmobile. For an overview of winter park activities and regulations, call park information, (307) 344-7381, and request a copy of the latest winter edition of Yellowstone Today.

The Albright Visitors Center at Mammoth Hot Springs stays open year-round, (307) 344-2263. The Old Faithful Visitors Center, (307) 545-2750, stays open through the winter season, then closes in spring until the roads re-open in May. During the winter season there are ranger-naturalist programs at both the Old Faithful Visitors Center and in the Map Room of the Mammoth Hot Springs Hotel.

Adjoining Areas

NORTH: **Bozeman and Environs**

SOUTH: **Grand Teton National Park; Jackson Hole**

EAST: **Red Lodge**

WEST: **West Yellowstone and the Madison Valley**

inside out

Scenic Drives

Like it or not, you're going to do a lot of driving in Yellowstone. We've highlighted below the four major attractions—Mammoth Hot Springs, Old Faithful, Yellowstone Lake, and Grand Canyon—driving in a clockwise direction from the north entrance. The Yellowstone Association publishes a series of informational pamphlets about the various special features of the park. Pick them up for a quarter each at any visitors center or at the individual sites. *Yellowstone Today,* the park's free newspaper available at each entrance and visitors center, is also a helpful guide.

Make use of your auto time by listening to TourGuide, (800) 247-1213, a creative **audio tour** available for rent at any park activity center. The all-in-one CD unit plugs into your cigarette lighter and plays through the FM radio. Though it sometimes borders on the hokey and may not be technical enough for everyone, generally TourGuide does a fine job of employing radio theater, sound effects, and music to provide an overview of Yellowstone's complex history, geology, flora, and fauna.

Yellowstone is best known for its 10,000 **thermal features.** With the exception of Mammoth Hot Springs (see below), the Mud Volcano, and the Sulphur Caldron, most of these thermal attractions are accessible by road and are located between Norris and West Thumb.

While you can't actually sit and soak in **Mammoth Hot Springs** (too disruptive to the natural processes, not to mention too hot), you do get a chance to see beautiful travertine terraces. Underneath the surface, ground water seeps downward through sedimentary limestone and comes into contact with carbon dioxide gases rising from a hot magma chamber. The resulting acidic solution dissolves the limestone, carrying it through the rock layers until it reemerges onto the hot springs' terraces in colorful displays. Once exposed to the outside air, the carbon dioxide escapes, leaving the limestone solution to form a solid mineral known as travertine. You can walk along the lower and upper terraces, or drive along the upper ones. These features are continually changing; the hot springs deposit as much as 2 tons of travertine a day.

The most famous of Yellowstone's thermal features is, of course, **Old Faithful.** For more than a century, the aptly named geyser has erupted every 75 minutes or so (actual intervals range from a half-hour to as much as 2 hours). The best time to see Old Faithful is early, before the hordes arrive. If you don't mind a seat in the outfield, avoid the crowds entirely by watching from the second-floor balcony of the Old Faithful Inn.

The staff at Old Faithful Visitors Center keep tabs not only on Old Faithful but also on several other fairly predictable geysers; they should be able to help you schedule yourself accordingly. Lots of people like to take the easy 5-mile round-trip hike to **Lone Star Geyser,** which erupts every 3 hours. The trailhead to Lone Star is located 3 1/2 miles southeast of Old Faithful, just east of the Kepler Cascades turnout.

What's a geyser? Basically, it's a wine-bottle shaped underground pool of water superheated by molten rock and covered with a cap of cooler water. As the pool fills, pressure rises. Despite water temperatures of 300°F to 400°F, the cap of cooler water prevents the release of steam. Eventually, though, the water level rises to a critical point where the trapped steam breaks through the cold water cap, allowing the hot water to spurt out. Voila!—there's your geyser. A similar super-heating process is responsible for **fumaroles,** which vent steam rather than water (look for them along the south shore of Yellowstone Lake). If a fumarole's acid gases have decomposed rocks and mud into clay, you get a **mud pot.** A simple **hot spring** results if the water never gets pressurized.

You'd have to be blind or on the parks' north end to miss **Yellowstone Lake,** the nation's largest lake above 7,000 feet. Certainly it's one of the most beautiful, with the craggy Absaroka Mountains as a backdrop in the east and the Red Mountains mounded to the south. About 20 miles long and 14 miles wide, the lake annually provides wildlife and anglers alike with half a million fish, including native Yellowstone cutthroat. For more information on the lake, see Boating/Canoeing, below.

There are numerous vantage points from which to view either the upper or lower falls of the **Grand Canyon** of Yellowstone. Granted, it's not *the* Grand Canyon, but it's pretty spectacular in its own right. Our favorite spot is the brink of the Upper Falls, where you can stand just above the water as it pours over the lip of the 109-foot drop. Eagles sometimes soar along the rim of the canyon by Artist Point, as the Yellowstone River flows 1,000 feet below. By the way, it wasn't the yellow banks of these canyon walls that inspired the river's name, but rather the yellow banks where it meets the Missouri River, farther north.

Hiking/Backpacking

It used to be that you could venture 500 yards off the road in Yellowstone and find yourself in total solitude. With backcountry use skyrocketing, that's no longer the case; in summers, trailhead parking lots are often nearly full, and virtually all backcountry campsites are taken. Still, a hike is a good way to escape the majority of the crowds and to absorb the essence of Yellowstone.

There are 1,100 miles of trails within Yellowstone. Since much of the park is located within a basically level caldera, many trails are suitable for novice hikers. Each visitors center has brochures detailing day hikes in that area. Rangers tend to be most familiar with the area where they're stationed. There are short ranger-led hikes as well; check the *Yellowstone Today* newspaper you received when you entered the park for schedules. The best hiking guide to Yellowstone is *Yellowstone Trails: A Hiking Guide,* by Mark Marschall, published by The Yellowstone Association and available at park visitors centers or by mail order (The Yellowstone Association, Box 117, Yellowstone National Park, WY 82190; (307) 344-2293).

Yellowstone is, of course, major grizzly country. If you are unfamiliar with bear-country practices, request a **bear information** brochure from visitors centers. (Also see the Wildlife section in the Northern Rockies Outdoor Primer or the Glacier National Park chapter for basic information on bear-safety procedures.) You'll need a free permit to camp in Yellowstone's backcountry. You may obtain a permit in person up to 48 hours in advance from any backcountry office at the park's ranger stations (the earlier, the better within that 48-hour period). You'll have to watch a video and listen to a short orientation before you can obtain your **back-**

country permit; you must have a permit even if you already have confirmed backcountry reservations. Allow half an hour for the entire process. Sixty percent of the campsites, however, can be reserved by mail from April 1 through the summer season (there's a $15 charge for the service). If you know where you want to go, it's better to request your campsite via the US Postal Service (not over the phone or by fax) as early as you can. Sites on Yellowstone Lake and Shoshone Lake go particularly quickly. You may obtain information about the sites and trails from the Backcountry Office, (307) 344-2160. Ask for the Yellowstone National Park Backcountry Permit Information packet. Mail requests for reservations to the National Park Service, Attention: Backcountry Office, PO Box 168, Yellowstone National Park, WY 82190.

The best comprehensive backcountry **map** to Yellowstone is the Earthwalk Press Hiking Map and Guide, though some editions do not mark backcountry campsites. The backcountry maps published by the American Adventures Association are also very good, but are split into two maps: North Yellowstone Park and South Yellowstone Park. Once you've decided where you're going, you can also order the appropriate Yellowstone Quarter Section Maps, published by the Yellowstone Association. All are available through the park's visitors centers and at area bookstores.

The 6-mile round-trip hike up **Mount Washburn** (elevation 10,243 feet) may be the quintessential Yellowstone trail; it offers panoramic views, and, in the heart of summer, stupendous wildflowers and bighorn sheep to boot. There are two possible routes: both the Dunraven Pass and Chittenden Rd parking lot trailheads are on the Canyon Tower Rd, and both trails climb 1,400 feet in 3 miles. Weather on 10,000-plus foot Mount Washburn is windier and colder than at the trailheads and can shift in a hurry; bring rain gear and a fleece or sweater. The trailheads are midway between Canyon and Roosevelt–Tower.

The lower elevation of the 18-mile **Yellowstone River Trail** at the park's north end makes it a good early or late season hike through the river's spectacular Black Canyon. Be sure to check with rangers about water levels before you attempt to ford Hellroaring Creek; when conditions are dangerous you should detour 3 1/2 miles to cross a stock bridge. You can access the Yellowstone River Trail from the Hellroaring Trailhead, 3 1/2 miles west of Tower on the Tower-Mammoth Rd, or from the Blacktail Creek Trailhead 7 miles east of Mammoth.

There are several ways to access **Shoshone Lake,** Yellowstone's largest backcountry lake and home to one of the park's nicest backcountry geyser basins on its southwest tip. The **Delacy Creek Trail** is the shortest route to the lake, 6 miles round-trip. A more scenic hike leaves from the Dogshead Trailhead and follows the **Lewis River Channel Trail** from Lewis Lake to Shoshone Lake, then loops back on the **Dogshead Trail,** for a total of 11 miles round-trip. Both of these routes are described in the Grant Village/West Thumb area day hike brochure. Neither of them, however, access the geyser basin, which is too far for a day hike. The shortest route there is 8 ½ miles along the Shoshone Lake Trail, which departs from the Lone Star trailhead just south of Kepler Cascades on the Old Faithful-West Thumb Rd. Stay on the trail; during the fires of 1988, a careless off-trail hiker was burned to death.

A very popular overnighter leads 8 miles through a burn area to **Heart Lake.** You can continue farther along several different trails, but be forewarned: there are numerous stream crossings that can be very dangerous. You'll want to do this trip in August or September, when the mosquitoes have left and the water-level has dropped.

The **Thorofare Trail** leads 32 miles along the east side of Yellowstone Lake and down to the very remote Thorofare Ranger Station. This is one of the few places in the park where it's possible to find some solitude—but you'll have to work for it, fording streams and risking bear encounters. The really scenic part of the trip doesn't even start until after the first 15 ½ miles. The trail exits Yellowstone on the southern border; for a really extensive trip, you can follow it all the way to the South Fork of the Shoshone River.

Camping

With the exception of backcountry camping (see Hiking/Backpacking, above), camping in Yellowstone is not so much an aesthetic experience as a practical one. Campgrounds are crowded and sites are very close together. There are five huge, 200- to 400-site reservation-only campgrounds run by Amfac Parks and Resorts, and another seven operated on a first-come, first-served basis by the National Park Service. Campground openings and closings vary; in general the season runs from May through September with the exception of Mammoth, which stays open year-round.

The **Park Service campgrounds** (Indian Creek, Lewis Lake, Mammoth, Norris, Pebble Creek, Slough Creek, and Tower) are smaller and more scenic, but they don't have showers or other amenities—and of course you take a chance without a reservation. Nicest, because of its central location and forested campsites, is the **Norris Campground;** unfortunately, at press time it was closed due to budget constraints. Check to see if it's reopened. The rest of the campgrounds are on the park perimeters; choose yours depending on what you want to be nearest to. If you're fishing, you might want to camp creekside at **Slough Creek**

Campground; boaters will head for the **Lewis Lake Campground**. Checkout time is 10am, but many people leave much earlier, so show up by 9am to get a site, especially in July and August. Get more details through park information, (307) 344-7381.

Of the **reservation campgrounds** (Bridge Bay, Canyon, Fishing Bridge, Grant Village, and Madison), **Canyon Campground** is probably the nicest, with a good central location and tree-cover at the sites. **Madison Campground** is also pretty, though the closest shower facilities are at Old Faithful, 16 miles south. **Fishing Bridge Campground** is open only to RVs. Avoid Bridge Bay if at all possible—it's like sleeping in a parking lot. If you choose to stay at **Grant Village Campground**, which is pretty but out of the way, ask for sites 316 through 322, which are quieter and near the lake. You'll want to reserve at least 6 weeks in advance, especially for July and August. Amfac Parks and Resorts, (307) 344-7311.

Fishing

Anyone 12 or older must purchase a Yellowstone National Park **fishing permit** (state permits and regulations do not apply). Ask at any visitors center or Hamilton Store within the park for a copy of Yellowstone fishing regulations; inside there's a map detailing which species live where. The park has implemented a nontoxic fishing program outlawing leaded tackles; live bait also is illegal. None of the waters are stocked.

Most park waters are restricted to catch-and-release fishing, and there are strict limits on those that aren't. There is one major exception: in an attempt to eradicate illegally introduced lake trout in Yellowstone Lake, park officials actually require that you keep any you catch and present them to a ranger for identification (don't panic; the rangers give the fish back). This mandatory keep-rule also applies for any lake trout caught in backcountry Heart Lake.

The Hamilton Stores within the park sell fishing equipment, or you can rent at Bridge Bay Marina. Because employees are seasonal, it's hard to say whether the store employees will have good advice. Try the rangers in the Backcountry Office at Grant Village Visitors Center; they're avid fishermen and very knowledgeable. Ask for Dick Lewis or Roy DeWalt. We also recommend the Mountaineers' *Lakes of Yellowstone,* by Steve Pierce, for information about lake fishing. From mid-June through mid-September, Amfac Parks and Resorts, (307) 344-7311, offers **guided fishing trips** on Yellowstone Lake, some equipment included. Numerous outfitters based outside the park also offer guided fishing trips. For a list of licensed Yellowstone outfitters, call park information, (307) 344-7381.

Fish **Yellowstone Lake** for its native Lake Yellowstone cutthroat (and nonnative lake trout); the best shore fishing is between West Thumb and Bridge Bay, where the shoreline drops abruptly. Three blue-ribbon trout streams course through Yellowstone—the **Yellowstone, Madison,** and **Firehole Rivers**—and all are good bets for fly-fishing for Yellowstone cutthroat, particularly during the salmonfly hatch, late June through mid-July. There's plenty of stream access, but some places are closed; check the fishing regulations. You'll find brown and lake trout in **Lewis Lake,** which is best early and late in the season. In the heart of summer, **Slough, Pebble,** and **Lamar Creeks** in the northeast corner of the park offer good fishing for rainbows and cutthroats.

Boating/Canoeing

One of the nicest ways to view Yellowstone Lake is from a boat; the 1-hour **Scenicruiser Rides** on Yellowstone Lake are indeed very scenic, and you'll get some history and geological information about the area, too. The cruises leave from Bridge Bay Marina every 1 ½ to 2 ½ hours; we prefer the evening cruises, when the light hits the mountains just right (after mid-August the last cruise leaves at 4:30pm). You'll want to make reservations, generally 24 hours in advance; you can do so at the activities desk at any of the park's lodging facilities or through Bridge Bay Marina, (307) 242-3876.

You must purchase a **permit** to operate a boat within Yellowstone National Park; the season runs from May through October. Boats larger than 40 feet are prohibited. Motorboats are allowed on **Yellowstone Lake** and **Lewis Lake,** but Yellowstone Lake has restricted areas and seasonal closures. With the exception of the Lewis River Channel (see below), boating is not allowed on any of the rivers within the park due to wildlife and fisheries concerns. Jet-skis are prohibited in the park. Pick up a copy of the park's **boating regulations** from any visitors center or through park information, (307) 344-7381. There are special campsites designated for backcountry boaters, but you'll need a backcountry permit; see Hiking/Backpacking, above. Camp at least 100 feet from shore.

Rent rowboats and outboards at **Bridge Bay Marina,** (307) 242-3876, on Yellowstone Lake. No advance reservations are accepted.

Snake River Kayak and Canoe School, (800) 529-2501 or (307) 733-3127, of Jackson, Wyoming, runs overnight **sea-kayaking tours** on Yellowstone Lake.

You can canoe or sea kayak from Lewis Lake to Shoshone Lake via the very pretty 3-mile **Lewis River Channel.** This is a popular trip, despite the fact that you have to tow your boat the last mile. You'll want to make advance reservations for a campsite. Obtain information about the sites from the Backcountry Office, (307) 344-2160.

Biking

With the exception of about 20 miles of dispersed trail riding (pick up an informational bicycling brochure at visitors centers for details), bikes are not allowed off-road anywhere in the park—and road riding is fraught with the usual dangers associated with high-traffic areas. The danger is exacerbated in Yellowstone because of the many large motor homes, whose external mirrors, coincidentally, are exactly the height of a cyclist's head. Add to that the fact that many drivers are distracted by the park's natural features and wildlife, and you can see why park officials generally discourage cycling within Yellowstone (though, ironically, the Park Service sets asides special campsites for anyone arriving via bicycle). There have been bicycle fatalities within the past few years. For every rule there's an exception, however, and listed below are two rides on the park's north end that are a lot of fun.

Ride the **Old Stage Road** from Gardiner to Mammoth Hot Springs, a tough 6-miler on gravel with a 1,500-foot elevation gain. This is a good place to see pronghorn antelope, elk, and bison without having to deal with too much automobile traffic.

Ambitious bikers can pedal the historic **Yellowstone Highway** (a gravel road) from Mammoth northwest along the northern boundary of the park, which follows the Yellowstone River until it ends at US 89 at Point of Rocks, 25 miles one way. This is a good intermediate ride with a few challenging hills. At **Yankee Jim Canyon,** about 18 miles northwest of Mammoth, look up to the west and you'll see an old roadbed 100 yards above. Leave your bicycles down below and hike up to the road to find turn-of-the-century advertisements painted on the rock walls of the canyon.

Horseback Riding

Though they are not well-publicized within the park, nearly two dozen outfitters offer day and multi-day **horsepack trips** into Yellowstone. Sometimes these trips are combined with fishing expeditions. For a list of Yellowstone outfitters with park permits, call park information, (307) 344-7381.

Weather permitting, 1- or 2-hour **trail rides** leave frequently from Mammoth Hot Springs, Roosevelt Lodge, and Canyon Village. These are your basic head-to-tail rides, but the ones out of Roosevelt Lodge and Canyon Village are very scenic. Children must be at least 8 years old and 48 inches tall; children 11 and younger must be accompanied by someone aged 16 or older. **Stagecoach rides** also depart five times a day from Roosevelt Lodge. It's not nearly as exciting now that they've switched from stagecoaches, which were known to tip over, to more stable wagons, but it's just as pretty. You can also experience Amfac Parks and Resorts' version of an **Old West Cookout,** which leaves from Roosevelt Lodge; you'll either ride horseback or in a horse-drawn wagon to an outdoor picnic site for a steak dinner. It's plenty touristy, but what did you expect? Make reservations at any activities desk or call (307) 344-7311.

Snowmobiling

Snowmobiles are allowed on most roadways (but roadways only) throughout the park, with the exception of the Gardiner-Mammoth Rd and the Mammoth-Cooke City Rd, which are plowed for automobile traffic. There's a maximum speed limit of 45 mph. Concerned about the high traffic (as many as 2,000 snowmobiles enter the park daily during winter) and the number of accidents involving young drivers, park officials now require snowmobile operators to have a valid driver's license; those with learner's permits must remain within sight (and no farther than 100 yards) of a licensed driver who is 21 years or older.

Bison present a real threat to snowmobilers; be sure to give them the right of way. Check with park rangers for further safety tips. In any case, snowmobiles are hard on wildlife, so please be respectful.

Rent snowmobiles at either Old Faithful or Mammoth Hot Springs through Amfac Parks and Resorts, (307) 344-7311, or through private vendors outside the park. Amfac also offers snowmobile tours of the park; so do numerous other companies. Call the Backcountry Office, (307) 344-2160, for a list of approved winter operators within the park.

Snowcoaches operated by Amfac Parks and Resorts, (307) 344-7311, run between Mammoth Hot Springs, West Yellowstone, Flagg Ranch (near the park's south entrance), and Old Faithful. This is not the Pony Express; the rides include stops at various park features and a narrated tour, and most take about 4 hours to reach their destination. Amfac Parks and Resorts also offers shorter snowcoach sightseeing tours departing from Old Faithful or Mammoth Hot Springs. Several private snowcoach companies operate out of West Yellowstone (try Yellowstone Alpen Guides, (800) 858-3502 or (406) 646-9591) and one operates out of Flagg Ranch.

Cross-Country Skiing

Trails are marked, though not groomed. Unfortunately, skyrocketing snowmobile use means the experience often is not as serene as you might have hoped. Snowmobiles are allowed only on roadways, whereas skiers can veer off onto marked trails, but the insistent droning of snowmobiles travels a long way. Old Faithful is snowmobile central; ski other areas of the park if noise bothers you. If you want absolute quiet, either stay out of the park or be prepared to ski a long way into the backcountry and camp. You'll need a **backcountry permit** to do so; they're free and available 48 hours in advance. Contact the Backcountry Office, (307) 344-2160, or stop by either the Old Faithful or Mammoth Ranger Stations or the West, South, or East Entrances to the park. In any case, before you set out you should stop by a ranger station to discuss trail conditions.

Skiing little-trafficked areas of the park is an expensive and complex proposition, because you'll have to **access** the park by snowmobile or by hired snowcoach. The Backcountry Office keeps a list of independent snowcoach companies and also has brochures describing routes in five distinct areas. Amfac Parks and Resorts runs shuttles from Mammoth Hot Springs Hotel to several nearby trails, including those in the Tower area, and from Old Faithful to the Fairy Falls or Continental Divide areas. If you want to ski the Canyon area independently, you'll have to arrange shuttle service through an independent snowcoach operator.

Amfac Parks and Resorts, (307) 344-7311, offers ski rentals, lessons, and guided day tours of the park; tours depart from both Mammoth Hot Springs and Old Faithful. Yellowstone Expeditions, (800) 646-9333 or (406) 646-9333, based out of West Yellowstone, offers small, guided multi-day trips in the Canyon area. Guests rough it in comfort, staying overnight in wood-stove heated huts (even the outhouse is heated!) and enjoying gourmet meals.

Most skiers take day trips out of **Mammoth** and **Tower,** which are accessible year-round by automobile. Novice skiers easily can master the **Upper Terrace** at Mammoth Hot Springs. More advanced skiers can continue on to **Snow Pass,** another 2 ½ miles of steep uphill (and therefore steep downhill), or hook up with the **Bunsen Peak Road** for an 11-mile full-day trip (watch out for the wind, which can be brutal). From Tower, the ski to **Tower Falls** is gorgeous and easy.

There is nice day skiing out of the Canyon area—try the **Canyon Rim Trail** or the **Roller Coaster Trail,** which loops around the campground)—but it makes for a long day trip. You can go with Amfac Parks and Resorts or hire a snowcoach from either Mammoth or West Yellowstone and ask for a drop-off, then camp overnight, since no indoor overnight facilities are open.

You can base yourself out of Old Faithful Snow Lodge, but you have to ski a long way to get out of earshot of the snowmobilers—it's the busiest snowmobile destination. One option is the nice, fairly level trail that leads from Old Faithful 10 miles (one way) to **Shoshone Geyser Basin**; you can camp nearby with a backcountry permit.

You can also ski to **Heart Lake** on the park's south end (8 miles in, and you may have to walk through a thermal area) but you'll have to take a snowcoach from either Old Faithful or Flagg Ranch and ask for a drop-off.

Wildlife

Barring the Discovery Channel, Yellowstone provides unrivaled wildlife-watching opportunities. It is virtually impossible to travel through the park without seeing some of the 35,000 **elk** or 3,300 **bison** that live in the Greater Yellowstone ecosystem. You may even glimpse some of the 250 **grizzly bears,** and several dozen **gray wolves** that live there, the latter thanks to a wolf reintroduction program begun in 1995. The easy sightings come partly because the animals have become so habituated to humans. Park rangers can tell you about recent sightings. For an overview of wildlife in the park, pick up a copy of Todd Wilkinson's *Yellowstone Wildlife: A Watcher's Guide,* published by NorthWord Press and available at park bookstores.

The Hayden Valley, between Canyon and Yellowstone Lake, is the park's top wildlife watching area. From turnouts, you can spot bison, elk, grizzlies, and **coyotes.** Look on the river for **trumpeter swans, pelicans,** and **eagles.** In the early summer, stop at LeHardy Rapids to watch **spawning trout** swim upstream.

You'll see bison, **mule deer,** coyotes, **badgers, mountains lions,** and, in winter, Yellowstone's largest elk herd in the Lamar Valley in the northeastern section of the park. But the big draw here is the occasional sighting of gray wolves.

The thermal features of the Upper Geyser Basin in the Old Faithful area attract **calving elk and bison** each spring. Grizzlies occasionally feed upon carcasses there. Look for **sandhill cranes** in the grasslands. In winter, watch for trumpeter swans and bald eagles along the Firehole and Madison Rivers, which don't freeze over because they're fed by thermal features.

Visit Mammoth Hot Springs in the fall to **hear bull elk bugle** their distinctive mating call. On the cliffs and benches north of Mammoth, look for **pronghorn antelope, bighorn sheep,** and mule deer. South of Mammoth look in the marshlands by Beaver Ponds, Obsidian Creek, and Indian Creek for **moose,** elk, deer, trumpeter swans, coyotes and grizzlies.

Other Activities

During winter season, you can lace up a pair of **ice skates** on a pond behind the Mammoth Hot Springs Hotel. Rent skates at the hotel; you can also rent a hot tub by the hour, a fine place to escape from the often excessive cold of Yellowstone.

You can actually immerse yourself in naturally hot water at the so-called Boiling River, where **hot springs** meet the Gardner River. A rock wall prevents you from being swept away by the current, and crowds prevent you from going nude. Bring water sandals. The springs are on the north end of the park, near the sign for the 45th parallel, 2 ½ miles from the north entrance; it's about a quarter-mile walk upriver from the parking lot.

Attractions

Several of the visitors centers in the park offer museum exhibits. The **Yellowstone and Fire exhibit** and 30-minute video at Grant Village Visitors Center goes a long way toward explaining the 1988 fires and fire ecology. It plays every hour. The Albright Visitors Center at Mammoth features an exhibit about early **Yellowstone history.** Check to see if the Norris Geyser Basin Museum has reopened; it houses an exhibit about **geothermal features.**

Attend one of the **ranger-naturalist programs,** which meet at various locations throughout the park and cover a wide variety of topics. This is a fine way to slow down and focus on one aspect of the park. The free programs run from 20 minutes to 1 ½ hours; you'll find a schedule and description of them inside *Yellowstone Today,* the newspaper you received on entry to the park, or call any of the visitors centers listed at the end of this chapter.

Obtain more in-depth information through the highly esteemed **Yellowstone Institute,** which offers multi-day courses in a wide range of topics, from wildflowers to fly-fishing, nature photography to winter backcountry camping. Founded in 1976, the institute is based at the historic Buffalo Ranch in the Lamar Valley, but conducts courses throughout the park, including many that take place in the backcountry. Some courses are designed specifically for families and children. Yellowstone Institute, PO Box 117, Yellowstone National Park, WY 82190, (307) 344-2294.

Summer concerts at the Lake Yellowstone Hotel, (307) 242-3700, feature a string quartet or pianist. Order a cocktail and settle down in the lovely sun room for a civilized end to the day. Music runs from 6:15pm to 10pm nightly.

Free guided tours of the remarkable **Old Faithful Inn** run four times daily. This enormous turn-of-the-century log structure is as much a must-see as the geyser for which it was named. Call (307) 344-7381 and ask for Visitor Information Services.

In summer, you can take **drawing and painting classes** through the artist-in-residence program. The 2-hour classes meet at the Canyon Visitors Center; there's a fee for the classes but art walks (for adults or kids) are free. You'll find information in the *Yellowstone Today* newspaper or call the Canyon Visitors Center, (307) 242-2550.

The **Junior Ranger** program encourages kids ages 5 to 7 and 8 to 12 (age range is flexible) to learn about the Yellowstone environment through a series of activities. Kids who complete a set of written exercises receive a Junior Ranger patch. The program materials are available at all visitors centers.

Calendar of Events

Each August 25, the National Park Service celebrates its founding in 1916 with a fee-free day; visitors arriving that day receive a free entrance pass good for a week.

Restaurants

All restaurants within the park (with the exception of the lunch counters at Hamilton Stores) are operated by Amfac Parks and Resorts. The ambitious gourmet menus vary slightly at each hotel dining room, but the food is comparable in quality, ranging from adequate to very good. The **Lake Yellowstone Hotel,** (307) 242-3899, is hands-down the prettiest place to eat, with hardwood floors and views of the lake (request a window table), and it has a reputation as the best restaurant in the park, though it doesn't always meet expectations. Stop by to have a cocktail or after-dinner drink in the lovely foyer; from 6:15pm to 10pm there's live classical music, and the view of the lake or the Absaroka Range is sublime at sunset. Dinner reservations for any of the facilities are required, though walk-ins sometimes get lucky; front desk staff at any of the park hotels can make reservations for you.

The same all-you-can-eat breakfast buffet is served at all park hotels (or you can have eggs to order), but coffee lovers should know that the park's only espresso cart is located on the second floor of the Old Faithful Inn in summer, and in the Map Room at Mammoth Hot Springs Hotel in winter.

Lodgings

All lodging within Yellowstone is handled exclusively by **Amfac Parks and Resorts**, (307) 344-7311. Reservations can be made up to 2 years in advance; any less than 6 months and you're pushing it, though there are always cancellations. Persistence often pays off, since there's no wait list. Phone lines are often busy, especially during May and June; try calling weekends or evenings. For same-season reservations, you can call direct to the individual park facility, where staff are more knowledgeable about specifics—though they may refer you back to Central Reservations if they're extraordinarily busy. It is also possible to write for reservations; address your request to Central Reservations, PO Box 165, Yellowstone National Park, WY 82190.

The only lodgings open during winter (December through mid-March) are **Mammoth Hot Springs Hotel** (upper-floor, odd-numbered north-side rooms have the best views; don't take Rooms 101–120, which are located near the housekeeping and accounting offices), and the **Old Faithful Snow Lodge.** Both are rather spartan, but a new Snow Lodge is scheduled to open by 1998 (call Amfac for updates, (307) 344-7311). Flagg Ranch Village (bordering the park's south entrance) also stays open year-round.

You may camp at Mammoth Campground and at Canyon Campground (no indoor facilities in winter, but you need a backcountry permit to camp at Canyon). There are 24-hour warming huts at Canyon, Fishing Bridge, Indian Creek, Madison Junction, Old Faithful (day-time only), and West Thumb. Most have vending machines; there are also light meals available at Canyon.

Lake Yellowstone Hotel ☆   When it was constructed in 1891, the Lake Yellowstone Hotel emerged as a plain, undistinctive squat structure, with only its location along the shores of magnificent Yellowstone Lake to recommend it. Two renovations, one in 1903 and one in 1929, transformed the Lake Hotel from the park's ugly duckling into a graceful neoclassical swan, with ionic columns, false balconies, hardwood floors, portico, and sun room. Further renovation in the 1980s made the Lake Hotel the most elegant place to stay in the park. Avoid the annex and request upper-floor front rooms with a view (some are blocked by trees); they were remodeled in 1988–1989 and all come with private bath. Staff won't guarantee a view but they'll do their darndest. The hotel's east wing has elevators, so if stairs are a problem be sure to mention it. Lake Yellowstone Hotel is closed November through April. *On the north shore of Yellowstone Lake; (307) 344-7311 for Central Reservations, or (307) 242-3700 to Lake Hotel, May through October, for same-season reservations; AE, DC, DIS, MC, V; local checks only; $$-$$$.*

Old Faithful Inn ☆   Built from native lodgepole pine and stone quarried from within the park, this historic turn-of-the-century structure is unrivaled in terms of sheer character. The 85-foot high central lobby, the massive three-story stone fireplace, and the twisted branch supports on the banisters make staying at the Old Faithful Inn a unique experience. Rooms in the original building have the most personality (and a lower price tag), but are often noisy due to loud radiator thumps and proximity to the mezzanine. Many of the rooms in the original building also share a bath. If you decide to risk a good night's sleep in favor of historic integrity, then request a room farther down the wings to avoid disturbances, and ask for a room with two double beds (though equal in price, rooms are not uniform in size; those with two beds are more spacious). Recently remodeled rooms in the slightly newer east and west wings are nice, though more generic; they all come with private bath. For a view of Old Faithful, make sure to request a room in the front side of the East Wing, and specify that you want a view (not all the rooms there have one). No one will guarantee a view, but reservation staff will do their best. Old Faithful Inn is closed November through April. *At Old Faithful Geyser Basin; (307) 344-7311 for Central Reservations, or (307) 545-4600 to Old Faithful, May through October, for same-season reservations; AE, DC, DIS, MC, V; local checks only; $$-$$$.*

More Information

Albright Visitors Center, Mammoth: (307) 344-2263.

Amfac Parks and Resorts: (307) 344-7311.

Canyon Visitors Center: (307) 242-2550.

Fishing Bridge Visitors Center: (307) 242-2450.

Grant Visitors Center: (307) 242-2650.

Lake Yellowstone Hotel: front desk, (307) 242-3700; dining room, (307) 242-3899.

Old Faithful Inn: front desk, (307) 545-4600; dining room, (307) 545-4999.

Old Faithful Visitors Center: (307) 545-2750.

Roosevelt Lodge: (307) 344-5273.

Yellowstone Association: (307) 344-2296 or, to order books and maps, (307) 344-2293.

Yellowstone National Park General Information: (307) 344-7381.

YNP Backcountry Office: (307) 344-2160 or (307) 344-2163 for recorded information.

YNP Special Services Office (for information on wheelchair-accessible facilities): (307) 344-2019.

Grand Teton National Park

Including the Grand Tetons, Jackson Lake, Jenny Lake, and the Snake River Valley.

Today, you could not get away with naming a mountain range "The Large Breasts," which is the English translation of what 19th-century French trappers named the Grand Tetons. It should come as no surprise that there once was talk of changing the name of Grand Teton National Park to Teewinot, a significantly less-offensive Native American term meaning "many pinnacles." Semantics aside, however, few visitors to the Rocky Mountains' geologically youngest range would deny that these imposing peaks of rugged, pointed beauty can take your breath away.

Rising 7,000 feet straight up from the valley floor, the north-south wall of granite that separates Wyoming from Idaho thoroughly dominates the surrounding landscape, with the 13,770-foot peak Grand Teton as its centerpiece. Glacial lakes lie at the mountains' base, and the Snake River meanders through the sagebrush-covered plains to the east. Nearly 30 miles from northerly tip to southerly toe, Grand Teton National Park averages 12 miles across and comprises 310,000 acres of the west's best scenery and wildlife habitat. Wildlife—moose, elk, bison, pronghorn, mule deer, coyotes, black bear, and numerous birds—is so prominent that the park often feels like an American version of a safari; this is one time you don't want to forget your binoculars. Nearly three million visitors annually descend upon the Tetons to enjoy the tremendous hiking, wildlife watching, and climbing opportunities. Even beginners can scale Grand Teton after passing a 2-day beginner course. Though, indeed, crowded, the Tetons have a decidedly less frenetic atmosphere than their northern neighbor Yellowstone, perhaps because the landscape as a whole, rather than various individual features, is the major attraction.

The enormous vertical relief of the Teton Range is due to a fault line that runs parallel to the eastern edge of the mountains and is the site of a series of earthquakes that began five to nine million years ago. Each of these violent quakes caused the mountains to rise 1 to 4 feet, while the valley floor simultaneously sank up to four times as much. Geologists believe a remnant of sandstone they found at an elevation of 6,000 feet on Mount Moran once was part of a sandstone layer that now lies an esti-mated 24,000 feet below the valley floor. Ice Age glaciers that scoured the range also created broad, U-shaped canyons and dragged immense amounts of rock to the mountains' base, where the debris dammed up the lakes that draw so many accolades today.

When Grand Teton National Park was dedicated in 1929, only the mountains were protected. The park now contains an entire ecosystem, from valley floor to mountain summit, due to oil magnate and philan-thropist John D. Rockefeller. Using the Snake River Land Company as a front, Rockefeller secretly bought up 35,000 key acres on the valley floor from ranchers, who, he suspected, might have been reluctant to sell to East Coast money. Nearly 30 years passed before Congress, in 1950, accepted Rockefeller's offer to donate the land to the existing park. As a consequence of this piecemeal land acquisition, 2,300 acres of private land still dot the park, including a 1,100-acre spread south of Phelps Lake that belongs to the Rockefeller family—modest compensation in exchange for leaving such a vast public legacy.

Getting There

Grand Teton National Park is tucked into the northwestern corner of Wyoming, between Jackson to the south and Yellowstone National Park to the north. The Jackson Hole Airport lies 4 miles south of Moose, within Grand Teton National Park boundaries. US Highway 89/191 runs north-south through the park.

Entrance fees for Grand Teton National Park also cover Yellowstone National Park, though time constraints apply. There are three visitors centers within the park: Moose (a half-mile west of Moose Junction on the Teton Park Rd at the south end of the park), open year-round; Jenny Lake (8 miles north of Moose Junction on the Teton Park Rd), open seasonally; and Colter Bay (a half-mile west of Colter Bay junction on US 89/191/287), also open season-ally. Visitors centers have brochures on just about every conceivable outdoor activity, from bird-watching to bicycling, climbing to backcountry camping. Be sure to check with rangers about your interests. There is also an information station at Flagg Ranch, 15 miles north of Colter Bay, midway between Yellowstone National Park and Grand Teton National Park, (800) 443-2311 or (307) 543-2861. Grand Teton National Park, PO Drawer 170, Moose, WY 83012-0170, (307) 739-3600.

The Teewinot newspaper you receive on entrance details park services; use the map on the back or the accompanying National Park Service map to orient yourself.

Adjoining Areas

NORTH: **Yellowstone National Park**

SOUTH: **Jackson Hole**

WEST: **Boise and Sun Valley**

Hiking/Backpacking

There are more than 200 miles of trails in the park, with plenty of possibilities for loop trips. Novice hikers should stay on the valley floor, especially on the level trails around Colter Bay. Experienced hikers should head up any of the canyons. Be aware that much of the high country remains snow-covered through late summer. You can camp on the snow, but you'll want a good tent and sleeping pad. Passes require an ice ax as late as July. The visitors centers have free copies of day-hike brochures, and rangers know the trails well.

You'll need a **backcountry permit** to camp overnight, available 24 hours in advance at all backcountry stations at the visitors centers. About 30 percent of backcountry campsites are now reservable in advance from January 1 to May 15; this is highly advisable, especially if you're planning to visit the park in July and August. Requests are accepted by mail, fax, or in person at the Moose Visitors Center. Even those with reservations must pick up a permit, available at the Moose or Colter Bay Visitors Centers or the Jenny Lake Ranger Station. (In winter, only the Moose Visitors Center remains open.) There is a limit on camping: you may stay in one campsite zone or lakeshore site for 2 consecutive nights (3 on Jackson Lake), and you may only remain in the backcountry 10 days (5 in winter). Submit your itinerary, including your name, address, daytime telephone number, number of people in your party, and preferred campsites and dates, along with a backup plan, to: Grand Teton National Park, Permits Office, PO Drawer 170, Moose, WY 83012; call (307) 739-3309, or fax (307) 739-3438. You can pick your permit up the day before your trip, but you *must* pick it up by 10am the day of your trip or it will be given away (call if you're running late).

The park's "Backcountry Camping" brochure includes a basic map listing all campsites by name and number, as well as many hiking suggestions, but you'll want a better **map** for your hike. Both the Earthwalk Press Recreation Map for Grand Teton National Park and the Trails Illustrated Map of Grand Teton National Park indicate camping zones, lakeshore sites, mileage, and topographical information; they're available at visitors centers. Earthwalk is better for topographics, but Trails Illustrated has more exact mileage. We also recommend the thorough *Teton Trails: A Guide to the Trails of Grand Teton National Park,* by Kate Duffy and Darwin Wile, published by the Grand Teton Natural History Association, for anyone considering a backcountry trip. Maps and books are available at park visitors centers or by mail order, (307) 739-3606. An order form is included in the park's backcountry information packet.

The quintessential Teton hike is the 1-miler to **Hidden Falls** and **Inspiration Point,** which begins with a boat ride across Jenny Lake. The trail climbs at a fairly steep rate to Inspiration Point, then levels off to a moderate slope as it continues up Cascade Canyon to Lake Solitude (or, for an overnighter, loops around to Paintbrush Canyon). The lake is poorly named, however; you're not likely to find much solitude here. On a summer day, you may pass 200 to 300 people in the canyon. No kidding. On the other hand, the falls are impressive, and the canyon is really pretty—plus it's one of the best places in the park for seeing black bears. Look for moose in the swampy areas. Boats run every 20 minutes all day, every day, June through late September. The last return boat leaves the far side of the lake at 6pm, so unless you want to hike all the way around the lake (an additional 2 1/2 miles), you need to time it right. Pick up the boat at the dock near the Jenny Lake Ranger Station; there's a $4 round-trip charge.

The not quite 5-mile (one-way) trail to **Surprise and Amphitheater Lakes** gains 3,000 feet from the valley floor to these two cirque-enclosed lakes. It's not easy, but assuming you're in good shape and have acclimated to the altitude, it's worthwhile; you'll be rewarded with stunning views of the valley as you go into the heart of the Tetons. It can be hot on this trail, so get an early start to avoid midday sun as you switchback across open slopes. The trail begins at the Lupine Meadows trailhead just south of Jenny Lake.

Many variations of multi-day backpack trips run along the **Teton**

Crest Trail. This trail is best explored by devising a shuttle, which allows you to loop back down one of the drainages to the valley floor without having to retrace your steps. You can save yourself a lot of time and trouble by taking the Aerial Tram at Teton Village (there's a fee) to the South Fork Trail. It's nearly 40 miles from the top of the tram north to Cascade Canyon and the String Lake Trailhead; you can shorten your trip by exiting out a closer drainage, or lengthen it by dropping west into Alaska Basin. This high-altitude trail should be hiked in August, after snowmelt.

Just about the only place to avoid people in the Tetons is on the **remote trails** in the north end of the park, on the west side of Jackson Lake. Logistically these are much harder hikes: the trails receive little maintenance and can be hard to distinguish from game trails. You'll want a topographical map and good compass reading skills. Numerous stream crossings can be difficult in high water, and you may want to bring a pair of extra shoes you don't mind getting wet. You'll either have to hike in from **Grassy Lake Road,** north of the park boundary, or get yourself across the lake; arrange a $45 round-trip boat shuttle (four people, additional charges for more passengers) from Signal Mountain Lodge Marina. If you've got a boat, one easier option is to camp at **Wilcox Point** and day hike. This is serious bear country, with both black bears and grizzlies; you'll want to take all the proper precautions. Other wildlife you're likely to spot are bighorn sheep, elk, moose, and harlequin ducks.

From Flagg Ranch Village, north of the park, you can hike to **Huckleberry Hot Springs,** about a mile long. The front desk at Flagg has photocopied maps with directions.

Climbing

People come from all over the world to climb the Tetons. Not only do these mountains provide classic, traditional, unbolted climbs rated from 5.4 to 5.12, but also the range boasts some of the most spectacular scenery on the planet. Be forewarned, though: even a seemingly basic climb can get tricky in the Tetons, due to high altitude and long approaches, and it's easy to lose your way on the climbs. Anyone considering climbing in the Tetons should have a copy of *The Complete Climbers' Guide to the Teton Range,* by Renny Jackson and Leigh Ortenburger, available at visitors centers in the park or through the Grand Teton Natural History Association, (307) 739-3403.

June through September, get **climbing information**, conditions, and register for backcountry sites at Jenny Lake Ranger Station, (307) 739-3343; off season call the Moose Visitors Center, (307) 739-3400. The rangers have photographs of all the mountains and can show you the routes.

You will need a **backcountry permit** for all overnight climbs (see Hiking/Backpacking, above). Registration, however, is not required for day climbs and off-trail hiking. As always, solo climbing is not advised. The park does not track you or check that you got out safely.

Moosely Seconds at Dornan's in Moose, (307) 739-1801, rents climbing shoes and sells equipment; it's open summers only. Its sister store, Moosely Seconds in Jackson, (307) 734-7176, is open year-round. The American Alpine Club operates the Climbers Ranch just south of Jenny Lake, (307) 733-7271, a dorm-style hostel where climbers and their families can bed down cheaply.

Even neophytes can climb the 13,770-foot **Grand Teton** with a 2-day crash course offered by Exum Mountain Guides and School of American Mountaineering, (307) 733-2297, or Jackson Hole Mountain Guides and Climbing School, (307) 733-4979. You have to qualify, but most people do, as long as they're in good shape. The 2-day **guided climb** up the peak itself isn't very technical—it's rated 5.4 to 5.6. Mostly it takes a lot of determination and some good fortune to succeed, though weather plays a serious factor in who makes it and who doesn't. There's also an easier fourth-class route.

Climbs are led year-round; expect snow until mid-July and again in September. Both Exum and Jackson Hole Mountain Guides offer private guide service up all peaks in the Teton Range. Exum is based within the park at Jenny Lake; Jackson Hole Mountain Guides are at 165 N Glenwood in Jackson.

There's good **ice climbing** much of the year on the north side of the Grand and the north side of the Enclosure area.

Boating/Canoeing/Rafting

You must purchase a **boating permit** for either motor or human-power crafts, including Jet-skis and windsurfers; permits are available at the Moose or Colter Bay visitors centers. Motor boats are permitted on Jackson, Phelps, and Jenny Lakes (with a 7 ½ hp maximum on Jenny). Sailboats, water skis, windsurfers, and Jet-skis are permitted on Jackson Lake only. Overnight buoys are available at Colter Bay Marina and Leek's Marina, both on Jackson Lake. Canoes, kayaks, and other human-powered boats are allowed on the three aforementioned lakes plus Emma Matilda, Two Ocean, Taggart, Bradley, Bearpaw, Leigh, and String Lakes, as well as the Snake River. Jackson or Jenny Lakes are favorites, because of their size and scenery. A Yellowstone National Park boating permit is also valid for Grand Teton National Park.

The park's boating brochure covers most questions; pick one up from any visitors center or phone the park, (307) 739-3300, to request one.

Rent canoes and kayaks at Adventure Sports, (307) 733-3307, at Dornan's in Moose. Rent motorboats and canoes at Colter Bay Marina, (307) 543-2811, ext. 1097. The marina at Signal Mountain Lodge, (307) 543-2831, rents rowboats and canoes, fishing boats, pontoon boats, and deck cruisers.

Rangers from the Colter Bay Visitors Center sometimes lead weekly **interpretive canoe trips** on Jackson Lake; rental canoes are available. Days and times of the half-day trips vary. There's no charge, but reservations are required. Colter Bay Visitors Center, (307) 739-3594.

Highly recommended is a commercial **float trip on the Snake River.** These are flatwater trips that concentrate on scenery, geology, and wildlife (particularly birds). You'll find a list of all the commercial floaters who operate within the park in the park's free *Teewinot* newspaper. We recommend owner-operated Solitude Float Trips, (307) 733-2871, and Barker–Ewing Float Trips, (800) 448-4202 or (307) 733-1000, both of which leave from Moose; or try Grand Teton Lodge Company, (307) 543-2811, whose trips originate at either Colter Bay or Jackson Lake Lodge. The river can be very busy. Ask how many other float trips are running concurrently with yours and schedule yourself accordingly.

For scenery and good swimming and picnicking, **sea kayak or canoe** either Jenny or String Lakes. Don't be deceived by the seemingly innocuous flatwater of the Snake River; its logjams and channels have been known to trip up even experienced boaters. With the exception of Oxbow Bend (see below) boating is not recommended on the Snake unless you're with someone who knows the river.

For wildlife watching, though, head to **Oxbow Bend,** 1 mile east of the Jackson Lake junction, where the meandering river attracts bald eagles, osprey, waterfowl, and moose. Put in at Cattlemen's Bridge, but make sure the water isn't so high that you can't paddle back upstream.

Narrated **scenic cruises** depart in summer from Colter Bay Marina, (307) 543-2811, ext. 1097. Breakfast cruises leave every day but Saturday; dinner cruises operate Monday, Wednesday, and Saturday; shorter scenic cruises leave several times a day. The ranger-led Fire and Ice Cruise is a good way to learn about geology. Breakfast cruises are lovely, since the lake's still quiet and wildlife is more abundant. Plus you'll get a huge breakfast of trout, pancakes, eggs, and hash browns. Dress in layers and bring bug repellent. Advance reservations advised.

Fishing

You'll need a valid Wyoming fishing **license**, available at the marinas, Signal Mountain Lodge, and Fish Moose at Dornan's. Pick up a copy of park fishing regulations from any visitors center. Rent fishing equipment from Fish Moose, (307) 733-3699.

Guided fishing trips on the Snake River are available through the Moose Village Store, (307) 733-3471. Guided fishing trips on Jackson Lake are available through Colter Bay Marina, (307) 739-3594, and Signal Mountain Lodge, (307) 543-2831.

From July through mid-October, fish the **Snake River** for native cut-throat. Fishing is notoriously good below the dam, especially early in the season. Often it's combat fishing; try early morning or evening. You can also access the shoreline from the Moose Visitors Center, or drive east on the RKO Rd (just south of the Jenny Lake turnoff from the Teton Park Rd) until you hit the river.

You'll find lake trout averaging 16 to 24 inches, as well as a few Snake River cutthroat, some browns, and whitefish on **Jackson Lake.** Fish from shore early in the season; it's best right after the ice melts, usually in late May. From June through September you'll want a boat. Mid-July and August, it's usually too hot to catch much. Look for shore access points on the Park Service map you received upon entrance to the park. The same general rules apply for **Jenny Lake,** which has lake trout and some Snake River cutthroat.

Camping

All five National Park Service campgrounds operate on a first-come, first-served basis, which means you'll want to get there pretty early in high season; there's a 2-week maximum stay. Entrance stations and visitors centers have current information about campground status; call Grand Teton National Park information, (307) 739-3300.

Colter Bay Campground is a half-mile west of Colter Bay Junction on US 89/191/287; **Gros Ventre Campground** is on the southeast edge of the park midway between the Gros Ventre Junction and Kelly; and **Signal Mountain Campground** is midway between Jenny Lake and Jackson Lake Junction on the Teton Park Rd. The tents-only **Jenny Lake Campground** (8 miles north of Moose Junction on the Teton Park Rd) generally fills by 8am in July and August and has a 7-day limit. Late arrivals should try the equally pretty **Lizard Creek Campground** (off US 89/191/287 on the north end of the park); it's out of the way, but peaceful.

The basic and relatively inexpensive ($24/night) tent-cabins at **Colter Bay Village,** (307) 543-3100, offer a reasonable alternative to the campgrounds, particularly in poor weather. A tent-cabin consists of two wood walls and two canvas walls with a canvas roof; inside, there's a wood stove (you have to purchase the wood) and metal frame bunks. Bring your own bedding. (The mattresses are skimpy, so you may want to bring your own mattress or pad, too.) There are pay showers on-site. One-half mile west of Colter Bay Junction on US 89/191/287.

Biking

Park visitors centers have bicycling brochures covering regulations. Bikes are allowed only on roadways; the **Teton Park Road** sports wide shoulders but lots of traffic. Obviously, early mornings are the best time to see the park from a saddle. There are a couple of decent short loop rides within the park, but serious mountain bikers will want to explore nearby Forest Service terrain, including the **Shadow Mountain** area, due east (see Biking in the Jackson Hole chapter).

Rent bikes at Adventure Sports at Dornan's in Moose, (307) 733-3307. The employees there have a small brochure highlighting area rides, and can steer you to a suitable one. They sell their own *Adventure Sports Ride Guide*, as well as *Mountain Biking in the Jackson Hole Area*, a **map** recommending rides both in and out of the park, published by Adventure Cycling, the national bicycling advocacy organization based in Missoula, Montana.

Horseback Riding

Hour-long, half-day, and breakfast and dinner **trail rides** leave from Colter Bay and Jackson Lake Lodge. Height, weight, and age restrictions apply, and advance reservations are advised. Grand Teton Lodge Co., (800) 628-9988 or (307) 543-2855.

The Tetons don't lend themselves well to horsepacking; the terrain is too steep and snow-covered much of the year.

Cross-Country Skiing/Snowshoeing

Rent touring or telemark skis and get information in Jackson at Skinny Skis, (307) 733-6094, or at Teton Mountaineering, (800) 850-3595 or (307) 733-3595.

With the exception of a riparian zone along the Snake River, you can cross-country ski anywhere in the park; trails are marked but not groomed. **Avalanche danger** is very high in the canyons, so only very experienced skiers well-versed in avalanche safety and equipped with beacons should think about attempting it. You'll need a permit to camp and can do so anywhere in the park, as long as you're on snow and at least one mile from a trailhead or road.

The most popular place to ski is along the trail leading to **Taggart Lake,** because you can drive to the trailhead (the Teton Park Rd is unplowed from Taggart Lake to Signal Mountain). You can also ski along the road to Jenny Lake.

Exum Mountain Guides, (307) 733-2297, leads backcountry Nordic ski tours and extreme alpine descents of the Tetons. Backcountry experts ski what locals call **10,552** (that's the elevation), also known as Mount Albreck. Don't bother trying to find it on the Forest Service map, as it's not there; you'll want a USGS topographical map. The **Maverick Bowl** area just north of there is also a favorite backcountry spot. Locals often refer to this entire area as the **Buck Mountain massif.** This is for experts only, with experience and good avalanche skills.

Beginning in January, rangers lead twice-weekly **snowshoe hikes** from the Moose Visitors Center, with an emphasis on natural history. Snowshoes are provided (they're old, but they work). These are relatively easy trips, either along the road or on other easy trails; no experience necessary. Moose Visitors Center, (307) 739-3399.

Snowmobiling

Forty-three miles of roads in Grand Teton National Park remain unplowed and open to cross-country skiers and snowmobiles. Additionally, the **Continental Divide Snowmobile Trail (CDST)** is open on an experimental basis, connecting Dubois, Lander, and the Togwotee Pass areas with Yellowstone National Park, following US 26/287 from the east park boundary to Moran Junction, then connecting with US 89 north to Yellowstone. The section that lies within Grand Teton is about 20 miles long. The Moose Visitors Center, (307) 739-3399, has snowmobiling brochures with more information; those interested in touring the CDST should request a second handout detailing special regulations there.

Wildlife

Check in the *Teewinot* newspaper for additional suggestions. Ranger-naturalists at any visitor station can provide the most up-to-date wildlife movement.

The willow flats behind Jackson Lake Lodge are prime **moose** habitat; you can often see them from the verandah behind the lodge. Thursday through Saturday and Tuesday evenings between 6:30pm and 8:30pm, a ranger comes armed with a powerful spotting scope to help you locate moose and other wildlife. It's free, and you don't have to be a lodge guest to attend.

Moose and **trumpeter swans** hang out on the lily-covered Swan Lake, an easy half-mile hike from the Colter Bay Marina. You can make another easy 3-mile loop by walking past Heron Pond, where you'll often see **white pelicans.** Ask at the Colter Bay Visitors Center for a map of the area.

Pronghorn antelope aren't really antelope at all, but rather a distinct genus of their own. In any case, you'll see these gazelle-like creatures in the open, sagebrush flats throughout the park; look for their white rumps and telltale forked antlers.

The Snake River claims the park's best bird-watching opportunities. To see **osprey, bald eagles, great blue herons,** and even occasional **sandhill cranes,** try the slow-moving channels of Oxbow Bend (park at the turnout on US 26/89/191/287, just east of the Jackson Lake Junction). Even better, take one of the commercial float trips that cruise down the Snake (see Boating/Canoeing/Rafting, above).

outside in

Attractions

Stop by the **Indian Arts Museum** at the Colter Bay Visitors Center for a look at David T. Vernon's superb collection of 20th century Plains Indian beadwork, pottery, and basketry. The museum is small but visually stunning. In summer, an artist-in-residence program brings various Native American artists to the museum on a weekly basis to show their wares and demonstrate techniques. Admission is free. Guided tours of the museum are offered at 4pm every day; on Tuesdays and Thursdays at 1:30pm you can attend a ranger-led program on Native American art and culture. Colter Bay Visitors Center, (307) 739-3544.

The self-guided interpretive trail at **Menor's Ferry** on the south end of the park is a must for anyone who wants to know more about how the Snake River valley came to be preserved. No longer in service (it's been replaced by a bridge), the ferry bore the name of homesteader William Menor, who in the 1890s capitalized on the need for a route across the Snake. The site's historic value was upped by Maude Noble, who purchased the ferry in 1918, doubled its price for out-of-staters, and spearheaded the movement to preserve the valley along with the mountain range. The buildings are furnished with terrific old photographs and period pieces.

Sign your little one up for the National Park Service's **Young Naturalist Program,** which encourages children to study the natural world. Their job is to successfully complete an activities brochure and take a vow to protect the environment. Your job is to pay a buck for the patch your kid earns, then—no rest for the weary—sew it on. Suitable for kids ages 8 to 12, the program is available at park visitors centers.

The park's free *Teewinot* newspaper lists the extensive schedule of **ranger-led activities** offered during the summer season. The Colter Bay Visitors Center also operates additional programs not listed in the paper; call for more information, (307) 739-3594.

Located on the site of a former dude ranch on the east side of the park, the privately run **Teton Science School** has been offering 1- to 5-day natural science seminars for 30 years. Courses are designed for a variety of ages, from young children through adult. Academic credit is available for some courses. Teton Science School, Box 68P, Kelly, WY 83011; (307) 733-4765.

Calendar of Events

To celebrate the anniversary of the creation of the National Park Service in 1916, the government waives entrance fees each August 25, and visitors centers offer free "birthday" cake.

Restaurants

The **Aspens Restaurant at Signal Mountain Lodge,** (307) 543-2831, along Jackson Lake in Moran (see Lodgings, below), serves great, casual breakfasts and espresso, too; go for the Garden Skillet (scrambled eggs, veggies, and three kinds of cheese) or the blackberry french toast. In the evening, grab a seat on the outdoor deck at the lounge there, well-known among park employees for its terrific margaritas and enormous portions of nachos, the Grand Teton of Tex-Mex food. The restaurant at **Leek's Marina** (in Moran, (307) 543-2494), has very good pizza and calzones. **Dornan's Grocery Store** (at Moose, 12 miles north of the town of Jackson near the south gate, (307) 733-2415), is a bona fide gourmet grocery store, with huge take-out sandwiches and wonderful baked goods, including killer brownies. The wine store has the best selection of wines in the valley.

Jenny Lake Lodge ☆   With its seven-course, $37.50 prix-fixe dinners and intimate atmosphere, Jenny Lake Lodge has long prided itself on its reputation as the park's premier dining spot. The graciousness of the log dining room provides a welcome respite from the usual frantic pace of the park. Unfortunately, it's difficult to maintain high standards when you're dealing with young, seasonal employees. Our waiter, for instance, was so inexperienced and eager (a thoroughly frightening combination) that he made us nervous. Our appetizers were quite good, but one of our entrees—the lodge's unusual seafood sausage—was delivered cold. Our waiter obligingly took it back to the kitchen, and returned it hotter, but this time it had been thrown together in a haphazard manner, the mark of an irritated chef. A better bet is the less pretentious breakfast ($12.50 for a sit-down, all-you-can-eat meal); the extensive menu includes berries and crème fraîche, trout and eggs, and smoked salmon and trout with a bagel. The Sunday night buffet, which changes weekly, is reputed to be consistently wonderful. Lunches are more simple and less costly, à la carte soup, salad, and sandwich kinds of affairs. Staff is very eager to please, which makes any mistakes easier to forgive. Reservations are recommended for breakfast and lunch, required for dinner. Jackets are suggested for male dinner guests. *1 mile off Teton Park Rd from the N Jenny Lake turnoff; PO Box 240, Moran; (800) 628-9988 or (307) 543-2855 off-season, (307) 733-4647 in season; breakfast, lunch, dinner every day June through Sept; AE, MC, V; checks OK; $$$.*

Lodgings

The three main lodgings in the park, Colter Bay (rustic cabins and tent cabins), Jackson Lake Lodge (hotel rooms and condo-like cottage rooms), and Jenny Lake Lodge (duplex cabins) are run by the Grand Teton Lodge Co., (800) 628-9988 or (307) 543-2855, or (307) 733-4647 for Jenny in summer. Two other private companies operate cabins in the park: Signal Mountain Lodge (cabins) and Dornan's in Moose, (307) 733-2522. All but Dornan's close off season.

Dornan's Spur Ranch Cabins ☆☆   Built in 1992, these plush custom log cabins are located along the Snake River at the south end of the park, with views of the Tetons; the best one-bedroom is Cascade, which has a straight shot of the Grand Teton through the living room window; the best two-bedroom is Larkspur, which has a view of the Grand from both bedrooms. All 12 back-to-back duplex cabins are furnished with lodgepole furniture, and come with a fully equipped kitchenette, down comforters, tiled bathrooms, and patio with barbecue. One-bedroom cabins sleep a maximum of four; two-bedrooms sleep six. Set in a courtyard below Moose Village, these are some of the park's most private lodgings, yet within easy walking distance of a gourmet grocery store and wine shop. They are also the park's only year-round accommodations. Housekeeping is on a weekly basis. No smoking. The cabins use environmentally friendly, biodegradable cleaning products. There's a flexible 2-night minimum stay in summer. *12 miles north of Jackson, on the south end of the park, just across the bridge from the Moose Visitors Center; PO Box 39, Moose, WY 83012; (307) 733-2522; AE, DIS, MC, V; checks OK; $$$.*

Jackson Lake Lodge ☆☆   This very modern, full-service resort claims one of the park's best locations, on a bluff overlooking Willow Flats with the Tetons rising in the background. (Though, ironically, Jackson Lake itself is obscured from the ground floor.) The two-story, 60-foot high picture windows in the lobby offer astounding views, and moose are such a common sight from the back veranda that ranger-naturalists set up spotting scopes there several times a week (see Wildlife, above). Even if you're not staying here it's worth stopping in for a peek; there's a nice bar, and the Pioneer Room lunch counter has some terrific historical photographs. Jackson Lake Lodge offers two types of accommodations: 37 large, comfortable hotel rooms and another 348 "cottage rooms," which resemble condo housing. None come with television or radio, but the lodge does have a large outdoor pool (also available to registered guests at Colter Bay Village and Jenny Lake Lodge). The lodge's gift shop is a cut above most, with an impressive collection of Native American jewelry and pottery.

Rooms with a view are spacious and tasteful and come with refrigerators and down comforters; unfortunately there are no balconies. Ask for rooms numbered 18 through 30, which are quieter. Cottage room clusters are spaced out over a square mile around the hotel; they have either a balcony or a patio and are much larger and offer more privacy than rooms in the main hotel. At press time, their decor had just been changed and was disappointingly mismatched. Unless stairs are a problem, request upper floors in the cottages; the recently remodeled 900 series is a bit more private than the rest. The lodge begins taking phone reservations in mid-November for the following season; written requests are processed as much as a year out, in the order they are received, but not until after the lodge closes down for the season in October. List a second choice if possible. Open mid-May through mid-October. *20 miles south of Yellowstone National Park, 5 miles north of Moran Junction on Hwy 89; Grand Teton Lodge Co, PO Box 240, Moran, WY 83013; (800) 628-9988 or (307) 543-2855; AE, DIS, MC, V; checks OK; $$$.*

Jenny Lake Lodge ☆☆   Billed as the park's most exclusive—and most expensive—resort, Jenny Lake Lodge certainly exudes old-world class. Set off by themselves on Jenny Lake Rd, 37 small, attractively decorated log cabin units are clustered around a main lodge where guests congregate for gourmet breakfasts and dinners that are included in the nightly rate. Cabins are decorated with custom furniture and appointed with unusual extras such as walking sticks and umbrellas, as well as terrycloth robes, luxurious toiletries, and patios with Adirondack chairs. The nicest cabins are Violet, Fireweed, Lupine, Chokecherry, and Columbine, though these original rustic log cabins are slightly darker and less spacious than the newer cabins constructed in the early '90s. The central lodge, with its huge fireplace and comfy couches, is a good place to relax with a book, and staff is notoriously ready to bend over backwards for guests' comfort. If you take advantage of everything included in the rates—enormous meals, bicycles, horseback trail rides, and free admission to the pools at either Jackson Lake Lodge or the Jackson Hole Golf & Tennis Club—prices seem more reasonable. The lodge has developed a devoted following of guests who return year after year, often for a week or more. Apparently, they understand that exclusivity has its price, especially within a national park.

Jenny Lake is the best place to eat in the park (see Restaurants, above), if somewhat inconsistent, and guests may also dine at Jackson Lake Lodge's Mural Room or at the Strutting Grouse Restaurant at the Jackson Hole Golf & Tennis Club. Repeat guests receive first priority for reservations; neophytes should write well in advance for next season and can phone beginning in December. Take heart, though; there's always the possibility of a cancellation, and Jenny Lake Lodge keeps a waiting list. The lodge is open June through September. *1 mile off Teton Park Rd from the N Jenny Lake turnoff; Grand Teton Lodge Co, PO Box 240, Moran, WY 83013; (800) 628-9988 or (307) 543-2855 off season, (307) 733-4647 in season; AE, MC, V; checks OK; $$$.*

Signal Mountain Lodge Of Signal Mountain's 78 units along Jackson Lake, we much prefer the older, less expensive log cabins. They have more character than the newer, rather generic lakefront four-plexes, which come with a kitchen that's not of much use since no utensils are supplied. Of the older cabins, the best are 136 through 144, which feature lakefront locations but aren't billed as such. Staff is neither as knowledgeable nor as helpful as we might wish. Signal is open mid-May through October. *At the south end of Jackson Lake, midway between Moose and Yellowstone; PO Box 50, Moran, WY 83013; (307) 543-2831; AE, DIS, MC, V; checks OK; $$$.*

More Information

Adventure Sports: (307) 733-3307.
Backcountry Weather and Avalanche forecast: (307) 733-2664.
Colter Bay Visitors Center: (307) 739-3594.
Dornan's: (307) 733-2415, or (307) 733-2522 for cabin reservations.
Grand Teton Lodge Co.: nonreservation calls, (307) 543-2811; reservations, (800) 628-9988 or (307) 543-2855.
Grand Teton National Park: (307) 739-3300.
GTNP Permits Office: (307) 739-3309; fax (307) 739-3438.
Grand Teton Natural History Association: (307) 739-3403.

Jenny Lake Lodge: (307) 733-4647.
Jenny Lake Ranger Station: (307) 739-3343.
Jenny Lake Visitors Center: (307) 739-3392.
Moose Visitors Center: (307) 739-3399.
Signal Mountain Lodge: (307) 543-2831.

Jackson Hole

Including Jackson, Wilson, Teton Village, and the Gros Ventre, Bridger, and Teton Wilderness areas.

Jackson used to be just another tiny western town with a stupendously fortunate location, surrounded by the Teton Mountains to the west and the Gros Ventres to the east. Now, though, Jackson (city pop: 5,700, county pop: 13,330) is one of the biggest tourist draws in the west, with three million visitors yearly. Most of them come in summer and use Jackson and Jackson Hole (you'll hear these terms used interchangeably, but technically the town is simply Jackson, while the entire valley is Jackson Hole) as a jumping-off point to Grand Teton National Park or, during winter, to massive Jackson Hole Ski Resort. Both are just 12 miles from town.

There are enough guest rooms in the valley for every single Jackson resident, and then some. Tourism is the community's lifeblood and everyone in Jackson knows it—which means no one's going to try to ride you out of town, like they might in other more xenophobic western locales. On the other hand, we have heard locals joke that they can spot the tourists pretty easily: they're the ones wearing spanking new cowboy hats, outrageously expensive fringed leather vests or dusters, and cowboy boots that have never come within a mile of anything even resembling a cowpie. Real cowboys wear baseball caps and Wranglers, and never—*never!*—fringed leather vests.

Once you accept the fact that Jackson isn't the real West but rather a cleaned-up version of the same, you can relax and have a good time in fantasyland. Polo, Benetton, the Gap, Orvis, and London Fog are among the national chains with outlets in Jackson, and few other western towns can boast two sushi restaurants. Most western communities host an annual rodeo, but Jackson boasts two a week during the summer, and stages a shoot-out nightly in the town square.

At its best Jackson has a lot to offer, including terrific restaurants, good art galleries such as the impressive National Museum of Wildlife Art, and (we have to admit it) some good shopping opportunities. But mostly, what Jackson offers is proximity to some of the most breathtaking scenery in the nation and some of the finest outdoor playgrounds. Although you can't actually see the Tetons from town (they're hidden by East Gros Ventre Butte), it's only a short drive until they come into view. Jackson also sits on the edge of the Gros Ventre Wilderness and the National Elk Refuge. In fact, 97 percent of the county is public land, and only 2 percent of the land remaining is still available for development—which explains the astronomical price of property (modest homes with views run into the high six and sometimes seven digits).

Founded in 1897 and named after fur trapper Davey Jackson, the seat of Teton County is now home to only the very wealthy or those who share cramped, Manhattan-priced apartments. More and more "modem cowboys," including some pretty heavy-hitters, are packing up their Powerbooks and relocating from New York or LA to Jackson, where they can enjoy the tremendous scenery and outdoor activities by day and still have their pick of gourmet restaurants by night. Jackson Hole has gotten so expensive (the average price of a home is $225,000, with apartment rents ranging from $800 to $1,200 per month) that an entire group of professionals now live in a community of yurts—Mongolian domed tents with canvas walls and no electricity—in nearby Kelly.

With the cost of living so high, it's no wonder that just about every service you could possibly imagine is available here. From dogsledding to hot air ballooning, sleigh rides to guided hikes, and mountain bike rides to horseback trips or wildlife safaris, Jacksonites are ready to cater to your every whim. Which makes Jackson the perfect destination for people who have only a short amount of time and want to make the most of it.

Getting There

Jackson is served by the Jackson Hole Airport in Grand Teton National Park. At the junction of US Highway 26/89/189/191 and Hwy 22, the town lies 12 miles south of Grand Teton National Park and 12 miles east of the Wyoming-Idaho border.

Adjoining Areas

NORTH: **Grand Teton National Park; Yellowstone National Park**

WEST: **Boise and Sun Valley**

Hiking/Backpacking

Most people who come to Jackson come because of its proximity to Grand Teton National Park, and it's there that most people venture onto the trails. But surrounding Jackson is the massive Bridger–Teton National Forest, at 3.4 million acres the second-largest national forest in the Lower 48, and it's there that locals head when they want to get away from the crowds. Three designated wildernesses—the Gros Ventre, the Bridger, and the Teton—lie within the Bridger–Teton National Forest, with trailheads within easy driving distance of Jackson. For instance, the boundary of the Gros Ventre Wilderness lies just a mile east of town.

Three **maps** cover the Bridger–Teton National Forest. For the area immediately surrounding Jackson, you'll want the one that covers the Buffalo and Jackson Ranger Districts. For the Wind River Range, you'll want the Pinedale Ranger District map. The Big Piney, Grays River, and Kemmerer District map covers the area south of Jackson. The Bridger–Teton National Forest Supervisor's Office, (307) 733-5500, and the Jackson Ranger District, (307) 739-5400, are located next door to each other at the north end of downtown Jackson on Cache Street as you head toward Grand Teton National Park. Buy maps at the Jackson Ranger District or at Teton Mountaineering (170 N Cache, (800) 850-3595 or (307) 733-3595). The ranger district also has a free "Day Hiking Trip Planner" with good descriptions, but mediocre maps, of numerous area trails.

Also recommended: *Jackson Hole Hikes* (formerly *Fifty Jackson Hole Hikes*), by Rebecca Woods, which covers Grand Teton National Park and the Targhee and Bridger–Teton National Forests. For detailed information about the Wind River Range, try *Walking the Winds: A Hiking and Fishing Guide to Wyoming's Wind River Range,* also by Rebecca Woods; or *Climbing and Hiking the Wind River Mountains,* by Joe Kelsey. All three books are available at the Jackson Ranger District and at area outdoor stores. Rent sleeping bags, pads, and tents from Leisure Sports, (307) 733-3040, or Skinny Skis, (307) 733-6094.

Camping **restrictions** imposed in much of the national forest require you to camp at least 200 feet from most waterways and lakes (and where it's not regulated, it's at least encouraged). You are also encouraged to eschew campfires in favor of backpacking stoves; if you must make a fire, please use existing fire rings. Be sure to check with the appropriate ranger district about regulations for your destination. And remember that this is bear habitat, both black and grizzly (the latter especially in the northern part of the forest); make sure you know—and practice—all the proper precautions.

The Hole Hiking Experience, (307) 739-7155, offers **guided half-day and day hikes** in the Bridger–Teton and Targhee National Forests, complete with lunch. Clients rave. For a different approach, try hiking with **llamas.** Black Diamond Llama Expeditions, (800) 470-2877 or 307-733-2877, offers day hikes with gourmet lunches Mondays, Wednesdays, and Fridays. Four-person minimum.

Just inside the Gros Ventre Wilderness, **Goodwin Lake** is an intermediate-level, easily accessible 6-mile (round-trip) day hike from Jackson. The trail starts high and continues up a ridge, where it levels out and continues to the little lake, situated below the ramparts of Jackson Peak. Bring water. There are also several overnight possibilities in the area; you can loop around and come out **Cache Creek** (you'll want a shuttle, and watch for mountain bikers when you exit the wilderness), or bear east to **Turquoise Lake,** 7 miles past Goodwin Lake (there's no water on the trail), then come out at Granite Hot Springs, where you can soak your tired tootsies (and the rest of you, too; see Attractions, below). To get to the Goodwin Lake Trailhead, take the Elk Refuge Road at the east end of Jackson and follow the signs to Curtis Campground. The road dead-ends at the trailhead, about 3 miles past the campground. The total distance from Jackson to the trailhead is about 11 miles.

Known locally as the Sleeping Indian, because in profile it resembles an Indian lying on his back, headdress pointed southward, the **Sheep Mountain** area northeast of Jackson is another area popular for day hikes. Most people head for **Grizzly Lake,** an 8-mile round-trip hike suitable for families (there's fishing there, too). If you're willing to expend the extra effort, choose the **Blue Miner Lake Trail,** which leads to the belly of the Indian inside the Gros Ventre Wilderness; it's a steeper and longer hike, 12 miles round trip, but you won't see as many people and you'll get a great view of the Tetons from the top. You don't actually wind up at the lake but rather on a ridge overlooking it. By the way, Sheep Mountain was the site of the 1996 plane crash that killed several members of President Clinton's entourage. Watch for bighorn sheep and, during fall, elk (and elk hunters) along both of these trails. The trailheads for Grizzly Lake and Blue Miner Lake are located on the Gros Ventre Rd northeast of Kelly, about 2 miles and 5 miles, respectively, past Atherton Campground.

You can call it cheating, but we call it smart. You can save yourself a lot of time and effort (4,139 vertical feet, to be exact) by taking the **aerial tram** to the top of 10,450-foot **Rendezvous Mountain.** From there, access the **Teton Crest Trail,** which heads north through the park. Sure, you'll see other hikers, but it's the classic overnight trip in the area. If you want to avoid the cost, you can hike up the **Granite Canyon Trail** in the park (about 12 miles one way) and ride the tram down for free. You can also hike down the 7 1/2-mile trail as it switchbacks down the mountain, but it's much better to hike the high trails. (See Hiking/Backpacking in the Grand Teton National Park chapter for more details.)

The 1 1/2-mile hike to **Ski Lake** in the Tetons, a glacial cirque lake surrounded by granite cliffs, is popular with families because of its easy accessibility. It's particularly lovely in late spring and early summer, when wildflowers are out in force. To get to the trailhead, take Hwy 22 west through Wilson; about 2 miles before you reach the top of Teton Pass, you'll see a four-wheel-drive road to your right. Park and hike the road about a quarter-mile, where you'll then see the trail bearing left. The trail forks again shortly afterwards; bear left again.

The most spectacular hiking in the Bridger–Teton National Forest region is within the 428,000-acre **Bridger Wilderness,** along the Continental Divide on the west slope of the magnificent **Wind River Range** southeast of Jackson. The wilderness claims 1,300 named glacial lakes (and many more unnamed), cirques, U-shaped valleys, and hanging troughs to explore, as well as huge peaks, including 13,804-foot Gannett Peak, Wyoming's highest (a popular climbing destination). The Wind River Range also claims 7 of the 10 largest glaciers in the Lower 48. Remember to camp at least 200 feet from trails or lakeshores. Campfires are permitted below timberline only, using downed fuel. You'll want to stay at least overnight, possibly longer. There are nine primary trailheads; **Big Sandy** and **Elkhart** trailheads are the most popular, with easy access to great views, but don't expect much solitude. Choose another trailhead if you want a wilder experience. Over 80 percent of Bridger Wilderness users come from out-of-state or foreign countries. Two notes: There are grazing allotments within the Bridger Wilderness, so you may well see sheep or cattle (district rangers can tell you how to avoid them), and there have been problem black bears in the wilderness; make sure you check with rangers before heading out on the trails. Contact the Pinedale Ranger District, (307) 367-4326, for more complete information.

Located in the north end of Bridger–Teton National Forest, the 585,500-acre **Teton Wilderness** is known for its broad valleys, high plateaus, and long approaches, which is why pack trips account for 95 percent of its use. If you do hike along trails here, you can expect to run into pack strings and see a lot of horse impact. Consequently, the best hiking is on the trailless plateaus; you should be experienced with a compass and familiar with no-trace camping etiquette. This is big bear country, too, with both black bears and grizzlies. One recommended and unusual moderately difficult day hike is the 15-mile round-trip hike to **Gravel Ridge,** which overlooks the eerie blowdown scene of the highest altitude tornado ever recorded (in 1987). The trailhead leaves from Box Creek, 46 miles northeast of Jackson. From Jackson, drive north on US 287, following it as it bears east at Moran Junction, then turn left onto Buffalo Valley Rd and drive another 8 miles to the Box Creek trailhead. Buffalo Ranger District, (307) 543-2386.

Camping

There are 18 Forest Service campgrounds in the Jackson area, 12 of which have sites you can reserve in advance by calling (800) 342-2267. The Jackson Ranger District, (307) 739-5400, has a list of the campgrounds that includes descriptions of sites and amenities; RV travelers should check to see that the campground can accommodate their vehicles. The general season runs from Memorial Day through Labor Day, though some of the campgrounds stay open in the fall at no charge.

The biggest plus about the 52-site **Granite Creek Campground** is also its biggest drawback: it's just down the road from Granite Hot Springs. Despite the crowds, this is a pretty place to stay. It's 35 miles southeast of Jackson; take US 189/191 southeast for 25 miles and turn left (north) at Granite Creek Rd.

The 13-site **Atherton Creek Campground** sits near Lower Slide Lake, which was formed on June 23, 1925, when part of Sheep Mountain slid into the Gros Ventre River and dammed it up. You can swim here, if you dare. A few miles farther down the road you'll find more solitude at **Red Hills Campground** (five sites) and **Crystal Creek Campground** (six sites). This is a fascinating, beautiful area and a great place to see bighorn sheep. It's about 20 miles north of Jackson; from Jackson, take US 189/191 north to the Gros Ventre junction, then bear right on the Gros Ventre Rd through the town of Kelly and turn right at the signs.

There's a series of five campgrounds within 5 miles along the Snake River south of Jackson, beginning with **Cabin Creek Campground,** 19 miles south of town on US 26/89. Cabin Creek doesn't have water available, but the rest of them do.

Fly-Fishing

The Wyoming Game and Fish Department puts out the *Wyoming Fishing Guide,* which gives a very good overview of access and fish inventories. Pick one up at the Wyoming Game and Fish Department in Jackson, (800) 423-4113 in-state only or (307) 733-2321, at 360 N Cache St, next door to the Jackson Ranger District, or at the Wyoming Visitors Center at 532 N Cache St. Get regulations and licenses through the Wyoming Game and Fish Department or area outdoor stores.

Rent equipment, including float tubes, and obtain advice from Westbank Anglers, (800) 922-3474 or (307) 733-6483, located on the Teton Village Rd midway between Jackson and Teton Village. Arrange half-, full-, or multi-day **guided fishing trips** on the Snake River, the South Fork of the Snake, or the Green River, through Westbank Anglers or Upstream Anglers, (800) 642-8979 or (307) 739-9443. Westbank Anglers also guides in Yellowstone and Grand Teton National Parks and offers half-, full-, and multi-day fly-fishing clinics. Upstream Anglers concentrates on waters in the immediate Jackson area. A good investment for anyone fishing Wyoming's waters is *The Wyoming Angling Guide,* by Chuck Fothergill and Bob Sterling.

There's good fishing for native Snake River cutthroat (also known as fine-spotted cutthroat for the fine black spots that cover its body) on the **Snake River** from mid-July through mid-October, with the best fishing after Labor Day. Expect fish to average 12 to 15 inches. This is big, classic holding water, suitable for both wading and floating. A gravel road follows the dike on the west bank of the river from the Wilson Bridge (between Jackson and Wilson on Hwy 22) south about 3 miles, providing good shore access. A good all-day float starts at the Wilson Bridge and ends at the South Park Bridge on US 26/89/191, a distance of about 13 miles. This section of the river has a lot of braiding; check with local fly shops about conditions. An easier float runs from South Park Bridge to Astoria Hot Springs, about 10 miles.

The **Green River,** about an hour's drive east of Jackson, yields up rainbows, browns, brookies, and Snake River cutthroat averaging 14 to 15 inches. The Green usually clears a couple of weeks before the Snake, and it's well-known for its gray drake hatch in early July. The Green is floatable early in the season, but you can find good shore access from Warren Bridge on US 191/189, 20 miles northwest of Pinedale. A Bureau of Land Management (BLM) road on the north side of the highway runs for about 10 miles along the river, offering a dozen access points; the first three are suitable only for high-clearance vehicles, but the rest you should be able to negotiate in a regular car.

August through October, you can fish **Lower Flat Creek** in the National Elk Refuge between the Old Crawford Bridge site and the McBride Bridge along US 191, where you'll find Snake River cutthroat and small numbers of brookies. This can be exceptional fishing, but beware: it's tough sight-casting, suitable for experienced anglers only. Boats are not permitted.

There's good lake fishing early in the season in Grand Teton National Park, just after ice-out. See the Fishing section in the Grand Teton National Park chapter.

Biking

Mountain bikers can rent bicycles and obtain advice in Jackson from Teton Cyclery (175 N Glenwood, (307) 733-4386) and Wilson Backcountry Sports, (307) 733-5228, in Wilson. Get yourself a copy of Adventure Cycling's *Mountain Biking in the Jackson Hole Area*, which has detailed descriptions, including mileage charts, and a map of nearly two dozen area rides. It's widely available at local bike shops. And don't forget you can ride on the National Elk Refuge, which is pretty level though it can have heavy traffic; you'll want to go early in the morning. Uncomfortable with do-it-yourself rides? Teton Mountain Bike Tours will take you on a guided ride suited to your ability. Call (800) 733-0788 or (307) 733-0712 for details.

A popular and scenic 23-mile ride that begins close to town is the **Cache Creek–Game Creek Loop,** suitable for intermediate to advanced riders. Start on Cache Creek Rd just east of downtown Jackson, and follow it as it turns into a trail and skirts the Gros Ventre Wilderness. Bear right onto the Game Creek Trail, which winds up on US 189/191. Follow the highway north back to town.

The 14-mile **Shadow Mountain Loop,** on the east edge of Grand Teton National Park, is highly recommended for its views of the Tetons, Jackson Lake, and the Slide Lake area. This intermediate-level ride begins where Antelope Flats Rd turns north, 3 1/3 miles east of US 26/89/191. Follow the paved road as it turns into gravel where a sign announces "National Forest Access," then after slightly more than 2 miles bear right onto Forest Rd 3034. Follow this road as it climbs past Shadow Mountain, but don't forget to turn around and admire the view of the Tetons. Follow the main road down as it veers left and into the park; at about 10 miles you'll turn off the main road and bear left through a gate onto a double-track path that will take you back to the dirt road you came in on.

Advanced riders should head west of Jackson to Wilson, where they can follow the Old Teton Pass Rd up, then make loop trips out of either the **Phillips Canyon Trail** to the north or the **Black Canyon Trail** to the south. The 15 ½-mile Phillips Canyon Loop is described in detail in Adventure Cycling's *Mountain Biking in the Jackson Hole Area.* A national forest map is also useful.

Road **cyclists** should pick up the *Wyoming Bicycle Guidance Map,* a state map highlighting routes, shoulders, prevailing winds, and average daily traffic volume for cross-state bicycle travelers. It also includes information on bicycle shops and possible camping locations. Call the Wyoming Department of Transportation in Cheyenne, (307) 777-4719, for a copy.

Kayaking/Rafting

Lots of companies offer **whitewater trips** through Snake River Canyon south of Jackson. We recommend Barker–Ewing River Trips, (800) 448-4202 or (307) 733-1000; Charlie Sands Wildwater, (800) 358-8184 or (307) 733-4410; or Dave Hansen Whitewater, (800) 732-6295 or (307) 733-6295. The latter runs smaller, eight-person boats. All trips begin about the third week of May and finish up in mid-September.

Snake River Kayak and Canoe School, (800) 529-2501 or (307) 733-3127, teaches half-day and full-day **kayak and canoe classes;** instruction begins in an indoor, heated pool that simulates a 4 mph current, then moves onto the river. The school also offers inflatable kayak trips on area rivers and guided **sea kayaking** overnights on Yellowstone Lake. Rent rafts, canoes, and inflatable kayaks, as well as wet suits and accessories through Leisure Sports, (307) 733-3040.

The most popular stretch of whitewater around Jackson is the 8-mile run through **Snake River Canyon,** also known as Alpine Canyon, about 25 miles south of town, which has solid Class III rapids, without too much technical knowledge needed. Early in the year watch out for the Lunch Counter, about midway through the run; in lower water the Big Kahuna, just above the Lunch Counter, is the rapid of which to be wary. Put in at West Table Creek and take out at Sheep Gulch. River flows and maps of the Snake River or, specifically, of the Snake River Canyon are available through the Snake River Canoe and Kayak School (see above).

Expert kayakers head for the **Gros Ventre River** from Slide Lake to the boundary of Grand Teton National Park for a short but fun 2-mile ride through solid Class IV waves. The river is usually unrunnable by mid- to late-August.

Climbing

Jackson is conveniently located between two of the best climbing areas in the country: the **Tetons** to the north (see the Climbing section in the

Grand Teton National Park chapter) and the **Wind River Range** to the southeast, home to **Gannett Peak,** at 13,804 feet Wyoming's highest peak. Both Exum Mountain Guides, (307) 733-2297, and Jackson Hole Mountain Guides, (307) 733-4979, lead climbs in the park and the Wind Rivers.

For practice or advice, stop by the Teton Rock Gym (1116 Maple Way, (307) 733-0707). Also pick up a copy of *Climbing and Hiking the Wind River Mountains,* by Joe Kelsey, or contact the Pinedale Ranger District, (307) 367-4326.

Climbs in the Wind River Range run the gamut from beginner routes to challenging 5.13s. The most popular climbing areas are the **Cirque of the Towers** and the **Fremont Peak** area, which is home to Gannett Peak. Expect long approaches and plenty of fellow climbers.

Horseback Riding

With its history as dude ranch central, Jackson has plenty of companies specializing in horseback trips. The Jackson Ranger District, (307) 739-5400, keeps a complete list of outfitters and packers permitted in the Bridger–Teton National Forest. Two we hear good things about are Spring Creek Riding Stables, (307) 733-9209, and Mill Iron Ranch, (307) 733-6390. Both companies offer a range of rides, from 1 hour to all day, with or without meals.

With 30 years in the **horse packing** business, Gilroy Outfitting, (307) 733-4314, is a good choice for either overnight trips in the Gros Ventre Wilderness or longer 6-day trips into the Teton Wilderness (it's the only company with a base camp there). These trips put an emphasis on lots of riding, fishing, and scenery. Families welcome.

Golfing

Jackson is home to two championship golf courses, both semiprivate: the Arnold Palmer/Ed Seay-designed Teton Pines Country Club (4 miles south of Teton Village off the Teton Village Rd, (307) 733-1733) opens to the public mid-morning; the Jackson Hole Golf and Tennis Club, (307) 733-3111, is located on the way to Grand Teton National Park, with knockout views.

Swimming

The **Teton County/Jackson Parks and Recreation Center** (155 E Gill St, (307) 733-9025) has a 25-yard indoor pool with a great diving board, a "leisure pool" with waterfall, and a terrific 185-foot water slide. The center schedules both lap swims and open swims.

Downhill Skiing

The vast majority of tourists still show up before the snow flies, but with three ski areas within an hour's drive, Jackson has become a national destination for skiers in search of steep and deep. Want to try all three area resorts? Buy a $215 "Ski Three Multi-Area Lift Voucher," a book of five tickets good for one week at any of the local areas. Redeem a voucher at Jackson Hole and get a tram pass free; redeem one at Grand Targhee and get either round-trip bus service from Jackson or a group ski lesson; those redeemed at Snow King come with a free dinner.

About 12 miles north of the town of Jackson, the world-class **Jackson Hole Ski Resort** at Teton Village pretty much has it all: a 4,139-foot vertical rise; 7 chairlifts plus an aerial tram and surface lift; 62 runs on 2,500 acres; an average annual cumulative snowfall of 384 inches; and some of the toughest skiing in the country. About the only thing missing from the ski area is novice terrain; even the so-called intermediate runs are rated relatively, which means they often are as steep or steeper than runs rated expert at other resorts. Real experts enjoy (or pretend to, anyway) jumping off the 10- to 20-foot cliffs at the top of the tram into the steep and narrow Corbet's Couloir, or tracking up the powder early in the day in the Hobacks. Less confident skiers should stay off the tram altogether and stick to the Casper Bowl and Apres Vous Mountain areas on the north end. True beginners shouldn't bother showing up at all. (A measly 10 percent of the runs are green-rated). Services offered at Jackson Hole include a free mountain-host program to orient you (meet at 9:30am at the host building); a more exclusive (it costs extra) ski guide service, (800) 450-0477 or (307) 739-2663; NASTAR races four times a week; a Kids Ranch program for child care or ski school; and a "Ski with Pepi" program, in which you can join Olympian Pepi Steigler, the head of the ski school, for free ski tips (Monday through Friday at 1:30pm at the top of Casper Chairlift). There's even a photo/video company (Powder Shots, (307) 733-7142) that will immortalize your downhill adventures. Teton Village at the base of the ski area has a myriad of shops and restaurants to cater to every possible consumptive need, and on-mountain accommodations are available (see Lodgings, below). Ski season at Jackson Hole usually runs from the first Saturday in December through the first Sunday in April. Call (800) 443-6931 or (307) 733-2292 for information, and (888) 733-2291 or (307) 733-2291 for current conditions.

Beloved by powder-hounds, **Grand Targhee Ski & Summer Resort** boasts 42 feet (!) of snow annually. In fact, the area is so confident of its conditions that it offers a snow guarantee: if you're dissatisfied with the conditions, turn in your lift ticket and receive a voucher good for another day. About 40 miles northwest of Jackson on the west side of the Teton Range (you'll have to access it by driving over Teton Pass, through Driggs, Idaho, and back into Wyoming), the laid-back Grand Targhee area has less attitude than its upscale competitor on the other side of the Tetons, but no shortage of altitude. It boasts a 2,200-foot vertical rise and three chairlifts and one surface lift serving over 1,500 acres of terrain, though only 300 acres are groomed—leaving the rest pure, unadulterated powder. Don't miss the snowcat powder skiing on Peak Mountain; it costs extra but the privacy—you access an additional 1,500 acres—is worth it. Powder skis are available for rent. December through March, the Targhee Express bus provides transportation service from Jackson and Teton Village; take it when the weather's bad, even if you've got your own wheels. At lunch, head to Snorkel's on the mountain for enormous roast beef (and other) sandwiches, fresh baked scones, and cinnamon rolls. Ski season runs mid-November to mid-April; the best powder skiing is usually in January and February. Call (800) 827-4433 or (307) 353-2300 for more information; snow report is revealed at (888) 766-7466.

Founded in 1939 in the town of Jackson, the historic **Snow King Resort** is where the locals working regular day jobs at regular wages ski. Lift tickets are nearly half the price of those at Jackson Hole Ski Area, and there's night skiing on a portion of the mountain. Local ski teams train here, as 55 percent of the mountain's two dozen slopes are rated advanced-expert, with 15 percent boasting a slope of 45 to 51 degrees. Considerably smaller than its competitor to the north, Snow King has a vertical drop of 1,571 feet, three chairlifts, and a ropetow on 500 acres. Because of its lower elevation, Snow King doesn't get the snowfall of Jackson Hole Ski Area (120 inches compared to 200, though it does have snow-making capability) and is often icy, cold, and windy because it faces north. But locals like its convenience—the resort is located six blocks from the town square—and its flexible rates; you can pay by the hour if you want. Bill Briggs, the first man to ski the Grand Teton, directs Snow King's Great American Ski School, which guarantees success. The ski season generally runs Thanksgiving through the first week of April. Call (307) 733-5200 or (800) 522-5464 for information or (307) 734-2020 for the ski report.

Cross-Country Skiing

There are enough groomed cross-country ski trails to keep you occupied for a few days, but it's the **telemark skiers** who really have a heyday around Jackson. Rent touring skis and get advice from Skinny Skis, (65 W Deloney, (307) 733-6094). Rent tele equipment and get backcountry advice from Teton Mountaineering, (170 N Cache, (800) 850-3595 or (307) 733-3595). Jackson Hole Mountain Guides, (307) 733-4979, and Rendezvous Ski Tours out of Driggs, Idaho, (208) 787-2906, lead back-country ski tours. Call the **avalanche hotline** at (307) 733-2664 before heading out.

Recommended books are *50 Ski Tours in Jackson Hole and Yellowstone,* by Richard Dumais, for general touring, and *Teton Skiing,* by Thomas Turiano, for backcountry and mountaineering.

The **Jackson Hole Nordic Center** at Teton Village, (800) 443-6931 or (307) 733-2292, keeps 17 kilometers of groomed trails, suitable for diagonal stride and skate skiing. Rentals are available on the mountain. **Spring Creek Resort Nordic Center** (4 miles northwest of Jackson off Spring Gulch Rd, (800) 443-6139 or (307) 733-1004) has 14 kilometers of groomed trails. The **Teton Pines Country Club and Resort** (4 miles south of Teton Village on the Teton Village Rd, (307) 733-1005) also has 14 kilometers of groomed trails, with rentals available.

There's easily accessible backcountry skiing in the open bowls off **Teton Pass.** It's best to leave a shuttle at the bottom, but lots of people just use skis to climb up and yo-yo the bowls, or hitchhike back up to their cars left at the top. Another option is to hike up Mount Glory (there's usually a good boot-packed trail) from the top of the pass and ski or snowboard to the base of the west side. Be sure you know what you're doing, in terms of both skiing and avalanche skills.

Real backcountry hounds head into **Grand Teton National Park;** see the Cross-Country Skiing/Snowshoeing section in the Grand Teton National Park chapter.

Snowmobiling

The vast majority of snowmobiling in this area goes on within Yellowstone National Park, but there are several good options closer to Jackson. Pick up a Bridger–Teton National Forest/Teton Division Winter Travel Map from the Jackson Ranger District, (307) 739-5400; the map indicates snowmobile routes. It's best to take a tour if you're not familiar with the terrain.

Rent snowmobiles through Leisure Sports, (307) 733-3040. Cache Creek Snowmobile Tours, (800) 522-0035 or (307) 733-4743, or Jackson Hole Snowmobile Tours, (800) 633-1733 or (307) 733-6850, offer single- and multi-day tours of the Jackson area and Yellowstone National Park. The Jackson Ranger District keeps a complete list of companies operating in the Jackson Hole area.

Two popular day tours are the 11-mile drive into **Granite Hot**

Springs, where you can have a soak before venturing out (swimsuits and towels available for rent), and the **Gros Ventre Road** northeast of the National Elk Refuge, which leads through prime winter range for bighorn sheep, moose, and elk.

Wildlife

Great Plains Wildlife Institute, (307) 733-2623, leads great wildlife tours of the National Elk Refuge and Grand Teton National Park and surrounding wildlands. Tours are led by wildlife biologists, with spotting scopes provided.

About 7,500 **elk** migrate from Grand Teton National Park and surrounding public lands to winter on the 25,000-acre **National Elk Refuge** that borders Jackson to the north, where they're fed by the US Fish and Wildlife Service. The snowy white background makes for excellent photo opportunities. You can drive through the refuge or see the animals from the highway bordering it, but the best option is to take a sleigh ride offered late December through March by the National Wildlife Museum, (307) 733-5771. Tickets are available on a first-come, first-served basis at the museum, 2 1/2 miles north of Jackson on US 26/89/191. Wear very warm clothing. By the way, you can't pick up shed antlers from the refuge; that privilege is reserved for the Boy Scouts, who sell them at a local auction and give part of the proceeds back to the refuge.

Also, late spring through fall, be sure to stop at the turnout just north of town along the refuge border to see lots of waterfowl, including **trumpeter swans,** on Flat Creek.

Other Activities

The Wyoming Balloon Company, (307) 739-0900, takes clients for a bird's-eye view of Grand Teton National Park in **hot-air balloons.** It's stunning, but very popular; don't expect to have the basket to yourself. Grand Valley Aviation, (800) 472-6382 or (208) 354-8131, just over the border in Driggs, Idaho, offers two-person (you and the pilot) **glider rides** in the Tetons and Yellowstone areas. Rides range from 15 minutes to an hour (the latter cruises at 12,000 feet, nearly eye-level with Grand Teton) and are much quieter than a hot-air balloon (no burners). Grand Valley Aviation also offers **passenger-plane sightseeing tours** for up to three people.

With an emphasis on participation (you'll get to drive the sled yourself), Iditarod-veteran Frank Teasley's Jackson Hole Iditarod Sled Dog Tours, (800) 554-7388 or (307) 733-7388, offers **dogsledding** trips. These rides are so popular you'll have to book well in advance; some tours are sold out as much as 4 months beforehand. Half-day ($130/person), full-day ($225/person), and overnight ($500/person) trips are available. The half-day tour includes a modest lunch; the 22-mile full-day tour includes midday stop at Granite Hot Springs and a huge lunch spread featuring steak or trout and cheesecake. Overnights head into the Greys River area and stop over at a remote lodge. All tours include supplemental warm clothing.

So what if there are fewer than 6,000 residents of Jackson. This town has everything, including a full-size, indoor **ice skating** rink at the Snow King Center, (307) 733-5200. Skate rentals available. The center is closed between late spring through summer; call for public session schedules. On Snow King Ave six blocks south of the town square.

outside in

Attractions

In Jackson **window shopping** can drive your heart rate into the aerobic zone as easily as any hike or ski—particularly if you insist on seeing every store (or investigating prices). Jackson's town square has become a kind of western-themed equivalent to LA's Rodeo Drive, with items ranging from the ridiculous to the sublime. Here is everything you never needed and maybe a few things you do: just follow the boardwalks for cowboy hats and elk ivory jewelry, oriental rugs, fringed vests, southwest Indian pottery, T-shirts, pillows, shot glasses, wind chimes, baseball caps, and wildlife art galore. Polo, Benetton, and London Fog have factory outlets in Jackson, and the Gap and Pendleton are there, too, plus a number of very good art galleries (and some not so good).

They quit reenacting the hangings (too gruesome), but Memorial Day weekend through Labor Day you can see the **town square shoot-out** in downtown Jackson, complete with victims falling off buildings. Monday through Saturday at the town square. Jackson Hole Chamber of Commerce, (307) 733-3316.

The courteous folks in Jackson don't want you to miss out on any western fun, so they've scheduled the **J. H. Rodeo** every Wednesday and Saturday evening at 8pm from Memorial Day through Labor Day, and possibly into mid-September. It's not part of the pro-circuit, but there's all the action you would expect: bronc riding, bull riding, team roping, etc. At the Teton County Fairgrounds on Snow King Ave; contact the Chamber of Commerce, (307) 733-3316, for more information.

Sure, it's plenty touristy (and a little pricey), but that doesn't diminish the magnificent views from **Teton Village's aerial tram,** (307) 739-2753, leading to the top of Rendezvous Peak. It's often windy at the 10,450-foot summit; bring a fleece and, if you plan to hike, rain gear (the weather can change on a dime). Trails begin from the top of the tram (see Hiking/Backpacking, above); you can get packages that include rental hiking boots and sack lunches. Should you come totally unprepared and find yourself peckish upon arriving at the summit, don't worry: Corbet's Cabin, a snack bar, eagerly awaits your business. From the end of May through mid-September, trams leave every 20 minutes; it takes 12 minutes to ride to the summit.

Wildlife art doesn't have to be hokey, and if you don't believe it stop by the **National Museum of Wildlife Art,** (307) 733-5771, a massive 51,000-square foot building that houses some 2,000 pieces of the nation's best wildlife-inspired works. Among other things, the museum claims the nation's largest collection of works by artist Carl Rungius, a gallery devoted to bison art, and an interactive children's gallery. It's off US 26/89/191, 2 ½ miles north of Jackson on the way to Grand Teton National Park, across from the National Elk Refuge. During winter, the museum offers sleigh rides through the refuge (see Wildlife, above).

Head to **Granite Hot Springs,** (307) 733-6318, an old Civilian Conservation Corps project, for a soak in the pool and a pretty setting. You can rent towels and swimsuits. The springs are open year-round except for late fall and late spring, when the road is too muddy for visitors. Avoid the crowds by coming on a weekday. From Jackson, drive 25 miles southeast on US 189/191, then turn right (north) on Granite Creek Rd and drive 11 miles.

It's hard to imagine getting bored in Jackson, but if you or your kids need a quick, man-made recreation fix, the **Alpine Slide** at Snow King Resort, (307) 733-5200, offers a few minutes of safe, adrenaline-pumping diversion. Using a hand brake, you control the speed of your individual sled as it careens down the 2,500-foot course.

Calendar of Events

The **International Rocky Mountain Stage Stop Sled Dog Race** begins in downtown Jackson at the beginning of February and ends in Teton Village 10 days later. Mushers blow through nine other Wyoming communities on their 430-mile journey. Call race headquarters, (307) 734-1163, for more information.

The end of February ushers in the **Cowboy Ski Challenge** at Jackson Hole Ski Area. The two-day event features novelty ski races and rodeo events in the snow, a Dutch-oven cook-off, cowboy poetry, and a barn dance. Jackson Hole Ski Area, (307) 739-2706.

Hundreds of snowmobilers converge on Jackson the third weekend in March for the **World Championship Snowmobile Hill Climb,** a race to the top of Snow King Mountain. Jackson Hole Chamber of Commerce, (307) 733-3316.

Jackson celebrates its western heritage every Memorial Day weekend with **Old West Days,** a 4-day event featuring a mountain-man rendezvous, rodeo, street dances, Indian dances, and a country-western concert. With 15,000 to 30,000 spectators, Old West Days is Wyoming's second-largest event. Jackson Hole Chamber of Commerce, (307) 733-3316.

For more than 35 years, the **Grand Teton Music Festival,** (307) 733-1128, has been bringing together musicians from the nation's premiere orchestras to present classical concerts. The festival runs July through August. Full orchestra concerts are presented Fridays and Saturdays; chamber music concerts are held Tuesdays and Thursdays. All concerts take place at the Walk Festival Hall at Teton Village.

Restaurants

Jackson has more fine dining spots than you can shake a sun-dried tomato at. In addition to those reviewed below, try **Sweetwater Restaurant** (on the corner of King and Pearl, (307) 733-3553), especially good for soups and sandwiches at lunch, and **The Cadillac Grille** (on the town square, (307) 733-3279) for upscale, California-inspired entrees. Among Jackson's few modest-priced eateries, we recommend **The Bunnery** (130 N Cache, (307) 733-5474) for baked goods and breakfast, and **Bubba's Bar-B-Que** (515 W Broadway, (307) 733-2288) for huge, delicious breakfasts and hearty, filling, high-quality barbecue ribs, beef, and chicken.

Locals (and savvy tourists) flock to **Nora's Fish Creek Inn** in Wilson (6 miles west of Jackson on Hwy 22, (307) 733-8288), a rustic looking institution with both counter and table service, for enormous pancakes and terrific huevos rancheros. The **Mangy Moose** at Teton Village, (307) 733-4913, has a huge, if rather standard, salad bar, a lively atmosphere and good red meat (don't bother with the pastas or fish).

Stiegler's, (307) 733-1071, at the Jackson Hole Racquet Club (on Teton Village Rd 4 miles south of Teton Village) serves very fine Austrian food. Follow the signs to the Jackson Hole Racquet Club at The Aspens.

Skip the overpriced dinners at **The Granary** at Spring Creek Resort, (800) 443-6139 or (406) 733-8833, but make sure you get there for lunch or a drink and appetizers (you can sit on the outdoor lounge deck) for a truly astounding view of the Tetons.

The Blue Lion ☆☆☆   Located in an old house away from the hustle of the town square, this intimate, consistently excellent restaurant is a favorite of locals (unlike many of its competitors, The Blue Lion stays open even off season). You can't go wrong at The Blue Lion, but we highly recommend the roast rack of New Zealand lamb, a house specialty, served with a peppercorn-rosemary cream sauce. There's something for everyone here, including fresh fish specials and unusual vegetarian entrees (tempeh crepes, for one). The mushrooms stuffed with cream cheese, crab, and Courvoisier are superb. The Blue Lion has outdoor dining in season, and is closed Tuesdays in April and November. *Between Deloney and Gill, 2 blocks west of the town square; 160 N Millward, Jackson; (307) 733-3912; dinner every day; AE, DIS, MC, V; local checks only; $$$.*

Snake River Grille ☆☆☆   Very LA—people watching is great either in the log-walled dining room, which sports white tablecloths and a hand-painted ceiling, or on the outdoor deck. But the superb, innovative food and professional service are the real reasons to come to the Snake River Grille. Fish is flown in fresh from California (the chef hails from there), and used in creative presentations, but meat and potato lovers shouldn't fret: beef and pork are well-represented on the menu and show up in large cuts with either mashed potatoes or thin-cut french fries. Don't miss the signature potato pancake appetizer, smothered with Atlantic smoked salmon, or the terrific fried calamari with chili-citrus mayonnaise. This is one place we don't hesitate to eat raw or rare fish; the tuna sashimi is sheer heaven. For inside dining, request either one of the booths or the table by the stone fireplace. The Snake River Grille is closed in April and November. *On the southeast corner of the town square, upstairs and behind The Nature Company; 84 E Broadway, Jackson; (307) 733-0557; dinner every day; AE, MC, V; local checks only; $$$.*

The Range ☆☆   Just about everything at Chris McShane's and executive chef Arthur Leach's New York-influenced eatery is elegant, from the spare, modern decor to the typeface on the menu. And when things are good, they're terrific, though we have heard The Range can be inconsistent. Chef Arthur's elaborate menu changes seasonally, but always emphasizes regional American cuisine, fresh ingredients, and unusual combinations. Everything is prepared in the open kitchen within full view of the dining room. Start with the artichoke and red pepper pâté with lobster butter and garlic mayonnaise, then move on to the pan-seared tournedos of beef, wild mushrooms, sun-dried tomatoes, and oven-roasted potatoes, or roasted duck breast, sun-dried berries, and jalapeño spaetzle.

There are numerous highly original salads from which to choose, such as a red cabbage, bacon, and walnut warmed in vinaigrette, and one with fresh cactus, red pepper, and mango. Leave your Birkies and baseball caps behind; this is a place for sleek, black knit dresses and designer jeans. The Range is sometimes closed in April and November—call ahead to check. *2 blocks north of the Jackson town square, upstairs; 225 N Cache, Jackson; (307) 733-5481; dinner every day; AE, MC; local checks only; $$$.*

Calico   With its regular ol' pizzas (no duck sausage or venison toppings, though there is one goat cheese appetizer-size option), and very good pastas and salads, Calico offers a casual, unpretentious, modestly-priced alternative to the demiglaces and sun-dried whatevers that dominate most Jackson menus. New owner Jeff Davies has remodeled this Jackson staple (it's been open since 1966) so that it's bright and modern, and has greatly expanded the selection of pastas, but he still uses produce and spices grown in the restaurant's garden. Pizzas, served medium crust with all the usual toppings, are consistently good. Or try the delicious fettucini with wild mushrooms. Going crazy with the kids? There's a 1 ½-acre lawn where children belonging to Calico diners or diners at next-door Vista Grande can play. Weather permitting, outdoor dining is available. *On Teton Village Rd, midway between Hwy 22 and Teton Village; 2650 N Moose-Wilson Rd, Jackson; (307) 733-2460; dinner every day; AE, MC, V; local checks only; $.*

Lodgings

Compared to other western communities, accommodations in Jackson are extraordinarily expensive, with many standard motel rooms going for well over $100 a night. **Jackson Hole Central Reservations,** (800) 443-6931 or (307) 733-4005, can provide information and make reservations. Ask for their accommodations guide, an extensive listing of area lodgings.

Teton Village has a range of accommodations, from hotel rooms to condos and houses. Upper-floor rooms with balcony and view at the Best Western **Inn at Jackson Hole,** (800) 842-7666 or (307) 733-0844, are very nice, but be sure you don't get stuck in the cinder-block ground-floor (the rates are identical). Don't forget to ask for nonsmoking rooms if that's a concern. Condos are handled by three separate property management companies: Teton Village Property Management, (800) 443-6840 or (307) 733-4610; Jackson Hole Property Management, (800) 443-8613 or (307) 733-7945; and Alpine Vacation Rentals of Jackson Hole, (800) 876-3968 or (307) 734-1161. Condo units are individually owned and therefore a bit different; newest and nicest are those in the Teewinot, Rendezvous, and Nez Perce buildings, but these are all two-bedroom and larger. Winter rates are significantly higher. Ask for valley views in summer; mountain views in winter (since the valley is often socked in with temperature inversions).

Spring Creek Resort ☆☆☆   This 1,000-acre property atop East Gros Ventre Butte boasts Jackson's finest—and priciest—accommodations. Whether you stay in one of the resort's 200-plus hotel rooms ($200/night), condos ($210–$750/night), or freestanding homes ($950/night), you'll find yourself in the lap of luxury, with fireplaces, lodgepole furniture, terrycloth robes, and a truly astounding view of the Tetons. All the rooms face the mountains, though some have better views than others: best views are from units in the 2103–2104, 2203–2204, 2107–2108, or 2207–2208 buildings. The resort also has an outdoor swimming pool and hot tub and tennis courts, as well as an on-site stable (riding costs extra). In winter, Spring Creek offers sleigh rides. Various packages are available, including honeymoon, mountain-bike tour, and downhill or cross-country ski deals. In the shoulder seasons, a gourmet breakfast is included at the on-site Granary Restaurant; in summer and winter you'll have to spring for your own meals. But face it: if you have to worry about paying extra for meals, you can't afford Spring Creek Resort. *4 miles northwest of Jackson—drive southwest on Broadway, bear right on Hwy 22, then right (north) on Spring Gulch Rd, finally turn right on Spring Creek Dr; 1800 Spirit Dance Rd, PO Box 3154, Jackson, WY 83001; (800) 443-6139 or (406) 733-8833; AE, DIS, MC, V; no checks; $$$.*

Alpine House ☆☆   Run by two former Olympians, nordic skier Hans Johnstone and his biathlete wife Nancy, this airy, Scandinavian-style B&B offers a welcome respite from the usual faux-West decor of Jackson, as well as a break from the town's very high prices. Seven spacious rooms, all with private bath and balcony, are tastefully decorated with simple country furniture, heated tiled floors, and down comforters. Breakfast—a hearty combination of an extensive cold buffet and a hot entree—is served downstairs, where the Johnstones also keep a large inventory of outdoor reading material. Still avid outdoorspeople (Hans guides for Exum Mountain Guides, and Nancy coaches the local cross-country ski team), the Johnstones are walking encyclopedias about the possibilities around Jackson. In winter, they offer backcountry and cross-country ski tours; winter mountaineering and ice climbing trips (in conjunction with Exum); and downhill ski packages. Alpine House may be closed for the months of April and November—call to check. *2 1/2 blocks northwest of the town square, between Gill and Mercill; 285 N Glenwood, PO Box 20245, Jackson, WY 83001; (800) 753-1421 or (307) 739-1570; MC, V; checks OK; $$$.*

Nowlin Creek Inn ☆☆   Run by fourth-generation Jacksonite Mark Nowlin and his wife Susan, a former designer for the Smithsonian Institute, this lovely western-themed B&B on the east edge of town features overstuffed couches and original wildlife art and historical prints. All five bedrooms are individually decorated by Susan and come with private bath. A full breakfast includes home-baked breads and pastries and hot entrees. There's also a hot tub on the outdoor deck. *4 blocks east of the town square; 660 E Broadway, PO Box 2766, Jackson, WY 83001; (800) 533-0882 or (307) 733-0882; AE, DIS, MC, V; checks OK; $$$.*

Rusty Parrot Lodge ☆☆   There are no views to speak of, no fitness center, and no Jacuzzi in the room unless you pay extra. But folks continue to ante up the $200-plus standard room rates for the spacious quarters, faux-West decor, oversized bath tubs, and accommodating service at this 32-room hotel on the edge of downtown. The gourmet breakfast included in the rates is served in the small lobby/sitting area downstairs; it comes with a cold buffet and your choice of hot entree, made on an open grill. For an additional $20 (a relatively small amount, considering), you can get a fireplace and double whirlpool bath in your room. The Body Sage, an on-site masseuse service, offers enticing "treatments"; there's also a small, outdoor hot tub. Children under 12 are discouraged. *3 blocks west and 1 block north of the town square; 175 N Jackson, PO Box 1657, Jackson, WY 83001; (800) 458-2004 or (307) 733-2000; AE, DIS, MC, V; checks OK; $$$.*

A Teton Tree House ☆☆   Although it's not a treehouse in the strict sense of the word (it's hidden in the trees, not literally built in one), this secluded four-story B&B outside Wilson (8 miles west of Jackson) is a lot of fun. Five of six bedrooms have private balconies, and the Mountain Maple, Douglas Fir, and Aspen Rooms have window seats with a view. But you're more likely to spend time curled up next to the fireplace in the two-story living area, reading one of the inn's many books, or on the outdoor hot tub overlooking the valley and the Gros Ventre Mountains beyond. Owners Chris and Denny Becker, avid outdoorspeople, serve hearty, meatless, low-cholesterol breakfasts. Note: The 95 steps leading from the parking area to the front door make the Teton Treehouse obviously not suitable for the elderly or handicapped. And in winter, a four-wheel-drive (or at least a front-wheel) vehicle is recommended. Reservations are required. *¾ mile outside Wilson off Hwy 22; 6175 Heck of a Hill Rd, PO Box 550, Wilson, WY 83014; (307) 733-3233; MC, V; no checks; $$$.*

Wildflower Inn ☆☆   Built by Vail refugees and B&B veterans Ken and Sherrie Jern, this log home is situated on 3 private acres, a nice break from the crowds at nearby Teton Village. All five rooms come with private bath, television, log-framed beds, and down comforters; four of them include a private balcony, and one of them has a large tub and fireplace. A nice extra is the solarium with hot tub. Now a climbing guide and ski instructor and contractor, Ken Jern can offer advice for outdoor pleasures. Sherrie Jern can arrange a custom package of outdoor activities prior to your arrival. Breakfasts are served, weather permitting, on the back deck overlooking the pond. *Off Teton Village Rd, 2 ½ miles from Hwy 22 and 4 miles south of Teton Village, on Shooting Star Lane across from Westbank Anglers (the sign is hidden); PO Box 11000, Jackson, WY 83002; (307) 733-4710; MC, V; checks OK; $$$.*

Jackson Hole Racquet Club Resort ☆   Only 4 miles south of Teton Village, the Jackson Hole Racquet Club Resort is actually 120 spacious, reasonably priced (for Jackson) condo units, all with fully equipped kitchens, washer/dryers, and fireplaces, plus on-site tennis courts, a very good fitness center, a grocery/deli/liquor store, and a gourmet restaurant (Steigler's). Some units have views (best from the 2100 or 2200 buildings); one-bedroom units are all on the ground floor. There is a small fee for court time, but condo guests get a complimentary membership to the Aspens Athletic Club, which has a good weight room with Nautilus machines, racquetball courts, a heated outdoor swimming pool (summers only), and an indoor and outdoor hot tub. In winter, the resort runs complimentary shuttle service to and from Jackson Hole Ski Area. Rates during ski season and summer run from a high of $185 for a spacious one-bedroom to $349 for a three-bedroom, but drop significantly off season, early and late summer and all fall. *Off Teton Village Rd, 4 miles south of Teton Village (look for the sign to the Jackson Hole Racquet Club at The Aspens); 3535 N Moose-Wilson Rd, Star Route Box 3647, Jackson, WY 83001; (800) 443-8616 or (307) 733-3990; AE, DIS, MC, V; checks OK; $$$.*

The Wort ☆   Tudor on the outside, western on the inside, The Wort is a Jackson landmark. Built in 1941 by the descendants of Charles Wort, who as early as 1915 dreamt of putting a luxury hotel in Jackson ("Ridiculous!" mocked critics at the time), and rebuilt after a devastating fire in 1980, this 60-room hotel offers spacious, comfortable digs in a centralized location. At $165/double, it's overpriced, but what isn't in Jackson? The hotel's Silver Dollar Bar often features live music; request rooms in the north wing, away from the harmonies. *1 block west of the town square; 50 N Glenwood, PO Box 69, Jackson, WY 83001; (800) 322-2727 or (307) 733-2190; AE, DIS, MC, V; no checks; $$$.*

Ranches and Resorts

Lost Creek Ranch   Why, you ask, would a family of four pay darn near $9,000 for a week's vacation? We asked the same thing when we got to Lost Creek Ranch, which sits on 90 acres sandwiched between Grand Teton National Park and the Bridger–Teton National Forest 22 miles north of Jackson. The answer, we were told, lies in the astounding location (with a straight shot of the Tetons, the ranch borders the filming location for *Shane*), the exquisite gourmet food (no hot dogs and beans here), the accommodating staff, and the plethora of organized ranch activities included in the cost: scenic floats on the Snake River; trips to the Jackson rodeo; cookouts; cowboy poetry; astronomy presentations; and— we're not making this up—boot branding. Besides the scenery, the main draw is the riding, and at Lost Creek Ranch each guest is paired up with a horse for the week, then grouped according to ability so that advanced riders can canter into the sunset, while beginners remain content to stroll across the sagebrush flats of Grand Teton National Park (the ranch has permission to ride within park boundaries). There's even a gymkhana (a mini-rodeo), for guests at the end of the week. Children are well catered to, with special kids' rides and even a special menu, so they don't have to eat "all that fancy stuff." The ranch also has a tennis court, a small outdoor heated pool, and a hot tub to soak those poor, tired city-slicker muscles. The main lodge is filled with taxidermy and wildlife art, but the 10 cabins (maximum occupancy: 60) are more modest. But few guests spend much time in their quarters. Everyone deserves to play cowboy for a week, so if you can afford Lost Creek (rates of $3,960 per couple, $8,980 for a family of four cover Sunday-to-Sunday stays), well, pardner, mount up. The ranch is open June through September. *8 miles north of Moose and 10 miles south of Moran on Hwy 189; PO Box 95, Moose, WY 83012; (307) 733-3435; no credit cards; checks OK.*

More Information

You'll have to stop by the **Wyoming Visitors Center** (532 N Cache St, just north of downtown Jackson) in person to find a myriad of written information, plus representatives from the Jackson Hole Chamber of Commerce, the US Fish and Wildlife Service, and, on summer weekends, the National Park Service.

Backcountry avalanche hazard and weather forecast: (307) 733-2664 or http://www. wyoming.com/avalanche.

Bridger–Teton NF Supervisor's Office: (307) 739-5500.

Bridger–Teton NF, Buffalo Ranger District: (307) 543-2386.

Bridger–Teton NF, Jackson Ranger District: (307) 739-5400.

Bridger–Teton NF, Pinedale Ranger District: (307) 367-4326.

Jackson Hole Central Reservations: (800) 443-6931 or (307) 733-7182.

Jackson Hole Chamber of Commerce: (307) 733-3316.

National Elk Refuge: (307) 733-9212.

Teton Mountaineering: (800) 850-3595 or (307) 733-3595.

Wyoming Game and Fish Department: (800) 423-4113 in-state or (307) 733-2321.

Wyoming Travel Commission: (800) 225-5996 or (307) 777-7777.

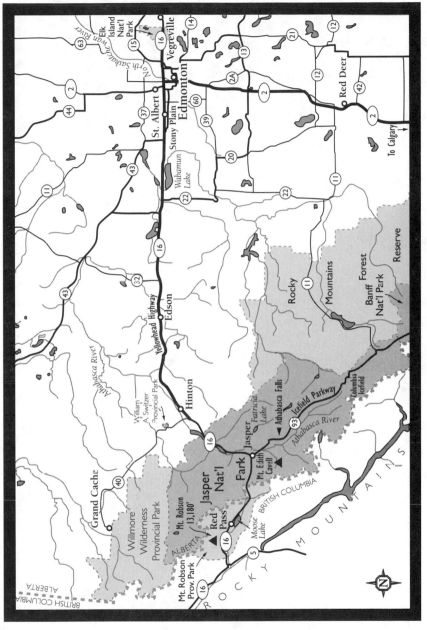

Northern
Canadian
Rockies

Northern
Canadian
Rockies

Edmonton
and Environs

Including the North Saskatchewan River Valley, and Elk Island National Park.

Alberta's big northern city, Edmonton, lives in the shadow of larger and more aggressive Calgary, to the south. The two cities are very different, however. A fort just before the turn of the 18th century, Edmonton quickly became a major settlement handling furs pouring in from the north and west. By the 19th century, the railroad had arrived, and thousands rushed through the area on their way to gold fields in the Yukon. A land rush followed, and in 1904 the city of Edmonton was chosen Alberta's provincial capital. In 1947, oil was found at nearby Leduc and, overnight, Edmonton became the Oil Capital of Canada. Today, there's not much visible that speaks to the city's fur-trading and gold rush heritage, but the oil refineries of Refinery Row are a permanent part of the southeast Edmonton skyline.

The development of the North Slope oil and gas fields in the late '70s and early '80s brought boom times to Edmonton. The influx of money rebuilt the downtown of this blue-collar city, adding towering glass skyscrapers and giving cultural arts, such as the resident ballet, opera, and symphony companies, a jump-start. The National Hockey League's Edmonton Oilers brought home the championship Stanley Cup five times on the sticks of hockey greats Wayne Gretzky, Mark Messier, and Grant Fuhr, while the Canadian Football League's Edmonton Roughriders won the championship Grey Cup—and Edmonton adopted the motto "City of Champions." But then came the bust. The development of the oil fields ended, and workers left for other boomtowns and stopped fueling the Edmonton economy. Even hockey fans felt the shift, since the Oilers traded away their great players, started losing, and, save for a last-ditch effort to sell thousands of season tickets in 1996, were days away from moving to one of the US cities vying for an NHL franchise.

After all that, the city of 850,000 is left with a calmer demeanor and plenty to show for its '80s party—the clean, contemporary downtown crowded with office buildings; a world-class botanical conservatory; and West Edmonton Mall, which draws tourists from all over the world to pump shopping dollars into the economy.

The glass skyscrapers of downtown Edmonton hug a river—the North Saskatchewan—where the banks are protected from development with broad green areas that run the length of the city on both sides of the water. Known locally as the Ribbon of Green, it's the longest stretch of urban green space in North America. Edmonton is within a parkland habitat, a zone where boreal spruce forest meets quaking aspen trees and prairies, separating the short-grass prairies to the south and the Arctic tundra to the north. What visitors might notice first about Edmonton is the light: in summer there's a lot of it, averaging 17 hours of daylight each day in June, while in winter there's hardly any daylight at all—December is dark from after 3pm until nearly 9am. Summer temperatures average a pleasant 72°F (22°C). Winters are apropos to the latitude: January daytime temperatures average 14°F (-10°C) and average annual snowfall is 51 inches (130 cm).

During daylight or dusk hours, Edmonton has a lot to offer those willing to leave Calgary behind and explore farther north.

Getting There

Edmonton is 320 miles (514 km) north of the US-Canada border, 184 miles (294 km) north of Calgary, and 226 miles (362 km) east of Jasper. From Calgary, drive north on Canada Highway 2 through Red Deer to Edmonton; from Jasper, drive east on the Yellowhead Hwy (Hwy 16) to Edmonton; from Saskatchewan, drive west on the Yellowhead Hwy to Edmonton.

Edmonton is served by two airports, Edmonton Municipal Airport, just north of the downtown, (403) 496-1747 (one-way cab fare to downtown is about $8); and Edmonton International Airport, 18 miles (29 km) south of the city, (403) 890-8382 (one-way cab fare to downtown is about $35). Grey Goose Lines provide shuttle bus service to Edmonton, $11 one-way, $18 round-trip. Rental cars are available at Edmonton International.

VIA Rail (10004 - 104 Ave, (800) 561-8630) serves Edmonton on the Canadian route that runs from Toronto west to Winnipeg, Saskatoon, Edmonton, Jasper, and Vancouver.

To navigate the city, Edmonton Transit, (403) 496-1611, runs bus and light rail transit systems. The light rail trains run 6 2/5 miles (10.3 km) from the University of Edmonton campus southwest of downtown to the northeast portion of the city, a convenient way to get to the Northlands Exhibition Grounds for events or hockey games. Fares are $1.60 in peak hours, $1.35 otherwise.

Visitors can contact local offices for more information: Edmonton Tourism, 9797 Jasper Ave, No. 104, Dept. F, Edmonton, AB T5J 1N9, (800) 463-4667 or (403) 496-8400, fax (403) 425-5283; Gateway Park Visitors Information Centre, Gateway Park/2404 Calgary Trail Northbound SW, Edmonton, AB T6W 1A1, (800) 463-4667 or (403) 496-8400; and Travel Alberta, Box 2500, Edmonton, AB T5J 2Z4, (800) 661-8888 or (403) 427-4321, (800) 222-6501 in Alberta.

All prices quoted are in Canadian dollars.

Adjoining Areas

SOUTH: **Calgary and Environs; Banff National Park**

WEST: **Jasper National Park**

Hiking/Walking

The 19-mile (30-km) walking and biking **Ribbon of Green Trail System,** along both sides of the North Saskatchewan River in the city, is still being developed and is the longest stretch of such a parkland in North America. Although there is a trail that extends the entire length of the system, some of it is only a narrow dirt path. Still, long sections are finished and the Edmonton Parks Department (PO Box 2359, Edmonton, AB T5J 2R7, (403) 496-4999) has published a **map** of recommended loop routes for walkers and cyclists. Information about the Ribbon of Green also is available from the River Valley Outdoor Centre, (403) 496-7275.

One of the best ways to get the flavor of Edmonton is to walk the streets and paths of the city. We recommend any of six **city walking tours,** ranging from a downtown walk (maps available at the Edmonton Planning & Development Dept., 10310 - 102 Ave, second floor, (403) 496-6160) to the **Heritage Trail Walking Tour,** a tree-lined 30-minute walk along the fur traders' route from Fort Edmonton to Old Town (begin at 108 St and 99 Ave and follow the red brick sidewalk). The 1-hour **Original West End Walking Tour** begins at the 1913-vintage Buena Vista

Building, 124 Street and 102 Ave, and explores the 1912–1914 boom area of Edmonton (maps at 124 St Business Association, (403) 482-5552). Another 1-hour walk is the **Highlands Walking Tour,** which flanks the river valley and leads through an early-1900s neighborhood of mansions and gracious homes (maps at La Boheme Restaurant, 6427-112 Ave, (403) 474-5693). The **Old Strathcona Walking Tour** includes the trendy shopping district of the same name, and the **River Valley Walking Tour** uses the valley trail system.

Primarily an education center for children, the **John Janzen Nature Centre,** named for the former director of the Edmonton parks department who spearheaded the movement to set aside natural areas in the city, has several pleasant trails for walking. The shortest, about a 10-minute walk, circles the nature center and grounds; the longest, about an hour's walk, goes around the perimeter of Fort Edmonton's grounds (see Attractions, below). The center has a gift shop and a small pond as well as an auditorium. Find it at Whitemud Drive and Fox Dr, (403) 496-2910; open daily, admission's free. Follow the signs off Whitemud Dr to Fort Edmonton, which shares a parking lot with the nature center.

West of Edmonton, University of Alberta horticulture students maintain the **Devonian Botanic Garden,** (403) 987-3054. The Buchart Gardens of Edmonton this is not. Where the famous Victoria, BC, garden is trim and formal in the best British tradition, Edmonton's Devonian Garden plays to the climate and to the region. It's the most northerly botanical garden in North America, established in 1959 by the University of Alberta. Wear your hiking boots to these gardens—they sprawl over 80 acres, landscaped with several water features and forest paths. The paths connect with an additional 110 acres of the **Bobby Cyde Nature Area,** which in turn afford views of the Imrie Wetland Ecological Reserve. Gardeners could spend hours here, but those out for an pleasant walk will be satisfied, too. One route leads through a boggy area with natural wetlands plants to a large pond with an elevated boardwalk across one end. The site also includes a garden with plants indigenous to Alberta, a Native Peoples' garden, and another large area with alpine plants. In addition there are the requisite rose, Japanese, peony, primula, herb, lilac, lily, water, and perennial gardens, as well as a shrub and tree zone. Most plants are well marked with their botanical names, so gardeners should bring pencil and paper for note taking. Be sure to save time for the **butterfly garden,** a conservatory full of unruly plants and dozens of brilliantly hued butterflies representing 30 species. The charming insects flit about the conservatory feeding at flowers or drinking water droplets on leaves. To get there, drive west 5 ½ miles (9 km) on Hwy 16 from Edmonton to Hwy 60, then go south 8 miles (14 km); the Devonian Gardens are 3 miles (5 km) north of the town of Devon, named for the rock formations nearby in which oil was found in the 1940s. The gardens charge for admission and are closed mid-October through April.

Cycling

Walking is allowed on the trails on both sides of the **North Saskatchewan River** in Edmonton, but cycling is not (see Ribbon of Green Trail System in Hiking/Walking, above). Cyclists can ride several nice loops along the length of the trail system, but some of the routes are on residential streets with no separate lane for bikes. Blue signs indicate scenic bicycle routes. These routes are not always synonymous with the river trails—rather, they are cycling routes through the city that are used to complete the river trails. An excellent map of the River Valley Parks Leisure Loops is available by calling (403) 496-7275. The map indicates on which of the river valley trails bikes are not allowed. By law, all bicycles must be equipped with a warning bell or horn to be used when passing pedestrians or in-line skaters. Bikes are allowed on Light Rail Transit trains (use the middle doors, regular fares apply), except weekdays during peak hours, 7:30am–8:30am and 4pm–5pm. Mountain bikes can be rented at any number of places in Edmonton; one outlet that rents not only mountain bikes but also tandem bikes, in-line skates, and canoes is AusCan International Recreation (Kinsmen Sports Centre, 9100 Walterdale Hill, (403) 439-1883; open daily). Guided half-day and full-day River Valley **bike tours** can be arranged.

In **Elk Island National Park,** about 45 minutes east of Edmonton (see Wildlife, below), cyclists can take the paved road running through the park, which is the only suitable bicycling route. Bicycles are not allowed on the trails.

Fishing

While **Lesser Slave Lake** is just 157 miles (251 km) north of Edmonton on Hwy 2, and plenty of anglers head there to try their luck, those who are serious about catching big fish on the north tundra book a flight for the Northwest Territories and **Great Slave Lake,** well north of Edmonton. Commuter flights leave Edmonton regularly for Yellowknife on the northern shore of Great Slave Lake, a mecca for fishers seeking trophy-sized native lake trout. The size that qualifies as trophy is relative to the lake, but in nearby **Great Bear Lake,** the record lake trout caught was 66 pounds. One of the lodges that caters primarily to anglers who want to catch trophy lake trout is Frontier Fishing Lodge, (403) 465-6843, located 115 miles (192 km) east of Yellowknife at the mouth of the Stark

River (see Ranches and Resorts, below). There are other fishing lodges, some located at remote lakes just a float plane trip away from Yellowknife. For more information about Great Slave Lake and fishing in the region, contact the Northern Frontier Visitors Association, PO Box 1107, Yellowknife, NT X1A 2N8, (800) 661-0788 or (403) 873-3131.

Canoeing/Kayaking

Bennett Lake is the heart of the **Strathcona Wilderness Centre,** (403) 922-3939, and only nonmotorized boats are allowed on this shallow lake. Weekends, canoes can be rented by the hour and instruction in canoeing and kayaking can be arranged through the center. The perimeter of the lake is flanked by dense cattails and other water plants, ideal for nesting waterfowl. The red-necked grebe is common here but an uncommon bird most other places farther south. To get to the Strathcona Wilderness Centre, drive east from Edmonton on Hwy 16 to Brookville Rd, then turn south and follow the signs, or drive east on Baseline Rd or Wye Rd (82 Ave) and follow the signs.

Canoeing and kayaking on the **North Saskatchewan River** through Edmonton is not advised due to dams and weirs. Tandem Canoe Tours, (403) 496-2966, runs guided canoe tours west of the city, from the town of Devon.

Golfing

The golfing season may be short in Edmonton, but there is still a strong contingent of golfers and courses on which to play. And why not? Edmonton's so far north that, in June, there's still plenty of daylight to hit balls down the fairways at 10pm. The Ribbon of Green flanking the river in Edmonton includes three public golf courses: **Victoria Golf Course,** 12130 River Rd, (403) 496-4900; **Riverside Golf Course,** 8630 Rowland Rd (east of Dawson Bridge), (403) 496-8700; and **Rundle Golf Course,** 2909 - 118 Ave, (403) 496-4926.

Golfers will find the nine-hole **Elk Park Golf Course,** (403) 998-3161, which flanks Asotin Lake in Elk Island National Park (see Wildlife, below), challenging unless they like narrow, treed fairways and water hazards. The course has a small restaurant, used by hikers in the national park as much as golfers.

The **Devon Golf Course,** (403) 987-2064, is a short drive out of Edmonton to the west and is adjacent to the University of Alberta's Devonian Botanic Garden (see Hiking/Walking, above).

Swimming

Edmonton's Parks and Recreation's 13 **swimming pools** are open to visitors as well as city residents (only 1 is outdoors and closed winters). For a schedule and location of pools, call (403) 496-SWIM.

Cross-Country Skiing

Edmonton is distant enough from the Rocky Mountains that it doesn't get the warm chinook winds that sweep off the slopes and melt the snow in Calgary. In fact, much of Edmonton's weather comes from systems moving in from the Northwest Territories, bringing snow and arctic-tinged temperatures. Because of this, the city is a wintry playground, snow-covered much of the season. Edmonton residents often ski the **river valley trails,** some of which are even lighted for night skiing. The trails are groomed regularly. All except those at Terwillegar Park are accessible via an Edmonton Transit bus, and trail conditions are available through the Nordic Ski Line, (403) 493-9000, ext. 3446. All trails are marked for level of difficulty. There's a **drop-in ski clinic** Saturday afternoons, run by River Valley Parks, (403) 496-2966. Cross-country ski **lessons** can be arranged through AusCan International Recreation at the Kinsmen Sports Centre, (403) 439-1883. The city trails are open for skiing until 10pm. Local skiers often ski by moonlight and the aurora borealis, although that's certainly not predictable. Trail grooming is done at night, however, so night skiers should watch for and yield the trail to grooming machines. Dogs are not allowed on the trails.

Access **Gold Bar Park** trails from the parking lot east of 50 St and north of 109 Ave, or from the Goldstick parking lot, one-quarter mile (one-half km) east of 50 St off 101 Ave. Trails range from the Lakeside Loop, a beginner route lighted for night skiing, to the S-bend Loop for advanced skiers.

To ski at **Capilano Park,** use the parking lot on the south bank of the river west of 50 St. Riverside/Capilano Link and Gold Bar/Capilano Link are connecting trails rated for intermediate skiers.

Riverside Golf Course is at Rowland Rd and 84 St, on the east end of Dawson Bridge across the river from downtown Edmonton. Skier parking is available on the south side of the road, across from the clubhouse; use the walkway underneath the bridge. Trails begin just below the hill next to the clubhouse. Riverside/Capilano Link is the connecting trail here, and there is a River's Edge Loop for beginners.

Mill Creek Ravine runs from Argyll Park to Conners Rd with access from Argyll Park, 69 Ave at 88 St; at the Mill Creek Swimming Pool parking lot, 82 Ave at 95A St; and from Muttart Conservatory, 98 Ave and 96A

St. There is one trail, rated for beginners, and this is one of the last areas to be groomed.

To ski at **Kinsmen Park,** use the Kinsmen Sports Centre parking lot or the lots along the river at the base of Walterdale Hill on the south side of the 105 Street Bridge. Of the two trails, **Putter's Loop** is lighted for night skiing.

William Hawrelak Park access is from the lot on the west side of Groat Rd, south of the Groat Road Bridge. Beginners will find the Perimeter Loop, which flanks the Mayfair Golf Course, to their liking since it's flat. No skating is allowed on this route.

To get to **Terwillegar Park** follow Rabbit Hill Rd west until it turns into a gravel road and drops into the river valley; the Terwillegar parking lot is at the base of the hill. Large enough for a half-day or full-day ski, Edmonton's newest park is located in Riverbend at the west edge of the city. The ski trails follow the river's edge for much of the route. Trails in the large central area are groomed, as are the more difficult trails through wooded areas at the south and east edges of the park.

During summer, the hiking trails at the well-developed, 550-acre **Strathcona Wilderness Centre,** (403) 922-3939, are ordinary and there are better places to see both wildlife and aspen forest. But in winter, the relatively flat trails make ideal cross-country skiing routes. About 10 miles (15 km) of trail are groomed, winding through the aspen forest and following the **Bennett Lake** shore. The visitors center is open through the winter with trail maps, rental equipment, and a waxing service. There is a small trail fee. A pine lodge at the center can be rented by a large group; it features dormitory-style sleeping quarters and a common kitchen, a dining room, and a sitting area with a fireplace. To get there, drive east from Edmonton on Hwy 16 to Brookville Rd, then turn south and follow the signs. Or drive east on Baseline Rd or Wye Rd (82 Ave) and follow the signs (the route turns several times on country roads that are otherwise unmarked). Snow conditions are recorded on the Sno-Line, (403) 467-5800.

Eight of the 12 major trails at **Elk Island National Park,** (403) 992-2950, are groomed in winter for cross-country skiing. The terrain is relatively flat with some dips and short uphills, and the sometimes narrow trails wind through heavily wooded areas. Bison live here during the winter, as well as in summer, so guidelines about not approaching the big buffalo apply (see Wildlife, below). The 11 3/5-mile (18.6-km) **Wood Bison Trail** offers the best possibility for sighting bison. To get to the ridgeline, which is still at a low elevation, take the 10 1/2-mile (16.8-km) **Tawayik Lake Trail,** which overlooks Tawayik Lake, winds along Adamson Lake, and joins the Shirly Lake Trail before heading back to the parking lot.

The 2-mile (3.3-km) **Lakeview Trail** along Asotin Lake is open to **snowshoers** but not cross-country skiers. Information about trail conditions for all users is available at the park information office, (403) 922-5790.

Wildflowers

Local bird-watchers tout the **Wagner Nature Reserve,** a small natural area west of Edmonton, as an ideal place to see birds. Indeed, the habitat, which includes an area of grassland, dense mixed aspen and spruce forest, and bogs and ponds, would seem ideal for attracting a plethora of bird species. Outside the heat of migration, however, it's an area better-suited for seeing wildflowers. Because of the variety of habitats, an abundance of wildflower species grow here, and it's not unusual to see hikers with magnifying glasses and cameras examining one flower or another. Some come nearly every week through spring and early summer to watch the different flower species bloom. Species include ragwort and bog orchids, shooting stars and violets, elephant ear and yellow lady's-slipper orchids. Constantly walking, the loop route takes about 45 minutes. Wear hiking boots or shoes that you don't mind getting wet until the boggy areas dry in midsummer. To get there, drive about 30 minutes west of Edmonton on Hwy 16X; 1 1/4 miles (2 km) west of the Villeneuve overpass turn left (south) on Rd 270 and, almost immediately, turn east on a dirt road that parallels Hwy 16X about a quarter-mile to the parking lot and trailhead.

Wildlife

The best way to see the parkland habitat is by hiking through the dense quaking aspen forests on the 80 miles (100 km) of hiking trails at **Elk Island National Park,** (403) 992-2950, about 45 minutes east of Edmonton on the Yellowhead Hwy (Hwy 16). The park was created in 1926 when 25 square miles (41 square km) were set aside to protect elk from over-hunting. Beginning in 1926, additions were made to the park: in 1947, to protect a herd of wood bison; in 1957, to include hay fields to feed the bison; and in 1978, to include Shirly Lake. Hiking trails radiate from the paved road. Elk and bison aren't the only wildlife to see here, though. Other species commonly seen include **coyotes, moose, deer, beaver,** and **muskrats.** And more than 230 species of birds have been sighted here.

The 8-mile (13-km) Moss Lake hike near the northern edge of the park offers the most scenic walk over predominantly flat terrain. The trail passes three ponds in which **waterfowl** such as blue wing teal, American widgeons, and redheads spend the breeding season. The deciduous forest is rich with other bird life, especially **warblers** that breed in this boreal forest. The park is also thick with **plains bison,** which graze the open areas and are heavy users of the hiking trails.

The **wood bison** herd is confined to the south end of Elk Island National Park. Wood bison are the largest native land mammals on the continent, with the bulls averaging 1,866 pounds (840 kg), significantly larger than the plains buffalo bulls. Incidents between hikers and bison are not rare, and warnings are issued frequently along the road to not approach the bison. Bison are particularly aggressive during the rutting season, late July to late August. The most prudent action when encountering bison on the trail is to simply yield the trail to these huge animals; park officials recommend keeping a distance of at least 330 feet (100 m) at all times and to never enter a herd of bison. Dogs are not allowed on park trails since they may provoke a bison attack. For the best opportunity to see wood bison, take the 11 3/5-mile (18.6-km) Wood Bison Trail, one of the longest in the park, which is open to cross-country skiers as well as hikers. The trailhead is on the south side of Hwy 16 (when you see the sign to turn into the park on the left, take a right instead).

Bird-watchers shouldn't miss the three-fifths of a mile (1-km) walk on a paved path to Beaver Bay on Asotin Lake at the northern edge of the park. The birds on the lake include **white pelicans, common loons,** and **red-necked grebes,** which nest on high spots in Beaver Bay as well as on the islands in the lake. Information about specific birding hot spots is available at the interpretive center in the Asotin Recreation Area, (403) 992-6392.

Fishing is not allowed in Elk Island National Park lakes; swimming is not recommended since the lakes have leeches. However, canoes, sailboards, and sailboats are allowed on Asotin Lake—a boat launch and dock are available at the north end of the recreation area. The Tawayik Lake picnic area has a **viewing platform and spotting scope.** A day-pass to this national park is $4, and there is a driving tour to an area most heavily populated by wood bison.

Attractions

West Edmonton Mall is the place to mega-shop, but the **Old Strathcona Historic District,** the heart of which is between 103 and 104 Aves on 82 St, is the urban alternative to the suburban mall. Many buildings here date to

1891, the year the railroad arrived. It's also the place to head if you want to shop at what has been deemed the best bookstore in Canada by the Canadian Booksellers Association, **Greenwoods' Bookshoppe** (10355 - 82 Ave, (403) 439-2005). The children's book section is actually around the corner in another building, Greenwoods' Small World, (8133 - 104 St, (403) 439-5600), adjacent to the Greenwoods' Calendars store, (8123 - 104 St, (403) 439-4471). And, Greenwoods' Volume II is nearby at 12433 - 102 Ave, (403) 488-2665. Espresso bars in this district are nearly as thick as they are in the heart of Seattle. Between shopping and lattes, interesting browsing sites include the **C & E Railway Museum,** 10447 - 86 Ave, (403) 433-9739; **Old Strathcona Model & Toy Museum,** 8603 - 104 St, (403) 433-4512; and, in summers on Tuesday and Saturday afternoons, the **farmers' market** on the corner of 83 Ave and 103 St, (403) 439-1844. Old Strathcona district walking tour maps are available at the historic district office, 8331 - 104 St, (403) 433-5866.

Edmonton residents flock to the **Muttart Conservatory,** 9626 - 96A St, (403) 496-8755, for a sampling of spring throughout the long, cold winter months. These picturesque pyramid greenhouses, which opened in 1976, are south of the North Saskatchewan River. The complex is impressive for the diversity of habitats. Each of three pyramids has a different climate—desert, temperate, and rain forest; the fourth has revolving displays of flowering plants. A new orchid greenhouse is in the planning phase. The whole is well done and worth a visit, summer or winter. The conservatory is open daily, admission charged.

Edmonton also boasts Canada's largest planetarium dome, at the **Edmonton Space & Science Centre,** 11211 - 142 St, (403) 451-7722. The dome has laser and star shows, and the center includes an IMAX theater, plenty of science demonstrations, and, despite Canada's lack of an ambitious space program, a simulated space station and mission control. It's open daily, admission charged.

The flagship of the province's museums and galleries is the **Provincial Museum of Alberta,** 12845 - 102 Ave, (403) 453-9100 or (403) 427-1786. The usual geology and wildlife exhibits are here, as well as displays about Native Peoples, fur-trading, and pioneer history, plus a cursory glance at prehistoric Alberta. Those wanting an in-depth look at dinosaur and fossil exhibits will find much better exhibits at the Royal Tyrrell Museum of Paleontology in Drumheller east of Calgary (see Attractions in the Calgary and Environs chapter). The Provincial Museum is open daily, July and August; Tuesdays–Sundays otherwise.

Those who want a guided tour of Edmonton can arrange for half-day and full-day **city bus tours** through Royal Tours, (403) 424-8687. **Hot-air balloon flights** over the city rise daily, an hour after sunrise and 2 hours before sunset (weather-permitting), flown by Windship Aviation, (403) 438-0111. The **Edmonton Queen cruises** on the North Saskatchewan River summers, departing from a landing on the south side of the river at 97 St and 98 Ave (just north of the Muttart Conservatory). For cruise times and reservations call (403) 440-4600, fax (403) 440-4090.

Adjacent to the John Janzen Nature Centre (see Hiking/Walking, above), **Fort Edmonton Park,** (403) 496-8787, a replica of the fur-trading post circa 1846, is Canada's largest historic park. Fort Edmonton is open May through September.

Whether shopping is on your agenda, or you simply want to take a look at Edmonton's best-known and biggest tourist attraction, be prepared to walk at **West Edmonton Mall,** (800) 661-8890. The world's largest shopping mall when it was built, it is now eclipsed by Minnesota's Mall of America. From the outside, the size is deceptive—it's surrounded by parking garages with 20,000 parking spots. (Remember the number of the mall entrance you came in so you'll be able to find your vehicle again.) But pick up a map at the first kiosk you run across inside, and wear your walking shoes. The two-level mall is eight city blocks long and three blocks wide.

Even if you don't pause at any of the 800 stores during your walk, there are interesting stops along the way. Watch future Olympic ice skating hopefuls practice triple jumps at the year-round indoor **ice rink.** If the figure skaters or youth hockey teams haven't booked the ice, it's open for public skating; the Edmonton Oilers also put in some practice time here. The **Deep Sea Adventure** wing has water deep enough for mini-submarines, which take visitors on a ride below the surface to the Sea Life Caverns. It also holds a replica of Columbus's *Santa Maria* and a dolphin lagoon, with dolphin shows throughout the day and evening. Under the towering atrium of the 5-acre **World Waterpark,** swimmers lounge in chairs on the concrete beach or ride the artificial waves in the wave pool. Others bungee jump from a tower near the glass ceiling. And the **Galaxy Amusement Park** in one wing contains a monster triple-loop roller coaster—the Mindbender—that climbs up the side of a wall then races down five stories and up and around at terrific speeds. The other two dozen rides pale in comparison, except for the Drop of Death, which seems popular with teens. Those looking for calmer play head for **Pebble Beach,** an 18-hole miniature golf course.

With 110 eateries, there are plenty of places to stop during your walk for sustenance; the better restaurants are on Bourbon Street.

Easter eggs aren't usual tourist draws, but in the case of **Vegreville,** a small town 62 miles (100 km) east of Edmonton on the Yellowhead Hwy, a single Easter egg is. Vegreville is home to the world's largest pysanka (painted Easter egg). More than 25 feet long, 18 feet wide, and 31 feet high (7.5 m by 5.4 m by 9.3 m), the egg was erected in 1974 as a tribute to the Royal Canadian Mounted Police (the town, which is Ukrainian by heritage, is also home to the **International Police Museum,** (403) 632-7650, which contains a display of worldwide police memorabilia). The **Ukrainian Pysanka Festival** is held the first week of July; for information, contact the Vegreville Chamber of Commerce, PO Box 877, Vegreville, AB T9C 1R9, (403) 632-2771.

The oldest settlement in Alberta, **St. Albert,** is just north of Edmonton proper (the city has spread out to this community) on Hwy 2. The site already had a settlement of Metis people, who were half-Indian and half-French, when Father Albert Lacombe established a mission there in 1861. The mission is at **Vital Grandin Centre,** (403) 459-2116, open daily mid-May to early September. Across the Sturgeon River Valley from St. Albert is the **Musee Heritage Museum,** (403) 459-1600, with artifacts of the Metis people, open daily June through August.

A 30-minute drive west of Edmonton, the small town of **Stony Plain** draws thousands of visitors to see the Heritage Walk Outdoor Murals. Fifteen murals tell the town's history, from a Stoney Indians' encampment here to homesteader days. The **Andrew Wolf Wine Cellars,** (403) 963-7717, located in a castle-style building in Stony Plain, uses traditional European-style winemaking methods (the grapes are imported from California and aged here); guided 1-hour tours are available, but we recommend spending your time tasting the wine instead. It's open daily. The **Stony Plain Multicultural Heritage Centre,** 5411 - 51 St, (403) 963-2777, includes a settler's cabin, homesteader's kitchen, and handicraft store; open daily, with guided tours available. (For Alaska-bound travelers, Stony Plain is at the intersection of the Yellowhead Hwy and Hwy 43 to Dawson Creek, BC, and at mile 0 of the famed Alaska Highway.)

Four hours to the west of Edmonton, **Edson's** claim to fame is the site of the largest slow-pitch softball tournament in North America and, as such, touts itself as the Slo-pitch Capital of Canada. Every July more than 250 teams compete for thousands of dollars in prize money. In addition to plenty of softball diamonds, Edson also has an 18-hole golf course and an indoor pool, and nearby in the foothills of the Rockies there are provincial parks for camping and hiking. Edson information is available from the Edson Chamber of Commerce, RCMP Memorial Park, (403) 723-4918.

The **Yellowhead Highway** runs 1,911 miles (3,185 km) from Winnipeg, Manitoba, to Vancouver, British Columbia—across 4 provinces and past 5 national parks and 11 provincial parks. It's open year-round and connects with the famous Alaska Highway in the Yukon Territory at

Stony Plain. The Yellowhead Highway was named for Pierre Bostonais, an Iroquois hunter, trapper, and guide. In the early 1800s, European fur traders searched in vain for a pass through the northern Rocky Mountains until they met Bostonais, whom they called Tete Jaune, or Yellowhead, because of his blond hair. He showed them a pass and they named it Tete Jaune (Yellowhead) Pass in his honor. The Yellowhead route travels through the mountains, not over them, with only four major elevation changes, all less than 400 feet (122 m) elevation. The highest point on the Yellowhead is Obed Summit west of Edson at 3,818 feet (1,163 m).

Calendar of Events

When Edmonton isn't claiming itself the City of Champions, it uses the moniker City of Festivals. To this end, it stages a plethora of festivals year-round.

The annual **Jazz City International Jazz Festival** runs the last week of June and first week of July. Call (403) 432-7166 for information.

The Works: A Visual Arts Celebration, features the artwork of Canadian artists in galleries and building foyers throughout the city for the first 2 weeks of July; call (403) 426-2122.

For 10 days in mid-July, downtown Edmonton is filled with street performers as part of the annual **Edmonton International Street Performers Festival.** Call (403) 425-5162 for details.

The largest summer festival, **Klondike Days,** (403) 479-3500, celebrates Edmonton's gold rush past. The event epicenter is at Northlands Park in northeast Edmonton, where visitors will find the oldest casino in Canada, a dance hall, gold panning, a crafts and country fair, agricultural exhibits, and a midway. Klondike Days is held the last 2 weeks of July with a parade, entertainment, and a Sourdough Raft Race, (403) 426-4055.

Held just days after the end of Klondike Days, the **Edmonton Heritage Festival** focuses on the singing, dancing, and arts and crafts of its various ethnic groups. For more information, call (403) 488-3378.

The annual **Edmonton Folk Music Festival** in early August is a 4-day outdoor celebration of folk, blues, Celtic, bluegrass, gospel and world music. For information on specific performers and dates, call (403) 429-1899.

A 10-day **Fringe Theatre Event** in mid-August includes new and old plays, mime and street entertainment, and is touted as the largest alternative theater in North America; call (403) 448-9000.

Restaurants

La Boheme ☆☆☆   For more than a decade, La Boheme's been a fixture on the corner of 112 Ave and 64 St, serving up French cuisine that draws everyone from the premier of the province to the city mayor to Edmonton Oiler hockey players. The reputation is well-deserved. The corner cafe-style eatery focuses on traditionally prepared French fare that's heavy on creamy sauces and butter. The menu doesn't have many surprises—the entrees range from chicken to fish—and you should be prepared to read a little French since that's the language of choice here (although the servers will cheerfully explain the menu in English on request). Located on the main street of one of Edmonton's oldest residential districts, the building housing La Boheme has some history. A few of the hotel rooms on the second floor are operated as a bed and breakfast but they fall short of the standards set by the restaurant itself. *In the Highlands District; 6421-112 Ave, Edmonton; (403) 474-5693; lunch, dinner Tues–Fri and Sun, dinner only Sat; AE, MC, V; no checks; $$$.*

Block 1912 ☆☆   The desserts in this European cafe in the heart of Edmonton's tony Old Strathcona District overshadow everything else on the menu. And who can blame the fans who flock here for sweets just about any time of day? While the offerings change regularly, there's always a selection of cheesecakes flavored with such things as chocolate or pineapple, tortes (pray they will have the raspberry cream and white chocolate torte the day you visit), cakes, and other rich goodies. Indulge in a piece of cheesecake and a latte while relaxing on one of the comfortable sofas set around a European stove, taking the chill off cold Edmonton days. The cafe also stocks newspapers from around the world so travelers can catch up on news from home. The casual menu includes a selection of salads, most with an ethnic flair (beware: when the description says spicy, it's serious), a quiche of the day, and tasty grilled Italian sandwiches, which are substantial enough they easily can be shared by two. *In the Old Strathcona District; 10261-28 Ave, Edmonton; (403) 433-6575; lunch, dinner every day; MC, V; no checks; $.*

La Boheme's Moroccan Room ☆☆   In 1996, the owner of La Boheme opened a Moroccan restaurant next door. Although the two restaurants are connected through a doorway, the food comes out of two kitchens. Diners seated in La Boheme can order from the Moroccan menu, but it's more fun to sit on ottomans in the Moroccan room and eat spicy lamb and vegetable couscous while Moroccan music plays on the sound system. The menu is westernized only in that it explains the primary ingredients in each dish. An impressive selection of wines is available, but we recommend the sweet mint tea. The dinner is served in the traditional manner—guests are offered a handwashing at the table prior to the meal—but at this Moroccan restaurant the food is served complete with eating utensils. *In the Highlands District; 6421-112 Ave, Edmonton, AB; (403) 474-1204; lunch, dinner Tues–Fri and Sun, dinner only Sat; AE, MC, V; no checks; $$.*

Lodgings

Holgate House ☆☆☆   Edmonton's premier bed and breakfast is located in a 1912 mansion that overlooks the North Saskatchewan River Valley and is on one of the city's scenic drives. Like most local mansions, it's located in the residential area called the Highlands, which was once grand but now is one of the least affluent districts of Edmonton. Gentrification has begun, however. The various owners of Holgate House took care to maintain the mansion through the years and, unlike many large homes, it was never divided into apartments. Now it's under the auspices of the Edmonton Historic District, and any restorations must remain true to the period. Much of the original woodwork of this Arts and Crafts-style mansion remains, including a finely crafted staircase and hardwood floors throughout. What's more impressive are the original murals painted on nearly every wall and on the ceiling of what's now the music room. In one room the painter told the history of Alberta; in the dining room, berry bushes are depicted, in metallic paint, through the four seasons. Guests have their choice of four sitting rooms, including a cozy den that's really a large landing off the stairs, but they have a choice of just two guest rooms. Neither will disappoint. Both are at the front of the mansion and overlook the Highlands Golf Course and the river valley. One is the original guest room of the mansion and has a pedestal sink, though the spacious bathroom is down the hall. The tiled bath has an oversized 6-foot bathtub (no shower), pedestal sink, chair, and marble-topped buffet. The other guest room is the original master bedroom and has a marble fireplace and an adjoining bath with 6-foot soaker tub and two-way shower as well as a private breakfast porch. Long summer evenings can be spent walking the river valley trail, which runs right in front of the mansion; relaxing on the broad wraparound porch; or playing croquet on the lawn. Breakfasts are continental-style, but the muffins, croissants, and scones are made fresh by innkeeper Jeanie Vanderwell. *In the Highlands District; 6210 Ada Blvd, Edmonton, AB T5W 4P1; (403) 448-0901; MV, V; checks OK; $$.*

The Straw Bed Bed and Breakfast and Livery Stables ☆   Those traveling with horses will especially like this bed and breakfast in a new house built on 75 acres in the country northwest of Edmonton. The entire acreage is covered with aspen forest, but owners Helen and Martin Schiebel have created several pastures where guests can turn out horses during their stay. Even the horseless will find this country B&B quiet and comfortable. The Straw Bed has three rooms, and its owners plan to build a separate cottage for more guests. Martin, who is a veterinarian, spends leisure time woodworking; he built the furniture in one guest room—a country pine sleigh bed with matching nightstand, quilt trunk and coffee table. It's in the only room with private bath (shower only, down a flight of stairs). For cross-country skiers who want to ski on a farm in the country, this is the place. There are 5 miles (8 km) of wide loop trails around and through the 75 acres, but what seem like gentle hills on foot can be intimidating on skis. Cleared fields adjacent to the trails can be skied, and there's a recreation area nearby with groomed trails. Guests can use the hot tub in the solarium that looks across the yard to the aspen forest or, winters, sit in front of the fire in the living room. There are resident cats and dogs, and guest pets can be accommodated with advance notice. *West from Edmonton on Hwy 16X about 12 ½ miles (20 km) to Hwy 779, north on 779 6 miles (10 km) to secondary Hwy 633, west ½ mile (1 km) to gate; 15622-111 Ave, Edmonton, AB T5M 2R7; (403) 963-1646; MC, V; no checks; $$.*

Fantasyland Hotel   Fantasyland Hotel is not a normal luxury hotel, but what hotel at a shopping mall is? Aside from being at a mall with a theme park, what sets this 355-room hotel apart is that 125 of its rooms also have themes. Guests can choose from the Truck Room, where the bed is in the back of a pickup truck and decor includes antique gas pumps and automobile seats, or the classic Roman Room with a round velvet-covered bed with silk draperies and a round Roman spa-tub. Or try the Igloo Room, where guests sleep in an igloo surrounded by tundra with a spa-tub in an iceberg. It's just in fun—for more serious guests, there are standard hotel rooms, too. Some packages include free admission to the rides at the mall. *At West Edmonton Mall; 17700-87 Ave, Edmonton, AB T5T 4V4; (800) 661-6454 or (403) 444-3000, fax (403) 444-3294; AE, DC, MC, V; no checks; $$-$$$.*

Streetside Garden Bed and Breakfast   Those who seek lodging in a quiet, older residential area with tall trees and well-groomed yards will find Streetside Garden accommodating. It's in the heart of the Highlands District of Edmonton, 10 minutes northeast of downtown. There's just a single guest room but plenty of areas to roam about the house, which showcases artwork of regional artists in the Sitting Room Gallery. Since innkeeper Ruth Carr is also an artist, the B&B nods to the creative—or at least those with appreciation for the arts. Its perennial garden was created for those who might want to sit and paint a bit. Breakfast is served on the sun deck, weather permitting. *In the Highlands District; 11318-63 St, Edmonton, AB T5W 4E8; (403) 474-7046; V; no checks; $$.*

Ranches and Resorts

Frontier Fishing Lodge   The Frontier is one of the lodges that caters primarily to anglers who want to catch trophy lake trout. It's 115 miles

(192 km) east of Yellowknife at the mouth of the Stark River. Amenities include a lodge with six bedrooms, log cabins, and a conference center with seven bedrooms. All meals are included. You can rent aluminum fishing boats with motors; a list of recommended equipment you need to bring along is provided. Open mid-June to mid-September but the fishing's best in June and July. *At the mouth of Stark River; 5515-82 Ave, Edmonton, AB T6B 2J6; (403) 465-6843; no credit cards; checks OK.*

More Information

Edmonton Eskimos (football): (403) 448-3757.

Edmonton Oilers (hockey): (403) 451-8000.

Edmonton Parks and Recreation: (403) 496-4999.

Edmonton Tourism: (403) 496-8400.

Edmonton Trappers (baseball): (403) 429-2934.

Elk Island National Park: (403) 992-2950.

Gateway Park Visitors Information Centre: (403) 496-8400.

Northlands Coliseum box office: (403) 471-7373.

Northlands Park (horse racing): (403) 471-7379.

Ribbon of Green/River Valley Outdoor Centre: (403) 496-7275.

Strathcona Wilderness Centre: (403) 922-3939; office (403) 922-6099; Sno-Line (403) 467-5800.

TicketMaster: (403) 451-8000.

Travel Alberta: (800) 661-8888 from out of the province or (800) 222-6501 within Alberta.

University of Alberta Devonian Botanic Garden: (403) 987-3054.

Weather report: (403) 468-4940; winter road reports (403) 471-6056.

West Edmonton Mall: (800) 661-8890 or (403) 444-5300.

Jasper National Park

Including the town of Jasper, the Icefield Parkway, and Mount Robson Provincial Park in British Columbia.

In Canada's largest Rocky Mountain park, it's easy to get to the middle of nowhere fast. Jasper National Park covers 4,200 square miles (10,878 square km), and like its sister park to the south, Banff, it straddles the spine of the Rockies. It boasts the same stunning scenery, glaciers, frigid turquoise lakes, hot springs, and wintry playgrounds as Banff National Park. But unlike Banff, which is near enough to Calgary to draw crowds of visitors who drive out to the mountains for the day, Jasper is a destination park. It isn't near anything. Edmonton is a 4-hour drive to the east (longer when the roads are snowy) and the nearest city west is Kamloops in central British Columbia.

Perhaps because Jasper National Park is so big, the three million visitors who come here every year don't seem to overrun the place; even during peak seasons the hiking trails and ski runs in Jasper seem less crowded. Hike a few minutes beyond any trailhead, and you'll find yourself alone in some of the most beautiful terrain on earth. Mountain chickadees sing in the stunted alpine spruce trees, and there's a constant soft rush of sound as streams melt off snowfields.

During winter, what you may notice first is the silence. The landscape and its sounds are frozen by deep, dry snows. But sunny winter days aren't rare in Jasper. Farther south in the Rockies, weather systems arrive from the coastal region, laden with moisture dropped on the western slopes and creating stiff (and often warm) winds on the eastern slopes. The weather systems in Jasper blow in from the Arctic, making for more consistent weather, deep powdery snow, and blue skies.

North and west of the town of Jasper, the hub of this national park, the terrain is rugged and not easily accessible. But the crown jewel of Jasper National Park is Highway 93, better known as the Icefield Parkway. It cuts due south from Jasper to Lake Louise through countryside that resembles a frozen moonscape more than mountains. Thick glaciers conceal mountain tops and fill valleys. Huge snowfields cover hundreds of square miles as waterfalls crash into glacier-scoured valleys. The visual texture is the rough rubble left by receding glaciers and the floods that sweep the valley floors clean each spring. A drive along the Icefield Parkway past the huge Columbia Icefield is stunning enough, but those who leave their vehicles and interact with the landscape may find it a once-in-a-lifetime experience.

Explorer and trapper David Thompson opened up the Jasper region looking for a northern route to the Pacific Ocean. The fur-trading companies quickly followed Thompson into the area in the 1700s and early 1800s, serving as collection and shipping agencies for trappers who harvested furs from beaver, coyote, wolf, bear, mink, and other animals. Activity was concentrated in the Jasper area and along the easy route through the mountains that is now Yellowhead Pass. Only after the railroad arrived and began bringing well-to-do passengers to spend their summer vacations in the mountains was the route south along the Athabasca River opened and developed. The Icefield Parkway was a relief-work project begun during the Depression years of the 1930s and completed in the early 1960s. Place names along the parkway are from groups of people who visited the area, from Native Peoples to fur-traders, mountaineers, explorers, and packers.

Jasper town is not on the Arctic tundra, but you can almost see it from here. Or maybe it just seems that way because it's so far north—at 53 degrees latitude, it's only 7 degrees from the Arctic Circle. Less a resort town and more a place to supply stop for mountain treks, Jasper retains the flavor of its roots. It's the last stop before entering the heart of the Rockies, and truck traffic rumbles past as it climbs over Yellowhead and Red Passes, both in Mount Robson Provincial Park, before reaching the next gas stop, the tiny community of Robson Junction, British Columbia.

Jasper's growth parallels the laying of railroad tracks up the Athabasca River valley and over Yellowhead Pass. After the Grand Trunk Pacific Railway arrived in 1911, Jasper boomed from the tiny community it had been for a century to first a fur-trading center, then a place to get supplies during gold rushes to the north and the west. In 1907, the region was established as a national park. Now, Jasper's population has settled in at about 5,400, and any development is under the restrictive jurisdiction of Parks Canada.

While the upscale jewelry stores and sushi bars that line the streets of downtown Banff remain absent here, Jasper nevertheless is a town in transition. Reindeer hides (and sometimes those of beaver, wolf, and raccoon) are still sold in a few shops, harking back to the heyday of fur-trapping in the region, while one taxi service in town now uses a Mercedes to ferry tourists to their destinations in style.

Some locals here lament what Banff has become since it boomed in the 1970s, citing its upscale restaurants and clothing stores, ski lift lines, and year-round crowds as downfalls of growth. But despite apprehensions of similar growth, Jasper still has none of that glittery image; it remains a quiet, rugged mountain town, remarkably similar to what Banff used to be.

Getting There

The Yellowhead Highway (Hwy 16) cuts through Jasper National Park. Edmonton is 220 miles (362 km) to the east; Kamloops is 265 miles (443 km) to the southwest. From Banff, drive west on TransCanada Hwy 1 to Lake Louise and turn north on the Icefield Parkway; Jasper is 172 miles (287 km) north of Banff, 139 miles (232 km) north of Lake Louise. Rental cars are available in Jasper. During winter months snow tires or chains are required on the Icefield Parkway and on access roads to all ski areas in Jasper National Park.

Jasper/Hinton Airport is 38 miles (64 km) east of Jasper and is served by charter flights and, some summers, by commuter airlines.

Rocky Mountaineer Railtours, (800) 665-7245, operates 2-day rail tours between Vancouver and Jasper or Vancouver and Banff/Calgary, mid-May to October. The tours stop overnight in Kamloops, BC.

The Parks Canada Information Centre, in a decades-old stone building that's quintessentially Northern Rockies, is perched on a square block of lawn much like an old town square and anchors Jasper. Contact the Jasper National Park Visitors Centre (mid-May to October only) at 500 Connaught Drive, Jasper, AB T0E 1E0, (403) 852-6176. Or contact Jasper Tourism, PO Box 98, Jasper, AB T0E 1E0, (403) 852-3858, fax (403) 852-4932.

Adjoining Areas

SOUTH: **Banff National Park**

EAST: **Edmonton and Environs**

inside out

Scenic Drives

If you were limited to one destination in the Canadian Rockies, we would recommend the **Icefield Parkway.** It's that spectacular. Sure, most parts of the Northern Rockies boast stunning snow-covered peaks, glacier-carved hanging valleys painted with beargrass, paintbrush, and penstemon in July, and turquoise-hued alpine lakes milky with glacial flour. The Icefield Parkway has all this *plus* miles of evidence of the sheer power of glaciers scraping across the earth—narrow deep canyons carved by water; valleys littered with boulders, rocks, and sand rather than wildflowers. In some respects, the Parkway is stunning for its barrenness rather than its beauty. The 143-mile (321-km) road from Jasper to Lake Louise should be traveled slowly. Though the distance can easily be covered in a half-day, this route passes viewpoints and side trips well worth extra time. The northern portion of the Parkway is in Jasper National Park; Sunwapta Pass is the boundary where travelers cross south into Banff National Park, although there is no noticeable difference in the terrain. However, the gem of the Parkway—the place where the Athabasca Glacier flows off the Columbia Icefield nearly to the highway—is in Jasper. The huge icefield also sprawls south into Banff and west into Hamber Provincial Park in British Columbia, but in both parks it's less accessible.

The **Columbia Icefield,** up to 1,000 feet (33 m) thick in places, is the largest on the continent outside Alaska and south of the Arctic Circle, covering 233 square miles (389 sq km). The icefield feeds eight major glaciers, three of which—Athabasca, Dome, and Stutfield—are visible from the Parkway. Meltwater from the icefield flows into three oceans, the Pacific, Arctic, and the Atlantic, a phenomenon called a hydrological apex and one of only two such triple divides in the world (the other is in Siberia).

Except for winter snowstorms that periodically close the road, the Icefield Parkway is open year-round. Travelers, however, should remember that services along the road are scarce. Although gasoline is available at Saskatchewan Crossing on the Icefield Parkway (91 3/4 miles/153 km south of Jasper), it's prudent to fill your tank in Jasper or Lake Louise. During winter (November to April) visitors will find no services open between Lake Louise and Jasper (135 3/5 miles/226 km) and should be prepared for winter driving conditions. Vehicles should contain a shovel, sleeping bag, warm clothes, and extra food. For a winter road report, call (403) 852-6161, or contact the Icefield Parkway Visitor Centre (May to mid-October only), on the Icefield Parkway at Athabasca Glacier, (403) 852-6560.

Hiking/Backpacking

Jasper's still a little rough around the edges, with folks more interested in which trails are snowfree than the political correctness of selling reindeer hides. Hikers come off a several-day backpack trip and head for the town's eateries still wearing dusty hiking boots and a 3-day grunge, and no one thinks it unusual. Summer days, the place is quiet as visitors are out on the trails. Evenings, however, hikers comparing trail maps litter the lawn around the Parks Canada Centre like robins listening for worms. Inside, the information counter is a buzz with queries about trail difficulty and condition, the best destinations to see wildlife, and how to get backcountry camping permits. By reputation, Jasper National Park is the destination for serious interaction with the backcountry. The town supports that pursuit.

Hiking in Jasper National Park and along the Icefield Parkway ranges from easy strolls of a few minutes to challenging multi-day backpack trips. Full-day **heli-hiking** trips can be arranged through Canadian Mountain Holidays, PO Box 1660 Banff, T0L 0C0, (800) 661-0252. The Jasper Park Service conducts free guided **interpretive walks** daily at a variety of trails in the park, including a walking tour of Jasper town; a schedule is available at the Parks Canada Information Centre, 500 Connaught Dr (in the historic stone building). **Personalized walking tours,** such as bird-watching or beaver-sighting walks, are offered by Jasper Adventure Centre, (403) 852-3127, and Walks & Talks Jasper, (403) 852-4945. Half- and full-**day hikes** in the Columbia Icefield area are offered by All Things Wild, (403) 852-5193, and White Mountain Adventures, (403) 678-4099.

Most summertime gondola rides to mountain tops can only be found at ski resorts. This isn't the case with the **Jasper Tramway,** a summers-only 7-minute ride to the top of 8,333-foot (2500-m) Whistlers Mountain. The mountaintop, named for the whistling marmots that live on its sides, allows views of six major mountain ranges (all part of the Rockies), the Athabasca and Miette Rivers, Jasper, and on very clear days Mount Robson. Hikes off the mountaintop abound, but they are all downhill going out and uphill coming back for the return gondola ride. We recommend an afternoon spent walking on the mountaintop looking at the wildflowers and views, then a sunset dinner at the terminal's restaurant (though the menu has no surprises and expect to pay a bit extra for the view). Jasper Tramway, (403) 852-3093, is a 10-minute drive (1 ¾ miles/3 km) south from Jasper on Hwy 93. The tram runs March to October. (The lifts at nearby Marmot Basin run winters only for skiers.)

The power of the Athabasca River is best seen at **Athabasca Falls,** where the river pounds through a narrow gorge and has carved potholes in the cliff walls. The parking lot is 14 1/5 miles (32 km) south of Jasper on the Icefield Parkway. A bridge directly over the falls is only a short stroll from the parking lot. Across the bridge, small decks hang out over the thundering falls and paths lead downstream to where the gorge opens again into a river. Winters, the frozen falls are spectacular and a few of the trails are accessible to cross-country skiers.

Because it's relatively easy for hikers to get close to a glacier quickly at **Mount Edith Cavell,** the area's popular with even the least-experienced walkers. The road to the trailheads, built in 1924, is narrow and in places broken up with frost-heaves. Many with RVs would find navigating the winding roadway difficult, and towed vehicles are not allowed. Between mid-June and mid-October, only one-way traffic is allowed (vehicles can only drive up one hour and drive down the next) between 8am and 9pm, which can mean a wait of an hour in the parking lot at the bottom of the road. The views of Mount Edith Cavell and Angel Glacier are worth the wait. Several trails begin at the upper parking lot. We recommend the 2-mile (3-km) hike up the valley to the base of **Angel Glacier** and the small lake in the cirque below the glacier. The trail winds through and around glacial rubble. In midsummer the glacier calves into the lake. Hikers should not approach the edge of the lake, since it is rimmed with ice, some of it concealed by gravel, which can break off into the icy waters. Climbing the snowfield beneath the glacier is also ill-advised, since the calving glacier creates avalanches of ice chunks the size of cars. The crevasses of the glacier can be seen well from a safe distance out in the valley, and those who remain quiet long enough should be able to hear the glacier groan and crack as it flows down the slope—at a glacial pace, of course. Allow about 1 1/2 hours for this hike (remembering that traffic is allowed downhill only during certain hours). Linger longer for the hike up one of the glacial moraines into high-elevation **Cavell Meadow.** The area's deeply snow-covered most years until July, when the wildflower display is spectacular. (Both hikes require proper footwear that you don't mind getting wet, since the streams coming off the snowfields are swollen in early summer and sometimes must be forded.) The trailhead is 17 2/5 miles (29 km) from Jasper.

Those not in the mood for a rigorous day hike can spend the morning on a more leisurely loop stroll around **Lac Beauvert.** A 4 1/5-mile (7-km) walk takes you around the lake. To get to the trailhead, take the Old Fort Point exit off Hwy 93A (across the train tracks from Jasper) and continue to a parking area at the barricade.

A short hike—4 ²/₅ miles (7.4 km)—up **Maligne Canyon** affords constant views into the deep limestone gorge that contains the Maligne River. The trail crosses five bridges along the way. The trailhead is 3 ³/₄ miles (6.5 km) up the Maligne Lake Rd east of Jasper off the Yellowhead Hwy.

The 2 ³/₄-mile (4.8-km) walk around **Patricia Lake** is a must-do for avid bird-watchers, especially those wanting to see common loons. Patricia Lake is just up the hill east of Jasper town, so this is a great early morning or early evening walk for those staying in or near there. The easy trail follows the shore of the lake and dips through Cottonwood Slough. In addition to a variety of waterfowl and songbirds, you may see deer, bear, moose, and beaver. The trailhead is at Pyramid Stables parking lot on the Pyramid Lake Rd.

Despite the name, the **Pyramid Lake Loop** trail doesn't circle Pyramid Lake but it does flank the shore nearest Pyramid Lake Resort. And after the trail leaves the lake it affords clear views of the Athabasca Valley about midway through the 10 ²/₅-mile (17.4-km) hike. Ambitious hikers can start the hike at Jasper town (in the parking lot opposite the Jasper Aquacenter) or pick up the trail along the road to Pyramid Lake. Stay on the marked trails, though, since numerous unmarked trails branch off the main Pyramid Lake Loop. The trail to the **Palisades,** an impressive ridge of slab mountains, cuts off the Pyramid Lake Loop at the end of the lake. The climb to the end of the trail is more ambitious than an ordinary day hike, but an easier walk up just a portion of the trail is still worthwhile for the mountain views and time spent above the tree line.

The distance to **Parker Ridge**, 1 ³/₄ miles (3 km) round trip, may sound like a cakewalk, but there's some elevation to this hike which climbs from 800 feet (245 m) to 7,570 feet (2,271 m) at the ridgetop. Much is taken via switchbacks. In late July and early August this is a great place to see some of the low-growing, less spectacular wildflowers such as heather. Near the top of the ridge where the trail crosses broad flat rock, pause and look down for fossils, evidence of a former inland sea. Take a jacket, hat, and gloves—it's always windy atop the ridge, but the view of Saskatchewan Glacier is gorgeous. The toe of the glacier flows off the Columbia Icefield from the north and Parker Ridge overlooks it and the deep valley scoured by the glacier and subsequent runoff. The trailhead is at a marked parking area on the Icefield Parkway 67 ³/₄ miles (113 km) south of Jasper, 70 ¹/₅ miles (117 km) north of TransCanada Hwy 1.

Those who have seen the Saskatchewan Glacier from above on Parker's Ridge might also want to see it from below via the **Saskatchewan**

Glacier Trail. The 4 3/4-mile (8-km) trail follows the North Saskatchewan River to its source, right up the valley beside the river. The trailhead is 10 miles (16.8 km) south of the Icefield Visitor Centre at an old concrete bridge on the southeast side of the Icefield Parkway, just past the Big Bend. The trail begins in the trees to the immediate right on the southeast side of the bridge. For a distance, the trail is on an old fire road, then it becomes less distinct but generally follows the outwash plain on the south side of the valley clear to the glacier. Look for cairns built by previous hikers along the way.

There is one reason to see **Peyto Lake**: it is picturesque. Not that the hundreds of other lakes in the Canadian Rockies aren't; it's just that Peyto Lake is thick with glacial flour, which lends it a milky turquoise hue as it laps against Mistaya Mountain, which plunges straight into the water. Up the valley toward Peyto Glacier are Mount Jimmy Simpson and Peyto Peak. Just north of Bow Pass is the trailhead for those who want to walk to the lake, a half-day hike for those who want to linger, otherwise just a brief excursion. For those who want to look down on the lake, there's a generous-sized parking lot at the turnoff from the Icefield Parkway at Bow Pass. From the parking lot it's a 15-minute gentle uphill walk on paved paths to the Peyto Lake overlook. Those wanting a full day's hike can continue on the trail from the overlook south and down into the valley. From there a trail follows the valley that's strewn with glacial rubble right up to the toe of Peyto Glacier. At the end of the hike, you will have to climb back up the mountainside to the Peyto Lake overlook, so don't expend all your energy early on in this hike.

An easy day hike that gets you near a glacier is the trail to **Bow Glacier** beyond Bow Lake. The trail begins at the Bow Lodge parking lot and flanks the lakeshore to the terminal moraine at the southwest edge of the lake. From there the trail follows the river melting off the glacier, moraine after moraine. Hikers climb through a narrow gorge into the glacial cirque via a set of steep switchbacks and a short steel ladder bolted into the cliff, the only seriously steep part of the hike. The shorter branch of this trail ends under Portal Peak; the longer side trail, which branches off to the left, goes to the valley under St. Nicholas Peak. The 4-mile (6.6 km) walk through glacial rubble is interesting, and the waterfall coming off the toe of the glacier into the cirque is mesmerizing. Note that this area is frequented by grizzly bears, more so than some other areas of the parks. If your trip allows only one hike, this shouldn't be it, but those with several days for hiking can combine this route with another activity or another short hike and have a satisfying day in the mountains. Bow Lake is 20 2/5 miles (34 km) north of TransCanada Hwy 1.

As a casual day hike, return transportation will be required for the 7-

mile (12-km) **Wilcox Pass** route that begins at the Wilcox Creek Campground about 1 ¾ miles (3 km) south of the Columbia Icefield Visitor Centre, on the north side of the campground entrance just beyond the firegate. Most hikers travel from south to north. The rewards are views of Athabasca Glacier across the valley and 7 of the 25 highest mountains in the Canadian Rockies. Wilcox Pass is almost 4 miles (6.5 km) from the trailhead. The trail ends at Tangle Falls, where Tangle Creek flows into the Sunwapta River. As a destination, Wilcox Pass alone is worth the walk for those without a second vehicle to drop at the other end of the trail. Bird-watchers should look for white-tailed ptarmigans, which nest at the pass.

Guided **ice walks** can be arranged through Columbia Icefield Tours, (403) 762-6735. Mount Athabasca, an 11,000-foot (3,300-m) peak at the south side of the glacier, is a favorite north face route among **climbers,** with a 40- to 50-degree, 1,500-foot (450-m) ice face that affords outstanding views from the top of the Columbia Icefield. The climb, however, requires expertise and climbing equipment. Get more information from the Parks Canada office.

Mount Robson Provincial Park, BC

The Rocky Mountains don't stop at the Alberta-British Columbia border and neither do the parks. Due west of Jasper National Park, the mountainous terrain continues deep into British Columbia, but at the border between provinces the park changes from Jasper to **Mount Robson Provincial Park.** It has the same mountain peaks and hanging valleys as Jasper, but there are fewer access points. The only town in the park, Robson Junction, 57 miles (88 km) west of Jasper, is little more than a refueling point for trucks making the long haul on the Yellowhead Hwy, and has a visitors center, three campgrounds, and a couple of cafes. The primary reason to come here is to see Mount Robson, which is impressive, indeed, as the highest peak in the Canadian Rockies at 13,180 feet (3,954 m). Even at the visitors center it's in your face, with glaciers spilling from the slopes to meet the forest that crawls up from the valley floor.

Backpackers come to Mount Robson to do the 3-day (round-trip) hike to Berg Lake, which sits at the base of Berg Glacier and high on the slopes of Mount Robson. The **Berg Lake Trail** is the most popular backpacking route in the Canadian Rockies, a 12-mile (20-kilometer) hike one way. The trailhead is 1 ⅕ miles (2 km) on a paved side road adjacent to the Robson Junction Visitor Centre. An ambitious day hike will get you to the **Valley of a Thousand Falls** and back. A backcountry camping permit is available at the visitors center for those extending beyond a day hike, given on a quota system; call (604) 566-4325 for information.

Keep in mind that **mountain bikes** are allowed on the first 5 ²/₅ miles (9 km) of this trail; **horses** are allowed on the length of the route. Beyond the Valley of a Thousand Falls is **Emperor Falls,** which plummets 200 feet (60 m) in one span. At Berg Lake, late-summer hikers will be able to hear and see the ice calving off Berg Glacier into the turquoise-hued waters. Those who don't want to hike all the way can opt to **fly in** and hike out. Mount Robson Adventure Holidays is licensed to fly hikers to the lake on a helicopter and drop them off for a more leisurely hike out (downhill, of course). Contact Mount Robson Adventure Holidays, Box 687, Valemount, BC V0E 2Z0, (604) 566-4386, fax (604) 566-4351.

Many backpackers extend their hike to see Robson Glacier via the **Snowbird Pass Trail,** which is rated as strenuous and requires a full day hike. Check with the visitors center.

Camping

The only campground open year-round in Jasper National Park is **Wapiti Campground,** 2 ⁴/₅ miles (4 km) south of Jasper town on the Icefield Parkway. There are no showers, but there is hot and cold running water and sites with electrical connections.

The campground at the **Columbia Icefield Campground** used to be walk-in only and was frequented mostly by bicyclists; now vehicles are allowed at most sites, but it's still restricted to tent camping (no trailer tents). The terrain's far from hospitable, but alpine spruce and a few aspen surround the actual campsites on the mountainside across the valley from the Athabasca Glacier. Where else can you boast in-your-face views of a glacier from the doorway of your tent? It can be cold with winds blowing off the massive Columbia Icefield, but the setting alone is worth it. Perhaps because of the barren landscape surrounding the campground and its remote location, this campground doesn't fill up as early in the day as others, and outside the peak tourist season, spaces can be found here even in early evening. The campground is 75 miles (125 km) north of Hwy 1, 63 miles (105 km) south of Jasper. Open mid-May to October and on a primitive basis until snow falls.

Even if its allotted campsites are full, the overflow sites at **Mosquito Creek Campground** (one of the designated overflow campgrounds) are some of the best campsites on the Icefield Parkway. There are just two overflow campgrounds in the area; the other is just east of Lake Louise on Hwy 1, a large, open site used to store gravel for winter use on the TransCanada Hwy. The overflow sites at Mosquito Creek are beside a rushing little river. Granted, they, too, are in an open, graveled parking lot, but at least the lot is surrounded by trees. Those who get there early camp mere feet from the stream. The campsites are all in dense forest, allowing maximum privacy, but they tend to be chilly and damp. This area is also frequented by grizzlies, more so than some other areas in the parks. Mosquito Creek is a 14 ⅖ miles (24 km) north of Hwy 1 on the Icefield Parkway.

Those wanting to stay near Jasper town in a campground that might seem more civilized than the Columbia Icefield Campground should opt for **Wabasso Campground,** south of Jasper on the Icefield Parkway (take the turnoff for Mount Edith Cavell, then turn for Wabasso Campground). You won't be alone at Wabasso, regardless of the season—the 238 sites tend to fill up early in the day during peak tourist periods. But the campground is well down in the Athabasca Valley, so stands of spruce and aspen offer privacy at some campsites. Six walk-in sites offer tent-only camping. Among those who travel with trailers and RVs, this is the campground of choice in Jasper National Park. Open May through September.

Not our favorite destination in July because of the mosquitoes, **Waterfowl Lakes Campground** makes a great August and September base from which to explore the Icefield Parkway trails and other attractions. The campground, with 116 sites, is beside the lower lake and is well off the Icefield Parkway between Bow Pass and Saskatchewan Crossing.

Because of its centralized location on the Icefield Parkway, about midway between Jasper and Lake Louise, we like **Wilcox Creek Campground.** It's just south of the Columbia Icefield Visitor Centre and has 46 sites, although this campground is not serviced. But that just makes it less crowded. Self-contained RVs and trailers are allowed here, and it's a good base from which to explore the Parkway trails.

Campers or those looking for an excursion from Hinton can drive north on the Bighorn Hwy (Hwy 40) to **William A. Switzer Provincial Park,** (403) 865-5600, where there's exceptional hiking, fishing, canoeing, and, for the hearty, swimming. Those with time can take a side trip farther north (87 miles/145 km) to the town of **Grand Cache.** Get gas before heading that way, however, since there are no services between Hinton and Grand Cache. The town has a nine-hole golf course, but visitors come here to day hike, horseback ride, fish nearby trout-stocked lakes, and gain access to the **Willmore Wilderness Park,** (403) 723-7141, a remote and rugged area on the northern border of Jasper National Park. There are no roads into the wilderness area and trails are not maintained, so be prepared for serious backpacking with plenty of elevation; get a topographic map of the area. This is the winter range of mountain caribou and, year-round, gray wolves. You can flirt with the wilderness area from a campground in a spectacular canyon where the Smoky and Sulphur Rivers meet, 3 ⅗ miles (6 km) north of Grand Cache on Hwy 40. **Hell's Gate Campground** is practically at the door of the Willmore Wilderness Park.

Biking

Mountain bikes are allowed on designated trails only in Jasper National Park. A brochure of trails on which biking is allowed is available at the Parks Canada Information Centre in Jasper. Trails may change from year to year. The center can also provide information as to which trails are snow- and mud-free; many trails are flooded in sections during spring run-off, well into July. Biking is not allowed on the Skyline, Tonquin, Lake Annette, Maligne Canyon (from the first to fifth bridge), or Mount Edith Cavell Trails.

Although there are few trails on which mountain bikes are allowed or even recommended in Jasper, biking is a fine way to get around town or make excursions to nearby lakes such as Pyramid and Beauvert. As evidence of the lack of mountain biking opportunities, the one shop in town that rents bikes, the Sport Shop (414 Connaught Dr, (403) 852-3654) has only touring bikes available. But they are fine for riding paved roads. The shop also has in-line skates available, although those prove less popular because of the lack of appropriate terrain.

One of the routes that's snow-free early in the season is in Maligne Canyon to Maligne Falls (bicycles are not allowed beyond that point on the road to Maligne Lake). The route goes almost 7 miles (11.5 km) from Jasper. Several later-season routes utilize fire roads, but are rated for only the most experienced bikers looking for grueling rides.

Fishing

Boats with 7 hp motors can be rented for fishing at Pyramid Lake at the resort office, 3 3/5 miles (6 km) from Jasper, (403) 852-4900. The lake has trout, but fishing pressure is heavy.

There is a public boat launch on Maligne Lake (drive past Maligne Lake Lodge to the public access) and those with their own boats (or canoes) can fish here for rainbow and Eastern brook trout. National parks fishing licenses are available at the Maligne Lake Boathouse. Maligne Tours, (403) 852-3370 (see Canoeing/Rafting, below), offers guided fishing trips and a van shuttle service between Jasper and Maligne Lake from May to mid-September. Canoes and rowboats are available for rent at the Maligne Lake boathouse.

In addition to Maligne and Pyramid Lakes, fishing is allowed throughout Jasper National Park, but catch-and-release fishing is encouraged. Fish include pike, whitefish, and dolly varden (April is the peak time these would be found in Jasper's rivers), and rainbow, brook, and lake trout (May through October, most often fished for in lakes). Boats and canoes can be rented at Maligne River Trading (416 Connaught

Dr, Jasper, AB T0E 1E0, (403) 852-5650), but the licensed **guide service** at the shop, Currie's Guiding, has boats and tackle already at the lakes for use by its guided clients. The guide service operates at Maligne Lake most often, but also guides fishing excursions to more than 20 other lakes and major rivers in 21-foot cedar strip freighter canoes. Fly-fishing instruction is also available.

Horseback Riding

Horses are available by the hour at the stables near **Pyramid Lake,** (403) 852-3562. Follow the signs to Pyramid Lake and look for the turnoff to the stables; nearby trails are through the woods and along the shores of Pyramid and Patricia Lakes. Guided half-day horseback trips begin at the Maligne Lake Chalet and climb to the 7,000-foot (2,100-m) summit of the Bald Hills and the site of an old fire lookout. Reservations are through Ridgeline Riders, 626 Connaught Dr in Jasper, (403) 852-3370, or at Jasper Park Lodge, (403) 852-3301. Year-round guided multi-day rides can be arranged through Skyline Trail Rides, Box 207, Jasper, AB T0E 1E0, (403) 852-4215.

Those who want to ride and hike can arrange 5-day **horse-packing trips** into the Tonquin Valley, which include time for hiking and trout fishing in the backcountry, through Jasper Tonquin Valley Pack and Ski Trips, Box 550, Jasper, T0E 1E0, (403) 852-3909.

Those who want to do several horseback day trips might choose lodging at one of the guest ranches outside the park boundaries. The ranches abound farther south along the eastern slopes of the Rockies just north and just south of Calgary. Near Jasper, we recommend the Black Cat Guest Ranch, (800) 859-6840 or (403) 865-3084, near Hinton, which has been operating since 1935 (see Ranches and Resorts, below).

Canoeing/Rafting

High-elevation **Maligne Lake,** the second-largest glacier-fed lake in the world, sits in Maligne Canyon at 5,500 feet (1,650 m) elevation, a 29-mile (48-km) drive from Jasper. The lake is 13 ⅓ miles (22 km) long and 320 feet (97 m) deep. Canoes and rowboats are available for rent at the Maligne Lake boathouse. There is a public boat launch here, too; drive past Maligne Lake Lodge to the public access.

Waterfowl Lakes, actually in Banff National Park on the Icefield Parkway, is a popular destination for those wanting to canoe. Upper Waterfowl Lake is flanked by wet meadows, which are good habitat for moose. As indicated by their names, both Upper and Lower Waterfowl Lakes provide opportunities to see a variety of ducks.

Boaters ply the waters of **Moose Lake,** 33 miles (55 km) west of Jasper on the Yellowhead Hwy. Fishing is allowed, but canoeing is an equally popular activity since a variety of wildlife—wolf, moose, deer, beaver, and muskrat—can be seen in the marshy fringes of the lake.

In Mount Robson Provincial Park, activities include whitewater rafting. The Fraser River flows west out of Mount Robson Provincial Park and morning or afternoon **float trips** down this relatively gentle river are available August to mid-September only (to see the Chinook salmon run upriver) through Mount Robson Adventure Holidays, Box 687P, Valemount BC V0E 2Z0, (604)566-4386, fax (604)566-4351.

Maligne Tours, at 626 Connaught Dr in Jasper, (403) 852-3370, or Jasper Park Lodge, (403) 852-3301, runs 8-mile whitewater rafting trips down the **Maligne River,** which drops at 66 feet per mile (33 m per 1.6 km), June to September, water level permitting. They also organize guided fishing tours on Maligne Lake.

Canoeing and rafting down the **Athabasca River** is not advised for anyone but those most experienced with whitewater. In addition to rapids, the water, clouded with glacial flour, hides boulders and other obstructions. Because it's glacial-fed, the water is extremely cold—hence hypothermia can occur quickly to those who fall in. Guided rafting trips can be booked through Brewster Transportation and Tours, (403) 852-3332. Tours, guided by a national parks-licensed guide, run mid-May through September and depart from Jasper Park Lodge for guests there, and from the Brewster Bus Depot, 607 Connaught Dr, Jasper.

Cross-Country Skiing

Since Jasper is situated in a broad valley, terrain appropriate for cross-country skiing abounds right around town. For current **trail conditions,** check with the Parks Canada warden's office, (403) 852-6157. Call (403) 852-6177 for recorded snowpack conditions and avalanche forecasts. A wilderness pass is required for those camping in the backcountry any time of year; backcountry skiers should always carry an avalanche transceiver, a shovel, extra food, and extra clothing. Training in avalanche rescue is recommended.

One of the popular destinations for Nordic skiers is **Maligne Lake,** a 29-mile (48-km) drive southeast of Jasper town. Skiers can cover as much of the 13 1/5 mile-long (22 km) frozen lake as time and energy allow.

Portions of the **old Icefield Parkway (Hwy 93A)** south of Jasper are not plowed winters and the highway is a pleasant—and flat—cross-country ski route. Not all of the portions are groomed, but there are enough resident cross-country skiers that there are always tracks in which to ski. Take the Marmot Basin turnoff from Hwy 93. Since the plowed areas vary even through the winter, check with the Parks Canada Information Centre in Jasper town as to which sections are open for cross-country skiing.

Downhill Skiing

By Banff ski resort standards, **Marmot Basin,** (403) 852-3816, is a modest downhill area. The resort has just one high-speed quad chairlift, one triple chair, and three double chairs serving 52 runs. Still, Marmot Basin boasts the same dry, powdery Rocky Mountain snow as the mega-ski areas to the south, but with fewer crowds. Skiers do have 1,000 acres of groomed terrain to explore. Marmot Basin isn't a destination resort and there's no lodging on the mountain, but for those who head to Jasper in the winter, it's a great day-use ski area to add to the repertoire of wintry activities. It's 11 ²⁄₅ miles (19 km) southwest of Jasper on the Icefield Parkway.

Attractions

Exploring downtown Jasper involves browsing the shops along three blocks that flank the Yellowhead Highway through town. Dining is done most often at motel and lodge dining rooms, although the cafes in Jasper offer the usual fare of sandwiches and salads, and a few have begun making espresso drinks. A vegetarian restaurant has a juice bar. Souvenirs abound for those seeking memorabilia.

On summer days, Jasper is quiet since visitors are hiking and biking the trails, out exploring glacial moraines, or looking for fossil evidence of the time this area was covered by a shallow inland sea. The **Parks Canada Information Centre,** 550 Connaught Dr, is worth a visit just to appreciate the historic stone structure that holds it. Inside there's a wealth of information on all aspects of playing in this national park. Call (403) 852-6176.

Those wanting a swim can head for the **Jasper Aquatic Centre,** 401 Pyramid Lake Rd, (403) 852-3663, which is open daily (and well into the evening year-round) for public swimming in the competition-size pool. When hot springs are in order, Jasper National Park has those, too. **Miette Hot Springs,** (403) 866-3939, are the hottest natural springs in the Canadian Rockies. The water coming from three springs collected at the hot pools is 129°F (54°C). Two pools, cooled to 104°F (40°C), are situated on a broad open-air deck on a mountainside in the Fiddle River Valley. There's a snack bar here, and locker rooms. Drive east from Jasper 26 miles (44 km) on the Yellowhead Hwy and south 10 miles (17 km) on Miette Rd. Open daily May through August.

The **Jasper Tramway,** (403) 852-3093, offers a 7-minute ride to the top of 8,333-foot (2,500-m) Whistlers Mountain during the summer; see Hiking/Backpacking, above, for details.

The second-largest glacier-fed lake in the world, **Maligne Lake,** is a 29-mile (48-km) drive from Jasper. Scenic 90-minute **boat cruises** include a stop on Spirit Island and run mid-May to mid-October hourly throughout the day; reservations are recommended. Contact Maligne Tours, 626 Connaught Dr, (403) 852-3370, or Jasper Park Lodge, (403) 852-3301.

Athabasca Glacier draws so many visitors that the historic stone **Columbia Icefield Visitors Centre,** (403) 852-6560, was outgrown. In 1996 the park opened a new stone chalet-style visitors center. In addition to the bigger gift shop and cafeteria areas, rooms for overnight lodging were added, and the Brewster Snowcoach Tours office was moved into the visitors center. As handsome as the new stone building is, the real show is still the **Athabasca Glacier.** We recommend getting up close to the ice by driving to the parking lot at the toe of the glacier (take the road across the highway from the visitors center). Almost as interesting as the glacier itself is the rate at which it has receded in this century, noted with signs posted along the road marking the edge of the glacier as the decades rolled by. Another way to interact with the glacier is via the 3-mile (5-km) round trip **Snowcoach Tours,** (403) 762-6735, which take a restricted road built along a moraine on the south side of the glacier (not open to the public) and park out on the Athabasca Glacier so tourists can get out and walk. (Allow about 1 ½ hours for the tour and wear a coat and appropriate footwear.) Walking out on the glacier beyond the Snowcoach lot or from the glacier toe is discouraged by parks officials and is dangerous. Deep crevasses often are snow-covered and people have fallen into them and died. Still, visitors ignore the warning signs every time we've been there; a well-used path leads from the end of the trail at the glacier toe well up onto the glacier, and snowboarders have discovered the year-round snowy slope. Canadian Rockies Icefield Skytours, (403) 762-8252, actually lands on the Columbia Icefield in a Cessna **ski-plane.**

The Columbia Icefield Visitors Centre is 63 miles (105 km) south of Jasper, 113 miles (189 km) north of Banff. Snowcoach Tours operate May to mid-October and reservations are not required; however, there may be a wait for those wanting to take the tour between 11am and 5pm during the peak tourist season.

The town of **Hinton** calls itself the Gateway to the Rockies and, indeed, when driving the Yellowhead Hwy west from Edmonton, Hinton is the beginning of serious mountains and the end of the undulating aspen-covered parkland. Those who don't want to stay in Jasper National Park but prefer a town outside the park, choose Hinton just 15 minutes away. The town has its amusements, which include a nine-hole golf course, public tennis courts, and an indoor pool. When visitors tire of looking at the mountains from Athabasca tower, they can join guided coal mine or pulp mill tours. Nearby, the best day hike that offers terrain different from that in the national park is on **Wild Sculpture Trail,** which most take to see the sandstone hoodoos sculpted by wind and ancient floods that raced out of the Rockies as the last Ice Age ended. For more information, call the Hinton Chamber of Commerce, (403) 865-2777.

Restaurants

Jasper Park Lodge ☆   The lodge offers four dining rooms for guests, but all are open to the public, as well. The Edith Cavell Room has garnered dining awards from various Canadian tourist associations, but it's as much for the view of Lac Beauvert as it is for the food. For a traditional Canadian menu, choose the Moose's Nook. The Beauvert Room offers Continental cuisine, the Meadows Cafe offers light and casual fare, and the Edith Cavell Room is formal. Reservations are recommended for dinner and are mandatory during tourist season. (See also Lodgings, below.) *Turn off the Maligne Lake Rd east of Jasper on the Yellowhead Hwy; PO Box 10, Jasper Park Lodge, Jasper; (403) 852-6052; breakfast, lunch, dinner every day; AE, DC, DIS, MC, V; checks OK; $$-$$$.*

Maligne Canyon Restaurant ☆   The busloads of tourists who crowd the parking lot here to see the falls can be daunting, but if the dining room isn't thick with people (outside the usual mealtimes), this can be a good choice for an informal meal. The menu ranges across the usual fare (don't look for an adventure in dining here or at any of the tourist-driven eateries) from pasta to sandwiches to barbecue. The experience is pleasant, as is the view of Maligne Canyon. Open April through October. *On the Maligne Lake Rd at Maligne Falls; PO Box 544, Jasper; (403) 852-3583; breakfast, lunch, dinner every day; MC, V; no checks; $-$$.*

Lodgings

Hostel-style lodging can still be arranged in dozens of private homes, and throughout the modest residential areas of Jasper, signs are posted on front lawns noting Approved Accommodations and vacancy status.

Alpine Village ☆☆☆   Log cabins surrounded by manicured lawns (groomed frequently by grazing elk), with pots of geraniums and petunias scattered about for color, beside a rushing glacial-fed river deep in the Rocky Mountains—what more is there? Alpine Village is situated on a gentle bend in the Athabasca River 1 ½ miles (2.5 km) south of Jasper on the Icefield Parkway (Hwy 93), which is really the only fault we can find with this resort; some of the cabins are adjacent to the highway, which lends less lodge-in-the-mountains ambience to those particular cabins. Cabins along the river have the best views, but all cabins are situated in the woods and offer pleasant surroundings. All have kitchens, private barbecues, decks, and wood-burning fieldstone fireplaces, welcome even in midsummer since nighttime temperatures can dip. Furnishings are appropriately lodge-style. Newer cabins are all one-bedroom; the older log cabins and lodge suites have been recently renovated, however. After a day of hiking, visitors can soak in the 16-foot outdoor whirlpool on a log deck with mountain views. Or spend hours sitting on the banks of the Athabasca River, watching the rafters float by. We're disappointed this lodge is not open winters, since there's plenty of nearby terrain suitable for cross-country skiing; but the cabins aren't winterized. It's open only May to mid-October. *South from Jasper on the Icefield Pkwy (Hwy 93); PO Box 610, Jasper, AB T0E 1E0; (403) 852-3285; MC, V; no checks; $$-$$$.*

Jasper Park Lodge ☆☆☆   More so than in the other Canadian Rockies parks, the historic lodge here—Jasper Park Lodge—presides over all other lodging options. The experience doesn't come cheap, however. Perhaps because it doesn't get the tourist pressure of lodges to the south in Banff National Park, Jasper Park Lodge retains some of the grandeur of the era in which it was built (1922). It seems less polished than, say, the Banff Springs Hotel or the Prince of Wales in Waterton National Park, and that's good. The lobby has been remodeled to the point it's lost that hunting-lodge feel, but gracious sitting areas look out on Lac Beauvert. There are plenty of patios, picnic areas, and sandy beaches on which to sit and smell the mountain air. Room decor is contemporary mountain rustic with plenty of wildlife icons. Those expecting a lodge tucked against a mountainside will be disappointed; Jasper Park Lodge is within walking distance of the Athabasca River, which explorer David Thompson paddled up in search of the Pacific Ocean nearly 200 years ago. While most lakes in the Rockies have frigid waters, Lac Beauvert and nearby lakes Edith and Annette are connected to the same underground water source that feeds the area hot springs; although they aren't lukewarm, swimming is a realistic option. Guests can book tee times on the adjoining 18-hole golf course mid-May to mid-October. Guests also can canoe Lac Beauvert, swim in the pool, play tennis, or book heli-hiking, horseback riding, fishing, or bicycling excursions (the lodge has all the needed equipment and guides). Winters, there's skating on the lake, cross-country skiing on groomed trails near the lodge, and heli-skiing or alpine skiing at Marmot Basin. The lodge even offers what's called a Canyon Crawl, a guided tour through the frozen waterfalls in Maligne Canyon. *Turn off the Maligne Lake Rd east of Jasper on the Yellowhead Hwy; PO Box 40, Jasper, AB T0E 1E0; (800) 441-1414 or (403) 852-3301, fax (403) 852-5107; AE, DC, DIS, MC, V; checks OK; $$$.*

Marmot Lodge ☆   Jasper's small, which makes any lodging right in town seem part of the summer tourist bustle. But winter's a different story. Marmot Lodge is one of the few lodges to remain open during the winter months, and it's a good one. The newer rustic-style lodge is set back a couple of blocks from the Yellowhead Hwy, which means that the truck traffic and trains that run through town will seem removed from your lodging. The rooms are on the ordinary side, but are clean and adequately sized. Some have gas fireplaces. Facilities include an indoor pool, sauna, and whirlpool. The lodge offers all necessary winter amenities in terms of ski storage, an on-site restaurant, fireplaces, and a shuttle to the ski hill. *At the east end of Jasper town, 2 blocks north of the Yellowhead Hwy; Mountain Park Lodges, PO Box 1200, Jasper, AB T0E 1E0; (800) 661-6521, fax (403) 852-3280; AE, DIS, MC, V; no checks; $$-$$$.*

Pine Bungalow Cabins ☆   The small, older cabins at this resort on the Athabasca River call up memories of family vacations—station wagons and all—in the '50s. They aren't log cabins, but they're sided with perfectly rounded log slabs, so the effect's the same. The older cabins with bright red doors are really charming, but we recommend staying in the new log cabins that are larger, more comfortable, and, well, more '90s. The resort is a 5-minute drive from Jasper. Its motel-type units are near the office and have none of the ambience that the cabins do. The cabins have kitchens, and most have fireplaces. The paved walkway along the river has plenty of benches for sitting and drinking in the scenery. Those bent on staying riverside should ask for Cabins 1 or 3, which are at the end of the road; they afford privacy and a view. Open about May 1 to Canadian Thanksgiving (early October). *Just east of Jasper town and across the Yellowhead Hwy; Box 7, Jasper, AB T0E 1E0; (403) 852-3491, fax (403) 852-3432; AE, MC, V; checks OK; $$.*

Columbia Icefield Chalet   When the Columbia Icefield Visitors Centre was rebuilt, overnight lodging was included in the new stone structure. Lodging is limited to 32 rooms on the upper floors. The rooms are standard hotel-style. Less expensive rooms look out on the mountainside behind the visitors center; the rest have views of Athabasca Glacier. The deluxe rooms are at the corners of the building. Columbia Icefield Chalet is open from early May to mid-October. *1 hour south of Jasper on the Icefield Pkwy, at Athabasca Glacier; PO Box 1140, Banff, AB T0L 0C0; (403) 852-6560 summers, (403) 762-6735 winters; MC, V; no checks; $$-$$$.*

Ranches and Resorts

Black Cat Guest Ranch   Guests spend the day in the saddle riding the forested trails of the Front Range. In July and August, raft trips and line dancing are offered once a week. And after a day out riding, the quintessential ranch-type barbecue is served up along with home-cooked fixings. Specialty offerings include writing and watercolor painting workshops, side trips to the Cadomin Cave, and a western-style New Year's Eve party. Black Cat Guest Ranch will shuttle guests from the train or bus in Hinton. *8 2/5 miles (14 km) north on Hwy 40; Box 6267, Hinton, AB T7V 1X6; (800) 859-6840 or (403) 865-3084, fax (403) 865-1924; MC, V; checks OK.*

Pyramid Lake Resort   Those who want to escape the fray of tourist-laden buses, trains, trucks, and souvenir shoppers in Jasper town can head to Pyramid Lake Resort. Everything you need is available at this year-round resort—food, newly renovated rooms with gas fireplaces, hiking/skiing trails, and lake and boating-type toys. The resort's only 3 3/5 miles (6 km) from Jasper (all uphill for those inclined to walk into town for dinner) but it could easily be miles in the backcountry, tucked at the end of a hanging valley up against major mountains. A variety of hiking trails wind around Pyramid Lake, going deep into adjoining valleys and up the mountainsides. Guided hikes are offered May to mid-October; inquire at the office where maps are available. The resort restaurant offers standard, adequate fare and will pack hikers' lunches. Boats with motors, canoes, kayaks, rowboats, pedal boats, catamarans, pontoon boats, and sailboards can all be rented through the office. Fishing licenses and supplies are also available. Winters, a portion of the lake is cleared for skating. Cross-country skiers can ski across and around the lake on groomed tracks. Rooms are in chalet-style buildings and some have kitchenettes (and the best views of the lake). Ask for an upper-level room so the cars in the parking lot won't be in front of your view. *On Pyramid Lake Rd, north of Jasper; PO Box 388, Jasper, AB T0E 1E0; (403) 852-4900, fax (403) 852-7007; MC, V; no checks.*

More Information

Icefield Parkway Visitors Centre: (403) 852-6560.
Jasper National Park Visitors Centre: (403) 852-6176 or (403) 852-6162.

JNP Warden: (403) 852-6156.
Jasper Tourism: (403) 852-3858.
Parks Canada emergency: (403) 852-6161.
Road report: (403) 852-6161.
Royal Canadian Mounted Police: (403) 852-4848.
Weather report, Environment Canada: (403) 852-3185.

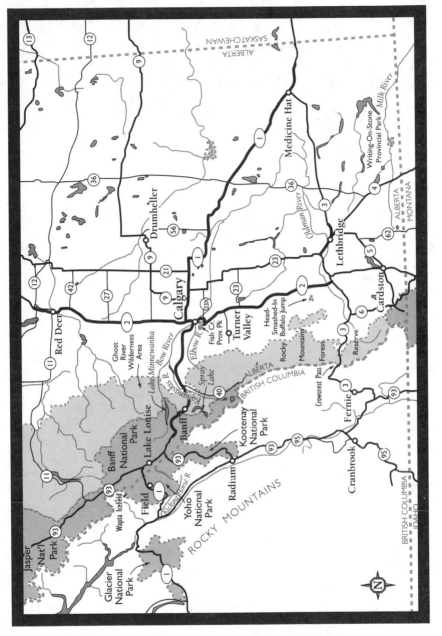

Southern Canadian Rockies

Southern Canadian Rockies

Banff National Park

Including Canmore, Kananaskis, the town of Banff, Lake Louise, and Yoho and Kootenay National Parks in British Columbia.

Banff National Park is the most popular destination in the Canadian Rockies, not only because it's so accessible but also because it claims some of the most stunning scenery in the world. Nearly four million people visit Banff each year, and Calgary residents view the park as their own playground; it's little more than an hour's drive west of Calgary on TransCanada Highway 1.

Banff National Park holds a sprawling mass of high, sharp mountain ridges and deep valleys. This is a place for skiing and hiking—downhill skiers have more than 5,000 acres of high-elevation terrain covered with deep, dry snow, and summer visitors can walk hundreds of hiking trails. Nestled in the middle of this array of 8,000- to 10,000-foot (2,400- to 3,000-m) peaks, right up against Tunnel Mountain, is the town of Banff. Serious about tourism, Banff takes advantage of the terrain, with its glacier-fed rivers and the hot springs that pop out of Sulphur Mountain above. An attempt by three Canadian Pacific Railway workers to stake a claim to the hot springs prompted Canada to establish Banff as its first national park in 1883. Along with four adjoining mountain parks, more than 5,200 square miles (13,520 square km) of the Northern Rockies have been preserved. The United Nations declared the area a World Heritage Site in 1985.

At Lake Louise, summer activities include a hike to a teahouse for lunch, paddling in canoes, or exploring low-elevation trails by horseback. Chateau Lake Louise dominates the lake itself, but non-guests are free to stroll the wide paved trail along the water's western edge. Benches along the trail allow hikers to rest or just sit still and breathe in the scenery. Winters, groomed cross-country ski trails around the lake are also open for public use.

The citing of the 1988 Olympic Nordic events had more to do with the growth of Canmore than any other factor. The town, just east of Banff National Park, boomed with the Olympic games, and the growth continues as motels spring up along the roads and residential areas. Because it's not in the park and lacks Banff's ambiance, fewer tourists stay here. But Canmore is well-situated as a base for recreating in both Banff and the nearby Kananaskis area, as many visitors are increasingly realizing.

The Kananaskis area stretches south from Hwy 1, encompassing 2,667 square miles (4,000 square km) of the foothills of the Rockies, including three provincial parks. The region has 150 miles (250 km) of paved trails and 276 miles (460 km) of unpaved trails open to mountain biking—more than any area in Alberta. The Kananaskis area is accessible through Bragg Creek, but the heart of the region is better reached through Canmore.

Some hiking trails don't observe provincial boundaries and freely cross into Yoho National Park in British Columbia. Yoho is not as large a park as Banff and, unlike Banff and Jasper, has no developed tourist town. What constitutes the community in this park is Field, BC, little more than a way-stop for truckers and vehicles needing fuel and food. The Rocky Mountains continue in wave after wave of mountain peaks and valleys west through Yoho and deep into British Columbia. The west sides of the icefields that line Banff's Icefield Parkway are in Yoho and a few Banff hiking trails get close to Yoho's Waputik and Wapta Icefields.

Those who have traced the Columbia River to its source say the glaciers and snowfields that feed the river's headwaters are in Kootenay National Park, also in British Columbia. There's not much difference, terrain-wise, between Kootenay and Banff. But while tourists flock to Banff year-round, Kootenay remains relatively unknown. For hikers, backpackers, and others who relish solitude, that's good news. There is no town in Kootenay, making it a camper's park, though campgrounds may seem scarce. But there's no shortage of hiking trails, many to pristine alpine lakes. Winters, Hwy 93 through the park is closed, but those who want to stay in Radium, just south of the park boundary, can cross-country ski and snowshoe on park land.

Getting There

Take TransCanada Hwy 1, which runs through Banff National Park, west from Calgary. Hwy 93 from Cranbrook, BC, connects with Hwy 1 just west of

Banff. During winter, snow tires or chains are required on Hwy 93 from Radium to Hwy 1 in Yoho National Park, and on the access roads to all ski areas in the parks.

Calgary International Airport is served by major airlines from the United States, Europe, and Japan. The airport is a 90-minute drive from Banff. Rental cars are available at the airport.

Rocky Mountaineer Railtours, (800) 665-7245, operates 2-day railtours between Vancouver and Jasper or Banff/Calgary, mid-May to October. The tours stop overnight in Kamloops, BC.

Visitors can get additional information from a variety of sources: Banff National Park, Box 900, Banff, AB T0L 0C0, (403) 762-1550; Banff/Lake Louise Tourism Bureau, PO Box 1298, Banff, AB T0L 0C0, (403) 762-8421 or (403) 762-0270, fax (403) 762-8545; Yoho National Park, Box 99, Field, BC V0A 1G0, (604) 343-6324; and Kootenay National Park, Box 220, Radium Hot Springs, BC V0A 1M0, (604) 347-9615.

Adjoining Areas

NORTH: **Jasper National Park; Edmonton and Environs**

EAST: **Calgary and Environs**

SOUTH: **Lethbridge and the Border**

inside out

Hiking/Backpacking

Spring comes late in the Northern Rockies. Even though snow may have melted in Banff townsite by April, storms regularly dust the town with snow into early July, and it starts again in late August. Hiking trails at low elevations are usually snow-free by mid-May but remain muddy into mid-June; trails into the high country sometimes aren't passable until July, and even then hikers will need to cross snowfields. Weather is always an element to be dealt with. Switchbacks are common to cut the steepness of the grade and most trails cross talus slopes regularly—sometimes a challenge. Before starting out, check with the Parks Canada Information Office in Banff (224 Banff Ave, (403) 762-1550) for **trail status** and information, as well as campground information. Trail closures due to bears and the weather are posted, and the rangers freely offer advice about hiking, backpacking, biking, and skiing routes. You'll need a **backcountry permit** to camp, available here, too.

A variety of **guide services** offer hikes in the Banff area; among them

White Mountain Adventures, (403) 678-4099, which offers early spring half-day walks guided by a park naturalist, and moderate half-day hikes that focus on wildlife in the Bow Valley. Mountain Quest Adventure Co., (800) 269-8735, leads custom hiking (and skiing) tours in the Banff region as well as in the Kananaskis area, including guided wildflower walks and hikes with biologists tracking animals or visiting spawning beds for research purposes. For a schedule of guided interpretive walks in Banff, call (403) 762-1550; at Lake Louise, call (403) 522-3833. For a list of hiking tour companies, contact the Banff-Lake Louise Tourism Bureau, (403) 762-8421.

Try the summer version of heli-skiing, **heli-hiking.** A helicopter drops hikers off deep in the backcountry for some prime hiking through remote alpine meadows and on otherwise inaccessible ridges. One of the heli-services, Alpine Helicopters, (403) 678-4802, runs heli-hikes to the **Three Sisters** area near Canmore.

One of the few trails that's snow-free in the spring, the **Stewart Canyon Trail** offers a variety of terrain and sights and gets you deep into the mountains fast. The trailhead is past the Lake Minnewanka marina and is marked. Those wanting just a short stroll can stop at Stewart Canyon, about a 10-minute walk to a straight-walled gorge through which Stewart Creek gushes into the lake. In late May, look for blooming lady's slipper orchids under the aspen stands across the bridge and up the hill. An hour's walk will take you to the talus slopes above the lake with good views of the mountains. More ambitious hikers and those who want a long day hike can continue to Aylmer Canyon and, midsummer, to **Aylmer Pass,** which pierces the **Ghost River Wilderness Area,** a 7 4/5-mile (13-km) hike.

Nearly any time Banff township is snow-free, the **Bow River Trail** will be, too. The trailhead is on Buffalo Street (past the cemetery and southeast of town). Walk just a few minutes to get a view of Bow Falls. From there the easy trail climbs the side hill of Tunnel Mountain, with plenty of views of the Bow Valley, and ends 3 miles (5 km) later at the resorts and lodges on Tunnel Mountain Drive.

Hikers are likely to see elk at the upper reaches of a modest 1-mile (1.8-km) hike up Tunnel Mountain on the **Tunnel Mountain Trail.** This hike offers a few nice views of town and samples of surrounding flora and fauna. The trail leaves from a marked parking area on St. Julien Road.

The **Sulphur Mountain Gondola** is for sightseers and hikers only—there are no ski runs down this mountain that rises from the south end of Banff Ave. From downtown Banff, drive past the Banff Upper Hot Springs to the Sulphur Mountain Lower Terminal at 1,526 feet (1,538 m). An 8-minute gondola ride ends at the Summit Observation Deck and

Restaurant at 7,500 feet (2,285 m). The most popular walking route is **Vista Trail** to Sanson's Peak, accessible to hikers of all abilities. The gondola, (403) 762-2523, runs year-round.

From June to October, the **Lake Louise Ski Resort gondola** becomes a sightseers' and hikers' transport. It takes visitors on a 12-minute ride to the lodge atop Whitehorn Mountain. The side of the mountain continues to rise beyond Whitehorn Lodge, but it's plenty high for views clear across the Upper Bow Valley, Lake Louise, and the snow-capped mountains to the south. Hikers can roam the ski runs, which are considerably less groomed than they appear when snow-covered; look for an explosion of wildflowers in late July and early August. Meals are available at the lodge, and during peak summer months the gondola and lodge are open through dinner hours. Call (403) 522-3555 for details.

The **Mount Norquay Gondola**, (403) 762-4421, is also part of a ski resort in winter, but in summer even nonskiers can take the 7-minute ride up to the 7,000-foot (2,313-m) level. It's a 20-minute drive north of the town of Banff and operates mid-June through August. Meals are available at the mountainside lodge, but the gondola runs only until 5:30pm.

We think the custom of backcountry teahouses is highly civilized, and even if the trails to the two teahouses near Lake Louise weren't so spectacular, we'd recommend them. Luckily, the trails are worth the walk even without food and tea at the end. Perhaps the most-hiked trail in Banff National Park is the 2-mile (3.5-km) walk—although some consider it a climb—to the **teahouse at Lake Agnes.** The elevation gain is 1,333 feet (400 m) and most of that comes in the second half of the trail. The first half climbs the forested side hill above Lake Louise (the trailhead is adjacent to Chateau Lake Louise; take the paved trail around the lake and you can't miss it). After Mirror Lake it gets significantly steeper. The teahouse, first built in 1901 but reconstructed in 1981, is perched at the edge of a glacial cirque above a waterfall that plunges over the cirque wall out of Lake Agnes. The menu is usually limited to hot soup du jour, fresh-baked bread, tea or coffee, and fresh-baked cake, all made by the resident staff. There is limited seating inside the tiny lodge, but we recommend sitting out on the deck regardless of the weather. There are better glacial lakes in the Rockies, but after the climb Lake Agnes always seems stunning. The teahouse also affords great views of Lake Louise, the Upper Bow Valley, and the Lake Louise Ski Area. Food and tea are served from lunch through about 6pm; hours vary seasonally, so ask at the visitors center. Meals are cash only—a typical lunch is about $10.

The other teahouse near Lake Louise is at the end of a hike through the **Plain of Six Glaciers,** a gentler but longer 4-mile (6.7-km) hike up the valley at the end of Lake Louise. The trail climbs the hillside with a few switchbacks near the teahouse, built in 1924 as a base camp for mountaineers. Overnight accommodations are no longer available, but a menu similar to that at the Lake Agnes teahouse is served (with similar prices and hours). The teahouse is just beyond the reach of avalanches that rumble off the glaciers hanging over the surrounding cliffs. After a meal and a breather at the teahouse, we recommend that hikers extend their hike 1 mile (1.6 km) up a lateral moraine for an excellent view of **Lower Victoria Glacier.** The moraine trail is rocky and at times narrow, so wear appropriate footwear.

Some locals swear by a September hike in the **Valley of Ten Peaks** but avoid it during the summer. The spectacular scenery, gained with a hike requiring only moderate exertion, draws crowds of tourists during the peak summer months. Hikers who frequent the trails in Banff also know that fall color in **Larch Valley,** accessible via this trail, can't be bested. When September frosts have turned the larch needles golden, and the soft autumn sunlight is shining, photographers rise early and head here. The trailhead for the Valley of Ten Peaks is at the Moraine Lake parking lot, just east of Lake Louise.

The hike to **Sentinel Pass,** elevation 8,703 feet (2,611 m), is an easy 3 ½-mile (6-km) hike to the highest point reached by maintained trails in the Canadian Rockies. We recommend extending this hike to include **Eiffel Lake,** a small turquoise lake in a glacial cirque where solitude is easier to come by even during peak hiking season. The trailhead is at the end of Moraine Lake, on the road to Lake Louise.

Yoho National Park

The best-known and perhaps most popular hike in Yoho National Park begins at **Takakkaw Falls**—one of Canada's highest waterfalls with a free fall of more than 800 feet (250 m)—and heads up the Yoho River Valley to **Twin Falls.** To get to Twin Falls and back in a day would be a stretch even for the strongest hikers, but the walk up and back the Yoho Valley as far as time or energy allows is pleasant. Those with time limitations should opt for the Iceline portion of this trail, which also heads to Twin Falls. The **Iceline Trail** gets you above the tree line fast (just 1 ½ miles/2.5 km into the hike). The reward for the steep climb is some of the best views of alpine lakes and glaciers in the region. The trail parallels **Emerald Glacier.**

If you are prepared for an overnight in the backcountry, spend it at the Twin Falls Campground. After setting up camp, head back down the trail to the junction with the trail to **Yoho Glacier** and extend your hike to the glacier's terminal moraine. Those with time and inclination for a several-day sojourn into the backcountry would not be disappointed if they spent it here. Other trails that loop off the **Yoho Valley Trail** and the **Whaleback Trail** lead within shouting distance of Waterfall Valley; there's also a loop trail that leads from Yoho Pass to Emerald Lake, over Burgess Pass and back to Yoho Lake.

Kootenay National Park

Many of the hikes in Kootenay National Park are at a lower elevation than those in the national parks to the north. Hikers walk through dense fir and spruce forests rather than above tree line where vistas are plentiful. But for an array of walks to mountain lakes—ranging from only a few hundred yards to **Olive Lake** to a pleasant full-day hike to **Floe Lake**— this is a place you could spend several days on the trails in relative solitude. Contact the park, (604) 347-9615, for information and conditions.

Native peoples discovered a place where springs bubbling up from the hillside reacted with the minerals in the clay, turning it brilliant colors of ochre and red. They used the clay to decorate implements and as war paint. Later settlers began mining the colored clay and shipping it to Calgary, where the pigment was extracted for use in paint. The **Paint Pots** can be reached after a 15-minute walk on a well-developed trail that crosses a suspension bridge over the Kootenay River. The trail then crosses a bog fed by runoff from the springs uphill, where the clay is stained brilliant colors. The bubbling, brightly colored ponds are worth the short climb. The trailhead parking lot is 1 ⅕ miles (2 km) south of Marble Canyon Campground in Banff National Park.

The hike to **Stanley Glacier** is one of our favorites. The trailhead on Hwy 93 is well-marked. The trail climbs gently the first couple of miles through a reforested area that burned more than three decades ago. After that it heads up the canyon and across moraines with constant views of the glacier. The trail officially ends well short of the glacier and across the canyon from several high waterfalls. Hikers have picked their way to the waterfalls and the base of the glacier. Only experienced hikers, however, should continue up the canyon to the glacier, since the trail is difficult to follow in some places (look for cairns built by other hikers) and crosses steep and unstable talus slopes. A round-trip trek to the end of the official trail can easily be done in a morning. The trailhead is not quite 2 miles (3 km) north of the Marble Canyon Campground.

Canoeing/Kayaking

Banff and Jasper National Parks aren't destinations for those wanting to spend significant time on the water. These are hikers' parks. But canoeing and kayaking are allowed on Banff's lakes and rivers, and a pleasant few hours can be spent paddling around **Lake Louise** and nearby **Moraine**

Lake. To reach Lake Louise, take the signed exit from Hwy 1 and head up the hill (south), past Lake Louise village and several lodges. There's plenty of parking, and the lake's only a short walk away—a dauntingly long walk, though, for those who want to use their own canoes or kayaks instead of renting boats at the marina. There is no public launch at either Lake Louise or Moraine Lake, which is farther up the hill and to the left and which has the same length walk from parking lot to lakeshore.

The winds are nearly constant on larger, less-protected lakes such as **Lake Minnewanka** and **Bow Lake,** creating sizable waves. Canoes can be rented in the town of Banff at the boathouse at Bow Ave and Wolf St.

About an hour's drive west of Calgary on Hwy 1, Hwy 40 punches south into the **Kananaskis** area. This is where those serious about white-water head. **Canoe Meadows** is a day-use area where some put in and ride the rapids downstream to the takeout just north of Hwy 1 (look for the parking lot just north of the freeway off Hwy 40). Others put in at **Widowmaker** day-use area at the outlet of **Barrier Lake** (a man-made reservoir) and paddle through the Class II and Class III rapids between Widowmaker and Canoe Meadows. Be aware that water in the river can rise and fall rapidly and without warning as the dam at Barrier Lake is opened and closed.

For more quiet canoeing and kayaking, **Upper Kananaskis Lake** has miles of scenic shoreline and islands to explore. Several campsites are accessible only by boat (at the end of the lake, and up the Kananaskis River and Three Isle Creek). To get to the lake take the Elkwood turnoff from Hwy 40 and follow the signs.

Rafting

Banff National Park is hardly a mecca for whitewater rafters, but it does have a few rapids and companies that conduct guided trips. Most white-water rafting in the park is down the **Kicking Horse River** between Lake Louise and Golden. Half-day, full-day, and 2-day **trips** are offered May through August by Wet 'N' Wild Adventures, (800) 668-9119; Alpine Rafting Co., (800) 663-7080 or (604) 344-5016; and Wild Water Adventures, (403) 522-2211. Shuttle service is available from Banff, Lake Louise, Radium, and Golden.

With Class III rapids, the **Kananaskis River** isn't the place for novices running the river on their own. But a guided tour will get you safely down the best 7 1/5 miles (12 km) of the river. Three-hour tours depart Kananaskis Village twice daily (10am and 1:30pm), May through October, run by Kananaskis River Adventures, (403) 591-7773, or (403) 678-4919 in Banff. The same guide service operates a 1-day cycle and raft tour that includes a 21-mile (35-km) downhill ride from Highwood Pass (some on dirt roads) and the Kananaskis River raft trip.

Biking

Only a few of the trails in Banff National Park are open to **mountain biking,** and these change from year to year. Many of the park's trails are simply too steep and have extensive switchbacks or cross broad talus slopes. Check with the Parks Canada office on Banff Ave in the town of Banff, (403) 762-1550, before heading out; the trails approved for mountain biking are listed in the free "Trail Bicycling Guide" available there.

Trails around the town of Banff, some of which are paved, are open to **cycling,** as are all paved roads. For pleasant rides along the Bow River, take the **Bow River Trail** (start at the trailhead just north of the resorts on Tunnel Mountain for a route that's mostly downhill) or the **Fenland Trail** (park just west of the museum on Buffalo St, or at an area on Vermilion Lakes Dr). Another popular route is the **Spray Lakes Fire Road,** which is also the hiking trail to Spray Lake (park at the north end of Spray Ave). Mountain bikes can be rented in Banff townsite at The Ski Stop, 203A Bear St, (403) 762-1650, a ski shop-turned-mountain bike shop in summers; The Ski Stop at the Banff Springs Hotel, (403) 762-5333; and Bactrax at the Ptarmigan Inn, 339 Banff Ave, (403) 762-8177. Rental is by the hour and includes a helmet and water bottle.

The trails around **Canmore** range from easy rides along the river to loop rides to Banff and back. One of the more popular is the **Goat Creek Trail** to Banff. Those planning to do loops will need a trail map since few trails are marked and seldom connect directly. Many of the campgrounds in nearby **Peter Loughheed Provincial Park** are connected by the **Lodgepole, Wheeler,** and **Lakeside Trails,** about 7 1/5 miles (12 km) of paved trails open to bicycles. Maps and mountain bike rentals are available in Canmore at Altitude Sports, (403) 678-0009; Spoke 'n Edge, (403) 678-2838; Trail Sports, (403) 678-6764; Rocky Mountain Cycle, (403) 678-6770; and at Peregrine Sports, (403) 591-7453. **Guided trips** can be arranged through Cycle Tours in Kananaskis, (800) 215-2395, and Trailmasters Mountain Bike Guides in Canmore, (403) 678-0384.

Fishing

You'll need a **license** to fish in any of Canada's national parks, available at all Parks Canada offices. Regulations are available, as well; note that some streams are catch-and-release only.

The glacial-fed streams and rivers in Banff National Park aren't the best for fishing; most gush down streambeds and through gorges and are cloudy with glacial flour. Most fishing is done on **Lake Minnewanka,** where 16-foot boats with outboard motors are available for rent at the marina from mid-May to Labor Day.

Our favorite fly-fishing spot is along the **Bow River** on a broad gravel bar where the river makes a gentle S-curve, a 30-minute hike in. The water is shallow and there are riffles and pools for the trout to hide. Since the river often sweeps the gravel bar free of shrubs during spring melt, there's also plenty of room for your backcast. To get to the trailhead, drive south from the town of Banff past the Banff Springs Golf Course club-house and continue to where the road curves and heads back toward the Banff Springs Hotel. At the end of the curve, there's a wooden kiosk with a trail map and room to park a couple of vehicles. Take the trail along the riverbank and walk upstream about 25 minutes. After the trail crosses a talus slope, look down to the left and you'll see the gravel bar.

Ice Fishing

Not everyone thinks fishing is a summers-only activity. For those who want to sit in a hut and fish through the ice, the lakes west of Calgary are a natural destination, primarily because they freeze over early and stay frozen a long time. **Spray Lake,** 15 miles (22 km) south of Canmore, is fished for lake trout and whitefish; **Upper Kananaskis Lake,** 45 miles (67 km) south of Canmore, has rainbow trout. It's best to hire a guide unless you already know someone with a hut. Banff Fishing Unlimited, (403) 762-4936, puts heated huts at various lakes in the Banff and Kana-naskis areas for its clients and claims, "You catch 'em, we cook 'em." Each guided outing includes fish sandwiches and hot beverages, as well as all gear and spare clothing.

Camping

Lake Louise Campground is downhill from Chateau Lake Louise off TransCanada Hwy 1 and not actually on the lake. (Moraine Lake is a day-use area only.) The Parks Canada Information Office in Banff at 224 Banff Ave, (403) 762-1550, has more detailed campground information, includ-ing data on seasonal closures and campsite availability.

In Kootenay National Park, we prefer **Marble Canyon Campground** for its centralized location, access, and size, which makes it easier to get a campsite later in the day. Camp loop roads continue deep into the for-est; sites farther from the highway obviously have less traffic noise. The alpine trees aren't so tall that they block views of the surrounding moun-tains. One of the pleasant things to do here in the evenings is to sit back and watch the last light of day play off the mountain faces. Naturalists give programs at dusk in the amphitheater on most nights. Those inspired to take a short evening stroll can drive south just 1 mile (2 km) to the Paint Pots, while the Stanley Glacier trailhead is just 1 ½ miles (3 km) north of the campground.

Climbing

Expertise and equipment are required for any mountain or ice climbing in Banff, and those who have not climbed in the area should have a guide. Registration is not necessary but is recommended—in Banff call (403) 762-1550 and at Lake Louise call (403) 522-3833. **Guided trips** and instruction can be arranged through the M & W Guides office in Canmore, (403) 678-2642, fax (403) 678-4861.

Mount Yamnuska, a 1,500-foot (450-m) rock face, offers numerous routes and great views of the Front Range of the Rockies and the Alberta prairies. The weather is often favorable for climbing here. It's west of Canmore on Hwy 1 near the town of Exshaw.

The north face of **Chinaman's Peak** is a 1,500-foot (450-m) rock face with dramatic views of Canmore from on top. Find it southeast of Canmore near Spray Lakes. The **Grand Sentinel,** a 300-foot (90-m) quartzite pinnacle, rises near Sentinel Pass in the Valley of Ten Peaks near Lake Louise. Sport climbers often try the rock walls ringing the southern end of **Lake Louise.**

Ice climbers like the Louise Falls, adjacent to Lake Louise, and the Weeping Wall on the Icefields Parkway.

Boating

Sightseeing cruises of man-made Lake Minnewanka are offered summers only throughout the day, leaving from the marina. Lake Minnewanka Tours sail mid-May to October five times daily. For reservations call (403) 762-3473, fax (403) 762-2800, or e-mail at minntour@bowest.awinc.com. Transportation to Lake Minnewanka from the town of Banff is available through Brewster Transportation, (403) 762-6767.

Golfing

The best course in town is the **Banff Springs Hotel Golf Course,** (403) 762-6801, with 27 holes, all of which afford stunning—even distracting—mountain views. Elk love to graze the fairways, so golfers may need to play through herds. Take care not to approach the big animals, especially in spring when they defend their young elk from flying golf balls. From Banff townsite, follow the road to Bow Falls off Spray Ave.

The golf course at **Canmore** is challenging and scenic; 6 of the 18 holes flank the Bow River and Policeman's Creek. Add the course's seven ponds, and the theme here is clearly water hazards.

Horseback Riding

Horseback rides can be arranged at the Banff Springs Hotel, (403) 762-2848, and at Martin Stables Recreation Grounds, (403) 762-2832. Guided **trail rides** can be arranged throughout the park, as can **wilderness cookouts,** through Banff Trail Rides, Trail Rider Store, 132 Banff Ave, (403) 762-4551.

Downhill Skiing

Banff National Park ski resorts offer the dry powder that comes with high elevation. In fact, Banff's powder is so dry and its slopes so steep that it requires extreme snowfall before snow sticks to the highest runs. This means Banff's resorts may open a few weeks later than those in the Cascade and Sierra mountain ranges in the western United States, but they still have plenty of great snow well into May. It may take you several days to acclimate to the high elevation of the ski areas; some runs top out at more than 8,900 feet (2,700 m), which can cause shortness of breath and lightheadedness. And bring sunscreen, since it's easy to sunburn at these elevations.

All of the resorts in the park offer ski schools, private instruction, ski equipment rental, day care, and food service at the lodges. Skis can also be rented in the town of Banff at The Ski Stop, (403) 760-1650 or at The Ski Shop's store in the Banff Springs Hotel, (403) 762-5333, or fax info to (403) 762-8038 to reserve skis. A Ski Banff/Lake Louise Pass, (800) 661-1431, is a multi-day lift pass good at Mount Norquay, Sunshine Village, and Lake Louise and includes ski bus transportation between Banff hotels and the ski areas.

Until 1996, **Sunshine Village** had a reputation as an old, crowded, family ski resort, frequented mostly by skiers from Calgary. That was before the resort embarked on an aggressive expansion program and installed a high-speed quad chairlift on Goat's Eye Mountain. Now the runs cover three mountains, and Goat's Eye has a vertical drop of 1,900 vertical feet (570 m). The terrain now also includes open bowls and treed glades, plus a snowboard park. It's improved to the point that some visiting skiers are starting to talk up Sunshine. Getting to the ski area requires a 22-minute gondola ride. Call (800) 661-1676 or (403) 762-6500, fax (403) 762-6513; write to Sunshine Village Ski Resort, Box 1510, Banff, AB T0L 0C0.

Lake Louise Ski Resort has long been the choice among local skiers who sought lots of terrain, long runs, and steep slopes. It offers 17 square miles (27.4 square km) of terrain, and 62 miles (103 km) of trails. With 3 lodges, 11 lifts (including 3 quad chairs), and ski runs that sprawl across four mountain slopes, the crowds can really spread out. The parking lot is often full, even on weekdays, so expect to park on the service road and walk to the lodge. There are lockers in the lodge to store extra gear. The front side of the ski area is often crowded with beginning skiers or those in the plethora of ski classes run at the resort. We recommend taking the lifts to the top right away (especially if it's morning) and skiing in the sunshine on the eastern slopes, which are always less crowded. You can follow the afternoon sun back around the mountain to the western face in late afternoon when you are ready for some cruising runs. North of Lake Louise, across TransCanada Hwy 1; PO Box 5, Lake Louise, AB T0L 1E0; (403) 522-3555.

Mount Norquay boasts night skiing 1 night a week, proximity to the town of Banff (a 20-minute drive), and steep runs, but locals prefer the larger Lake Louise. Beginners should choose another area, since less than 15 percent of the terrain here is rated for beginning skiers, with the rest divided evenly between intermediate and black diamond runs. If there's any doubt that the runs rated intermediate in Canada would be marked with black diamonds in the United States, this area will convince you. We find the intermediate runs challenging; the diamond runs are, well, radical. The area has 25 runs served by 5 chairs, including 2 quads. It's north of Banff townsite across Hwy 1; PO Box 219, Suite 7000, Banff, T0L 0C0; (403) 762-4421, fax (403) 762-8133.

Those serious about **heli-skiing** often head for the Bugaboo and Purcell Mountains in British Columbia, but there are opportunities near Banff for those who want to be flown to the top of steep heights and rack up some major vertical feet. The heli-skiing center for the Banff area is in Golden, BC. Drive an hour west to the Esplanade Range of the Selkirk Mountains. The helicopter picks up skiers early in the morning; some services make arrangements with backcountry lodges, and most have a 4-day minimum. The heli-skiing season is best late December to mid-March, but it runs mid-December through April. These tours are for very strong skiers experienced in skiing ungroomed powder on steep slopes. Among the companies offering heli-skiing tours is Golden Alpine Holidays, PO Box 1050, Golden, BC V0A 1H0, (604) 344-7273. Or contact one of the backcountry lodges at which heli-skiers stay: Purcell Lodge, (604) 344-2639; Selkirk Lodge, (604) 344-5016; or Sorcerer Lake Lodge, (604) 344-2326.

Cross-Country Skiing

Canmore Nordic Centre, (403) 678-2400, just a few minutes drive south of Canmore, warrants a visit. The trails on which Olympic Nordic skiers raced around in 1988 are maintained in prime condition for hikers and mountain bikers when free of snow, and for cross-country skiers in winter. Roller skiers and in-line skaters can use the single three-fifths of a mile (2-km) paved trail near the center. Most trails have difficult and challenging sections, so pick up a **trail map.** Olympic athletes still train here, so at times portions of the trail system are closed for competition and workouts. Miles of trails, most of which climb the mountain above the Nordic Centre, wind through the forest and back to the Olympic stadium. About 1 ½ miles (2.5 km) of track are lighted for evening skiing. The center has a cafeteria, fitness room, and sauna. Bike and in-line skate rentals are available from Trail Sports, (403) 678-6764. The Nordic Centre is a 2 ½-mile (4-km) drive up the mountainside from Canmore.

Nordic trails abound near Banff and along TransCanada Hwy 1 to Lake Louise. Not all are groomed, however, and trail conditions vary. For information about trail snow and **grooming conditions,** ask at the visitors center at Banff or Lake Louise. The booklet "Nordic Trails in Banff National Park" is also available at both visitors centers.

A loop trail around the perimeter of frozen **Lake Louise** is groomed frequently and is perhaps the best beginners' trail in the park. It's totally flat, there are no obstructions, and the scenery doesn't get any better than this. At the upper end of Lake Louise, there's plenty of prime terrain for skiers ready for moderate backcountry skiing. Climbers frequent Louise Falls at the end of the lake, scaling the frozen ice. Watching climbers scrambling around on the face of the frozen waterfall is always a good excuse to pause in the fresh mountain air.

Skiers who leave the groomed trail to ski the **Plain of Six Glaciers** at the end of the lake should be prepared for backcountry skiing with appropriate equipment, avalanche skills, and a transceiver. The ski up the valley toward the teahouse (closed winters) can be a premier experience. Expect deep powder snow. Skiers frequent this valley, so there will be trails unless you're the first skier in after a snowfall. It's easy to spend an entire day skiing the snow-covered moraines deep into the Plain and standing in awe at the silence and glaciers spilling over the mountainsides.

Lake Louise Ski Resort grooms more than 50 miles (80 km) of trails for cross-country skiers of all abilities. Nearly a dozen are named trails with trailheads and maps posted near the resort lodge. These trails tend to be more crowded, naturally, since they are near the resort, but they are perfect for families who want to ski both downhill and cross-country at one location. Some cross-country skiers also ski at **Mount Norquay,** but the ski area does not set tracks so most trails are set only by the skiers themselves.

Wildlife

Those who want to hike the Rocky Mountains and Front Range with a purpose can participate in a **wildlife tracking hike** with a wildlife biologist. The hikes focus on tracking **wolves, cougars,** or **grizzly bears,** so the destination and route are decided by the biologist-guide and by the animals being tracked (for photo and research purposes only, of course). Mountain Quest Adventure Co., (800) 269-8735 or (403) 270-0000, will arrange such guided hikes, as well as hikes with interpretive guides who take you to trout spawning beds in mountain creeks or to see alpine meadow wildflowers.

When the highway through Banff National Park was widened in the early 1990s, **wildlife underpasses** were built as part of the road construction. Elk and deer used the underpasses, but wolves, cougars, and bears did not, so further construction in 1996 included two 15-foot (50-m) overpasses; watch for animals using these, their own bridges, as you're driving west of Banff townsite to Lake Louise.

Other Activities

Winter fun isn't limited to skiing. **Dogsledding** (about $40 for a half-hour), **canyon hiking, snowmobiling,** and **snowshoeing** are other options. Hotel ski shops can make arrangements and rent the necessary equipment. Guided half-day and full-day snowmobile tours (with hot chocolate and cookies or lunch atop a mountain) in the Kicking Horse Canyon are offered by Wet 'N' Wild Adventures, (800) 668-9119 in Alberta and BC, (604) 344-6546 elsewhere.

Seek out other recreation activities at the Canmore Recreation Centre, (403) 678-5597, and adjacent Canmore Golf and Curling Club, (403) 678-4784, fax (403) 678-2671. Both are open to the public. At the rec center there's an indoor swimming pool, weight room, and, July through April, an indoor **ice rink.**

Although sled-dog touring isn't really all the rage in the Canadian Rockies, it's yet another way to see the mountains. From Canmore, 1-hour, half-day, moonlight, and overnight sled-dog tours can be arranged through Snowy Owl Sled Dog Tours, (403) 678-4369. Mountain Quest Adventure Co., (800) 269-8735 or (403) 270-0000, will arrange 2-hour, half-day, and full-day sled-dog tours, as well as overnight tours spent in an **igloo** (a lesson in igloo building is included). **Ski-joring,** a hybridization of dogsledding and cross-country skiing, is gaining a following, and Mountain Quest will arrange a ski-joring outing on Spray Lake. Skiers are pulled along trails groomed for dogsledding by a team of sled dogs for a cross-country-ski-with-speed experience.

outside in

Attractions

The few blocks that constitute the main street through **Canmore**—Eighth Avenue—resemble a strip mall more than a true downtown, and there's little shopping other than those businesses that support the pervading spirit of outdoor recreation. Mountain bikers, snow boarders, and skiers hang out at an espresso bar, the **Coffee Mine,** Seventh Ave and Eighth St, (403) 678-2241, and will freely offer tips about trail conditions and their favorite routes. The focus in Canmore is on the mountains that rise from the south edge of the community. A group of peaks—the Three Sisters—are the mountains Canmore claims as its own.

The town of **Banff** knows its niche and makes the most of it, even going so far as to name its streets Buffalo, Wolf, Caribou, Otter, Fox, Beaver, Squirrel, Marten, Wolverine, and Bear. They all radiate off Banff Ave, which must weigh in as the most international street in the Rocky Mountains. Groups of people speak German and French, and everywhere there are Japanese tourists—in sufficient numbers to convince many locals that Banff National Park is Japan's mountain playground. Postcards, calendars, and guidebooks are all printed in Japanese, and many of the shop clerks are fluent in both English and Japanese. Despite its location in a national park, development within Banff townsite (as it is also referred to here) continues at a rigorous pace with more lodges for tourists and more condominiums for residents. Evenings, shoppers crowd the sidewalks and most stores accommodate by staying open until 10pm year-round. In winters, ski suits are the attire of choice, even for shopping and dining; summers, high-tech hiking boots seem almost mandatory. A chalet-style mall and peeled log balconies and window frames complete the town's image, as do the elk that wander through Banff year-round, grazing on trees and lawns.

Banff is a town in which fur coats and jewelry stores far outnumber espresso bars, but those in need of java should head for **Fine Grind** on Caribou St, (403) 762-2353, which also has breads and pastries perfect for assembling a hiker's or cross-country skier's lunch. The best selection of books of regional interest, guidebooks, and a decent selection of general interest books can be found at the **Banff Book & Art Den,** 110 Banff Ave, (403) 762-3919.

The **Banff Upper Hot Springs,** (403) 762-1515, on the side of Sulphur Mountain, are newly renovated, but the architecture remains true to the mountain style of stone buildings. The pool affords some of the best views around of the Bow Valley. There's a steam room as well as the hot mineral pool. Take Banff Ave south and follow the signs up the mountain, about a 10-minute drive. The parking lot is a short walk downhill from the hot springs, but there's a shuttle. Snacks are available, but we recommend heading downtown when you're relaxed and hungry.

Lake Louise Village is just off Hwy 1 and consists mainly of a small shopping mall, gas station, a couple of restaurants, and the **Lake Louise Visitors Centre,** which is particularly good. Its interpretive displays include a geologic history of the region and information about the flora and fauna, along with a small gift shop. Lake Louise itself is a drive south up the hill and past several lodges.

The town of **Radium,** in British Columbia, is little more than a support system for area vacation developments—a collection of gas stations, cafes, and a string of motels. But people don't come here for the town. In winter two ski areas—Fairmont and Panorama—are within easy driving distance. But the main attraction here is the **Radium Hot Springs,** which are within the boundaries of Kootenay National Park. Hot water that gushes from the mountainside is captured in a large hot pool, but unlike some hot springs, these waters are not odorous with sulfur or other minerals. The water temperature varies with the season—in winter and spring the snowmelt cools the thermally heated water, although it's still comfortably warm even in the coldest temperatures. Those staying in Kootenay or Banff National Parks overnight just need to show their park entrance and overnight-use receipts to use the springs; an additional $1 use-fee is charged by the springs for those not staying in the park (but still bring your park entrance receipt). Swimsuits and towels are available for rent at the hot springs if you've forgotten to pack yours. (See Lodgings, below, for additional information on the resort.)

Calendar of Events

There is always plenty of snow and ice for the **Banff/Lake Louise Winter Festival**, held the last week of January. Call (403) 762-8421 for details.

The Banff Centre on St. Julien Rd, (403) 762-6300, hosts the **Banff Arts Festival** every year from early June through August. The festival brings world-class musicians, dancers, actors, and artists to Banff to teach workshops and classes and to give public performances. The workshops change through the summer, so call ahead for a schedule. Entertainment continues year-round, but is less regular than when the festival is going on. For more information call (403) 762-6100.

The winners of an annual competition have their films shown at the annual **Banff Festival of Mountain Films,** held in November. For details, call (403) 762-8421.

Restaurants

Coyotes Deli and Grill ☆☆   The menu borrows heavily from the American Southwest—chili peppers permeate the menu, from the caesar salad to the British Columbia salmon. We don't usually order salmon when we're two provinces away from the ocean, but in this case, the fish doesn't suffer from geographic distance. The salmon fillet is grilled and topped with a spicy honey glaze, served on a bed of rice flavored with chopped peppers and sautéed summer squash. For the most part, the fare's a refreshing twist on what would otherwise be standard cafe cuisine. Presentation helps. Entrees come garnished just right with a dusting of cheese, herbs, or red bell pepper. Microbrews followed espresso into the Canadian interior; the menu here offers a modest selection from Calgary microbreweries. *Downtown, a half-block off Banff Ave; 206 Caribou St, Banff; (403) 762-3963; breakfast, lunch, dinner every day; AE, MC, V; no checks; $$.*

Cilantro ☆   This cozy cafe is located at Buffalo Mountain Lodge but it's a good choice for anyone wanting dinner with a casual edge. The menu, which leans toward Southwest fare, ranges from pizza to pasta to chicken and seafood entrees but we recommend one of the pizzas from the wood-fired oven. The crust is crisp and the ingredients, which change seasonally, are usually innovative and work well together. The ambience is created by rustic peeled logs and wood paneling. When the weather allows, there's dining on a small patio outside. *3 miles (4.8 km) from downtown Banff on Tunnel Mountain Rd; PO Box 1325, Banff; (403) 760-3008, lunch, dinner every day; AE, DC, DIS, MC, V; no checks; $-$$.*

Hard Rock Cafe ☆   The Hard Rock Cafe brought its reputation for raucous dining to the Canadian Rockies and renovated a former outdoor clothing store on a prime corner in downtown Banff. Diners eat upstairs in the two-story restaurant; on the street level there's an extravagantly large entrance where diners queue up for souvenir Hard Rock T-shirts. The space given to souvenir sales seems at the expense of the bar, which is jammed in the back. For dining in quiet—or at least at a low enough din level to discuss the day's goings-on—this isn't the place. Here diners eat to the thump of hard rock music while looking out wall-to-wall windows at the peaks. The menu offers no surprises, nor does it disappoint. Entrees range from gourmet burgers to pasta primavera to grilled chicken breast to caesar salad, which can be washed down with a selection of microbrews from Calgary. The selection of late night spots in Banff is limited, so this is the place to be seen. *In the center of downtown Banff; 137 Banff Ave, Banff; (403) 760-2347; lunch, dinner every day; AE, MC, V; no checks; $-$$.*

Sherwood House   Other than the restaurants at the motels, Sherwood House is one of the few choices for finer dining in Canmore. It's a contemporary building designed to look old-lodge, and for the most part it works. A generously sized patio offers picnic-table seating, perfect on warm summer days. The menu focuses on regional fare—an Alberta peppercorn fillet, Alberta buffalo broil, baked rainbow trout, and British Columbia salmon—but the entrees are more complicated than they sound. The buffalo broil, for example, is topped with onions and bell pepper and served on garlic toast, the combination of which overshadows any subtle flavor the buffalo may have had. *At the west end of Canmore's main street, at 8th St and 8th Ave; 838 8th St, Canmore; (403) 678-5211; breakfast, lunch, dinner every day; AE, MC, V; no checks; $$.*

Lodgings

Emerald Lake Lodge ☆☆☆   Summer or winter, you'll be well taken care of at this lodge in the heart of Yoho National Park, surrounded by the Rocky Mountains and stunning views. Part of a trio of Rocky Mountain lodges (which includes Deer Lodge at nearby Lake Louise and Buffalo Mountain Lodge in Banff), the Emerald Lake Lodge complex now includes 24 buildings (four-plexes and a few duplexes) as well as the main lodge, which has accommodations upstairs. Winter here is nearly as popular as summer: each room has a fieldstone fireplace, and decor includes twig chairs for curling up with a book on snowy winter days. Cross-country skiing and walking/snowshoeing trails circle the lake and the glacial basin beyond. There's a nice trail around the lake, as well as more serious hikes nearby to Sherbrook Lake and Takakkaw Falls. Hikers can order a sack lunch from the dining room.

Some rooms also have a balcony, large enough for a couple of chairs when the weather is warm. The lakeside buildings have the best views; buildings 32 and 33 offer the most privacy. The big lodge, now remodeled, still retains the feel of an old parks lodge. In a building called the club house, there's a hot tub and sauna; upstairs in the main lodge is a billiards room. The dining room menu boasts plenty of wild game—medallions of venison, buffalo, and caribou—as well as domestic fare such as veal, steak, and chicken entrees. Smoking and children are allowed, but there are no TVs. There's also no parking at the lodge—visitors leave their cars at a parking lot and call the bellhop for transport in a van. *5 miles (8 km) north of the Trans-Canada Hwy in Yoho National Park; PO Box 10, Field, BC V0A 1G0; (604) 343-6321; AE, MC, V; checks OK; $$$.*

The Lodge at Kananaskis ☆☆☆   The Lodge at Kananaskis was built in 1988 on the same mountainside as Nakiska, a ski area built on Mount

Allan for the Olympic alpine ski events, and a 5-minute shuttle ride away. Today most serious skiers head for Fortress Ski Area, almost 17 miles (28 km) south on Hwy 40, where there's more consistent snow and a better variety of runs that accommodate skiers of all abilities. Nakiska was not built without controversy and the naysayers' claims weren't without merit: the ski area is located in an area that typically receives less snow and less frequent snowfall than other areas, and severe chinook winds blow out of the mountains regularly. (Nakiska compensates by having enough snowmaking equipment to cover 85 percent of the ski runs.) The Lodge at Kananaskis offers ski packages that include vouchers to ski both Nakiska and Fortress, but the shuttle only runs to Nakiska. Summers, golfers play two 18-hole golf courses, which are challenging with narrow, tree-lined fairways and rolling greens.

The lodge lives up to the expectations for a Canadian Pacific Hotel, both in luxury and price. The site on the mountainside is nothing short of spectacular, there are indoor and outdoor whirlpools, an indoor pool, a sauna, a steam and exercise room, half a dozen tennis courts, and six restaurants with fare ranging from French bistro to Greek. Rooms have fieldstone fireplaces and some have private whirlpools. This is a favorite place for cross-country skiers who drive to the point the highway is closed (south of Fortress, Hwy 40 closes in winters) and simply ski up the road. Summers, mountain bikers ride over the pass, preferring the north-to-south route since it's a gentle uphill on the north side of the pass and a more severe downhill on the south side. *60 miles (110 km) west of Calgary on Hwy 1—turn south on Hwy 40 and drive 14 miles (23 km) to the Nakiska turnoff (adjacent to Nakiska Ski Area); Kananaskis Village, Canmore, AB T0L 2H0; (800) 441-1414 or (403) 591-7711, fax (403) 591-7770; AE, DC, DIS, MC, V; no checks; $$$.*

Post Hotel ☆☆☆   While the Post Hotel cannot boast uninterrupted mountain views, its location in the village is central and the Pipestone River flanks its grounds. It's a smaller, more quiet alternative to Chateau Lake Louise—charming, yet subdued without tourist groups tromping through the lobby. Built in the 1940s as a backcountry lodge near Lake Louise, the Post was purchased in the late 1970s by Swiss brothers George and Andre Schwarz. A decade later, they renovated the lodge into a restaurant and lobby area and built an addition, which now has 98 rooms. The hotel retains the ambience of a country inn with rustic pine and timber construction, but is also elegant and contemporary in style and feel. Rooms have luxurious touches, such as heated slate floors in the bathrooms, wood-burning fieldstone fireplaces, balconies (some with views), down quilts, or whirlpool tubs, and range from standard to loft suites.

There are also two riverside log cabins available, which are more romantic, private, and spacious. The hotel's kitchen is overseen by Chef Wolfgang Vogt, whose menu combines regional ingredients with international influences. The Post Hotel is one of the few inns in Banff that is independent of larger hotel chains (the Schwarz brothers also own Storm Mountain Lodge in Kootenay Provincial Park). The hotel is closed from mid-October to mid-December. *In Lake Louise Village adjacent to TransCanada Hwy 1; 200 Pipestone Rd, Lake Louise, T0C 1E0; (800) 661-1586 or (403) 522-3989; MC, V; checks OK; $$$.*

The Rimrock Resort Hotel ☆☆☆ When it comes to luxury lodging in Banff townsite, the historic Banff Springs Hotel certainly isn't the only game in town. In several ways, we prefer the Rimrock. It doesn't have the history and reputation of an old elegant hotel, but the Rimrock has a graciousness that befits a fine hotel, and it's well-designed for guest convenience. And the view simply can't be beat if you book a room that looks out on the Bow Valley. The hotel is surrounded by forest but is perched on the sidehill of Sulphur Mountain, directly below Banff Upper Hot Springs (although a walk up the road to the hot springs would be a hike) and a 10-minute drive to the town of Banff. The rooms in what's considered the back of the hotel have views of Sulphur Mountain. The hotel offers all the expected amenities, including aerobics, squash courts, an indoor swimming pool, and, when the weather accommodates, a broad sun deck. The Rimrock's restaurant, Ristorante Classico, specializes in Northern Italian cuisine. Skiers should ask about the ski storage service and ski packages that include lift tickets at local ski areas. *On Mountain Ave, a 10-minute drive southeast of Banff townsite; PO Box 1110, Banff, AB T0L 0C0; (800) 661-1587 or (403) 762-3356, fax (403) 762-4132; AE, DIS, MC, V; no checks; $$$.*

Banff Springs Hotel ☆☆ The century-plus old Banff Springs Hotel looks like a castle, even more so in winter when it's surrounded by snow-covered trees and mountains. The thick stone walls and castle-style hallways speak to the Scottish Baronial design, and 828 rooms further lend the impression. The hotel suffers from a reputation for grand public rooms and small and sometimes neglected guest rooms, but recent renovations have spiffed up the rooms and added a state-of-the-art spa facility. Still, by contemporary standards the rooms are modestly sized and the views from most are hardly commanding. Those seeking privacy and cozy intimacy in the public sitting rooms and lounges will probably be disappointed, since the hotel is on the must-see lists of many non-guests. From the public parking areas far down the road, tourists constantly stream through the lobby or indulge in a drink at one of the lounges just for the opportunity of a look-see. And overnight lodging here is included on many of the hundreds of bus tours to Banff National Park. *Along the Bow River on the outskirts of Banff townsite; PO Box 960, Banff, AB T0L 0C0; (800) 441-1414 or (403) 762-2211, fax (403) 762-5755; AE, DC, DIS, MC, V; checks OK; $$$.*

Chateau Lake Louise ☆☆   The chateau by the lake that is its namesake was built in 1890 but underwent a multi-million dollar renovation in the early 1990s. Like those of the Banff Springs Hotel, most of the Chateau Lake Louise's 515 rooms are modestly sized, and this hotel, too, is on the itinerary of many bus tours through the area. Its reputation lures hundreds of non-guests to cruise through the lobbies and linger in the lounges just to get a taste of luxurious living. Winters afford more privacy, although that, too, is relative—any winter we've been here, the lakeside and hotel are thick with tourists. A stay here is a sampling of elegance; be prepared to pay a premium for rooms with a view of the lake. Among the activities is ice skating on Lake Louise (some winters the makeshift rink surrounds an ice sculpture of a castle). The hotel provides hot chocolate and a bonfire at rink side. Those with a romantic streak can take a moonlit tour around the lake in a horse-drawn sleigh. *At lakeside on Lake Louise; Lake Louise, AB T0L 1E0; (800) 441-1414 or (403) 522-3511, fax (403) 522-3834; AE, DIS, MC, V; checks OK; $$$.*

Radium Hot Springs Resort ☆☆   It's apparent golf is the show at this resort—nearly all the rooms look out onto fairways or greens of the 18-hole course. Non-golfers can sit on the balcony of their rooms and watch the players; relax on the patio outside the swimming pool (which is indoors); or use the tennis, squash, or racquetball courts. The resort has 118 guest rooms including many two-bedroom condominiums. The condos and the rooms the resort calls villas are a vigorous walk from the full-service dining room. In summers, the choice of eateries is plentiful in Radium, a 10-minute drive north. Many restaurants and other tourism-based businesses close during winter, but the resort has a bed-and-breakfast package. Golf and ski packages are also available. *South of Radium on Hwy 93; Box 310, Radium Hot Springs, BC V0A 1M0; (800) 665-3585 or (604) 347-9311, fax (604) 347-9588; AE, DIS, MC, V; no checks; $$$.*

Storm Mountain Lodge ☆☆   Although technically located in Banff National Park, the boundary between that park and Kootenay National Park in British Columbia is just down the highway from Storm Mountain Lodge. This is the place to stay if it's remote lodging that you want—remote but still accessible by highway. Located on Vermilion Pass at an elevation of 5,600 feet (1,708 m), the lodge was built in 1922 by the Canadian Pacific Railway. It's rustic, but loaded with alpine ambience.

Each of the 12 single-room log cabins has a wood-burning fireplace, and the fire's kept blazing often throughout the summer in the main lodge. The bighorn sheep head hanging above the lodge fireplace is supposedly the second-largest sheep ever shot in the early days of the park when hunting was still allowed. The lodge dining room serves up appropriately hearty fare, and will pack a hiker's lunch. It also serves afternoon tea. Fifty miles (80.5 km) of hiking trails originate near the lodge. True to the name, the winds howl across Storm Mountain and Vermilion Pass late into spring and early in fall, so the beds come with down comforters. The lodge is open late May to early September, but at press time, the lodge was closed until the 1998 season. *At Vermilion Pass on Hwy 93; PO Box 670, Banff, AB T0L 0C0; (403) 762-4155; AE, MC, V; $$$.*

Buffalo Mountain Lodge ☆ As the town of Banff spreads up Tunnel Mountain, lodges that used to afford a bit of privacy because they were comfortably outside town are now losing that nicety. Still, it's pleasant to stay up out of the main Banff tourist fray and feel like you are at a lodge in the mountains. Buffalo Mountain Lodge is lodge-style to a fault, with all the appropriate trappings—peeled log structure, imposing fieldstone fireplace surrounded by lodge furniture, mounted animal heads on the walls, and plenty of stunningly beautiful photos of the national park. The lodge is run by Canadian Rocky Mountain Resorts, as is the Emerald Lake Lodge in Yoho National Park to the west. Rooms at Buffalo Mountain are in newer and renovated buildings, leftovers from a previous lodge. We recommend the newer rooms, which have wood-burning fireplaces, twig chairs, and private balconies, but are otherwise standard motel-style. Rooms numbered in the 700s–900s offer the most privacy from Tunnel Mountain Rd. Ask for an upper-level room so vehicles are not parked directly outside your door. Outside the peak tourist seasons we've found upkeep on the rooms spotty, but reported shortcomings have been quickly remedied. *3 miles (4.8 km) from downtown Banff on Tunnel Mountain Rd; PO Box 1326, Banff, AB T0L 0C0; (800) 661-1367, fax (403) 762-4495; AE, MC, V; no checks; $$$.*

Lady Macdonald Country Inn ☆ Not large enough to be a lodge yet larger than a traditional bed and breakfast, the Lady Macdonald Country Inn might be just the right size for those seeking personalized service and a home-style ambience, but a greater sense of autonomy than sometimes comes with a B&B stay. The Lady Macdonald has 11 rooms, some of which have views of the mountains, fireplaces, or lofts for family accommodations; two have sitting areas in turrets. The largest turret room affords a view of the Three Sisters mountains. Breakfast is served in a solarium. Downtown Canmore is an ambitious walk from the Lady

Macdonald and while some would consider the location of the inn on Bow Valley Trail (the old Hwy 1) that parallels TransCanada Hwy 1 a plus, those who would be disappointed to be staying just off a major road should look elsewhere. *On Hwy 1A in Canmore; Box 2128, Canmore, AB T0L 0M0; (800) 567-3919 or (403) 678-3665, fax (403) 678-7201; AE, MC, V; checks OK; $$-$$$.*

Wedgewood Mountain Inn ☆   Sandwiched between the seventh fairway of the Canmore Golf Course and the Bow River, the Wedgewood specializes in privacy—and breakfast, which is what the guests here most often talk about. Innkeepers Kathy Claxton and Frankie Michaluk claim they can serve a month's worth of breakfasts without ever repeating the menu, a claim that earned them the designation of the best B&B in Alberta by a regional food magazine. The famed breakfasts include homemade granola with spiced apple yogurt, fruit such as gingered peaches, and entrees like the Wedgewood version of eggs Benedict—poached eggs on a croissant with tomato, bacon, and mornay sauce. Sometimes there's stuffed French toast and strawberry and banana chocolate chip muffins. The 1980s-vintage house looks much older, with rough-cut cedar siding. Decor is eclectic country collectibles and antiques. There's a TV room and a living room for guest use, but when the weather accommodates it's much nicer to relax in the backyard, which backs onto the river. The three guest rooms all have private baths. The innkeepers know why visitors come to Canmore, so their garage is available to store mountain bikes, skis, or even to dry out your tent if you've fled the campgrounds for more civilized accommodations. *West of the Canmore Recreation Centre; 1004 Larch Place, Canmore, AB T1W 1S7; (403) 678-4494, fax (403) 678-5017; MC, V; checks OK; $$-$$$.*

Westridge Country Inn ☆   Despite its name, the Westridge Country Inn is more motel than country inn. But along what has become motel row in Canmore, this one stands out for its charm, trying hard to be more inn-like than motel-like. The Westridge opened a new building with plenty of peeled log appointments in 1996. The 30 rooms in the new building have fireplaces and balconies, some with a view of the Three Sisters. Continental breakfast is included, and the dining room is pleasant. Skiers will appreciate the sauna and ski room to store equipment between excursions. Ask for a room on the second level in the new building. *On Hwy 1A in Canmore; 1719 Bow Valley Trail, Canmore, AB T0L 0M0; (800) 268-0935 or (403) 678-5221, fax (403) 678-3352; AE, DC, MC, V; no checks; $$-$$$.*

Backcountry Cabins

The **Shadow Lake Lodge and Cabins,** west of Banff on Shadow Lake, are open summers to hikers or mountain bikers, but we think it's more fun to cross-country ski into the lodge during winter. The log cabin accommodations are heated and have feather down comforters to ward off frigid nights. Expect rustic conditions (i.e., outdoor plumbing). The route in is a 9-mile (14.5 km) ski from the Red Earth parking lot, 12 miles west of Banff on TransCanada Hwy 1. The lodge is also accessible for hikers via the Gibbon Pass Trail from Hwy 93. The full meal plan includes afternoon tea, and, like Skoki Lodge, is pricier than most US Forest Service cabins at more than $100/night per person ($85 for each additional person). The lodge opens to skiers for the December holiday season and again mid-February to mid-April, snow permitting. Summer season is late June to mid-October. For reservations write PO Box 2606, Dept S, Banff, AB T0L 0C0; or call (403) 762-0116, fax (403) 760-2866.

Built more than 65 years ago as one of the first ski resorts in Western Canada, **Skoki Lodge** is still servicing cross-country skiers (and hikers) willing to take the 6 ³/₅-mile (11-km) trek over moderate to difficult trails to the inn. The lodge is in the backcountry northeast of Lake Louise Ski Resort, and the trailhead is at the Lake Louise Ski Area—from there the trail crosses Boulder Pass to Ptarmigan Lake and heads up Deception Pass to the lodge. Transportation to the trailhead at Temple Lodge in the back bowl of Lake Louise Ski Area is included in the overnight fee (which, at more than $100/night per person, is steeper than most US backcountry cabins, but does include all meals). Since the trail is over two mountain passes, skiers should have backcountry skis; skins are also recommended. Those booking reservations here, summer or winter, should be in reasonable physical condition and have some experience in mountainous backcountry. Cross-country skiers would be wise to carry transceivers and be aware that avalanches are always a possibility. This is a mountainous region frequented by grizzly bears in summer. Hikers and skiers should carry their own water. The lodge and cabins are rustic—no electricity, no indoor plumbing—but the lodge has a wood-fired sauna. Meals and afternoon tea are included in the rate. Write PO Box 5, Lake Louise, AB T0L 1E0; call (403) 522-3555 or fax (403) 522-2095, for reservations or information.

More Information

Banff/Lake Louise Tourism Bureau: (403) 762-8421 or (403) 762-0270.

Banff National Park: (403) 762-1550.

Kananaskis Country: (403) 297-3362 or in Canmore at (403) 678-5508.

Kootenay National Park: (604) 347-9615.

Royal Canadian Mounted Police: (403) 762-2226 in Banff; (403) 522-3811 in Lake Louise.

Weather report: (403) 762-2088.

Yoho National Park: (604) 343-6324.

Calgary
and Environs

Including Drumheller, and the Bow River Valley.

More than any other Canadian province, Alberta boasts varied terrain—from mountain ridges at the western provincial border, which rise to 12,136 feet (3,700 m), to the shortgrass prairies and eastern badlands. During the ice ages, vast ice sheets covered the area and when the latest sheet receded 10,000 years ago, it left the land scoured, its prairies interrupted here and there by glacial debris hundreds of feet deep. Meltwater from the receding ice gouged deep channels, called coulees, and swept away soil—leaving regions such as the badlands east of Calgary near Drumheller.

Calgary is a sprawling city of the Alberta plains, although you can see the mountains from here. The city sits poised on the edge of prairies still cut by rivers fed with today's meltwater from the Rockies. Here and there on undeveloped land are erratics, huge boulders brought hundreds of miles from the north by flowing ice sheets in the last Ice Age, left behind when the glaciers melted. In north Calgary there's Nose Hill, a glacial moraine elevated above the surrounding shortgrass prairie, now the best vantage point from which to see the whole cityscape.

With a climate much more forgiving than that of Edmonton 4 hours farther north, Calgary's weather systems sweep out onto the plains from the Rockies, which stop the systems long enough for snow and heavy rains to be dumped on the western mountain slopes and for temperatures to moderate. It snows in Calgary, which is at 3,500 feet (1,050 m) elevation, but almost as soon as the white stuff's on the ground, a chinook wind—temperatures can warm more than 20°F (6.6°C) in a few hours—sweeps in and melts the snow. When Calgarians want to play in the snow, most drive an hour west to Kananaskis or Banff.

Like Edmonton, Calgary boomed with the development of oil fields. The huge Leduc oil field was discovered in 1947, and discovery of other oil and natural gas repositories soon followed. The city's population doubled to more than half a million people between 1959 and 1979. Oil workers frequented Edmonton, but oil executives worked in Calgary, earning the city a reputation as a white-collar counterpart. Oil money flowed into the city in the early '70s, and with it came the glass skyscrapers that dominate downtown. Gone is the cow town image, along with the sprawling railroad yards that once served as the center from which Alberta beef and wheat were shipped east. Today's Calgary has some glitz and is poised to lead western Canada into the next century. Bank buildings went up in Calgary to handle all that money rolling in off the oil fields, beginning the era of the downtown shopping mall: Toronto-Dominion Square spreads across several downtown blocks via a skywalk system.

The annual Calgary Stampede in mid-July lures thousands of cowboys and tourists to see the biggest rodeo on the continent. The stampede began in 1912 as a one-time event, financed by four local wealthy ranchers. (That was the same year the famous US industrialist Andrew Carnegie built Calgary's first public library, which is still in use.) The stampede was revived in 1919 and in 1923 became an annual event. Now, it's a citywide party, as much as it is a chance to ride buckin' broncs.

The province of Alberta boasts huge wheat farms, cattle ranches that ship famous Alberta beef, and logging industries through the forested northern and western mountains. The Rockies here draw millions of tourists to the region to see alpine lakes, glaciers spilling off the edges of icefields, rivers milky with glacial flour, delicate wildflowers that thrive at high elevations, and jagged peaks defined by wind and ice. While Alberta's premier city is distanced from the range, Calgary takes advantage of its terrain much as the province as a whole does. It's a city of trails—even its freeways have names such as Deerfoot Trail, Blackfoot Trail, and Crowchild Trail. But the most impressive trails are the 100 miles (160 km) of graveled or paved walking and cycling paths that flank the Bow and Elbow Rivers, which cut through Calgary's neighborhoods and downtown. Through decades of growth, Calgarians protected the riverbanks by creating flowing green public areas laced with trails and plenty of benches. The confluence of the two big water arteries is just east of the downtown area in the Inglewood District, and where the Bow River curves around the southeast portion of the city, Fish Creek Park was created as a broad forested buffer on both sides of the river. Visitors will find plenty of natural beauty to appreciate in Calgary—not just the distant view of the Rockies.

Getting There

TransCanada Highway 1 runs east and west through Calgary; Hwy 93 is the main road north to Edmonton (176 miles/294 km) and south to the US border (151 miles/244 km). Most major airlines serve Calgary International Airport, a 20-minute drive northeast of the city center.

Those who want to recreate but didn't arrive in the Calgary area with their own equipment can still be well-outfitted. The University of Calgary Outdoor Centre rents equipment that ranges from tents, backpacks, sleeping bags, camp cooking stoves, car racks, and topographical maps to rafts, canoes, sea and river kayaks, wet suits, rock and ice climbing equipment, in-line and hockey skates, bikes, and skis, both downhill and cross-country. The office is open daily except major holidays and equipment can be reserved; call (403) 220-5038. The rental office is at the University of Calgary, 2500 University Drive NW, and the best access for gear pick-up and return is from the south via University Gate (off 24 Avenue NW); drive by the Dining Centre on to the Outdoor Centre, just east of the Speed Skating Oval. Park in the 15-minute loading zone.

Get more information about Calgary by contacting the Calgary Visitors & Convention Bureau, Suite 200, 237-8 Ave SE, Calgary, AB T2G 0K8, (800) 661-1678 or (403) 263-8510, fax (403) 262-3809; e-mail: destination@visitor.calgary.ab.ca. Or check out their Web site on the Internet: http://www.visitor.calgary.ab.ca.

Adjoining Areas

NORTH: **Edmonton and Environs; Jasper National Park**

SOUTH: **Lethbridge and the Border**

WEST: **Banff National Park**

inside out

Horseback Riding

Alberta is horse country and abounds with numerous **guest ranches** and outfitters offering **horse-packing trips**. The largest concentration of ranches is southwest of Calgary where the prairies butt up against the foothills of the Rockies; but there are guest ranches all along the eastern edge of the mountains from the US-Canada border to far northern

Alberta. Some outfitters have ranches where permanent cabins and lodges serve as a base camp, and guests either take day rides into the mountains or set out on a several-day stay, riding into the backcountry for a couple of nights in tent camps maintained by the outfitter. Some have dance halls where guests dance the night away; others have moving camps, where the tents are erected nightly in different areas in the backcountry and cooking is truly done beside campfires. See Ranches and Resorts, below, for more information on working ranches.

In Calgary, Happy Trails Riding Stable, (403) 251-3344, offers guided and self-guided trail rides, as well as hay and carriage rides through **Fish Creek Park.** To get to the stables take 37 Street SW south from Anderson Road S, and turn east on 130 Ave. Past Woodpath Rd, look for the stable signs.

The heart of Albert's ranching country is the **Turner Valley** in the Kananaskis Country, southwest of Calgary. The following **outfitters** come well-recommended:

Alberta Frontier Guiding & Outfitting sets up base camp—tents, sauna, and bonfire pit—just a short walk from Eagle Lake at the edge of **Banff National Park.** The setting's bucolic with a creek running by the base camp; day rides extend above the tree line with lunch on the trail. Evenings, dinner is at fireside. Box 1868, Sundre, AB T0M 1X0, (403) 638-2897, fax (403) 638-2594.

Anchor D Guiding & Outfitting runs rides by the hour, day, weekend, or week through the mountains in the **Kananaskis area.** A seven-day Great Divide Ride is mostly in the high country; a six-day Lost Trail Trip is limited to experienced riders only. The ranch is a 45-minute drive southwest of Calgary. PO Box 656, Black Diamond, AB T0L 0H0, (403) 933-2867, fax (403) 933-2255.

Bar JJ Outfitting offers day rides, as well as pack trips, with champion rodeo cowboy Jim Kelts, who runs the ranch with his wife, Connie Kelts. Trail and backcountry rides are arranged to fit particular preferences. Guests can also participate in **brandings** and **cattle drives.** Box 141, Millarville, AB T0L 1K0, (403) 931-2537.

McKenzies' Trails West combines multi-day trail rides into the mountains northwest of Calgary with **fishing** and backcountry camping. Evenings are spent around the campfire; days are spent riding and fishing. Box 971, Rocky Mountain House, AB T0M 1T0, (403) 845-6708, fax (403) 845-4389.

Sunset Guiding & Outfitting has been taking visitors into the mountains northwest of Calgary for 20 years. Base camp for riders is a 90-minute drive northwest of Calgary, where there is a cookhouse, heated sleep cabins, hot tub, and shower. From there riders can sign on for 3- to

7-day **mountain pack trips** with tent camping. Box 340, Cremona, AB T0M 0R0, (403) 637-2361; Sunset Base Camp (summers), (403) 637-2576.

Those who want to drive cattle can sign on for a 3-day **cattle drive** every July, moving 200 head of cattle to summer pastures with Buffalo Head Cattle Drive. They provide the experience, you drive the cattle into the Canadian Rockies. Box 96, Longview, AB T0L 1H0, (403) 558-2345.

A brochure listing members of the Alberta Outfitters Association, along with details about the amenities and offerings at various ranches throughout Alberta, is available from Box 277, Caroline, AB T0M 0M0, (403) 722-2692.

Biking

Calgary is a city of fitness enthusiasts; nearly any time of day the paved paths through the city are being used by cyclists, joggers, walkers, and in-line skaters. To indulge its interest in outdoor exercise, Calgary built and maintains 130 miles (210 km) of paths within the city. Most cycling shops rent bicycles, about $20 for an afternoon, and a **bike trail map** is widely available for $1. One of the most convenient rental shops is in downtown Calgary—R N' R/Tech Shop, (403) 266-3606, at Eau Claire Market—from which a number of trails can be accessed. Bike rental is by the half- and full-day; in-line skates are available by the hour. Skates are also available at the Sports Swap, (403) 261-8026, 11th Ave and 7th St.

Cyclists can take their bikes with them on the front and rear cars of light rail transit trains between 10am and 3pm only; it's a convenient way to get to the suburbs where there are pleasant bike rides. The $1.50 one-way-fare tickets are available from the machines on the train platforms, exact change required. Light rail's easy to navigate: the Brentwood train goes to northwest Calgary, the Anderson train goes to south Calgary, and the Whitehorn train goes to northeast Calgary.

A favorite route of local cyclists is around **Glenmore Reservoir** in south Calgary, a man-made reservoir with two yacht clubs and the largest inland sailing school on the continent. Take the light rail to Heritage Dr and ride west to the reservoir. There's a biking/walking path around the reservoir. For a long half-day or leisurely full-day ride, start downtown and ride the trail along the winding **Elbow River** to the reservoir, then around the reservoir and back. Cafes along the way are plentiful and convenient for a lunch stop.

For a full day's ride, take the **Southern Loop Trail** that rims Calgary to the southeast, starting at downtown Calgary. Ride east along the Bow River and keep going to **Fish Creek Provincial Park,** an unmaintained park at the southern edge of town (although suburbs already are growing beyond the park). The trails through Fish Creek are dirt and some don't connect, so those not wanting to find their way through the park should take Canyon Meadows Dr to 14 St SW and north to Glenmore Reservoir. Continue up the east side of Glenmore Reservoir, unless you're looking for more distance, then ride around the reservoir and back to the Elbow River and continue north on the path on one side to downtown. Riding constantly, the tour requires 5 to 6 hours.

Biking/walking paths flank the **Bow River** on both banks through the length of downtown Calgary. A nice way to tour the central city is by simply riding east from downtown to one of the many bridges that crosses the river—we like the route to 12th St SE, where the trail crosses to St. George's Island Park and the Calgary Zoo, then to Memorial Dr. From there, ride back toward downtown to 10 St NW and the Kensington District, where there's a bridge back across the river. But pause long enough to browse the shops and espresso bars of Kensington, Calgary's yuppie area.

Mountain bikers head to **Nosehill Park;** the trails aren't official or mapped, but the area is used enough that trails lead to all parts of the park. There are no roads through the park, but there are access points off 14 St NW and John Laurie Blvd, where parking is allowed.

Canoeing/Kayaking

Both the Bow and Elbow Rivers are navigable for canoers and kayakers. In most places the banks are gentle, and since walking trails flank the river, the put-ins and take-outs are numerous.

A pleasant 2-hour canoe trip begins at **Shouldice Park** in northwest Calgary; take Bowness Rd west and park at the Shouldice Park Community Centre parking lot. The canoe launch is just downstream of the Bowness Rd bridge. Take a longer canoe trip by putting in at **Bowness Park** farther west; continue on Bowness Rd and the park will be on your left just before you cross the Bow River. Local canoers also put in at **Bearspaw Dam** upriver; take Bearspaw Dam Rd west from Bowness Rd and put in below the dam. The river is broad, so stay near one of the banks to see the best variety of birds and wildlife. Canoers can take out west of **Prince's Island Park**; pick a place with enough beach to drag the canoe up to the trees and lock it to a tree with a cable chain. Those with two vehicles should park one in a lot near Eau Claire Market or on the street just west of the market. (You can take out at Prince's Island Park but the portage to the parking lot there is significantly longer.) Another take-out that's accessible is east of downtown on the north side of the river at

St. Patrick's Island, just short of the Calgary Zoo (you'll see the 12th St bridge to the zoo and a broad sandbar on the left bank, except in very high water). There's a parking area up the bank.

Those wanting longer day of canoeing can take out at **Inglewood Bird Sanctuary,** or at **Fish Creek Provincial Park** at the confluence of Fish Creek and the Bow River. Both of these take-outs require portage around a weir just downstream from St. Patrick's Island (watch for the signs since the weir is very dangerous; the portage takeout is marked). Allow 6 to 7 hours from Shouldice Park to Fish Creek Park, less if paddling steadily.

The section of the Bow River that actually passes through Fish Creek Park is also navigable, but put-ins and take-outs are less plentiful because much of the park is undeveloped. Trails crisscross the park, but roads do not.

Hovercraft tours of the **Red Deer River** near Drumheller are offered by Canadian Hovercruise daily during the summer months, by reservation otherwise. For information call (403) 823-5100.

Hiking/Walking

An unmaintained fenced area in north Calgary, **Nosehill Park** is one of the few remaining protected areas where the prairie retains its environment from before it was plowed and developed (though part of the area is a former gravel pit). The hill is actually a moraine left by the ice sheet that pushed out of the Rockies and down from the north during the last Ice Age. Two glaciers met here, leaving a ridge of rock and gravel. Glacial erratics can be seen in the park. Outside the old gravel pit, there are alder and aspen stands, prairie grasses, and plants indigenous to Alberta. Take a magnifying glass, since prairie grasses grow densely, sometimes a couple of hundred species to a square yard. Several varieties of birds that prefer prairie habitat can be seen here, including long-eared owls, rock wrens, and lazuli buntings. The hill also affords good views of Calgary, the Front Range to the west in the Bragg Creek area, and the Rockies proper due west. There are no roads through the park, but there are access points off 14 St NW and John Laurie Blvd where parking is allowed.

Mountain bikers flock to the dirt trails through **Fish Creek Provincial Park**—the largest urban wilderness area in Canada—but we prefer walking. The park is also the largest in Calgary at 11 2/5 miles (19 km) long. It protects both sides of Fish Creek where it flows east across the southern edge of Calgary and into the Bow River. Because of the water access and the variety of terrain, which ranges from grassland and open deciduous woodlands at the eastern end to riverine willow and white spruce growth at the western end, this is good **bird-watching** habitat. Raptors such as American kestrel, red-tailed hawks, and Swainson's hawks are common; great horned and barred owls also have been sighted here. Local birders say this is the best location in the city to see yellow-bellied sapsuckers. Watch for sora and common yellowthroat in the marshy areas, clay-colored and savannah sparrows in the grasslands. Fishing is allowed in Fish Creek, although the area is so heavily used year-round that avid anglers who actually want to catch fish should head else-where.

Wildlife

Calgary is situated where the Rocky Mountain foothills meet the prairies, which means birds that favor both types of terrain are here, as are raptors. The mountains also act as a natural barrier for **bird migrations**, which means Calgary gets a lot of birds flying by on their way north to breed in the spring, and returning south in the fall.

One of Calgary's best-kept secrets, as far as bird-watchers are concerned, is **Inglewood Bird Sanctuary,** which is rich in the bird species that frequent the region. Along the Bow River just east of downtown Calgary, this sanctuary was set aside in 1929. Since then nearly 250 bird species (and 300 species of plants) have been sighted along the 1 ⅕ miles (2 km) of trails. The Calgary Parks & Recreation Department administers the sanctuary, and one way to find birds fast here is to hire a guide. Experienced birders, also well-versed in the geologic history and flora and fauna of the area, are available by the hour ($25) to walk the sanctuary trails pointing out birds; call (403) 269-6688 for details on these guides. Bird-watchers still needing **Baltimore orioles** for their life lists won't be disappointed here. The bright orange birds—the most colorful in the sanc-tuary—nest here; listen for their flute-like territorial calls in late spring or look for their striking plumage in the trees along the river. The best bird viewing times are the last week in April through May or mid-August through mid-September, with the peak migration period the last week in August when as many as 20 varieties of **warblers** pass through the area. A new visitors center was completed in 1996, and maps are available for self-guided tours. Take 9th Ave SE west past Blackfoot Trail to Sanctuary Rd.

Fish Creek Provincial Park is also a haven for bird-watchers; see Hiking/Walking, above.

Fishing

Some of the best dry-fly trout fishing in the world is done on the **Bow River** south of Calgary. Most fly-fishing is done from a drift boat because of the preponderance of private property along the river, where access points are limited. Most guided fishing trips on the Bow are full-day excursions; two outfitters who specialize in this area come highly recommended: Rainbow & Brown, (403) 256-9622, which offers guided float trips for rainbow and brown trout (transportation, streamside lunch, and casting instruction included); and Bow River Troutfitters, (403) 282-8868, which operates guided mountain stream walk-and-wade trips as well as float trips on the Bow River (equipment, transportation, and lunch included).

Camping

Good campground options near Calgary can be found in the Drumheller area, including **Dinosaur Trail Campground**, (403) 823-9333, and **River Grove Campground**, (403) 823-6655.

Golfing

Calgary's golf courses include three 18-hole courses, three par-3 courses, and two 9-hole courses, maintained by Calgary Parks & Recreation. Walk-ons are accepted. To book a tee time through the golf booking computer, call (403) 221-3510.

Other Activities

Like most Canadian cities, Calgary's thick with community centers, many of which have **outdoor ice rinks** that are maintained in winters. Visitors can pay single-visit fees at most of the community centers and use the **pool, weight room, tennis courts,** and other facilities. The largest and best-equipped is the Lindsay Park Sports Centre, (403) 233-8393, which has all of the above as well as an indoor running track and a cafe. Southland, (403) 251-3505, and Village Square, (403) 280-9714, leisure centers both have **indoor beaches,** with wave pools and water slides.

   Ice skaters can also enjoy the city's 17 ice arenas open for public use; at Jimmie Condon Arena music is dished up by a deejay, with scented fog and colored lights for the skaters. In winter, skaters head for the **lagoon at Bowness Park** which remains frozen and is maintained by the parks department. Call Calgary Parks & Recreation, (403) 268-3888, for public hours, seasonal openings and closings, locations, and admission prices.

outside in

Attractions

With several miles of paved paths, the 6-acre **Calgary Zoo, Botanical Garden, and Prehistoric Park,** (403) 232-9372, is a great place to walk. In addition to the 1,200 animals, there are 3,000 plant varieties on the grounds and in a large conservatory, which doubles as a bird aviary. There's also a butterfly aviary, where big graceful butterflies are as inclined to land lightly on your shoulder as on the blooming hibiscus or other butterfly-friendly flowers. The zoo is organized by habitat more than by animal, and it's ideally organized for the various ecozones of Alberta. The zoo paths wind through aspen woodlands into a Rocky Mountain zone with mountain goats, then to northern boreal forests, Arctic shores, and a shortgrass prairie. The showcase of the zoo, however, is the **dinosaur area,** impressively large, with a replica of what Alberta looked like during the period that dinosaurs roamed these plains. Accurately sized dinosaur replicas stand in ponds and on volcanic cliff sides. The zoo is open daily and best accessed from Memorial Dr at 12th St SE.

The best-preserved of Calgary's historic buildings can be seen on the **Heritage Walking Tour** in the Connaught-Beltline District. The tour can be divided into two 1-hour self-guided walks; district boundaries are 14 St W and First St E, and 17 Ave S and 12 Ave S. The area is a high-density, inner-city neighborhood and many of the larger buildings, once grand single-family homes, are now apartments. The walking tour offers a snapshot of what Calgary was like just after the turn of the century. A building-by-building booklet is available from the Calgary Planning & Building Department, PO Box 2100, Postal Station M, Calgary AB, T2P 2M5, (403) 268-5333.

Not much remains the city's early days, except the historic 40-acre **Fort Calgary Historic Park,** (403) 290-1875, which houses memorabilia from when the settlement was a Northwest Mounted Police fort, built in 1875. In the intervening century, the city grew to more than 750,000.

Hosting the 1988 Winter Olympic Games provided the impetus to spiff up the city and build new public buildings. The **Saddledome,** home of the National Hockey League Flames, was built to host the Olympic hockey and skating events. Downtown, a light rail transit system started for Olympic tourists now reaches the far-flung suburbs; a new riverfront shopping/restaurant mall provides a focal point in an effort to draw people to downtown Calgary. Condominiums have been built adjacent to the mall, which includes a YMCA and an IMAX theater as well as a huge warehouse with shops, a food court, and a market with fresh food. Nearby are plenty of walking areas and wading pools. A footbridge connects the mall with **Prince's Island,** a well-maintained green area where walkers share the paths with Canada geese.

When the Games were held, the site of the bobsled, luge, and ski-jump competitions was well to the west of the city on the gentle foothills of the Rocky Mountains. The **Canada Olympic Park,** (403) 286-2632, is now within the suburbs as housing developments have crawled west toward the mountains. The Olympic Park is still popular with visitors, less so with Calgarians for the same reason that plagued the Olympic events: no snow. There's snowmaking equipment at the site, which allows for **downhill ski and snowboard lessons,** and the bobsled and luge runs are kept frozen thanks to refrigeration. But most who visit the Olympic Park do so to see the well-stocked museum and for thrills. Visitors can take the last five turns of a **luge run,** or take a **bobsled run** in a special sled—the Bobsled Bullet—that doesn't need a brake man or driver. Those wanting to see the sights in a more gentle way can take a guided tour to the top of the 300-foot (90-m) **ski jump tower** or have lunch, tea, or Sunday brunch in the Naturbahn Teahouse at the top of the ski jump (reservations required, (403) 247-5465). To get to Canada Olympic Park, take TransCanada Hwy 1 west from Calgary and exit at Bowfort Rd.

Oil money funded and inspired resident cultural organizations, and Calgary boasts the credible **Calgary Philharmonic Orchestra,** (403) 571-1070, which performs at Jack Singer Concert Hall; a ballet company, **Alberta Ballet,** (403) 245-4222, which splits its performance schedule between Calgary and Edmonton; a variety of theater companies under the umbrella of **Alberta Theatre Projects,** (403) 294-7475; and an opera company, **Calgary Opera,** (403) 262-7286, which performs at Southern Alberta Jubilee Auditorium.

Those who live in rural Alberta flock to Calgary to shop, and while this central Alberta city doesn't boast a mall of the scale of the West Edmonton Mall, there are still plenty of opportunities to browse. Oil money flowed into downtown Calgary in the late '70s and several of the skyscrapers—on Seventh Ave between First and Third Sts SW—were connected with a skywalk. When it was built, **TD Square,** as it became known, was the showpiece of the new downtown. The crown jewel was the building-top atrium that housed a botanical garden and a public ice skating rink. Two decades later, the **Devonian Botanic Garden,** (403) 268-3830, remains open limited hours; the ice rink gave way to a food court dominated by franchise fast-food eateries. Still anchored by Canada's big department stores, Hudson's Bay (simply The Bay to Canadians) and Eaton's (both have parking garages on lower levels), TD Square is worth a visit; but as a center of small boutiques and shops, it's

been eclipsed by Eau Claire Market, only a few blocks north on the riverbank and 20 years newer.

Gentrification of the district of 17th Ave between Third and Fourth
Sts, known as **Uptown 17,** also has lured shops, boutiques, cafes, and
espresso bars. The small area south of downtown Calgary has gained a
reputation for interesting dining and upscale shopping. The installation of
Eau Claire Market as part of the early-'90s riverfront renovation put a dent
in the escalation of Uptown 17 as a shopper's mecca; however, the bookstore most widely recognized as the city's best, **Sandpiper,** (403) 228-
0272, is still headquartered nearby. Sandpiper opened a second store,
(403) 233-7150, in Eau Claire Market, as well.

Eau Claire Market, (403) 264-6460, Second Ave and Second St,
anchors a hearty expanse of Calgary's waterfront, renovated with a mixture of public green areas and walking/biking paths, condominiums with
prime river views, restaurants, the YMCA (which draws clumps of office
workers with gym bags hurrying to an after-work workout), and shops
gathered in a new warehouse building designed to look aged or at least
pre-used. Eateries in the mall-warehouse are plentiful and change often,
although regional fare is always represented in one form or another,
whether it's New Orleans-style Cajun cuisine or French fare with an eastern Canadian influence.

At the east edge of the market is the new **Calgary Chinese Cultural
Centre,** 197 First St SW, (403) 262-5071, an ornate building with a six-
story blue turret inspired by the Temple of Heaven in Beijing. The center
houses a Chinese restaurant, an arts and crafts shop, and a museum with
artifacts and ceramic arts, and hosts ongoing exhibitions, festivals, and
special events marking Chinese holidays.

More than 150 million years ago **dinosaurs** roamed and soared over
the plains of Alberta—then swampy and more temperate. Archaeological
finds date the human population of Alberta to about 11,000 years ago,
like most of the rest of the North American continent. But for much of the
millennia, the province was covered by inland seas, which advanced and
retreated over the region 10 times. During the Cretaceous Period—the
heyday of dinosaurs—the Bearpaw Sea extended north from the Gulf of
Mexico across the midwestern United States and Alberta. Dinosaurs were
particularly abundant in what is now central Alberta, and when they died
their bones were imbedded here in mud and sand.

In 1884, geologist Joseph Burr Tyrrell found the skull of
Albertosaurus in the badlands of the Red Deer River Valley near
Drumheller and sparked a paleontologic boom in the area. Thousands of
dinosaur bones have since been uncovered, and in 1985 a museum,
named for Tyrrell, opened on the 4,000 square foot (11,200 square m)

site. A decade later, with interest prodded by movies such as *Jurassic Park,* the **Royal Tyrrell Museum of Paleontology** draws almost a half-million visitors each year. The dinosaur gallery contains 35 complete dinosaur skeletons, the largest collection in the world. Wear your walking shoes, because the site where the museum sits is out in the badlands. Visitors can spend a day digging in a dinosaur quarry near the museum, daily in July and August (reservations required; daily fees are $85, $55 ages 10–15, lunch included; minimum age is 10). Those who just want to walk can take a guided tour to the dig site; make reservations for one of the three daily tours in July and August (may be fewer tours the rest of the year; admission $12, $8 youths; suitable for all ages). Those wanting more intensive digging can join a team of scientists for a week at one of the field research sites at the **Dinosaur Provincial Park** near Brooks, working beside the paleontologists. The week costs $700-$800, including meals and accommodations; minimum age is 18. Allow 3 hours for a museum visit. The Royal Tyrrell is open daily June through August, but closed Mondays during the rest of the year. From Calgary take Hwy 2 and Hwy 72 north, then Hwy 9 east to Drumheller and follow the signs. It's about a 90-minute drive from Calgary, 3 1/2 hours from Edmonton. Royal Tyrrell Museum of Paleontology, Box 7500, Drumheller, AB T0J 0Y0, (403) 823-7707, fax (403) 823-7131; e-mail: rtmp@dns.magtech.ab.ca or visit their home page at http://tyrrell.magtech.ab.ca.

Come to the farm! Much of Alberta is farmed, and not all of it is planted in wheat or grazed by cattle. Market gardens sell produce in season to visitors or offer **u-pick orchards** and berry patches. The vegetable and berry farms in Alberta are organized as the Alberta Market Garden Association, which produces a first-rate guide to 150 of the province farms that sell everything from asparagus to squash, strawberries to saskatoon berries. The farms range from Lethbridge in Southern Alberta out east to Medicine Hat and north to Calgary, Red Deer, Edmonton, and beyond. The guide has maps and lists farms by location, directions, phone number, produce grown, and the seasons it's available, and other features such as trout ponds and whether the produce is grown organically. Call (800) 661-2642.

Calendar of Events

The **Calgary Winter Festival** is held in February and includes all the usual wintry activities—ice sculpturing, skating, and skiing. Call (403) 543-5480 for dates and information.

The city hosts two summer music festivals, the **International Jazz Festival** that runs the last 2 weeks of June and into the first of July, (403) 233-2628; and the **Calgary Folk Music Festival,** held in July, (403) 233-0904.

The main event in Calgary is, of course, the **Calgary Stampede,** staged the first 2 weeks of July. Parades, rodeo events, street dances, chuckwagon races, concerts, and a carnival bring nearly a million people to Calgary for the 10-day Stampede. For details on this historic annual party, call (800) 661-1260 or (403) 263-8510.

Restaurants

River Cafe ☆☆☆   This cafe would make it on location alone—it sits on the riverbank of Prince's Island, accessible only by footbridge from Eau Claire Market or by water. The 60-seat restaurant is round with enough windows that it seems like an open-air gazebo. The decor is quintessentially Northwest Territories, with birch-bark basket lights, fishing creels hanging from the walls, and slate floors. The food matches the decor both in style and quality. It favors the Pacific Northwest with generous influences from southern Alberta traditions and ingredients; there's an entire menu section of flatbreads—reminiscent of Indian fry bread. We liked the flatbread topped with candied salmon, mild goat cheese, and blueberries. Other seasonal offerings may range from cedar-planked salmon to wilted dandelion greens. All of the entrees arrive beautifully garnished. The cafe closes for a couple of winter months while the chefs research new recipes and ingredients and reopens in March. *On the south bank of Prince's Island Park; 200 8th Ave SE, Calgary; (403) 261-7670; lunch, dinner every day; AE, DC, MC, V; no checks; $$-$$$.*

Mescalero ☆☆   The menu boasts food served in the spirit and traditions of the West and Southwest, and the decor is thick with Southwest flavorings. There's also a nod to cowboy tradition here, a natural for the city since the Calgary Stampede brings thousands of cowboys to town for the biggest rodeo on the continent. The building is decades old and holes in the plaster become part of the casual atmosphere. For a city on the prairies this close to the Arctic Circle, we think the menu leans a little heavily on tacos and tostados. The tostados are more like Mexican pizzas—flatbread rather than a tortilla topped with combinations such as black beans, jack cheese, smoked chicken, and freshly made salsa. And there's also an eclectic portion of the menu, featuring grilled lamb chops with peanut chipolte sauce or blackened red snapper with salsa. Salads are à la carte and, like the entrees, don't follow traditional lines. The brunch menu might include items such as pumpkin pecan waffles with wild boar sausage, huevos con chorizo ratatouille, and fresh-baked scones. *Just south of downtown; 1315 1st St SW, Calgary; (403) 266-3339; lunch, dinner every day; AE, MC, V; no checks; $$-$$$.*

Hard Rock Cafe ☆ If you've seen one Hard Rock Cafe, you've pretty much seen them all, and this Calgary version follows the formula that offers a broad cross-section of fare and a raucous atmosphere. Its main feature is its location at the center of the Eau Claire Market downtown along the banks of the Bow River. As with other Hard Rocks, you can hardly go wrong with the menu whether it's a cheeseburger, a Caesar salad, or a pasta entree that interests you. *In Eau Claire Market, downtown; 119 Barclay Parade, Calgary; (403) 263-7625; breakfast Sun, lunch, dinner every day; AE, DC, MC, V; no checks; $$.*

Joey Tomato's Kitchen ☆ Imagine a raucous sports bar, a family pizza joint, a hot spot for young professionals at the edge of an urban core. This is Joey Tomato's Kitchen. It's one of several tony restaurants at Eau Claire Market, but from the crowds you'd think it was the only eatery around. The dinnertime lines don't seem to trouble the staff at this busy restaurant, since the wait at the door to be seated is brief and those not wanting to hang around the entrance or wait in the bar are handed a pager. They can wander the adjacent market and will be beeped when their table is ready. The bar's thick with those getting off work from nearby downtown office buildings and chatter drowns out the sports play-by-play on the big screen TV. In fact, the entire eatery is loud, so don't plan on intimate table talk here. There's an array of pasta dishes—lasagna, fettuccine, and such—and a couple of real entrees like salmon and chicken, but the show is the pizza. The combinations are imaginative and utilize fresh ingredients such as spinach, tomatoes, and basil. The pizzas are baked in a wood-fired oven and emerge with a crisp crust. *In Eau Claire Market, downtown; 208 Barclay Parade SW, Calgary; (403) 263-6336; lunch, dinner every day; AE, MC, V; no checks; $$-$$$.*

Red Robin ☆ At the north end of the 10th Street Bridge, this Red Robin, from the outside, looks like a high-end eatery, with wall-to-wall windows through which diners can look out on the Bow River and the towering buildings of downtown Calgary. Inside, though, it's decidedly family dining, in the tradition of the chain that grew out of a single restaurant in Seattle. The menu follows the Red Robin tradition of burgers, fish and chips, and some Mexican entrees. Those familiar with Red Robin elsewhere will be happy here, too. And, really, with one of the best views in the city, how can you possibly go wrong? The eatery is on a busy intersection, though, so plan to look for a parking spot on the street at a meter. *Memorial Dr and 10th St NW, in the Kensington District; 1110 Memorial Dr NW, Calgary; (403) 283-9600; lunch, dinner every day; AE, MC, V; no checks; $$.*

Lodgings

During the Calgary Stampede, thousands of visitors flock to Calgary and fill the 10,000 hotel, motel, and bed and breakfast rooms in the city. All the major hotel and motel chains are represented in Calgary, and several dozen bed and breakfasts operate here, some under the auspices of the Bed & Breakfast Association of Calgary. Innkeepers in some B&Bs are fluent in languages other than English. The Calgary B&B Association will make reservations for you, (403) 543-3900, fax (403) 543-3901, as will the Big Country Bed & Breakfast Agency, (403) 533-2203. Outside the few weeks of the stampede, lodging is plentiful at all of the major chains located in all of Calgary's districts, including downtown.

Inglewood Bed and Breakfast ☆ Innkeepers Valinda Larson and Helmut Schoderbock built this Victorian-style home in the early 1990s as a bed and breakfast. The amenities are strictly late-20th century, though room decor is true to the Victorian period. A small parlor serves as the only common room for conversation and breakfast. One of the four guest rooms includes a round sitting nook with wraparound windows affording views of the Bow River, just beyond the backyard. A dirt access road and green area separate the yard from the path along the river, which is perfect for a walk or jog. The Calgary Zoo is a 5-minute walk south along the trail and across a footbridge; the downtown core is a 15-minute walk north, and Stampede Park is easily reached in about 12 minutes.

The B&B is located in an older but gentrified neighborhood—Inglewood—so neighborhood cafes, espresso bars, bookstores, and antiques shops are a few blocks away. Inglewood was the core of Calgary's first business district. The main street through the area is just a block away (used car lots and light industrial areas), but the residential buffer is sufficient to make this a quiet place along the river. *Just east of downtown in the Inglewood District; 1006 8th Ave SE, Calgary, AB T2G 0M4; (403) 262-6570; no credit cards; no checks; $$.*

Mountain View Bed and Breakfast ☆ Most of Calgary's bed and breakfast homes are located in residential areas; Mountain View is not. This small B&B is west of Calgary in what resembles a rural setting; it's on a 2-acre lot, with room for tennis courts. Amenities include an indoor pool and a game room. Guests also have use of a sitting area with fireplace. *Near Canada Olympic Park; Box 6, Site 24, RR 12, Calgary, AB T3E 6W3; (403) 246-4838; no credit cards; no checks; $.*

Ranches and Resorts

Guests can stay at working ranches throughout Alberta and participate in ranch work or just relax in the country. Other resorts offer a Western experience—trail rides, barbecues, singing around a campfire—along with amenities such as saunas, swimming pools, volleyball courts, and well-appointed individual cabins. At working ranches guests participate in activities ranging from collecting eggs to mucking out the barns to mending fences and tending cattle. Winters, most ranches boast cross-country skiing and snowshoeing opportunities. At some ranches, guests stay in the main ranch house, much like a bed-and-breakfast inn; at others they bunk in separate cabins or lodge buildings. The animals also vary—if you'd rather spend time with sheep than cows, ask the ranch owner. Some ranches also offer guided hunting trips in season. A list of members of the Country Vacations Association is available from Box 217, Trochu, AB T0M 2C0; (403) 442-2207. For information on guest ranches, hotels and motels, also try the Drumheller Tourist Information Centre, (403) 823-1331. (See also Horseback Riding, above.)

Tomahawk Mountain Outpost is located where the Red Deer River flows out of Banff National Park. Guests eat in the main lodge but sleep in log cabins. Day rides are taken into the Rockies. Contact PO Box 1709, Cochrane, AB T0L 0W0, for more information, or call (403) 432-7833, fax (403) 932-7933.

Few outfitters operate deep into Banff National Park, but **Warner Guiding and Outfitting** is among them. The guide service operates out of Trail Rider Store, 132 Banff Ave, Banff, and runs horse-packing trips from overnight to 6 days—or guests can stay in either the Banff Sundance Lodge or Halfway Lodge, operated by the guide service. The same outfitter offers barbecues and barn dancing in winters, as well as sleigh rides and cross-country skiing tours in the area. Contact PO Box 2280, Banff, AB T0L 0C0, for more information, or call (403) 762-4551, fax (403) 762-8130.

More Information

Alberta Ballet: (403) 245-4222.
Alberta Theatre Projects: (403) 294-7475.
B&B Association reservations: (403) 543-3900.
Calgary Cannons (baseball): (403) 284-1111.
Calgary Centre for Performing Arts: (403) 294-7455.
Calgary Flames (hockey): (403) 777-4646.
Calgary Opera: (403) 262-7286.
Calgary Parks and Recreation: (403) 268-3888.

Calgary Philharmonic Orchestra: (403) 571-1070.

Calgary Stampede: (800) 661-1260 or (403) 261-0101.

Calgary Stampeder (football): (403) 289-0205.

Calgary Transit: (403) 262-1000.

Calgary Visitor & Convention Bureau: (800) 661-1678 or (403) 263-8510.

Canada Customs: (403) 292-8750.

Devonian Botanic Gardens: (403) 268-3830.

Drumheller/Big Country Tourism: (403) 823-5885.

Fish Creek Provincial Park: (403) 297-5293.

Inglewood Bird Sanctuary: (403) 269-6688.

Stampede Park Harness & Thoroughbred Racing: (403) 261-0101.

TicketMaster: (403) 299-8888.

Lethbridge
and the Border

Including Writing-On-Stone Provincial Park, Cardston, and Crowsnest.

Southern Alberta is renowned for expansive wheat and cattle farms, short-grass prairies and big sky, but its windy prairies are hemmed in by the slopes of the Rockies. Even miles to the east, where the peaks are no longer visible on the horizon, the Rockies call the shots. The mountains stop weather systems that dump rain and snow on the western slopes, leaving their eastern edge, the foothills, and the prairies dry. But the prairies get the winds that sweep east from the mountains—black mesh netting hung from tall poles surrounds some farm houses to cut the constant winds; less expensive alternatives are walls of straw bales. In some areas, the wind blows more than 85 percent of the time. The Alberta prairies also are shaped by geologic history. Thick ice sheets flowed south across these prairies into Montana, and when the ice receded, floods carved enormous coulees into the prairies and left erratics—boulders that still dot the fields like lawn ornaments.

A small prairie city whose claim to fame is a single-span iron railroad bridge from the 1920s, Lethbridge sells itself short. The massive coulee that the railroad bridge spans is the real treasure of this southern Alberta city, and impressive steps already have been taken to preserve this natural resource. Nature trails, some paved, crisscross the coulee, a deep broad valley carved by rivers gushing out of the receding ice sheet when the last Ice Age ended. The coulee, with the modest Oldman River that flows down it, defines and divides the city. West of the coulee are new subdivisions that continue to spread toward the Rockies; east are more established residential areas, although Lethbridge is not old enough to have a truly historic district. The most visible connection between east and west Lethbridge is the famous High Level Bridge, the longest and highest single-span bridge in North America, which looms over Indian Battle Park and the nature trails below.

Getting There

Access to the mountains from the southern Alberta prairies is limited to the major roadways punched through the few mountain passes as railroad and, later, trucking routes. From the east, exit TransCanada Highway 1 at Medicine Hat to Hwy 3 and Lethbridge. Hwy 3 continues west to Fort Macleod and over Crowsnest Pass to Fernie and Cranbrook in British Columbia. From Waterton Lakes National Park, drive northeast on Hwy 5 through Cardston to Lethbridge. From Calgary, drive south on Hwy 2 to Fort Macleod and east on Hwy 3 to Lethbridge.

Adjoining Areas

NORTH: **Calgary and Environs**

SOUTH: **Glacier National Park**

WEST: **Banff National Park**

Hiking/Walking

The largest city in southwest Alberta, Lethbridge boasts miles of walking paths. A free **Pathways Brochure** with details about Lethbridge parks and the 36 miles (60 km) of walking and bicycling paths in the city is available from the Lethbridge Parks Department, City Hall, 910 Fourth Avenue S, (403) 320-5222, ext. 2795.

The **Helen Schuler Coulee Centre and Nature Reserve**, (403) 320-3064, anchors the system of trails in a deep coulee that divides east and west Lethbridge. The cut in the prairie was carved by the meltwater from the ice sheets that covered Alberta during the ice ages; now much of the coulee has been preserved in Indian Battle Park. Maps and interpretive brochures for several self-guided trails can be picked up at the nature center, where a garden focuses on plants native to the coulee. Despite the Oldman River and thick vegetation at the bottom of the coulee, the hillside habitat is surprisingly desert-like; prickly pear cactus grows in abundance. A visit in early June will be just in time to see the cacti bloom in soft peach hues, prompted by spring rains and longer days. Hikers should watch for prairie rattlesnakes. The coulee can be accessed at a number of places along its length through Lethbridge, with parking areas and marked trails. **Guided nature walks** from the Nature Centre are conducted Sundays at 2pm. The trails at the Nature Centre connect with trails through adjacent **Indian Battle Park** and **Botterill Bottom Park** to the south. To reach the Nature Centre, take Scenic Drive north to Sixth Ave and turn down into the coulee. The center is part of the 196-acre **Lethbridge Nature Reserve and Elizabeth Hall Wetlands** and is open daily June through August, closed Mondays the rest of the year; admission is free.

Alberta is known for prehistoric sites with a plethora of dinosaur bones, but one of the lesser-known gems is preserved in **Writing-On-Stone Provincial Park,** (403) 647-2364, southeast of Lethbridge and Milk River. The most extensive collection of **petroglyphs** and **pictographs** in North America—thousands of figures in more than 50 sites—can be seen on the sandstone cliffs in this 4,400-acre park. Native peoples considered the site sacred and a source of spiritual strength. Hiking trails wind through sandstone hoodoo formations, towers of stone carved by wind, ancient floods, and the Milk River. Access to the majority of rock art is limited to guided tours, available mid-May through August only. Guided walks to the rock art begin daily at 2pm with additional tours during peak season; the walks are free but tickets must be picked up from the Visitor Services Office 1 hour before the tour begins. From Milk River, drive 20 miles (32 km) east on Secondary Road 501, then south 6 miles (10 km) on Secondary Rd 500.

Camping

The **Henderson Lake Campground,** (403) 328-5452, a pleasant, small treed area, is adjacent to Henderson Park near the Lethbridge Exhibition Grounds, which host the annual Whoop-Up Days and Powwow in early August. The **Writing-On-Stone Provincial Park** (see Hiking/Walking, above) has 75 camping sites with pit toilets, shower facilities, wood, fire pits, and water.

Rafting

The prehistoric sites at Writing-On-Stone Provincial Park (see Hiking/Walking, above) can also be seen during rafting trips down the **Milk River,** a popular destination for rafters and canoers. There are no rapids beyond Class I, but those unfamiliar with the put-in and take-out points can explore the river most easily with a guide. Guide service, including all equipment, can be arranged through Milk River Raft Tours, PO Box 396, Milk River, AB T0K 1M0, (403) 647-3586. An interpretive map of the river (notable as the only river in Canada that flows into the Gulf of Mexico) is available from the Milk River Canoe Club.

Fishing

Guided fishing trips, in drift boats on the **Crowsnest, Castle,** and **Oldman Rivers** and at **Alpine Lakes** in the Crowsnest Pass area west of Lethbridge, can be arranged through the Crowsnest Angler, located on Hwy 3 near Bellevue, (800) 267-1778 or phone/fax (403) 564-4333.

In Lethbridge itself, fishing is allowed at **Henderson Lake** (an Alberta fishing license is required) in Henderson Park, at North Parkside Dr and Mayor Magrath Dr.

Golfing

With Lethbridge's dry summer days, golf is a popular activity. The best-maintained course is the **Paradise Canyon Golf and Country Club and Lodge,** located in the Oldman River Canyon. Accommodations are typical motel fare, but golf/lodging packages are available, (800) 661-1232. Tee times can be made 3 days in advance by calling (403) 381-7500. Those with more modest golfing ambitions can try **Bridge Valley Par 3,** (403) 381-6363, or the **Henderson Park Golf Course,** (403) 329-6767.

Downhill Skiing

Downhill skiers in Southwest Alberta usually head for the most developed downhill ski area in the region, **Snow Valley,** (604) 423-4655, which is just west of the Alberta-British Columbia border at Fernie, a mining town turned ski resort. That the snows are deep in Fernie, there is no doubt. Average snowfall is 350 inches (875 cm), compared with an average of 142 inches (355 cm) at Lake Louise. Snow Valley boasts a vertical drop of 2,400 feet (720 m)—from a 5,900-foot elevation (1,770-m) at the top. It's still a modest area by most standards, with just two triple chairs and one quad. And the mountain is so steep and rocky, it takes a considerable amount of snow for coverage, which makes for an early-December opening despite the elevation. On-mountain lodging includes the Griz Inn Sport Hotel/Condominiums, (604) 423-9221; Timberline Village Condo miniums, (800) 667-9911; Fernie Homes and Chalets, (604) 423-9284; and Wolf's Den Mountain Lodge, (604) 423-9202. The town of Fernie is 3 miles (5 km) east of the ski resort on Hwy 3. Lodging reservations can be made through Fernie Central Reservations, (604) 423-9284, fax (604) 423-4588. The nearest airport is in Cranbrook (Air BC), an hour's drive west.

For downhill skiing, the **Powder Keg Ski Hill,** (403) 562-8952, at Crowsnest Pass is a family ski area with predominantly easy and intermediate runs. Some runs are lighted for night skiing. More challenging runs can be found at **Westcastle Park,** (403) 627-5101, near Pincher Creek, which is also a day area only. Crowsnest Pass also boasts a **luge run.**

Cross-Country Skiing/Snowmobiling

Snowmobilers head for the high country fast on the system of 750 miles (1,200 km) of well-maintained snowmobiling trails that radiate from **Crowsnest Pass** on Hwy 3, one of three major passes through the Canadian Rockies west of Lethbridge. Most are well above the tree line, so the vistas seem endless and the snow is consistently powder. Crowsnest Pass also has groomed cross-country ski trails near the community.

More than 24 miles (40 km) of **cross-country ski trails** are groomed at the **Allison Recreation Area,** which connect with unmarked trails through the forest reserve. The **Syncline Area** also has groomed trails. Trail maps for snowmobiling and cross-country skiing, and snow conditions, are available from Chinook Country Tourism, (800) 661-1222 or (403) 329-6777.

Cross-country ski and **snowshoeing** day trips can be arranged through Roger's Outdoor Adventures, Box 24022, Centre Village PO, Lethbridge AB T1H 0E4, (403) 329-1374; or through Magic Mountain Tours, Box 10, Pincher Creek, AB T0K 1W0, (403) 627-5919. Snowmobiling, backcountry skiing, whitewater rafting, and hiking trips can be arranged through Adventure Shop in Fernie, BC, (604) 423-3515.

Wildlife

In mid-July the Helen Schuler Coulee Centre and Nature Reserve stages the **Butterfly Bash and Count** (the bash is the party and doesn't involve the butterflies). The 203-acre natural area is rich in bird life since it offers water, food and shelter; an impressive number of **warbler species** as well as **rock wrens** live in the coulee through the summer months.

The prairie terrain east of Lethbridge lends itself to soaring and hunting raptors, so a birds of prey center seems a natural. The **Alberta Birds of Prey Centre,** (800) 661-1222 or (403) 345-4262, is 6 ⅗ miles (11 km) east of Lethbridge at Coaldale and features **hawks, falcons, eagles,** and **owls.** When the weather accommodates, the birds are put through their paces in live flying shows. Otherwise, they can be seen on perches and in natural habitat. Open daily, May through early October.

Other Activities

Swimming in Lethbridge city lakes is prohibited, but **swimmers** can use the Henderson Pool; recorded information about Henderson Pool and four other public swimming pools in Lethbridge is available by calling (403) 320-5222, ext. 7896.

Like many Canadian cities, Lethbridge has a number of community centers with public **ice skating**; call (403) 320-5222, ext. 7897.

outside in

Attractions

The main artery through the southern Canadian Rockies is Hwy 3 over Crowsnest Pass, most famous for the Frank Slide of 1903. Before dawn one morning in April, 82 million tons (30 million cubic m) of limestone slid off the summit of Turtle Mountain, burying part of the town of Frank, Alberta. More than 1 1/5 square miles (3 square km) of the town were buried in less than 2 minutes, killing 70 people. The **Frank Slide Interpretive Centre,** (403) 562-7388, built above the slide, is open daily except major holidays. Those interested in getting underground can don a hard-hat and walk 1,210 feet (365 m) into a re-timbered mineshaft where the only light is from head lamps. The mine operated from 1903 to 1961. The **Bellevue Underground Mine Tour** can be arranged summers only at the Frank Slide Interpretive Centre; wear warm clothing and sturdy footwear.

The **Fort Whoop-Up Interpretive Centre,** (403) 329-0444, is in the Oldman River coulee just south of the nature center in Indian Battle Park. Fort Whoop-Up was a trading post built in 1869 by Montana traders, who came north to take advantage of the lucrative buffalo robe trade. Years of lawlessness at the post forced the North West Mounted Police to take control of the fort in 1874. Indian Battle Park commemorates the last battle fought between the Cree and the Blackfeet in 1870. Much of the battle took place in Indian Battle Coulee on the west side of the river.

Townsfolk in Lethbridge, a city of 65,000, celebrated their centennial in 1967 by building the **Nikka Yuko Japanese Garden,** (800) 661-1222 or (403) 328-3511, open mid-May to late September, in Henderson Park at North Parkside Dr and Mayor Magrath Dr. Henderson is a lovely 117-acre green area (including the Henderson Golf Course; see Golfing, above) surrounding a small lake.

A survey of the last century of life in southern Alberta can be seen at the **Sir Alexander Galt Museum,** Fifth Ave S and Scenic Dr, (403) 320-3898, open daily with free admission. Winters, the Western Hockey League **Lethbridge Hurricanes,** (403) 320-4040, play at the Canada Games Sportsplex, 2510 Scenic Dr S, also the site of other major entertainment events. For a schedule, call (403) 320-5222, ext. 7898; for tickets, call (403) 329-7328. Other **cultural events** are staged at the University of Lethbridge Performing Arts Centre, (403) 329-2616.

Attempts have been made to renovate the original downtown district of Lethbridge with street lamps, a clean and pleasant city-center park (Galt Park), and a brick walking street, but the shopping traffic heads for the mall—**Park Place,** 501 First Ave S, (403) 320-0008—which is at the north edge of the downtown area. Still, this pleasant city is charming in a smaller city way.

Horses played a big role in the farming history of the Alberta prairies and **Remington Centre,** (403) 653-5139, in Cardston houses the largest collection of 19th-century horse-drawn carriages, coaches, sleighs, and wagons on the continent. It's worth a side trip if you're going near Cardston anyway. (Cardston is a 50-minute drive west on Hwy 3 from Lethbridge, 2 1/2 hours south of Calgary.) The center has an 85-seat theater and offers interpretive tours and, perhaps best, leisurely **carriage rides** through Lee Creek Park. It may be the only park in Alberta where carriages join bicycles, in-line skaters, and pedestrians on the trails. Cardston's small, so the preponderance of signs for the Carriage Centre ensure you can't miss it.

Visit **Writing-On-Stone Provincial Park,** (403) 647-2364, southeast of Lethbridge and Milk River, to see the most extensive collection of petroglyphs and pictographs in North America (see Hiking/Walking, above, for more information).

One of the more interesting interpretive centers is located far from any city, where the Alberta prairie meets the sandstone Porcupine Hills. The seven-story **Head-Smashed-In Buffalo Jump Interpretive Centre,** (403) 553-2731, is built directly into the cliffside, a credit to the designers and to those who had the foresight to commemorate these historical hunting grounds of Native Peoples who lived in the area as long ago as 5,700 years. Well before the pyramids were built in Egypt, the tribes in this area constructed elaborate lanes down which they drove herds of buffalo over a cliff as a method of killing large numbers of the beasts for food, hides, and tools fashioned from the horns and bones. This site and another nearby were used intermittently until the 1800s when the Native Peoples acquired horses and rifles with which to hunt. The site was discovered in the 1930s, and eight subsequent excavation projects have uncovered evidence of thousands of buffalo killed and butchered at the

base of the cliff. The interpretive center, built in the 1980s, offers histories of the hunting methods and the Indians in the area, plus an excellent
explanation of the habitat and native flora and fauna. A 1-mile (2-km)
paved trail ends at the jump site. Apropos to the site, the cafe in the center serves buffalo burgers, which don't really taste all that different from
Alberta beef burgers. Those wanting an overnight experience can spend
the night in a **Blackfeet tepee,** camped at the base of the Head-Smashed-
In Buffalo Jump, June through August, $35, (403) 553-2731. The site is
open daily year-round, until 8pm in summers. Admission is charged.
Head-Smashed-In Buffalo Jump is almost 11 miles (18 km) northwest of
Fort Macleod on Secondary Rd 785 or 105 miles (175 km) south of
Calgary on Hwy 2 and SR 785.

Calendar of Events

The annual **Alberta Winter Games** are staged in Lethbridge and west in
the mountains the last week of February. For dates and details, call (403)
381-1996.

As a nod to its heritage, Lethbridge holds a 1-day **Great Buffalo
Hunt,** a reenactment of the tradition, in late March at Fort Whoop-Up. In
early April, a **Traders Day Camp,** which actually lasts 3 days, is also held
at Fort Whoop-Up. Call (403) 329-0444 for information.

Whoop-Up Days and Powwow are in early August, held at the
Lethbridge Exhibition Grounds. Events include a Whoop-Up Parade;
(403) 328-4491.

Restaurants

O-Sho Japanese Restaurant ☆   In a small city in the heart of Alberta's
farming region, a Japanese restaurant that serves up authentic sushi, wonderfully light tempura, and teriyaki is a real surprise. This is Alberta beef
country, after all, and platters of prime beef abound. This Japanese cafe is
popular with the locals, however, and Friday and Saturday nights there's
often a short wait for a table. From the outside, there's not much that
would draw passersby off Sixth Street; indeed, it is downright easy to miss
the place. It's worth finding, though. The sushi arrives on a lacquered
platter, beautifully presented. There's also a sushi bar where, from a stool,
you can watch the sushi chef at work. The tempura-battered vegetables
and prawns, chicken, or beef arrive hot, served with rice and dipping
sauce. Order sake for an authentic Japanese dinner, or opt for green tea.
*Just east of the downtown district; 1219 3rd Ave S, Lethbridge; (403) 327-
8382; lunch, Mon–Fri, dinner every day; AE, MC, V; no checks; $.*

Lodgings

Forsyth House   This house is just what you would expect to find on the prairies, a farmhouse with Victorian touches here and there. The 1906 house overlooks the coulee and the University of Lethbridge on the far side of the valley, a modern building that's layered into the cliff. Outside, the house is ordinary in an older neighborhood of ordinary prairie-style homes. Inside, the original woodwork and wood floors are a perfect backdrop for the pine antique furniture innkeeper Helen Haynes brought with her from Toronto when she retired and moved west. Both guest rooms are on the second floor and share a tiny bath with a claw-footed tub but no shower. While the room at the front of the house has views of the coulee, the other room is the brighter and cozier of the two. Breakfast is served in the dining room and usually includes muffins made from one of Haynes's own recipes. *Just south of the downtown district; 715 3rd St S, Lethbridge, AB T1J 1Z4; (403) 320-5344; no credit cards; checks OK; $.*

More Information

Alberta Birds of Prey Centre: (800) 661-1222 or (403) 345-4262.

Chinook Country Tourist Association: (800) 661-1222 or 403-329-6777, fax (403) 329-6177.

Head-Smashed-In Buffalo Jump Interpretive Centre: (403) 553-2731.

Lethbridge Hospital: (403) 382-6111.

Milk River Country: (403) 647-3773.

Royal Canadian Mounted Police: (403) 329-5010.

Writing-On-Stone Provincial Park: (403) 647-2364.

Index

Inside Out:
Northern Rockies
Report Form

Based on my personal experience, I wish to recommend the following trail, route, waterway, area, guide, outfitter, organization, or establishment; or confirm/correct/disagree with the current review.

_____

_____

_____

(Please include address and telephone number of your recommendation, if applicable.)

Report:

Please describe the aspects of your experience that made it memorable; for example, the type of trail, outstanding natural features, best season to go, etc. Continue on the other side if necessary.

_____

_____

_____

_____

_____

_____

I am not concerned, directly or indirectly, with the management or ownership of this guide, outfitter, organization, or establishment *(if applicable)*.

Signed _____

Name *(please print)* _____

Address _____

_____

Phone Number _____

Date _____

Send to:

Inside Out: Northern Rockies
c/o Sasquatch Books
615 Second Avenue, Suite 260
Seattle, WA 98104

Or email your report to: books@sasquatchbooks.com

About the Authors

Susan English has skied and hiked in the Northern Rockies for more than two decades. She works as a writer and editor at The *Spokesman-Review* in Spokane, Washington, and teaches writing and ethics courses at Gonzaga University and Eastern Washington University. She has contributed to the *Best Places* guidebook series for more than a decade and also writes for the Fodor's travel series. When not exploring the backcountry of the Canadian Rockies, Susan retreats to a family lakeside cabin in the Selkirk Mountains. She lives with three cats and a Siberian Husky.

Kathy Witkowsky is a freelance journalist and travel writer based in Missoula, Montana, where she writes frequently about issues affecting the region. A former reporter with the city news bureau of Chicago and the Spokane *Spokesman-Review*, she has traveled extensively on magazine assignments—both throughout the Rocky Mountain region and beyond. Ms. Witkowsky holds an MFA degree in Creative Writing from the University of Montana. She is also producer/writer/director of "Bella Vista: An Unseen View of World War II," an award-winning historical documentary produced for public television.

Did you enjoy this book?

Sasquatch Books publishes high-quality books and guides related to Alaska, the Pacific Northwest, and California. Our books are available at bookstores and other retail outlets throughout the region. Here is a partial list of our current titles:

TRAVEL/OUTDOORS

Inside Out: Washington
A Best Places Guide to the Outdoors
Ron C. Judd

Take a Walk
100 Walks Through Natural Places in Puget Sound
Sue Muller Hacking

Northwest Boat Dives
60 Ultimate Dives in Puget Sound and Hood Canal
Dave Bliss

Northwest Best Places
Restaurants, Lodgings, and Touring in Oregon, Washington, and British Columbia
Edited by Stephanie Irving

Alaska Best Places
Restaurants, Lodgings, and Adventure
Edited by Nan Elliot

Northern California Best Places
Restaurants, Lodgings, and Touring
Edited by Rebecca Poole Forée

Seattle Best Places
Restaurants, Lodgings, Shopping, Nightlife, Arts, Sights, and Outings
Edited by Nancy Leson

Vancouver Best Places
Restaurants, Lodgings, Shopping, Nightlife, Arts, Sights, and Outings
Edited by Kasey Wilson

Portland Best Places
Restaurants, Lodgings, Shopping, Nightlife, Arts, Sights, and Outings
Edited by Kim Carlson

Native Peoples of the Northwest
A Traveler's Guide to Land, Art, and Culture
Jan Halliday and Gail Chehak

LITERATURE

**I Don't Know Why
I Swallowed the Fly**
My Fly-Fishing Rookie Season
Jessica Maxwell

Voyage of a Summer Sun
Canoeing the Columbia River
Robin Cody

Alaska Passages
20 Voices from Above the 54th Parallel
Edited by Susan Fox Rogers

Way Out Here
Modern Life in Ice-Age Alaska
Richard Leo

FIELD GUIDES

Field Guide to the Bald Eagle

Field Guide to the Geoduck

Field Guide to the Gray Whale

Field Guide to the Grizzly Bear

Field Guide to the Humpback Whale

Field Guide to the Orca

Field Guide to the Pacific Salmon

Field Guide to the Sasquatch

Field Guide to the Slug

For a complete catalog of Sasquatch Books titles, or to inquire about ordering our books, please contact us at the address below, or visit our website at www.sasquatchbooks.com.

SASQUATCH BOOKS

615 Second Avenue, Suite 260, Seattle, Washington 98104
(206) 467-4300 or (800) 775-0817 Fax (206) 467-4301